AF657658

JAINISM
History, Society, Philosophy and Practice

LALA SUNDERLAL JAIN RESEARCH SERIES

VOLUME XXIV

JAINISM

History, Society, Philosophy and Practice

REVISED EDITION

AGUSTÍN PÁNIKER

Translated from the Revised Spanish Edition by
DAVID SUTCLIFFE

MOTILAL BANARSIDASS
PUBLISHING HOUSE • DELHI
Email: mlbd@mlbd.in • Website: www.mlbd.in

2nd Revised Edition : Delhi, ***2022***
2nd Reprint: Delhi, 2021
First Edition : Delhi, 2010
First Published in Spanish as
EI. Jainismo: Historia, sociedad, filosofia y práctica
by **editorial Kairos**, *Barcelona, Spain in 2001*

ISBN: 978-81-948578-7-7 (Hardcover)
ISBN: 978-81-948578-6-0 (Paperback)

This book has been translated and published with a subsidy of the Dirección General del Libro, Archivos y Bibliotecas del Ministerio de Cultura de España (Ministry of Culture, Spain)

Printed & Published by
Rajendra P Jain *for*
Motilal Banarsidass Publishing House
A-44, Naraina Industrial Area, Phase I,
New Delhi–110 028 (INDIA)
Email: mlbd@mlbd.in
Website: www.mlbd.in

CONTENTS

LIST OF TABLES, FIGURES AND ILLUSTRATIONS

TABLES

FIGURES

PLATES AND ILLUSTRATIONS

(Figures 1 to 21 are placed between pages 158 and 159)

(Figures 22 to 48 are placed between pages 326 and 327.)

FOREWORD

I deem it a great honour to write a foreword to the English version of Professor Agustín Pániker's well-known work on Jainism. The original book was written in Spanish in 2001 and the revised edition in 2008. This edition is translated into English from the revised Spanish edition by David Sutcliffe. The three editions in ten years' time show their popularity among the scholars.

The author is an acute and versatile scholar, and his present treatise is an all-comprehensive, outstanding contribution to the subject of Jainism. The author, in his book, has covered varied and sundry subjects on Jainism, which are not usually found in one volume. The author has selected 12 topics of importance and each of his selections is unique in its presentation. All of the important and comprehensive subjects are put in one volume, so that the readers can thoroughly grasp the subject. It deals with the history, mythology, philosophy, religion, and the Jain society systematic ally. The cosmology of Jainism, though difficult to present clearly, has been discussed in a scholarly manner. The development of Jainism in different parts of India is delineated from a historical perspective. The Jain orders, Iconography, and worship are all done befittingly. Even the topic soteriology is depicted from a scientific outlook. In one word, the book is one-in-all and all-in-one.

The style of the translation is simple, lucid and poignant. The translator has not unnecessarily made his style cumbersome and difficult to understand. The exposition of the subject is straightforward and easy to comprehend.

I must congratulate Shri N.P. Jain for publishing this book in his series for the benefit of the readers, and I also believe that the scholars will derive much knowldge from this book. I recommend this volume strongly to the reading public.

SATYA RANJAN BANERJEE
Quondam Professor of Linguistics
University of Calcutta

19th February,
Kolkatta,

JAINISM

INTRODUCTION

Jainism is one of the great religious traditions of India. Nonetheless, it is little known outside South Asia. For those few who have heard of the Jains, they simply form a part of the fabulous and exotic tapestry of India—an intrinsic part of a dream-like landscape, which over the course of centuries, the West and its imagination have steadily moulded around ideas like "India" or "the East".

It all began with the Greek chronicle. Later came the Phoenician and Roman traders, Subsequently the Arabs, the Portuguese navigators, the Christian missionaries, the German Romantics, the orientalists, the British colonisers, the hippies and flower power people... down to the tourists we see today. Every generation,. including those who travelled to India, and those who never set foot on its soil, have played their part in weaving a tapestry portraying a fantastic, deep, exotic, and distant India. Educated Indians, on their part, have deliberately embellished this picture.

The Indian landscape is replete with luxuriant jungles; rimmed by inaccessible mountain ranges. Here, hot spices and aromatic herbs grow; great elephants, cobras, and Bengal tigers have their dwelling. These are lands scourged by tropical storms and networked by extremely sacred rivers. Among the paddy fields, there are dusky eyes and colourful saris. There have been reports of incredible palaces inhabited by immensely rich maharajahs, whose treasures beam with shining rubies, pearls, and amber. An estimated 300 million gods and goddesses inhabit this land, each with his or her temple, where incense burns incessantly. India, or rather, the Indie *continent,** as an object of desire, has always

* At the present time "India" is identified with a politically and legally defined country dating from its foundation in 1947. However, the place I refer throughout this work is much bigger and incredibly more ancient than the modern nation-state. In fact, until 1947, India was never a nation-state, a concept which is in any case pre-eminently European. The area that I refer to is the Indian civilisation, or if you prefer, that of South Asia (India, Pakistan, Bangladesh, Nepal, Sri Lanka, Bhutan and the Maldives) an extremely complex tectonic plate of humanity which in no way can be reduced to a mere nation. It comprises a myriad of cultures, religions, languages, social groups, ethical values, political notions, etc. Accordingly, in this volume, when we use the terms "Indian civilisation", "South Asia" or "Indian continent" (let us do away once and for all with the *sub*-continental idea) I am not referring to a political entity but rather a civilisational one.

been a constant in the horizon of the Western imagination. Hegel (1837: 272) already observed this was so.

Of course, there are other Indias that have been imagined that are less fantastic or evocative. The India of famines and grinding poverty filth and lack of hygiene. The overpopulated India teeming with boys and girls with no future, flooded by the monsoons and devastated by drought, the scenes of catastrophic accidents, the India mortgaged by social injustice and gender violence, the India of inter-religious conflicts, fanaticism, and war. Indians could be as spiritually trascendent or as incorrigibly superstitious. Although these stereotypes are much later, excessively promoted as they are by media interests and the yellow press, they too have fed into, and helped mould, the images of India we— Indians and non-Indians—continue to create. The mystical and exotic India of the Romantic view contrasts with the ugly India of the Utilitarian view.

Notwithstanding, Jainism rarely forms a part of this miserable, third-worldish and moribund version of India. If it is imagined at all, Jainism is filed, so to speak, under a subheading of the fabulous and prodigious India, the India of wisdom, the India that has long seduced the Europeans. Let us return, then, to the fabulous picture.

At the top of some mountain, on the fringes of a village, beside a river, perhaps within an abandoned temple, extraordinary mystics meditate. Quiet, serene, the archetypes of the anonymous wisdom of the remote past: the yogis with supernatural powers; the priests versed in sacred litanies (*mantras*), the fakir on his bed of nails; the over-zealous holy men, smeared in ashes; the dauntless ascetic, entering into total ataraxy. It is in this last category, that of the proverbial yogis, the Jains fit into. Were not the Jains those mysterious naked philosophers (*gymnosophistés*) that the forces of Alexander the Great (4th century BC) came upon during their Indian campaign?

Alexander's chroniclers deserible the meeting between the commander and a group of holy men, whose wisdom was already legendary at that time. Of the gymnosophist Kalanos, it was said that he was immune to pain and pleasure, and of Dandamis that he did not dare to leave India. The way of life adopted by these naked ascetics, their way of facing death, their indifference to social conventions, all left a deep impression on the Macedonians. Later, the Stoics saw in them the practical culmination of all their theories concerning immunity to pleasure and pain (Halbfass 1988: 435). While not everyone accepts these naked ascetics as Jains (von Glasenapp 1925: 163-165), it remains a likely possibility (Drew 1987: 147). This curious state of affairs: the first Indian monks to capture the West's imagination, were precisely those whom it then forgot almost completely. Even Diogenes Laertius (3rd century) spoke of these wise men, and wondered to what extent they had affected the Hellenic philosophy (Halbfass 1988: 3). There was sparse mention centuries later, from the lips of the missionaries, or some German intellectual, but gradually, the references disappeared. Today, if Jainism appears at all on the West's horizon, it has to do with India populated with strange ascetics that fascinated the Greeks. The initial image formed has endured and remained with us, ever more obscure and lost amidst legends.

I think it is quite legitimate and healthy that fables are spun out of these stereotypes, and the imagination is left to free-wheel. After all, India has long been the land of fables and legends and has always stimulated a healthy vein of day-dreaming. But, at the same time, I think that a measure of correct information would also be valuable. My argument is that knowledge is one of the few cures that we have for healing intercultural respect and for approaching the daunting complexity that is India. Reviewing the clichés in this way is not in any sense a cold, soulless reappraisal of the scene, but rather a more stimulating, deeper comprehension of an extraordinary tradition.

BASIC INFORMATION

On a more prosaic level, this book aims to fill in the gaps, the lacunae of information that we have where this religion is concerned. In following the dynamics and the development of Jainism, I have sought to cover its main aspects: its cosmology, mythology, origins, and transformations, its perception of history, major figures, main religious groups, castes, scriptures, philosophies, ritual practices, and its soteriological ways, aims and objectives, ethics, iconography, connexions with other religious traditions, and sacred geography. What I seek to do is provide a manual of *basic information* for a general readership, not necessarily specialised in this material.

In a world of dialogue, it becomes indispensable to have knowledge of the values and referents of the different cultures on this planet. To understand a society as intricate as the Indian one, knowledge of its religious expression is fundamental. If only for its historical importance, readers should familiarize themselves with the cardinal practices and teachings of the Jains.

DYNAMICS AND HISTORY OF THE TRADITION

The study of other cultures should form a part of the general education provided in schools, and the first thing that should be taught is that, in a planetary situation, dialogue between cultures is totally asymmetrical; it takes place in a Western medium, using a Western language, and in fact the very concept of intercultural dialogue sounds suspiciously Euro-American. Never the less, the rest of the world has no choice than to undergo what is known as westernisation or modernisation (on the ideological, technological, economic and political levels) as ambiguous, and in need of qualification, as these concepts might arguably be. To palliate the effects of ravaging globalisation, a good antidote is precisely the learning and understanding of the "others". This book fosters and expands this understanding. At the same time, the journey toward modernity means that each culture will have to rediscover and reinterpret their own identity.

The entire history, as in the case of any other tradition, has to be seen in the context of continual dialogue with the other; it defines itself, it struggles, it opposes, it is stimulated, and it reconsiders. Let us take a look.

Jainism is an ancient religion, with at least 2,500 or 3,000 years of more or less recorded history, and with infinite aeons of other history, nowadays usually termed "mythical". Originally, the members of this community were known as "bondless ones" (*nirgranthas*), a label which reflects the ascetic nature of this religion. Its historical and mythical leaders were called by the strange name of "fordmakers" (*tīrthaṅkaras*). Fords? Yes, crossing places in rivers that would enable others to cross over to the farther shore of liberation (*nirvāṇa*). A synonym for *tīrthaṅkara* is the word *jina,* which means "victorious", or "spiritual victor" (Monier-Williams 1899: 421). The *tīrthaṅkara or jina* is, one who vanquishes his passions, who rids himself of attachment, who attaines enlightenment, and preaches the Jain path by which others can reach the further shore of salvation. The last of these perfect guides was Mahāvīra (6th-5th centuries, BC), *the jina* of our times. Jainism is, as its name suggests, the religion that these *jinas* gave to the world. All followers of this path marked out by the *jinas* are known as *jainas* or Jains.

At the origin, the Others in relation to which Jainism began to define itself were Vedic Brāhmaṇism and a series of religious groups referred to as Śramaṇic, the foremost of these being Buddhism, and in fact the group to which Jainism itself pertained. For many centuries, Buddhism constituted this other at one and the same time sister and rival, a religion with which Jainism both struggled and learned, and also fed. Later, the Other took the form of devotional Hinduism, especially the Śaiva and Vaiṣṇava persuasions. Then, came Islamic India. In the 19th and 20th centuries, there was the British Raj. Today, Jainism has to respond to modernity and Hindu nationalism. In all cases, Jainism has had to transform itself and create a new discourse. This long history of *interaction* this book. Jainism is not a sacrosanct monolith, but a tradition that has transformed itself in response to the ever-changing social conditions in relation to the Others. It may be, that in its journey to the *new,* Jainism—and Indian traditions as a whole—possesses more resources and capacity for adaptation than we think.

For decades, observers have had the impression that Jainism had reached the fag end of its existence; it was an unchanging tradition with no real developments (von Glasenapp 1925: 163-165), which remained utterly conservative. I hope to show, however, that although the tradition has placed particular emphasis on faithfulness to its principles, it was not and is not as static as it is made out to be. For that reason, I believe that the *historic approach* I have partially adopted, and the incursions into other ways of understanding the religious in other Indian traditions, are clearly relevant. From this point of view, one comes to understand that all traditions are *dynamic* phenomena, in perpetual motion and contact with the others. Only thus, can we realise the value of the immense role played by Jainism in constructing theIndian civilisation. I believe that the study and popularisation of South Asian history has placed too much emphasis on Brāhmaṇic, Vedic and Sanskrit elements, to the detriment of other factors—Buddhist, Jain, Tantric, Hindu devotional, Tribal, Muslim, Sikh and Christian. This work aims to restore Jainism to its appropriate place in the construction of Indian civilisation. Let us look at an example.

The present-day Jain community is not large. It numbers about 4.5 or 5 million practising faithful and has remained within the confines of the country of its birth, India, with just small enclaves of Indian Jains in Africa, Europe, America, and other points of Asia. However, in former times, it was a religion with innumerable followers, especially between the 5th and 12th centuries, when it quite successfully rivalled the other Indian traditions. Its influence on the values and practices of Hindus and Buddhists was considerable. Jainism has, for example, been the religion that put greatest emphasis on such issues as vegetarianism or non-violence (*ahiṃsā*) which are today the heritage of millions of Indians and the Indie religions. The doctrine of *ahiṃsā* gained such prestige that Brāhmaṇism raised it to the status of the cardinal virtue. Its entire system of worship, based on the sacrifice of animals stipulated in the holy scriptures, had to be drastically revised. It is not surprising that the two greatest monarchs of India, the Buddhist Aśoka (3rd century BC) and the Muslim Akbar (16th-17th centuries), were visible proponents of the doctrine of non-violence. Today, Hindu devotional worship (*pūjā*) is invariably vegetarian, and the slaughter of animals has been prohibited in many indian states. Thanks to Gandhi's message, the ethics and praxis of non-violence have reached every corner of the planet.

The above will serve to challenge the widespread cliché—well dissected by John Cort (1998: 3)—that the Jain religion is something like the poor and more or less insignificant relation of Hinduism or Buddhism.

Indeed, if we examine the treatises on South Asian spirituality, Jainism appears—invariably in the *shadow* of Buddhism—when the wave of spiritual unrest afflicting northern India in the 8th-4th centuries BC is considered. The treatises speak of the intellectual and social changes of this crucial time, and of the new traditions of renunciants-of-the-world (*śramaṇas*) lead by charismatic leaders like the Buddha and Mahāvīra. Then, from this point onward, the Jain religion disappears from the treatises. Jainism is identified only with its most ancient formulation and its weight is recognised only as the challenge it represented for the Vedic and Buddhist traditions, some centuries before the Common Era. Authors like Kundakunda (2nd century), Umāsvāti (3rd-4th centunes),

Haribhadra (8th century), Jinasena (9th century) or Hemacandra (12th century), whose genius had a tremendous impact on Indian philosophy and spirituality are not even mentioned. Similarly, neglected is the influence Jainism had on the Gaṅga, Rāṣṭrakūṭa, Hoysala or Solaṅkī dynasties, in the post-Gupta period (middle ages). Scarcely studied, too, are the practices of worship in the temples, or the ideals and practices of the lay community—not to mention the enormous impact that Jainism had on the development of the vernacular languages: Tamil, Kannada, Marathi, Hindi, or Gujarati. Yet another aspect scarcely mentioned, is the powerful influence that Jainism had on Indian literature and art. Moreover, the general tone of many Western scholars borders on the scornful. Jainism is presented as marginal, as being of little to no consequence to modern society; alternatively it is depicted as a washed out, atheist, and irrelevant sect (Hopkins 1898: 296). At best, the only interest Jainism is seen to hold is in its having preserved an archaic, pre-philosophical, and pessimistic vision of the world.

INDOLOGISTS VERSUS SOCIOLOGISTS

Obviously, the real experts know the importance of this tradition. There is a long tradition of Jain studies.

The pioneers were European missionaries and army officers like Thomas Colebrooke, Horace Wilson, Otto Böthlingk, or Father J. Stevenson, who translated the first Jain texts into the European languages in the first half of the 19th century. At the end of that century, came the first serious studies by Indologists and Sanskritists of the stature of Albrecht Weber, Georg Bühler, and Hermann Jacobi. In the 20th century, another generation of scholars like Walther Schubring and Ludwig Alsdorf, contributed to enrich our knowledge. The general introduction by Helmuth von Glasenapp, *Der Jainismus,* published in 1925, represented an important advance in the dissemination of this tradition for the intelligent lay reader. Of course, I am referring to the works of Western authors writing for a *Western* audience. I do not include here the numerous studies by the Jains, so liberally drawn upon by the Indologists.

The next milestone in the dissemination of knowledge of Jainism was the splendid introduction by Padmanabh Jaini, *The Jaina Path of Purification,* published in 1979. The problem with Jainology is the fact that its works tend only to bc known by scholars, and are not so accessible to a common reader.

Most studies of religions tend to concentrate on the spiritual virtuosos and their path (monks and nuns, renunciants, saints and prophets) while tending to forget or dismiss the spirituality of the great majority. Jainism is no exception to this. One only needs to leaf through most of the authors mentioned above to see they have concentrated on Jainism's written tradition, transmitted by ascetic monks whose work is based on the concerns and characteristics of the monastic community. As a result, Indologists have bequeathed us a rather arid, androcentric and ascetic picture of Jainism. With few exceptions, the vision that is offered is excessively concentrated on textual study or on historical details. Significantly, there are many more treatises that deal with the ancient history of the Jains than of the living Jainism of today. The experts have bequeathed us the unfortunate cliché that only ancient India has anything to teach us.

Although the viewpoints of the Indologists and Sanskritists are of fundamental importance in understanding the Jains, they more than any others have encouraged the classical stereotypes attributed to the community: that of their excessive sobriety, austerity and tendency to go in for ordeals. Without denying the importance that asceticism has for members of the community, all of us who have lived with members of this community will agree with me—and John Cort (1991: 213)— that Jains are no less lively than the ever-extrovert Hindus, nor are their rituals less eye-catching or sensual even, than those of their neighbours. There is a yawning gulf between the monastic view of Jainism and the living religion practised by the lay people. The same can be said about Hinduism in general, and hence the great disillusionment of enthusiasts when they travel to India only to find out that the country does not square with what they have read or studied (Said 1978: 122-123)

The language of the historians and Indologists has to be complemented by that of the sociologists and anthropologists, who are able to offer us a more up-to-date picture of the tradition. Textual study is essential to get to know the *religious thought* of a people, but this is insufficient for determining their *religious behaviour.* Precisely, by putting somewhat less emphasis on textual study and combining it with field work, new writers have emerged like Ken Folkert, John Cort, Paul Dundas, Caroline Humphreys, James Laidlaw, Christopher Chappie and Lawrence Babb, who have provided a richer and livelier view of Jainism. I believe it is important to make available anthropological information that explains the tradition as lived by the great majority of its adherents. The Jainism of lay people, let us state this once and for all, *is not* an inferior, dilute or popular version of a true or authentic Jainism practised by the monks and nuns (we could say the same of Buddhism). Lay Jainism is an integral way of life, and is a path for spiritual progress which follows the same lines, in the same direction, as those of their virtuoso ascetic counterparts. However, they integrate the values, aims and traditional metaphysics in a different way.

Although as a general rule I shall maintain the impersonal voice of the Indologists (not because of any presumed objectivity, but as a way of recognising my appropriation of the ideas and evaluations of the experts) and I am equally indebted to the work of the sociologists, this work is based also in my direct experience with different Jain groups in Delhi, Rajasthan, Gujarat, Maharashtra, and Karnataka.

WHAT JAINISM CAN TEACH US

Intercultural dialogue should not lead to a mutual comprehension out of courtesy. The sagacity to learn from and draw on humanity's traditions of wisdom, the next of the purposes implicit in this work. The traditions of India should not just be made known to a wider audience because they are practised by millions of people, or that they represent the world view of millions of people, or because the world has shrunk, but because they have something to contribute to all corners of the world. Jainism can *teach us*.

Asia would not be what it is without the great Jain contribution of non-violence (*ahiṃsā*), channelled marvellously by Buddhism: the virtue of not harming any living being, or more exactly, the righteous state of mind ever mindful not to inflict harm on any such creature nor on oneself. *Ahiṃsā* is the fundamental feature that would characterise the Jain community as a whole and Jainism as a religion. This ethic has inspired all sections of the community for centuries and has served to carry the classic forms of Jainism down to the present. The virtue of *ahiṃsā* is the epicentre of what could be a Jain way of life, and the world would do well to put this virtue in pre-eminent position, and adopt a more Jain-like vision of our environment, human relations and the beings around us. Jain teaching on non-violence constitutes one of the most powerful and committed solutions to the problem of violence in the world.

From the Indian perspective, we take part in the same flow of life *(saṃsāra)*. Nature and society are not in opposition. Simultaneously, India has to take on the challenge of modernisation. And modernism invariably brings with it consumerism, aggressive capitalist viewpoints, the exploitation of the environment, the use of invasive technology, and so on. The future, from a global point of view (an overall anthropological, cultural, environmental, psychological and sociological point of view), is not looking good. Nonetheless, India has its own resources for dealing with these problems, and one of these, resides in the country's renunciant traditions. For many centuries, the renunciants of India (Buddhists, Jains, Śaivas) have preached silently, by example, the virtues of frugality, non-attachment, non-violence and non-consumerism. There are many ways to adapt and reinterpret the ethics and spiritual values of Jainism to help to palliate modern social and environmental ills. A more compassionate attitude to animals, ethically—if not necessarily in dietary terms—more vegetarian, with less attachment to possessions, could bring about much good for society.

Jainism, at the same time, promotes the doctrine of non-absolutism *(anekāntavāda)* a concept that could be translated as philosophical pluralism. A reconciliatory pluralism that seeks to avoid all extremes. I believe that an acute perspectivism such as we find in Jainism could help to bring about a world, an existence, that is more healthy, more understanding and more intelligent. And it could be a good antidote to the tendency, precisely, in many religions, to become hide-bound in dogmas or fundamentalisms of various kinds (Chapple 1993: 93).

What I want to show with these examples is that one can *live* the idea and the practice of non-violence or pluralism in the Jain way. What is more, all those who have familiarised themselves to some extent with Jainism have become Jains *sui generis.* Perhaps, much of Jain teaching may sound strange, distant, exotic and even impracticable. It is not a question of conversion to any religion, or dressing up as saints. I am aware that is not always easy to incorporate an ascetic and soteriological path into our modern and secular contexts. This book is an invitation for each of us to interpret Jainism—or, while we are at it, any spiritual tradition—in a creative and fertile way. It is only by having other reference points that the possibility of revising one's own convictions becomes available.

For me, the experience of Jainism has been supremely enriching. This is an only partially academic book. Above all, it has been my own personal study, the fruit of my sympathy and attunement with many of the teachings of this tradition.

HERMENEUTICS

The learning of other wisdoms is no simple matter. It requires the audacity to surrender ourselves to be taught by others, while yet not renouncing a critical spirit or convictions that we consider valid. I am conscious that reinterpreting the traditions, plucking a little from here and a little from there, could emerge the classic pot-pourri of beliefs *à la carte* without any kind of solid structure. It requires a certain acuteness and intelligence, to know how to discriminate between what we can learn and what will be irreconcilable with our background; and a certain lucidity and imagination so as not to lapse into shallow superficialities or passing fads.

Freeing oneself of Eurocentric modes—whether one is Western or Indian— is a much more difficult task than it may at first seem, but we can open up an intercultural focus that will prove fruitful. To open oneself up and to learn a new "language," we first have to listen to it. For that reason, I also present this work as a point of departure so that readers who are already familiar with Indian religions can move beyond the basic facts. This book is also an *invitation to study* the traditions of India: to study its philosophy, its art, its ways of life, its way of going into the world, its way of leaving the world... in short, its way of engaging with the spiritual dimension of life within Indic traditions and more particularly the Jain tradition. For that reason, I have gone beyond merely providing information or historical facts to give deeper insights and considerations. I have sought to explain the meaning of some of these religious aspects and symbois:

what does this or that goal really mean, how does the tradition perceive its own history, how it can be that a deity is lesser than an enlightened being, what is a sacred text, what feeding a monk means, etc.

Every anthropological, indological, historical, or sociological study of South Asia is a work of *interpretation.* There are points where readers may have the impression that I have forsaken my approach of writing for the intelligent lay reader and have ventured onto ground only suitable for experts. That is not my intention. My basic working assumption is that readers want something more stimulating than a mere compilation of facts. They will want to know about the deeper meaning of the spirituality and anthropology of a civilisation. To do so, they must (if they are not from an Indian or Indologist background) submerge themselves in an unfamiliar world and allow themselves to be impregnated by a mentality that understands things from what is at times a radically different perspective. To be able to interpret the thinking and behaviour of India, it will be necessary to empty the mind of certain constructs, categories, ways of understanding the world or religion, that are typical of the Western traditions.

INTRODUCTION TO JAINISM

A good way of introducing all these considerations is to outline the basic postulates, the scale of values and the fundamental basis from which the Jain religion starts out. Readers who are already familiar with the concepts of Indian thought will find numerous elements in common with Theravāda Buddhism or Sāṃkhya philosophy, two of the most prestigious Indian philosophical systems. My intentions, however, are didactic rather than comparative. Let us put ourselves in the skin of an adult Jain. What will he or she have in their mind when thinking about their religion? What is their cultural baggage?

RELIGION AS SOTERIOLOGY

The point of departure is spectacular. The first maxim of Jainism has it that each and every individual, by their own efforts, without help from the gods, and with the guidance of the teaching of the *jinas,* is capable of making their own way along the spiritual path seeking the highest of goals: liberation (*mokṣa, nirvāṇa*).

The Jain religion does not intend simply that men and women should become integrated into society and the cosmos (a functional aspect of all religion). At the same time, it constitutes soteriology (the mystic aspect of all religion), which intends that the practitioners disengage themselves from the phenomenological world. This point might seem strange to secularists or monotheists, who are unused to conceive religion as a spiritual path or way. Asiatic traditions in general, and the Indian traditions in particular, are difficult to fit into the Western concept of "religion" since, as Frits Staal (1990: 390) has noted, the emphasis is not on doctrines and beliefs, but rather on ritual and mysticism. For Indians, existence is inadmissible without this concern with spiritual progression, purification or the quest for emancipation. This is what India has named *yoga.* Following a typically Indian pattern, Jainism insists that gnostic knowledge together with ethical, ritual and contemplative practices can lead us to the highest realms. What the enlightened *jinas* teach us is not simply *communicable,* it can also be *realisable.*

Historically, the Jains were pioneers in boosting mysticism and *yoga.* Admittedly, they were not alone in this. They acted side-by-side with teachings of the Vedic Upaṇisads, the doctrine promulgated by the Buddha, and the researches and discoveries of other religious groups who would share this revolutionary view of meaning of the life. The interaction between these different vectors was the order of the day, but of all the world's philosophical-religious systems Jainism was the first to map out, in clear bold terms, a path to salvation that was *free from all supernatural intervention.* The *jinas* or spiritual victors were human masters who reached enlightenment (*kevala-jñāna*) or infinite knowledge and preached the path to liberation. For that reason, the Jains do not need God, and are strictly speaking atheists. For someone used to the the-ist environment of Semitic religions, the religious atheism of the Jains and the Buddhists appears frankly impious. Hence, the classical observation that religions that are atheist are not religions; philosophies perhaps. Philosophies?

THE BASIC AXIOM

The aim of Jainism, which it shares with most Indian religions or philosophies, is liberation, release, or spiritual salvation, which Jains tend to refer to interchangeably as *mokṣa, mukti, nirvāṇa,* or *kaivalya.* But, what do Jains liberate or emancipate themselves from? From the condition of alienation or contingency of *being human.* Jains and Hindus in general, aspire to transcend the human condition, to rid themselves of language, to go beyond the bondage which are the ties of this world, and its inevitable consequence— and this, too, is important—of rebirth into another life of attachment.

Indeed, traditional Indie thought has been very averse to limiting the notion of the human being to one life. For classical Indian thought, there is no substantial difference between birth and rebirth. The Jain, the Hindu, and the Buddhist see this existence as just one more in an infinite chain of existences. As many readers will know, rebirth is caused by action (*karma*), particularly those actions committed under the influence of ignorance (*avidyā, mithyādṛṣṭi*) and desire (*kāma, tṛṣṇa*). The question here is obvious. How daes action lead to rebirth? How does reincarnation come about? India has always considered that action, whether physical, verbal, or mental, is not an independent event bereft of consequences. Alls actions leave a seed, a trace, a transcendental effect (*bīja, vāsanā, saṃskāra*), which will appear sooner or later. A key aspect of this question is that the effect is not confined to the present life, but—attached in a subtle way to the agent—continues after physical death, and has transmigration as its most tangible consequence. In the case of the Jain religion, the theory of *karma* maintains that the valency of the action adheres to the soul (*jīva, ātman*) in the form of highly refined *matter,* which casts a pall over its qualities. Action is the cause that returns us again and again to a new contingent life, since the "action" has adhered materially to the agent, condemning it to yet another existence. This materialistic view of *karma* is unique to Jainism. The new existence will be powerfully conditioned by the moral merit (*puṇyd*) and demerit (*pāpa*) of actions in preceding incarnations, and given that all living beings act with attachment and ignorance of their situation, the chain can be extended indefinitely. By extension, the law that governs the whole of this process is called the law of *karma* or law of cause-and-effect, and the wheel of transmigration, *saṃsāra.*

Even though the conditions of the new birth will be determined in part by the quality of the actions committed, there is room for free will (the cards are already dealt, but the player is free to play them how he or she will). Hence, the concept of *karma* does not lead to absolute fatalism and the path of spiritual progress takes on its complete meaning.

This formulation eliminates the necessity of any divine intervention. There is no "fall" to state in which we currently find ourselves. The world is what it is, and living beings are what they are, thanks to the retributive force of *karma.* The formulation is pretty subversive for the Western mind, since it turns out that the inequality of existence is rationally explained by the mechanics of an impersonal law.

This scheme is the origin of the most important soteriologies of India. It was shared, with varying adjustments and shades of meaning, by Mahāvīra, the Buddha, the Vedic sages of the Upaniṣads and an infinity of other Indian masters from the same period. It forms a part of the cultural baggage of the Indian people as a whole.

Who or what is it that transmigrates? Here, Jainism parts company with Buddhism and converges with certain Brāhmaṇic sages. Jainism postulates that the world is teeming with living beings (*jīvas*), the latter being the Jain way to name what Hindus call soul (*ātman, pursuṣa*). Although there are differences here with the Hindu-Brāhmaṇic notion of *ātman,* for the moment it will be enough to say that, according to Jainism, the infinite number of souls incarnate in the different types of living beings, from the most minute bacteria to the men and women of this world. This spiritual conception taking in all living beings provides the backdrop to the Jain doctrine of non-violence. For Jains, these beings can just as easily be human beings, animals, creatures of hell, as angelic beings from the celestial realms. There is continuity between the many and varied forms of life. While *essentially,* the soul is pure consciousness, infinite bliss and unequalled energy, it is trapped within a prison of matter due to the actions committed. Given that the agent acts attached to the mundane, beginning with the body, which *karma* itself has constructed, the state of bondage (*bandha*) is none other than the connection between soul and matter. What Jainism seeks to do is nothing less than free the soul from the cycle of birth and death in the material world. Jains seek to free themselves from the *saṃsāra* conditioned by their own acts. They wish to break out from the prison of eternal corporalisation. To achieve this, they purify their being of all that is foreign to their essential nature. Those who achieve liberation are those who *become one* with themselves: the consciousness uncontaminated by selfishness, language, passion, and ignorance. Being pure knowledge (*jñāna*) and pure vision (*darśana*), actions cease to be rooted in ignorance and attachment, and they become, karmically speaking, innocuous, neutral. This realisation is *nirvāṇa*—literally, "blown", "extinguished" (Monier-Williams 1899: 557). What is it that extinguishes itself? The flame of *karma,* the engine that drives the wheel of transmigrations. Without *karma* to bind them, those who attain liberation leave the cycle of death and rebirth, and thus it is legitimate to say that liberation is emancipation from death (*māra, mṛtyu*). And indeed, how can anyone die who has freed themself from the artificiality of an "I"? Having eliminated any identification whatsoever with the ego (attachments, thoughts, emotions) there is no "me" and no "death", only the *consciousness of being.*

THE PATH

No Indian spiritual tradition fails to mention how one advances towards liberation. What is more, the practical and yogic teachings are always ahead of the doctrinal teachings. What does a Jain have to do, therefore, to achieve liberation? The path that leads to liberation, the Jain path of purification, finds its most concise and abbreviated expression in the so-called Three Jewels (*tri-ratna*): (1) right vision (*samyak-darśana*), (2) right knowledge (*samyak-jñāna*), and (3) right conduct (*samyak-cāritrd*).

To become aware of the state of bondage in which we find ourselves is difficult and arduous. Difficult because of our lack of essential knowledge of the nature of the soul and the cosmos, and arduous because our actions and desires—with the attachment they involve—cloud the pristine nature of the soul, cloud its own clairvoyance (its perfect vision and knowledge), and induce us to act in an ignorant way, fuelling the chain of *saṃsāra* yet again. We find ourselves caught up in a vicious circle. What the Jain path sets out to do, in the first place, is dynamite our ignorance and thus break our vicious circle. With the necessary wisdom it will be possible to combat attachment, and prise the soul free from its attachment to the mundane.

First, the Jain tries to "see" (*darśana*), to have confidence in Jain teachings, which encapsulates the jewel of right vision. Then, the Jain seeks to "understand" (*jñāna*), to eliminate faulty understanding and grasp the full meaning of the teaching. This is the second jewel. Then, there will be nothing for it but to "behave" (*cāritra*) in accordance with this knowledge. To adopt the ethical, ascetic and meditative practices which millions of Jains have followed; and this is encapsulated in the third jewel. This conduct is known as Jain *asceticism* and distinguishes Jains from other religious persuasions in India.

What does this asceticism consist of? To take the correct steps along the path of liberation, Jains undertake a series of ascetic exercises, which normally consist of fasting and dietary restrictions, confessions, penitences, limitation of activities (in the case of monks this will include sexual abstinence and abstinence from possessions) and a series of meditative practices (contemplation, worship of the *jinas)* designed to impede the entrance of more *karma* and burn the *karma* already accumulated. Burn *karma*? Yes. As I have already said, Jainism considers that action literally materialises in the form of very subtle karmic atoms that infiltrate into the soul and weigh it down. So what is needed, then, is to avoid more karmic material entering, and also eliminate the karmic particles already adhering to the soul. What Jains set out to do is to *purify* their soul, cleanse it of the contamination of the ego, the desires, and ignorance. The backbone of this spiritual mastery is non-violence (*ahiṃsā*) toward all living beings, accompanied by the practice of austerity (*tapas*), non-attachment (*aparigraha*) and mental concentration (*dhyāna*). Whoever succeeds in controlling their desires? to the point of *disassociating themselves* from all action, will be an omniscient (*kevalin*), someone who will have burnt all traces of *karma,* and their soul will not have to reincarnate ever again. No longer will they be a human as such, but rather a liberated soul (*mukta*) and a perfect one (*siddha*). With the onset of physical death, the spiritual monad will dwell in its original purity, characterised by infinite consciousness, knowledge, energy and bliss.

OTHER-WORLDLY JAINISM VERSUS MUNDANE JAINISM

Is this spiritual mastery possible? The Indian or Jain response is loud and clear: the search for this perfection is not only possible, but is the only really essential thing in life. Yet it is clear that not everyone can achieve it, or even pursue it. The statistics speak for themselves. There are in India some 11,000 Jain monks and nuns who have renounced the world and devote themselves body and soul to the path. The number of *ascetics* (in the Jain context, more apt a term than monk or nun) is relatively great, but insignificant compared with the millions of lay persons who have not decided upon renunciation. And the immense majority of Jains, rather than seeking liberation, aspire to generate enough religious favour (*puṇya*), sufficient good *karma,* to be reborn as a divinity or a human being, perhaps as a very advanced being who would be able to take the path of the renunciants in a future life. For the rest, Jainism is not just soteriology, and the fact is, it could not just be soteriology, since without the community of lay Jains, which maintains it with donations, the renunciant lineage could not be perpetuated.

At first sight, there seems to be a contradiction between the otherworldly and renunciatory values of the path followed by ascetics who aspire to liberation (the path perfectly idealised in the lives of *the jinas)* and life in this world and the human aims and objectives of lay men and women, who seek religious merit. If to this discord, we add the fact that the Jain lay community is, in terms of wealth, one of the most powerful and influential in India, the question becomes paradoxical in the extreme. How can these two ways of life and two sets of objectives be reconciled? How can we take on board such impractical recommendations as complete non-attachment, radical non-violence, or the stark privations designed to liquidate *karma*? What to do with the ideal of *nirvāṇa*)

As we shall have the occasion to see, the community has devised many tools (ideas, institutions and practices) for the ascetics' path subtly to impregnate lay practice (and vice versa) and for these "impossible" values to find a place in the lives of men and women who have not decided to renounce the things of this world. The recommendations of confidence, wisdom, and conduct prescribed in the Three Jewels, for example, dominate the lives of the lay people in the same way as they do the ascetics, perhaps with a difference of degree. Simply put, the lay population cannot enter into a life fully dedicated to enlightenment, given their excessive involvement in mundane affairs, but if lay men and women do not aspire to liberation in this life, they are nonetheless set on that same goal. Liberation is the beacon that lights up their existence.

For the lay community, rather than *yoga* or a set of theories and doctrines that ought to be put into practice, Jainism is an ethical and ritual tradition? The concern here is to imbue oneself with ascetic values, which is the sure way to generate good *karma* and give depth to the present life. Nor should the soteriological dimension of Indian religions be overly emphasised. Jainism is not only a path to liberation (*mokṣa-mārga*). As John Cort (2001: 9) puts it, *mokṣa-mārga* is an ideology, an universal truth, but the ordinary Indian in the street is less otherworldly than he is frequently made out to be. He or she is as concerned about practical and material needs of this world as a European or an African. It is true, however, that they never forget the ultimate aim of transcending the human condition. But the ordinary Hindu, Jain or Buddhist in the street is in no hurry to reach *nirvāṇa.* They have a long chain of future existences stretching before them to devote to the question.

THE CONCEPT OF RELIGION

Let us return now to the question, which we posed few pages earlier. Is Jainism a philosophy? Personally, I do not think the sketch I have outlined can represent a philosophy. Of course it contains philosophical concepts, but it also has a clear ethical dimension, and a ritual and a social one. It includes a soteriological, meditative and ascetic path which has precious little to do with the Eurocentric idea one has of philosophy. Furthermore, for the great majority of lay people, the philosophical tenets are secondary. Jains do not strictly follow the theoretical premises delineated by their masters, clerics, and scriptures. This feature is particularly strongly present in India, where there is a healthy anarchy between the directives and the religious practices. Thus, it is plain that Jainism cannot be *only* a philosophy. But then, is it a religion?

Naturally, if we restrict the term religion to a belief in God, a revelation through Scripture, a monopoly of the Truth under the aegis of a particular doctrine, plus an obligation to undergo conversion to the faith and reject any otherness, then Jainism clearly is not a religion. I would go further: religions of this type do not exist in most of the world. This definition is a projection of the major features of the Abrahamic religions. In fact, Jainism lacks even a Church, so that the notion of orthodoxy, heterodoxy, or heresy is strictly speaking impossible. Notwithstanding, I think Jainism *is* a religion, and is so beyond etymological considerations of the term "religion" (Latin: *religio*) and the meanings which it would be given by Cicero or Lactantius. The fact that the concept is used inaccurately, and the word often made to apply indiscriminately across the board to any spiritual tradition—see Wilfred Cantwell Smith (1978: 48)—does not, I think, oblige us to eliminate it. I subscribe to the idea that the so-called great religions of the world are nothing more than useful categorisations for the administration and journalistic interest (Larson 1995: 279-280). In my opinion, religion is—like the concepts "culture" , "language", or "society"—a dimension which interpenetrates the individual, the society and the culture, and not a watertight compartment *within* culture, society or personal choice. Obviously, this does not mean that we cannot choose reference points and even be "converted"—if that suits. What I want to say is that, strictly speaking, we are all *homo religiosus.* Jainism is, from this perspective, more than a religion that possesses immutable dogmas, fixed cannons, sacrosanct practices or closed institutions. It is a particular dynamic and dimension of Indian genius, a dynamic that we might call "religious" not because it—etymologically—*re*-binds us with God, but, as Raimon Panikkar (1996: 175) has written, referring to Buddhism, because it *un*-binds, because it liberates.

THE JAIN IDENTITY

Jainism is an intrinsically Indian product, and should be contemplated as such. It possesses innumerable points in common with what has come to be called Hinduism, or the sister tradition of Buddhism, and the fact is that the borderlines between religions are very diffuse in South Asia. Except in the case of the professional religious (ascetics, monks and nuns, clergy, and renunciants) the notion of conversion hardly exists in India.

All of this does not mean that Jainism lacks specific characteristics that make it unique. Jainism is not a stream within a Hinduism river, but one of Indian culture's points of view and particular sensitivities. There is a Jain way of understanding the world, of ploughing the furrow of one's life. More exactly, there are numerous Jain ways of understanding the world and imagining what Jainism itself is. It is not just a case of the tradition bequeathed by ascetic-monks, it is also the tradition of Jain poets, kings, architects, women, philosophers, bankers, farmers and so on. All of these form part of Jainism or Jainisms (Cort 1998: 13). Using the plural here is appropriate, as in India what is more important than the religious labels are the lineage of the masters, the traditions of worship, the divisions and groupings of caste. In fact, many Jains who follow the so-called Śvetāmbara tendency in northern India, have more affinities, points in common with and even affection toward Vaisṇava Hindus, with whom they frequently have matrimonial ties, than with the Jains of the Deccan, who follow the Digambara tendency. However, these observations must not lead us to the typical post-modernist idea that Jainism, given its plurality, does not exist, it is but a category invented by the experts. This is something that is often repeated—with some justification, in fact—about Hinduism (von Stietencron 1989: 32-53), and we will deal with this in due course. In the case of Jainism, it is plain that the Jains have been questioning themselves, and have been asking about what in fact Jainism is, and who the Jains are, for over 2,000 years (Cort 1998: 13).

A NOTE ON LANGUAGES AND ROMANISATION

The oldest Jain scriptures are written in various Prakrit known as semi-Magadhi (*ardha-māgadhī*). Later on, they began using other varieties of Prakrit such as Maharashtri-Jaina (*mahārāṣṭrī-jaina*) or Shuraseni (*śaurasenī-jaina*). The use of Sanskrit was common from the 6th and 7th centuries onward. In later years, Jainism was not averse to using modern languages, such as Gujarati (*gujarātī*), Hindi (*hindī*), Marathi (*mahārāṣṭrī*), Tamil (*tamil*) or Kannada (*kannaḍa*) to expound their doctrines, make commentaries about sacred texts or compose hymns. Following a style much used in modern works—save those for highly specialised purposes—I have chosen to use Sanskrit nomenclature and terminology. Its use brings Jainism closer to the public already familiarised with Sanskrit terms.

For the Romanisation of Sanskrit, I have used internationally accepted forms. I am aware of the fact that the use of diacritical marks may make the reading heavier going, but their use is inevitable if one wants to maintain a certain rigour. Eliminating such mark in Sanskrit is like omitting an accent in Spanish or French. After all, it is rare for a word to become incomprehensible owing to these marks and once familiarised with them it is relatively easy to have an idea of its pronunciation. Even Sanskrit terms, which have been anglicised (such as pundit or brahmin) or have come into English (as karma or yoga) are given in their italicised or current transliterated forms (*paṇḍita,* Brāhmaṇa, *karma, yoga,* and soon).

A couple of pragmatic exceptions need to be taken into account. The first is the treatment given to plurals. Here I follow the Anglo-Saxon rule, that is to say adding an *-s* to the end of the word. Although the formula is not grammatically correct, it is very extended, even in academic circles.

Another exception in the transcription has to do with certain proper names. For obvious reasons of simplicity I have omitted the scientific transcription of place names (countries, states, rivers, cities) or of languages and religions, given that the use of the modern, international form creates no conflict and usually we are dealing with terms that have already come to form part of our general knowledge.

A few recommendations in pronunciation are necessary: *c* is always pronounced like "ch"; *g* is always a hard sound, even when followed by "e" or "i"; *ṣ* or *ś* is pronounced "sh" as in English. As for the rest, the phonetics of Sanskrit vowels are very similar to those of Italian or Spanish. The macron over the vowels (*ā, ī, ū,* the *ō* and *ē* from Tamil) indicates a long sound with grammatical force.

Since I have not followed the phonetic transcription, an additional consideration must be taken into account. The mute *-a* in Sanskrit at the ends of words is not usually pronounced in vernacular languages. In Hindi, Mahāvīra is pronounced *mahaaviir,* the city of Jodha-pura, *jodhpur,* and a Jaina or follower of Jainism is simply a *Jain.* The same applies for a Osavāl(a), a Digambar(a), the practice of *dān*(*a*), and so on.

ACKNOWLEDGEMENTS

I am grateful for extremely helpful suggestions and recommendations from Florence Carreté, David González Raga, Joaquim Martínez Piles, George Kurian and, specially, Javier Rodríguez Ganuza, who is responsible for the book Index. I also wish to recognise my debt to Rajeev P. Jain and Jainendra P. Jain of Moti-lal Banarsidass. My deepest gratitude to David Sutcliffe, who had the arduous task of translating the Spanish original to this slightly updated English version.

Lastly, I should particularly like to express my enormous debt to the sources upon which I have drawn in the realisation of this work. The References bears eloquent witness to this.

Part I
Cosmology

Every society has its way of remembering what it considers important from its past. In ancient India, the task of compiling and registering history fell mainly on the Hindu Epic tradition (Itihāsas) and the Ancient Chronicles (Purāṇas), along with Sermons (Sūtras) of specific religious groups, such as the Buddhists and Jains. The latter also have their Chronicles (Purāṇas) and Biographies (Caritas) that compliment their Sūtras. This huge body of texts, which we could generically call *itihāsa-purāṇa-sūtra,* contains and covers almost all Indian history.

Now, it does happen that the historical sense of these texts is scarce and unreliable. This was already commented upon by the Central-Asian traveller al-Bīrūnī (11th century), without a doubt the most illustrious "Indologist" of ancient times. In a sentence, which now has become famous, al-Bīrūnī (49.208) expresses his frustration at the Indians' sparse historical knowledge and enormous propensity to flights of fantasy:

> "Unfortunately, the Hindus do not pay much attention to the historical order of things, they are very careless in relating the chronological succession of their kings, and when they are pressed for information, they invariably take to tale-telling".

Although, al-Bīrūnī was exaggerating somewhat (after all, Indians had compiled hundreds of Purāṇas and Caritas) it certainly is true that at the first excuse they lapse into storytelling.

The first thing that one notices is that Indian authors never deliberately set out to write "objective" history. It is plain that they only wanted to emphasize on those aspects from their past that they considered basic, even though, these events were not always historically verifiable. These vital aspects did not precisely entail enumerating political events, but in revealing the *mythical* plot of past times in a precise cosmological context. In fact the Sanskrit word *itihāsa* means "tale", "legend", "tradition" or "history", all at the same time (Monier-Williams 1899: 165). This is exactly as in the Greek *historía.* For Herodotus (cited in Klostermaier 2000: 3), the term is simultaneously the record of events and tales or legends. The Indian historiographic sense, like the Greek, is always to be seen within a wider framework, and this is made up of myths of origins, legends from the past and a coherent cosmological and cosmographical frame-work.

This "history" reflects values around which society is organised, codifies beliefs, controls the proper carrying out of rituals... in short, it makes sense of the present. This is what al-Bīrūnī was referring to when he trotted out what he said about "tales".

The absence of a Chinese or Western style historiography has led to the widespread notion that the Indian people do not have a sense of history. Many 19th century Indianists exploited the idea, largely misguided as it was, of the cliché promoted by G.W.F Hegel (1837: 281), that Indians were not just inept at historiography, but that India had furthermore always lain outside history. India was a stationary, vegetative world, without evolution or revolutions, dominated by despotic rulers (Lewis and Wigen 1997: 63-64). In short, the Indian people are fantasy mongers, mystic, a-historic, submissive and irrational, with the good and bad that this entails. In Hegel's opinion (in Halbfass 1988: 2), India had never reached philosophic or scientific levels, these being uniquely and genuinely European achievements. In clear contrast to the Indians are the Westerners, who are scientific, expansive, pragmatic and rational people with a sense of history.

It is true that India has held reason for suspicion, but in no way do they lack the power of reasoning. These stereotypical contrasts drawn between an *Oriental being* and a *Western one* (Said 1978: 61-63) blinds us to the sharply practical sense of Indian sciences (*vidyās*). One only needs to take a look at their sciences of mathematics, grammar, architecture, astronomy, logic, ritual, and philosophy to become aware of this. It also obscures the historical nature (albeit *sui generis)* of the Indians' ancient chronicles.

Indian *history* is that of the enormous cosmic periods, of the birth of the humanities, of the genealogy of their royal houses, of the transmission of their religious lineages, of the deeds of their gods and goddesses, and those of men and women who embodied the ideals and models of wisdom. Tradition called the latter saints (*sādhus*), awakened ones (*buddhas*), victors (*jinas*), not to mention divine incarnations (*avatāras*). In remembering their enlightened ones, saints, gods and virtuous kings, Indians ignore individual peculiarities and latch on to the a-temporal truth these figures embody and represent. For Hindus, their archetype is found in gods such as Rāma, Kṛṣṇa, and the wise seers of ancient times (*ṛṣis*). Buddhists have their model in the Buddha, the Awakened One. The model of the Jains is Mahāvīra, the Great Hero. And if a master (*ācārya*) or preceptor (*guru*) embodies this same truth and same ideals, none in India will hesitate to describe him (or her) as a divinity (*guru-deva*), worthy one (*arhat*) or universal master (*jagad-guru*).

Similarly, political events are only considered relevant if and when they express the same ideal as in mythical times. Kings who identified themselves with Pṛthu, the first monarch to organise the world and human affairs according to the Brāhmaṇic model, or with Bharata, the mythical Jain king who embodied the ideal of universal monarch (*cakravartin*), would then be remembered in a *sūtra* or *purāṇa,* else, they would be forgotten. Just as David Kinsley (1982: 26) pointed out, what is cosmic, eternal, or true is worth remembering; what is merely individual, biographical, and historic, is not. As expressed by Edward Dimock (cited in Kinsley 1982: 26): if an individual's life has cosmic significance, then their private affairs have no relevance, and if their private affairs are important, then the life of this individual is not worth writing about.

We moderns are so impregnated with a sense of history, that the classical Indian perspective seems anachronic, but Indians depend much less on the arrow of time. For that reason, they have known how to preserve and cultivate, more than any other people, a sense of the a temporal, a sense of the timeless. Hence all Indian traditions would say that the order of things (*dhartna*) is immutable, immune to changes of the ages and the passing of time. Perhaps it would be correct to say, after Garma Chang (1971: xiv), that Jainism is, like Buddhism, a *trans*-historical religion. It is not that historical deeds have no value. On the contrary, Jainism gives great significance to history because it is the process needed to achieve the perfection of living beings. *Tradition* always has to anchor itself in the present. As we shall see, Simultaneously, Jainism reminds us that *human* history is not the only significant history, nor is the Earth the only place where history evolves.

Therefore, if we want to be fair to the Jain tradition, we must tackle the subject according to its frames of reference. In the three chapters that make up this part, first [chapter 1] we will talk about the Jain cosmic periods or ages, within which framework their mythical scheme is inserted. Immediately following this [chapter 2] we will describe those worlds where "histories" are to be set. We will then go on to the "biology" of the universe [chapter 3]. Without this cosmological, cosmographical and biological framework traditional Jain "history" lacks meaning. We will leave the lives of *jinas* and the sublime persons of ancient humanities, the only biographies that were really worth remembering, for the following section. The script for the Universal History (the concept in itself is not from Jainism but from the Indological scholarship) as Jainism has conceived it, begins with an introduction to their traditional cosmological framework.

1. COSMOLOGY

THE CYCLIC AND ATHEISTIC VISION

Fundamentally, the stereotype of lacking a sense of history in the Indian people is due to their characteristic way of understanding time (*kāla*) in terms of cycles. For Indians, history is not something unique and unrepeatable. Therefore, it is something which has a relative value. This perception, by the way, which the Greeks along with other peoples from ancient times also had, is common to all Indian systems. It is clear that the cyclic models of Hinduism, Buddhism, and Jainism stem from the same cultural trunk. In all probability, the cyclic theories of time arose from observation of natural rhythms: lunar cycles, the solar year, seasons... as is very well shown in hymns of the *Ṛg-veda* (1.168.2), the most ancient of the Vedic texts. It is the awareness that there is a *rhythm,* an order, that the wise men of the *Ṛg-veda* called *ṛta*; its most authentic expression being found in the annual calendar replete with rites, sacraments, and festivals, which are repeated over and over again year after year.

THE ETERNITY OF THE UNIVERSE

Unlike the Indian vision, the Christian viewpoint is completely linear. Starting with creation, followed by Adam and Eve, then the Jewish prophets leading via Jesus Christ to the final judgement. This escatology has no parallel in India.

In Jain cosmology, the universe has no beginning or end. An infinite repetition of cosmic cycles unfolds. Time is represented by a wheel with six spokes (or eras) that make it turn. When time is ascending, knowledge, behaviour and scope increase in human beings. When time descends, these same barometers dwindle. At the end of each ascendant or descendant cycle, one moves directly onto the next. A complete rotation is known as a *kalpa* [see Fig. A]. Unlike the Hindu conception, there is no period of dissolution of the universe (*pralaya*). After an ascendant cycle (*utsarpiṇī*), there is another descendant one (*avasarpinī*), with no break. Neither is there any divine intervention (Viṣṇu does not descend to reorder the cosmos, destroy the world to later recreate it). In Jainism—as in Buddhism—the wheel spins by itself, eternally. There was not a time when *kāla* did not exist, nor will there be a time in which it does not exist.

The cosmological and cosmographical concepts in Jainism, must have been weaned off the idea of a creator from a very early age. Perhaps, it never subscribed to a creationist solution and aligned with the rationalist, mechanicist tendency in Indian materialism. In the opinion of Jains, change and diversity exist because of simultaneous cooperation of the conditions of time (*kāla*), one's own nature (*svabhāva*), need or concatenation of causes (*niyati*), action (*karma*) and the desire to be and do (*udyama*). All these causes, also known from certain Upaniṣads (*Śvetāśvatara-upaniṣad* 1.2), simultaneously operate on all substance whether material or spiritual. Just as the great philosopher Umāsvāti (3rd-4th centuries) states, the cosmos is a mechanism, with its own uncontrolled and uncreated forces, which permanently transforms due to the origination, destruction, and permanence of what exists (*Tattvārtha-sūtra* 5.29).

JAIN ATHEISM

Understandably, Jains do not accept the notion of a *Big Bang* before which there would have been no time, or the idea of God the creator (*īśvara*) that, just like the Abrahamic one, set the universe in motion at one given moment, *ex-nihilo,* from nothingness. This statement comes from an important, ancient Jain *sūtra:*

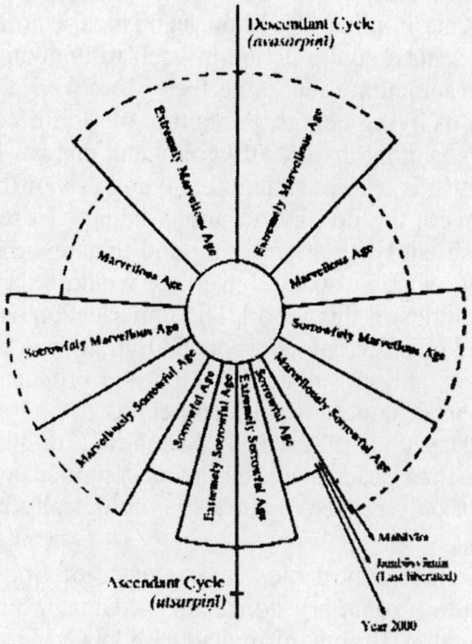

Fig. A: *A rotation or cycle* **(kalpa)** *with the eras of time that make it up. Rotation is in a clockwise direction. The arcs consisting of dotted lines indicate very long periods.*

"Those who on arguments of their own maintain that the world has been created, do not know the truth. Nor will [the world] ever perish" (*Sūtrakṛtāṅga* 1.1.3.9).

No all-powerful Lord has created, governs, nor would destroy the universe. It exists by its own nature, without any support, suspended in space, uncreated, un-governed. History is no drama produced by God, but the result of collective *karma* of living beings. Why should a prime cause intervene? Even accepting that the world is the effect of a prime cause, why should it be intelligent?

Jain philosophers of the style of Jinasena (9th century), Malliṣeṇa (13th century), and Guṇaratna (14th-15th centuries) devoted themselves to biting refutation of the thesis that logically and rationally sustained the idea of an eternal agent of creation and destruction. They had the medieval atomists (the Vaiśeṣikas) and logicians (the Naiyāyikas) in their sights. For the Nyāya-Vaiśeṣika Brāhmaṇic philosophy, God is like a cosmic potter who put the first atomic combination into action. The world is composed of atoms as a material cause and has God as its effective cause. This position, similar to that of Christianity, was to be adopted by quite a few Vaiṣṇava and Śaiva groups. Against this, Jains argued that creation could not come about without the *desire to create.* But, how could it be that a non-creator God suddenly becomes creative? Doubtless as a result of desire... but the desire to create implies a volition, egotistical-emotional activity, imperfection, which represents a contradiction in itself of the notion of God, which by definition should be something that is perfect. Moreover, if the theory of *karma* controls the destiny of living beings, the notion of God becomes unnecessary. If god is incapable of changing the law of *karma,* and this law governs the world in spite of Him, what use is it to postulate the hypothesis of the existence of God? Even if God did govern the destiny of human beings, He would then be shown as a cruel and selfish entity, their suffering and unhappiness being well known. For the same reason, what we would have here would be an imperfect being: as the producer of all things in this world, His imperfection as a creator is clear. If even then we concede the idea of a corporeal God, governor and destroyer of the world, one must inevitably postulate that God is a product, as his activity cannot take place without changes, which compels us to find a cause for God, and so on *ad infinitum* (Dasgupta 1922:1,204). Kumārila (7th-8th centuries), the main philosopher of the Mīmāṃsā system, maintained similar positions. For him, the idea of God was not only repulsive but also ontologically irrelevant (*Śloka-vārtika* 16.68).

The Jain doctrine, not only denies the existence of God, but also rejects the notion of an Absolute (*brahman*), typical of Vedānta, which is the most influential philosophy within Brāhmaṇism and Hinduism. For Vedāntins, such as Śaṅkara (8th-9th centuries) only the Absolute is real (*sat*); the phenomenal world is an illusion (*māyā*). To which Jains interpose: Is cosmic illusion inherent in or different to the Absolute? If *māyā* is real and inherent to the Absolute, all that it produces (ignorance, unorthodoxy, evil) belongs to the nature of the

Absolute. If *māyā* is something different, and has joined with the Absolute (or any of its manifestations) it is right to ask whether this union takes place according to God's will or contrary to it? If it took place according to God's will, then God/Absolute *desired* something, and in that case we are confronted with an impure being. If it took place without consent, then we barely have an omnipotent being. If we believe what scholars of Vedānta suggest—that *māyā* is unreal (given that only *brahman* is real and nothing else exists outside *brahman)*— then between the Absolute and the phenomenal world.

Then, we have those who proclaim that God revealed himself in their texts, against which the astute Malliṣeṇa (13th century) argues:

> "Revelation is done either by him or by someone else. If he has done it, then it proves his omniscience; then his majesty ends up in smoke, because it is not proper of majesties to proclaim their own advantages...
>
> But if the revelation comes from someone else, then it is to be asked whether he is omniscient or not omniscient. If he is omniscient, then they have to be two, an this would, therefore, exclude his uniqueness which was proclaimed before...
>
> But if he is not omniscient, who would trust his words?" (cited in von Glasenapp 1925: 246).

If to these incongruities, we add the countless supposedly revealed texts, all of them contradicting each other, the notion of a "scriptural revelation" (read the Veda, the Bible or the Qur'ān) ends up being superfluous.

Jainism is consistently atheist. Not only does it consider the existence of God or any other external agent incompatible with the law of *karma* but it understands the very concept of a personal God as a product of the ego, and as such, a creation of ignorance (Nahar and Ghosh 1917: 237-238). In short, we are not in debt to any God for existence. Such an idea is a futile invention of theologians. As Hemacandra (*Yoga-śāstra* 4.103) sums up:

> "This *loka* has not been created by anyone; it is not even sustained by anyone."

This radical atheism must be explained in more detail. In the Indian context, an atheist is not what in the West is commonly referred to as an unbeliever. Indian atheists are simply those who do not identify any particular supreme being as a creator or ruler of the universe in particular, but nor do they set out to demonstrate such a being's non-existence or deny the spiritual nature of all beings. Transtheist, as Heinrich Zimmer (1951: 182) suggested, would be a better, or at least less misleading, term. Notice that Jainism has never denied the existence of certain supernatural or luminous beings (*devas*, *devatās*), or certain demonic or titanic beings (*asuras, nārakis*). The word "divinity" to translate *devatā* (Monier-Williams 1899:495) should not confuse us. A *devatā* is not

God. In fact, one of the translations proposed by Ananda Coomaraswamy (1934: 9) is "angelic being", a concept which expresses the nature and position of deities of India better—because these intra-cosmic divinities are not immortal or omniscient. The so-called *devatās* are no more than spiritual monads, essentially identical to the rest, who are provisionally enjoying the merit or spiritual worth that they have gained for their perfect conduct.

As in Buddhism, Jain atheism provides an authentic path to emancipation. If the universe does not depend on any external cause, then human beings are truly *free,* and all action can reinforce the inherent liberty of existence.

THE DESCENDANT CYCLE

There is no Creation in Jainism. In its place, there is an infinite succession of rotations or cosmic cycles (*kalpas*). As we have mentioned, each descendent half-rotation (*avasarpiṇi*) contains six waning ages, and each ascending half-rotation (*utsarpiṇī*) contains six other waxing ages. Since we find ourselves in an *avasarpiṇī,* it would be pertinent to begin with this era.

THE EXTREMELY MARVELLOUS AGE

The first descendant period in the *avasarpiṇī* half-cycle, which is repeated over and over again whenever the descendant cycle begins, is known by the illustrative name of the Extremely Marvellous Age (*suṣamā-suṣamā*). As can be imagined, the Extremely Marvellous Age is the Jain equivalent of utopia: the age of truth and virtue, happiness and joy.

As the happiness of each period is directly proportional to its temporal duration, it is said that this age, the happiest of all possible ages, lasted for the mind-boggling number of 400 billion oceans of years. The unusual concept of "ocean of years" (*sāgaropama*) is equivalent to a hundred million times a hundred million *palyopamas,* and each *palyopama* is an incommensurable period of years. At first sight, it seems totally illogical that a *palyopama* should be beyond all possible calculation, given that its name indicates an uncountable number. If to this we add the scant unity that exists among Jain treatises in this respect, the whole thing gets decidedly tricky,* but the numbers are the least important consideration here. In reality, the *sāgaropama* and *palyopama* are nothing more than an approximation to the notion of *infinity,* A concept which Indian mathematicians have worked with since very ancient times. This would indicate that this type of formulation has to be taken as soteriological rather than

* Some say that the *palyopama* is nothing more and nothing less than the time needed to empty a barn, which measures 15 kms in diameter by 15 kms in height, full of extremely fine hairs, taking one out every 100 years. Truly an uncountable number of years.

scientific. What it means is that the Extremely Marvellous Age was that incommensurable and very distant time when the greatest happiness abounded.

To express human happiness and virtue in each of its ages Jains resort to other rather unusual measures: height, number of ribs, and human longevity. In the Extremely Marvellous Age, humans measured nearly 10 kilometres in height, they had 256 ribs and they lived for up to 3 *palyopamas.*

Life conditions were those of utopia. When people wished for something, they only had to go to the fantastic "trees that fulfilled desires" (*kalpavṛkṣas, kalpadrumas*), which supplied every need. One tree yielded health and happiness. Another bestowed all kinds of food and drink. A third tree gave delicious fruit. Another, marvellous music. A fifth tree illuminated darkness. Another tree flowed with out-of-this world jewellery. Another, shelter, pots and pans and other useful things. There was a tree that made people beautiful. And one outstanding tree that shone like the Sun, meteorites, and fire. There was no need to plough the land or hunt animals. The water in the rivers was sweet and refreshing. There were no social differences or political authority, no religion, family, illness or poverty. Births were always twins (girl and boy). After a few weeks, the twins lived as a couple and procreated another set of twins. Accordingly, in the pre-social times of humanity, not even incest was taboo. A very short time after the birth of a new generation, the previous one would disappear. Overpopulation was unheard of. In fact, India was then called the Land of Enjoyment (*bhogabhūmi).* Heaven was here on Earth.

THE MARVELLOUS AGE

The second descendant age is known simply as the Marvellous Age (*suṣamā*) and was exactly half as happy as the previous age. Logically, it lasted somewhat less: 300 billion oceans of years. Human height descended to 6 kilometres, the number of ribs decreased to 128 and life span decreased to just one *palyopama.* While human appetite increased, the trees that fulfilled desires continued providing every need for a happy existence.

THE SORROWFULLY MARVELLOUS AGE

The third period of the cycle is known as the Sorrowfully Marvellous Age (*suṣamā-duhṣamā*) and, as one can suspect, things got worse, conditions deteriorated. Human height decreased, the number of ribs decreased, as well and life was shorter. Even then the water in the rivers continued to be delicious and the magic trees had not run out of good things. When they died, human beings went to the heavens of the gods, but little by little, rebirths as human beings and animals began to occur. This meant that the goodness in the people had declined considerably. Hate, greed and conflict had appeared on the face of the Earth. Given that this disorder began to spread, people decided to join together in families (*kulas*) beneath the direction of family heads (*kulakaras, manus*). These proto-rulers established rights, punishment and property limits, and in short took care of the maintaining of law and order. Progressively the magic trees stopped fulfilling people's needs, and people began to struggle amongst themselves over food, work and shelter. Each *kulakara* had to teach human beings new knowledge to make up for the absence of the magic trees. It is said that the last *kulakara,* one Nābhi, taught people how to plant and harvest fruit. It was around this time that it rained for the first time in this cosmic cycle. The mythical history of Jainism, the Universal History, explains that Nābhi's son was the *tīrthaṅkara* Ṛṣabha. The concept of the *tīrthaṅkara,* which we have already come across in the Introduction, is of the greatest of importance.

THE *TĪRTHAṄKARAS*

Jainism speaks about 24 fully enlightened beings who showed the Jaina path, the first of whom was Ṛṣabha [see FIG. 33]. The apparition of the first *tīrthaṅkara* in the Sorrowfully Marvellous Age implies that virtue had decreased to such an extent that a spiritual guide was necessary. But, what is a *tīrthaṅkara*?

In India there are certain places, usually rivers—although occasionally forests, temples and mountain tops also—which are known figuratively as "fords" (*tīrthas*). It is thought that deities descend to these places and that from these places transit beyond the conditioned world is relatively much easier. According to Jain thought, *tīrthaṅkaras* are makers (*kāra*) of the ford (*tīrthd*) by which everyone else can cross the river or ocean that leads to liberation (*nirvāṇa*). In other words, the *tīrthaṅkaras* were those who crossed to the farther shore from the phenomenal world (*saṃsāra*), and indicated the path so that everyone might liberate themselves. loan Couliano and Mircea Eliade (1990: 205) have underlined the similarity between the Sanskrit *tīrthaṅkara* and the Latin *pontifex,* which appears to mean "bridge maker". The *tīrthaṅkaras* are, in summary, the guides of Jainism.

As we have seen, *tīrthaṅkaras* can also be called conquerors or victors *(jinas).* Jains must also overcome *karma* in battle and conquer passions. Those who have achieved this are the perfect ones (*siddhas*), worthy ones (*arhats*), omniscient ones (*kevalins*). The perfect ones that showed the world how to do the same, are the *tīrthaṅkaras* or *jinas.*

Jain scriptures remind us over and over again that these omniscient ones were human in every way. They are not to be treated as gods or divine incarnations, but as virtuous human beings who, thanks to their prolonged efforts over many lives, achieved the condition of *jina.* This poses no obstacle for tradition to venerate them with the same admiration and honour as others when they pray to their gods. It is the *tīrthaṅkaras* (and to a lesser extent the ascetics who emulate them) rather than the gods, who define and focus Jain worship and delineate the ideal to follow.

To what extent are *tīrthaṅkara* to be seen as sublime? Every *jina* is quite simply perfect. It is said that they possess superhuman cognition, their breath has the fragrance of lotus flowers, they have awesome bodies, with a diaman-tine constitution (needed to support the rigours of asceticism) and endowed with the 1,008 auspicious marks of a sublime being. Eight marvellous signs (*prāti-hāryas*) accompany them all the days of their lives, wherever they go: a throne, three parasols, showers of flowers that rain all around them, a drum, a divine halo or aura, a magic sound, numinous geniuses who accompany them with fans, an emblematic tree that is always close by and celestial music that can be heard in their presence. *Tīrthaṅkaras* can also be recognised by other signs, the result of their absolute non-attachment: they remain sitting in a lotus position (*padmāsana*) or standing (*kāyotsarga*) always impassive, immobile, totally indifferent to what is happening around them [see FIG. 1]. They never frown or smile, joke or get angry. They are not attached to anybody or anything, they do not need masters or preceptors. They do not hate anything or anybody. They know no fear. They overflow with compassion and show no trace of sexual appetite. They can live without food, they never sleep, and their eyes do not even blink. Their hair and fingernails do not grow, and their bodies do not cast a shadow. Thanks to their omniscience, they oversee everything in all four directions; they make plants and trees grow in all seasons; the sound "victory, victory!" (*jaya, jaya*) echoes in the space surrounding their presence; they reduce to nothing any violent tendency in those who come near; they impede droughts and famines within a radius of 800 miles; they speak a multitude of tongues... In short, *tīrthaṅkaras* are those who, after annihilating the last trace of passion and selfishness, have become one with their deeper spiritual essence and, in consequence, emanate the power of absolute knowledge and have bodies which reflect their inner purity.

The biographies—or better, hagiographies—of the 24 *tīrthaṅkaras* or *jinas* are exemplary and fabulous. All such beings were conceived and born into royal families (Kṣatriyas). Later, they would renounce the world, dominated action (*karma*), thanks to asceticism (*tapas*) and meditation (*dhyāna*), and would have achieyed full enlightenment (*kevala-jñāna*), from which there is no turning back. After escaping from the cycle of death and rebirth (*saṃsāra*), each one would have expounded the eternal doctrine (*dharma*), re-establishing Jain-ism in the era in which they had to live. When they felt death approaching, they would have retired to the summit of a mountain, where after a final meditation, their luminous soul was extinguished (*nirvāṇa*). Their spiritul monad (*jīva*) left their body and ascended to heights of the heavens, never to be reborn again. As we shall see, these traces are duplicated in Māhavīra's biography that echoes in the depths of the ages.

A similar idea would, possibly somewhat later, also be used by Buddhists (Parrinder 1970: 181), proclaiming a series of 25 previous *buddhas* to Gautama, the Buddha. Professor Bhagchandra Jain (1972: 22-23) has shown that many of the names of these ancient awakened ones (*buddhas*) and solitary awakened ones (*pratyekabuddhas*) proclaimed by Buddhism correspond to the

Jain *tīrthaṅkaras.* According to Dines Sircar (1971: 37), the important later Hindu doctrine of the incarnations (*avātaras*) of Viṣṇu similarly seems to be derived from the Jain notion of the 24 *tīrthaṅkaras.* This makes sense: the message that Mahāvīra expounded was for his followers the only Truth *(satya),* the path that leads to final emancipation. Just as in the Veda of the Brāhmaṇas, this Truth must have existed from the beginning of time. It was extremely unlikely that it had not been discovered until Mahāvīra came along. Therefore, Jainism understood that this Truth, the Jain doctrine, was realised and revealed by *tīrthaṅkaras* in different cosmic eras for the benefit of generations of humans. In one sense, Jains replaced the notion of a Supreme Lord (*īśvara*) with this infinite and uninterrupted succession of human masters (Jaini 1978: 15). Furthermore, the formulation emphasises the antiquity of Jainism, something that Jains have maintained with ardent insistence. In which case, Jainism would be prior to any Indian religion, and more particularly, prior to the Veda, the body of scriptures of the Brāhmaṇas. That is if we do not opt for the view of Hemacandra (12th century), for whom the Veda was originally expounded by the emperor Bharata (son of the *jina* Ṛṣabha) and consisted of hymns to the *tīrthaṅkaras,* which unscrupulous Brāhmaṇas would later pervert (cited in Fynes 1998: xxv). In one way or another, Jainism is advanced as the true eternal religion (*sanātana-dharma),* periodically propagated by the *tīrthaṅkaras.* This Truth may be forgotten from time to time, but with the apparition of a new *tīrthaṅkara,* it would once again be expounded and practised. Human insignificance and meaningless seen against these gigantic scales of infinite time are abolished, given that the *tīrthaṅkaras* proclaim the possibility of liberation from reincarnation (Thapar 1978: 253). For this reason, the *tīrthaṅkaras* are the real protagonists of the Universal History. When devotees visualise them, they bring a piece of eternity into their lives.

THE MARVELLOUSLY SORROWFUL AGE

Let us continue with the descendant cycle. In the fourth age, the painfulness and unpleasantness of existence outdoes the happy aspects. It is known as the Marvellously Sorrowful Age (*duhṣamā-susamā*) and it lasted almost 100 billion oceans of years. Human height was much less. They only had 32 ribs and their life span had diminished considerably.

In spite of the unhappiness of this period, it is when the other 23 Jain *tīrthaṅkaras* who once again proclaimed and spread the eternal religion lived and preached. Not only these superior beings, but also a series of traditional heroes from stories in the Universal History, who in all represent a total of sixty-three sublime men (*śalākā-puruṣas*), who stood out in these intermediate ages of the cycles. According to Jain chronology this age ended exactly in the year 522 BC. Mahāvīra, the last *jina* achieved liberation just 3 years before the beginning of the fifth age.

One main fact in Jain cosmology is that liberation is only possible in the 3rd and 4th periods, precisely when the *tīrthaṅkaras* lived. In these intermediate periods (neither excessively happy nor too sad), is when human beings have unsatisfactory and reasonably short lives, but enough for them to be able to grasp the impermanence of things and the alienation of existence, necessary conditions to urge men and women to accept the Jain ascetic path. Therefore, although these lesser marvellous ages do not have the Utopian nature of the previous ones, they possess the insuperable value of allowing the unconditioned state *(nirvaṇa).* An obvious corollary of this idea is that gods and angelic beings that live in the bliss of heaven do not have the sufficient amount of dissatisfaction or the short lifespan needed to aspire to liberation. In conclusion, *nirvāṇa* can only be achieved on coming from a human rebirth.

Jains believe that numerous followers of these *jinas* reached enlightenment during these periods. They are known as omniscient ones (*kevalins*), perfect ones (*siddhas*), and worthy ones (*arhats*), but not *jinas.* The reason is not only the fact that they did not become propagators of the Jain doctrine but that except in cases of solitary awakened ones (*pratyekabuddhas, svayamsiddhas),* all of them needed the help of the *jina* to achieve the perfect condition.

THE SORROWFUL AGE

The fifth period, which is the one we now find ourselves in is known as the Sorrowful Age (*duhṣamā*). As an indication of the unhappiness in these times, it is said that they would only last for 21,000 years. This number is exactly the space of time that, according to the *Vyākhyā-prajñāpti* (20.8 [792a]), Jain wisdom would survive. The longevity of human beings has decreased in a spectacular way, as has their constitution. In this age, there are now no more *tīrthaṅkaras* or sublime beings, nor will anyone achieve the highest goal, liberation, without having gone through another human rebirth. It is related that the last liberated person on this Earth was the saint Jambūsvāmin, who reached the *summum bonum* around 460 BC, according to traditional chronology. The present-day mission of the community is, to maintain contact with the times of the *tīrthaṅkaras.* In spite of the fact that these awakened ones are now no longer among us, their teachings can continue to be transmitted thanks to the ascetic community that traces its lineage back to Mahāvīra. It is because of this, the masters who emulate them (*ācāryas, upādhyāyas,* and *sādhus*) are also known as "supreme ones" (*parameṣṭhins*).

Even though, at the beginning of this era, things were not intolerable (not in vain did Jambūsvāmin liberate himself a short time after its commencement) we find ourselves now in a ramshackle intermediate phase. Inevitably, the world will go on deteriorating. The cities will be like crematoria (for Indians impure and chaotic places par excellence). Governors will be cruel as Yama, the god of death. Corruption will overrun politics and justice. Material wealth will be the only source of devotion. People will turn their back on morality. Disciples will not obey their preceptors. The gods will refrain from visiting the human world, and little by little, an unquestionable sign of the general deterioration in this Sorrowful Age, we shall see the gradual disappearance of the Jain religion. This conception of eras of a successive deterioration of things, evidently resembles the Buddhist idea of the gradual decline of Buddha's doctrine, along with the Hindu notion of the successive eras of decadence that lead up to the present Corrupt Age (*kali-yuga*) of misery and chaos (*Viṣṇu-purāṇa* 4.24). Again, what we have here is a recurring pattern that runs through all Indian cosmologies.

This notion shows that the conception of time is not only cyclical, but what is truly relevant in the ages that make up these cycles is that there is a change in the quality of morality in each of them. Given this perception, one can explain, even if simplistically, the situation of suffering in our contemporary world.

THE EXTREMELY SORROWFUL AGE

The present Sorrowful Age will lead on to the final descendant era, the Extremely Sorrowful Age (*duhṣamā-duhṣamā*), which will also last for 21,000 years. People will only measure 45 centimetres, they will not have more than eight ribs and they will not live for more than 20 years.

With a sharp futuristic instinct, Jain theologians have not skimped in describing these future eras. There is a desolate landscape. There will be no milk, fruit, mangoes, or flowers. Days will be unbearable, beneath the burning Sun; the Moon will give off insufferable cold temperatures and there will be frozen nights. People will live in caves, scavenging fish and tortoises. Hunger and illness will take hold on society. The rule of the strongest will prevail. The last Jains will die four years before the cycle comes to an end. When the limit of chaos is reached the descendant cycle will be detained and the ascendant cycle will commence. Since the cycle began, the chilling number of 100 million times, 100 million oceans years (*sagaropamas*) will have passed, and this is only half a complete rotation.

THE ASCENDANT CYCLE

The ascendant phase of the cycle will begin with five floods, a universal symbol of the influx of chaos and of a new beginning. The first era will be just as extremely sorrowful as the previous one, and will also last 21,000 years. But as it advances through time things will begin to get better. Little by little, the Earth will return to having flowers germinate and human beings will grow in all senses. Then, in the next Sorrowful Age, human beings will leave their caves, stop hunting turtles and eating fish by reinstating vegetarianism. In this way we shall reach the third age of the ascendant cycle, during which the *tīrthaṅkaras* and sublime beings will reappear. The first saviour will be Padmanātha, who will again announce the arrival of the Jain religion. The Truth, the Jain religion, as we know, is eternal.

The future *jina* Padmanātha will not be alone in proclaiming the eternal truth: if we recur to traditional Buddhist cosmology, we find that he will be contemporary to Maitreya, the future *buddha.* A brief comparison between the *bud-dha* Maitreya and the *jina* Padmanātha will clearly show the similitude and the difference there is between Buddhism and Jainism.

For Buddhists, Maitreya is provisionally enjoying celestial bliss until the moment comes to be born again as a *buddha.* On the other hand, Padmanātha, who is none other than the reincarnation of king Śreṇika of Magadha, contemporary to Mahāvīra, is expiating his bad *karma* in hell owing to his committing suicide when depressed, after his son had taken over the throne. Meanwhile, Maitreya is a *bodhisattva* (one "on the path of buddhahood"), an extremely sacred being for Buddhists everywhere, the object of popular worship. Jainism, on the other hand, has not developed any kind of worship for its future *jina.* Even in the case of Padmanātha being in heaven he would not merit better treatment than what is reserved for a mendicant ascetic. All this has much to do with the special relationship that Jains maintain with their *tīrthaṅkaras,* a matter which we shall be looking at later on in the book. The *tīrthaṅkaras* are so free from attachment that they disregard any prayers or petitions from their devotees.

After Padmanātha will come Suradeva. Again, the succession of *tīrthaṅkaras* will continue up to the 24th and last one, Svayambuddha. Sublime beings will again appear, beings such as the 12 *cakravartins,* nine *vāsudevas,* nine *prativāsudevas* and nine *baladevas,* to complete the total of 63 excellent men in the Universal History. Human beings will again grow in size, magic trees will reappear. The successive eras of ascendant happiness will lead to the completion of the *utsarpiṇī* cycle. The wheel of time (*kālacakra*) will continue turning toward the beginning of a new descendant cycle, and so on to infinity.

* * *

This vision of eternity in perpetual rotation, drawing souls down to be reincarnated as different forms of life, is something that can only be detained by liberation. To this end, there is the universe and eternity: by their means souls trapped in this cycle can free themselves to become fully liberated. This teleological position is quite close to the Brāhmaṇic Sāṃkhya philosophy *(Sāṃkhya-kārikā* 57). The inanimate would seem to exist so that the soul can be aware of itself, of its loneliness or complete isolation, and can achieve liberation.

2. COSMOGRAPHY

THE WORLD VIEW

The stage where the Universal History takes place is the cosmos (*loka*). For Jain philosophy the cosmos is a reality and is called substance (*dravya*), and the Jain view of this cosmic substance is also very singular. Normally, it is said that the universe is a three-dimensional space formed by three worlds (*tri-loka*), but in reality it is made up of four: the Lower World, Middle World, Upper World, and Abode of the Liberated Souls [see FIG. B].

Beyond the cosmos, there are three atmospheric membranes with increasingly rarefied airs. Beyond that the infinite, the ultra-cosmos or non-world (*aloka*), which surrounds the universe. The texts are not precise about what this impenetrable void is like (*Vyākhyā-prajñāpti* 1.6 [78b]). Here, there is nothing except, apparently, hurricane winds.

Jains have been pleased to conceive this universe in iconographic terms as various objects: a drum, cymbal, boat, etc., where each piece represents the different fractions or worlds of the cosmos (*Vyākhyā-prajñāpti*: 11.10 [521b]). From the 16th century onward, it became common to represent the cosmos as a Cosmic Being (*Loka-puruṣa*), frequently with the body of a woman [see FIG. 2]. Although this representation as Cosmic Mother is late, it is nonetheless a reflex of the classical notion of the "mother" who carries the world in her body. But this is a mother without a spouse, without a male. The Jain universe is not the result of the union between a cosmic couple along the lines of Tantric Hinduism, nor does it exist by virtue of some "golden embryo" (*hiraṇyagarbha*) as in Brāhmaṇism. The Cosmic Being is simply the organism, which comprises all life and matter, the spiritual (*jiva*) and the non-spiritual (*ajīva*). The *Lokapuruṣa* is identical to the universe, uncreated and indestructible.

THE MATHEMATICS OF THE COSMOS

Three important works that describe the traditional vision of the cosmos are the *Bṛhat-saṃgrahanl* by Jinabhadra Gaṇi (6th century), the *Jambūdvīpa-saṃgrahaṇi* by Haribhadra Sūri (12th century), and Candra Sūri's *Trailokya-dlpikā* (13th century). These authors deployed enormous mathematical rigour in calculations and measurements of the different parts of the Cosmic Being. They spatial units such as the *yojana,* which is roughly 15 kilometers, or the string (*rajju*), which is the distance covered by a divinity in six months' uninterrupted flight at a speed of two million *yojanas* per second. For Collette Caillat (1981: 20) this would represent some 10 million leagues. I rather tend to think it would be a very much greater distance than that. At all events, it is reminiscent of the light year employed by present-day astrophysicists.

For Digambara Jains, the universe is of a precise size: 14 strings high, with a volume of 342 square strings (somewhat smaller for Śvetāmbara Jains). Statistics of this sort, like the cycles of time, that seemed pure fantasy to the European scholars and missionaries of the 19th century, have a powerful psychological and soteriological value. What matters to the Jain cosmologists is to emphasise the utter immensity of the cosmos, and the singularity of human destiny. Thus, it would be foolish in the extreme to waste human incarnation, the only one that offers us the possibility of liberation.

The technicalities of Indian cosmography, which we need not go into here, do not set out to describe the universe scientifically, but rather to describe it *cos-mologically.* In other words, they do not try to describe the abstract laws of the universe, but to provide a framework or context into which life and people's spiritual path can be placed.

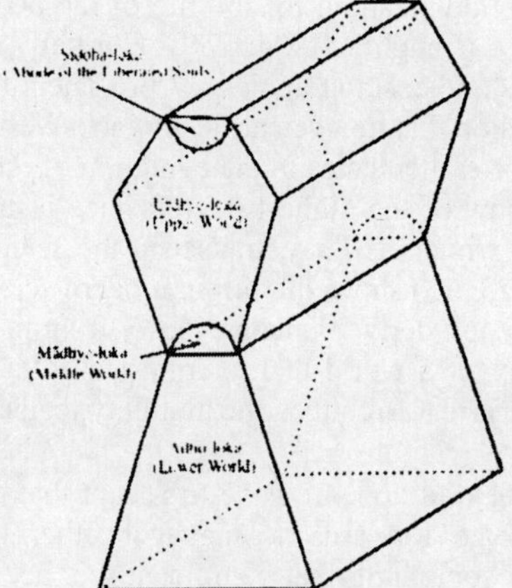

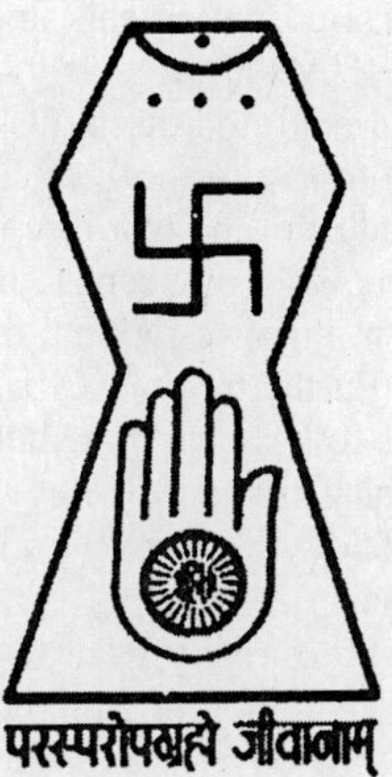

FIG. B (left): *The Worlds of the universe according to the traditional conception.*

FIG. C (right): *The* Jaina pratīka, *the symbol of the Jain religion adopted in 1975. In the palm of the hand is inscribed the word* ahiṃsā. *The* svastika, *the three dots and the half Moon symbolise respectively the four possible births, the Three Jewels* (triratna) *and the Abode of the Liberated Souls.*

Jainism invariably speaks of a moral universe in which symmetries can be established with spiritual progress. The cosmos is conceived in relation to the organisms which dwell therein; thus, rather than a coldly static cosmos, we have to do with a living universe, with a living superorganism. It is not the physical description which counts, but the destiny of human beings and other beings. The task in hand is always to provide a general sketch of the cosmos and its immensity, within which souls transmigrate from one bodily situation to another. In other words, the *loka* is the stage, almost infinite as it is in extension, where the continual flow of incarnations in infinite cosmic cycles take place. The beings in their becoming, affect it and qualify it constantly. Ethics, via the doctrine of *karma,* are an integral part of physics and metaphysics. Whether this vision corresponds to the facts is not important, provided it serves for what is really important: preparation for the non-conditioned state or *nirvāṇa.* For this reason, in 1975 the Jain community adopted a stylised representation of the *loka* as the symbol of their faith [see Fig. C]. Recently, the community has constructed scale replicas of the Jain cosmogram in Hastinapura and Palitana. This fact reflects the enormous significance that this concept holds for Jains.

This is an important point to grasp. We need to have the courage to admit that modern scientific cosmology is only one of the possible cosmologies, however precise it might be. In fact, science's vision of the world would need to be termed quasi-cosmological, since it does not provide meaning for the life of the people who live in the cosmos which is depicted (Laughlin 1994: 259). Normally, the rational mind discounts other cosmologies and cosmographies as "pre-scientific", not to say "primitive". There is an impression that non-scientific and non-Western models of the world represent backward or earlier states in the evolution of ideas. This is a ethnocentric and reductionist view of the highest degree since it judges in empiric-rational terms cosmologies which, as I say, transcend the scientific. Furthermore, as Alfred Whitehead (1925: 13) showed, faith in modern science has to be seen, nonetheless, as a phenomenon derived unconsciously from medieval Christian theology. The very concept of a world that is empirically knowable derives from the Christian idea of the Great Architect, the almighty legislator God.

If we really want to understand another tradition, we have to accept that other cosmologies and cosmographies can go forward in languages other than that of physics and mathematics. This is something that significantly is accepted by leading-edge scientists. Knowing that they do not possess the monopoly on knowledge and that scientific cosmology is always *provisional* (hence its strength) many have recovered other forms of knowledge: art, symbols, intuition. And such is the case of India, where, cosmologically speaking, soteriolog-ical language is what prevails. Forms of language where arithmetic yields to metaphysics, in the words of Colette Caillat (1981: 32). As Frank van den Bossche (2007: 1) has shown, Jainism is very holistic; it organises all elements of the human and non-human world into an integrated whole of which cosmography and geography are fundamental parts. Emphasis is put on the place and the spiritual situation of the beings that inhabit the cosmos, and not on its atoms. The *loka* is a web upon which human life can be structured and make complete sense. This, in turn is no reason why Indians, and Jains in our particular case, cannot subscribe to modern cosmology for their everyday lives, at the *same time* as they maintain the symbolic, traditional cosmology, which is what provides meaning to their spiritual dimensions. This typically Indian agility in changing register offers a richness, which ought to be emphasised. Indians can be in two worlds, in two universes of discourse, simultaneously. Science and myth can be complementary explanations, provided that no dogma is made out of either. And this is something that Indians, familiar as they are with the paradoxical nature of reality, are completely comfortable with. In India, unity of thought has never been held up as a virtue—and proof of this is that no ideology or philosophy has ever cornered the monopoly of the truth. The paradoxical, the contradictory, the plurality of approaches, are valued. Given the tendency to swallow up and assimilate everything, Indians coexist with astonishing familiarity with logical and spiritual thought, myth and science, the rational and irrational, the traditional and the modern.* Taking the retro-progressive model put forward by Salvador Pániker (1987: 39), it could be said that Indians are paradigmatically retro-progressive, the simultaneous movement toward the new and the old, toward complexity and toward origins. As a result, the Indian people have shown themselves much better prepared than the Biblical ones for assimilating the chronological mutation, which the scientific evidence of Darwin and of astrophysics have visited upon us in this modern world.

THE LOWER WORLD

The Lower World (*dho-loka*)forms the lower limbs of the Cosmic Being. It is the vastest of all the worlds. It consists of seven infernal levels (*narakas*) where dwell the foetid demonic beings (*nārakis*). The images are more terrifying as one goes down. The mildest hells are places of fire, the direst are of pure ice. The living conditions are miserable, the stench is pestilential, hunger and thirst prevail. These levels are inhabited by those who, having committed truly criminal and perverse acts, accumulated *karma* that ensured them rebirth as *nārakis.* When they are not beset by titans (*asuras*), they spend their day inflecting torments

* India maintains values, references and visions rooted in Brāhmaṇic, Jain or Buddhist antiquity, alongside values and so on deriving from Islamic, Christian or Anglo-Indian modernities. Not one of these layers has replaced any of the preceding layers. All of the phases of Indian history have been kept up. Seemingly, only Europe feels the need to eliminate traditions, forms of worship, beliefs, customs or languages in the name of so-called progress. The majority of civilisations, and Indian civilisation in particular, have tended to amalgamation.

on each other (*Tattvārtha-sūtra* 3.4). Some hang from tridents, some are roasted over a slow fire; there are those who have a millstone hung from their neck and are thrown into water (*Sūtrakṛtāhga* 1.5.1.9-12) or who are crushed in a sugar mill or devoured by wild dogs (*Uttarādhyayana-sūtra* 19.53-55). Ofentimes, the torture fits the crime. Adulterers have to couple with incandescent copper statues of women, meat eaters are obliged to eat the minced flesh of their own bodies and drunkards are forced to drink molten lead. Quite a number of Jain manuscripts contain illustrations that show the aggression and suffering one is subjected in the infernal regions. It is said that the seventh inferno is so unspeakable, the suffering so great, the horrors so abominable, that no women is capable of sinning so intensely as to be reborn there. Only men—and certain fishes!—are capable of visiting such horrific regions.

The levels above the first hell, known as Ratnaprabhā, are also inhabited by a type of semi-divine being known as "residents in mansions" (*bhavanavāsīns* [see page 49]), able to move between the Lower and Middle worlds.

Given that all is subject to the impersonal law of action-and-retribution, no one is condemned to live eternally in these hells. What is more, despite the horrors suffered in these Dantesque regions, *nārakis* do not retain the individuality, humanity or personality of their former existence. They are, in fact, other beings, or rather the same spiritual monads (*jīvas*) incarnated in low and unworthy forms. It may be that one *nāraki* or other will remember the actions that brought about their current condition, but in general they are in a state of total ignorance and attachment. Fortunately, their condition is provisional. Recall that Padmanātha, the future *jina* of our world, is expiating his bad *karma* in the seventh hell. Even the most evil beings will have their opportunity for better reincarnations. If it has to be a human being or an animal with five senses (which is obligatory for *nārakis,* since consecutive rebirths in infernal regions are not possible) this will take place in the Middle World.

THE MIDDLE WORLD

Indeed, humans and animals can only be reborn and carry out acts in the Middle or Intermediate World (*mādhya-loka*), iconographically situated at the waist of the Cosmic Being. Unlike the other worlds, the Middle regions are represented as a disc seen frontally [see Fig. 3]. It is the smallest of the worlds, but undoubtedly the most important. Here, live humans and the animals; *tīrthaṅkaras* are always born here, and here is where one can aspire to liberation. The Middle World is the centre of gravity of the Cosmos, where those who in their previous lives were in heaven or in hell are reborn. The Middle World is also the abode of those known as "stellar" gods (*jyotiṣkas* [see page 49]), that is, the deities that inhabit the Suns, Moons, planets, stars and constellations.

The Middle World is formed of islands or rings of land (*dvīpas*) separated by oceans (*samudras*). In the centre of this disc, rises the *axis mundi,* Mount Meru. While this mountain is gigantic, in the immensity of the Middle World it is an insignificant protuberance. It is surrounded by a first ring of land called Rose Apple tree Island (Jambūdvīpa), which always has a prominent place in Jain cosmograms. The second ring is the Island of the Grislea Tomentosa tree (Dhātakīkhaṇdadvīpa); the third is Lotus Island (Puṣkaradvipa)... the eighth Nandīśvaradvīpa... up to an uncountable number of island. Interestingly, each island has its own independent astronomy, with its Moons, Suns and constellations. In a sense, each island is a universe within the Middle World. The texts give many of details concerning the dimensions of each island, its continents, its distance from other islands, or the oceans that surround them.

The islands of the Middle World are also inhabited by semi-divine beings known to all Indian religions: *yakṣas, gandharvas, rākṣasas, bhūtas* or *piśācas* [see page 49]. Given that they are able to move from one world to another, they are known by the generic name of "interstitial ones" (*vyantaravāsīs*). On occasions, the divine beings of the Upper World [see below] descend to the Middle World to venerate *tīrthaṅkaras* at crucial and auspicious moments of their lives. Of special interest is the eighth island, the Isle of Nandisvara, replete with gardens graced with splendid statues of the *tīrthaṅkaras,* which the deities come to worship.

Rebirth as an animal or human being is limited to the central part of the Middle World, specifically the Rose Apple tree Island, which is our world [see Fig. 4]; and the contiguous Grislea Tomentosa Island and Lotus Island. The latter is divided in two by a high mountain chain beyond which human beings cannot be born nor even live. Beyond these mountains, in fact, the concept of time ceases to exist.

JAMBŪDVĪPA

The one island out of all those mentioned above that really interests us is the Rose Apple tree Island (Jambūdvīpa). The Jain description of this island is very similar to what we find in Buddhism and Hinduism, even down to tiny details. Very probably they all stem from the same origin. Nonetheless, when we connect the Jain explanation of the cosmos and Jambūdvīpa with their vision of the Universal History (with their cosmic ages *Jinas,* sublime men, etc.) the resulting picture is consistent solely with the values of Jainism.

A work that gives an account of the sacred geography of Jambūdvīpa is the *Jambūdvīpa-prajñāpti* of Amitagati (10th-1 1th centuries). The text puts an effort to describe the mountain chains, rivers, cities, lakes, palaces, or sanctuaries. The descriptions are purely mythical, while they do relate to a certain extent with the known topography of ancient India.

Jambūdvīpa is a disc-shaped island centred around Mount Meru. It takes its name from a gigantic stone apple tree situated near the top of the mountain. The island is surrounded by a high wall, with four gateways, each guarded by a semi-divine being. Beyond that, the Salt Ocean (Lavaṇasamudra). It consists of seven continents (*varṣas, kṣetras*) separated not by seas, but by mountain ranges [see FIG. 5]. These are, from South to North: Bharata, Haimavata, Hari, Videha, Ramyaka, Hairaṇyavata, and Airāvata.

The description of the physical geography of Jambūdvīpa, as detailed as it may appear in the texts and illustrations, is not the most relevant consideration. What is fundamental, let us stress yet again, is the moral and soteriological geography. Let us explain.

Of these seven continents, only two and a half are spheres, where actions lead to results (*karmabhūmis*), that is to say areas subject to ascending and descending cycles, and places where, consequently, the *tīrthaṅkaras* preach Jainism. The remaining areas of Rose Apple tree Island, and of the Cosmos, are not affected by a slow moral decline. Conditions there remain constant, according to the *Tattvārtha-sūtra* (3.28) and chronology is unknown. Neither virtue, nor size of body, lifespan, climate, or vegetation are subject to positive or negative variation. The eternal prison of *karma* is restricted, therefore, to the portion of Jambūdvīpa known as *karmabhūmi.* This point is of the greatest importance. It is in these regions that human beings have to work and act to get by, and consequently it is where the law of *karma* imposes retribution according to action. Fortunately, it is precisely in these regions that humans can have recourse to asceticism to be able to "burn" *karma,* attain enlightenment and final liberation. The rest of Jambūdvīpa's four and a half continents are Lands of Enjoyment (*bhogabhūmis*), each one in a permanent state of the Extremely Marvellous Age or Marvellous Age. Humans who have the great joy of being born in these blissful regions live in the same condition as they did who lived those blessed cycles in the *karmabhūmis.* They live in paradise. However, given that humans cannot practice asceticism in such Utopian surroundings, the *tīrthaṅkaras* don't come to the *bhogabhūmis* to preach Jainism. Thus, liberation is not possible in here.

All the accuracy and precision in delimiting the heavens, hells, islands, continents, arises out of the need to delimit the areas of the continents where liberation is possible [see FIG. 5] (Caillat 1981: 34). It is plain that the immensity of cosmos and the relative smallness of the *karmabhūmis* or places where liberation is possible, serve to underline the incalculable value of human rebirth in a *karmabhūmi.* These are the places where humans have the possibility of trascending *saṃsāra.* Parallelisms with the Brāhmaṇic concept that we find in the Purāṇas is evident (*Visṇu-purāṇa* 2.3.24-26).

Let us confine ourselves to the two and a half continents making up the *karmabhūmis.* The largest of these is Videha, also known as Mahāvideha owing to its great dimensions. It is situated in the centre of Jambūdvīpa, surrounding Mount Meru. Half of this gigantic continent is not a *karmabhūmi,* but rather a *bhogabhūmi,* where the inhabitants live permanently in the Extremely Marvellous Age. The other half is a *karmabhūmi.* This region is crucially important since it is thought that the effects of our descendant cycle do not reach here. Time stands still in this part of Videha *(Vyākhyā-prajñāpti* 20.8 [791b]), which means that it is a permanent *karmabhūmi* undergoing the conditions of the third period (the Sorrowfully Marvellous Age), where at any one time there is a *tīrthaṅkara* showing the way, and where at all times the human beings reborn there can attain liberation. It is said that the *tīrthaṅkara* Sīmaṅhara, venerated by different sections of Jainism, is now preaching in Videha.

The other two *karmabhūmi* continents are Airāvata and Bharata. They are completely symmetrical. Airāvata is simply the northern replica of Bharata. As in half of of Videha, there too *tīrthaṅkaras* preach.*

Let us continue to home in on this space and concentrating on Bharata-varṣa, the southern continent of Jambūdvīpa, separated from the rest by the Himalaya mountain range (Himavan, Himavat).

A chain of mountains, which runs parallel to the Himalayas, known as the Vaitāḍhya mountains, divides the continent horizontally in the northern and southern regions. In turn, two very well-known rivers descend from the Himalayas, the Indus (Sinddhu) and the Ganges (Gaṅgā) which clearly delimit a western, central and eastern zone. In all, Bharata-varṣa is divided into six regions.

All these regions, with the exception of the south-central one, are known as ignoble (*anārya*) and are populated by barbarian races (Mlecchas). Ignoble in this case means where knowledge of Jainism has yet to penetrate. The central southern region is the land where the noble ones dwell (Ārya-khaṇḍa) whose capital is Ayodhyā. As one can expect, this land of Ārya-khaṇḍa is none other than India, although many Jains say that it also includes Europe, America, Africa, Asia, and Oceania. At all events, the whole continent takes the name of the first enlightened governor (*cakravartin*) of the Universal History, Bharata the son of the *jina* Ṛṣabha, who came to rule over the six zones of Bharata-varṣa.

If one contemplates the cosmos from the locality in Ārya-khaṇḍa, the issue becomes clear. Vast is Ārya-khaṇḍa, the land of the nobles, but small in comparison with the rest of Bharata. And this continent is just the southern extreme of the gigantic island of the Rose Apple tree, and that in turn is just one of the countless islands that form the Middle World. This Middle World is ridiculously small in comparison with the cosmos, and there is no God here to latch onto. Jains have a lead of many centuries over modern man anguished by existential solitude ushered in by the scientific vision of the universe. The positive side to this insignificant situation is that perfection and liberation are possible,

* Similarly, Dhātakīkhaṇdadvīpa and Puṣkaradvīpa, the two islands contiguous to Jambūdvīpa, where human beings can also be reborn, consist of four and a half continents that are *bhogabhūmis* and two and a half that are *karmabhūmis,* where *tīrthaṅkaras* preach the way.

precisely, in this portion of the cosmos, seeing that it is the place where the cause of our suffering, action *(karma)* exists and, moreover, can be eliminated. While in Bharata, we human beings can no longer reach liberation in this Sorrowful Age, we can be reborn in Videha or in one of the two contiguous islands and there reach liberation.

THE UPPER WORLD

The Upper World (*ūrdhva-loka*) is located at the summit of the mythical Mount Meru, the hub of the cosmogramme, and above the stars. Iconographically speaking, we find ourselves in the upper part of the Cosmic Being.

This world consists of twelve celestial levels or *kalpas*, each one more beautiful than the one before. Here live the deities known as the *vaimānikas* , since all of them drive celestial vehicles (*vimānas*). The divinities are increasingly serene, long-lived and pure as one goes up and the level is increasingly paradisical. Occasionally, the *vaimānikas* descend to the Middle World to visit friends from previous existences, to console us unfortunate ones who suffer the consequences of our actions or to give homage to the *tīrthaṅkaras.* The most sublime among the gods is the grand Indra (Śakra in the Jain scriptures). This god has a type of replica which presides over each celestial level.

Above these 12 levels are the fourteen "unsurpassable" heavens (*kalpātītas*), the highest heavens of the Upper World. They are the abode of the "unsurpassable" and ethereal gods devoid of all passion. Undoubtedly, these *kalpātītas,* followed the Jain path, and such was their freedom of attachment that they enjoy the greatest beatitude. Even these divinities that dwell in the 14th ultra-heaven will, if they want to escape from the wheel of eternity, have to pursue this from human incarnation.

Everything seems to indicate that, as in Buddhist cosmology, this succession of levels—from the infernal to the celestial—correspond to the different states of psycho-spiritual experience (*dhyānas*) of the yogi. As the Jain meditator progresses through the higher degrees of concentration, she or he not only visualises more ethereal and more pure realms, but also acquires the corresponding divine conditions. The meditator and the object of meditation are one. Hence the Indian yogi is able to develop the same powers as the divine beings and be comparable to the gods. Traditional Indian cosmology is as rooted in myth and philosophy, as it is in meditation and yogic experience. Nevertheless, yogis must also transcend all meditative states if they want to attain the highest level of existence, that of the unconditioned or *nirvāṇa.*

THE ABODE OF THE LIBERATED SOULS

The unconditioned realm is located at the apex of the cosmic diagram. It is called the Abode of the Liberated Souls or the World of the Perfect Ones (*siddha-kṣetra, siddha-loka*), and said to be as white as milk and takes the shape of a gigantic parasol. For that reason, it is also known as the Slightly Curved Place (*iṣatprāgbhāra*), which is usually depicted as a half Moon, slightly turned on one side, in the forehead of the Cosmic Being. It is said that the liberated ones go there. No *jīva* that has ever ascended to this point at the top of the cosmos has ever been born again in any other world.

For Jainism, the liberated ones do not transcend the cosmos. Such beings will enjoy eternal beatitude in the Siddha-kṣetra, above the heavens, on the frontier with the empty realms. According to Ananda Coomaraswamy (1914: 4), the concept of a place of purity where the perfect souls go was perhaps a contribution from Indian materialism, an influential tendency at the time of Mahāvīra. In this, Jainism clearly differentiates itself from Buddhism. The *nirvāṇa* of Buddhism has never been considered a *place,* and those who attain *nirvāṇa* do not go to any particular space. The dissident opinion of Coomaraswamy (1914: 4) is that the true field of the liberation is the non-world (*aloka*) and this would thus correspond to the Buddhist void (*śūnya*), and to the unconditioned plenitude *(brahman)* of Hinduism. Nobody can say. However, the Jain *Uttarādhyayana-sūtra* (36.56-57) is quite forceful on this point:

> "Where do the perfected souls reside? Where do they leave their bodies, and where do they go, on reaching perfection?
>
> Perfect souls are excluded from the non-world [*aloka*]. They reside on the top of the world. They leave their bodies here [below], and go there, on reaching perfection".

3. BIOLOGY

SAMSĀRA

Traditional cosmology and cosmography make up a conceptual setting in which the Universal History takes on its full meaning. Before proceeding with the biographiies of the *tīrthaṅkaras,* it would make things clearer if we concentrated on the protagonists of cosmic flow: living beings (*jīvas*). The coming and going of these beings over these infinite cycles and in these immense worlds, is what Jains call *saṃsāra,* one of the most recurring words in Indian spiritual tradition. It is formed by the prefix *saṃ* and the root *sṛ*-, "to go about", "to flow" (Monier-Williams 1899: 1119). *Saṃsāra* is something, which is in constant movement, something, which is perpetually flowing.

The principal mechanism that governs the destiny of *saṃsāra* is the law *of karma,* which we will talk about at length later on [see chapter 25]. Here we are simply emphasing its essential postulate: the quality, quantity, duration, and intensity of all action *(karma)* conducted by a living being leaves an invisible trace (*vāsanā, saṃskāra*) that, attached to the agent's subtle body (*sūkṣmū-śarīra*), drags the spiritual soul (*jīva*) down to a new existence. For that reason, birth and death are only doors the soul passes through on its wandering throughout the cosmos.

And Bharata-varṣa is a permanent battlefield for all action at ego levels (aggression, lust, greed, and hate). The general situation of existence can be summed up in one idea: dissatisfaction, pain, suffering, frustration, contingency; everything, in other words, expressed by the *duḥkha* concept, well known in Buddhism and the Sāṃkhya and Yoga philosophies.

Jains have a bleak view of the cycle of transmigration; or that is what we gather from their scriptures. Infinite living beings find themselves involved in a material world since beginningless time, and will remain indefinitely in such a distressing state of dissatisfaction, from rebirth to rebirth. Indian philosophies say that bondage is without beginning (*anādi*). Bondage has no *history.* There is no Fall in the *duḥkha* condition. The Cosmic Being in whom the life monads dwell is magma of space-time-matter, shaped by the activity and vitality of organisms trapped like insects in the web of matter. Perhaps, the image which best illustrates this situation is the wheel of life (*Bhava-cakra*) from Buddhism, a graphic symbol of *saṃsāra* conditioned by actions.

All Indian philosophies use the word *saṃsāra* to describe this mundane world in which beings suffer pain.

THE FOUR DESTINIES

Logically, the Indian notion of the transmigration cycle takes the view that all living beings are susceptible to living through any type of existence. What is more, the *Vyākhyā-prajñāpti* (12.7 [580a]) maintains that every spiritual monad or soul *has passed* through *and will pass* through all the possible types of incarnation. A *jīva* can be reborn as a caterpillar, blade of grass, human being, or a deity, depending on its overall computation of actions in previous lives. India has never established rigid borders between the divine, human, animal, and vegetable realms. The main teaching in the doctrine of *karma* is that everything is interconnected and that all forms of existence are interrelated.

It is said by way of instruction, for example, that an animal rebirth will have been heavily preconditioned by acts of cowardliness and dishonour. Similarly, rebirth in hell is the fruit of unrestrained conduct when in pursuit of power, or the consequence of activities marked by cruelty and violence. On the other hand, a heavenly rebirth will have been determined by acts of charity and penitence. It is maintained that human rebirths are fruit of a certain moderation in all activities. However, these explanations should not be taken literally. Just as Padmanabh Jaini (1979: 116) has it, these perceptions go beyond a system of retribution proportional to the acts. There is another intention behind them: that of encouraging desirable behaviour and placing it in a comprehensible context. The idea that one must retain is that beings are responsible for the conditions of their own existence.

Accordingly, the notion of *saṃsāra* implies that the interrelation between all forms of existence is total and complete. In the infinite stream of *saṃsāra* no living being can exist without having been the father, enemy, king, or servant of each and every other being, and so one is a part of a brotherhood with all the rest of living beings that have been born (*Vyākhyā-prajñāpti* 12.7 [581a]). The Buddhist *Laṅkāvatāra-sūtra* (245) uses the same metaphor almost verbatim. Or as Hemacandra *(Yoga-śāstra* 4.66) says, there is no atom in the universe that has not been occupied by the soul in its infinite cycle of existences. One goes through the immense range of incarnations until, tired of millions of meaningless rebirths, she or he takes the path proclaimed by the *jinas,* and puts an end to all this peregrination.

Jains have spent much effort in classifying types of beings according to different criteria. The first order of difference is found between liberated beings (*muktas*) and those who are still incarnated (*saṃsārīns*). Within this second category, which is the one that concerns us, there are multiple classifications. For example, according to whether they are mobile (*trasas*) or static (*sthāvaras*), a distinction, which is the one most commonly encountered in older texts; or depending on the number of senses (*indriyas*), or the number of breaths taken (*prāṇas*), or according to their colour (*leśyā*), and so on. Here, we shall take our cue from the most habitual and generic of these classifications. And this postulates four major categories of incarnations or rebirths (*gatis*). One can be reborn as: a divine being (*deva*), a human being (*manuṣya*), a hell being (*nāraki*), or as an animal or plant (*tiryañca*). It is said that one of the meanings for the swastika (*svastika*), a symbol much cherished by the Jains [see FIG. C], represents these four possible destinies by each of its arms.

DIVINE INCARNATIONS

The highest order of rebirth is as a deity or divinity (*deva, devatā*), a type of being that comes into the world as a "manifestation", suddenly, bereft of any material base, but according to its *karma,* should do so. From birth until death, these angelic beings live in a perpetual state of youth. Their long life is reckoned in oceans of years. Thanks to "a metamorphic or transformation body" [see page 391], they can alter their appearance, something which can also allow them develop certain supernatural powers. Something which is not so surprising if we consider that gods' bodies do not possess bones, flesh or even blood. Theirs is a body of sublime beauty; *luminous* and brilliant—one of the literal meanings of the word *deva* (Panikkar 1996: 320)—free of illnesses. Their high level of consciousness matches their extremely high level of spiritual purity.

In short, the gods enjoy immense religious worthiness, but they are faced with one problem: they are not able to attain liberation. The reason is clear. The path leading to *nirvāṇa* is based on asceticism. In their permanent state of bliss, the deities cannot become ascetics. So blessed is their existence (comparable to an existence in Marvellous Age) that there is no yearning for liberation, and no possibility of asceticism. All their desires are fulfilled *ipso facto.* They have no place for self-discipline. Moreover, their bodies are so luminous and ethereal (so much so that they are called discarnates) that they cannot fast (gods do not eat) or deprive themselves of pleasure. To practice asceticism, one cannot enjoy paradise. Their happiness, then, has to be seen in context. Their bliss is immense, but transient. Sooner or later, gods are reborn as humans or animals. Deities are no more than trapped souls, condemned to transmigrate to refined and privileged forms of existence. A great god is as subject to *karma,* as much as a snake (*Sūtrakṛtāṅga* 1.2.1.5). When the *karma,* which has brought about this luminous existence runs out the karmic valences of previous lives will drag them back to this world in a less ethereal form.

GODS "DWELLERS IN MANSIONS"

The lowest gods are "dwellers in mansions" (*bhavanavāsīns*). These are usually called demigods. Among them, we come across demons *(asuras),* divine serpents (*nāgas*), fire divinities (*nāgnis*), wind deities (*vāyus*), divine eagles (*suparṇas*), etc. The *asuras* live in Ratnaprabhā, the upper level of hell. Others, like the *nāgas,* dwell in the Middle World. In general, all the *bhavanavāsīns* have the facility of transiting from one level to another. In appearance they resemble young princes, thus the suffix *-kumāra,* meaning "prince", is added to their name. They are governed by the 16 *indras.*

"INTERSTITIAL" GODS

Certain slightly higher ethereal beings are called "interstitial ones" *(vyantaravāsīs*). They take their name from the place they occupy in the cosmos: between the first hell and the Middle World. Interstitial ones are heavenly musicians (*gandharvas*), geniuses of the earth *(yakṣas),* bird men (*kinnaras*), titans (*rākṣasas*), ghosts (*bhūtas*), imps (*piśācas*), etc. The first-mentioned usually help human beings. The last, on the contrary, are not so benevolent. They are also governed by the 16 *indras.*

"LUMINOUS" GODS

The third type of deity are the "luminous ones" (*jyotiṣkas*), comprising divinities that inhabit Suns, Moons, dark Moons, planets, the trillions of stars and constellations. They are governed by various *indras.*

As in all Indian tradition, Jainism has been concerned with the study of astronomy and astrology, and their contribution to the development of these sciences has been valuable. The quintessential texts in this respect are the *Sūra-prajñāpti* and the *Jambūdvīpa- prajñāpti* of Amitagati (10th-11th centuries).

The knowledge of astrology continues to be fundamental for pinpointing the moment and place of all important religious ceremonies (initiation of ascetics, consecration of images, pilgrimages, festivals). The technical knowledge of orbits, conjunctions, in relation to months, years, is admirable. According to Jain astronomy, even though in Bharata-varṣa we might be able to see only one Sun and one Moon, in reality there are two Suns and two Moons in Jambūdvīpa. This notion has no parallel in any other Indian system.

GODS "THAT DRIVE VEHICLES"

Finally, we have the major gods, "those that drive heavenly vehicles" (*vaimānikas*), that dwell in the 12 heavenly paradises (*kalpas*) and in the 14 insuperable ultra-heavens (*kalpātītas*). It is said that the conditions on these planes are similar to those of the Extremely Marvellous Age. Their eyes only behold beautiful things, they enjoy sublime fragrances, taste delicious tastes, their minds always in a clairvoyant state, difference between day and night, is unknown. Each of the 26 heavens is governed by one or two *indras.*

The *indra* that appears prolifically in Jain mythology is Śakra, regent of the Saudharma heaven. His role in the *tīrthaṅkaras'* history is important. Each time a *jina* is to be born in Jambūdvīpa, Śakra's throne booms, and the king of gods alerts all the other divinities that a great event is about to take place. He ascends to a mountain on the island of Nandīśvara and, from there, he points to the house where the *tīrthaṅkara's* birth will take place. As we shall see, Śakra also appears on the scene at other auspicious moments in the *tīrthaṅkara's* career.

The gods of the fifth heaven, Brahmaloka, stand out, being destined to end their earthly existence very shortly—in divine calendar terms. Goddesses are only found on the first and second levels, precisely in the heavens where divinities indulge in sexual relations. At higher levels divinities are androgynous.

Among those who dwell in the 14 *kalpātītas* we find divinities with such curious names as "those who are a joy to observe", "those who are a delight for the mind", "those who are universally benign" or "those who are completely fulfilled" (Campbell 1962: II, 262-263). As we go up levels the *devas* are smaller, more luminous, more powerful, purer, happier, live longer lives and their cognitive faculties are superior.

* * *

Each order of divine incarnation, whether that of the *yakṣas,* the heavenly bodies, or the different types of *vaimānikas,* are organised like an Indian kingdom. We invariably find a royal authority at the head (*indra*)*,* with his female consort (*indrāṇī*) and with a series of princes (*sāmānikas*)*,* civil servants (*trāyas-triṁsas),* noble courtesans (*pāriṣadyas*)*,* guards (*ātmarakṣasas*)*,* protectors (*lokapālas*)*,* warriors (*anīkas*)*,* citizens (*prakirṇakas*) and even servant gods (*ābhiyogyas*)*.*

All deities will know of their end six months beforehand. From this moment on, stress takes possession of the divinity, in view of the millions of eons of enjoyment and happiness that are about to come to an end. Terrified by their future incarnation, some divinities commit atrocities, which can condemn them to an inferior rebirth.

INFERNAL INCARNATIONS

The gods have more than a little in common with the beings born in the lowest levels of all: the infernal beings (*nārakis*)*.* In a way, the *nārakis* constitute a mirror image of the *devas.* While the former suffer the consequences of their unworthiness, the others enjoy the reward for their merits, the latter enjoy the reward for their merits. In this, Jainism resembles Christianity and its concept of angels and devils. Both types of beings share the same constitution. Like the gods, hell denizens are not born, but appear suddenly, out of the blue. Their life span cannot be measured in human terms, but rather in oceans of years, for this reason their suffering is horrifyingly long. The *nārakis* are always asexual and are particularly deformed and lop-sided. As we have already seen, they are subjected to all kinds of torture during their stay in hell. The farther they are down the hell, the greater the size of the body, and harsher and more prolonged the torment. Once the *nāraki* has passed through the range of sufferings prescribed by their *karma,* death comes to them, without any apparent cause. Fortunately for the *nārakis,* they are always reborn on the human plane, or the plane of animals with five senses.

HUMAN INCARNATIONS

Humans are those beings with five senses that also have the faculty of thought, long life, physical strength, power of speech and respiration. These characteristics serve to differentiate them from the rest of the animal kingdom. It is not because animals cannot have them (elephants, cows, and tigers for example, possess the faculty of thought) but they cannot have all of them simultaneously.

Basically, humans are divided up according to the zone of the Middle World they can be reborn into. Those that interest us are those who live in continents where action is rewarded (*karmabhūmis*), since all of us inhabit this Earth are such. And among us humanity is divided up into persons of noble lineage (Āryas) or barbarians (Mlecchas).

The sublime beings (*śalākā-puruṣas*) are among the most elevated of noble human rebirths. As we know, each ascendant era and each descendent era produce seventy-three sublime beings. The 24 *tīrthaṅkaras* are of this number. The remaining thirty-nine constitute a type of near divine hero, many of whom are well known in Hinduism. On the one hand, we have the 12 universal monarchs (*cakravartins*), such as the great ones Bharata, Sagara, Sanatkumāra and Padma, who got to govern over the six regions of Bharatavarṣa. Next come the nine *vāsudevas,* beings such as Kṛṣṇa, Nārāyaṇa (Viṣṇu) or Lakṣmaṇa. They are heroes who vanquish a *prativāsudeva,* a villain who is a "governor of half the world" (*ardhacakrin*), that is to say, three quarters of Bharatavarṣa. Within this category we have Bali, Prahlāda, and Rāvaṇa, the main villains of the Hindu epics. Then come, the nine *baladevas,* stepbrothers and companions of the *vāsudevas,* such as Balarāma or Rāma (Padma). These three characters appear when there is not a *cakravartin* governing in Bharatavarṣa. In Jain mythology, it is the *vāsudeva, baladeva's* younger stepbrother, who kills and overcomes *prativāsudeva* and, consequently, becomes the "governor of the middle world". Invariably, the *vāsudeva* and the *prativāsudeva* will have to be reborn in hell, due to the violence committed during the war. On the contrary, on the death of his stepbrother, *baladeva,* a more mystic character, will enter the Jain order, practice asceticism, and attain *nirvāṇa.*

Likewise, Jain traditional mythology talks about other notable souls: the nine *nāradas,* the 24 *kāmadevas,* the 24 fathers of *the jinas,* the 24 mothers of the *jinas* or the 14 *kulakaras* or governors of presocial times. All these remarkable beings lived in this descendant cycle in Bharata. But similar beings existed in Videha, Airāvata, and the *karmabhūmis* of Dhātakīkhaṇḍadvīpa and Puṣkaradvīpa.

The importance of a human incarnation lies in the fact that it is there where karmic computation can bring about any of the four possible destinies. A human being can be reborn as a divinity, an infernal being, another human or an animal. And vice versa. The path leading to the human state can be long and arduous for an animal, but it can eventually attain this treasured rebirth. Moreover, the human condition is crucial because it is *only* from this rebirth that one can acquire the necessary self-discipline and consciousness to achieve salvation. Human incarnation is like the interchange from which one can set off on the path of non-violence, purification and compassion. Humanness is the form of life that is *potentially* liberating. Apart from this quality, humankind is not particularly praised or exalted in Jainism. Moreover, human existence in these sorrowful times is characterised by dissatisfaction and frustration—not to mention poverty, old age, slavery, or illness, but rebirth as a human being is rare, so it would be a pity to waste it. It is rarer still to have the benefit of instruction in the Jain religion and all the more exceptional was having enough energy to practise self control. Regrettably, the upshot of all these limitations is that only a few choose the path and thus Jainism will slowly disappear from the face of the Earth.

ANIMAL INCARNATIONS

Animals represent the last possible destiny. They share with us humans beings one important characteristic: after death, animals can be born in any of the four possible destinies.

Jainism considers "those that walk horizontally" (*tiryañcas*) as an extremely wide range of beings. According to Umāsvāti, all those beings which are not humans, divinities or infernal beings are animals (*Tattvārtha-sūtra* 4.28). Accordingly we have all the animal and vegetable kingdoms. One peculiarity in Jainism is that it is considered that souls can be reborn in inorganic objects like stones, flames, drops of water, or gusts of wind. Their consciousness is nonexistent, but they exist in a latent form. These beings also come under the heading of "animals". What we have here is clearly an animist outlook. The continuum of life stretches from angelic to mineral.

THE *NIGODAS*

The most minute of all beings are the infinitessimal *nigodas,* entities which do not possess a body and unite in colonies, inhabit all the worlds of the universe.

Moreover, they occupy other beings' bodies in the form of parasites; notably the bodies of human beings, certain animals and bulbous plants. Their numbers are infinite. They occupy the lowest rung of the ladder of spiritual progession (*Vyākhyā-prajñāpti* 19.3 [765b]). Their soul is so dense and opaque that it is said that they have not even begun their spiritual development. It is thought that infinite numbers of *nigodas* will remain perpetualy in the lowest of conditions and will never achieve salvation. This has its own particular logic. There is a problem for all traditions that postulate liberation from the cycle of existences. As beings are being liberated, the world of *saṃsāra* would be emptying, as Jinabhadra Gaṇi (*Viśeṣāvaśyaka-bhāṣya* 1827-1830 [*Gaṇadhara-vāda* 279-282]) admits. In a certain sense, Jains replace liberated souls with this infinite reserve of *nigodas*. And so the danger of disappearance of the *saṃsāra*— and therefore of eternity— is averted.

Nonetheless, for another indefinite number of *nigodas,* the path of progression towards an eventual human rebirth is not barred. Every time a *jīva* attains liberation, it allows some *nigoda* to rise in the order of things. Similarly, any other being can regress to the state of a *nigoda* due to unworthy *karma.* There is a Digambara tradition that affirms that Maskarīn Gośāla [see pages 162-163], Mahāvīra's disciple and rival, was reborn as a *nigoda* for the frustrated attempt to murder Mahāvīra. (On the other hand, another Digambara tradition assures that thanks to a sincere act of repentance he is enjoying an existence as a deity!)

Although technically speaking, *nigodas* are classified as "vegetable beings with one sense and of an immobile type", as a result of their tendency to association and their peculiarity of being able to live in all possible worlds, they can be considered to be another category. They constitute, as Walther Schubring (1934: 203) expressed, the opposite pole to the liberated ones.

THE *EKENDRIYAS*

The second most insignificant type of beings are "animals" that similarly only possess one sense (*ekendriya*), that of touch. In fact, we can define a "soul" or *jīva* simply as a living being that experiences pleasure and pain through its single sense of touch (Wiley 2002: 38). Here, we are dealing with subtle and immobile incarnations of earth, fire, water, and air. Since they are subtle and invisible, nothing much is said about them.

Next, we have the beings referred to as coarse—that is, visible—*ekendriyas.* Among the incarnations of the earth we have, for example, specks of dust, grains of sand, precious stones, rocks, diamonds or metals. Among those consisting of water we find seas, rivers, raindrops, snow, dew, sweat, clouds, mist or the monsoons. In the incarnations of fire, we find flames, coals, meteorites, or lightening. *Ekendriyas* of the air are gusts of wind, inhalations and exhalations of living beings, cyclones or tornadoes.

It is not a case of a drop of water containing microscopic animals, which in fact, it does, but that drop of water is in itself a *jīva* denominated "water body with only one sense" (*apakāya-ekendriya*). Therefore, a glass of water is formed by a colony of *apakāya-ekendriyas.* This perception, unique to Jainism—and derisively called archaic animism, when it would be more accurate to call it hilozoism (Basham 1989: 61)—has enormous implications. It underlines the spiritual and animate presence in all manifestations. As Kristi Wiley (2002: 43) writes, whenever matter in the form of earth, water, air, or fire is embodying a soul, it constitutes a living being, which breathes, nourishes the body, and sustains life in its body; and it feels pleasure and pain through the sense of touch. Like a glimpse of the the Gaia theory Jainas suggest that there is no hard and fast barrier between the apparently inert and the vital. The chain of life is an interconnected whole, and it extends beyond the merely biological. Nothing exists in the universe without a degree of consciousness (this is the essential characteristic of all *jīvas).* There are ethical implications here. The Jain ascetic will try, by every possible means, to avoid destroying these lives. The cloth muzzle with which some monks cover their mouths [see FIG. 31] is worn not to harm the invisible bodies in the air. It is a symbol of their determination to respect even the lowest forms of life—not to avoid swallowing insects, as is commonly said. The Jain animism may be archaic, but nonetheless valid and more refined than the blatant anthropocentricism of other traditions.

Although the existence of the *ekendriyas* is not so horrible as that of hell beings, their situation is deplorable. The bodies of the earth are continually stepped upon by elephants and horses, bodies of water are martyred by the Sun, and those in the wind annihilate themselves by crashing into one another when storms collide.

VEGETABLE INCARNATIONS

The next rung on the stairway of complexity is that of "immobile animals with two senses"—touch and taste. This class is formed entirely by the vegetable kingdom.

Vegetables come in two categories. Those that are composed of a single *jīva,* and others which are made up of colonies of *jīvas.* Among the first, we have all the trees, grasses and bushes. Among the second, potatoes, onions, garlic, carrots or figs. This is an important classification from the dietetic point of view. Following the vow of non-violence many Jains abstain from eating these plants that contain *jīva* colonies. This feature constitutes one of the clearest distinguishing signs of the Jain community.

For Jains, vegetable souls have consciousness or knowledge of themselves and the world that surrounds them. How, otherwise, would they know when to germinate? The Jain concept of plants grants them almost human characteristics. For example, desires for nutrition, for reproduction or even emotions like fear or possessiveness. According to the *Vyākhyā-prajñāpti* (14.8 [652b]), Mahāvīra preached that some trees and branches of trees would achieve salvation.

ANIMAL INCARNATIONS

The rest of animals with two senses are composed of different mobile beings: worms, caterpillars, cockles or shell fish. While common people cannot be as particular as ascetics in avoiding the accidental killing of *ekendriyas*, the vow of non-violence for lay persons technically begins with this category of beings. One can say that all Jains with the minimum of consciousness scrupulously avoid bothering any mobile soul (*sthāvara*). Therefore, all Jain families, apart from their dedication to religious practices, are invariably vegetarian.

With three senses (touch, taste and sense of smell) we have ants, flees, earwigs and ticks. With four senses (touch, taste, smell and sight) there are flies, wasps, scorpions, butterflies and mosquitoes. Finally with five senses (touch, taste, smell, vision and hearing) we have dolphins, crocodiles, fish, elephants, lizards, geese and bats.

Although animals cannot achieve liberation in their condition, they can listen to the sacred doctrine, be awed by it and act in accordance. Not in vain does tradition also attribute the sense of reason *(manas)* to the higher animals. This is a pan-Indian feature. There are numerous fables in which animals take vows, fast, show respect to ascetics or practice non-violence. Thanks to that they can work towards human or divine rebirth. Which was the case for the elephant Udāya, to give an example, which had previously been an *asura* and in its subsequent incarnation was born human, achieving salvation in Videha *(Vyākhyā-prajñāpti* 17.1 [720a]). Or the chief of a band of monkeys who thanks to the compassion shown towards an ascetic in the forest, was reborn as a deity with a handsome and resplendent body (cited in Balbir 1990: 20). Mahāvīra himself had been born a lion [see page 131] and was instructed in the religion of nonviolence, thanks to which the seed of right vision (*samyak-darśana*) was awoken inside him which was to catapult him through the course of various lives until reaching the state of *tīrthaṅkara.* Of course, Jainism projects human values on animals to exemplify the mechanisms of *karma* and to promote the principals of non-violence and compassion, but there is no doubt that as a result Jainism has been, out of all the religions in the world, the most respectful for all other beings. This degree of equivalence between human and animal behaviour reflects the same equivalence of each and every soul. Although in spiritual progression there are great differences between beings, qualitatively speaking, all souls are identical. Hence, all life, is not just sacred (the Hindu option) but inviolable (the Jaina option).

TAXONOMY

Jain intellectuals have also investigated the morphology, anatomy and reproduction of living beings. The text that delves most deeply into human anatomy and at greatest length is the *Ta ulavaicārika.*

Jain anatomic explanations principally focus on enumerating organs, veins, and bones or in delimiting size, symmetry, or structural firmness of beings. Much is said about the forms of being born, sexual behaviour or potential life span. The medical viewpoint comes close to the *āyurveda* or traditional Indian medicine.

However, Jain biological interest is fundamentally taxonomic. What is important is not so much the physiology, but the situation of beings in the order of things and their capacity to liberate themselves or not. In all, 8,400,000 possible types of birth are mentioned. This is a commonly encountered number and is best rendered to be understood as "umpteen types". At all events, it is said that Jain biologists succeeded in identifying some tens of thousands of species. To be frank, their lists of birth categories are incredibly arid and their obsession for numerical classifications could be described as mind-bending. According to some authors, the origin of Jain taxonomy dates back to periods prior to Mahāvīra, given that the biological systematisation of the Ājīvikas, a religious group contemporary with ancient Jainism, was similar.

In the light of present day knowledge, the zoological and anatomical rigour of all these lists is debatable, but the systematisation is nonetheless impressive. Recall that the biological knowledge of Aristotle did not exceed five hundred species. And, I repeat, the aim here is never merely scientific. According to Pad-manabh Jaini (2000: 126) these levels of spiritual existence reflect a scale of awareness (*upayoga*). Texts are explicit in recommending the intellectual study of living beings to understand what *ahiṃsā* means and be able to practice non-violence leading to *nirvaṇa* (*Sūtṛakrtāṅga* 1.11.11). When one knows where beings come from and where they go to, when one grasps the mechanism and structure of *saṃsāra,* one can take steps to escape it. That is the opinion of the *tathāgatas, arhats* and *tīrthaṅkaras,* the venerable *Ācārāṅga-sūtra* (1.3.3.2) proclaims. Jaina biology goes hand-in-hand with the practice of Jainism. The latter, as we shall see time and time again, is based firmly on not harming any living being.

The apparent pessimism of Jainism is never absolute. Jains not only consider that a human incarnation is the best one possible, but that every incarnation, however low it may be, is susceptible to improvement. No *jīva* possesses a fixed place in the hierarchy, for those who are now human, may be a deity or a denizen of hell in a future existence. All spiritual souls are in constant and perpetual flux, which is exactly what the idea of *saṃsāra* expresses. A soul embodied as a *nigoda* may be reborn as a human being and attain *nirvāṇa* in its first and only embodiement as a human. If instead of classifying the possible types of births from the *jīva's* perspective, we look at them in terms of *saṃsāra,* what we see is an interconnected web of fluxes, a series of different graduations of matter, the denser the concentration, the lower the spiritual pureness. Even in the coarsest of cases, the qualities of the soul (awareness, bliss and energy) do not completely disappear. They can be utterly obscured but almost never irreparably so. The potential for spiritual progress, called *bhavya* (and also for retrogression, admittedly), is never eliminated. One of the most important Jaina *sūtras* states:

> "An earth-, water- or plant-being with a darker spiritual hue [*leśyā*] may in its next existence be a human being, reach the *kevala*-knowledge and consequently attain liberation" (*Vyākhyā-prajñāpti* 18.3 [739b]).

It is true that in all classes of beings, there are *jīvas* incapable of liberating *themselves* *Jīvas* that find themselves in a situation called *abhavya;* souls that are not displeased with *saṃsāra* (*Uttarādhyayana-sūtra* 3.5), that feel good in a bodily state because they know no better, and consequently, they will never reach liberation. Aside from these allusions to "predetermination"—possibly a very ancient Śramaṇic survival (Jaini 2000: 102-105), which does not preclude these *jīvas* attaining the fourteenth ultra-heaven (von Glasenapp 1925: 269)—the fundamental Jain thesis is that every living being is susceptible to forging the path that leads to *nirvāṇa** Every *jīva,* in the words of N. Shāntā (1985: 290), is on the way to becoming a *siddha.*

What Jain taxonomy really intended to show is the extreme rarity of a human birth. We have had the immense good fortune to have passed through the horrifying life of the infinitely tiny *nigodas*... we have been, millions of times, one of a 1,000 million *ekendriyas*... we have gone through umpteen lives in a colony of uncountable *jīvas* in a bulb... we have been reborn a violent carnivore whose subsistence inevitably leads to infernal reincarnation... we have spent aeons in hell... Once we have finally attained a rebirth which will put an end to the nightmare of eternity, are we going to be so stupid as to not take advantage of it? Are we going to waste this virtually unique opportunity? Moreover, we as human beings have the opportunity to live in times when Jainism still exists on the face of the Earth. Are we going to live a life without a goal that can send us back at a stroke to any of the lower existences? Are we going to continue being violent to other living beings in the knowledge that the entire universe displays various degrees of awareness? Are we going to continue wandering aimlessly in the web of *saṃsāra* without a goal or an end?

* According to Padmanabh Jaini (2000: 130), the Jaina doctrine of *karma* is a late addition— albeit a very old one—over a linear-evolutionary framework, remnants of which are discernible in "inconsistencies" like the *nigodas* incapable of liberation. Jaini suggests a possible common background with the Ājīvika tradition.

Part II

Mythology

The narrative that unfolds in the Universal History, history Jain style, concerns this descending cycle and does so only in that part of the cosmos where human life is relevant: Jambūdvīpa. It is based mainly on the hagiographies or exemplary lives of the *tīrthaṅkaras,* and to a lesser extent on those of the other sublime beings. The texts most representative of this genre are the immense *Mahāpurāṇa* by Jinasena (9th century) and Guṇabhadra (9th century) and the no less monumental *Triṣaṣṭiśalākapuruṣa-caritra* by Hemacandra (12th century). The first is an account from the Digambara perspective, and the second from a Śvetāmbara point of view.

It is true that the idea of 24 "historical" *tīrthaṅkaras* is not accepted by the scholarly community. In fact, all Jain formulations of the Universal History are relatively recent. They began to emerge around the 2nd century BC, when Mahāvīra's biography began to take on mythical tones. Even the notion of the twenty-four *jinas* is not that ancient, perhaps dating from the 2nd century BC to the 1st century CE, the period to which the *Kalpa-sūtra* and the *Āvaśyaka-niryukti* are assigned, these being the first texts to mention them. The Universal History as such did not acquire its classic form until the advent of Jinasena and Hemacandra. This being so, the experts only accept the historical existence of Mahāvīra and, in somewhat hypothetical vein, Pārśva, the lastjma but one.

With the Universal History, Indian cyclic sensitivity becomes myth-like. The mythical history takes us back to a time both remote and palpable: the deeds of ancient times thanks to which human beings are what they are. Myth is a symbolic history, inserted into the cosmology and the universal events.

For many, the mythical account cannot be considered "history" in any sense, since it cannot be verified, cannot be subjected to criticism or to the archaeological record. This perception is a clear consequence of the dissolution of *mythos* by Western philosophers, but Indian thought has never felt the need to break with the mythical vision.

Each age interprets history in its and way, ours is no exception. We believe we can go back to the spirit of an era and be able to capture it objectively, a crass error. History with a capital letter is a fascinating literary genre, but it is still a *narrative* (White 1973: 14). So, the *myth* of historical objectivity itself, characteristic of historicism and rationalism, needs thorough revision. As Hans-Georg Gadamer (1975:I,367) wrote, we have to recognise distance in time and not attempt to abolish it. We should allow history, any form whatever of *story,* to penetrate our horizons.

So, in the single chapter that makes up this part, we will save ourselves from having to investigate whether the *myth* has a historical basis in the conventional sense. The thing is to grasp the way in which the past has been perceived and *lives* in Jain tradition, and this too is history. History does not just consist of "events"—the way in which a culture or tradition understands itself can be as valid or more valid than the chronology of the wars, dynasties and annals of the community in question. Even present-day Indian political discourse makes frequent use of the language of myth. The concept of the past, be that what it may, forms part of our society and our way of understanding the world. In this function, mythical history is as powerful as its conventional counterpart. In reality, mankind is the outcome of mythical events and presuppositions. Our psyche *consists* of myths and cannot live without communicating by means of symbols, and that is why it is so difficult to see, to perceive, the myths of one's own tradition. We find it easy, on the other hand, to recognise the myths of others, since for us they are not invisible.

Every mythical narrative is complex. It is *philosophical and scientific,* as well as *ritual and soteriological.* It does not set out just to reveal truths in the rational sense of the word. Myth is always transrational. Hence its enormous symbolic richness—and the importance of myth in religion. A mythical explanation contains the wherewithal to re-bind us (*religio*), or unbind us—whether by means of offerings, rites, *yogas,* worship, art, crafts, study, and so forth. Myth ends up being the fundamental premise on which the ideas, beliefs and practices of the present are based. Plainly, myth cannot be the path to self-realisation, but it can be a support. A myth, which does not guide spiritually, is nothing more than a pseudo-philosophical point of view, which all too easily becomes dogma, and likely to be seen as mere fantasy.

4. THE UNIVERSAL HISTORY

THE 24 *TĪRHAṄKARAS*

The jinas were those humans whose lives were worth recounting. They constitute the archetype for all Jain ascetics to emulate (which to a certain extent they replicate) and the model which all lay people are aware of. Most Jains have learnt the essentials of their tradition through the *jinas'* hagiographies. With these perfect models, Jains come into contact with the supreme bliss that one day they hope to achieve.

Generally, the previous incarnations of each *tīrthaṅkara* are enumerated. In addition, their parents' names are given, as well as their place of birth, their sign of the zodiac, some physical characteristics, type of tree under which they achieved enlightenment, number of disciples they had, guardian spirits (*śāsana-devatās*) which accompanied them, date and place of their *nirvāṇa,* and amount of time that passed before the appearance of the next *jina.* Distinctive emblems (*lāñchanas*), colours and guardian spirits form the basis of iconographic recognition [see TABLE 1]. The symbolism involved can vary slightly according to the Jain tradition in question. As can be seen in the chart, the title "lord" (*nātha*) is added to their names.

We are not only delving into a symbolic and mythical history, but into the mind and imagination of any Jain alive today. Given that the two Jain streams (Śvetāmbara and Digambara) do not agree on certain details in the Universal History, I shall present a neutral reconstruction as possible, indicating dissident versions when needed.

RSABHANĀTHA

The first *tīrthaṅkara* of the Universal History was Lord Bull (Ṛṣabhanātha), also known as the Bull God (Ṛṣabhadeva) or Self-existent (Svayambhu). This character, much loved by the whole community, has the privilege of having been the first to expound Jainism in this *avasarpiṇī,* in this *karmabhūmi* of Bharata.

As we know, Ṛṣabha lived in the closing stages of the Sorrowfully Marvellous Age. Consequently, his physical dimensions were colossal and his life span

TABLE 1: The 24 *tīrthankaras*

n°	jina	*colour*	*emblem* (Śvet.)	*guardian spirits* (Śvet.)	*place of birth*	*place of* nirvāṇa
1	Ṛṣabhanātha	yellow	bull	Gomukha and Cakreśvarī	Vinītānagara	Aṣṭāpada (Kailāśa)
2	Ajitanātha	yellow	elephant	Mahāyakṣa and Ajitabalā	Ayodhyā	Sameṭa-Śikhara
3	Saṁbhavanātha	yellow	horse	Trimukha and Duritārī	Śrāvastī	Sameṭa-Śikhara
4	Abhinandana	yellow	monkey	Nāyaka and Kālikā	Ayodhyā	Sameṭa-Śikhara
5	Sumatinātha	yellow	red goose	Tumburu and Mahākālī	Ayodhyā	Sameṭa-Śikhara
6	Padmaprabhu	red	red lotus	Kusuma and Śyāmā	Kauśambī	Sameṭa-Śikhara
7	Supārśvanātha	yellow	*svastika*	Mātanga and Śāntā	Vārāṇasī	Sameṭa-Śikhara
8	Candraprabhu	white	Moon	Vijaya and Bhṛikuṭī	Candrapura	Sameṭa-Śikhara
9	Suvidhinātha	white	crocodile	Ajita and Sutārakā	Kānaṇḍīnagara	Sameṭa-Śikhara
10	Śītaḷanātha	yellow	*śrīvatsa*	Brahmā and Aśokā	Bhadrapura	Sameṭa-Śikhara
11	Śreyāṁsanātha	yellow	rhinoceros	Yakṣeṭa and Mānavī	Simhapura	Sameṭa-Śikhara
12	Vāsupūjya	red	buffalo	Kumāra and Caṇḍā	Campā	Campā
13	Vimalanātha	yellow	wild boar	Ṣāṇmukha and Viditā	Kampīlya	Sameṭa-Śikhara
14	Anantanātha	yellow	falcon	Pātāla and Aṅkuśā	Ayodhyā	Sameṭa-Śikhara
15	Dharmanātha	yellow	lightning	Kinnara and Kandarpā	Ratnapurī	Sameṭa-Śikhara
16	Śāntinātha	yellow	deer	Ganiḍa and Nirvāṇī	Hastināpura	Sameṭa-Śikhara
17	Kunthunātha	yellow	goat	Gandharva and Balā	Hastināpura	Sameṭa-Śikhara
18	Aranātha	yellow	*nandāvartta*	Yakṣeṭa and Dhaṇā	Hastināpura	Sameṭa-Śikhara
19	Mallinātha	blue	pitcher	Kubera and Dharaṇapriy ā	Mithilā	Sameṭa-Śikhara
20	Suvrata	black	turtle	Varuna and Naradattā	Rājagṛiha	Sameṭa-Śikhara
21	Naminātha	yellow	blue lotus	Bhṛikuṭi and Gandhārī	Mathurā	Sameṭa-Śikhara
22	Neminātha	yellow	shell	Gomedha and Ambikā	Saurīpura	Girnār (Girinagara)
23	Pārsvanātha	blue	snake	Dharanendra and Padmāvatī (Laksmī)	Vārāṇasī	Sameta-Śikhara
24	Mahāvīra	yellow	lion	Mātaṅga and Siddhāyikā	Kuṇḍalapura	Pāpā (Pāvāpuri)

was astounding. Mythology informs us that he was a prince of the city of Ayodhyā (Vinītānagara), son of the last of the *kulakaras,* Nābhi, and his wife Marudevī.

In those already less marvellous times, people began to break the laws established by the *kulakaras.* Important men in that society approached Nābhi petitioning him to impose more strict law and order. The chief crowned his son Ṛṣabha king *(rājā).* It is revealing that the first *jina* and the first *rājā* should have been one and the same. As we shall have the occasion to see, the association between Jainism and royalty has been constant throughout history.

As in ancient times, Ṛṣabha married his twin sister Sumaṅgalā, although according to Digambara Jainism she was not his twin. From this marriage was born his first-born son Bharata, the latter's twin sister Brahmī and 98 other brothers. Ṛṣabha married a second wife, Sunandā. It is related that her twin brother died when a coconut fell on his head (in fact, this was the first violent death of the whole cosmic cycle!). Out of this union, Bāhubali and his twin sister Sundarī were born. At this juncture, Ṛṣabha broke with the institution of marriage between brothers and sisters, introducing the union by marriage between members of different families. When forming this new marriage pattern, Ṛṣabha put society in order according to the system of castes (*jātis*) and of socio-spiritual classes (*varṇas*).

To maintain order, Ṛṣabha introduced the state, justice, punishment, and taught the 72 sciences to men and the 64 arts to women. The former included: agriculture, grammar, arithmetic, rhetoric, singing, astronomy or the training of elephants. Among the latter, there were: dance, painting, intelligence, hypocrisy, commerce or the peculiar art of composing verses with the last syllable of a word.

One day, after the sudden death of his favourite dancer, Ṛṣabha opted to abandon palace life. He decided to launch himself upon the search of eternity. He divided his kingdom up into one hundred parts (giving them to his hundred children) abandoned life-in-the-world and devoted himself to asceticism for a thousand million years—twelve months in human calender terms? (Mehta 1993: 10). Obviously, being the first renunciant ascetic of this cosmic cycle he was also the first to beg for food, and in receiving a donation (*dāna*) from a lay person, a most important event for the Jain community, which is still commemorated with much feeling these days. After prolonged asceticism and meditation he achieved enlightenment beneath a fig tree. Following that, he dedicated himself to the teaching of the path of non-violence and self control for billions of years. His followers formed the first communities of Jain ascetics, led by his grandson Puṇḍarīka. His daughter Brahmī, patron of the sciences, arts, and knowledge (equivalent to the Brāhmaṇic Sarasvatī) and her half sister Sundarī, headed the first communities of Jain nuns.

As can be seen, Ṛṣabha is considered to be the father of civilisation as well as being the first one in promulgating the spiritual path that leads to salvation [see FIG. 33]. For that reason, he is also known as First Lord (Ādinātha) or Lord of the Age (Yugādīśa). He attained liberation on mount Aṣṭāpada, which tradition identifies as the famous Kailash, in the Himalayas, just before entering into the fourth age of the descending cycle.

THE STORY OF BHARATA AND BĀHUBALI

Bharata and Bāhubali's lives were just as significant as that of their father, the first *jina.* The biography and figure of the former, represent a model of an enlightened universal ruler (*cakravartin*); those of the latter [see FIGS. 8, 9] represent the ideal of a Jain hero *(vīra).* Moreover, according to Jainism, both constitute the origin of the Indian dynasties. All Indian kings trace their genealogy back to a common ancestor, via two birth-lines, one "solar" (*sūryavaṃśa*) and the other "lunar" (*candravaṃśa*). The descendants of Bharata formed the solar genealogy of the Indian dynasties. The lunar lineage was formed by the descendants of Bāhubali. The first formal report of their story is found in Jinasena's *Ādi-purāṇa,* the main Digambara writings on the origins of civilisation. The narration more or less goes like this.

Bharata ruled over one of the kingdoms ceded by his father. He was such a master in politics that his chaplains recognised that the art of government had fully manifested itself in him for the first time. They were experts in the Books of Laws (Śāstras), but there was no one who knew how to apply justice with such versatility as Bharata. Bharata also possessed a magic war disc, a *cakra* (the symbol of all *cakravartins*), which transformed him into an invincible warrior. Thanks to his bravery in battle and mastery in the art of government, Bharata conquered all the noble regions of Bharata-varṣa, one by one. Crossing the river Indus (Sindhu), he appropriated the ignoble lands (those beyond the pale of civilisation). Towards the North, he overcame the *vidyādhara* kings who lived in the Vaitāḍhya Mountains that cut Bharata-varṣa in two. He also conquered the Ganges (Gaṅgā) and with great pomp was crowned emperor. Well aware of his power, the young king sent messengers to the last princes with a clear message: "Your elder brother, the emperor, is worthy of your veneration and should be honoured in all ways" (in Strohl 1990: 219), and that is what they did.

The brothers took to the ascetic path that their father Ṛṣabha preached to the world for the first time in this cosmic cycle. They set off for the lonely forests. In India, the image of a forest conveys that which is borderline, dangerous and uncivilised, but which is open to endless possibilities. Jungles are infested with imps or devils thirsty for human blood; all is impregnated with the mysterious murmur of owls. The howling of jackals echoes from all directions, but ascetics are not afraid of the dismal places in which they have to spend the night, or the lions or wild elephants roaming around nearby. The only fear for the ascetic is the mere thought of the endless flow of *saṃsāra.*

The renunciation of Bharata's brothers left his stepbrother Bāhubali, who governed in Taxila (Takṣaśilā), as the only one not to have handed over his kingdom.

He was given the same message: surrender or be exiled along with the group of ascetics in the forest. Bharata's perceived greed was intolerable to Bāhubali:

> "Clearly he desires to possess the land Our father granted Us. Would it satiate his greed if We acquiesced? O messenger, that respected Lord has no shame, for he desires to take from Us the family land Our father bequeathed Us" (in Strohl 1990: 227).

War was inevitable, but the ministers of both sides exhorted them to solve the dispute with a triple combat between the two brothers, a more Jain form of contest which would not lead to unnecessary bloodshed. The loser would have to accept defeat without rage; the winner, without pride.

Bāhubali won the first two contests, the staring duel and the combat in water. Finally, it was the turn of the wrestling match. After a fierce confrontation, Bāhubali managed to lift his stepbrother contemptuously above his head. The crowds on Bāhubali's side claimed victory, while Bharata's allies bowed their heads in sign of respect. It was too humiliating for Bharata. Overcome with anger, he let fly his lethal magic disc at his stepbrother, thanks to his powers of concentration, but instead of decapitating him, the *cakra* circled three times around Bāhubali's neck, in celebration of his triple victory. Repentant, Bharata knelt down before his step brother, offering him his kingdom. In the precise moment that Bāhubali began to proclaim the greatness of his heroic feat, he became aware of the futility of seeking what was ephemeral. He understood the selfishness and attachment of one who was avid for power and converted the victory over his brother into a victory over attachment. He renounced the throne and decided to take the path of asceticism. Following the example of his father, he retired from the world. For a whole year, Bāhubali remained standing still (*kāyotsarga)* in a state of permanent fast. Creepers began growing up his legs, cobras used the saint's feet as their dwelling place, but he kept his gaze fixed on the North, in an internal battle to overcome his ego, determined to arrest the terrifying cycle of *saṃsāra* [see FIG. 8]. Meditating on Jain truths, he progressed through gnostic levels. Wild beasts curled up meekly beside him. The tigress, which had just given birth, kissed an old jackal on the head, and let its puppies suckle her milk. Elephants carried water on lotus leaves to sanctify the sacred place where the saint meditated. The whole forest became a paradise of serenity and peace, shot through with the majesty of the Bāhubali's composure, and the author of the *purāṇa,* Jinasena, proclaimed in praise:

> "Oh, is not asceticism peace-inducing?" (in Strohl 1990: 241).

After a year of asceticism, Bāhubali awoke to enlightened reality. According to Digambara tradition, he achieved *nirvāṇa* even before his father Ṛṣabha. Thus, even without being a *tīrthaṅkara,* the saint Bāhubali has the honour of having been the first liberated one in this descending cycle. Legend has it that the emperor Bharata came to worship the enlightened one. Thanks to his sincere attitude he eradicated many of his faults.

If Bāhubali represents the spiritual warrior par excellence, Bharata is the model of the enlightened ruler, the *cakravartin,* which is also a well-known ideal in Buddhism and Brāhmaṇism. Just as with all *cakravartins*, Bharata possessed the beauty, strength, intelligence, and the distinctive physical and mental features that characterise monarchs who succeed in conquering the six parts of Bharata-varṣa. After overcoming his opponents and reuniting all the kingdoms into a single empire, Bharata governed for a long time. Jains named India after him, giving the continent the classical name of the land of the descendants of Bharata (Bharata-varṣa). It is said that it was he who had the true Vedas (*Ārya Veda*) composed, where the cult of the *tīrthaṅkaras* and the path of the Three Jewels are proclaimed. The custodians of the Vedas were called Brāhmaṇas—which we must not confuse with the false Brāhmaṇas who populate India today and confuse the issue mumbling a heterodox Veda.

If the *tīrthaṅkara*'*s* lives all follow the same pattern (since there is only one way that leads to unconditioned reality) the *cakravartins*' lives on the other hand can vary a great deal, especially where their ends are concerned. Some *cakravartins* opted for renouncing the world, and some even became *tīrthaṅkaras',* others ascended into the heavens after death, and there were still others who descended into hell owing to the crimes and misdemeanours committed during their lifetimes. In Bharata's case, Hemacandra tells us that one day while the emperor was looking into the mirror he suddenly realised that a ring had slipped off one of his fingers. The sight of his ugly, bare finger knuckle shattered him, so much so that for the first time he *grasped* the transitory nature of things. He immediately attained omniscience (Laidlaw 1995: 37). Other sources stress the fact that his sadness overwhelmed him when he realised that most of his family and friends had departed this life. Bharata accordingly decided to renounce the world. After sublime penances, he attained enlightenment or omniscience on the summit of Mount Kailash (von Glasenapp 1925: 296).

In the Śvetāmbara version of Jainism, the honour of being the first liberated human being does not fall to Bharata or Bāhubali, or even Ṛṣabha, but to the latter's mother, queen Marudevī. Having become aware of Ṛṣabha's omniscience, she went one day with her grandson Bharata to worship the new worthy one (*arhat*). The sight of her son's glory caused her to rise through all the levels of knowledge that destroy ignorance. She achieved the knowledge known as unique (*kevala-jñāna*) and then, leaving her body, achieved liberation (Balbir 1990: 66).

THE SUBLIME BEINGS THAT FOLLOWED

Ṛṣabha and Bharata were the only sublime beings of the Sorrowfully Marvellous Period. The remaining 61 exemplary human beings lived in the third Age, the Marvellously Sorrowful Age.

The second *tīrthaṅkara* was Ajita. His nephew Sagara was the second *cakravartin.* Then came the third *tīrthaṅkara,* Sambhava—and so on until the ninth *jina,* Suvidhi. With his death, Jainism completely disappeared from Bharata-varṣa for a quarter of a *palyopama.* The 10th *tīrthaṅkara* was the first one to revive Jainism. But once again, after his emancipation, Jainism again disappeared. The 11th *jina,* Śreyāṁsa, restored it. The first *baladeva,* Acala, the first *vāsudeva,* Tripṛṣṭa, and the first *prativāsudeva,* Aśvagrīva, came on the scene during this period. These sublime beings succeeded one another. Numerous Jain accounts provide profuse details of their lives. In all cases, these are didactic and interspersed with legends and folk-tales. We then come to the 16th *tīrthaṅkara,* Śānti, from which point the Jain religion would not be interrupted again. Before renouncing the world, this *jina* had been the fifth *cakravartin* of the Universal History. After conquering the six parts of Bharata-varṣa and enjoying his kingdom for 25,000 years, he renounced the world, awakened, and went forth to propagate Jainism, thus becoming a *tīrthaṅkara.* The same happened with Kunthu, the sixth *cakravartin* and 17th *tīrthaṅkara,* and with Ara, the seventh universal monarch and eighteenth *jina.*

As the Universal History unfolds, each succeeding *tīrthaṅkara* is of slightly lesser stature and does not live as long as the one before. In the same way, the time intervals that separate their lives continue to decrease.

MALLINĀTHA

We come to the time of the nineteenth *tīrthaṅkara,* a character whose life deserves close attention. According to Śvetāmbara tradition, Malli was a woman. However, Digambara tradition has it that Malli was male, just like all other *tīrthaṅkaras.* Obviously, it is the Śvetāmbara story, which interests us most. Not because it is maintained by a majority within Jainism, but because it brings up some interesting issues. How was it that a *tīrthaṅkara* come to be born in the body of a woman? The Śvetāmbara version goes like this.

In an earlier existence, Malli was king Vaiśramaṇa. As with many virtuous monarchs, he one day renounced the world and, along with some friends, embraced Jainism. The group of mendicants agreed to practice asceticism, all with the same intensity and for the same lapse of time. Vaiśramaṇa excelled himself in fasting, and through this he generated the valuable *karma* that would vouchsafe him his next existence as a *tīrthaṅkara.* Nevertheless, for not being true to his group of friends, he gained himself other, additional *karma,* which would be visited upon him in his next existence: female *karma* (*strī-karma*) or birth as a woman.

With this burden, princess Malli was born in Mithilā, the capital of Videha, a kingdom in northern Bihar. She was brought up in the palace and as all admired princesses do, she grew into a maiden of unequalled beauty. Legend has it that there were six princes from six neighbouring kingdoms who all asked for her hand in marriage. Acting in accordance with his daughter's wishes (something certainly not usual in India) the king rejected all the princes' petitions. Given such a snub, the princes had reason to declare war. The king implored his daughter to accept, as Videha's army would not be able to contain the mighty enemy forces. Malli thought up a scheme. She proposed sending a messenger to each of the six kingdoms with the message that she would finally concede her hand in marriage, and this was what was done. A few days later the princes began arriving in Mithilā, each one by a different road, and through a different gate, and as such unaware of the other princes in the palace. In the part of the harem visible to the outside world, she had a life-size replica of herself sculpted and set up. From their apartments, the princes could see the statue and smell the garland of flowers that surrounded it, which filled them with pleasure and eagerness. One day Malli had the flowers removed. A nauseating smell wafted out from the interior of the statue, and reached the astonished suitors. It was then that Malli spoke to them, in more or less these words: "Below this statue I have placed a little food everyday. With the passing of time it has become a mass of putrefaction. The same thing happens with one's body... So then, beloved of the gods, do not look for human beings for your gratification. Do not be creatures of passion, guided by desire, and do not let attachment dominate you" (Shāntā 1985: 102). Enlightened by the princess's wisdom, the suitors abandoned the idea of marriage and opted to take the path of renunciation. Malli and her disciples were initiated into the Jain order and it is said that the ascetic nun attained supreme knowledge that very same day. She had become Mallinātha and from that moment on she preached the eternal path of the *jinas.*

The story of Malli contains various interesting teachings: the intrinsically impure nature of food, the inherent ignorance of all passionate activity, etc. Undoubtedly, the main teachings are the determination, independence and wisdom of the princess. In a patriarchal society such as India, Malli's tale has a powerful impact: the way of spiritual progress and the possibility of a higher goal is within everybody's reach, whether man or woman. We shall have the opportunity to look at this question in more detail in chapter 12.

EPICS WITH A JAIN SLANT

After Malli, well-known characters from pan-Indian mythology begin to appear in the Universal History. The legend of the eighth *baladeva,* the eighth *vāsudeva* and the eighth *prativāsudeva,* is by far the most significant. The eighth *baladeva* was Padma, known in Hinduism as Rāma. Lakṣmaṇa, his stepbrother, was the eighth *vāsudeva.* The eighth *prativāsudeva* was the villain, Rāvaṇa. This last would kidnap the beautiful Sītā, Padma's wife, who would then be rescued by Lakṣmaṇa and the generals Hanumān and Sugrīva. The plot and characters are well-known to those familiar with Hinduism, being the protagonists of one of India's most popular epic poems (Itihāsas): the *Rāmāyaṇa.*

Soon enough, Jainism felt the need to adapt to legends, epics, and stories from popular tradition to a Jaina context. A logical step, if Jainism were going to integrate into the vast Indian culture. If, at the same time, it could manage to "Jainise" the epics (give them a Jain slant) its tradition would succeed in maintaining its independence and its particularities would be perceived. This is a feasible (and very common) process in India, where legends and myths have never ceased to change. India never had a Homer or a Hesiodus who would petrify these into a definitive pantheon. All the stories are susceptible to reinterpretation, to assimilating other legends and even to modification. Professor A.K. Ramanujan (1991: 46) said that the cultural area in which Rāmāyaṇas are endemic has a pool of signifiers that include plots, characters, names, geography, incidents, and relationships. Every author dips into it and brings out a unique crystallisation, a new text with a unique texture and a fresh context. The fact speaks for itself that we have no less than 30 versions of the Hindu *Rāmāyaṇa*—Vālmīki must have composed the embryonic version around the 4th and 3rd centuries BC (Winternitz 1907:1,480-494). We find Rāmāyaṇas in all Indian vernacular languages, in Chinese and in Indonesian. Jains also composed their own Rāmāyanas, of which more than a dozen have been passed down to us.

In chronological order, the first *Rāmāyaṇa* to Jainise the story of Rāma was the *Padma-carita* by the poet Vimala Sūri (3rd-4th centuries). Following the plot of the classical *Rāmāyaṇa,* Vimala purged the story of excessively Brāh-manical elements and endowed it with a more Jain spirit. He also purged the narration of implausible aspects, giving it a more realistic touch. Vimala found it inconceivable for the great Indra to be Rāvaṇa's captive, or for monkeys (Hanuman and Sugriva) to be victorious over the troops of the *prativāsudeva.* All this was changed. The violent acts of Rāma (Padma) are not mentioned, nor is much interest taken in portraying the wickedness of the titan Rāvaṇa. In fact, Rāvana emerges as a quite heroic villain. He is a sublime being, devoted to the *tīrthaṅkaras,* whose only weakness and perdition arising from his uncontrollable love for Sītā. For Vimala, the titan Rāvaṇa is not a human-devouring monster. He is a lord of a semi-divine type of being known as *vidyādharas,* who are highly civilised and strict observers of the vow of *ahimsā* (Kulkarni 1952: 78). Curiously, in the *Padma-carita* it is Lakṣmaṇa and not his brother Rāma who kills the titan and rescues Sītā, since in the Jain Universal History it is always the *vāsudeva* who annihilates the *prativāsudeva.* Owing to his violent act, Lakṣmaṇa had to go to hell, while Rāma remained faithful to Jainism and achieved liberation.

The complete Jainisation of the *Rāmāyaṇa* came about with the *Padmapurāṇa* by Raviśena (7th-8th centuries). Raviśena basically follows the *Padmacarita,* but with certain modifications to fit in with the Digambara point of view. Here, too, the titan Rāvaṇa assumes the role of a virtuous Jain ruler who reigns in a peaceful kingdom. In the end, Sītā becomes a Digambara nun (*āryikā*) and seeks the classical death by fasting (*sallekhanā*), as a result of which she would be reincarnated as a deity. Rāma renounces the world; he becomes an ascetic and attains enlightenment. In his omniscience, he predicts that Sītā will be reborn as a universal ruler and Lakṣmaṇa and Rāvaṇa would have to go to the fourth hell—where to the best of my knowledge they still are—owing to their violent deeds. Nevertheless, they will be reborn as sons of Sītā, and in that same life will achieve liberation.

Another good example of the Jainisation of pan-Indian mythology was the adaptation of the other great Hindu epic: the *Mahābhārata.* The principal version, known as the *Harivaṃśa-purāṇa,* was the work of Jinasena Sūri (8th century). The chronicle centres on the lives of the *tīrthaṅkara* Nemi [see the following] and his cousin, the sublime Kṛṣṇa, ninth *vāsudeva* in Jain mythology. Here again a similar ruse is used as in the *Padma-carita* to adapt it to Jain teachings: Kṛṣṇa is not the hero and virtuous defender of Jainism—perhaps his warlike and amorous conquests prevented him from changing his role so drastically. He is presented in a rather immoral light, and it is his brother Balarāma rather who is the hero.

In this process of Jainisation, the influence of Kṛṣṇa-centred and Viṣṇu-centred Hinduism is patent. Rāma, Kṛṣṇa, Balarāma, Sītā, Laksmana or Hanumān are deities of the first order for the Vaiṣṇavas (followers of Viṣṇu). The symbols, which the *vāsudevas* display are the classical ones of Viṣṇu: the shell, disc, sword, and hammer. In fact, 27 of the 63 Jain sublime beings are related to the legends of Kṛṣṇa. The popularity of Kṛṣṇa and Balarāma— characters always associated with the *tīrthaṅkara* Nemi—is significantly much greater amongst the Jains of Gujarat and Rajasthan. It is noticeable that Jains and Vaiṣṇavas in these regions have always maintained good, close relations. So if it is true that Jainism has decisively influenced Vaiṣṇava doctrine on incarnations (*avatāras*), Vaiṣṇava mythology has equally played a major role in the mythology of the Universal History. Do not read this as a kind of Hinduisation of Jainism, but in fact the other way round: as a way of integrating potential converts.

NEMINĀTHA

Neminātha was the 22nd *tīrthaṅkara,* also known as Ariṣṭanemi [see FIGS. 1, 46, 47]. Tradition has it that he originated from the region of Saurashtra, in Gujarat. He belonged to the Yādava clan, a famous lineage that had always been linked with Kṛṣṇa, and like his cousin, the *Uttarādhyayana-sūtra* (22.5) mentions Nemi as being of a dark complexion (*kṛṣṇa*). Afraid that Nemi would usurp his kingdom, the not very charitable Kṛṣṇa arranged for him to marry the fair Rājīmatī. With the operation of *karma,* on the very day of the wedding, young Nemi was deeply moved on hearing the pitiful cries of the caged animals that were going to be slaughtered for the wedding banquet. He decided on cancelling his wedding, gave all his possessions to his coachman, and left Dwarka to go to Mount Girnar, in the Kathiawar region. With his renunciation, Nemi emerges as Kṛṣṇa's opponent, at least to the Kṛṣṇa who was attached to luxury, weapons, and women, who appears in the Hindu Purāṇas. Nemi begins a new life, as a dedicated ascetic in the caves and forests of the sacred mountain. After some weeks of ascetic practice, Nemi gains infinite knowledge at the summit of the mountain, beneath a majestic banyan. Today at Girnar, one can find some of the most splendid Jain temples [see FIG. 41] and the sacred mountain has inevitably remained linked to the figure of *the jina* Nemi. It is said that he died at the age of 1,000 years.

PĀRŚVANĀTHA

We finally come to the last but one *tīrthaṅkara* of this descending cycle. Tradition maintains that Pārśva was born in the year 817 BC, in the city of Benares (Vārāṇasī), exactly 84,000 years after the *nirvaṇa* of his predecessor, Nemi. This nearness to our time is responsible for Pārśva's nearly normal size and the fact that he lived for only one hundred years.

Pārśva is usually represented as dark blue in colour and is the only *jina* who possesses a distinctly recognisable sign evident at first sight: a many headed cobra [see FIG. 10] always protects him. These days he is still the most worshipped of all *tīrthaṅkaras.* Not for nothing does the *Kalpa-sūtra* (149), the first text in relating his biography, nickname him "the people's favourite" (*purisādāṇīya*), the celebrated one.

Pārśva's hagiography follows the same recurring pattern found in all *jinas'* lives. It is another replica of the life of Mahāvīra that is lost in the remote past. Nevertheless, the account has some peculiar features, which are not found in those of the other *tīrthaṅkaras.*

As in the case of most Indian sages, saints and gods, Pārśva's biographers—for instance, Vādirāja (10th-11th centuries) or Bhāvadeva Sūri

(13th century) authors of the respective *Pārśvanātha-caritas*—did not limit themselves in narrating his last life, but details many of his previous incarnations. The intention behind the inclusion of these tales of previous lives is clear. On one hand, we learn of the inevitable consequences of action. On the other hand the different patterns of virtue are described that can be adjusted to the needs of different people. No Jain expects to achieve liberation in this life—which in any case is not possible in Bharata—but to seek to generate enough worth to be reborn in superior spiritual circumstances, perhaps on another continent where even today humans can attain liberation. The accounts of Pārśva's previous incarnations illustrate many of the values and doctrines of Jainism.

A characteristic feature of his biography is the pronounced duality existing between him, all goodness and non-attachment, and his brother, who represents his *alter ego,* his wicked, darker side. Heinrich Zimmer and Joseph Campbell (1951: 185-186), who both considered the Jain religion to have pre-Aryan and pre-Vedic origin, note a possible influence on Zoroastrian dualism. The matter requires further consideration. In this dual relationship, the virtuous one ascends, life after life, until literally becoming a worthy one (*arhat*), while the luxuriant, malignant one continues sinking further and further into misery and wickedness. It could be said that the course of the latter exhibits almost fatalist determination. Notwithstanding, the protagonists are responsible for their own actions. It is ignorance that seems to dissipate freewill rather than make it impossible. Let us take a look at how this worked. We shall learn, like any young Jain, how to class action and what the career of a future *tīrthaṅkara* is like.

The first episode narrates the vicissitudes of the brothers Marubhūti and Kamaṭha, sons of one of king Aravinda's ministers. Marubhūti is the character that would be Pārśva nine existences later on; Kamaṭha is his *alter ego.* Convinced of the transitory nature of existence, the good-hearted Marubhūti opted to renounce the world. The passion-dominated Kamaṭha took advantage of the situation and committed adultery with his brother's wife. When the king became aware of this offence he asked Marubhūti to be the one to dictate sentence. The future *jina* implored forgiveness for his brother, but the king decided to punish him with exile. Devoid of his belongings, Kamaṭha devoted himself to solitary asceticism. His aim was not to purify himself but to acquire supernatural powers (*siddhis*) thanks to the spiritual ardour kindled by the asceticism *(tapas).* When Marubhūti learned of his penitence, he went to do him homage, believing that his reasons were healthy and pure. At the moment, Marubhūti knelt down to kiss his feet, the irate ascetic struck him on the head with a rock and killed him. Kamaṭha continued his life of crime and wickedness until, in due course, he died. Death in India does not represent an end. The continuity between life and death, between one personality and another, all is dissolved in the light of *karma.*

The following legend takes us back to king Aravinda. Now old, he decides to renounce the throne and take the path of contemplation and asceticism along with other hermits. One day, while all were deep in meditation, a wild elephant charged into the place where they were meditating. Filled with panic, the hermits fled. All except Aravinda, who stood firm in a deep contemplative state. Seeing the serenity of the ascetic the elephant calmed down and, lowering its trunk, bent his two front legs in a sign of obeisance. Aravinda questioned it: "There is not a greater sin than harming another being. Your incarnation in this animal form is a result of the unworthiness acquired at the moment of your previous violent death. Abandon these unworthy deeds; take vows; a happy state will begin to germinate within you". Aravinda's harangue enabled the elephant to realise it had been Marubhūti in its previous existence. Owing to his violent death and the bad thoughts that flourished at the moment of the mortal blow, he had been reborn in that inferior condition. On hearing the ascetic, the elephant remembered sequences of its previous life as the son of the king's minister; it took the vows of an ascetic and received religious instruction from Aravinda. From that moment on, it followed a vegetarian diet, led a life of austerity and meditation. One day, when taking a drink of water at a nearby lake, an immense *kukurṭa,* a creature that is half cockerel half serpent (the incarnation of Kamaṭha) killed it. The antagonistic opposition between the brothers had happened again, this time in the form of two animals. At the moment of this new death, it did not forget its ascetic's vows. Its serenity earned it an incarnation in the highest of heavens.

After a few thousand years in a heavenly condition, this spiritual soul was reborn as the devoted ascetic Agnivega, who was also bitten by a snake and was to die without blinking or losing his inner balance. The snake—of course—was the incarnation of his ex-brother, who after some aeons in hell had returned to the Middle World.

The stories follow one after another. One goes to heaven, the other to hell, but their destinies converge again and again in Bharata-varṣa. In every rebirth in the Middle World, we can see one being more advanced in his spiritual progress. The other all the while sinks further into wickedness. This opposition is well illustrated in the first brother's incarnation as the devout Vajranābha, a ruler who renounces the throne accompanied by a hermit. The second brother is reincarnated as a tribal huntsman, a Bhīl, and ends up shooting a poisoned arrow at the saint. The former goes to the highest heaven; and the latter to the seventh and most horrific hell.

In the following and second from last incarnation, the future *jina* was born as the emperor Svarṇabāhu. In this existence, he acquired the valuable and unique *karma* that would result in a future rebirth as a *tīrthaṅkara.* His *alterego,* however, takes the form of a lion who comes to kill him for the umpteenth time. The future *jina* is then reborn in the 10th heaven, while the lion yet again goes to hell. In his heavenly existence, he who was once Marubhūti worshipped the eternal images of the *tīrthaṅkaras* that exist on the island of Nandīśvara.

Thus, the future *tīrthaṅkara* arrived at his last existence. All the gods came to share in the supreme bliss that accompanies the birth of a *tīrthaṅkara* upon the Earth. Like all mothers with *jina* sons, the queen had the auspicious dreams that precede the birth of an exceptional being. And in the month of April-May (Vaiśākha), the 23rd *tīrthaṅkara* of this descending cycle was born in Benares. He was son of king Aśvasena and queen Vāmā; and thus a member of the nobility (Kṣatriya), as all *jinas* should be.

Hagiographies tell of the day when the young Pārśva came across his grandfather Mahīpāla in the forest. The old man was cutting firewood to feed the five fires used in his penance, a common practice even these days among Brāhmaṇa ascetics. On meeting, the young man warned his grandfather not to chop any more logs as there were two snakes among the branches and he might kill them. The old man paid no heed and while cutting up the branches he chopped the two snakes in half. The youth exclaimed: "Don't you feel any compassion for them? Grandfather, you don't have knowledge. This penitence you practice is absolutely useless... The spirit of envy infects all your practices; and every day you kill animals with your fires... Abandon this meaningless mortification; take the path of the *tīrthaṅkaras* and undertake right action, right vision and right knowledge, as this is the only path that leads to salvation" (cited in Zimmer 1951: 198). The young man chanted some hymns to the dying snakes and both expired in his presence. After such a worthy death, the serpents were reborn in the subterranean world: the male as the *nāga* Dharaṇendra, the female as the *nāgiṇī* Padmāvatī (Lakṣmī). Some versions of this myth speak of only one snake, but the story of the two *nāgas* is the one that became more popular. As some readers will have guessed, the old man Mahīpāla was none other than his original brother incarnated as a false Brāhmaṇa after various births in hell. The irascible hermit continued in his stupid penitence and died. The young prince grew up to wed the princess Prabhāvatī, the daughter of king of Ayodhyā.

One spring day Pārśva saw an image of the *tīrthaṅkara* Nemi. *Ipso facto* his mind was seized with the spirit of renunciation. Fulfilling the predetermined course that actions in his past lives had earned him, at the age of thirty he renounced the world and became a homeless (*anagāra*) mendicant. He decided not to lose any more time swimming in the ocean of transmigration. The very gods came down to celebrate the auspicious event of his worldly renunciation.

The central episode of Pārśva's hagiography has to do with his victory over Death (Māra), the equivalent of omniscience (*kevala-jñāna*). Buddhism refers to the same theme in the life of the Buddha, which seems to be copied from the life of Pārśva(Coomaraswamy 1914: 15).

Pārśva meditated imperturbably in the heart of the forest. Gradually, he came to reach the highest levels of consciousness. One day, while he was sitting still, in meditation, a demon came to bother him. It was Saṃvara, also known as Meghakumāra. Although the demon was repelled by the ascetic's saintly halo, he was set on attacking the yogi. The demon then appeared as Death (Māra), but Pārśva remained impassive. Saṁvara was none other than the treacherous being that many incarnations before had been Kamaṭha. Summoning all his supernatural powers, he conjured up the forces of darkness and wind. He attacked Pārśva with colossal downpours, he assumed horrific forms, he incited him to kill, to be violent, without success. The earth shook and in the subterranean caverns, the *nāgas* Dharaṇendra and Padmāvatī perceived the danger threatening the saint who had illuminated their deaths, and brought about their benevolent condition. Both took up a position beside the sage and, adopting the form of a gigantic cobra, lifted the saint out of the water and covered him like an umbrella [see FIG. 10], protecting him from the torrential rain sent by Death. The apparition was so terrifying for Saṁvara that the demon was forced to retreat. Understandably, Pārśva's emblematic animal is the snake. Professor Zimmer (1955:1,56-60) has demonstrated that the story of the prince who renounces the world and becomes a contemplative sage, who is subsequently protected by a dragon or snake which acted as his parapet, is a pattern which dates back to very ancient times. Some think that these mythological and iconographic motifs stem from the Indus civilisation, but this is just speculation [see page 121]. In this connection, Jagdishchandra Jain (1947: 10-11) refers to the forms of worship of the tribal peoples of Bengal and Bihar, where the cult of the snake deity Manasā is very popular. At all events, it is undeniable that Jain mythology and iconography, filled as they are with serpents (*nāgas*), marvellous beings (*yakṣas*), sacred trees and yogic trances, hark back to practices and beliefs of thousands of years ago. Both Buddhism and Jainism have done none other than model their heroes' lives around these elements.

The sage continued meditating for seven weeks and finally attained omniscience beneath a *dhātaki* tree. He had eliminated all his destructive *karmas* and had become liberated in this life, one who was able to perceive the entire universe. In a state of complete and perpetual omniscience, Pārśva dedicated himself to proclaiming his doctrine and forming groups of followers. Tradition states that, like all *jinas,* he divided the community (*saṃgha, tīrtha*) into four groups: (1) renunciant men (*nirgranthas, sādhus*); (2) renunciant women (*nirgranthīs, sādhvīs*); (3) lay men (*śrāvakas*); (4) lay women (*śrāvakās*). At the head of each group there was a group leader (*gaṇadhara*), under the supervision of his chief disciple, Svayambhu. It is said that among his followers there were no less than a thousand omniscient ones (*kevalins*), and hundreds of scriptural experts (*śruta-kevalins*). Legend has it that Saṁvara himself turned up to listen to his message of peace and happiness. At a stroke, all his continued hate and hostility of the past million years and innumerable rebirths, evaporated upon hearing the message of non-violence. Woebegone and full of remorse, the demon bowed down before the sage's feet and wept. The infinitely good-natured Pārśva consoled him. Thanks to Pārśva's composure, Saṁvara's mind opened to right perception and he placed his feet on the unfailing path that leads to liberation.

For 69 years, men and women continued to flock to him to be converted and become disciples of the new *jina.* Finally, Pārśva retired to the South of Magadha, to the summit of Mount Sameta-Śikhara [see FIG. 40], a mountain that these days is known in Bihar as Mount Parasnath (Pārsvanātha) in the saint's honour. After prolonged fasting, the last and definitive penitence recurrent in the exemplary lives of many Jain saints, Pārśva attained *nirvāṇa.* It is said that eight of his chief disciples, headed by the great Śubhadatta, took charge of the order. The latter was followed by Haridatta, Āryasamudra, Prabha, and Keśīn. This last was Mahāvīra's contemporary [see page 154].

Part III

The Social and Religious Context

A classical prejudice has it that cyclic time, typical of India, is incompatible with the linear time that prevails in the West. With the steady secularisation of the concept of time in the 18th and 19th centuries, it took in the notions of change, of evolution and of progress. Marxist faith in progress or the scatological Christian faith look ever forward. From this point of view, we live in a clearly linear time, and one that is decidedly optimistic: civilisations progress, species evolve, societies advance and there are even those who say that mankind is improving.

Nonetheless, I believe that the cyclic notion of Hindu cosmologies does not necessarilly exclude other ways of perceiving time. The dichotomy between a linear-historical-rational-profane time versus another, which is cyclicd-ahistorical-mythical-sacred will not stand up to scrutiny. Following the historian Romila Thapar (1996: 9), it has to be accepted that both conceptions of time can coexist, at least in India. To illustrate this, the Indian mentality conceives time as a sort of segmentation within arcs, which in turn are inserted into greater cycles. This simultaneity of categories of time supposes an admirable degree of complexity and refinement.

It is for this reason that the *itihāsa-purāṇa-sūtra* tradition also took on those historico-linear particularities that it considered relevant. One of the preferred areas is formed by the royal genealogies and the associated myths. Perhaps, these genealogies are not completely accurate but, as the detailed study by Romila Thapar (1978: 198) shows, they reveal a landscape of migrations of peoples and interactions between cultures. The fact is that today the experts have recognised that they had all too blithely underestimated the exactitude of traditional Indian history (R.M. Smith 1973: 1). What is revealing is a clear notion of genealogical time inserted into the cyclic vision.

Inserted within these gigantic cosmographic spaces, within an infinite succession of ages, human life seems no more than a tiny accident. But this existential angst has its positive counterpart. If the future and the past stretch out into the infinity, what really has value is the *present.* Interestingly, this does not delete a projection into the future. Thanks to the notion that all action has its corresponding fruit that will ripen in a subsequent existence, this present life has a clear *raison d'être* for many Indians. One either expects an auspicious rebirth thanks to the merit of one's actions or a total break with the cycle thanks to *yoga* which leads to liberation. Indian cosmological notions, as nightmarish as they seem to be, would be devoid of sense without the proclamation that there is a way to be saved. This opportunity arises in the *here and now.* It is in this world and in this human condition that the experience of enlightenment can be attained. For Jainism, time is a means (a real one, not an illusion) by which this can be realised. Time *constitutes* reality. Hence, the Jain interest in biography, in micro-history and the lessons that history can bring us.

In Jainism, what corresponds to the genealogies and Purāṇic chronicals is to be found in the Caritas and Purāṇas that make up the Jain Universal History. The Buddhist Sūtras and Jātakas play a comparable role. These texts expound the biographies of their leaders and the history of the monastic communities they presided over. In the task of compiling this material, a process that lasted several centuries and which, in a sense, is still being carried on, the example of the Hindu Purāṇas and the need to counter them played their part. The Jain ascetics who transmitted these teachings show a more accentuated historical-linear sense of time than that of the Brāhmaṇical tradition. In fact, 6th, 5th, and 4th centuries BC, when Mahāvīra and the Buddha were living, are known by Indians as the historical period of their chronology. Both Jains and Buddhists began to date the happenings of their history from the time of the final release (*vīranirvāṇa, mahāparinirvāṇa*) of their respective leaders. The use of historical eras by the Brāhmaṇic tradition is surely the result of Jain and Buddhist influence.

Truth be teld, the Jain texts are not so much interested in political and social issues of the time of Mahāvīra, but in explaining and unfolding the framework in which to situate the exemplary and archetypical life of the last *jina.* They do not reflect upon the historical events or social relations. It would be a mistake to paint a picture of the Indian society of that time based on the Sūtras. Not only was that not their purpose, but it is in any case clear that these texts were compiled by a small elite. They do not represent the vision of society. Logically enough, they have nothing to say about the groups that were normally marginalised by the lettered intelligentsia: low castes, women, tribal peoples, and so forth. One way or another, the Jain texts, when examined critically and checked against Buddhist and Brāhmaṇical material, provide us with a clear historical picture with more or less diaphanous images. In no way do I wish to question the mythical aspects of the tradition, since I consider that mythology is as much history as the reviewing of the "facts" would be. My purpose is rather to contextualise the origins of Jainism, for the tradition is deeply rooted in a culture, society, time, and ways of perceiving the world. The teachings and the religious texts, even the most a-temporal and anonymous of them, were composed, compiled, listened to or recorded by human beings. Both the scriptures and their authors were children of their time. They supply information on ways of understanding the world, on the institutions, on practices and ways of perceiving oneself. It is important to, tell the micro-history because Jainism can only be understood contextually, in its perpetual relationship with Hinduism and Buddhism, with the political, economic, social and religious events of India. This is something that the Jain linear sense of time concedes and authorises.

Accordingly, before reviewing the life of Mahāvīra, the lasty *jina* it would be both justified and enlightening to insert here a section that looks at the sociopolitical context [chapter 5] and the religious context [chapters 6 and 7] in which Mahāvīra's life and that of his predecessor, Pārśva, fitted.

5. THE SOCIO HISTORICAL BACKGROUND

THE VEDIC NIGHT

Let's turn our attention to North India, more specifically, to the plains along the lower Ganges. At the present time, this area consists of Bihar, Uttar Pradesh, plus a portion of Bengal and Jharkhand. Today, this area is one of the most backward in the whole country. Overpopulation, deforestation, malnutrition, and communal conflicts are mortgaging its future. However, some 2,500 or 3,000 years ago, this was an eminently wooded and fertile land thanks to the alluvial deposits of the great river.

We are in the long period that historians have come to call, for better or worse, the Vedic Night. This term refers to the opacity of historical documentation. From 1,800 BC to 250 BC, that is to say from the last vestiges of the old script (of the Indus civilisation) to the reappearance of writing on Hindu soil (on emperor Aśoka's pillars) it is said that India voluntarily opted out of chronology and history. Not only are there no written records, but archaeologists have great difficulty in classifying and dating the materials that are dug up. Here, then, we are entering into a mysterious period that inclines to the imaginary.*

This murky historical lacuna has only reinforced the notion that Indian civilisation has no sense of history. Nonetheless, basing ourselves on the *itihāsapurāṇa -sūtra,* and on the research conducted archaeologists and historians, I think we can venture a feasible picture of what it was like.

* I cannot skim over the oldest strata of the Vedic society, and I shall leave that subject for another occasion (Pániker 2005: 113-194). It Suffices it to say that between 1,900 BC and 1,200 BC, which is the period known as Ṛg-vedic, a monumental and fascinating synthesis occurred between the Indo-European speaking nomadic people, others who spoke Dravidian languages (possibly the creators of the vanished Indus or Harappan civilisation) and still others from the Austro-Asiatic branch, clearly more peripheral but by no means less important. In the end, the first-mentioned imposed their languages in North India and channelled a good part of the cultured tradition of the continent.

SOCIOECONOMIC ASPECTS

It has been said, ingenuously enough, that the meditative-ascetic movements, including Jainism, Buddhism, Ājīvaka, Yoga or Sāṃkhya, all of which emphasise the condition of human suffering (*duḥkha*), imply a social environment of misery, increasing poverty and social conflict. Hence, the urgent need to flee, to escape this world of pain and poverty, by means of ascetic renunciation. As I see it, it is difficult to accept this line of reasoning. The Jain, Buddhist, and Brāhmaṇic renunciants do not speak of social misery. The suffering that the Sūtras refer to is existential (Pande 1984: I, 62); it is the realisation of the absolute finiteness of the human condition, which they tend to illustrate with images of illness, ageing, and death (*Uttarādhyayana-sūtra* 19.15). *Duḥkha,* like *saṃsāra,* has to do with the contingency, the alienation and dissatisfaction of *being* human. The mere fact of existing, of being subject to time, is *duḥkha.* The suffering is ontological not sociological. What is more, the social picture provided by archaeology and textual study, really shows the opposite. As far as we know, between the 9th and 5th centuries BC, the entire course of the Ganges saw spectacular economic, social and political development.

The archaeologists speak of a veritable urban revolution, on the northern plains, where several important cities have been uncovered [see FIG. 71. In the West, there was Taxila (Takṣaśilā), near present-day Rawalpindi, in Pakistan. In Punjab, Indraprāṣṭha, which stood roughly where modern Delhi now stands, as well as nearby Hastināpura. Certain western enclaves show evident connections with the culture—by that time totally disbanded—of the Indus civilisation. In central India, there was the communications nerve centre of Ujjain (Ujjayinī) Further to the East, in the area of the mid-Ganges, we find the most major concentration of urban centres: Śrāvastī, Kauśāmbi, Benares (known in ancient times as Kāśī) and Rājagṛha, close by the modern city of Patna.

The development of urban civilisation goes inseparably hand-in-hand with a surplus of wealth and complex economic and commercial activity. We know that in these prosperous cities, there appeared a wealthy merchant class, something unknown in ancient Vedic times. The use of coin money was already established in the 6th century BC and the texts mention the existence of merchant trades and guilds. Communications increased spectacularly. There is evidence of trade with Babylonia, Persia, the island of Ceylon and even the Mediterranean. While agriculture and the textile industry still constituted the main economic resources, it was at this time that a host of new trades and professions came into being: iron working, mining, skilled crafting of luxury items, money lending, and so on. In general, there was a qualitative leap forward in the quality of life.

The economic power was concentrated among the nobility (Kṣatriyas) and the merchants (Vaiśyas), while the liturgists (Brāhmaṇas) were relegated—or did they exclude themselves—to matters of ritual, study, and jurisprudence. This is significant, because in the ideology of such Brāhmaṇas, who had virtually the monopoly of the sacred [see next chapter], commerce was not well-regarded. The merchants were assigned a certain rank in terms of socio-spiritual class (*varṇa),* but not without reticence. Already the *Gautama-dharma-sūtra* (16.45), one of the most ancient Brāhmaṇic treatises on norms and duties, looked askance at the cities and said that according to some Brāhmaṇas recitation of the Veda was prohibited there. Indeed, for a time the Brāhmaṇic centre of gravity remained to the West of the Ganges, in the region where modern-day Delhi stands, and the plains of Punjab begin, the land that produced noble people (Āryāvarta), the homeland and cradle of Sanskrit, in which the treatises were written. From the Brāhmaṇical point of view, the urbanised, agricultural, mercantile, and politicised region to the East was a peripheral area. However, it was a frontier that they constantly turned toward. The pastoral and nomadic society of the Vedic Indo-Aryans was in constant movement... toward the East. Thus, this eastern region, which saw the birth of heterodox Jains and Buddhists, was a Brāhmaṇised area and *at the same time* a *frontier* region.

There is no doubt that the origins of Jainism have more than a little to do with the tension between the old tribal society and the emergent agrarian, mercantile and state society. We know for example, that 65% of the monks who formed the first Buddhist community came from urban areas far from the Brāhmaṇical centre, especially from Śrāvastī, Kapilavastu, Rājagṛha, and Vaiśālī (Gombrich 1988: 56).

It is clear that certain strata of the noble, landed, and military classes (all those that could be included under the heading of Kṣatriya) began to be aware of their power. It is not unusual to find mentions of Kṣatriyas ritually "purer" than their Brāhmaṇa counterparts. This is something that clashes head-on with Brāhmaṇical ideology and denotes a certain tension within the Kṣatriya-Brāh -maṇa "team" upon which society was sustained [see below]. Who knows if these instances of friction mark the transition from the old ideal of tribal loyalty to that of territorial loyalty, typical of state-orientated monarchism. With this state of affairs we should not be so surprised to find Buddhists and Jains claiming Kṣatriya origin for their great preachers, the Buddha, Mahāvíra, and the rest of the *jinas.*

These socio-economic and political aspects have their importance since Jainism emerged in the context of a series of clearly "individualistic" movements. People would enter into the Jain order of their own free will. This lack of conformity with the pattern established by more traditional Brāhmaṇism would not be feasible in a pastoral subsistence farming setting or a social organisation where the pivot was exclusively the clan. What is more, totally "unproductive" monastic orders can only emerge and perpetuate themselves by means of the economic surplus generated by mercantile activity plus the patronage of royalty. Obviously, we should not reduce Jainism to a set of production modes, tension between classes or particular political interests, as if the message of Mahāvīra were nothing more than an ideology, one that was the outcome, exclusively, of the development of agriculture, commerce, and a ruling class. In world history, many places have seen the development of agriculture and the emergence of ruling classes, without this producing Jainisms or Buddhisms. Having said that, I cannot rule out this aspect; as if Jainism were not anchored and rooted in a particular society nor depended on any factor. While the Jain Truth might be a temporal, the Jainism of historical times, like Buddhism, represented a new response to an environment, which was undergoing decisive changes.

In general, the first cities in the Ganges basin, besides being commercial centres, were ritual complexes. The urban centres came to represent royal power, which was, however, crowned by the solemn ritual of the priests. It is plain that the Brāhmaṇas, too, knew how to adapt to the new times.

Possibly, around the 8th and 7th centuries BC, the *brāhmi* and *kharoṣṭhī* alphabets of India were devised. The first surviving inscriptions do not pre-date the reign of Aśoka (3rd century BC), but there is little doubt that the writing system had been in use for centuries before they were used on this king's pillars. While this alphabet could have been developed by the merchants, its incredibly precise, scientific representation of Indian phonetics indicates its fostering among the learned priests and grammarians.

THE POLITICAL CONDITIONS

The development of urban life, writing, communications, metallurgy and the use of money, as well as the emergence of a merchant class, profoundly altered the old nomadic tribal society. With the surplus wealth, there came private property, unknown in the early Vedic period, and the first states appeared. According to the Brāhmaṇical texts the idea of a state ruled by kings had come about to protect property and a society ordered in socio-spiritual classes and castes (*Vāyu-purāṇa* 8.160-161). The Buddhist perception is similar: the social perfection of earlier times had become dislocated owing to private property, theft and family disputes (*Dīgha-nikāya* 3.93). The Jains, were of a similar opinion [see pages 29-30 and 65]. The state and the monarch emerge as an unfortunate but inevitable necessity. We go from the notion of a Utopian past to a sadder and more degenerate present.

ROYALTY AND THE STATE

It is during these times that the political treatises began to be written—of which the celebrated *Artha-śāstra* of the astute Kauṭilya (1st century) is the prime example. Although the *Artha-śāstra,* as we know it today, cannot be more than 2,000 years old, there is a consensus that its main outlines go back further (de la Peña 1992: 74-76). Basically, Kauṭilya's task was to impose a new state-orientated order on the old tribal one. The solution is totally Indian, since even today the Indian state has to coordinate discourse on modernity with powers and structures anchored in the past.

For this thinker, the state is the king (*rājā*), minister, territory (*janapada*), fortress, treasure, army, and neighbouring allied kings (*Artha-śāstra* 6.1.1). Indian kings have always ruled not so much over a territory as over a population, which is what the term *janapada* expresses: an undifferentiated whole consisting of people-in-a-territory. The classical theories of Indian political science always speak of an open state. The allusion to the neighbouring king leaves us in no doubt. He, too, forms part of the state. What is more, Kauṭilya gives us to understand the existence of an eighth component: the enemy.

Of course, the king's prime activity was war. The prime minister (*amātya*) had to be well-versed in the political and military arts. The role of the general (*senāpati*) was vital. The martial arts underwent fabulous development. No less important was the role of military strategy, of diplomacy, and of espionage. The ambition of every king was to conquer the six parts of Bharata and, true to the mythical models, proclaim himself universal monarch (*cakravartin*) or conqueror (*vijigīṣu*).

In times of peace the primordial function of the king was to administer the law. He was expected to impart government with justice and equanimity. To do so, kings were assisted by a minister of justice. A series of other ministers were in charge of other areas. Simultancously, there was a council of notables (*pariṣad*), including scholars versed in the Veda, in the local conventions or in political science. The notable known as the *śreṣṭhin* was also consulted; this was a wealthy merchant, responsible for the trades (*śreṇis*). On questions of local administration, authority was devolved on village headman (*grāmaṇī, yajamāna*) or the tax collector (*bhāgadughā*), who formed the liaison between the central government and the village. Although these times saw the beginning of a veritable urban revolution, the rural economy continued to dominate the scene.

Normally, on the death of the king, the first-born son succeeded him. On occasions, the monarch might put prospective candidates to the test. In the Jain *Vyavahāra-bhāṣya* (cited in Jain 1947: 65) a legend is told of a king who examined his three sons with aplomb. He offered them a splendid banquet and, while they were eating, unleashed a pack of furious dogs. The first prince left his plate and went haring out the door; the second stopped the dogs by dealing them blows with his stick. The third continued eating calmly and let the dogs eat with him. The king congratulated the third son for his attitude, and named him heir. Obviously, this story is from a later period, permeated by Jain notions of *ahiṃsā* applied to kingship, but it illustrates very well the Jain ideal of what a *rājā* should be. That man, who in some respects replicates the disposition of the *tīrthaṅkara*, is a worthy successor to the throne.

ROYAL AUTHORITY

Despite his central role, for Indian thought the position of the king is frankly ambivalent. The king is, in effect, the personification of order (*dharma*) (*Nārada-bṛhaspati* 18.20), and his sceptre (*daṇḍa*) symbolises the law. Through the rite of consecration, he is a sacred being who acquires great powers as a result of his renunciatory state (*dīkṣā*). Thus, the king is the perfect sacrificer in the complex Brāhmaṇical sacrificial apparatus. The religious aspect of kingship is undeniable. However, at the same time the law books (Dharma-śāstras) declare that the king is as malignant as a butcher who runs 1,00,000 slaughterhouses (*Manu-smṛti* 4.86). How does this contradiction come about?

For India, the *rājā* or king is an agent who lacks the *ultimate* legitimation and authority. He is not a free being. He depends on a complex network of social interconnections. As Robert Lingat (1967: 256) has said, the power of the king derives from his subjects. And that is not all. To maintain order (*dharma*) he lacks autonomy. The scriptures direct him to follow social customs, even where this would be contrary to the norms, which means that the transcendent order is not within his reach. As Jan Heesterman (1985: 115) observes, at all times the king must weigh up whether to proclaim his own mandate to be *dharma* or obediently follow what his subjects tell him is *dharma.* The lack of authority of the Indian ruler emerges with clarity. A good example of this is provided by the Brāhmaṇical texts: they recognise the fact that the king is simply the one who exercises power, irrespective of whether he is a Kṣatriya (Lingat 1967: 235).

The only option that remained open to the king to legitimise his authority was to commit *dharma* to the Brāhmaṇas. It is they who, basing themselves on the collective teachings of the society (the Veda), are familiar with the ultimate mysteries. The Brāhmaṇas are able to confer on the king the trascendent status of a renunciant thanks to which they can then involve themselves in the mundane spheres of government and deal with the world of conflict—at the same time enabling the Brāhmaṇas to reside in the realms of transcendence. Hence, the rites of enthronement (*rājasūya, abhiṣeka*), which need periodically to be brought up to date—and the royal donations to men who had gained independence from society: honoured Brāhmaṇas and leaders of religious movements. For this reason, that monarchs were advised by their Brāhmaṇa chaplain, the *purohita,* who Simultancously, acted as the royal *guru,* advised on statecraft, and actively took part in the rituals of enthronement.

Unlike the Egyptian, Chinese, or Christian worlds, Indian civilisation never placed temporal and spiritual power in one person. The classical Indian model is represented by the Kṣatriya-Brāhmaṇa dyad. The former needs the latter to legitimise himself, and the latter needs the king for his physical sustenance. Although it may be an exaggeration to speak of secularisation of the monarchic function in ancient Indian civilisation, as Louis Dumont (1979:

355-357) has maintained, there is no doubt that this separation between the political and the religious (common to the Brāhmaṇical, Buddhist, and Jain models) has been recurrent throughout Indian history.

THE SIXTEEN STATES

Let us turn now to the geopolitical picture. Tradition tells of 16 more or less powerful kingdoms or states, which coexisted in the region and vied for hegemony. While the Buddhist (*Aṅguttara-nikāya* 1.212) and Jain (*Vyākhyā-prajñāpti* 15.C8 [680a]) accounts differ on certain of their names, we can form an opinion of the political make-up of the 6th and 5th centuries BC [see Fig. 7].

Kāśī, which was located in the area of present-day Benares, was one of the most powerful states. It was rich, prosperous, and at that time one of the most important centres of learning in South Asia. In Mahāvīra's time, it was conquered by the mighty kingdom of Kauśalā.

Kauśalā, which constitutes the present-day region of Awadh in central Uttar Pradesh, was one of the great kingdoms striving for supremacy. Besides its capital, Śrāvastī, it possessed another great city: Sāketa, which would later be known as Ayodhyā. King Prasenajit of Kauśalā, Mahāvīra's contemporary, was one of the most respected monarchs of his time. He not only annexed Kāśī, but he also absorbed the Śākya and Kālāma confederations. His relations with the other great ruler of the time, Śreṇika of Magadha, were cordial. When Kūṇika ascended the throne in Magadha, the two powers went to war. After years of contention, Kauśalā fell to the Magadha forces.

In Mahāvīra's time, the kingdom of Magadha was restricted to what is now the modern Patna and Gaya districts of Bihar state. The ancient texts describe it as the land of impure people (*Atharva-veda* 5.22.14). In contrast to the lands of the mid-reaches of the Ganges, in these eastern regions, there was a Prakrit linguistic tradition which had begun much earlier. Or, and this comes to the same thing, they were far removed from the Sanskritic and Brāhmaṇical centre. In the 4th century BC, king Śreṇika (Bimbisāra in the Buddhist chronicles) and his son Kūṇika (Ajātaśatru for the Buddhists) made this kingdom the most powerful in the continent. In fact, on attaining supremacy, Magadha became the first Indian empire in the classical sense of the word. Magadha ended up by overwhelming Kauśalā, Kāśī, and the Vṛjjīs and subdued the kingdom of Aṅga.

Magadha's great expansion came about under Kūṇika's ruling hand (*Vyākhyā-prajñāpti* 7.9 [315b]). According to Buddhist writings, Kūṇika usurped the throne from his father, Śreṇika, after putting him to death. The Jain chronicles are somewhat more benevolent and state that he imprisoned his father, who took his own life in prison. For that reason, Śreṇika will have to spend several aeons in the Lower World before being reincarnated as the *jina* Padmanātha [see pages 34-35]. Having gained control of the entire region, the kingdom of Magadha sowed the seed that a century and a half later was to become the mighty Maurya empire [see pages 177-178].

Campā, the capital of Aṅga (present day Bengal), was an important commercial centre, renowned for its riches. After his awakening, Mahāvīra preached his first sermon in that city.

To the south of the Ganges, lay the great kingdom of Vatsā. Its capital Kauśāmbī, close to the present-day city of Allahabad (Prayāga), was ruled in the time of Mahāvīra by king Udayana.

Alongside these powerful kingdoms, the remaining political entities were a mosaic of small states more or less subordinated to one or other of the larger ones. Many of these minor entities were not known by a place name but by the name of the predominate tribe. There were, for example, the Mallas or Mallakīs, Kālāmas, Śākyas, Vṛjjis or Licchavis, and so on. In reality, these were tribal confederations *(gaṇas)* rather than states *(raṣṭras)* in the modern understanding of the concept. The chiefs werer chosen from the noble or warrior class (*Atharva-veda* 3.4.2), so that some writers speak openly of oligarchic republics (Kosambi 1965: 91). Nonetheless, the scholars who see the Jain and Buddhist communities of the time as constituting parallel democratic or communist societies (Bhattacharyya 1976: 84-85) are, I think, mistaken. Jan Heesterman (1985: 147) has shown that the difference between a "monarchic" system and a "republican" one is basically one of degree.

The most important of these confederations was that of the Vṛjjīs, comprising basically the Vṛjjī and Licchavī tribes, together with the Videha and Jñatrka clans. The capital of the state was Vaiśālī, the site of present-day Besarh. The city was divided into three wards: the Brāhmaṇical area, the nobles' area (where Mahāvīra was born) and the commercial district. The great rival of the Vṛjjīs— led by the king Ceṭaka (Mahāvīra's uncle?)—was the powerful kingdom of Magadha. As happened in other cases, the impetuous Kūṇika ended up conquering the Vṛjjīs.

Another important confederation was that of the Mallas, formed by nine clans and possessing two important cities: Kuśīnārā (where the Buddha died) and Pāpā. The fact that the Buddha and Mahāvīra visited Malla shows clearly that these religious movements were well established in this region. Soon after Buddha's death, Magadha annexed the territory. The confederation where the Buddha was born was that of the Śākyas, subordinated to the kingdom of Kauśalā. Other smaller confederations were those of the Koliyas and the Kālāmas.

Farther to the West, around the modern city of Delhi, lay the kingdom of Kuru, with its capital in Indraprāṣṭa, and with another important city in the territory, Hastināpura. Close by was the kingdom of Pañcāla, whose capital was Kāmpilya. These two kingdoms, in reality made up of a myriad of tribal chieftainships, formed the historical heart or *centre* of the old Vedic society.

There is little doubt that the most relevant event of the Vedic Night, recorded with unusual force by the tradition—it may well have inspired the central plot of the *Mahābhārata—was* the great civil war between the Kuru clan and their rivals the Pañcālas. The war putatively broke out in Kurukṣetra, near to Indraprāṣṭha, perhaps around 1,000 BC, although not everyone accepts this as historical fact. It was "remembered" with such insistence that it really matters little whether it took place "historically" or not. Professor D.D. Kosambi (1965: 91) was of the opinion that the incident must actually have been a pretty minuscule affair, but Indian literary tradition conferred on it the same importance as the Greeks did to the Trojan War, if not considerably more.

In the northern part of the present-day state of Rajasthan was to be found the kingdom of Matsya. Around the city of Mathurā, the city commanded by the Yādava warrior clan and the Vṛṣṇi scion, there was the kingdom of Śūrasena. In central India, today occupied by the northern regions of Madhya Pradesh, the flourishing kingdom of Avanti was to be found. The latter had two capitals Māhiṣmatī and Ujjain, important nuclei of Jainism since very ancient times.

The lower reaches of the river Indus belonged to the kingdom of Sauvīra. Further to the Northwest lay Gandhāra with the city of Taxila (Takṣaśilā) a seat of learning and a commercial centre of the first order. At the close of the 4th century, Gandhāra fell to the Persians. Lastly, we have the kingdom of Kāmboja, situated in Kashmir.

6. THE BRĀHMAṆIC TRADITIONS

THE VEDA

The period of the Vedic Night is, precisely, the time of gestation of the Veda. What is the Veda? What is Vedic religion? What relationship does it have with Hinduism? And with the Brāhmaṇas? It is clear we cannot answer these important questions in depth in one short chapter, but it will be worthy to provide a brief synopsis here.

The issue is an essential one. In the same way that Christianity is unintelligible if one ignores the Jewish and biblical context it came from, we cannot understand the meaning and impact that the Jain message had in ancient India if we do not familiarise ourselves with the system of practices and beliefs upon which it fed, with which it coincided and, against which it rebelled. And this system was, principally, the Vedic religion, fostered by liturgists, priests, and scholars by family tradition: in a word the Brāhmaṇas. This was the first "other" in the development of historic Jainism.

The Veda is a large body of teachings which took the form of four collections of Liturgical Hymns (Saṃhitās), to which were added Ritual Explanations (Brāhmaṇas), Esoteric teachings (Āraṇyakas) and Gnostic teachings (Upaniṣads). In the period we find ourselves, between the 10th and 5th centuries BC, the Veda was not complete (in fact, it has never been) as many of the mystic teachings of the Upaniṣads were still taking form. On the other hand, the oldest hymns, those of the *Ṛg-veda,* had been composed more than a 1,000 years before—if we do not opt for more daring chronologies, which date the beginning of the *Ṛg-veda* to around 4,000 years BC (Klostermaier 2000: 42). Later on, between the 6th and 1st centuries BC, another series of technical explanations of the Veda (Vedāṅgas) would be added. The most relevant auxiliary treaties were given the name of Threads of Aphorisms (Sūtras). It is important not to confuse these Brāhmaṇical Sūtras with those of Buddhists or Jains which, even if they have an equally aphoristic format, are recognised as the "sermons" or "discourses" of the Buddha or Mahāvīra.

No God revealed the Veda. It is said that the Word (Vāc) that it reproduces was heard by generations and generations of sage-poets (*ṛṣis*) who transmitted this cosmic vibration in the form of sacred hymns (*ṛ ks*) and religious teachings *(dharma)* always in the "perfectly constructed" language (*saṃskṛta*). Owin to of that, the Veda is considered eternal (*nitya*) and of no human authorship (*apauruṣeya*). Afterwards, the different priestly schools went on transmitting it orally, with astounding precision, up until our days. The Veda is the nearest thing to an Indian divine revelation (*śruti*).

THE RELIGION OF THE BRĀHMAṆAS

The religion of the Brāhmaṇas was entirely based on the Veda. For this reason, one can call it Vedism. It was the predominant religion in northern India between the 15th and 5th centuries BC. From then on, to a great extent due to plight of Jainism and Buddhism, Vedic Brāhmaṇism went on to evolve into what was to be Hinduism.

THE CONNECTION WITH HINDUISM

Perhaps this is not the appropriate place to question the meaning of the term "Hinduism", a newly stamped concept (19th century) which is used to denominate what is in reality an umbrella under which an infinity of ritual, textual or philosophic expressions are grouped. Then again, it is worth a slight reflection. More than a religion, Hinduism can be seen as a family of religions. There is more diversity (theological, textual, cultual, mythological) within what is called Hinduism, than in the great monotheisms (Judaism, Christianty, Islam). Obviously, these religions would not like it very much if we reduced them to a range of mere *sects* of an abstract "Abrahamic Religion", so there leaves us no alternative as to come to the conclusion that Hinduism is a greater entity than "a religion". And if Hinduism is more than a religion, then the grade of tolerance which India has promoted, in accepting the existence of an infinity of religions like Śaivism, Vaiṣṇavism, Śāktism or so many other *-isms* to be found on the continent, is praiseworthy. India admitted that from very early on that every individual or social group is free to choose the path that gives meaning to their existence. Therefore, when we refer to Hinduism in this book, we are approximately following Heinrich von Stietencron (1989: 48) and we do not consider it a "religion" on the Semitic model, but a group or family of Indie religions, a Hindu religiousness which has expressed itself within forms such as Vedism, Brāhmaṇism, classical Hinduism, Smārta tradition, devotional Vaiṣṇavism, Śaivism, Śāktism, Tantrism, neo-Hinduism, tribal traditions, etc.

Having said that, what is interesting to emphasise here is that there is continuity between polymorphous Vedism and heterogenic Hinduism; although if we compare religion of the mid Vedic period (10th century BC) with the classical Hinduism of the Gupta period (4th-5th centuries), to state two significant moments, they could be two entirely different traditions. That is why in some books it is also said that Hinduism was effectively born around the Common Era

(2nd century BC to the 2nd century CE) (Tardan-Masquelier 1999: 71). The connecting thread between Vedism and Hinduism was the weight of the Veda and Brāhmaṇical authority. It happens that the Veda is so extensive that an endless number of practices and beliefs could assimilate or be legitimatised within it. Just as Brian Smith (1989: 29) says, the Veda is a prototypical canon that can lend its authority to resembling counterparts. That is why Jan Gonda (cited in Klostermaier 2000: 9) simply defined Vedism as ancient or Brāhmaṇical Hinduism. Any tradition that does not recognise the power of the Brāhmaṇas together with the eternity and the transcendental character of the Veda would be a clear candidate for being dissident (*Manu-smṛti* 12.95).

VEDIC RITUALISM

Classical Vedism basically concentrated on a series of sacrifices, rites and sacraments well described in different sections of the Veda. The meaning is explained there, as much for the great public sacrifices (*śrauta*)—usually financed by kings and that needed the priests' knowledge owing to its enormous complexity and for its use of the sacred language—as for small domestic rites (*gṛhya*) that were at home, and did not necessarily need the presence of a priest. The male head of the family was—and is—the liturgist, accompanied by his wife. At the same time, the Veda provided multiple hymns to recite in every ritual and mythologies of the main deities. Just as in one type or another of rituals different offerings were made with the purspose of feeding the divinities. They made supplications to them to bring prosperity, offspring, long life, glory for the monarch, cure for an illness, etc. In the public rituals, they used three or more altars of fire. They could get to sacrifice dozens and up to hundreds of animals and consume the intoxicating beverage called *soma.* It is possible that in the oldest rituals they sacrificed human victims (Bhattacharyya 1975: 35). An integral part of sacrifice, above all the most archaic, were the verbal combats (*brahmodyas*), betting with dice and martial contests between the distinct participants, duels that emulated the cyclic generation and destruction of the cosmos and the warlike and nomadic character of the old Vedic society. Violence, provided it formed part of the sacrifice (*yajña*), was exalted. However, domestic rites were simpler and centred around the fireplace with the offering usually being milk. Sacraments (*samskāras*) were a special part of domestic rites of passage, which marked crucial moments in life (birth, initiation, marriage, funerals), a lot of which are still practised these days. Centuries later, Jainism also made a good part of them its own [see pages 447-450].

In classical Vedism, both great solemn sacrifices and modest domestic rites were designed for noble members (Āryas) of the society. Who were these nobles? In first place, the actual priests and reciters of the Veda (Brāhmaṇas); then come kings, the military and warriors (Kṣatriyas); finally, high ranking agriculturalists and merchants (Vaiśyas). In reality, these groups were at the same time subdivided into a multitude of castes (*jātis*) or endogamic units, but these never really interested theologians. The important thing is that the Veda and Vedic religion opened up to these three social-spiritual classes (*varṇas*) which formed the core of noble society. We will talk about these social-spiritual classes and castes in more depth in chapter 20. For now, a rough sketch.

The overriding, decisive factor according to Brāhmaṇical ideology is being born in one of the various classes and not what micro-history allots to each individual. Although a Brāhmaṇa might have to give up his traditional duties and devote himself to divination or administration, that would not mean the loss of his high status. He would surely go on to be considered a Brāhmaṇa of an inferior grade to a learned expert in grammar, and perhaps not as exempt from taxes as the other would, but he would still continue being a Brāhmaṇa. For Vedic texts, the important thing was establishing how a Brāhmaṇa should behave ritually and how he had to relate to the rest of society. So pivotal was the issue that the Vedic religion became to be known as—somewhat incorrectly, but not unreasonably — Brāhmaṇism. In fact, the other social-spiritual classes hardly interested the liturgists. But hierarchy did. And below the noble elite Brāhmaṇas ideally placed the bulk of peasants, artisans (Śūdras), and numerous tribal groups. At the heart of these very heterogenic collectives (farmers, artisans, musicians, servants, stock breeders, ironmongers, and hunters) Brāhmaṇical ideology began to define a "purity line," below which groups would be classified depending on their duties, resources, language and habits, to be impure amongst impure or exluded from society (*avarna*). Later, Vedic texts classed them all under the heading of Caṇḍālas. The mere sight of them, not to mention physical contact, polluted Brāhmaṇas to such an extent, that centuries later someone resorted to the concept of "Untouchable" to describe them.

Each of these collectives had to act socially and ritually accordingly to their nature. Social order depended on that each one accepted his or her role and position in society, and acted accordingly to the rules, duties and prohibitions, which were established in the Treatises on Duty (Dharma-sūtras, and Dharma-śāstras). The king and his ministry of justice took care of the maintenance of social order. If everybody chose duties and rules to suit himself, the result would be a totally chaotic society. Why? Because the social composition stratified into social-spiritual classes was a reflection of the very structure of the cosmos, of the *ṛta* or ordered course of the cosmos. The social-spiritual classes, as in reality the rest of rituals, would have emerged from the self-sacrifice of the Puruṣa, the mythical notion used to describe the *ṛta.*

In fact, it was thought that the rites, specially the great solemn sacrifices, emulated the primordial sacrifice undertaken by the demiurge, an entity that the priests first named the Male (Puruṣa) and afterwards Lord of the Progeny (Prajāpati). All rites accurately executed were susceptible to identifying with the self-sacrifice, which Puruṣa inflicted upon himself, and which brought on the manifestation and social organisation (*Ṛg-veda* 10.90). This is very explicit in the rite of the construction of the fire altar (*agnicayana*), which replicates the restoration of Puruṣa-Prajāpati. Thanks to the recurring Indian conception of the analogy and correspondence between the planes (*bandhu*), the solemn rites of the priests were capable of generating such a power, in olden times called *brāhman*, that the very cosmos came to depend on ritual sacrifice. Even the gods became divine by the grace of the sacrifices (*Taittirīya-saṃhitā* 6.3.10.2). It was the learned expert's responsibility to reproduce the very structure of the cosmos again and again in the sacrifice, to reconstruct Prajāpati (*Śatapatha-brāhmaṇa* 7.1. 2.2) to such an extent that the texts predicted that the Sun would not rise if the priest did not offer the sacrifice to the fire (*agnihotra*) in the early morning (*Śatapatha -brāhmaṇa* 2.3.1.5). So crucial was and is sacrifice (*yajña*) for Hindu thought that Madeleine Biardeau and Charles Malamoud (1976: 13) do not doubt in qualifying it as the organising principle of the world and of life.

Since a solemn ritual consisted of the regeneration of the universe, one would expect for the whole population to take part, but in classical Vedism, collective rites are conspicuous by their absence; rejected even (*Manu-smṛti* 3.151). Sacrifice is a strictly personal affair. The sacrificer, who is assisted by the expert Brāhmaṇas, is the patron and beneficiary of the rite, but it had not always been as such.

Jan Heesterman's thesis (1985: 28) is that in pre-classical Vedism the relationship between the Brāhmaṇa and the sacrificer (*yajamāna*) was different. The Brāhmaṇa'*s* function was to absorb the impurity of the death and exorcise the chaos. The Brāhmaṇa-*yajamāna* partnership maintained the continuity of the cosmos. This ritualism goes back to the Ṛgvedic society's nomadic period, when Brāhmaṇas were not expert priests, but warriors who proclaimed themselves Brāhmaṇas thanks to the ritual of consecration (*dīkṣā*). Even the king was called a Brāhmaṇa. In other words, social-spiritual class fluctuated. Originally, sacrifice did not require any professional from the priesthood. It was a thing for warriors, kings and chiefs of the Ṛgvedic society who competed for all types of material and spiritual wealth. One infers that the *purohita,* who was later to be the king's chaplain, was not originally so; before he was but the monarch's charioteer (*Pancaviṃśa-brāhmaṇa* 13.3.12), a figure which reminds us of Kṛṣṇa, charioteer of the warrior Arjuna in the *Bhagavad-gītā.*

Not everybody agrees with Heesterman's vision of this "pre-classical Vedic society" (Smith 1989: 40-44). In whichever case, in classical Vedic ritualism-probably when Indo-Aryan society became sedentary, settled all across the Ganges plains, the relational aspect of sacrifice was substituted by the absolute individualism of the ritual. No more combats, violence, orgiastic feasts. All competitions became liturgic operations. This is perfectly illustrated in the myth of the sacrificial duel between Prajāpati and Death. The prior succeeds in beating death thanks to his knowledge of symbolic equivalencies, thanks to science of ritual (Heesterman 1985: 91). The slightest error could lead to disaster. Therefore, ritualists ended up constructing a mechanicist universe, controllable, closed and guided by ritual. Catastrophe and doubt were replaced by the certainty of ritual (Heesterman 1985: 91). Vedism became an issue for professionals, and went on to evolve into a jealously guarded hereditary caste. When impurity and evil stop transiting from one participant to another, they become fixed beneath the different levels of hierarchy. The Brāhmaṇa, isolated in his purity, requires the rest of society to also observe social-spiritual divisionary lines (*varṇas*). In other words, we come to the beginning of the caste system ideology (Heesterman 1985: 35).

The highest ranking of these experts were not the king's chaplains, whose involvement in worldly affairs, made them from the Brāhmaṇical point of view excessively dependent. The highest and purest were those who had made themselves independent from social ties and resided in the purity of transcendence. The ideal Brāhmaṇa was—and still is—he who has stepped aside from the world and cultivates the Veda for its own sake. Exactly the opposite of the king, the Brāhmaṇa par excellence can only be a renunciant. For instance, the versed Brāhmaṇa (*śrotriya*), predecessor of the scholar (*paṇḍita*) of later periods. These sages were specialists in different branches of knowledge (grammar, etymology, astronomy, ritual, music, martial arts, and medicine) or the different transmissions of the Veda—necessary for the correct execution of rites. They ended up forming schools (*gurukulas*), where the children of noble families, once they had received initiation into the realms of ritual adulthood (*upanayama*), would study. The teacher (*guru*) well versed in his own branch of knowledge, adopted a pupil like his own child. Each *guru* helped by an advanced student formed an institution in itself. Some cities were converted into centres of knowledge of the highest category. Such was the case of Vārāṇasī, Pāṭaliputra or Takṣaśilā.

In spite of the priest's protagonism, the Vedic religion—as in present-day Hinduism—continued to be a family-centred religion. "He who stays at home" (*gṛhastha*), the head of the family (subsuming the rest of the family members) has always been the epicentre of the Vedic/Hindu religion. For the *gṛhastha*, the fulfilment of the rites meant harmonically organising oneself with society and the cosmos. In other words, the cosmological notion of *ṛta* became *dharma*, a concept with more practical or even legal connotations: bringing the law that governs all beings and religious and moral duty to a human level. The fulfilment of *dharma* became the hub of the *gṛhastha's* ritual and moral life.

A Vedic ordinance, which reflects this spirit very well, is the famous debt (*ṛṇa*) (*Taittirīya-saṃhitā* 6.3.10.5), Later on, inextricably linked to the five great sacrifices (*pañca-mahāyajñas*), a series of rites which all "twice born" (*dvija* or initiated) nobles would live out their lives performing daily. Still today these five sacrifices continue to form the backbone of the ritual life of the most devout members of the Brāhmaṇa class. We are dealing with the five rites considered to be obligatory by all Vedic schools. The first is aimed at the sacred power of sacrifice (*brahman*) and the sages of ancient times (*ṛṣis*). One pays this ritual debt through studying the Veda (*brahmacarya*) and through Vedic recitation. The second is sacrifice to the gods *(devas),* which one pays with offerings and oblations to fire, like the *agnihotra* or the *sarhdhyās.* Mastly, these days, worshipping the deity (*pūjā*) has come to be the sacrifice itself. The third is sacrifice to the manes (*pitṛs*), to be paid by means of funerary offerings (*śrāddhas*) and daily libations in their honour (*tarpaṇa*). The fourth is the sacrifice to living creatures (*bhūtas*), redeemed by the maintenance of domestic animals (especially cows) and looking after spirits. The fifth is the sacrifice to other human beings (*puruṣas*), which is paid with good treatment of guests, of the homeless and of religious mendicants.

He who follows these recommended rituals from the Veda, keeps in step with cosmic order through the rites and sacrifices, accepts Brāhmaṇic spiritual and liturgic authority, to him and his family will be the heaven of the gods.

VEDIC PANTHEON

The Indians' heaven has always been very populated. We already know the Jain viewpoint [see pages 48-50]. Now, we will take a look at the Vedic point of view.

It is commonly said that the Vedic pantheon consisted of 33 divinities, but there are far more deities than that mentioned in hymns. From among all of them, three clearly stand out. In first place, Indra, a very versatile deity, who received the title of "king of the gods". This god was the great protector of the noble society (*ārya*). Jain texts often mention ancient festivals held in his honour. Of all the Vedic deities he is the only one that Jains give a certain preeminence to; notably so to the great Śakra, one of the 64 or 100 *indras* conceived by their mythology. The second important Vedic deity would have been Agni, or fire. Perhaps, Agni was the most significant deity given his protagonism in all solemn or domestic rites. All offerings and petitions are carried by Agni from the altar of sacrificial fire to the heavens where the gods dwell. In third place, comes Soma, being a deity and at the same time an intoxicating plant (*soma*), and the prototype of all oblations. Nonetheless, in the later Vedic period *soma* was replaced by symbolic substitutes, notably by clarified butter (*ghṛta, ghī*), so that his position declined. More than half of the Ṛgvedic hymns are dedicated to these three deities.

Other significant divinities were the sovereign god Varuṇa, guardian of cosmic order (*ṛta*); Vāyu, the wind deity; Aditi, the infinite goddess; Uṣas, the dawn goddess; Bṛhaspati, the priest-god of creative power; Sūrya, the god who dwells in the Sun; and many others. Of particular interest were two lesser gods, Viṣṇu, the preserver, and the terrible Rudra, who continued to rise in importance over the years until they reached the rank of of supreme divinities. The first was assimilated to local deities such as Vāsudeva, Kṛṣṇa, or Nārāyaṇa; the second merged with Śiva. These transformations, already palpable at the end of the

Vedic period (5th-1st centuries BC), correspond to the beginning of Vaiṣṇavism and of Śaivism, the real driving force behind devotional Hinduism. At the time of Mahāvīra, the extremely important Puruṣa/Prajāpati was already becoming Brahmā. It is also worth pointing out the rising of the goddess Śrī (or Lākṣmī), the divinity of fortune and prosperity.

The opposite of these *devas* were the *asuras,* symbol of violence and destruction, beings who rapidly became demonic spirits, in perpetual combat with the *devas* fighting for the power of sacrifice.

Aside from these great gods, Hindu tradition was replete of lesser divinities called by the generic term of marvellous beings (*yakṣas;* fern, *yakṣiṇīs*). In Mahāvīra's time the cult based on these imps or spirits was extremely popular. They were invoked to protect villages, increase fertility in women, cure illnesses, or fulfil people's desires. Some *yakṣas* also caused harm. It is known that many of these genies were promoted to higher levels. In fact, in Vedic and Jain literature there is not much difference between a *yakṣa* and a *deva.* These genies had their own sanctuaries (*caityas*), situated in gardens or parks [see pages 215-216]. Both Mahāvīra and the Buddha along with many other heads of religious orders stayed at these popular sanctuaries. Other supernatural beings often propitiated were divine snakes (*nāgas*), of clearly tribal origin. In the popular pantheon, we also find ghosts (*bhūtas*), some of which could be extremely angry and dangerous. The whole of this range of "lesser" divinities were shared by Jainism in the form of "the mansion dwellers" or "interstitials" gods.

The gods form an equally integral part of sacrifice as priests or sacrificers. The offerings were taken up from humans to divinities and came back in the form of long life, beneficial rain, and offsprings. The reciprocity between gods and humans maintained cosmic order (*ṛta*). When everything was thoroughly ritualised and codified by priests, there was no longer room for the gods, with their transcendental character, to act in an independent manner. Only the invisible force of ritual (*adṛṣta, apūrva, brahman)* operated. In other words, the gods were trapped in the world of contingency (*saṃsāra*).

The atheism of Jainism, Buddhism or the Mīmāṃsā philosophy seems inseparable from the disenchantment of the world anticipated by Vedic ritualism. If in reality one can speak about an axial period on the planet, in India it was the time before the Upaniṣads (11th-9th centuries BC).

VEDIC SOTERIOLOGY

Although the ritualist type of Brāhmaṇism was the predominant religious expression in northern India, it was not the only one nor was it too homogeneous. Since no one person wrote the Veda (I would say it resumed collective spiritual experience of fifteen or twenty centuries of society which called itself Aryan) and the role of the reciter and transmitter of its teachings fell to clerical families,

Vedism and its prolongation, Hinduism, have always been open to integrating, developing or assimilating all kinds of religious beliefs and practices; all those that were not antagonistic. Vedicism/Hinduism is the religion without a founder, Church, without an official dogma, agreed canon, hegemonic god, or universal ethics. It could be described as the connecting thread of a series of rituals, beliefs, divinities and religious expressions that have gone on transmitting and influencing themselves upon different regional and social collectives. In this sense, more than one religion or meta-religion, Brian Smith (1989: 28) proposes describing it as a *process*. This rare process, then, has gone on opening and closing up to religious forms developed in tribal cultures or among non -Brāhmaṇical collectives, especially those of Śūdras and peripheral castes, not always well inserted in Brāhmaṇical orthodoxy. These marginal cultures have never ceased to contribute to mythology, cult forms and religious expression. At the same time, Brāhmaṇas have never stopped investigating, developing and encouraging new paths and approaches that, while not interfering with or questioning the authority of the Veda, they have gone on to enhance the wide range of practices and philosophies of Vedicism/Hinduism.

VEDIC GNOSTICISM

At the end of the Vedic period (8th-4th centuries BC), a period in which India experienced very creative religious dynamism, some Brāhmaṇical tendencies began to interpret ritual in a symbolic and esoteric manner. This is very obvious in the teachings known as Āraṇyakas. Logically enough, with the individualisation of sacrifice, the sacrificer sacrifices for himself and reunites within himself the opposite poles of life and death. The benefit of sacrifice is individual; the sacrificer identifies himself with Prajāpati and assimilates death. Therefore, he can attain immortality. There is only a small step from the individualisation to the interiorisation of ritual. Summing this up, we could say that there were some sages who understood that the sacrificial act had to take place within each being, with the flame of meditation, asceticism and study. Fire worship *(agnihotra)* was replaced by the sacrifice of internal fires (*prāṇāgnihotra* (*Kauṣītaki-brāhmaṇa-upaniṣad* 2.5). Now, it was not a matter of exorcising chaos, exalting existence or ritualising cruelty, like in ancient public sacrifice, but self-interrogation concerning the transcendence of oneself. It is the inrush of the way of knowledge (*jñāna -mārga*).

Many of the Upaniṣads, the last part of the Veda, were codified in this spirit. The emphasis shifts from ritualism to mysticism, from external activity (*pravṛtti*) to introspection (*nivṛtti*); so much so that some Brāhmaṇic groups, or some groups which shared this more gnostic spirit, ended up forming parallel spiritual movements. They were not so much dissident movements, but as orders or fraternities with different centres of interest. Some were very marginal, but others belonged to the mainstream Vedic tradition. In the next chapter, we shall see how one cannot draw a clear line between Brāhmaṇic and non-Brāh -manic groups, and even less try to qualify the teachings of the Upaniṣads as a break with the ideology of texts precisely called Brāhmaṇas (the ritualistic part of the Veda). Although their perception is different, the Upaniṣads maintain all the symbols and prolong the same ideology of sacrificial ritual. He who knows the equivalences, subsumes the universe within himself and undertakes sacrifice within with no need for exterior intervention. This is the sacrifice of the self (*ātmayajña*) (*Baudhāyana-sharma-sūtra* 2.10.18.8-9). The dualism of sacrifice is transcended. The sacrificer and the sacrificed are the same thing, the giver and receiver also, the world and transcendence are one. That is why the majority of mystics were Brāhmaṇas completely freed from the bonds that govern the world. Their purity is absolute, as they are no longer dependent on the interchange of sacrifice, nor the ties of life-in-the-world. The institution of renunciation begins to take shape.

The Upaniṣadic quest had to be carried out beyond the social group, away from the town, in the forest (*āraṇya*)*;* a place where the ritually organised society was under permanent threat, but a space of unlimited possibilities. The sage who had retired into.the forest knew perfectly well that, according to Brāhmaṇic ideology, there is a rite for each and every purpose. Those who desire prosperity, want descendants, yearn for a kingdom in peace, pursue a heavenly afterlife... must carry out the prescribed rite. Every rite has its own specific effect. The ascetic brought this reality, which he knew well, to its ultimate consequences. All ritual action (*karma*)*,* and any action of mind, speech or thought (*kriyā, karma*)*,* would always bring forth a result, fruit, and it is the union between action and its fruit that forms an individual life and feeds the world of continuity (*saṃsāra*)*.* The theory of *karma* was being proclaimed. Therefore, it became clear that Vedic sacrifice did nothing more than to sink human beings into the karmic cycle of cause-and-effect.

What was it that transmigrated? The most ancient Upaniṣads describe the individual as a material and mental continuum. The individual is a knot made up of five breaths (*prāṇas*)*:* respiration, speech, face, ears and mind. There is no ontological separation between the material sphere and that of thought. When a being dies the connection between the *prāṇas* is disconnected. But a *postmortem* existence is possible when the five breaths are grouped together again by the power or force of *karma*. Professor Stcherbatsky (1923: 116-118) thought that the sophisticated Buddhist theory of the five factors of personality (*skandhas*) could be a development of this old theory of the five breaths. In the intermediate Upaniṣads, a separation between the mind-matter continuum and an indescribable sphere (*nirguṇa*) of pure consciousness is articulated. Sages eventually came to the logical conclusion that in all beings *something* existed, a consciousness or an immaterial soul (*ātman, puruṣa, and jīva*) or a portion of divinity (*jīvātman*)*,* to give it a name, that transcended death, finitude and contingency. But as all acts perpetuated the cosmos and the individual, it was clear that all action also resulted in a perpetuation or transmigration of this portion of the divine. Action drags the soul back to the world of contingency and continuity.

This mysticism coherently began to question religion as merely carrying out ritual duties and prescriptions. Now, the issue was not putting oneself in order in the social web by carrying out the rites, but the opposite: abandoning any social ties (village, caste, family, ritual, and culture) to concentrate on the immanent, divine soul so that *it* would not ever return to the world of transmigration. What was meant was thoroughly investigating the soul (*ātman*), the divine self. The science of sacrifice gave way to the science of the knowledge of *brahman*. Instead of talking about the fire (*agni*) of the sacrificial altar that puts us in contact with the gods, these sages spoke of the spiritual ardour *(tapas)* that purifies within and leads us to absoluteness. The idea of release (*mokṣa*) was being revealed. The spirituality of the Upaniṣads and the distinct movements of mystics, logically shifted from the householder *(gṛhastha)* to the renunciant (*samnyāsin*): he who has renounced his position in society and the benefit of the rites. *Grosso modo,* two lines of investigation emerged.

One Brāhmaṇic tradition (which would give rise to the school that later would be called Vedānta Advaita) came to the impressive conclusion that the soul (*ātman*) and the absolute *(brahman)* were identical. There is no duality (*ad-vaita*). When, thanks to the true knowledge (*vidyā jñāna*), meditation (*dhyāna*), and asceticism (*yoga, tapas*), one becomes aware of the first principle (*ātman*), one grasps the ultimate principle *(brahman)* at the same time. This existential insight consisted of liberation (*mokṣa*) from any type of continuance in the world of the *saṃsāra,* because, how somebody is going to incarnate, having learned at all levels of being (*sat*), that there is no other thing but Being *(sat)*? The world of multiplicity and material objectivity dissolves; once the *āt-man/brahman* identity is realised the world becomes an illusion (*māyā*).

A second line of investigation (that would give birth to the school called Sāṃkhya) postulated a fundamental difference between the objective, material world (*prakṛti*) and the spirit or soul (*puruṣa*), which is pure consciousness. Through true knowledge (*vidyā, jñāna*), achieved by discrimination (*sāṃkhya*) and *yoga,* pure consciousness is attained in the form of disconnection from the material. Liberation constituted final solitude (*kaivalya*), once pure consciousness has been separated from whatever content, separated from the material and contingent. How would the soul that has become one with itself incarnate? The world of multiplicity is but a mere stage so that this solitude is produced.

As will be seen, Brāhmaṇical positions vis-à-vis the nature of the spirit or pure consciousness (*ātman*, *puruṣa*) are practically identical. The difference in here is in its interpretation of the material world. For Vedānta, everything that is not the One is illusory. On the other hand, for Sāṃkhya, the world is real. As we shall see, Jainism clearly opts for the line of thought proclaimed by the Sāṃkhya philosophy. And who knows if it did not precede it.

BRĀHMAṆIC RENUNCIANTS

Toward the end of the Vedic period, many Brāhmaṇas (as well as members of other noble classes too) opted for moving away from religion centred around ritual. They became what the literature of the period called hermits (*vā-naprasthins*), itinerants (*parivrājakas*) and, sometime later, renunciants (*saṃnyāsins*). Possibly, yogis had always existed, organised in religious orders. The *Ṛg-veda* (10.136), a much earlier collection than the Upaniṣads, already mentioned the enigmatic silent (*muni*) or unkempt (*keśīn*) who roamed aimlessly along desert paths endowed with supernatural powers (*siddhis*), with which he could levitate and talk with the gods. What we probably have here is the predecessor of the Śaiva renunciant. Another ancient text, the *Atharva-veda* (15.1-18), depicts a rather extravagant fraternity of mystics, the *vrātyas,* who seemed to be very numerous in Magadha. We will come back to these proto-renunciants.

The Brāhmaṇical tradition gradually included in its classical formation four ideal stages (*āśramas*) in the life of all members of the three upper classes: (1) the study and apprenticeship of the Veda; (2) the stage of householder who carries out domestic rituals and maintains society; (3) that of the hermit who retires into the.wilderness to interiorise ritual; and (4) the stage of total renouncement, when the hermit refrains from taking part in rituals and devotes himself to being a mendicant throughout the country, concentrated on the quest for liberation (*mokṣa, mukti*). With this nimble formulation, all the religious expressions of the Veda were perfectly interwoven. This theoretical and ideal model remains alive and is still valid in Hinduism. Brian Smith (1989: 193) is clearly quite right when he says that the Veda never died, but transmigrated to different bodies.

Brāhmaṇic, Buddhist, and Jain texts mention many different types of Vedic hermits and renunciants with an ascetic and mystical orientation. We know of reputed, itinerant sophists (*parivrājakas*), who were experts in the Veda and its auxiliary branches. They spent their time between their retreats (*āśramas)* and towns and cities where they would partake in discussions and expound their doctrines. These were undoubtedly the *śrotriyas,* the masters who compiled many teachings of the Upaniṣads and contributed enormously to the development of sciences such as grammar, ethics, history or the Brāhmaṇical philosophies.

We also have more eccentric offshoots, inheritors of the *keśīns,* and *vrātyas.* For example, the *disāpokkhīs,* of which there were many types. It seemed that they sanctified everywhere by pouring a little water as they went, and gathered flowers and fruit (Jain 1947: 301). Furthermore, we have knowledge of *tāvasas* of many different types, who devoted to meditation in the depths of the jungle, combining this with asceticism and study. Some renunciants were very strange, like the *carakas,* who never stopped moving, even when they were eating. Even more peculiar, were those who behaved like cows (*govvaias*). These followed cows at all times to identify themselves completely with their divine bovine nature, and only ate grass and leaves. We also have the mendicants called *paṇḍuranga,* who daubed ashes all over themselves, very much to the style of the Śaivas of later times. There were those who grew their hair in dreadlocks (*jaṭilas*), like the Kāśyapa brothers, the famous followers of the Buddha. Then there were itinerants, experts in other different philosophical tendencies, like the Sāṃkhyites, Yogins, Kapilas, and the Paramahaṁsas. In short, we enter to the full into a universe of mystic orders and fraternities of ancient times. One step more and the authority of the Veda, and of the Brāhmaṇas, would be transcended.

7. THE ŚRAMAṆIC TRADITIONS

THE ŚRAMAṆAS

As we have seen in the previous chapter, the interest of Vedism changed from a ritualistic to a mystical viewpoint and a section of Brāhmaṇism began to revolve around mystic and renunciant orders from all walks of life, but they were not alone. A particular series of groups consisted of a class of people known as "strivers" (Śramaṇas). This term refers generically to ascetics, someone devoted to *yoga* or spiritual practice after abandoning their role in society. This concept has always been used, and that is important to notice, only for non -Brāhmanic groups.

When Megasthenes, the famous Greek ambassador, visited the court of the emperor Maurya Candragupta, around 300 BC, he divided Indian philosophers into two groups, *Brachmanes* and *Sarmanes* (McCrindle 1926: 97-103). This shows that some movements had become aware of their distinctiveness and did not include themselves among Brāhmaṇas. The pillars of Aśoka confirm it. The pre-Islamic mystical traditions of India can be divided into these two great blocs: Brāhmaṇical and Śramaṇical. It is to this second bloc that we must now turn our attention.

Śramaṇas could be certain mendicants (*bhikṣus*), ascetics (*tāpasas*), yogis (*yogins*), renunciants (*saṃnyāsins*), bondless ones (*nirgranthas*), excellent ones (*sādhus*), silent ones (*munis*)... In all cases, the reference was to people who had abandoned the town (*grāma*) and, in the boundless space of the wilderness (*araṇya*), devoted themselves to experimenting and *searching* on their own or in small groups, aside from the public religion of the Brāhmaṇas.

RENUNCIATION

The most distinctive sign of these Śramaṇas was their renunciation (*saṃnyāsa*) and their indifference (*vairāgya*) to worldly affairs. For all of them, and most especially for the Nirgranthas (future Jainas), renunciation was not a way to perfection, but rather, as Raimon Panikkar (1981: 11) has said, renunciation in itself constituted perfection.

If, as the sages of the Upaniṣads knew, all action led to a new rebirth, the right thing would be not to act. In fact, the idea of total inactivity was not unknown to some Śramaṇas, and in some aspects Jainism is not far off this radical position (*Uttarādhyayana-sūtra* 24.37). At all events, the basic assumption here was that *social and ritual activity* resulted in the chain of rebirths. If, as we already know, rites sustained the universe and the continuity of individual life, what one truly had to renounce would be the domestic ritual (household, family), as well as the public one (cosmic, social). The solution: renounce the lifestyle of a householder who goes through life carrying out ritual duties. With an eye explicitly on the obligations (*ṛṇas*) of Brāhmaṇism [see pages 98-99], the Jain *Uttarādhyayana-sūtra* (14.12) decried Brāhmaṇic ritual:

> "The study of the Vedas will not save you; the feeding of Brāhmaṇas will lead you from darkness to darkness, and the birth of sons will not safe you".

THE ORIGIN OF RENUNCIATION

Perhaps the model for these mendicants was the Brāhmaṇic renunciant; for example, the reputed *śrotriya* turned hermit (*parivrājaka*). Hermann Jacobi (1984: I, xxxii) takes it that ascetics from a non-Brāhmaṇa caste would have been judged to be of an inferior order and separated from Brāhmaṇa ascetics. Perhaps non -Brāhmaṇa hermits tended to form sects inclined to dissidence. Jacobi deduces that it would be these ascetics who would have taken the step of abandoning the recitation of sacred litanies and hymns and breaking with Vedic tradition. Shantaram Deo (1955:44-56), for whom the Jain Śramaṇic movement consisted in an adaptation of the forms of Brāhmaṇic renunciation and asceticism, was of a similar opinion.

On the other hand, these days more and more researchers maintain that the groups of Śramaṇas, *all* of whom indisputably were renunciants, predate even the Vedic institutionalisation of renunciation. It could be that the Vedic stage of renunciation was nothing other than the adoption, or homologation, of renunciation practices initiated by non-Vedic or rather "non-mainstream" yogis, but which yet whose practices had gained prestige. Therefore, Śramaṇas could equally be tribal shamans, sophists, or members of orders like the *vrātyas, keśīns,* or *munis,* that is, the ecstatic ones mentioned in the previous chapter, who were rather marginal to primitive Vedic culture and followed an ascetic-yogic type of spiritual practice. Some argue—but needs further confirmation—for a linguistic link between the Sanskrit *śramaṇa* to the Siberian *shaman,* which in Tungus means "one who knows" (Rankin 2006: 29) We know that the *vrātyas* spoke Prakrit languages, did not study the Veda nor did they follow Brāhmaṇical rules and ceremonies shaping the order of life. For some observers, the mysterious *vrātyas* were the original Jainas of ancient times (B.C. Jain 1972: 21). For others, they marked the start of the devotional spirituality of Rudra-Śiva worship (Sergent 1997: 403-404).

The fact that these more or less unorthodox orders, to which should be added anti-ritualist schools within the Vedic tradition itself, would have developed in urban areas of Magadha, point towards a Prakrit or Magadhi, as opposed to a Sanskrit or Vedic, religiosity (Shāntā 1985:94). Patrick Olivelle (1993: 98) also thinks it is possible that the institution of renunciation was a fundamentally urban development. This would apply just as much to Brāhmaṇas as Śramaṇas open to new ideas gestated in the towns. It is even possible that a certain evidence of Kṣatriya protest existed, an anti-Brāhmaṇic feeling opposed to a degenerate clerical class (Deo 1955: 56). For Appaswami Chakravarti (1950: 27-28), the *jinas* clearly represent the Kṣatriya heretics mentioned in Vedic literature. These Kṣatriyas would have been the bringers of spiritual knowledge of the Upaniṣads, Jainism and Buddhism; anti-ritualistic teachings that sages such as the Brāhmaṇa Yājñavalkya would later incorporate into *mainstream* Brāhmaṇism. However, this reasoning should not be taken too far. Jan Heesterman (1985: 39-41) has already shown that the institution of renunciation cannot be conceived as an anti-Brāhmaṇic revolt, since, it was already implicit in ritual Vedic thought. In any case, this supposed reaction would not have had taken place within the social order, as Louis Dumont (1979: 362) has commented, but rather through renunciation, which is on a level that transcends the social. In actual fact, it does not matter if the institution of renunciation is Vedic or non-Vedic. In such issues, there are no hard and fast dividing lines. There are all kinds of overlaps between an orthodox and Vedic mainstream Brāhmaṇism, and a less mainstream fringe, less Brāhmanised and more unorthodox and open to dissidence. There have never been clear limits separating the Vedic from the non-Vedic and it would be wrong to construct a dichotomy in Indian society in terms of doctrinal or social adherence.

What is true is that the institution of renunciation gained so much prestige that not only many Brāhmaṇas went over to Śramaṇa movements, but that all their values such as non-attachment, non-violence, meditation, and *yoga*, came to be shared by high Indian spirituality. With the appropriation of renunciation the Brāhmaṇas introduced these values into the worldly lives of men and women in society. That synthesis was to bear fruit in Hinduism, but that is for another moment. The important thing to grasp here is that Śramaṇa movements were not necessarily a reaction against Vedism. If anything, they were against the spiritual monopoly of a certain Brāhmaṇas and their excessive ritualism.

It is possible that, in the institution of this model of a wandering lifestyle, social factors would have played their part. Given that the renunciant would reverse the values, identities and duties of caste, in certain cases joining a religious group could represent the only legitimate form of dissidence from the obligations of Brāhmaṇic *dharma.* Just as Romila Thapar (1989: 69) has written, the multiplicity of renunciants in India should not always be explained in terms of otherworldly aspirations. This issue does not end here. The wars between the kingdoms of the Ganges plains need to be taken into account. In fact, the groups of Jain and Buddhist renunciants took on such appellations as assembly (*saṃgha*) and troop *(gaṇa),* terminology which in ancient Vedic texts, were used to denominate Indo-Aryan military fraternities. If we add to this, the strict monastic codes and the requirements of physical health, one could be led to believe in a degree of continuity with these ancient warrior brotherhoods, just as Paul Dundas (1992: 15) maintains. Martial symbolism actually plays a very prominent role in Jainism. The ascetic is the hero (*vīra*), the victorious one (*jina*) who conquers the enemy: *karma* and ego. It is said that clear vision is his strength, austerity and self-control the bolt that locks the gate in his stone walls, and patience is his watchtower. With the weapons of asceticism, truthfulness and caution, he would be victorious in battle and be freed from the cycle of rebirth (*Uttarādhyayana-sūtra* 9.20-22). This martial symbolism has given Jainism its own name: the way of the followers of victors *(jinas).* This also would explain why warrior and aristocratic circles were associated from the beginning with the Śramaṇic movements. However, it is possible that the figure of the religious warrior who conquers *karma* and death may be a transformation of Indra's mythology (king of the gods, the warrior par excellence), victorious over Vṛtra the dragon, the key myth in the *Ṛg-veda* (1.32.4), another reason not to set up very firm barriers.

THE RELIGIOUS GROUP

A characteristic feature of Śramaṇic movements was the institution of religious orders, generally open to all types of individuals. Renunciants broke away from ritual immersion in the world, from name and family, socio-spiritual origin and caste. They entered into a parallel society, an alternative brotherhood with its different features and symbols, its rules of conduct, its spiritual practices and its diets. The life of the initiates followed an ethic code founded on the principles of non-violence and non-possession of wealth. In summary, renunciation produced a vital type of social group in India: the religious group or sect (*saṃpradāya, panth*). In contrast to ritual society, which was perpetuated through lineage and caste, the renunciant monastic society regenerated itself through initiation (*dīkṣā*). However, this dissidence was never so strict as to break ties with society. To underline the point once more, using the words of Louis Dumont (1979: 236), leaving society meant renouncing the role attributed to them in human society, but in no way meant ceasing to relate to other members of society. Not only did many of these renunciants "return" to the world, albeit free of attachment, to set out their doctrines and paths of salvation but masters were in any case always closely linked to society. Moreover, the brotherhoods and organisations were materially maintained by householders, and so they interacted—and still do—daily. The renunciant (Brāhmaṇic or Śramaṇic) is one who has become completely independent of sacrifice and of society, and so resides in the sphere of absolute purity. That is why in India all renunciants are considered to be a source of worthiness. They can accept donations of food from others without sullying their purity, just as long as, and this is a key factor, they maintain their independence and equanimity and do not interfere in worldly matters.

IGNORANCE + ACTION = TRANSMIGRATION

Most sages of the period accepted certain basic premises. We go back to the framework, which we noted earlier in the Introduction.

There is an entity beyond the individual that we could call soul (*puruṣa, jīva, ātman*) or consciousness (*caitanya, vijñāna*). This deep dimension of being is ageless and pristine, but owing to nescience (*avidyā, moha, mithyādrsti*), meaning ignorance of its existence, the human being continues to act (*karma, kriyā*) prompted by material and corporal desire (*kāma, tṛṣṇa, icchā*). It is not the soul that acts, it is its ignorant cladding: the ego, body and mind. All action *(karma)* bears its fruit (*phala*) returning us time and again to a new life (*saṃsāra*). The origin of this lack of knowledge is unknown (as is the relation between soul and body), but it is a fact that the cycle of existences is characterised by dissatisfaction, alienation, contingency and suffering (*duḥkha*). Even the search for emancipation is *duḥkha.* The axiom here is identical to that of Brāhmaṇical sages.

In India, the capital sin as it were, is very clearly ignorance. Ignorance is the mind trapped in a dual vision. A mind that considers that "my" thought is a consciousness separated from the objects. The illusory identification with "my" mind and "my" sensations produces the attachment to objects, in turn causing desire (violence, hate, negligence, greed); all that distorts emotional life. The result: *duḥkha.*

Fortunately, all the renunciant movements agreed that ignorance and attachment could be eliminated thanks to effort and gnosis. The destruction of ignorance would free action of dross, as one who acts with awareness would not be an individual, since there would only be one pure consciousness unfettered by any material dependencies. If there is no individual, there is no ego, volition, desire, nor is there any attachment. Any kind of activity would be karmically neutral, as there is only one *witness,* not identified with any action, truly *transpersonal.*

In one way or the other, such Śramaṇas were trying to overcome *karma,* the driving force in the wheel of transmigration, because halting the cycle represented liberation from bondage (*bandha*), from the condition of human suffering and rebirth. In summary, the problem would be:

Ignorance + desire	=	unworthy action > transmigration
(*avidyā*) (*rāga*)		(*apunya-karma*) (*saṃsāra*)

The answer:

Discrimination +	non-attachment	=	knowledge >	liberation
(*viveka*)	(*aparigraha*)		(*jñāna*)	(*kaivalya*)

The goal would be the equivalent of restoring faculties darkened by egotistical and ignorant activity; that is to say, restoring the soul to its innate state. This is what in India is called *enlightenment* or *awakening:* the non-dual way of experiencing the world, where there is no distinction between the knower, the known and the knowledge, where pure consciousness (*jīva*) simply *is.* The realisation of this form of experience, radically different to the common one, has been called solitude (*kaivalya*), extinction (*nirvāṇa*), emancipation (*mokṣa*) or liberation *(mukti).* Indian traditions have always distinguished between worldly and spiritual happiness. Except for Indian materialism, all renunciant movements and aimed at the second type of happiness. This goal, unknown to socially and ritually active religiousness derived from classic Vedism, was a revolutionary contribution in terms of the history of religions.

The idea of *karma-saṃsāra,* just as the Śramaṇas outlined it, is a complex idea. It implies that there is a being (spirit, soul, or self) that *seems* to act, but is distinct from the body, which is nothing but the result forged by past actions, and is the true active agent. *Karma* is just the connection between body and soul, between one incarnation and another, as action evokes retribution via corporal rebirth. As we know, there is no divine intervention. In consequence, many of these groups developed a clearly atheist attitude and a type of dualism between the soul (*jīva, puruṣa, ātman*) and matter (*prakṛti, ajīva*). The remedy for ignorance lies in discerning what is the soul and what is not. This is very palpable in Jain philosophy, Sāṃkhya, and Yoga.

Therefore, this notion of *karma* is ontologically individualistic, as it starts out from the point that all beings and all souls are separate from each other. That is how it is expressed in the Jain *Sūtrakṛtāṅga* (2.1.41):

> "Individually a man is bom, individually he dies, individually he falls [from this state of existence], individually he rises [to another]. His passions, consciousness, intellect, perceptions, and impressions belong to the individual exclusively".

Jainism states that there are as many souls (*jīvas*) as there are living beings (*jīvas*). In theory, there is no connection between one soul and another. It is only in the state of bondage in the world of *saṃsāra* that incarnated souls meet each other or have any interaction. It is from there that they would try to reach a state of solitude *(kaivalya).* We again quote the *Sūtrakṛtāṅga* (1.10.12):

> "Try to realise that you are single and alone; thereby you will obtain Liberation; mind, this is no false assertion!"

With an eye on the great Upaniṣadic maxim that says “Thou are That” (*Tat tvam asi*) (*Chāndogya-upaniṣad* 6.8.7), the oldest of Jain texts affirms: “I am I” (*Ācārāṅga-sūtra* 1.6.2.2). Only one who realises that he or she is the soul—not an intellectual absolute—and nothing else but the self-which-is-awareness, is the true Śramaṇa.

THE WAY

To purify the soul and free it from the wheel of time one would have to not only renounce ritual and social condition, but to undertake a greater sacrifice: that of the ego; that is, the world of attachment, desires and ties. How could one attain the state of *witness* when attached to things? (*Uttarādhyayana-sūtra* 35.4-5). Until the *persona* is unmasked, its attention is only fixed on worldly and material things; in other words, in what the soul *is not.* This is the great ignorance. And as a result of not taking heed of what is truly essential, we act. Only by sacrificing attachment, only by unmasking the ego can one coincide with the soul (*jīva, ātman*). This brings about an urgency in renunciation, and because of that there is a certain continuity with Vedic ideology. As Jan Heesterman (1985:42) has observed, it was not a matter of affirming or rejecting Vedic sacrifice, but in determining which was the authentic sacrifice. The Śramaṇas and the Brāhmaṇas of the Upaniṣads all came to the conclusion that authentic sacrifice came from within. The exoteric rite cannot solve the problem of suffering, nescience and human alienation. Only a greater sacrifice, the path of inner purification, could free us.

There were various accepted formulas for purifying the soul, as well as dispossession (*aparigraha*), spiritual power and the renunciatory nature of chastity (*brahmacarya*) were valued, along with the understanding that all being *is* soul and, for that reason, should not be have violence perpetrated on it (*ahiṃsā*). The Śramaṇa Mahāvīra, for example, established five major vows which all Nirgrantha ascetics should comply with: (1) not to kill, (2) not to lie, (3) not to steal, (4) have no possessions, and (5) not to have sexual relations. As the work of Kamala Jain (1983: 240) has shown, these five Jain vows (*pañca-mahāvratas*), the five precepts of Yoga (*pañca-yamas*) (*Yoga-sūtra* 2.30) and the five virtues of Buddhism (*pañca-śīlas*) (*Dīgha-nikāya* 3.182), which are virtually identical, constitute the foundation for the whole Indian moral and ethic codes. That is precisely how they are found in the doctrines of the Upaniṣads (*Chāndogya-upaniṣad* 3.17. 4).

Precepts and vows did not only shape ethics, but also represented real purifying agents. Whoever took these vows, never to break them, would be combating precisely the contrary actions (*karmas*) which bind us to the world: violence, lies, covetousness and material and sensual desire. If, as we already know, every action sows a seed that will at a later time bear fruit, the opposite action becomes a purifier; it counteracts it. Ethical conduct taken to the limits of rigour is what Śramaṇic traditions called asceticism *(tapas).* We shall go into this key concept in greater depth. Where does *tapas* originate from?

For India, one of the main instruments for freeing oneself from the ego-corporeal prison has been and still is asceticism. Since prehistoric times Indians have considered that ascetic practices generate such spiritual ardour or heat that the practitioner is capable of literally *burning* his or her bonds and passions. Mircea Eliade (1972: 233) relates *tapas* to shamanic techniques of mastering fire. Expanding on this, the ascetic practice that generates spiritual ardour is known as *tapas* and the ascetic *tāpasa.* In other tendencies, these terms would be replaced by those of *yoga* and *yogin,* but Jainism has remained faithful to its Śramaṇic origin and continues to use them on a normal basis.

Vedic-Brāhmaṇic ideology also claims that the god Prajāpati created the world inflamed by his own ardour taken to an extreme by means of asceticism (*Aitareya-brāhmaṇa* 5.32). The *Ṛg-veda* (10.167.1) affirms that Indra attained heaven through this fervour *(tapas).* Ascetic austerity also played an important part in the study and apprenticeship phase of the Veda. Sacrifice and *tapas* are interchangeable. When internalising sacrifice, the ascetic channels the sacrificial violence onto himself. All penitence, deprivation, the fact of being himself or herself the sacrificial oblation, enables the ascetic to accumulate impressive spiritual power. Internalised sacrifice converts the ascetic into a very powerful person, sought and feared even by kings. Moreover, the *Taittīriya-up-aniṣad* (3.5.1) said that through *tapas* one must find the absolute. *Brahman* is *tapas.* Therefore, the Veda already completely accepted the importance of *tapas.*

This fervour or spiritual ardour was produced by means of techniques such as breath retention, ingesting intoxicating substances, exposure to fire, exposure to the Sun. In the case of the Jains, the most frequently adopted practice was and still is fasting. But then again, as stated earlier, the ascetic way of life, guided by the five vows or precepts, is in itself an act of *tapas.* Jain asceticism does not extend to eccentric practices, or those consisting of ordeals, but rather involves care, control, rectitude and exertion (*śrama*) in all activities. Two ideas underlie these practices: (1) the transcending the ego-corporeal condition, to meet with the spiritual condition; and (2) literally the burning away of passions and bonds with the aid of spiritual ardour generated by penitence and strict conduct.

But this heating would be futile without control of the mind. To *tapas* one must add the practice of concentration (*dhyāna*) aimed at control of the mind. In this way it can lead to absolute equanimity (*sāmāyika*). Contemplative practice and ascetic practice must go hand-in-hand.

Coherently, for the Śramaṇas spiritual authority does not lie with professional liturgists, but with those masters who, spiritually qualified as they were, would have themselves experienced the path that purified the soul and freed them from the state of attachment and ignorance. The perfect man *jina, vīra, buddha, yogin,* mystic in the broadest sense, is above any cleric, as he is at one with himself and possesses the unlimited compassion and wisdom of the soul in its pure state. He is a superhuman, super-divine being on whom pleasure or pain, cold or heat has no effect. It is not surprising that someone who has transcended the human and divine condition would be exalted in the way as the Jains praise their *tīrthaṅkaras,* the Buddhists their *buddhas* and *bodhisattvas* or the Yogins their *yogins.* Thus, it is the experience of the awakened sage and his personal testimony and not an age-old memory of a revelation that defines religious authority. This feature directly relates to the historic nature of Śramaṇic movements. Spiritual truth depends on historical tradition and the possibility of personal verification (Pande 1984: I, 70).

In conclusion, in India there is a yogic-ascetic tendency, which goes beyond all affiliation and can be traced back to very ancient times. Later on it would issue in Vedic-Brāhmaṇic branches of Sāṃkhya, Yoga, and Vaiśeṣika, and in the Śramaṇic streams of Jainism and Buddhism. Masters such as Kapila, Patañjali, Pārśva, Mahāvīra, or the Buddha were their best exponents. Just as their peers demonstrate, these modes of thought and of liberation were not as clearly differentiated as they latter became with the passing of time. All of them formed part of a very old ascetic-meditative culture from the North of the continent.

Overall, the idea of *progress* in ancient India was clearly different to that of the modern world. It did not necessarily involve improving society (politically, socially, legally or technologically) but attaining transcendental wisdom. The West has invested enormous amounts of energy in dominating nature and controlling matter. Modernity says that human beings can change if their surroundings are controlled. Classical India, on the other hand, has used the same amount of effort and energy in mastering what lies within the human being. For many Indians, freedom is the search for oneself, within oneself. Only improving what is truly essential can lead to progress in society. Emphasis is always on personal enlightenment, before any other social consideration. It is not a case of saving the personality but of achieving absolute liberty—a freedom that requires sacrificing the human condition and personality. This does not lead to a fierce individualism, as the ethical basis of Indian religious movements (non-violence, truthfulness, not stealing, chastity, and lack of possessions) have immense social repercussions. In fact, whoever infringes these ethical principles is considered to bring evil upon himself and the rest of society (K. Jain 1983: 240). All mystics and saints in India (from Mahāvīra, Kabīr, or Tukārāma to Gandhi or Krishnamurti) have insisted, with astonishing unanimity, that without the search for this liberty or saintliness, there is no possible social change.

THE DIFFERENT SOLUTIONS

Those groups of renunciants, which distanced themselves once and for all from the Veda and did not recognise Brāhmaṇas' authority gave root to the unorthodox religious or non-Vedic traditions of the Śramaṇas. Other tendencies, on the other hand, ended up being incorporated into the polymorphous Brāhmaṇism; perhaps they never did split off entirely. Such must have been the case of the extremely important Sāṃkhya school and of those tendencies that would later crystalise as Yoga philosophy. As a result of the emergence of hetereodox paths, Indian religion ended up splitting into two major visions: the Vedic-Brāhmaṇic current which would slowly transform into what is now called Hinduism, and the Śramaṇic trend, which gave birth to Buddhism and Jainism.

Within the overall consensus on the basic premises, there were marked disputes and dissent among the Śramaṇas: What was the ultimate cause of *saṃsāra*? Action, desire, ignorance? What generated *karma*? What were the best ways to avoid the consequences of action? What was liberation? Who or what was it that was liberated? (Davis 1995: 15). Various answers emerged to such questions. Each answer would produce a different spiritual practice and doctrine. Hence the ever-present Hindu idea that there are as many ways to attain liberation as there are spiritual paths (*yogas, mārgas*).

Among the many groups that are mentioned in the scriptures, there are some six or seven, which must have rivalled each other from a position of considerable strength. Their masters are literally categorised as leaders of an order, founders of a religious group, well-known, respected for their saintliness, itinerant and elderly (*Dīgha-nikāya* 1.47-48). Although in texts, they seem to belong to well-defined movements, it is clear that their ideas spread from one tradition to another or were shared by all. Buddhist and Jain Sūtras never cease to talk about converts from one group to another. Buddha went so far as to instigate special rules to allow the integration of the followers of Nigaṇṭa Nātaputta (Mahāvīra) into his community, which goes to show that numerous Nirgranthas entered the Buddhist order (B.C. Jain 1972:44). If these crossovers achieved anything, it was to bring together ideas and practices. One only has to compare their analysis of the condition of bondage, their logical dialectic, their ethics, their cosmology or their techniques of meditation. If in time their differences increased, it is a fact that Buddhist and Jain Sūtras erroneously took Śramaṇas or specific practices of one group as examples of practices of some other group. I think it is worthwhile reviewing some Śramaṇic positions, as they form the second backdrop—after Vedic Brāhmaṇism—against which Jainism should be viewed.

ETERNALISTS

One of the most respected Śramaṇas of the period was Purāṇa Kāśyapa. His basic position was that of the theory of non-action (*akriyāvāda*) and non-causation. For Purāṇa no action led to worthiness or unworthiness. Not even Vedic sacrifice or control of the senses, or truthfulness, or giving alms or anything at all resulted in an improvement of the soul. The spirit is something absolutely impassive and nothing can affect it. This perspective is somewhere between nihilism and fatalism, but also sounds familiarly Vedāntic.

Another contemporary of Mahāvīra was Kakuda Kātyāyana, also highly regarded by his contemporaries. Just like Purāṇa, he maintained that the soul did not act upon anything or suffer any modification. Kailash Jain (1974: 159) has noted that Kakuda and Purāṇa were Brāhmaṇas by birth, so they would have been well versed in Upaniṣadic theory and rejected in a radical fashion that the soul could be altered by acts. When the Buddha and Mahāvīra referred to "eter-nalists", they had the doctrine of Kakuda in mind.

MATERIALISTS

One of the most polemical and influential masters among Śramaṇas was Ajita Keśakambala, the main exponent of Indian materialism (Cārvāka, Lokāyata). Historically, in India, the materialist tendency has been an anathema and the target of criticism from all sides.

Broadly we can say that under the name of materialism we find those systems of belief that consider that only sensory perception and empirical experience (*pratyakṣa*) are valid for acquiring true knowledge. Anything that cannot be perceived by the senses is invalidated. All belief in something supernatural must be rejected.

All Ajita's assertions were expressed through negation. There was no worthiness whatsoever in sacrifice, nor fruit born from action, nor anything that would transmigrate from one world to another or to a new rebirth. He did not accept the fact that Brāhmaṇas or Śramaṇas who had attained liberation existed. Ajita Keśakambala said that when the body dies, be it a fool or a sage, they die the same death. They do not survive after death (*Dīgha-nikāya* 1.55).

In the development of materialism one detects a strong component of reaction against Brāhmaṇic privileges and excessiveness. For materialists, all ritual was an invention of priests to perpetuate themselves in power.

SCEPTICS

Another giant of the 6th century BC was Sañjayin Vairaṭṭīputra. It is extremely likely that this Śramaṇa was Śāriputra's and Maudgalyāyana's master, two of the most outstanding of the Buddha's disciples.

Sañjayin was the main exponent of the doctrine of Indian agnosticism or scepticism (*ajñānavāda*). His philosophy is well illustrated in a famous section of a Buddhist *sūtra* (*Digha-nikāya* 1 .58). When king Ajātaśatru (Kūṇika) asked him if he thought that afterlife existed, or if there were supernatural beings, or a retribution for good and bad actions, or a perfect one (*siddha*) continued existing after death, Sañjayin answered each time that he could not say: not even (1) if it were so, nor (2) if it were not so, nor (3) if it were so and at the same time were not so, nor (4) if it were not so and were not not so. With the help of this four-pronged argument, one confidently rejects any affirmation about anything which escapes our experience (von Glasenapp 1958:147). These evasive questions, whose answers always remained in the field of speculation, deflected attention from the true sense of spirituality: the search, attainment and preservation of total equanimity.

Sañjayin's logical method must have had an influence on the development of Jaina and Buddhist logic, since it contains obvious similarities to Nāgārjuna's method known as *prasaṅga* or the Jain *syādvāda* [see pages 366-369].

FATALISTS

One of the most charismatic leaders of the period was the fatalist Maskarīn Gośāla, chief of the group of Ājīvikas or "followers of the path of life". The determinist ideas of Gośāla to some extent form the background from which Mahāvīra formulated important points of his philosophy, although both movements had many features in common.

It is quite possible that Gośāla gravitated around Mahāvīra and the Nirgranthas for years. After separating from them, he went on to be leader of the Ājīvika group. Therefore, he was not the founder of the Ājīvaka school, as texts mention that the sages Nanda Vaccha and Kisa Saṁkiccha were his predecessors.

Just as with the Jains, oral teachings of the Ājīvikas were known as Pūrvas— a coincidence that has been seen by some authors as having a common origin with those of Jain scriptures. However, since *pūrva* means "ancient", "tradition of the past", Ājīvika texts do not necessarily have to be the same as those of the Jains. One thing in common was that they maintained the existence of twenty-four *tīrthaṅkaras* before Gośāla, which demonstrates the antiquity of the notion of a chain of enlightened ones who preached one same truth.

Gośāla argued fervently in favour of the theory of change and transformation (*pariṇāmavāda*). For Ājīvikas, creation is like a gigantic cosmic laboratory in which spiritual monads, by a slow alchemic process, gradually transform, refine, enrich and purify themselves (Zimmer 1951: 267). Everything follows its course; the soul goes on purifying itself as it transmigrates. The salient point in the Ājīvika theory is—according to what Jains and Buddhists tell us—that the actor is in no wise responsible with respect to his or her acts. The quality of actions does not determine the reincarnation, but transmigration operates according to destiny. Nature is the course by which destiny (*niyati*) and time (*kāla*) operate. Every soul must pass through tens of thousands of existences, from the lowest forms of geological life to human existence. At the end of a cycle of tens of thousands of cosmic aeons liberation occurs spontaneously, without any effort involved, but only then. Everything is predestined. What must happen, will happen; a notion that even today is quite deep-rooted in the minds of many Hindus. Any attempt at freeing oneself in one's lifetime is in vain. The Jain or Buddhist insistence in forging a spiritual path is futile, and cannot be achieved by one's will o energy. Living creatures do not possess the will, strength, or vigour in themselves. They evolve by force of destiny (*Dīgha-nikāya* 1.53-54).

What we have here is a radically fatalist vision. Buddha came to say that the Ājīvaka was the worst among all doctrines and that no one person had discouraged so many people as Gośāla (*Aṅguttara-nikāya* 1.32). If Gosala foresaw a strictly determinism and had a belief in the total lack of willpower of human being, what did not follow at all, as Paul Dundas (1992: 26) has observed, is the idea that this philosophy could form a basis for any renunciant movement or any path towards liberation. In reality, there are well-grounded reasons to think that Gośāla's positions were deliberately distorted by Jains and Buddhists. This issue becomes more comprehensible, in the case of Jains, if we take into account that Gośāla and Mahāvīra shared years of spiritual practice together. Jain tradition has never been able to free itself from this genuine historic connection and perhaps tended to exaggerate the fatalistic nature of the Ājīvika doctrine and Gośāla's talents as a master in the art of supernatural powers. In this way Gośāla could be stigmatised and the Ājīvaka could represent the Other against which one could compare the originality of Jainism. The fact is that, just as in so many Śramaṇic movements, the Ājīvika shared many of the structural features of the groups of the period. The Ājīvikas owed much to the atomism of Kakuda Kātyāyana and the nihilism of Purāṇa Kāśyapa. A not inconsiderable number of scholars have detected his influence in the Jain doctrines on *karma* or practices such as nakedness *(acelaka)* (Jacobi 1884: II, xxix-xxx), and even death by starvation (Basham 1951: 127) [see pages 486-488].

The naturalist concept of the world inspired Ājīvikas to undertake interesting studies of nature and the laws of life. For Ājīvikas, nothing was deadnor did anything happen by chance. Moreover, they considered that human beings, as the highest form of life, had to behave in a manner coherent with the law of nature and approach all other beings with respect. Although their acts were futile and they could only wait passively for the end of the *kalpa,* human beings would have to demonstrate their position in the spiritual hierarchy of creation. Hence their ascetic and non-violent ethics. They had similar practices to the Jains: they abstained from eating certain fruits and bulbous plants, they practised certain restrictions, mortifications, and observed vows of solitude. Although Ājīvika asceticism did not have any purifying value, it was presented as a characteristic way of life for a being close to release. Pious and ascetic acts are not the cause of purification but the effect, signalling that liberation is near.

The Ājīvikas effected a curious classification of human beings into six groups *(abhijātis)* according to "colour": black for those who lived by killing animals, blue for ascetic monks who lived as thieves, red for Jains (Nirgranthas), green for the Ājīvika laity, white for Ājīvika ascetics of both sexes, and supreme white for Maskarīn Gośāla and his predecessors. This theory has quite a lot in common with the Jain theory of tints or *leśyās* [see pages 391-392].

AWAKENED ONES

We come to the most universal Śramaṇa of all, Gautama Siddhārta (563-483 BC, as the most commonly accepted dates), whom the world would come to know as "the Awakened One" (the Buddha) and who would organise the movement of enlightened or awakened ones (Bauddhas).

He was son of Śuddhodana, chief of the Śākya clan of Kapilavastu. His mother, Mahāmāyā, died seven days after giving birth. After an infancy and adolescence in court it is said that he decided to take the path of renunciation when he was suddenly confronted with the fleeting nature and pain of existence *(duḥkha)* in the form of a sick man, an old man, and a corpse. On meeting a peaceful saint, the young prince opted to become a Śramaṇa and search for the path that led to the non-conditioned. He learned the doctrines and practices of Sārçikhya, of Yoga, and the path of asceticism *(tapas).* After rejecting these solutions, he opted for a more moderate way, essentially through meditation. After weeks of concentration, he attained enlightenment *(bodhi)* beneath a fig tree, on the outskirts of Gaya, in southern Magadha. Buddhist awakening or enlightenment consists of the simultaneous perception of the three characteristics of existence: impermanence, *(anitya),* suffering *(duḥkha)* and selflessness *(anātman),* along with an understanding of the law of dependent co-origination *(pratītya-samutpāda)* that brings into being the samsāric cycle and shows the complete interconnection of what exists. The Buddhist way lies in re-enacting the experience of the Buddha's awakening.

The new *buddha* gave his first sermon at Sārnāth, just outside Benares and, after a short time, he congregated a good number of followers. It is said that rich merchants and powerful monarchs supported his doctrine and helped in sustaining his community of renunciants *(saṃgha).*

The main teaching of the Buddha is headed by his famous proclamation of the Four Noble Truths: (1) human existence is alienation, suffering *(duḥkha);* (2) the cause of suffering is desire, thirst *(tṛṣṇā);* (3) the extinction *(nirodha)* of desire ends suffering and alienation; this extinction is called the non-conditioned *(nirvāṇa);* and (4) the practical way that leads to the extinction of desire and, therefore the end of suffering, is the Noble Eight-fold Path. This eight-fold way is the Buddhist path: (1) right view; (2) right thought; (3) right speech; (4) right action; (5) right livelihood; (6) right effort; (7) right mindfulness; (8) right concentration.

Although in times Buddhism would concede great value to knowledge *(prajñā)*—perhaps to counteract devotional and yogic excesses—for the Buddha, philosophy was not of great value outside practice. The most ancient Buddhism (as in Yoga and Jainism), attributes enormous value to effort and personal experience. Above all, the Buddha was a great master of meditation *(dhyānin).*

The Buddha's biography is very similar to Mahāvīra's, and the structure of both religious groups is practically identical.

THE NIRGRANTHAS

Finally, we come to the Nirgranthas, the future Jainas. What we are considering here is to what extent the Universal History has anything to do with micro-history. Myths are usually connected to empirical deeds and to a context. To brand Jain mythology as mere fantasy without any connection to reality (Biardeau 1981: 9), seems to be, in my opinion, erroneous, at least insofar as affirming that all that hagiographies reveal can be confirmed by relevant archaeology, that any myth is nothing more than a conversion of real events into myths (Shendge 1977: 8). Myths are not a representation of empirical deeds, and so the historical basis of the myth is less significant than the religious or symbolic value. As such, it does not matter whether the *tīrthaṅkaras* existed or not, nor if they lived, as tradition says, thousands of oceans of millions of years ago. There is no reason to fall into the simplistic error of looking only for the *man* behind the myth. Let us not forget that for Jains, the *tīrthaṅkaras* were not people who simply attained liberation, but an integral and vital part of the order of things. Without ascendant and descendant cycles, the very idea of *tīrthaṅkara* makes no sense. However, if in any way we can bring history and myth together, the reach of our enterprise can be much greater. Giving a basis to the myth does not legitimise it, but it does help to put it into context and broadens our horizon.

It is something that can be done with Jainism. Despite all of its mythical content, Jain reasoning about their *tīrthaṅkaras* should not be dismissed at a stroke, at least *a priori.* In Jain thinking, myth and history are integrated to form a single schemata which impedes any kind of distinction. Moreover, in India what is age-old is never lost or forgotten. The past permanently intertwines with the present. The fact is that among all the *tīrthaṅkaras* the first (Ṛṣabha) and the last three (Nemi, Pārśva, and Mahāvīra) are those who are subject to special treatment and worship over and above the rest. This fact is not pure coincidence as their mythology shows signs that it could be due to historical nature, from the conventional point of view. Were these *jinas* Śramaṇas?

This line of investigation ties in well in with current Indian tendencies of legitimising religion *(dharma)* historically. Formerly, Indians frankly did not see the need of proving that their *avatarās* such as Rāma or Kṛṣṇa, or *jinas* such as Ṛṣabha or Nemi, existed historically. The classical temporal or eternalist vision has these days been somewhat sidelined. In contrast, a large proportion of Indians rack their brains (undoubtedly influenced by Christianity and historicism) delving into the past and pursuing traces of their *jinas, buddhas* or *avatarās;* and this is also now a part of Jainism. The way in which tradition today interprets its own history plays just as much of an integral part in Jainism as does its traditional vision. So, let us take a look at these central figures.

A SAGE CALLED ṚṢABHA?

What is historic about the mythology of Ṛṣabha? Could he have been the instigator of a proto-Jain tendency? Experts have mainly traced back in two fields of study.

The first possibility, synthesised by Joseph Campbell (1962: II, 251)—in Heinrich Zimmer's footsteps, although without excessive enthusiasm—says that if we can go back 23 generations prior Mahāvīra (one for every *tīrthaṅkara)* we would find ourselves in the mature period of Indus civilisation (2,500-1,900 BC). The thesis that Jainism along with a whole series of Indian religious practices stemmed from the Indus Valley civilisation has been supported by a great number of Indian and Western researchers (Bhattacharyya 1976: 51-56). Following similar reasoning to that of Hindu nationalism, Jyoti Prasad Jain (1951: 41-57) goes further in maintaining that Ṛṣabha preached the truths of Jainism no more and no less than 6,765 years before our era. Jain *dharma* was the religion of the Dravidians of the Indus civilisation and it was transmitted down through the Vedic period by mystic brotherhoods and other groups on the fringe. Doctor Jain comes to the conclusion that Jainism is the oldest living religion of the civilised world. Among Western researchers, Michael Tobias (1991: 54) holds that Jainism is the oldest religion in India, and possibly the oldest in the entire world.

The main argument in this train of thought is that in certain seals unearthed in Mohenjo-daro, one of the main cities of the Indus civilisation, there are meditators depicted sitting in a yogic posture, surrounded by emblematic trees, snakes and animals. All these motifs are found in the iconography of some of the *tīrthaṅkaras,* notably in that of Pārśva [see pages 76-77]. Other figures, surrounded by animals such as the bull *(ṛṣabha),* seem to be in the immobile standing posture *(kāyotsarga),* also typical of Jain iconography. Perhaps the seals represent a type of *proto-jina* or proto-yogic religion that later would become Yoga, Sāṃkhya, and Jainism. According to Mircea Eliade (1972: 258), yogic practices could go back as far as this pre-Vedic urban civilisation. Heinrich Zimmer considers that out of all unorthodox sects of itinerant monks the Jains would have been the ones that have most genuinely prolonged the yogic-ascetic persuasion in India. For Zimmer (1951 217-221) there was no doubt about the pre-Vedic nature of Jainism. Although the ancient and Indie nature of *yoga* is evident, its association with the seals and figures of the Indus Valley civilisation is debatable (Shah 1955: 3). The convincing thesis by Asko Parpola (1994: 248-250) points to a Mesopotamian origin of the figures. Therefore, although a fascinating speculation, it seems to be premature to bank on proto-Jainism in the Indus civilisation.

The second line of reasoning is based on textual study. In two very old Vedic texts, the *Ṛg-veda* (3.13-14) and the *Athvarva-veda,* there are references to a sage called Ṛṣabha, son of Viśvāmitra. Although, one cannot conclude with certainty that this sage was the same figure as the *tīrthaṅkara,* it is tempting to assume some kind of identification. In Jain literature, Ṛṣabha is called "the one with long hair" (Keśī) and is sometimes iconographically represented with curls. As we already know, the most ancient mystics mentioned in the *Ṛg-veda* are called the long-haired ones *(keśīns)* or silent ones *(munis),* this last term being the one which later would be inextricably associated with Jain masters and ascetics. According to Georg Feuerstein (1989:327), this would perhaps establish a relationship between the said Ṛṣabha and circles of yogis and ascetics from age-old times. Also of interest is the fact that a text such as the *Viṣṇu-Purāṇa* (2.1.27-32) relates a story of a wise king Ṛṣabha son of Nābhi, who renounced the world, decided to practise asceticism and went naked. The *Bhāgavata-Purāṇa* (5.3-6) even considers him to be a lesser incarnation of Viṣṇu.

So one cannot rule out a cultural memory of some great master who would have lived around 1000 BC, if not before, belonging to the ascetic-yogic tendency that would later lead on to Jainism. However, the proof is tenuous. The name of Ṛṣabha appears in the Veda representing something like an epithet of the god Indra and the ecstatic description of the *keśīn* plausibly points towards the orders of followers of the god Siva. The mentions of him in the Vaisnava Purāṇas clearly relate to a period when Jainism and Vaiṣṇavism were closely associated.

So although the idea that there was a proto-Jain Śramaṇa, cannot, as I say, be discounted, Ṛṣabha's life, modelled on that of Mahāvīra, like the other *tīrthaṅkaras,* would seem rather to be a structurally necessary argument for the Jain Universal History, as Paul Dundas (1992:35) argues. In his opinion, the list of 23 *jinas* previous to Mahāvīra appears to be a partial imitation of the list of the Vedic sages *(ṛṣis)* that are found in the Upaniṣads (Dundas 1992: 35). Myth and history do not seem to coincide.

NEMI AND KṚṢṆA

Some researchers (J.P. Jain 1951:22-23) also accept the historical evidence of the 22nd *tīrthaṅkara,* Nemi. The central thesis is that Nemi is identical to Ghora Aṅgirasa, the Brāhmaṇa sage that instructs the god-hero Kṛṣṇa in the *Chāndogya-upaniṣad* (3.17.6). The master speaks to him of the virtues of non-violence, truthfulness, austerity, charity, and rectitude, the very values of Śramaṇic ethics. Since Jain tradition states that Nemi and Kṛṣṇa were contemporary to each other, Nemi had, therefore, to have been the above-mentioned master of Krsna.

M. Hiriyanna (1945: 35) thought that Kṛṣṇa was a religious reformer of northern India, somewhat before Mahāvīra, who initiated a kind of theism which would later evolve into the Bhāgavata movement (one of the origins of Vaiṣṇavism). Popular worship ended up making him divine. This is certainly possible, albeit uncertain. In any case, none of this proves the historical existence of the *jina* Nemi. Moreover, Jain tradition points to a family connection, rather than a religious lineage. Such sources state that either Nemi was Kṛṣṇa's uncle or they were first cousins. In fact, a host of episodes associated with this *jina* are closely connected to the mythology of Kṛṣṇa. The association with Kṛṣṇa almost certainly owes much to socio-historical reasons. When followers of Kṛṣṇa crossed over to Jainism a relationship between Kṛṣṇa and Nemi was established (Radhakrishnan 1923:1,331). In the same way as followers of Viṣṇu adopted Ṛṣabha, Jains did so with Kṛṣṇa.

Once again, the important thing is that for many centuries the Jain believer has had no doubt that the omniscient Nemi proclaimed the doctrine of non-violence on the sacred mountain of Girnar. If we are searching for historic features of these first *jinas,* it is simply to put Jainism into context, and to give a sense of union between mythical perception and linear history. Nevertheless, at the moment we still have no hard evidence for this.

PĀRŚVA, FOUNDER OF JAINISM?

There is rather more consensus among scholars in recognising historical evidence of the 23rd *tīrthaṅkara,* Pārśva. The Universal History maintains that he would have lived some 200 years before Mahāvīra, between 800 and 700 BC, quite surprisingly reasonable dates.

The community of experts tends to consider him as the possible founder of Jainism (von Glasenapp 1958: 307), or at least its first historic exponent. Mahāvīra only would have reformed and expanded upon the work initiated by Pārśva (Jacobi 1884:1, xxxiv). Even the great Professor Jacobi, the first to prove the historical evidence of Pārśva, accepted that there was no certainty as to whether Pārśva would have founded Jainism.

The fact is that, given his antiquity, Pārśva is the first Śramaṇa we know of and his group would also be the most ancient, having the name of "bondless" (Nirgranthas), i.e., without *(nir)* bonds *(granthas).* Until the 1st century, Jains were still invariably called Nirgranthas. With the passage of time, this ancient Śramaṇa brotherhood ended up giving form to the *Jaina* phenomenon.

How can we prove that Pārśva was a historical character? Texts from the Buddhist canon on repeated occasions mention this group *before* the enlightenment of the Buddha. Moreover, Hermann Jacobi (1884: II, xx-xxi) detected that some of Pārśva's doctrines had been attributed to Mahāvīra, a mistake which could not have been made if Pārśva and his followers had not existed. Normally in India, scriptures of religious movements do not accord any rank to other rival groups unless they are well established. The mention of Nirgranthas demonstrates the antiquity of Jainism. On the other hand, there is not even a single mention of the Buddha in the most ancient Jain texts, which would seem to indicate that Buddhism evolved later on. The antiquity of Pārśva's proto-Jainism is also strengthened by the fact that other leaders such as Purāṇa Kāśyapa or Maskarīn Gośāla, who were also called *tīrthaṅkaras* by their followers, adopted doctrines and practices clearly based on a proto-Jainism (B.C. Jain 1972: 21). Moreover, in the classification of humanity into six types of human, according to Gośāla, the third was that of the Nirgranthas. Of course, these theories are reinforced by internal evidence in Jain texts. Jain Sūtras, time and again refer to ascetics from the lineage of Pārśva who were re-directed by the reforms introduced by Mahāvīra [see pages 154-155].

We know very little of Pārśva's doctrine. The core of it must have consisted a type of dualism between the spiritual *(jīva)* and the non-spiritual *(ajīva)*. Pārśva included apparently inert beings, typical of those in Jain biology, in the spiritual half. This clearly animist idea that all living beings *(jīva)* possess a spirit *(jīva)*, is perhaps an indication that this religion originated in extremely ancient times.

Its praxis would rest on the four vows *(cāturyāma-saṃvara)* that have been referred to: (1) not to harm *(ahiṃsā)'*, (2) not to lie *(satya)*; (3) not to steal *(asteya)*; (4) not to own property *(aparigraha)*. According to some medieval commentators the fourth vow would perhaps imply chastity *(brahmacarya)*, although theoretically the inclusion of a fifth vow must be regarded as the work of Mahāvīra. Although the great Jainologist Walther Schubring (1934: 247) doubted that Pārśva would have established clearly-defined monastic vows, this continues to be the mainstream view within Indologists as well as the Jain tradition. Details of the ascetic-purifying practices of the ancient Nirgranthas are not known, but we can be quite sure that the ideal would be to emulate the example given by Pārśva himself.

Pārśva was one of the first critics to question various key points in Brāhmaṇic ideology with success. On the one hand, he would have openly opposed the carnivorous diet and animal sacrifices of the Brāhmaṇas. Secondly, he would have criticised the Brāhmaṇical vision of society structured into socio-spiritual classes *(varṇas)*, especially with the spiritual authority and rank vested in them. Finally, he would not have recognised the authority of the Veda. Armed with these criticisms Pārśva would have definitively turned his back on Vedic religiosity.

Part IV

Mahāvīra

In Mahāvīra, we find mythical and linear time converging inexorably. The 24th *jina,* whose historical existence is beyond all doubt, was simultaneously, both the last *tīrthaṅkara* of the Universal History and precisely for that reason the first *tīrthaṅkara* of historical times.

Mahāvīra was not the founder of Jainism or of the groups of Nirgranthas. He was one of the propagators and the last to achieve omniscience of a chain of awakened masters who taught an ancient truth. The honour of having founded Jainism, is reserved for Pārśva, but even this is not certain. Most likely, no one ever founded Jainism. Like the Vedic tradition (or that of Hinduism), Jainism progressively constructed itself around charismatic masters, recurrent practices and prestigious doctrines, but it is not necessary to speak of any founder. The compulsion to look for founders of the great spiritual traditions of the world is a typical projection of the Abrahamic religions (Judaism, Christianity, and Islam). The Semitic style of founder or prophet is unusual or rare in South Asia. The Indian sage generally does not find invent, create, or write; rather he remembers an ancient teaching, perhaps fallen into disuse. This is applicable even to the Buddha. In Mahāvīra's case, tradition doggedly insists that he embraced a faith that already existed. After years of practice, he attained sublime wisdom that this community had already known, although at that time only in imperfect form.

In its origin, Jainism must have been just one more component in the ascetic culture of northern India of which we have seen so many examples. It would consist of a small group of Nirgrantha Śramaṇas who, with the passing of the centuries, increasingly became aware of their originality. Gradually, they came to mark the differences between themselves and other religious groups. Nevertheless, in its beginnings, Jainism tended to identify itself with, associate itself with and even seek legitimacy from, a series of teachings common to the sages of that part of India. A significant instance of this assimilative process is to be found in an obscure text, one which fell into disgrace early on within the tradition itself: the *Ṛṣibhāṣita.* This is one of the most ancient of the Jain texts, dating from around the 4th century BC. The intriguing thing about the *Rsibhāsita* is that it presents us with the teachings of Pārśva and Mahāvīra juxtaposed with the teachings of the seers *(rsis)* who would later be seen as rivals: the Upaniṣadic sage Yājñavalkya, two of the great disciples of the Buddha Sāriputra and Maudgalyāyana, the Hindu saint-god Nārada, and even the notorious evil one Maskarīn Gośāla. Paul Dundas (1992: 16) has demonstrated, interestingly, that the imagery used in this text is still sacrificial (that is, Vedic) and Mahāvīra's teachings are presented under his original given name Vardhamāṇa. It is logical that, with the passing of time, tradition would reject a text that tended to eclipse Mahāvīra's originality and connect him unduly with his rivals. The text is paradigmatic of the asceticism of ancient India, when the Śramaṇas were not clearly differentiated into Nirgranthas, Ājīvikas, Bauddhas and Yogins.

We do not know for certain to what extent Mahāvīra was responsible for Jainism's identifying features. Perhaps, he was a successful reformer who succeeded in bringing together and unifying diverse practices and doctrines which gravitated around the Nirgranthas. At all events, the tradition is unanimous in associating him directly with Pārśva, in this way setting up a link with all other *jinas* from prehistoric times. Mahāvīra showed the way for the difficult times of this cosmic aeon. It is for this reason that the tradition declares him to be the last *jina.* Until many thousands years into the future, no other *tīrthaṅkara* will appear on the face of Bharata-varṣa.

Consequently, we shall devote the whole of this Part [chapters 8 and 9] to relating the story and the teachings of Mahāvīra, the maestro par excellence of Jainism for the Sorrowful Age. Here, myth and history merge into a unique and exemplary narrative.

8. THE ASCETIC VARDHAMĀṆA

MAHĀVĪRA'S BIOGRAPHY

Mahāvīra's life story provides us with a model of the last incarnation of a *tīrthaṅkara.* This point needs to be emphasised. It is Mahāvīra's *last* life. An individual's biography makes no sense outside the context of the wheel of transmigration. At the same time, his life shows the pattern to follow for all Jain monks. For Jain ascetics, Mahāvīra is like the Buddha for Buddhists: the *archetype.*

The central episodes of his biography are described in several different texts. The soberest, most realistic and certainly the oldest account is found in the *Ācārāṅga-sūtra I* (5th-4th centuries BC). The *Ācārāṅga-sūtra II* and the *Kalpa-sūtra*, which are later (2nd-1st centuries BC), already show exuberant admiration. Subsequently, the biography was gradually expanded in many different commentaries, among which the most important are the *Niryuktis* (lst-3rd centuries CE). Even though the versions vary, there is unanimity in recalling five auspicious moments of the master's life: (1) conception *(garbha);* (2) birth *(janma)*; (3) renunciation *(samnyāsa, niṣkramaṇd)*; (4) enlightenment *(kevala-jñāna)*; and (5) death and liberation *(mokṣa, nirvāṇa).* These five episodes are still commemorated in some of the most important celebrations of the Jain community. They are considered unmistakably to mark out the last life of all the *tīrthaṅkaras* and define the ideal ascetic life. The same five moments are shared in identical fashion by the lives of Pārśva, Nemi, Ṛṣabha and all the other *tīrthaṅkaras,* above and beyond the details of their own particular biographies. In themselves, these five events taken together form a symbolic sacred structure.

Buddha's mythical biography is very similar. Similar too are those of certain Hindu gods and of other masters of that time. We are dealing with quite a recurrent pattern in Indian thought.

From the historiographer's point of view, his biography presents several inconsistencies and difficulties. It is just as difficult to reconstruct an "historical Mahāvīra" as an "historical Jesus", but this is hardly a problem. Just as the Gospel writer's interest is christological, that of the hagiographies of Mahāvīra is basically doctrinal. The latter's life and teachings are beyond historic accidents.

As David Snellgrove (1987: 7-8) so well observes, in the case of the Buddha, one cannot talk about a mere mortal who teaches a philosophy of life or simple ethics and later goes on to be deified as a result of his followers' enthusiasm. It is clear that the master was even in his own lifetime considered to be beyond the contingent and conventional. The "historical Mahāvīra" is not an isolated phenomenon. Mahāvīra is one more link in the chain of enlightened beings that appear periodically and preach the same doctrine.

Nevertheless, the Jain tradition also possesses a fine historical sense, and its texts never cease to alert us to the humanity, even if sublime, of its *last jina.* Mahāvīra was neither a god *(deva)* nor a divine incarnation *(avatāra).* For many readers, the miracles and fabulous episodes of his life may seem merely mythical stories. Behind all that they will look for the *man,* the sage who was the proponent of Jainism in historic times. These days it is Mahāvīra's, Buddha's, or Jesus' humanity which people are tending to value. What is interesting is that the tension between the biographical accounts and the hagiographies occur in the texts themselves at the heart of the tradition. As is habitual in India, one can choose: one can seek to see only the man and the master, or the super-divine victor, worthy of the most pious veneration. It is a personal question, but in the last instance, there is no clear-cut barrier between the two notions—since is not he or she who rises above the phenomena and the mundane, by definition, a supernatural being? Also, the knowledge of some of the features of the Jina's life-story is of great help in grasping how the majority of his future followers understood him and see him. Just as Richard Gombrich (1988: 21) has written (again on the subject of the Buddha) the interesting point is not in what the Buddha said, but in what his listeners must have heard, and what they have been hearing over the centuries. To adjust my prose to modern tastes, I have partially cleansed the biography of hyperbole. Without entirely rendering the narration un-mythlike, the end result is a reasonably believable biographic nucleus, since we shall not find anything here, which is not consistent with the life of that time and the development of Indian thought.

PREVIOUS INCARNATIONS

Since the future Jina reached his pristine, diamantine state thanks to the merits and virtues of previous lives, as in the case of Pārśva, many texts go on at very great length regarding Mahāvīra's previous incarnations. The monad of the future *tīrthaṅkara,* just as with all other *jīvas,* had gone through millions of births of different kinds. The stories trace a gradual, spiritual itinerary, presenting a model for spiritual progress for laymen and ascetics alike. Once the future *jina* obtains the right vision *(samyaktva),* or (and this amounts to the same thing) once he grasps the principals of Jainism, the seeds of perfection are planted. From then onward, spiritual progress is feasible. Even though for Jain lay-persons reaching liberation may seem a far-off goal, they possess a pronounced sense that progress is always possible, that in emulating these patterns they are on the right path, the path laid down by the *jinas*.

It is said that 26 incarnations earlier, the *jīva* that would be Mahāvīra was Nayasāra, a virtuous headman of a village, born in the continent of Videha (Ratna-Prabha Vijaya 1948: 1-I,71-86). His exemplary behaviour earned him an incarnation in the Upper World in his next life. After that, he was reborn as Marīci the heretic, the emperor Bharata's son, and thus Ṛṣabha's grandson. According to the story, Marīci heard how Ṛṣabha had prophesied that one of his grandsons would become the last *tīrthaṅkara,* and so devised a way that was a soft option, a path that deviated from the original premises. He taught this doctrine to the sage Kapila (Ratna-Prabha Vijaya 1948:1 -1,190-194), and this way became one of the classical Brāhmaṇical paths, heretical as it was from the Jain point of view.

Incarnation followed incarnation, almost always as a divinity or Brāhmaṇa, until arriving at the existence of the first *vāsudeva* Triprsta. As a consequence of the atrocities that all *vāsudevas* must commit when coming up against *apra-tivāsudeva,* the *jīva* whose final existence would be as Mahāvīra, visited the seventh hell. The next incarnation was as a fierce lion, which was to gain him another arduous reincarnation. In the chain of lives of all saints or *tīrthaṅkaras* there is always one in which the right vision (*samyaktava, samyak-darśana)* emerges, a heavenly flash of light that would plant the seed leading to liberation. In the case of Mahāvīra, this moment of enlightenment happened when he was reborn as a lion—later adopted as his emblem. It is said that just when the carnivore was about to devour a small deer, some Jain ascetics came along and the lion remembered its past lives, all the innumerable painful deaths and rebirths. He remembered that in one of these lives long ago he had heard the Jain Truth. This realisation would catapult him over the course of various lives directly to liberation.

These stories are full of religious instruction, mythical symbology, descriptions of society, and even popular tales. They are very similar to the previous lives of the Buddha, narrated in the popular Jātakas. Very many of the passages and stories are common to both (and to the Hindu Purāṇas) only varying in their context and the morals they express. India has always been an immense repository of myths, tales, fables, and legends, which have impregnated the hagiographies of their saints and gods and, for good measure, a good part of the world's ancient literature. Jains, better than most, have been able to preserve oral traditions and story telling mixed in with their doctrinal expositions and explanations of Universal History. With these stories, Jainism has offered both entertainment and doctrine to their followers. Tens of generations of Jain lay people have learnt the recommendations of the Jain way or the consequences of action through the tales of the previous lives of the protagonists of Universal History.

The previous incarnation to that of Mahāvīra was as an ethereal *vaimānika* deity. Even though the future *jina* showed himself to be indifferent to these elevated incarnations, for the common man who hears or reads the stories, these types of lives are of maximum importance. The message is clear: those who lead a life of meritorious actions *(puṇya)* will gain admittance to heaven; those who commit malignant actions *(pāpa)* will be rewarded with the miseries of hell. Keeping oneself firmly to the Jain path, the layman legitimately aspires to heavenly or sublime existences.

After various aeons, incarnated as a divine being, the soul who will become Mahāvīra feels that his life in heaven is (at last!) coming to an end.

CONCEPTION

After uncountable existences in the different worlds of this cosmos, there came to pass the first auspicious event in the life history of any *tīrthaṅkara.* The sources say that Mahāvīra was conceived in the womb of Devānandā, the wife of the learned priest Ṛṣabhadatta, residing in the Brāhmaṇical district of Vaiśālī, the capital of Vṛjjīs. Like all mothers of exceptional beings, the Brāhmanī Devānandā had a series of auspicious dreams. She related them to her husband and he immediately understood the meaning: Devānandā had a baby in her womb that would be an expert in the Veda, in the auxiliary sciences of the Veda and all the systems of Brāhmaṇical philosophy. Fortunately for the Universal History, the great god Indra (Śakra) had a hand in the matter. Using his clairvoyant knowledge, typical of gods and great yogis, from his vantage point in the Saudharma heaven he visualised all the continents of Jambūdvipa and he perceived that a great, auspicious birth was going to take place. But something unbelievable was happening, something that had very rarely taken place in the infinite *kalpas* of the universe: this exceptional being was growing in the womb of a Brāhmaṇī. Indra caused the embryo to be transferred from the Brāhmaṇī Devānandā to the princess Triśalā so that, like all *jinas,* the future *tīrthaṅkara* would come into the world in a noble aristocratic family (Kṣatriya). While the mothers were sleeping, the baby that Triśalā was expecting was transferred to Devānandā. This deed marks a small difference between the five auspicious moments of Mahāvīra and other *jinas.* We also come across this myth in the Kṛṣṇa legends *(Bhāgavata-Purāṇa* 10.2.8), and it has symbolic importance. On the one hand, it shows the exceptional nature of a birth of such a being. On the other hand, it demonstrates that of their own volition, the gods preferred a birth in the aristocratic class to one in the priestly class. Indra knew to perfection that:

> "It never has happened, nor does it happen, nor will it happen, that *arhats [tīrthaṅkaras], cakravartins*, *baladevas,* or *vāsudevas,* in the past, present, or future, should be bom in low families, mean families, degraded families, poor

families, indigent families, beggars' families, or Brāhmaṇical families" *(Kalpa-sūtra, Jina-caritra* 17).

The *sūtra* author's irony in placing purest of pure Brāhmaṇas in the same category as ignoble, lower class beings is absolutely perverse. The fact that Mahāvīra was conceived by a Brāhmaṇī can be explained by the consequence of the *karma* created by his pride when he was born as Marīci the heretic (Ratna-Prabha Vijaya 1948: 1-I,196-197). Even so, the Digambara tradition does not recognise the transference of the embryo.

The night of the proverbial transference, in a state between sleeping and waking, the new—and appropriate—mother had the 14 dreams (16 according to the Digambaras) that all mothers who are going to give birth to a unique being have during their pregnancy. Triśalā told them to Siddhārta her husband and he immediately understood what it meant: Triśalā was pregnant with a prince who was going to be a brave and gallant king (note the difference of interpretation with respect to that of the Brāhmaṇa Ṛṣabhadatta). So as not to waste the auspicious and propicious effect of the dreams, the coupler spent the rest of the night awake. The next day, Siddhārta called on astrologers and interpreters of dreams to reveal their full meaning. The verdict was unanimous: it was prophesied that a beautiful male child would come into the world; he would be an expert in all branches of knowledge and he would be either a universal emperor *(cakravartin)* or a spiritual victor *(jina),* Lord of *dharma* and of the three worlds. The interpretation of the signs (also found in the Buddha's hagiography) clearly shows a bifurcation. The *tīrthaṅkara* is he who could have been a universal monarch *(cakravartin)* but renounced royalty and earthly dominion to become an ascetic monk, a spiritual conqueror *(jina)* who would transcend the whole Earth.

BIRTH

In the Upper World, gods become sad when they see that their end is approaching. Millions of years of happiness and pleasure will be reduced to an animal or human existence. This is not so in the case of a future *tīrthaṅkara.* He casts off the divine way with indifference and prefers a human rebirth; the only one in which he can follow the eternal path of asceticism preached by *the jinas* and, ultimately, the one in which he can aspire to emancipation. According to old mythological stories, the *tīrthaṅkaras* know the destiny of their last incarnation. It is even said that the future *jina* decides the moment of his renunciation of the world before being born—in the case of Mahāvīra, after the death of his parents *(Kalpa-sūtra, Jina-caritra* 94). Despite that, Jain dogma insists that unlike the Buddhist *bodhisattvas,* the *tīrthaṅkaras* are never aware that they are beginning their existence as such (Jaini 2000: 114-115).

The majority of Jain traditions claim Mahāvīra was born on the 13th day of the waxing Moon in the month of Caitra. It was the year 599 BC near the end of the Marvellously Sorrowful Age *(duḥsamā-susamā).* According to the horoscopes, the Sun (Sūrya) was in Aries (Meṣa), his ruling planet was Saturn (Śani); his ascendant was Capricorn (Makara Rāśi), Mars (Maṅgala) was rising and the Moon (Candra) was in Virgo (Kanyā) (Jivanlal Doshi 1948: 166-174).

For many decades, scholars have indulged in endless speculation over Mahāvīra's "real" dates. This is a supremely complex task as it also depends on the Buddha's dates, given that the two figures were most probably contemporary. There are no less than 12 possible dates in the Buddha's case, spanning some two centuries. At all events, these days scholars are considering somewhat later birth dates to those hallowed by tradition. Most usually, it is calculated that the birth must have taken place around the year 539 BC. He was born into a noble family in the region of Videha/Vṛjjīs, in Kuṇḍalapura, the Kṣatriya district of Vaiśālī. The exact location of Kuṇḍalapura has not been determined, while the candidate for Vaiśālī continues to be Besarh, in Bihar state.

Vardhamāṇa was his name at birth, which literally means "prosperous". All *tīrthaṅkaras'* names are related to events during their mother's pregnancy. In this case it is said that from the moment of the embryo's transference, the family's wealth, along with that of their relatives and the entire kingdom, prospered in a miraculous way. Of course, we are told that innumerable marvellous signs accompanied the birth. Even the gods descended from heaven to celebrate this second auspicious happening of the last incarnation of the 24th *jina* of this cosmic cycle. It is said that when an event like this occurs, a radiant, pure light shines upon all sides. It is the only light that the beings from the shadowy Lower World have occasion to see in all their existence. Even their torments are slightly alleviated during an event of such cosmic significance

He was of the Kāśyapa lineage *(gotra),* of the Jñātṛ clan. Buddhist texts in Pali language refer to him as Nigaṇṭa Nātaputta *(Dīgha-nikāya* I.57), the Nirgrantha of the Jñātṛka clan. We know he had an older brother, Nandivardhana, and an older sister, Sudarśanā.

More than what we conventionally understand as kings and queens, his parents, Siddhārta and Triśalā were surely heads of aristocracies or feudal clans, as with Śuddhodana and Mahāmāyā, the Buddha's parents. According to Narendranath Bhattacharyya (1976: xvi), the birth lines to which Mahāvīra and the Buddha belonged were purely tribal. It would only be after Brāhmaṇas (ever attentive as they were to questions of socio-spiritual class) were converted to their doctrines, that Mahāvīra's parents would come to be treated as Kṣatriyas, in its traditional sense of princes or kings. Nonetheless, this does not rule out that Vardhamāṇa might perhaps have been related, on his mother's side, to king Ceṭaka of Vṛjjīs and the powerful Śreṇika of Magadha.

It is said that the newborn baby possessed a perfect, diamantine body, with the auspicious marks which all *tīrthaṅkaras* are known to have. This is also a well-known notion among Buddhists, being based on the universal monarch's *(cakravartin)* iconography. Perhaps the most emblematic sign is the wheel *(cakra)*; an old Vedic symbol associated with Indra, which all *jinas* have on the soles of their feet. These signs identify them ineluctably with the notion of great man *(mahāpuruṣa),* as foretold by the astrologers.

According to the hagiographies, all *indras,* with the great Śakra at the head, took the newly born baby to mount Meru to perform its first sacramental bath *(abhiṣeka).* To carry out the ablution, the gods brought the water from the very Milky Way, and from the most sacred rivers of the cosmos. Everything was done in an identical way as had been done with the 23 *tīrthaṅkaras* before that. This gesture is daily repeated in a multitude of Jain temples, in one of the most quintessential of Jain rituals.

YOUTH

The *Ācārāṅga-sūtra* (2.15.16) states that his parents were already Jains who worshipped Pārśva and the Śramaṇas. Although one could doubt the veracity of this statement, what counts is that for many centuries (at least 20) tradition had it that Mahāvīra was born the son of Jain lay people and received and education according to religious precepts from Śramaṇas followers of Pārśva. The city of Vaiśālī was unquestionably always one of the strongholds of the Nir-granthas. His infancy and youth took place peacefully against the background of palace life, although we know very little about these stages in his life. The only thing that we gather from later texts is that he learned all the arts and sciences that a prince should know, and he grew up to be a handsome young man. Stories tell of his deep erudition, his astounding strength or the hard tests that he was put through by jealous divinities. It is said that the gods gave him the name of Great *(mahā)* Hero *(vīra)* for his bravery, perseverance and self-control, and for his lack of love or hate he was already called renouncer *(Śramaṇa) (Kalpa-sūtra, Jinacaritra* 108).

As an adult, he complied with the duties of all Indians of his rank. That is to say, he married the princess Yaśodā and, according to Śvetāmbara sources, he had a daughter, Priyadarśanā. The Digambaras absolutely deny that any *tīrthaṅkara* would marry.

RENUNCIATION

The third auspicious event in the life of a *jina,* and indeed of any Śramaṇa, is the renunciation of ritual and social family life. Given the promise contracted by Vardhamāṇa, this crucial moment had to be postponed until the death of his progenitors. The legend narrates that his parents opted to put an end to their lives with voluntary euthanasia, by starvation *(Ācārāṅga-sūtra* 2.15.26). Here, we refer to one of the strictest and most sacred religious vows of Jainism [see pages 486-488].

However, Digambara sources do not accept the story linking the renunciation to his former marriage to Yaśodā and the death of his parents. They maintain that Vardhamāṇa took the path towards definitive renunciation from childhood, although his parents were initially opposed to the idea. When he became an adult he was duly given consent. According to Śvetāmbara sources, once he completed his duty as householder, it was his eldest brother and his paternal uncle who were to give him permission to take the path of renunciation. Nandi-vardhana insisted on his waiting for two years, until the pain from the death of his parents had subsided. It is told that in these two years Vardhamāṇa began to prepare himself: he abandoned all types of activities that might result in the destruction of life, he stopped drinking liquors, he maintained complete celibacy, he stopped grooming his body, he started distributing his substantial wealth and possessions. He took the vows of the Nirgranthas at a lay level. Stress is put on the enormous quantity of objects, desires and attachments he renounced. Because the more one has, the more heroic it is to renounce it (Laid-law 1995: 42).

All sources recognise that, finally at the age of 30 years, Vardhamāṇa formally initiated his renunciation *(niṣkramaṇa).* Indra himself, helped by his replicas and acolytes, carried him on a litter to a majestic *aśoka* tree in a nearby forest. To the shout of "victory, victory!" the gods urged him to take the step of renouncing the world, the deed that would establish anew the teachings of the sacred path for the benefit of the entire universe. Some gods in the party, the *laukantikas,* had a special interest in the event, as it is said that they are destined to liberate themselves as ascetic Jains in a future existence. They obviously could not do so until Jainism was once more proclaimed by the *tīrthaṅkara.* Vardhamāṇa fasted for two and a half days, he tore out all his hair from its roots in five yanks, he got rid of his last possessions, he worshipped the liberated souls and, swearing the vows of the Nirgranthas, undertook initiation *(dīkṣā)* as a mendicant monk. The gods rejoiced. The third auspicious moment of the last *jina's* career had taken place.

SPIRITUAL PRACTICE *(SĀDHANĀ)*

From that day Vardhamāṇa devoted himself to pilgrimage as a mendicant (*bhikṣu)* in the forests and paths of the Ganges Valley. He ended up immersing himself in the age-old Śramaṇic, yogic, and ascetic tradition of northern India.

He doubtlessly first lived as an itinerant Nirgrantha in the region of Videha/Vṛjjīs. Afterwards, he broke off all ties and connections with other Nirgranthas. After 13 months, he decided to leave off wearing clothes, garments, which had been donated by Indra himself on the day of his initiation. For the rest of his life, Mahāvīra went naked. This constituted the first break with the tradition transmitted by Pārśva (at least that is what we gather from the texts) and it would be an important disputed point in the future [see chapter 12]. According to the Digambara tendency, no authentic Nirgrantha, and much less someone who was one day going to become a *tīrthaṅkara,* could be attached even to a tattered rag. Consequently, according to the Digambaras, Vardhamāṇa laid aside his clothing the day of his initiation.

For over 12 years, he devoted himself strictly to asceticism *(tapas)* and meditation *(dhyāna).* To capture the essence of Jainism it is vital to understand the length these practices were taken to, something we already focused upon in the previous chapter.

TAPAS

Jain texts insist, again and again, that a true Śramaṇa is oblivious to hunger or thirst, fire or ice, dirt or lack of sleep, sexual appetite or the desire for clothing. In other words a Śramaṇa has to be independent from his body, the synthesis of that which is contingent, that which perishes; pertaining to the world of action *(karma)* and transmigration *(saṃsāra).* Indian traditions insist on the power of spiritual heat *(tapas)* for transcending the body, caused by different types of mortification or physical practices. In Vardhamāṇa's case, the most usual penitence consisted of fasting. Jain *tapas* hardly accord any value to ordeals— at least, in theory—but abide by the principal of *privation.* It is not self-mortification or insensibility to pain that counts, but the capacity to stand privation (the lack of food, insults from others, the absence of affection, etc.). Vardhamāṇa began fasting for two days, and gradually lengthened the periods of abstinence, until he was fasting partially for periods of up to eight months *(Ācārāṅga-sūtra* 1.8.4.5). Even these days, most Jains practice various types of fasting as an expression of their spiritual orientation. In doing so, they are seeking to emulate the years of asceticism that led the Jina to awakening.

As we know, in India, the prestige of the *tapas* dates back to ancient times [see page 113]. Hindu literature is full of tales about ascetics—and not a few demons—who had accumulated so much ascetic ardour that the very gods felt their position to be in danger. To curb this power, the gods usually send a maiden to tempt and confuse the thoughts of the ascetic one *(tapasvin, tāpasa).* Otherwise, with his miraculous powers *(siddhis)* the ascetic could force the divinity to come before him and make him concede favours. That is why in India, saints *(sādhus)* and yogis *(yogins)* have been feared for their supernatural powers obtained by means of their ardour or as a blessing from the gods. Within Jain tradition, Gośāla would be an example of the *tapasvin* being a master of supernatural powers, but trapped by his own magic. This is the great danger of *tapas.* The *siddhis* tempt the holy one with the vanity of dominion over the world (Eliade 1972: 136). Such ascetics become attached to *their* power and incapable of transcending their "divine" condition, and letting go of the ego. Asceticism as a means to obtain powers or gaining rewards in other lives was incompatible with Mahāvīra's vision.

In clear contrast to the image of the fallen magician, Jain tradition has collected a multitude of stories of monks that, seeking support in their ascetic heat *(tapas)* and magic chants *(mantras),* are capable of moving any object and— here is the difference—favour Jainism. The hagiographies of the Śvetāmbara *dādāgurus* of medieval times [see pages 266-267] and, indeed, those of almost any reputed master are full of references to ascetic ardour and the occult powers derived from the *tapas.* Bāhubali himself in his formidable asceticism, which lasted for a whole year, acquired such great supernatural gifts that his power was able to make the three worlds of the cosmos tremble (Strohl 1990: 239). The *tapas'* power is unimaginable. The same is true of *mantras.* Jain texts never cease to mention esoteric sounds, thanks to which monks can exorcise demons, defeat enemies, bring women good luck, favour victory in battle and even find hidden treasures. Notwithstanding, even though tradition constantly praises the supernatural powers of its ascetic monks, the mission of asceticism in soteriol-ogy is different. On the Jain path, the *tapas* is the highest *purifier* and protector.

In fact, for Jainism, the meaning of *tapas* is far from that of "ardour", "heat" or even "ascesis"; it means something more like "purification obtained by effort". Or translated into pan-Indian language, *tapas* is the equivalent to *yoga.* With the *tapas,* the ascetic burns his passions and his attachments and with the *tapas* he shields himself from them, as a breastplate that repels the arrows of passion and addiction (Granoff 1990: 145).

Asceticism is nothing other than independence from the body. Consequently, to the principle of privation Jain *tapas* adds the principles of absolute care *(samiti)* and control *(gupti)*when walking, speaking, sleeping, excreting, drinking, etc. Always making sure not to harm any living creature, not to be overcome with pride, covetousness, and anger. The strict conduct of a Jain religious is in itself an act of *tapas.*

DHYĀNA

Like other yogis of antiquity, Mahāvīra was not content simply with the privations of *tapas.* Apart from fasting and corporal control, he included the practice of reflection, the vow of silence or meditation. For Mahāvīra, asceticism without connection with internal purification via meditation *(dhyāna)* was fruitless.

What the ascetic monk must do is gradually free himself from the agent that desires (his ego) cultivating total equanimity *(sāmāyika),* which is the name habitually used in Jainism to refer to meditative practices. The ascetic monk who has withdrawn from society through initiation, who has transcended his body and his emotions by means of the *tapas,* must now overcome his psychic and linguistic contingency. Meditation involves withdrawing one's mind and feelings from all external objects and focusing attention on one single point, such that any kind of identification with the mind or body is eliminated. By transcending the human condition, yogis attain equanimity, expressed in the form of indifference towards external stimulation, and complete absence of passion.

Although Mahāvīra shared with Buddhism and Sāṃkhya their emphasis on meditation, for him this had to be complemented by total abnegation and control of one's passions. His position is similar to that of Patañjali, founder of classical Yoga. Mindfulness had to combine with the example of perfect austere conduct. *Dhyāna* along with *tapas.* Defeating the ego's mirages is a task of meditation; to put an end to corporal confinement one needs asceticism.

YEARS OF ASCETICISM AND MEDITATION

The stories of his years of pilgrimage are full of anecdotes. It is said that after two years of travelling as a Śramaṇa, when he was staying the night in Nā-landā, Gośāla (future head of the Ājīvikas) joined him. After sharing spiritual practice for six years, they separated. Solitude sits better with the spirit of Nirgrantha practice. Texts show an imperturbable, impassive man facing the inclemency of life. A multitude of jealous gods, evil men, perverse damsels, people from primitive tribes, fierce animals or little forest imps, bothered him and continually put him to the test, and always failing. Moreover when the inhabitants of a remote and wild region of Lāḍha (identified with central Bengal) stoned and attacked him, the great ascetic stood his ground, without budging an inch from his practices:

> "As water does not adhere to a copper vessel, or collyrium to mother of pearl [so sins found no place in him]; his course was unobstructed like that of Life; like the firmament he wanted no support; like the wind he knew no obstacles; his heart was pure like the water [of rivers or tanks] in autumn" *(Kalpa-sūtra, Jina-caritra* 118).

Always given to the most arduous privations and abstinence, practising equanimity, Vardhamāṇa conquered all physical and moral temptations *(parīsahas)* that in the future all Jain monks would have to overcome [see page 493]. When walking, he concentrated on not hurting the tiny creatures of the earth, since he, on scrutinising them, understood that they were imbued with life *(Ācārāṅga-sūtra* 1.8.1.12).

He never stayed more than one night in the same city and not more than five in a village *(Kalpa-sūtra, Jina-caritra* 119) to avoid any kind of excess of hospitality on behalf of the local people. Sometimes he would end up in a traveller's refuge, at other times in more out-of-the-way places: a graveyard, an abandoned house, underneath a tree *(Ācārāṅga-sūtra* 1.8.2.3). He stayed away from places where they told stories, where they had wrestling matches or put on theatre. Like other Śramaṇas, Vardhamāṇa only allowed himself to stay in one place during the rainy season, when the roads in India become impassable. With this rule, that later on the Buddha would imitate, and which is still observed by Jain renunciants, one seeks to avoid harming the infinity of life which appears with the arrival of the regenerating monsoons. He took great precaution on being given food by people: invariably vegetables, never food which had been specially prepared for him, always on the palms of his hands, etc. When people asked him who he was, and what he was doing there, he remained silent.

Someone like that is not a man.

9. THE *JINA* MAHĀVĪRA

ENLIGHTENMENT

Vardhamāṇa was unshakeable in his ascetic practices and meditations concerning the intimate nature of being. Purified by *tapas,* he had eliminated all trace of attachment to this world and any other world beyond. Set apart from the human condition by the *dhyāna,* his soul shone free of all karmic residue.

The *Ācārāṅga-sūtra* says his 12 years, 6 months and 15 days of wandering led him to the East of Magadha, to a region near Bengal, on the banks of the river Ṛjupālikā, on the outskirts of the town of Jṛmbhikagrāma. Not far from a small temple, below a tree, when then Moon was in conjunction with the constellation of Uttaraphālguṇi, in the second month of summer, sitting in a lotus position exposed to the burning Sun and concentrated in the deepest meditation, Vardhamāṇa achieved enlightenment, the unique *(kevala)* knowledge *(jñāna),* omniscience *(Ācārāṅga-sūtra* 2.15.25).

He had ceased to be Vardhamāṇa. He had become one with his soul, free from all mental and bodily impurity. He had become a victor *(jina),* omniscient one *(kevalin),* awakened one *(buddha),* hero *(vira),* worthy one *(arhai),* thus-come *(tathāgata),* sublime one *(bhagavat)...* From now on, he would be known as the Great *(mahā)* Hero *(vira).* All these epithets were common to the great awakened ones of this period. As the facts show that Gautama the *buddha,* was also proclaimed *bhagavat* and *tathāgata,* and the Ājīvika Gośāla was known as *jina.* With the virtual disappearance of the Ājīvika tradition and the unmistakable association of the title of *buddha* with Gautama, those of *jina* and *mahāvira* came to be synonyms of Vardhamāṇa. Toward the 1st and 2nd centuries the term *Jaina* must have become a popular way of naming the followers of the Jina, and, around the 9th century, it is recorded that Jains were no longer referred to as Nirgranthas, a name which was exclusively reserved for renunciant ascetics. Even though *mahāvīra* is technically an epithet and not a name, the universalisation in its application as such has virtually converted it into a proper name. He was the self-enlightened hero, without the mediation of gods or magic spells, who remained unmoved before what would make mortals shudder with fear: the annihilation of contingency. The arrival of such a being on earth is a very rare occurrence; so rare, that only a few have deserved the title of *jina* or *mahāvīra.*

MAHĀVĪRA'S INSIGHT

What is Jain enlightenment? What did Mahāvīra see or learn after so many years of asceticism and meditation? On what would he base his teachings? It is very difficult to conjecture on these questions. We only have Jain texts to help us elucidate them, the majority written many centuries after Mahāvīra's death. However, if we delve into the most ancient sources, those in the first sections of the *Ācārāṅga-sūtra* and the *Sūtrakṛtāṅga,* we can discern certain clues. This does not imply reconstructing a type of "original" Jainism, which would be an impossible task, but giving some kind of main outline that plausibly would lie behind the awakening and teachings of the Jina.

The first thing we need to understand is the nature of enlightenment. In general, Jainism recognises five types of valid knowledge: sensory, rational, supernatural, telepathic, and omniscient. In another section, we will go deeper into these epistemological subjects. What is important here is that, while his soul was being purified, Mahāvīra acquired these forms of knowledge. The more cleansed his *jīva* was, the higher the type of knowledge he obtained. At the moment when he coincided with his soul alone, Mahāvīra possessed unique or absolute knowledge *(kevala-jñāna),* which is inborn to all *jīvas,* but has always been obscured by karmic impurity. The clearest reference to his enlightenment declares:

> "When the Venerable One had become an Arhat and Jina, he was a Kevalin, omniscient and comprehending all objects, he knew all conditions of the world, of gods, men, and demons; whence they come, where they go" *(Ācārāṅga-sūtra* 2.15.26).

Enlightenment is the total vision that endows direct and simultaneous access to all things and and all relations in the universe. It is a gnostic event, and not exactly a minor one! Mahāvīra had succeeded in detaining his human condition to arrive at a plane, that of pure cognition, which allowed him to know the mechanisms of the universe, the situation of bondage that beings find themselves, and what is more crucial, allowed him to be fully conscious of himself. Buddhist texts confirm this:

> "Friend, the Nigaṇṭha Nātaputta [Mahāvīra] is omniscient and all-seeing and claims to have complete knowledge and vision thus: 'Whether I am walking or standing or asleep or awake, knowledge and vision are continuously present to me'" *(Majjhima-nikāya* 1.92-93).

This proclamation from a human being was unique in Vedic India. Buddhist tradition did not even consider that the Buddha in his awakening might know all the objects in the universe, at all times an in all their possible modifications. On learning the very nature of things Mahāvira penetrated all the principles that make up reality *(sat).*

THE FUNDAMENTAL PRINCIPLES

Traditionally, Jain dogma is usually summed up in seven truths or fundamental principles *(tattvas).* Of course, Jainism should not be reduced to this doctrinal construction. Furthermore, its formulation is relatively late (lst-2nd centuries) and its systematisation is very much due to Umāsvāti (3rd-4th centuries). However, it is possible that its content was based on Mahāvīra's experience. Except for the fifth principle, the rest are mentioned in the *Ācārāṅga,* in a different order.

The fundamental principles that the Jina apprehended or, failing that, tradition ended up ratifying because of the experience of Mahāvīra are:

1) the reality of the animate or soul *(jīva);*
2) and reality of the inanimate or non-soul *(ajīva);*
3) and inflow *(āśrava)* of karmic matter;
4) and bondage *(bandha)* of the soul to karmic matter;
5) and rejection *(saṁvara)* of more karmic inflow;
6) and extinction *(nirjarā)* of karmic matter;
7) the liberation *(mokṣa)* from the cycle of existence *(Tattvārtha-sūtra* 1.4).

As observed, the list is hetereogeneous, as it mixes ontological categories with others that are cosmological. Let's see how this extremely important scheme unfolds. Later [see chapters 24, 25, and 32], we shall be going more deeply into all of the principles. At this moment a brief sketch will suffice.

Mahāvīra apprehended, as did other Śramaṇas, that the world is replete with spirits *(jīvas)* or souls *(ātmans).** All living creatures *(jīvas)* are truly spiritual monads *(jīvas),* souls associated in a characteristic form with the non-spiritual *(ajīva)*; that is, the material body which gives them lodging, space and time. The comprehension of this dualism is the essence of enlightenment: the radical solitude of the spiritual nature and its false identity with body and mind. While this identification lasts, all actions are guided by body-mind, and so will be passionate and egoistic.

Even though the identity is false, the association is real. The soul is trapped in emotions, the senses, psyche, and language. This association is what Jains call the bondage *(bandha)* of spiritual monads. How does this bondage come about? Why is the soul trapped in matter? Due to inflow *(āśrava).* The

* Although the oldest Jain texts use the Prakrit *āyā,* which is the exact equivalent for the Sanskrit *ātman,* with the passing of time Jains preferred the *tevm jīva* to express their concept of spiritual monad, even though the use of *ātman* as a synonym has been common. In any case *jīva* has a more general connotation, denoting the animate, the incarnated being. *Ātman,* on the other hand, would correspond to the *spiritual potential* of all beings, specifically of the human nature. In this work it is advisable the use of *jīva,* as it is a specifically Jain term and it is free of other connotations that the term *ātman* has in Hindu tradition.

flow of what? Of *karma.* According to the Jain concept of *karma,* bodily, mental and speech activity *attracts* karmic powder that flows freely through the cosmos and impregnates the agent, the actor, dragging it into the world of transmigration. Actions causes its valency to adhere to the soul in the form of extremely subtle material particles. *Karma* infiltrates the spiritual monad and constructs a subtle body, which accompanies it through existence after existence. This forged association of the *jīva* with the *ajīva* is eternal, just as the universe itself. This material conception of *karma* is unique to Jainism (possibly taken from materialism). It is not found in Buddhism or Brāhmaṇism.

Through his years of asceticism and meditation Mahāvīra achieved the extinction *(nirjarā)* and rejection *(saṁvara)* of this *karma.* How? By means of the profound understanding of these truths or principles and consequent conduct in non-harming to all forms of life *(ahiṃsā)* along with non-attachment *(aparigraha).* Enlightenment is not an explosive vision; rather it is silent insight, self-consciousness, free from all mediation. Enlightenment is exemplary conduct. Mahāvīra made the effort to extinguish and eliminate the force of gravity of *karma* already accumulated and reject the inflow of new *karma.* The result being the total purification of his soul. Jain spiritual practice would come to consist of liberating the *jīva,* through purified conduct by means of asceticism and meditation, from its karmic, material bonds. The full awareness of *the jīva,* pure consciousness in its solitude, is liberation *(mokṣa),* authentic *freedom.*

Ancient Jain theories (in any case centuries later than Mahāvīra), liked to place these fundamental principles in opposing pairs. The first of these pairs would be the spiritual *(jīva)* and the non-spiritual *(ajīva).* The second one bondage *(bandha)* and liberation *(mokṣa).* The next one, virtue *(puṇya)* and unworthiness *(pāpa).* Followed by the inflow *(āśrava)* and rejection *(saṁvara).* Finally, the opposites of karmic experience *(vedana)* and the extinction of *karma (nirjarā).* As K.K. Dixit (1971: 5) has said, this scheme would be a sort of Jain Five Noble Truths, designed to counteract the Buddhist Four Noble Truths.

HIS PREACHING

If Mahāvīra once awakened had remained in his solitude, waiting for the last karmic traces to be extinguished in the final extinction *(nirvaṇa), he* would have gone on to be one of the infinitely perfect liberated ones from different cosmic aeons. But the Jina opted on staying in the world to organise, for the umpteenth time, a community of ascetics. Because of this, he was not just a perfect one *(siddhd)* or a solitary enlightened one *(pratyekabuddha),* but a founder of a community *(saṃgha, tīrtha),* a *tīrthaṅkara.* Like all *tīrthaṅkaras*, his noble mission was to proclaim the eternal Truth to all creatures.

THE SACRED ASSEMBLY

A Digambara tradition states that after enlightenment the Jina did not eat, speak, or sleep. Keeping to a vow he preached silence with a monotonic sound equivalent to the syllable *Oṃ* (Jaini 1979:42), as an omniscient one does not organise nor preach sermons. Such is his condition of non-attachment that nothing in the world can impel him to do so. As with the Buddha in the *Laṅkāvatāra-sūtra,* the word of the Jina is a non-word, as any sermon would not be more than a mental-linguistic construction. The Jina's silence is comparable to his freedom and transcendence of any conditioning. However, tradition says that a supernatural sound *(divyadhvani)* in the divine language without syllables *(an-akṣarī)* emanated from his body, was heard and interpreted by those who listened, who translated it into the local language. That is how the sermons (Sūtras) of Mahāvīra were composed. More pragmatically, the *Ācārāṅga-sūtra II* (the *I* says nothing of his *tīrthaṅkara* stage) tells us that out of compassion he preached the doctrine openly.

Once the divinities became aware that the new *jina* had achieved illumination, they congregated to celebrate this fourth auspicious moment in the life of the *tīrthaṅkara.* The versions of what happened vary, but we can provide a synopsis.

Immediately, the gods built a hall or a sacred assembly *(samavarasaṇa),* just as they had done on 23 previous occasions in this descendent cycle, so that the Jina could deliver his first sermon. This notion is of maximum importance to Jain art and iconography. It consists of a square stage (sometimes shown as round) closed in by a series of concentric balustrades connected by passages, which were occupied by different types of audiences. The final outcome, always richly decorated, is a mystic diagram *(maṇḍala),* a representation of the cosmos centred on the Jina [see FIG. 6].

This first sermon was given at night, on Mount Vipulācala, near Rājagṛha, in the presence of the gods. Since the divinities cannot form part of a spiritual community, in the end Māhavīra did not speak. On the following morning, he addressed the gods, human beings and animals alike. Situated in the centre of the hall, on a throne bearing the emblem of the lion and beneath an insignia tree, Mahāvīra turned to face East. Rapidly, the gods' consorts created three replicas of him so that the Jina should face all four directions and all the audiences could hear him perfectly. A divine halo appeared behind him. It is clear that the assembly equates the image of a temporal ruler *(cakravartin),* Lord of the four cardinal points, to that of a spiritual victor *(jina),* Lord of the three worlds. It is said that this second assembly took place in a sanctuary *(caitya)* dedicated to the *yakṣa* Pūrnabhadra, on the outskirts of Campā.

Padmanabh Jaini (1979: 196) says that all Jain temples are replicas of this sacred assembly, which in turn is the symbol of the enlightenment of the *tīrthaṅkara,* the emblem that represents the fourth auspicious moment in the life of all *jinas.* The motif of the sacred assembly is surely the best symbol of the

Jain community. In clear contrast to the Vedic sacrificial model, there everyone is congregated: monarchs, laity, divinities, and animals to hear the excellence of non-violence. The message is truly universal. Very few religions have as rich and alive symbolic expression of their community as the *samavarasaṇa.* Ken Folkert (1993: 147) has remarked that the most similar structurally and symbolically is the Buddhist *stūpa.* From the artistic and ritualistic point of view, the closest comparable image is that of the crucifixion in the Catholic world (Laidlaw 1995:31).

PREACHING YEARS

If Mahāvīra had preached previous to his enlightenment, it is possible that some of his teachings would have contained errors. After becoming omniscient, his sermons (translated so to speak by his disciples), would have always been impeccable.

It is said that the first converts were 11 Brāhmaṇas with a great reputation who had come to the area where the sacred assembly took place to participate in a great Vedic sacrifice. Each one of them was convinced by a sublime sermon on the reality of the soul *(jīva),* the reality of *karma,* the reality of our bondage *(bandha),* the reality of liberation *(mokṣa)...* that is, the seven fundamental principles of Jain doctrine.

The 11 Brāhmaṇas were initiated and were declared heads of school *(gaṇadharas).* Each time a Brāhmaṇa master was converted to the teachings of the Jina, he brought along all his pupils into the community. It is said that with the conversion of all 11 *gaṇadharas,* the order went on to number more than four thousand members. Among these *gaṇadharas* Gautama Indrabhūti [see pages 164-165], Mahāvīra's first disciple, was the one who stood out most. Gautama translated the Jina's unintelligible sounds into Magadhi, the Prakrit language of the region. Using a variety of Prakrit, the language of the common people, in place of the refined Sanskrit, illustrates well the desire to be understood by all and the rejection of Brāhmaṇical elitism.

For the following 30 years, Mahāvīra and the *gaṇadharas* wandered throughout the whole of northern India teaching the doctrine. It is told that his parents (Ṛṣabhadatta and Devānandā) were soon converted, along with his own daughter Priyadarśanā and her husband Jamāli. Later, his aunt Jayantī, king Udāyana and the merchants Sumanobhadra, Supratiṣṭha, and Ānanda followed suite. Texts also tell of debates had with Brāhmaṇa renunciants, Sāṃkhya mendicants, Buddhist monks, with the now leader of the Ājīvikas, Gośāla, and with the followers of the Nirgrantha order of Pārśva. It seems that Mahāvīra especially focused his attention on merchants and the educated aristocracy. At least these were the groups that were more open to listening to a new message. Among the merchants, an outstanding instance was the rich merchant Upāli, who made large donations to the order, as well as the banker Mṛgaragāra. Texts relate that the kings Śreṇika and Kuṇika of Magadha also supported him, although

Buddhists similarly claim them as "theirs" (by the name of Bimbisāra and Ajātaśatru). Truth to tell, the dignitaries of the period had the habit of giving reverence to various different leaders of orders and religious sects. One must treat with caution the Jain and Buddhist tales of kings "converted" to their beliefs. However, it is probable that Mahāvīra was related to the nobility of the Ganges. The very fact that Mahāvīra spent no more and no less than 14 monsoon seasons in Rājagṛha suggests that he must have exercised some kind of influence over the kings of Magadha. It is entirely possible that his uncle Ceṭaka, ruling king of Vṛjjīs (the confederation of his birth) would have openly financed the Nirgranthas and may even have been converted. Significantly, Ceṭaka is not mentioned in the Buddhist canon. Much of the prestige gained by the Śramaṇic movements came from their acceptance by queens and princesses. Some of them managed to bring princes and kings to the ascetic path. And so, with the backing of aristocracy the Jain religion extended through Aṅga and Magadha (J. Jain 1947: 13). Although the only region mentioned in the *Ācārāṅga* is the remote Lāḍha, the *Kalpa-sūtra (Jina-caritra* 122), composed at a later date, says that in his 12 years of asceticism and 30 years of preaching, Mahāvīra visited all the major cities on the Ganges plain [see Fig. 7], an area which now comprises the present-day states of Uttar Pradesh, Bihar and West Bengal (Yasovijaya 1974: 45-48).

ORGANISATION OF THE COMMUNITY

Primitive Jainism must have been a rather marginal movement along with being exclusively ascetic. Despite of the tales stories of merchants, bankers and kings having been converted, there was not a lay community to speak of. Although ascetics interacted with laity to be provided with food and shelter, the providers could not be considered "Jains". Richard Gombrich (1988: 75) has pointed out that in ancient India the duty of every householder was to feed any mendicant who knocked on their door. We have no knowledge of a "Jain" lay community until the 2nd and 1st centuries BC [see page 214], even though one must have existed before that.

As in Buddhism, initially Jainism revolved exclusively around its ascetics. This does not mean that there was a stable community of monks, much less a Jain Church. In the most ancient texts there is no mention of a monastic hierarchy. The only figure that is clearly defined is that of the instructor *(śāstā),* who must have simply been an ascetic that imparted the first teachings to young Śramaṇas. In fact, in the oldest texts, typical figures—in later organisation—like heads of school *(gaṇadharas),* masters, *(ācāryas)* or preceptors *(upādhyāyas)* are not even mentioned. Hence, K.K. Dixit (1978: 9) assumes that the habitual practice would be that of a solitary ascetic along with, perhaps, a small groups of novices accompanied by an instructor.

WHAT MAHĀVĪRA TAUGHT

Like many mystics, Mahāvīra did not creat any kind of doctrinal or philosophical system, but he gave practical recipes on how to liberate oneself from all action *(karma).* It is not surprising, that the most ancient texts do not devote much time to explaining the situation of bondage of beings, nor investigate cosmological principles. In fact, these subjects are dealt with so vaguely that hardly anything is mentioned about *karma* that could not also have been maintained in Brāhmaṇical and Buddhist theories (Dixit 1978: 9). Similarly, a characteristic trait of ancient Jainism is its lack of interest in mythological aspects. They do not speak about continents and islands in the Middle World, or the heavens, nor is there any trace of the 63 sublime beings that appear in the classic recensions of the Universal History. Inaddition the eulogistic tales about Mahāvīra are very austere. In contrast, practical instruction abounds in the *Ācārāṅga-sūtra I* and the *Sūtrakṛtāṅga I*, the two most ancient sections of the Jain canon.

RENUNCIATION AND ASCETIC HARSHNESS

The path that Mahāvīra proclaimed had to be strictly individual. His ideal was of solitary heroes that venture into unpopulated territories, jungles and mountain tops. Ancient Jainism convincingly insists that true Śramaṇas must reduce their contact with laity to a minimum. They cannot give sermons in return for food that is given by people-in-the-world. Moreover, in contrast to classical and contemporary Jainism, it was prohibited for Nirgranthas to go near to those who were their relatives before their initiation into the order.

Daily practice would not only include constant restrictions (generally fasting), but also mortification of the body. Ascetic life, as it appears in the first texts, was notable for its particularly harsh nature *(upasarga, parīṣaha).* Their meals and bedding had to be as rough as possible. No medicine was allowed. In the case of illness, a reduced diet was recommended; in the case of an incurable affliction, a definitive fast, which would lead to death. This practice has not yet completely disappeared.

This rigorous ascetic path may seem exaggerated, above all if we compare it with the Buddhist path. As readers may know, the Buddha proclaimed the Middle Way (Pali: *majjhimā-patipadā)* with a particular view to the extremes of self-indulgence (as among the nihilists) and self-mortification (typified by the Jains). Nevertheless, seen from the Jain point of view, the Buddha weakened. He left the path of interior purification that combined *tapas* and *dhyāna,* to be content with meditation alone.

ATTACHMENT, POSSESSION AND VIOLENCE

If there is a concept which sums up the essence of the Jain message, it is non-violence *(ahiṃsā).* The exceptional importance in the Jain path and ethics is surely very much due to Mahāvīra.

The notion of *ahiṃsā* is complexly linked to the concepts of attachment, possession and violence. For Mahāvīra, the two actions of an ignorant person, someone attached to the world, are possession *(parigraha)* and violence *(ārambha, hiṃsā).* The possession of, or attachment to, things is not bad in itself; but it is to the extent that obtaining possessions (material, emotional, and social) inevitably leads to a harmful and violent attitude towards others. One cannot preserve wealth or possessions without harming others. And thus all violent attitudes are more or less rooted in attitudes of attachment (Dixit 1978: 5). Violence, possession and attachment are the cause of all action which bind us to the world.

Ancient texts never cease to classify all the possible objects of attachment—material wealth, family, ideals, etc, and the possible objects of violence—mobile beings *(trasa),* such as human beings, animal and insects, and immobile beings *(sthāvara),* such as plants, bodies of water, fire, air and earth. Each time that the Sūtras refer to violence, it is taken for granted that the possible victims are *all* these kinds of *jīvas.*

Non-attachment and renouncement are inevitable if one desires to stop being violent towards the countless living beings that inhabit the cosmos. The life of attachment and possession *(parigraha)* emerges as ineluctably associated to the sphere of householders:

> "Know that it [property] entails pains in this world, and very great pains in the next. Who will lead a domestic life when he knows that everything must perish?" *(Sūtrakṛtāṅga* 1.2.2.10).

In the most ancient Jain texts (compiled by ascetics to be memorised by ascetics), the situation of laity is not well looked upon. If all activity bonds the spirit, people in the world, householders who never cease to act, are inevitably condemned to committing some degree of violence *(hiṃsā)* and transmigrating. They are spiritually ignorant beings, and this is reflected by their negligent, careless and ultimately violent behaviour. Laity is trapped in a vicious circle. They must take care of their material possessions and family. To do this, they must harm all types of beings. It is clear that for Jainism, attachment and possession are the equivalent to what Buddhists call "thirst" *(tṛṣṇa,* Pali: *taṇhā),* and what characterises a life of such ignorance is the lack of control.

CONTROL AND CAREFULNESS

Through their carelessness and negligence human beings *punish* their surroundings. Activity, as it is conceived by primitive Jainism—corroborated by ancient Buddhist texts *(Majjhima-nikāya* 1.372)—is better expressed by the term punish *(daṇḍa)* than by the classical term action *(karma),* which would be used by Buddhism and Jainism at a later time. Mahāvīra implies that all physical action (corporeal, mental and verbal) is harmful and punishes one's soul plus all other souls, however, good the intention. On the other hand, in Buddhism the negative nature *of karma* depends entirely on the intention. This position would later on be adopted by Jainism, but in ancient texts it was understood that all activity led to the inflow of karmic particles. It is true that ascetics could not avoid *accidentally* killing invisible *earth-ekendriyas* or the diminute air-*jīvas*. So this action, if occurring in the context of rigorous ascetic care, the *quasi-obsessive* behaviour of ascetics in not harming these beings, is karmically less significant than if it happens through carelessness or lack of control. The *Ācārāṅga-sūtra* (1.5.4.3) is very clear when it says that the virtuous ascetic will take all the punishments for these actions in his life, but if the action has been committed in disagreement with the rules the seriousness is much greater, and the penitence and repentance cannot be foregone. Hence the enormous difficulty of the Jain path and its tendency to total inaction, ataraxia, for which the *Ācārāṅga-sūtra* (1.6.4.2) declares:

> "A very severe religion has been proclaimed".

Which the *Daśavaikālika-sūtra* (6.5) was still later to echo:

> "This sort of highly difficult conduct
> For the world of human beings
> Is delineated nowhere save in *nirgrantha* philosophy.
> For those covetous of *mokṣa*
> Such conduct has nowhere been prescribed in the past
> Nor will it ever be prescribed in future".

THE CENTRALITY OF AHIMSĀ

Let us return to *ahiṃsā*. For the sake of convenience, the term is translated as non *(a-)* violence *(hiṃsā)*. However, according to Madeleine Biardeau (1981: 177), a more exact translation would be the absence of the will to kill. Negative meanings in Sanskrit are extremely rich. The negation of violence does not refer to absence of a quality but affirms a state in which the negated quality is excluded. If *hiṃsā* is simply "violence", "harm" or the badness inherent in the wish to kill, *ahiṃsā* is the fostering of qualities such as friendship, peace, compassion and doing good. It is a positive, affirmative term: the wish or desire not to wound, kill or cause harm to any living being, including oneself. In Jainism, this concept permeates all dimensions of the religion: ethics, philosophy, logic, diet, profession and art.

Where does this value come from? According to Louis Dumont (1979:191), although *ahiṃsā* was channelled by Jainism and Buddhism, these schools simply bore witness to a development on a grander scale: *ahiṃsā* goes back further. *Ahiṃsā* would be a shared cultural value in ancient India, which Jainism took to its extreme consequences or expressed in a more radical way. The concept comes from a Vedic ritual.

Vedic sacrifice required a great amount of violence (ritual combat, sacrifice of animals, war on ignoble people and perhaps archaic human sacrifice). Motivated by the aversion to the spilling of blood, Brāhmaṇas gradually went on to investigate valid substitutes charged with sacrificial essence *(medha),* appropriate for being destroyed and consumed in sacrifice. As the doctrine of *karma* developed, such substitutes and rites of expiation became more and more necessary, because, what benefit would there be in sacrifice if the retribution for killing living beings led to an unattractive beyond? It is true that Brāhmaṇas considered that the death of an animal in the context of sacrifice was not a truly violent act *(Manu-smṛti* 5.39-40), as in India violence is not conceived in moral terms in relation to the victim, but from the viewpoint of the consequences of the person who conducts it. Soon, it was seen that transpersonal action and renunciation could avoid the retribution of the acts and escape transmigration. It is no coincidence that *ahiṃsā* was first and foremost a development arising among renunciants, Brāhmaṇical and Śramaṇical. Instead of disguising violent sacrificial acts, renunciants would channel them, not outwardly but towards themselves. Boris Oguibénine (1993: 92) says they renunciants are those who sacrifice themselves, who make the sacrifice for themselves, within themselves. In the *Chāndogya-upaniṣad* (3.17.4), when the term *ahiṃsā* appears for the first time, the will not to kill is intimately linked to the interiorisa-tion of ritual. Non-violence forms part of the practice of abstention for renunciants, and since it is contrary to natural behaviour—it being a transcendental value, beyond the reach of society—it testifies to the autonomy, independence as well as the inwardness of those who have interiorised sacrifice (Oguibénine 1993: 93). Thus, Indian non-violence is focalised on sacrifice, and it is not an ethical reflection on the problem of violence. In the context of the renunciant, stress is placed on non-attachment and not on the situation of the victim. *Hiṃsā* becomes the *desire* to kill; hence *ahimsā* comes to symbolise the non-attachment of whom, having become aware of the impermanence and retribution of their acts, make a conscious effort to reach full self-independence.

Thus, it's important not to confuse *ahiṃsā* with a sort of pacifism or an animal defence movement. While *ahiṃsā* can be expressed in terms of *caritas,* it is based on other values and parameters. It represents the renunciant's full autonomy.

However, in Jainism, *ahiṃsā* is also intimately linked to an acute understanding, almost a naturalist's understanding, of reality and living creatures. Here Jain *ahiṃsā* takes on a component, which is absent in the Hindu counterpart. As Mahāvīra saw it, there was an infinite number of spiritual souls in the cosmos. A traditionally Jain trait, is the idea that nearly everything in the universe has a soul: from an *indra,* to a fern, to a bolt of lightening... that is to say, everything which they call life *(jīva).* The *Sūtrakṛtāṅga* says:

> "Earth-lives are individual beings, so are water-lives, and wind-lives; grass, trees, corn;
>
> An the remaining, [viz.] the movable beings...
>
> A wise man should study them with all means of philosophical research. All beings hate pains; therefore one should not kill them.
>
> This is the quintessence of wisdom: not to kill anything. Know this to be the legitimate conclusion from he principle of the reciprocity with regard to non-killing *[ahiṃsā].*
>
> He should cease to injure living beings whether they move or not, on high, below, and on earth. For this has been called *nirvāṇa,* which consists in peace" *(Sūtrakṛtāhga* 1.11.7-11).

Mahāvīra succeeded in integrating categories and notions like action *(karma),* transmigration *(saṃsāra)* and liberation *(mokṣa),* all common to other sages and Śramaṇas, into a lifestyle based on the analysis of the nature of the outer world and the different types of living beings. What labelled Jainism as a universal religion from the outset was, in Paul Dundas's words (1992: 39), the self-control and compassion generated by the awareness that all beings, to a greater or lesser degree, experienced the same kind of feelings as human beings. The world of *saṃsāra* is the permanent flow of billions and trillions of living beings, which are constantly born and then perish. Although human life is longer than that of the countless air-*ekendriyas,* the situation is identical. All living creatures are morally and ontologically equivalent. The Jain view of *ahiṃsā* regards any kind of violence to other beings as violence to self. In consequence, Michael Tobias (1991: 70-71) wrote that the *Ācārāṅga-sūtra* is the first and most profound psychoanalysis of violence that has ever been compiled. The psychological, moral, social, and ecological reach of this message is amazing, notably more powerful than the Brāhmaṇical *ahiṃsā.*

For example, Brāhmaṇical Vedānta philosophy (synthesis of the message in the Upaniṣads) bases non-violence on non-duality *(advaita).* According to the Advaita Vedānta, the difference between one *jīva* and another, is illusionary *(māyā),* as there are really no beings different from the One. Buddhism, on the other hand, does not accept *this jīva* or *ātman,* but since the ignorance of beings is such to the point of believing in the futility of this eternal soul, for this precise reason all life deserves compassion. Jainism accepts the differences between all *jīvas* and their state of complete ontological solitude, but at the same time maintains that the essence and potential of every *jīva* are identical. Consequently, considering that all life is sacred, every *jīva* has the potential for liberation. To kill another being is to kill one's equal. Moreover, the *Ācārāṅga* (1.5.5.4) says harming other beings is harming oneself. In fact, in various places, it states that liberation is non-violence in itself, as is repeated over and over again in the *Sūtrakṛtāṅga* (1.3.4.20). It is not a case of saving lives or minimising deaths. Jains are guided more by an aesthetic sensibility (and a certain repulsion towards the conception and fertility of the world) than by a moral sentiment. In India, compassion rests not on a universal morality, but on the knowledge that all life is infused with spiritual-consciousness plus the necessity to be purified from violent and attached action. *Ahiṃsā* raises Jains' moral stature and, given the interaction with all beings in the *saṃsāra,* heightens the moral profile of the whole community, in its broadest biotic sense (Bilimoria: 1998: 9). The typical imputation that Jainism takes *ahiṃsā* to childish extremes seems to me unfortunate. And equally unfortunate in my view is the idea of Jainism as a self-centered practice for individual liberation. Such critics forget that for the scholar Āśādhara (13th century), for example, compassion was the root of the whole sacred doctrine (cited in Williams 1963: 42).

One of the logical conclusions of the doctrine of *ahiṃsā* is vegetarianism. Jain and Buddhist renunciants alike initially accepted any sort of food offering, always provided that no animal had been especially sacrificed for them. With the passing of time, Buddhists stayed faithful to the principal that renunciants could not refuse food offered by laity, but Jains radicalised their position to a strictly vegetarian one. This is already palpable in the *Sūtrakṛtāṅga* (2.6.30-42), where the Jain prince Ārdraka condemns Buddhist laxity concerning *ahiṃsā.* In any case, it was Jainism and Buddhism that stimulated Brāhmaṇism to reconsider its posture concerning diet and its attitude towards living beings. Louis Du-mont (1979: 246-247) states that the Brāhmaṇas, in their process of re-absorption of Buddhist and Jain "heresies", under threat of being disqualified as spiritual leaders, had to take on the prestigious vegetarianism and non-violence of their counterparts. *Ahimsā* was progressively adopted by Brāhmaṇas, and the *Mahābhārata*(13.116.37-39) praised it as being the highest form of *dharma,* the best form of austerity, the best gift, best form of self-control, highest form of sacrifice, best friend, best truth and best teaching. Naturally, the medieval Brāhmaṇical exegesis sustained that the doctrine of *ahiṃsā* was Vedic and not Śramaṇical. While the Vedic origin of the notion seems to be real, as has already been mentioned, it were undoubtedly the Śramaṇical traditions, and Jainism in particular, that elevated it to an exemplary form of living. The first Brāhmaṇic articulation of *ahimsā* did not appear until the Dharma-śāstras *(Manu-smṛti* 6.40), later texts than the most ancient sections of Jain scriptures. And the Hindu tradition that most efficiently incorporated it was Yoga, which had always been close to the Śramaṇic movements. For Vyāsa *(Yoga-sūtra-bhāsya* 2.30), the great commentator on Patañjali, all the abstentions *(yama)* and disciplines *(niyama)* have their origins in *ahiṃsā.* In any case, it is extremely interesting that different philosophical perspectives, Jain, Buddhist and Hindu, all remain faithful to the principal of non-violence as being their primordial ethic virtue.

MAHĀVĪRA'S REFORMS

Although, according to tradition, the teachings of Mahāvīra were a prolongation of those preached by Pārśva, the Jina introduced some variants to the practice and philosophy of the ancient Nirgranthas.

In first place, Mahāvīra introduced nakedness, perhaps under the influence of Gośāla. In second place, he institutionalised the practice of repentance and confession *(pratikramaṇa),* still a central feature of Jain religious practice. Just like his predecessor he promoted four ascetic vows: non-violence, non-possession, truthfulness and refraining from stealing. But the Sūtras *(Uttarādhyayana-sūtra* 23.23) say that Mahāvīra added a fifth vow, the vow of chastity *(brahma, brahmacarya),* even though not all experts support this thesis (Jaini 1979: 17-18), given that the notion of the five great vows *(mahāvratas)* or basic vows *(mūlavratas)* are not found in the oldest layers of the texts.

The best account of the substitution of the old Nirgrantha doctrine for the five great vows of Mahāvīra is given in the *Uttarādhyayana-sūtra,* specifically in the episode of the conversation between Keśīn, a follower of Pārśva's ancient doctrine, and Gautama Indrabhūti, Mahāvīra's favourite disciple.* Both were masters who were almost omniscient. Keśīn inquires to Gautama: Why, if Pārśva and Mahāvīra represent the same truth, does one preach four vows and the other five? Why had Mahāvīra introduced nudity?

The main thread of the conversation was that, although Jain *dharma* was unitary, there were differences when it came to practical implications. The doctrine expounded by Pārśva was intended for beings living during more virtuous times. But in Mahāvīra's day, when ascetic were less wise, slower in understanding and more negligent *(Uttarādhyayana-sūtra* 23.26), a more rigorous conduct was necessary. Hence in more ancient periods ascetics could wear clothes and even adornment, while in Mahāvīra's times they were obligated to strictly respect chastity and nudity. This latter trait would become a distinctive sign *(liṅga)* of Jain renunciants that would be recognised by society *(Uttarādhyayana-sūtra* 23.32). For the followers of Pārśva, celibacy was taken for granted (implied in the vow of non-possession), and, therefore there was no need to place any special emphasis on chastity and nakedness.

Texts mention that the ascetics who followed the four vows of Pārśva went on to accept the five vows of Mahāvīra. The *Vyākhyā-prajñāpti* (5.9 [247b]) describes how Mahāvīra converted monks of Pārśva' s order by diligently enunciating cosmological subjects that Páráva had already put forward earlier. There

* Perhaps in these two incipient groups of Nirgranthas the seed of the important division that would take place some centuries later, is found [see chapter 12]. However it would be wrong to assimilate Śvetāmbaras with the followers of Pārśva and Digambaras with the followers of Mahāvīra.

was, then, a clear and evident connection between Mahāvīra and his predecessor. Everything seems to indicate that historical Jainism would seem to have absorbed a series of cosmological and philosophical beliefs coming from Pārśva combined with a more rigorous form of orthopraxis proposed by Mahāvīra (Dundas 1992: 28-29). With the passing of time, the relationship between the two would be perfectly established with their connection in the lineage list of *tīrthaṅkaras.*

Even though Mahāvīra may perhaps not have had as much impact on his times as the Buddha did—which in reality is debatable (Jacobi 1884: II, xxxii)—what he did demonstrate, as time would tell, was a very effective capacity for organisation. The rules he laid down for ascetics have survived 2,500 years and continue to form the support of the ascetic community.

FINAL LIBERATION

At the age of 72 years, after 12 years of asceticism and 30 years of preaching, the Jina reached *nirvāṇa.* He expired; he left this world. The event happened in Pāvāpurī (Pāpā), a few kilometres from Rājagṛha. Since then, the place is the destination for many Jain pilgrimages, and the Great Festival of the Dead (Mṛtyu Mahotsava) commemorates the event. At the main temple in Pava, his footprints *(pādukās)* sculptured in the rock, are venerated. The emblem of the footprints of the saint or divinity is one of the oldest in India; we also find it in Buddhism and Hinduism. They do not symbolise death, but the *conscious departing* from this world, the last of the five auspicious moments in the life of all *tīrthaṅkaras.*

This happened in the year 527 BC according to traditional sources. Many Jains count the years starting from this date, called "Liberation of the Hero" *(vīranirvāṇa).* It represents the longest continuous historical era in Indian chronology, starting some tens of years earlier than the Buddhist era and predating the Brāhmaṇical ones by various centuries. Most modern historians pinpoint the event as taking place around 467 BC, even though in Kailash C. Jain's opinion (1974: 84-88) the traditional date is correct. There are even others who, based on the reconstruction of the dates of the Buddha and Mahāvīra proposed by Heinz Bechert (1995: 11-36), situate it around 400 BC or 370 BC.

Some legends relate that the greater part of the community and the governors of all kingdoms had been invited by king Hastipāla to listen to the last great sermons of the Jina. On the seventh night, Mahāvīra gave his last sermon. Afterwards, while his audience was asleep, the Jina, aware that his final hour had come, sat down cross-legged on his throne with the diagram of the lion and the symbol of the wheel of teaching *(dharma-cakra)* and entered the most profound of meditative trances. Practically all his *karma* had been destroyed. He only had a small residue of neutral karmic matter left. First, he stopped all verbal and thought activity; then corporeal activity. With the suppression of breathing and beating of his heart, he penetrated the most elevated meditative trance of all. At dawn, he achieved final extinction *(nirvāṇa)* and his spirit soared up to the Abode of the Liberated Souls. At sunrise, the people understood that their master had died.

The gods attended to celebrate this last auspicious event and it is said that they lit an infinite number of small lamps to emulate the light which had recently departed. Jains say that the festival of lights (Dīvālī), a festival celebrated throughout the whole of India [see pages 432-433], has its origin in this auspicious happening.

He alone, with his own effort, had extinguished all *karma,* a *sine qua non* condition to avoiding rebirth, and had preached the path of salvation to the entire universe. Neither birth nor death could touch his soul; the wheel of transmigration had stopped for him. On this very same day, his disciple Gautama In-drabhūti attained omniscience.

MAHĀVĪRA AND THE BUDDHA

As an endnote to this section I'd like to briefly look more deeply into similarities and differences between Mahāvīra and the Buddha, the other great Śramaṇa of the period.

The first thing that strikes one is the remarkable parallelism that there is in their biographies. Neither Mahāvīra nor the Buddha belonged to the priestly class. Both were members of the tribal nobility in northern India. They renounced the world at the age of 28 and 30 years respectively. They went on pilgrimages to the same places and both practised asceticism *(tapas)* and meditation *(dhyāna).* They both achieved enlightenment *(kevala-jñāna, bodhi)* beneath a tree. Afterwards, they preached *dharma* for various decades and formed communities of renunciants *(saṃgha).* Finally, they both achieved *nirvāṇa* peacefully. Moreover, we know that the Buddha followed ascetic practices for some years. Buddhist references themselves leave no doubt. Gautama followed a virtually identical path to that of the Nirgranthas:

> "Such was my asceticism, Sāriputta, that I went naked, rejecting conventions... I did not accept food brought or food specially made or an invitation to a meal; I received nothing from a pot, from a bowl... I accepted no fish or meat, I drank no liquor, wine or fermented brew... I took food once a day, once every two days... once every seven days... I lived on forest roots and fruits; I fed on fallen fruits... I was one who puled out hair and beard... I was one who stood continuously, rejecting seats... I made a matress of spikes my bed... Such was my asceticism" *(Majjhima-nikāya* 1.78-79).

As late as the 10th century, the Jain master Devasena characterised the Buddha as the ascetic Buddhakīrti, a follower of the Pārśva lineage. Amitagati (10th-11th centuries) was of a similar opinion, describing the Buddha as a student of Pārśva (cited in Warder 1972: VI, 260), and attributed the origin of Buddhism to the wiles of Maudgalyāyana—one of Buddha's historical disciples (von Glasenapp 1925: 500). While the Chinese Buddhist pilgrim Xuanzang (7th century) considered Jainism to be a heretic offshoot of Buddhism *(Da Tang xiyou-ji* 3[Beal:I, 144-145]).

Considering the similarities in their lives and the connection—a schismatic one, admittedly—that their own followers attributed to them, it is not surprising that in the middle of the 19th century Western scholars got into all kinds of confusion over these two figures. Some thought that Mahāvíra was the Buddha's master, others that Jainism was an offshoot of Buddhism, and there were even some who thought that Mahâvīra and Buddha were the same person. However, as Hermann Jacobi (1884: I, xvii-xix) observed and corrected, neither their births, deaths of their mothers, the way in which they took the path of renunciation, their enlightenment, nor their deaths were the same. Since the studies done by H. Jacobi, G. Bühler and A. Guérinot, at the end of the 19th century, no one from the academic community has doubted the independence—not to say the greater antiquity—of Jainism.

The *nirvāṇa* of Mahāvīra pre-dates the Buddha's, and that is ratified by Buddhist texts themselves *(Dīgha-nikāya* 3.209-210), but no one has doubted that they were contemporaries (Mette 1995: 183). What is to a certain extent surprising is that while being reputed masters and having preached in the same regions, there is no news of them ever having met. Buddhist and Jain texts often talk about discussions and meetings of their leaders with other Śramaṇas. The reason for their having avoided each other remains a mystery. The matter is ripe for all kinds of speculation (K.C. Jain 1974: 72).

Their teachings share many typical Śramaṇical traits. Both Buddhism and Jainism reacted in the face of Brāhmaṇical ritualism. They rejected the revealed nature of the Veda. They opposed to the ideology of social-spiritual classes. They denied there was a prime intelligent cause. Neither of them sought wealth and worldly happiness, instead seeking the unconditioned. Both groups have an order of renunciant and celibate monks and nuns, both venerate their saints and masters, as well as basing their ethics on non-violence. Both their systems are based on the perfection attained by their respective masters, born as mundane human beings who renounced their kingdoms, attaining enlightenment and achieved *nirvāṇa.* For this reason, the Buddha and Mahāvīra are indistinctly both *called jina, buddha* and *Śramaṇa.* Jainism and Buddhism, in short, took *heterodox* paths—heterodox being a word preferred to *heretic* in India.

However, even though they share a similar position and their teachings have much in common, their doctrines differ notably. If the path laid down by the Buddha was the Middle Path, Mahāvīra preached a much harder and stricter path. In fact, the Buddha's rejection of *tapas* carne to be seen as the main difference between *bauddha-Śramaṇas* and *nirgrantha-Śramaṇas.* Buddha's personality as reflected in texts is that of a friendly almoşt naive man. He even allowed himself to be dined, if not wined. This was something unthinkable for a *tapasvin* such as Mahāvīra, a highly reprehensible concession to life-in-the-world. Undoubtedly, Mahāvīra was less prone to giving sermons and interacting with people-in-the-world. Buddhist texts are quite often ironic about the insistence of Nirgranthas on asceticism *(Majjhima-nikāya* 2.223). For their part, Jain references to Buddhism never cease to criticise its excessive mental-ist and even illusionist viewpoint. A famous verse satirises Buddhist monastic life as such:

> "A soft bed, food and drink, gambling and at the end of it all deliverance" (cited in Dundas 1992: 207).

From the Jain point of view, the Buddhist path is all but hedonistic: one of reprehensible materialism (Lokāyata), a synonym of ignorance. Jains consider that the Buddha weakened in pursuit of his mission and chose a much softer, easier one, in time leading to laxity and relaxation of the rules, a calamity for his monastic order.

What is more, properly speaking, Buddhism begins with the Buddha's teachings. Hence, its sermons are marked by clear rejection of other doctrines. In contrast, Mahāvīra was not the first one to expound the Jain doctrine. He accepted the *dharma* acquired from his family tradition, or sympathetically. If the Buddha had to form a community, Mahāvīra had to *reorganise* one. At a philosophical level, we find notable contrasts. If Buddhists professed the unreality of the soul (the doctrine of *anātman*), Jains maintained its reality. As professor Rad-hakrishnan (1923:1, 292) observed, the theories of the soul and of knowledge, so peculiar to Jainism and so different from those of Buddhism, could not have arisen from the other.

FIGURE 1: Image of the *tīrthaṅkara* Nemi and his escorts. Rajasthan, 11th century. Freer Gallery of Art & Arthur M. Sackler Gallery, Smithsonian Institution, Washington.

FIGURE 2: The cosmos incorporated into the Cosmic Being (Lokapuruṣa). The area of the legs is the Lower World. In the centre, is the Intermediate World. In the torso, the heavens of the Upper World. In the forehead, the half moon or Slightly Inclined Place, the Abode of the Liberated Souls. Gouache, 16th century, Gujarat.

FIGURE 3: Lokapuruṣa. The Intermediate World is disproportionately emphasised to show its innumerable islands *(dvīpas)* and oceans *(samudras)*.
Rajasthan, end of 19th century. Linden Museum, Stuttgart.

FIGURE 4: Jambūdvīpa and its continents. The second ring is Dhātakīkhaṇḍadvīpa. The third is Puskaradvīpa. Gouache on cloth. Northeast India. Carlos Cruañas collection. (Courtesy of Carlos Cruañas.)

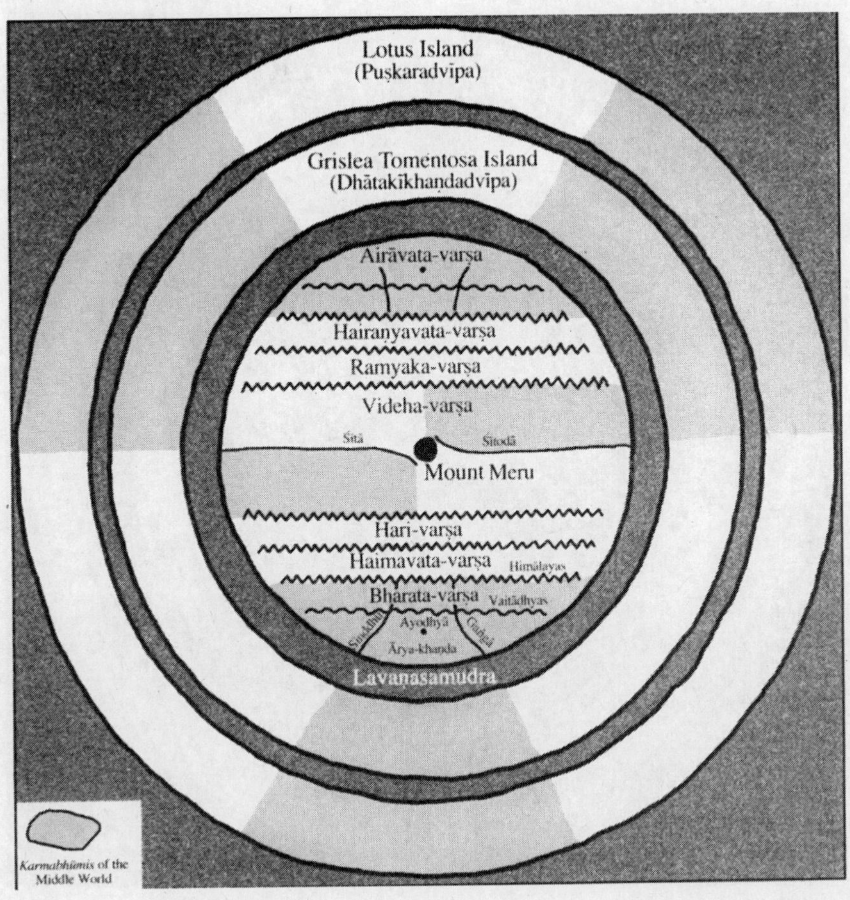

FIGURE 5: Schematic representation of Jambūdvīpa with its continents and certain important regions. Areas of the Intermediate World where liberation is possible are shown in grey. (Source: Agustín Pániker, based on FIGURE 4.)

FIGURE 6: The *samavarasaṇa-paṭṭa* or sacred assembly in the shape of a *maṇḍala.* Painting, Rajasthan, 1800.

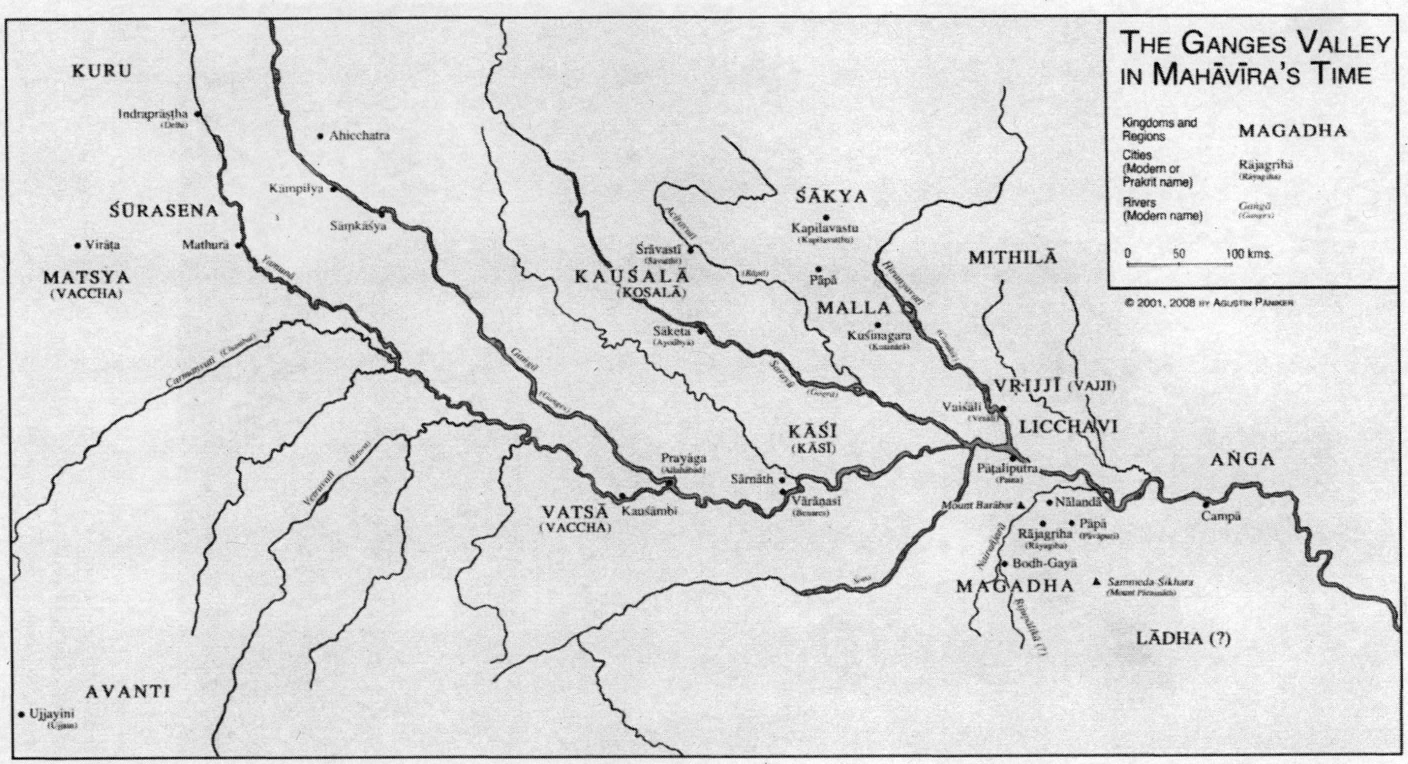

FIGURE 7: The Gangetic plains at the time of Mahāvīra, showing some of the cities an
(Source: Agustín Páníker, based on Lamotte, 1958.)

FIGURE 8: The imposing statue of Bāhubali at Shravanabelgola, Karnataka. Note the creepers entwined around the legs and arms. The saint assumes the classical posture of abandonment of the body *(kāyotsarga)*. (Photograph: Jaume Gurgui & Pilar Pichon.)

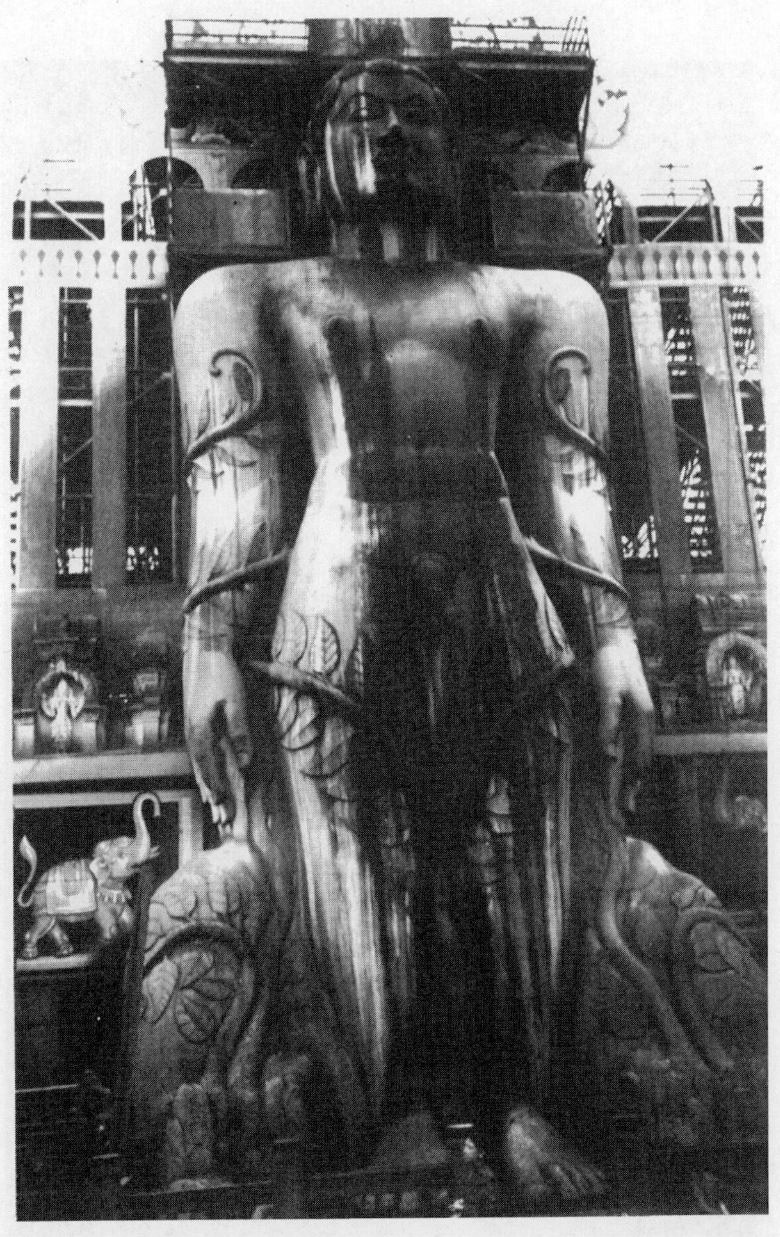

FIGURE 9: The statue of Bāhubali, also known as Gomateśvara, in the Digambara sanctuary of Shravanabelgola, Karnataka, soon after the Ceremony of Anointing in 1993. (Photograph: Agustín Pániker.)

FIGURE 10: Pārśva standing, protected by the 1,000-headed cobra and accompanied by Dharanendra and Padmāvatī. Bas-relief in the temple at Ranakpur, Rajasthan, 14th-15th centuries. (Photograph: Agustín Pániker.)

FIGURE 11: Naked Digambara ascetic on the road *(vihāra)*. His only possessions are his feather duster made with peacock feathers and a small pitcher of water. (Photograph: Kurt Titze. Courtesy of Motilal Banarsidass publishers.)

FIGURE 12: Śvetāmbara Mūrtipūjaka nuns on the road (*vihāra),* with the typical items allotted them: the three pieces of clothing, the feather duster, the stick and the begging bowl. (Photograph: Kurt Titze. Courtesy of Motilal Banarsidass publishers.)

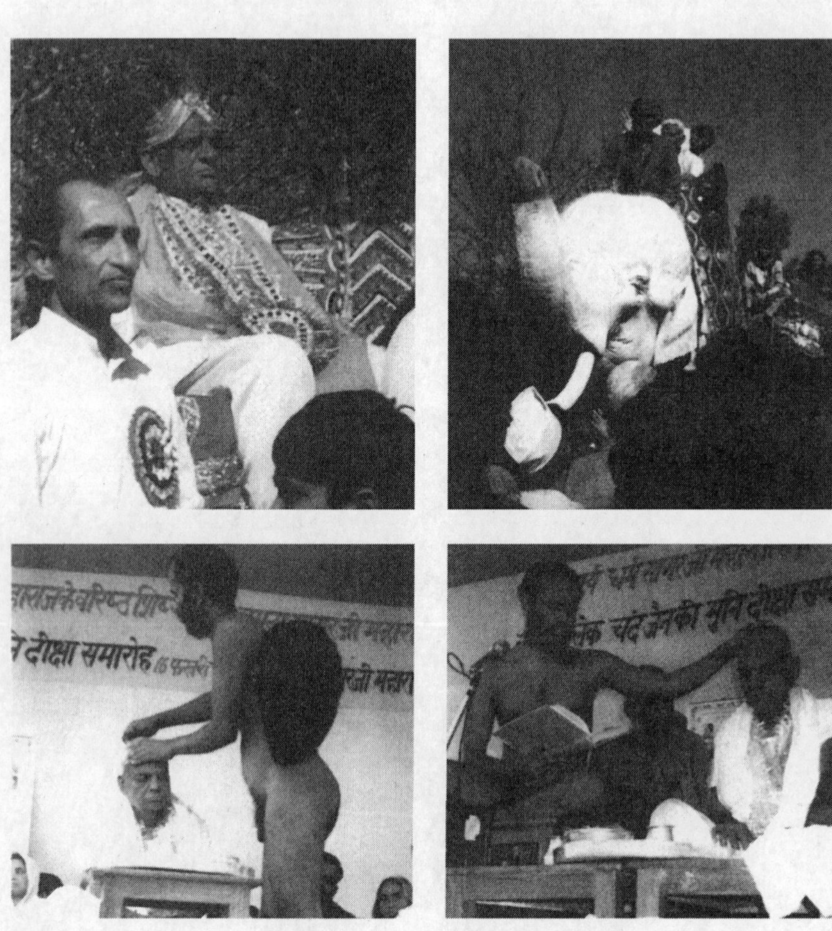

FIGURES 13-16: Scenes of a Digambara initiation in New Delhi. The day before, the candidate (an affluent 60-year old businessman) is carried in procession through the streets of the neighbourhood, dressed like a king. On the day of the initiation, he is transported by an elephant to the appointed place, where more than 6,000 members of the community will attend the ceremony. After assisting him in shaving his head the master conducts the ceremony using the ancient scriptures. (Photographs: Kurt Titze. Courtesy of Motilal Banarsidass publishers.)

FIGURE 17: The eight auspicious symbols. Kaṅkālī Ṭīlā site, Mathura, *circa* 1st century. State Museum of Lucknow. (Courtesy of Abhinav Publications.)

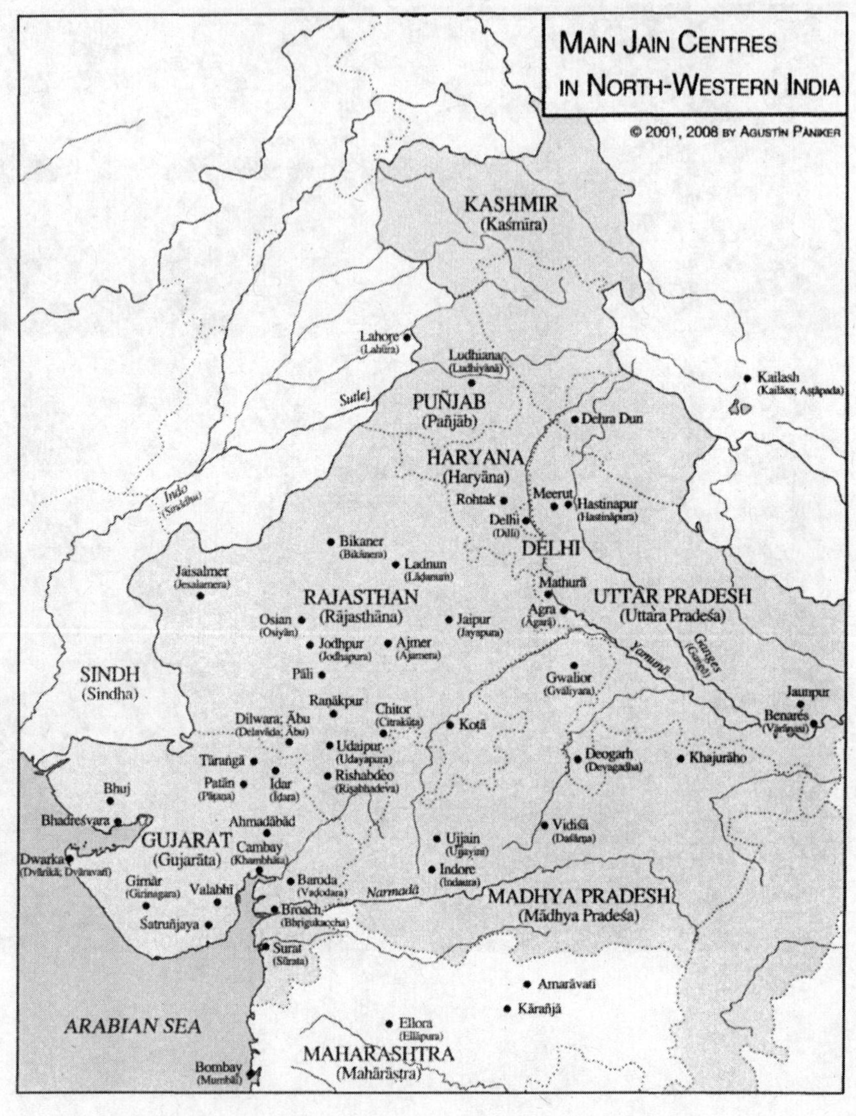

FIGURE 18: Principal nuclei of Jain settlement and centres of pilgrimage in Northwestern India. (Source: Agustín Pániker.)

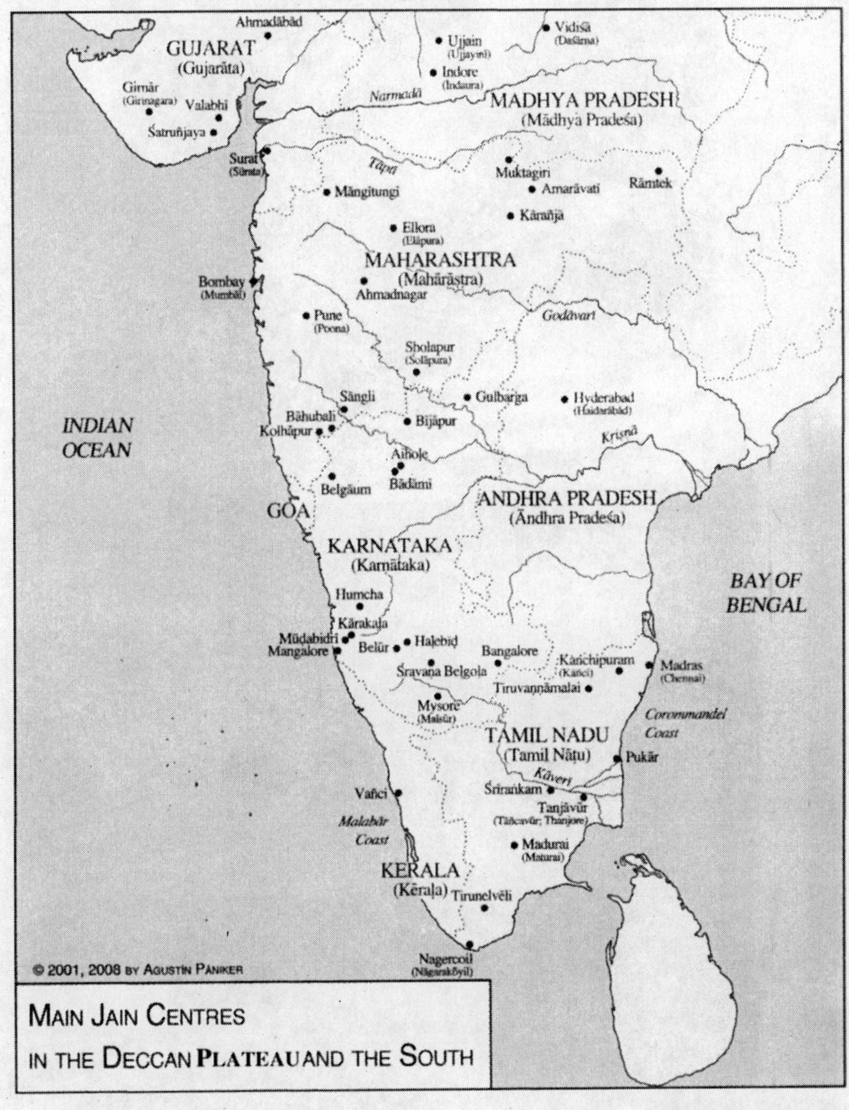

Figure 19: Principal nuclei of Jain settlement and centres of pilgrimage in the Deccan Plateau and the South. (Source: Agustín Pániker.)

FIGURE 20: "Beds" for Jain ascetics hewn out of the rock (3rd century BC). For centuries ascetics lodged in such refuges. Near Gingee, Tamil Nadu. (Photograph: Kurt Titze. Courtesy of Motilal Banarsidass publishers.)

FIGURE 21: Temple complex, residence of the *bhaṭṭāraka,* library and hostel at Humcca, Karnataka. (Photograph: Kurt Titze. Courtesy of Motilal Banarsidass publishers.)

Part V

The Formation of the Community

The life of Mahāvīra was for his disciples the archetype of one who knew how to lead others along the path to enlightenment. For that reason he was declared the 24th and last *tīrthaṅkara.* Under his leadership, the old order of Nirgranthas became a fully historical religion in the conventional sense. When he departed this world, the leadership fell to his disciples.

We shall devote the first two chapters of this Part [chapters 10 and 11] to the first generations of followers and the marked growth of the community from Mahāvīra to the 1st century CE. Thereafter, we shall be looking [in chapter 12] at one of the most important episodes in the long history of this tradition, the schism of Jainism when the movement split into two rival branches: the Digambara and Śvetāmbara persuasions.

We shall then devote the last chapter of this Part [chapter 13] in its entirety to explaining the organisation of the community of renunciants. The monks and nuns were and still are the epicentre of the Jain community. A clear understanding of ascetic-monastic Jainism is essential to be able to capture the essence of this tradition. We will move away, for a time, from the historical development of Jainism and focus on the question from the modern point of view.

A very brief explanation is needed. Jain renunciants have been called, variously, unattached *(nirgranthas,* fem.: *nirgranthīs),* mendicants *(bhikṣus,* fem.: *bhikṣuṇīs)* or benevolent ones *(sādhus,* fem.: *sādhvīs);* it is still even possible to call them strivers *(Śramaṇas,* fem.: *śramaṇīs).* A higher or superior category, restricted to male ascetics, is that of master *(ācārya).* The great masters are usually termed silent ones *(munis, sūris)* and their leaders of old were called by the venerable title of elders *(sthaviras).* All of these terms can be conveniently translated as "monk" or "nun", but a clarification is in order. Jain monks and nuns do not live in monastic reclusion, like their Christian or Buddhist counterparts, but instead spend eight months of the year walking about, without a fixed abode. They are called the homeless ones *(nirāgara, anāgāra).* They settle in one place only for three or four months of the year during the monsoon season. At this time they lodge in a retreat—something quite different from what is usually understood as a monastery—in constant interaction with the lay community. In this respect, they are very well-known public persons. Perhaps a better way of referring to them would be simple to call them *ascetics,* which is one of the terms most used in this book. In addition, we shall be using the modern terms *sād-hu* and *sādhvi,* which furthermore distinguish gender.

10. MAHĀVĪRA'S SUCCESSORS

THE ĀJĪVIKA GOŚĀLA

If we are to believe Jain traditions, Mahāvīra's first clearly distinguishable disciple was Śramaṇa Maskarīn Gośāla, whom we already know from chapter 7. The relationship is not in question. Simply, some people maintain that it was Mahāvīra who took Gośāla as a master. He would leave him in later years to found his own school of thought and to re-organise Pārśva's order of Nirgranthas (Barua cited in K.C. Jain 1974: 48). Hermann Jacobi maintained that, after some years of shared asceticism, Gośāla and Mahāvīra had tried to merge their groups of renunciants. Their experiment had not borne fruit.

Either way, the truth is that after six years of peregrination together, tradition has it that Gośāla acquired supernatural powers *(siddhis)* and he self-proclaimed himself victor *(jina)*. This deed would have deeply displeased Mahāvīra. He, the same as the great master of Yoga Patañjali *(Yoga-sūtra* 3.37-38) or the Buddha himself *(Dīgha-nikāya* 1.213), subscribed that the greatest danger for a yogi was attachment to the powers resulting from the practice of *tapas* or *dhyāna (Daśavaikālika-sūtra* 9.4.3-4). The tradition goes on to state that after a most grave error, Mahāvīra opted to separate from him. According to the account given by Jain texts, Gośāla maintained that:

> "According to our Law an ascetic, who lives alone and single, commits no sin if he uses cold water, eats seeds, accepts things prepared for him, and has intercourse with women" *(Sūtrakṛtāṅga* 2.6.7).

The mere idea of having sexual relations was inadmissible for a genuine ascetic. Maybe it was then that Mahāvīra decided to add a fifth vow of chastity to the already existing four of the Pārśva laws. Perhaps, the story is a mere strategy for stigmatising a character uncomfortably close to Mahāvīra—Buddhists, too, speak of such a legend. It is also possible that the mysterious Gośāla was immersed in the ancient Indian proto-Tantric currents, which have always used the strength of desire *(kāma)*, shall we say *homoeopathically.*

Once separated, Gośāla gravitated towards the deterministic postures typical of the Ājīvaka movement, of which he became leader [see pages 117-118].

Jain accounts tell us that quite a few years later, the impostor Gośāla actually tried to murder Mahāvīra. Peeved because Mahāvīra would not recognise his rank of *tīrthaṅkara,* Gośāla attacked him with yogic flames. The fire bounced off the genuine *jina*'s diamantine body and ended up returning like a boomerang upon Gośāla.

Around the 3rd century BC, the Ājīvikas formed one of the most influential groups in northern India, aided even by the Maurya emperors. Not only does Aśoka mention them but also his grandson Daśaratha donated some caves in Magadha for the use of monks. Gradually, the Ājīvaka lost support. The movement disappeared around the 14th century, and its last members were integrated into Vaiṣṇava groups, followers of Nārāyaṇa, and—perhaps—certain Digambara Jain groups (Basham 1951: 277). There are still those from these lat-test groups who consider that having sincerely repented for the frustrated homicide attempt, Gośāla is now in one of the heavens of the gods, waiting to be reborn as a *tīrthaṅkara* in a future age.

The relationship between Gośāla and Mahāvīra was prior to the Jina's awakening. Thus, he cannot be considered a genuine disciple. Nonetheless, their peculiar relationship is illustrative. On the one hand, Gośāla clearly appears to be an example of the ascetic who has strayed from the path. Gośāla failed to overcome being a magician; he did not resist the temptation of magic (Eliade 1975: 89-90). For Jainism, he became the model of the fallen monk. On the other hand, as an historical figure, he serves to contextualise the continual interaction/opposition between Jainism and the others. Borrowing between Śramaṇic tendencies was as much the order of the day as was strife. This ambiguity is well reflected by the position taken by some Jains, who see the Ājīvika as a future *tīrthaṅkara,* while others relegate him to the plane of an insignificant *nigoda,* beings who, as we already know [see pages 52-53], have their way to spiritual progression practically barred.

MAHĀVĪRA'S DISCIPLES

If Gośāla cannot be considered as a disciple, texts clearly show us that there were eleven headmasters *(gaṇadharas)* who directed the companies into which Mahāvīra divided his community. They were responsible for directing and organising the ascetics, since a *jina,* by definition, does not take care of these matters. We already know that the Jina simply emits a magic sound, but, this monotone manifests the meaning *(artha)* of his teachings, which will be translated into sermons (Sūtras) by the *gaṇadharas.* Therefore, the importance of these leaders is crucial when organising and structuring the Jina's teachings into sacred scriptures (Āgama). Śvetāmbara Jainism, orientated towards a more human conception of Mahāvíra, has maintained that the Jina's magic sound is divine in the sense that not only both humans from different regions and animals are capable of understanding it. In this case, the *gaṇadharas* would not be interpreters but compilers of the teachings and in charge of organising the community.

All the *gaṇadharas* came from Maghada and its vicinities. Interestingly, all eleven came from the clerical class, of well-known lineages *(gotras)* such as the Gautama, Vāśiṣṭha, Bhāradvāja, and Kāśyapa. All were Brāhmaṇas by birth. K.C. Jain (1974: 59) infers that there was an ideological revolution taking place among the Brāhmaṇas, a revolution which obliged them to abandon their arguments in favour of ritualism. Later on it was this *intelligentsia* of Brāh-manical origin which contributed to the extension of the doctrine.

Except for Gautama Indrabhūti and Sudharman, the other nine heads of companies achieved the supreme knowledge after 12 years of renunciation. They were omniscient *(kevalins)* in the full sense, but they were not surrounded by the series of miraculous phenomena that always accompany a *tīrthaṅkara.* From the moment they reached the state of omniscience they no longer devoted themselves to the community. They retained their title of *gaṇadhara* in a merely nominal fashion. The real community leaders during the so-called *kevalin* period were Gautama Indrabhūti and Sudharman, the only ones who still had not reached omniscience and who outlived Mahāvīra.

GAUTAMA INDRABHŪTI

Indrabhūti was a Brāhmaṇa from the Gautama lineage. He was well versed in the Veda. Everyone knows the episode concerning his conversion. Although there are various versions, the most cherished one says that the Brāhmaṇa had "summoned" the divinities during a solemn sacrifice. To his astonishment the gods began to concongregate around the newly awakened *jina* to listen to Mahāvīra's first sermon. Gautama went to the sacred assembly to refute and belittle it. Yet on the contrary, in the end he was convinced by the Jina's lucid explanation of the reality of the soul *(jīva)* and the virtues of non-violence *(ahiṃsā).* The good man Gautama lost all the arrogance that Indians attribute to Brāhmaṇas. He became one of the Jina's followers and was with him for forty years, dedicated to taking down his sermons, with absolute love and devotion for his master. We can find a similar archetype in the figure of Ānanda, the faithful disciple and right hand of the Buddha. So strong was the love, that Gautama felt for his master, that this attachment prevented him from achieving complete freedom from attachment. The great *gaṇadhara* already had accepted the idea of going through another human incarnation, in which, in the absence of his dearly beloved master, he would be able to aspire to the Abode of the Liberated Souls. Only with the death of Mahāvīra could Gautama conquer this love, and tradition is in fact unanimous in affirming that Gautama reached omniscience the very same day as Mahāvīra's death. That day, the Jina's sermon made the seed of true wisdom grow in his faithful follower. According to the *Uttarādhyayana-sūtra,* the sermon more or less went like this.

Mahāvīra urges and implores Gautama to take the definite step to break the ties between his actions and the soul. He shows him that one day, absolutely everything, ends up dying and transforming itself *(Uttarādhyayana-sūtra* 10.1). Life is just a mere instant in the infinite cycle of the *saṃsāra;* it is as brief as the time a caterpillar takes to climb to the top of a blade of grass. Only when the avatars of transmigration lead to a very rare human rebirth, can one at last be freed of the fruit of past actions. But that is not all:

> "Though one be born as a man, it is a rare chance to become an Ārya [noble]; for many are the Dasyus [slaves] and Mlecchas [barbarians]" *(Uttarādhyayana -sūtra* 10.16).

Even if one is an Aryan, not everyone has the opportunity to hear Jain doctrine, since there are those who follow masters who have gone astray. Even if we listen to the true *dharma,* we may not have enough strength to take the path of renunciation and devote oneself to meditation and asceticism. Now that Gautama has taken that path and gotten so far, Mahāvīra urges him to cut all trace of ties. He is already old, and beginning to deteriorate, but Gautama continues with his attachment:

> "You have crossed the great ocean; why do you halt so near the shore? Make haste to get on the other side; Gautama.
>
> Going through the same religious practices as perfected saints, you will reach the world of perfection, Gautama, where there is safety and perfect happiness" *(Uttarādhyayana-sūtra* 10.34-35).

The *sūtra* states that after hearing the sermon Gautama relinquished every last shred of attachment and achieved omniscience, from which no one can fall. The *Kalpa-sūtra (Jina-caritra* 127) maintains the version that it was not until hours later, once Mahāvīra had died, that Gautama reached supreme wisdom. Twelve years later, at the age of ninety-two, he reached *nirvāṇa.*

Gautama is one of Jainism's most loved figures. He is a benevolent character; loving—jolly, even—with a prominent paunch, which apparently does not square well with the high regard Jains have for fasting. During the medieval period, Gautama was an object of devotion *(bhakti)* by some tendencies within Śvetāmbara Jainism. A good part of ritual literature invokes his name, somewhat on the lines of Gaṇeśa of the Hindu tradition (with whom he shares not a few characteristics), as a mover of obstacles and a dispenser of miraculous powers. Gautama receives special veneration during the Dīvālī festival [see pages 432-433].

SUDHARMAN

After the death of Mahāvīra and omniscience of Gautama the responsibility for directing the order lay in the hands of the *gaṇadhara* Sudharman, the only head of school who had not obtained enlightenment.

Tradition states that Gautama related all Mahāvīra's sermons to Sudharman. Thus he was left as the sole custodian of the entire body of Jaina teachings. Later, Sudharman transmitted the teachings to his disciple Jambūsvāmin. That is why many Sūtras begin with the words spoken by Sudharman to Jambū:

> "O, long-lived! I have heard the following discourse from the venerable..." *(Ācārāṅga-sūtra* l.l.l).

JAMBŪSVĀMIN

The first generation of Mahāvīra's followers disappeared with the death of Sudharman. The direction of the community passed into the hands of Jambūsvāmin, son of a trader from Rājagṛha (and, thus, a non-Brāhmaṇa) and he led it for 24 years. Jambū has a special position in the list of Jain enlightened ones. It is said that he was the last person of the Sorrowful Age, and ultimately of the descendent cosmic cycle, to have reached liberation here on this earth (Hemacandra, *Pariśiṣṭa-parvan* 4.49-51). This event took place 74 years after Mahāvīra's *nirvāṇa.*

ANCIENT JAINISM

Let' s return to our scriptural study. If the *Ācārāṅga-sūtra I* and the *Sūtrakṛtāṅga I* could represent Mahāvīra's teachings, chronologically, the texts which come after are surely the *Uttarādhyayana-sūtra* and the *Daśavaikālika-sūtra.* In the form that they have come down to us, both texts are anthologies by different anonymous authors, transmitted down the ages. Nevertheless, the poetry is still predominant and Vedic metre is still used, all these features denoting great antiquity.

The *Uttarādhyayana* continues to be rather unconcerned with the world of lay people. We are still moving within an ascetic community. Yet, we are already-finding exceptions. For the first time it was said that after death, a pious layman could be reborn as a deity *(Uttarādhyayana-sūtra* 5.24). The idea of an auspicious rebirth (as a divinity or a fortunate human being) was unheard of in older texts. For old Jainism all that was not total liberation (*mokṣa, nirvāṇa)*, all that implied the mere idea of rebirth, was considered a failure. There is already a bifurcation in the *Uttarādhyayana.* Either a heavenly rebirth—for a good Śramaṇa or a perfect layman—or liberation—for a Śramaṇa ho excelled *(Uttarādhyayana-sūtra* 5.25). The idea of gradual progression over a series of rebirths begins to be insinuated.

In ancient India, there must have been an intense intellectual debate over whether the householder could lead an authentic religious life or not. Brāhmaṇical authors opted for an affirmative answer. The householder who follows the rites prescribed in the Veda will attain salvation. The Śramaṇical thinkers,

Buddhist and Jain, tended to answer in the negative. For the most remote Jain texts, the householder or head of family (a concept which includes all laymen) is still the "servant" *(upāsaka),* he who feeds the ascetic monk. The concept of "listener" *(śrāvaka),* which later on would be used to describe devoted lay people, had still not clearly emerged. Although the *Uttarādhyayana* shows a more conciliatory attitude toward the lay community, we still do not find teachings for the lay. The *sūtra's* tone continues to be exclusively monastic, and for the ascetic it is still insisted that solitary wandering and begging constitute the correct way of life *(Uttarādhyayana-sūtra* 2.18). The ascetic must live in solitude, emulating Mahāvīra. The classical concept of the twenty-two hardships *(parīṣahas)* that the *sādhu* must overcome (hunger, thirst, cold, heat, fear, dirt, ill treatment, etc.) are established. Nonetheless, the notion that during peregrination one could be accompanied by a preceptor is now mentioned, so that a minimum of monastic organisation must have begun to appear. The small group consisting of master and disciples is termed a "family" *(kula)* in the *Uttarādhyayana* (11.14).

The rigour of the ascetic life, which the *Uttarādhyayana* merely continues from the *Ācārāṅga I* and the *Sūtrakṛtāṅga I,* would have to compete with softer, easier practices in the future, and in the context of a better-organised community. As we move further from Mahāvīra and his direct disciples, we increasingly get the feeling that there were two types of ascetics. On the one hand, there were those of olden times, who wandered alone and braved the hardships of the ascetic life in the same way as the *jinas* (hence they were called *jinakalpins).* According to tradition, after the death of Gautama, Sudharman, and Jambūsvāmin, nobody else continued the Jina's path *(jinakalpa)* in the perfect way. Thus, there was only the other type of ascetic monk left, those of modern times who have to wander in the company of other monks and who need to learn from their masters. This model came to be called the way of the elders *(sthavi-rakalpa).* This stems from the idea of the slow decline of *dharma.*

In the *Daśavaikālika-sūtra,* we already find references to a key notion of Jainism. The ascetic must renounce five or six attitudes: violence, possessiveness, telling lies, lack of sexual restraint, stealing, and eating at night-time. Obviously, these restrictions represented the embryonic stage of the five great classical vows *(mahāvratas),* which would be instated in later times. This text abounds in details relevant to ascetics: the way to conduct oneself when meeting people, the correct ways of begging, ways of speaking, etc. The text is the precursor of the later disciplinary codes and shows evidence of a certain monastic organisation.

The next textual layer is surely that of the *Sūtrakṛtāṅga II.* K.K. Dixit (1978: 34) has noted that the second part of this text is clearly much later than the first, as it is mainly in prose and devotes considerable space to going over the pious layman's duties and makes frequent use of the technical concepts of classical Jainism. It is interesting to note that, in the relation to the layman's spiritual life, the *Sūtrakṛtāṅga II* already recommends the observation of monthly fasting *(pauṣadha)* and the renunciation of the same five harmful activities which required for ascetic monks. It also recommends a short, daily period of meditation, which it terms *sāmāyika,* or zeal in the application of *ahimsā* in geographically restricted spaces. We will see all these practices in their entirety in chapter 31; they will crystallise into a path of spiritual progression for laymen, composed of 11 states and 12 religious vows. Just as Dixit (1978: 35) has observed, the constant references to pious laymen's activities strongly contrast with the oldest texts. All this proves that at the time of the composition of the *Sūtrakṛtāṅga II* Jainism had ceased to be an exclusive religion for ascetics: the concept of the devout layman faithful to the path had emerged.

Similarly, it was during this period that much more elaborate texts began to be codified with respect to monastic conduct. The Cheda-sūtras of the Śvetāmbara canon (similar to the Buddhist Vinaya), constitute a good example. Although the idea of a solitary ascetic did not disappear, the emerging practice was that of a reputed master directing a company *(gaṇa)* or sub-order *(gaccha)* of ascetic monks.

THE FORMATION OF THE COMMUNITY

Tradition states that, just like his 23 predecessors, Mahāvīra again formed a community consisting of four pillars: ascetic monks, ascetic nuns, laymen and lay women. The story tells that at the time of his death, the community of monks numbered 14,000, that of the nuns 36,000, lay men numbered 159,000 and lay women 318,000. Obviously, a community structured in these sorts of numbers is of a later period. However, what we are interested in is going over the four collectives that form the Jain community *(saṃgha, tīrtha).*

MALE AND FEMALE ASCETICS

The collective of male ascetics *(sādhus)* have always carried the weight of the community. They all trace their monastic line *(paṭṭāvalī, sthavirāvalī)* back to Mahāvīra via Sudharman *(Kalpa-sūtra, Sthavirāvalī* 2). We will discuss the internal organisation of the ascetic-monastic community in considerable detail in chapter 13.

One point that stands out and which is surprising, is that right from the beginning the number of nuns (*sādhvīs, āryikās)* nearly triplicates that of the monks—something only maintained by the Śvetāmbaras. It would be worthwhile taking a closer look at this aspect.

One could doubt the accuracy of the figures—except of course that the wives of a new polygamous renunciant might well opt to become renunciants or feel obliged to do so, or the figures might have a purely sociological explanation—

even today there are some Jain nuns who are widows who prefer the ascetic way to a life of stagnation in the reclusion of their family home, or to life as paupers. Yet, the fact that tradition should choose this proportion is in itself revealing. One can hardly argue that all female ascetics who embraced the monastic path were motivated by social or domestic events. We can assume that women saw in this doctrine a way to spiritual progression that perhaps the rigid Vedic-Brāhmaṇical rules denied them. Let's consider this.

The Brāhmaṇical ideal of classical spiritual progression considers that all higher social-spiritual class members must go through distinct stages in life *(āśramas)* which culminate in renunciation *(samnyāsa).* However, even if Brāhmaṇism has greatly valued the way of asceticism and renunciation, it has never considered these as being the only path to liberation. In this sense, Brāhmaṇism has a wider reach than Jainism or Buddhism, for which renunciation is practically a condition *sine qua non* for achieving liberation. Given its more sociable character—not in vain is society a reflection of the macro-cosmos—Brāhmaṇism has never looked too favourably on women becoming renunciants and mendicants, not even in the case of widows. Marriage is virtually compulsory for Hindu women, as the prolongation of the lineage is in itself a ritual obligation. Female celibacy seemed repugnant to Brāhmaṇical theology (Olivelle 1993: 188-190). It is not that there have not been women renunciants within Brāhmaṇism. We know of quite a number in all kinds of different contexts (Teskey Denton 1991: 211-231). Well known are the monasteries for female renunciants of the Ramakrishna Mission. The thing is that Brāhmaṇic tradition has put ideological obstacles in the way of women who aspire to reaching liberation. Although in Mahāvīra's times the Brāhmaṇical position could have been more flexible, as the female sages of the Upaniṣads confirm *(Bṛhadāraṇyaka-upaniṣad* 3.8.1-12), it is a fact that around the first centuries of the Common Era the Brāhmaṇical society lowered the marriage age to pre-puberty. Meaning that women were barred from learning the Veda, and the very idea of liberation *(mckṣa).*

In contrast, in Śramaṇical traditions and incipient Hindu devotional movements, there is a degree of egalitarianism that we do not find in Vedic orthodoxy. The cornerstone of devotional Hinduism is the *Bhagavad-gītā,* which was composed sometime between the 2nd century BC and the 2nd century CE. The *Gītā* (9.32) mentions the possibility of spiritual liberation for women and also members of the lower social-spiritual classes—Vaiśyas, Śūdras. Of course, we are talking about soteriological equality, the fact of conceding that women might attain ultimate liberation *(mokṣa),* not questioning the power of the patriarchal society of the times. In reality, with their constant insistence on renouncement and the danger of sensual pleasure, Buddhist and Jain texts can—and normally do—tend to be more androcentric and misogynous than the Brāhmaṇical ones. Hence, when the Buddha agreed to the creation of an order for women renunciants, he did so against his will, towards the end of his life. But he accepted, and went on clearly to say that women were just as capable as men were of following the contemplative path and of reaching *nirvāṇa (Cullavagga* 10.1.3). With Mahāvīra, on the other hand, one can detect no hesitation. This fact has no precedent. On the contrary, it is said that he placed his first cousin Candanā, in charge of all the Jain *sādhvīs* as their spiritual mother. According to the *Vyākhyā-prajñāpti* (12.2 [556b/558b]), Jayantī, the king of Kauśāmbī's daughter, took her vows as a nun before Mahāvīra himself. Not all Jain circles accept this episode, but it is indisputably advanced that, according to the Śvetāmbara tradition, Mahāvīra had no hesitation in ordaining a female ascetic (Altekar 1956: 208). Even more importantly, it is conceded that, as soon as she was ordained, Jayantī reached liberation. And she was not the only one. According to the *Kalpa-sūtra (Jina-caritra* 144), during the Jina's lifetime, 1,400 women (compared to only 700 men) reached liberation. Note that, from the Brāhmaṇical point of view, also upheld by Digambara Jains, all women would invariably have to be reborn as a man to reach the highest goal.

Jainism has certainly not always maintained such a "liberal" attitude as that which prevailed in the times of Mahāvīra and the *gaṇadharas.* We shall be noting this shortly [chapter 12], since women's spiritual liberation has been the object of prolonged and lasting debate within Jainism. But it is also true that when the Buddhist order of nuns disappeared (around the 4th and 5th centuries), the Jain *sādhvīs* formed the only organised female monastic group in South Asia (Shāntā 1985: 90). Although the attitude in medieval times reflected the monks' misogynous prejudice (women embodied temptation for ascetic monks), a fact common to monastic traditions all over the world, throughout history there seems to have been more Jain nuns than monks. Today, their number triplicates that of male ascetics [see Table 2].

LAYMEN AND LAYWOMEN

The last two pillars of the community were the lay men *(upāsakas, śrā-vakas)* and lay women *(śrāvikas).* They formed (as they still do) the great mass of householders who did not opt to renounce the world, but sustained the *sād-hus* and *sādhvis* with their donations. Instead of taking the strict vows of the ascetics, they took a lighter version. For this reason, the first are called great vows *(mahāvaratas)* and the second ones, the little vows *(anuvratas).* It is said that in Mahāvīra's times Śaṅkha Śataka was responsible for organising them—which is obviously an addition. Originally, there was no special rite or formal external sign which proclaimed one as being a Jain. As in Buddhism, one only had to say that one was, and that was all.

Since the beginning, the great majority of lay people came from commercial and merchant classes. This social characteristic has remained up until the present time, perhaps reinforced by the Jain emphasis on *ahiṃsā,* which obliges one to work in non-harming occupations. The role of lay people consisted of offering food, shelter, and any other help to ascetics. In olden times, we find no evidence of the notion that offering *(dāna)* to an ascetic, was a way of acquiring religious merit, an idea which, is these days fundamentally important in maintaining the ascetic community.

Despite what we might gather from reading the texts, Jainism soon ceased to be a religion exclusively for ascetics. I would even say it was not so in its origins, for all the insistence in the *Ācārāṅga I* and the *Sūtrakṛtāṅga I* that the only path was that of the renunciant ascetic monk, and that the role of householder *(gṛhasta)* was merely to give material support *(Ācārāṅga-sūtra* 1.7.2). At all events, with the passing of time the layperson model came more strongly into focus, and as we have seen the texts increasingly devoted more attention to them. We even find a classical text, the *Upāsakadaśāh,* which as its name indicates, instructs laymen *(upāsakas)* on their spiritual duties in ten *(daśā)* chapters. Even though the possibility of a layman achieving liberation is not openly recognised in any of the old texts, the object of reaching heaven begins to be discernible.

11. THE EXPANSION OF JAINISM

THE UNIVERSALISM OF JAINISM

What would have been an insignificant Śramaṇic movement in time of Mahāvīra and the *gaṇadharas,* became a structured tradition. What initial factors influenced the success of Jainism? How could it break through Brāhmaṇical hegemony? We will try to answer these questions by attempting to cover the social scope that the Jain message would have had.

All Śramaṇical religions possessing a definite non-Brāhmaṇical, non-Vedic character is an established fact. But, what does that exactly mean? The subject has been quite badly interpreted; seen in terms of such modern values as social equality. The Śramaṇas' anti-Brāhmaṇism has to be properly understood. As we have seen, for the core of Brāhmaṇism, sacrifice *(yajña)* was what, in the last instance, enabled the maintenance of the world. To such a degree, that Brāhmaṇical orthodoxy did not consider any principle that was not useful to the sacrificial ideology. Denying the sacred power of sacrifice was tantamount to denying their very conceptionion of the universe, the authority of the experts in ritual (the Brāhmaṇas) and the legitimacy of the holy scriptures (the Veda) that had looked deeply into the matter of sacrifice. That is exactly what Jains and Buddhists did: they propounded a theory of the universe, reality, and the situation of beings without taking sacrifice into account (Dasgupta 1922:1,210); beyond ritual and its results. Mahāvīra's interpretation put so many vectors in doubt that Brāhmaṇas considered it to be a heterodox *(nāstika)* and non-Vedic *(avaidika)* teaching. Jainism does not perpetuate itself, nor transforms in relation to Vedic authority.

Neither its radical atheism, nor the abandon of the supreme gods, nor its decided experiential approach would have been a reason for the imputation of heterodoxy. After all, other Brāhmaṇical currents (the Sāṃkhya philosophy, for example, and sections of the Vedānta) proposed similar theses. Jain heterodoxy has to do with the rejection of Vedic ritual schematics as well as a reaction against the Brāhmaṇas' excess of speculation" (Eliade 1972:93). Explicitly, the statement is made that sacrifice is the cause of actions completely lacking in merit:

> "The binding of animals [to the sacrificial pole], all the Vedas, and sacrifices, being causes of sin, cannot save the sinner; for his works [or *karman*] are very powerful" *(Uttarādhyayana-sūtra* 25.30).

Jains criticised the Veda as being of the same human origin as any other literature. As Amitagati (10th-11th centuries) said (cited in Warder 1972: VI, 260), the violence of Vedicism is like that of the demons and the supposedly non-human and eternal nature of the Veda should be denied given that this is contrary to reason. Similarly, for the great Jain thinker Hemacandra (12th century), the Brāhmaṇa priests were monsters disguised as ascetics that, with the supposed idea that sacrificed animals are reborn as divine beings, seriously distort reality. For him, those who carry out these sacrifices will go to the vilest hells, and even a materialistic atheist (a Cārvaka) would have a better fate than the hypocrites who preach the *dharma* of cruelty *(Yoga-śāstra* 2.37-39).

Notwithstanding, Jain distancing from sacrifice is not complete. What Mahāvīra distanced himself from was the exoteric ritual in itself, but like the masters of the Upaniṣads, he retained all the symbolism. The sacrificial altar fire was insignificant compared to the fire and the heat generated by asceticism. Violence toward sacrificial objects is turned inwards, in the form of non-violence [see page 151]. The sacrifice is interiorised, as is clearly stated by the ascetic Harikeśa in the *Uttarādhyayana-sūtra* (12.44):

> "Penance is my fire; life my fireplace; right exertion is my sacrificial ladle; the body the dried cowdung; Karman is my fuel; self-control, right exertion, and tranquility are oblations, praised by the sages, which I offer".

At no point does Harikeśa condemn sacrifice but rather exhorts us to carry out the true sacrifice: the renunciant life of the monk *(Uttarādhyayana-sūtra* 11.40-42). We find the same idea in Buddhist monasticism *(Dīgha-nikāya* 1.127-149) and in the eclectic *Bhagavad-gītā* (4.25-30). This is a constant in South Asian spirituality: new ideas and doctrines can become intelligible if they are encoded under the old, well-known vocabulary of sacrifice. The issue, is to be homologous with Brāhmaṇical schemes and values. According to Jinab-hadra Gaṇi (6th century), when Mahāvīra converted the *gaṇadharas* he did not at any point seek to refute the Veda, but emphasised that its apparent contradictions arise from its being incorrectly interpreted *(Viśeṣāvaśyaka -bhāṣya* 1649 [*Gaṇadhara-vāda* 101]). What is involved is not declaring the Veda to be false, but of adjusting it to Jain truth. This audacity is typical of India. Only in this way, could Jainism make progress among the Brāhmaṇical *intelligentsia.* It is not surprising that Kumārila Bhaṭṭa (7th-8th centuries), the champion of medieval Brāhmaṇical orthodoxy, considered the heretics that rejected their origins (Vedic origins) like unnatural sons who repudiate their parents *(Tantra-vārtika* 1.3.3).

One of the most illustrative ways of denying the ritual edifice was to show that the greatest honour was to be born as noble (Kṣatriya) and not as priest (Brāhmaṇa), with the added plus of propagandistic *appeal* that this affirmation possessed. Recall the transference of Mahāvīra's embryo or the place accorded to Ṛṣabha (the first king and creator of civilisation) in the Universal History. Jainism used all the martial symbolism within its reach, to draw a very clear model: the true ascetic is the spiritual warrior who conquers the passions and the ego. Understood thus, it does not seem so paradoxical that the religion of non-violence par excellence was promoted by 24 Kṣatriyas. Buddhist scriptures even speak of a general called Sīha, a contemporary of the Buddha, who was a Jain layman *(Mahāvagga* 6.31.1). Accordingly, adherence to the principles of non-violence would have been necessary only in certain religious contexts. Jainism should not be confused with pacifism [see pages 246-248].

It should not be inferred from this that Jainism represents a Kṣatriya revolt against the Brāhmaṇas. It has perhaps been overstressed that the contributions of the Upaniṣads and the Śramaṇical movements were fostered among illuminated noble circles who looked for a way that would give them supremacy over the priests. It would be fatuous to reduce the complex inter-religious dynamic of India to a power struggle. Note that the first followers of Mahāvīra were all Brāhmaṇas by birth. Even while one can doubt the historicity of the *gaṇadharas,* the Jain tradition recognised them as Brāhmaṇas.

A brāhmaṇa, in the Jain context, no longer designates an expert in sacrifice and the holy scriptures, but refers to a quality acquired through behaviour and not through birth. The *Uttarādhyayana-sūtra* (2531-32) continues:

> "One does not become a Śramaṇa by the tonsure, nor a Brāhmaṇa by the sacred syllable *om,* nor a *muni* by living in the woods, nor a *tāpasa* by wearing [clothes of] *kuśa*-grass and bark.
>
> One becomes a Śramaṇa by equanimity, a Brāhmaṇa by chastity, a *muni* by knowledge, and a *tāpasa* by pennance".

For this reason, even Mahāvīra was called *māhaṇa (Sūtrakṛtāṅga* 1.9.1), the Prakrit form of *brāhmaṇa.* In fact, the compound *brāhmaṇa-Śramaṇa* to designate saints is recurrent in Jain literature. And as the Buddhist *Dhammapada* (26.4) shows, the position of Buddhism is practically identical: a brāhmaṇa is that one who is free of passions and who has reached the highest level of saint-liness. The antagonism between Brāhmaṇas and Śramaṇas, as depicted in the *Mahābhāṣya* of the grammatician Patañjali (2nd century BC), is a later development (Tatia and Kumar 1981: xxi). For the medieval philosopher Merutunga (14th century), "Brāhmaṇa-ness" is typified by truth, *tapas* and self-control. Thus, playing with the two senses of the term, he says:

> "The are Cāṇḍalas [Untouchables] in all *jātis* [castes]; there are Brāhmaṇas in all *jātis;*
>
> Even among Brāhmaṇas there are Cāṇḍalas, and among Cāṇḍalas, Brāhmaṇas" *(Ṣaḍḍarśana-nirṇaya* [Folkert 1993: 384]).

Rejection of the authority of the priests, and of all divine origin of their rank (backed up by some Vedic hymns), does not amount to rejecting the system of castes *(jātis)* of India. Especially since Jains were proposing the superiority of the warrior class. The caste society is a very complex reality which is based not just on the ideology of the socio-spiritual classes *(varṇas)* fostered by the Brāhmaṇas, but on a whole series of social, political and economic factors, critically entangled among themselves [see chapter 20]. Neither Jainism, Buddhism, nor—much later—the Hindu devotional movements, nor even Islam or Christianity wanted to dynamite the Indian social fabric. Where all these groups have coincided is in not recognising the authority of the Brāhmaṇas and, in some cases, attributing the status of Śūdras to Untouchables (Caṇḍālas). Although the notion of untouchability would have only been gestating in the time of Mahāvīra (Parasher-Sen 2004: 16-22)—notwithstanding, Louis Dumont (1979: 77) observed that the impurity of the Caṇḍāla was conceptually inseparable from the Brāhmaṇa's purity—we know that members of the groups that were considered very low or impure entered and formed part of the Jain order. This was the case with the above-mentioned Harikeśa, an untouchable (Śvapāka) by birth, praised by the gods:

> "The value of pennance has become visible, birth appears of no value! Look at the holy Harikeśa, the son of a Śvapāka, whose power is so great" *(Uttarād -hyayana-sūtra* 12.37).

The Buddhists have a very similar story to Harikeśa in the *Mātaṅga-jātaka* (15.497). This point is important because it shows that with the Śramaṇic movements the way of liberation became *universal.* Everyone, beyond their birth or gender, can aspire to release taking the Jain path. Caste is soteriologically irrelevant. Consequently, when joining the renunciant order, all trace of socio-spiritual rank that one might have had is lost—in theory, at least. This contrasts with Brāhmaṇical orthodoxy, who actually prohibited the study and recitation of the Veda in any village where untouchables were living *(Āpastamba-dharma-sūtra* 1.3.9.15). For Jainism, purity is not inherited (as the Brāhmaṇas maintained) but is attained through renunciation.

This universalist tune should not be confused with proselytism. The missionary zeal of the Jains has never been very strong. This can be seen in the fact that it barely spread beyond the frontiers of South Asia [see pages 303-304]. Possibly, among those religions that consider themselves universalists (i.e., Islam, Christianity, and Buddhism) the Jains are those who least have felt a vocation to seek converts. With their emphasis in non-intervention and in personal effort, its expansion was not so much propagandistic as strictly universalist.

THE PATRONAGE OF THE MONARCHS

This muted universalism would not have been sufficient to cause Jainism to flourish. On the other hand, we know that the Jain religion, like the Buddhist religion, made good and relatively rapid progress. All of the middle region of the Gangetic Valley was full of Jain communities in the 3rd and 2nd centuries BC. The second key aspect to grasp to be able to understand its development was the patronage that these two traditions enjoyed.

As these were strictly renunciant movements, both Jainism and Buddhism were obliged to form closer links with the elite that were their patrons. And what better source of material support than the aristocracies and the political powers. Hence the calculated emphasis that Jainism placed on the superiority of the princely classes (Kṣatriya) and to present itself in imperial terms (be it the description of Mahāvīra's omniscience, the use of martial and royal symbology, or the encyclopaedic and totalising tendency of some Sūtras). This fact would not have passed unnoticed by the leaders of the time, constantly subjected as they were to the ritual authority of the Brāhmaṇas. While the Brāhmaṇas neither governed nor accumulated riches like the kings, various factors put them in a very advantageous position of strength: their advice in matters of state (via the chaplains and preceptors of the kings), their ritual authority (effected through the rites of coronation), their legitimisation of the dynasty (thanks to the work of the genealogists), and their guarantee of legitimacy (embodying as they did the transcendence and independence that the monarch seeked to portray at all cost [see page 89]). The kings did away with their taxes, granted them lands, financed their institutions and organisations, and attended solemn rituals. While these very close ties between Brāhmaṇas and *rājās* were maintained for centuries, it is clear that many monarchs saw the advantages of playing the card of other groups and sustaining other *dharmas*. Buddhists and Jains (who, after all, were renunciants and similarly represented the independence from and transcendence of the social) formed alliances with particular kings and their monastic institutions flourished.

Some monarchs acted out of religious convictions, but others undoubtedly took advantage of the circumstances provided by these "heretical" groups and to strengthen their position vis-à-vis the powerful Brāhmaṇical apparatus. The versatility and astuteness of Indian kings and politicians on religious questions is well-known. This aspect should be emphasised properly to understand the success of the Śramaṇical movements.

THE GANGES VALLEY DYNASTIES

It is possible that Mahāvīra and his doctrine captivated king Śreṇika of Magadha, perhaps instigated by queen Celanā. Otherwise, it is difficult to explain the quantity of histories and legends that Jainism has accumulated concerning this king. Rājagṛha, the capital of Magadha, became the epicentre of Jainism. It should be remembered that at that time, Magadha was becoming the most powerful kingdom in the continent. Śreṇika's son, the usurper Kūṇika, openly favoured Buddhism. Nonetheless, Kūṇika did not close the door on other religions or Śra-manical movements, nor on the Brāhmaṇas. In fact, some Jain texts claim him as theirs, although his predilection for Buddhism is generally accepted.

All sources agree that after Kūṇika and his succesor Udāyin (apparently also a benefactor of Jainism) the Nanda dynasty came to power. According to Jain documents, its religious leaders knew how to ally themselves pretty well with the Nanda princes (later regarded by Hindu orthodoxy as *adhārmikas)* and Jainism continued to flourish. However, these same kings are claimed also by the Buddhist, so that once again one has to take with a pinch of salt the religious affiliations that Jains and Buddhists attribute to "their" kings. In fact, we must also emphasise that most of the Jain alliances with the monarchs must have been so insubstantial that we can hardly speak of "Jain" kings until the Gaṅga [see pages 223-226] and Solaṅkī [see pages 244-246] dynasties.

JAINISM UNDER THE MAURYAS

The Nanda dynasty soon came to an end. A little while afterwards, the first great empire in the history of India rose to power. Its dynasty was based in Patna, known in ancient times as Pāṭaliputra, the centre of what by then was the former kingdom of Magadha.

It is said that the first Maurya ruler, Candragupta (reigned 322-298 BC), came to be a disciple of the Jain master Bhadrabāhu [see pages 180-181]. And not just the emperor. The monarch's chief advisor, the machiavellian strategist Cāṇakya, the inspirer of the famous *Artha-śāstra,* was converted to become a pious Jain figure in the Jain popular stories collected by Hemacandra *(Pariśiṣṭaparvan* 8.194-469). Whether these—seemingly improbable— alliances really occurred, what is certain is that in the reign of Candragupta's grandson, Aśoka (reigned 269-232 BC), the empire continued to openly favour the Śramaṇas and their movements. Although the emperor Aśoka is associated with the promotion of Buddhism, and some Buddhist legends tell of the persecutions of Nirgranthas (Lamotte 1958: 268), the fact is that during his mandate all forms of religion were tolerated and even encouraged. Aśoka made generous donationsto all religious formations. Most probably, at the beginning, he favoured Ājīvaka, emulating his father Bindusāra. Later, he went on to sponsor Buddhism (and this was surely his preferred religion) not as a "convert", but as a tolerant ruler. What is referred to in his edicts as *dharma* do not have the typical features of Buddhism. This *dharma* takes up a position between Buddhism, Jainism and Brāhmaṇism/Hinduism. It is a genuinely suprapersonal, universal *dharma,* and was engraved upon pillars throughout the territory (Smith 1909: 9-10). In a sense, like a modern political leader, Aśoka could do without Brāhmaṇical authority, since the *dharma* that legitimised him was beyond any affiliation. His system included the principle of royal law *(rājadharma),* conceived in terms of a paternalist, protector state, and the Buddhist principle of "conquest through *dharma"* in opposition to conquest through war. The emperor wished to follow the classical Indian pattern of the universal monarch *(cakravartin)* in its highest sense. In this way, during Aśoka's reign the country benefited from a large number of public works (hospitals, canalisation, wells, etc.). His ethics inculcated respect for the elderly, for the Śramaṇas and Brāhmaṇas, charity for the less fortunate, the principles of truth, humility, purity, and non-violence towards living beings. Indeed it has only been from his reign onward that we can speak of "India" as a political entity.

Thanks to Aśoka's just and even-handed rule, Buddhism, Jainism and Ājīvaka extended throughout North India. However, the Cheda-sūtras, texts that may even post-date the Maurya dynasty, delimited a geographic area whose limits Jain ascetics should not cross, under peril of entering into the worlds of the barbarians (Mlecchas). The Sūtras mark as a limit the region of Aṅga in the East, the city of Kauśāmbī in the South, Sthuṇā to the West and Kuṇāla in the North. This means that, beyond this area, Jainism would have been very marginal. This area covers approximately the same regions as those "visited" by Mahāvīra: all of the present-day state of Bihar, good part of Uttar Pradesh, as well as some of Jharkhand and Bengal. We are still, then, in the Gangetic Valley. Thus, there are reasons to think, with Paul Dundas (2003: 135), that early Jainism did not receive any significant royal patronage.

Aśoka's son was blind, so that control of the empire passed to his grandchildren. If Daśaratha, who ruled over the eastern portion, showed a certain preference for the Ājīvikas (to whom he gave the caves of Barābar), Jains maintain that Aśoka's other grandson, Samprati, favoured the expansion of Jain doctrine throughout the Centre and South of the continent. According to his sources, Samprati ruled over the eastern portions from Ujjain, today in Madhya Pradesh, advised at all times by his tutor Suhastin, one of the great masters of ancient Jainism. During his reign, Jainism became strong in Avanti. It is said that in the capital, Ujjain, there were 500 retreats for ascetics *(Āvaśyaka-cūrṇi* 2.196; cited in J. Jain 1947: 422). The legends say that Samprati was very liberal with the Śramaṇas, prohibited the sacrifice of animals, fed the needy, had many monuments to be built (J. Jain 1947:469) and, like Aśoka with Buddhism, he caused Jainism to expand throughout Gujarat, Kashmir, Maharashtra and the Deccan. However, Paul Dundas (2006: 394) has styled Jainism from 3rd century BC to 4th century CE as a "nonimperial" religion.

JAINISM IN BENGAL AND ORISSA

Jainism also became solidly implanted in the lower Gangetic Valley. In the 7th century, the Chinese pilgrim Xuanzang observed that Nirgranthas formed the most numerous sect in Puṇḍravarddhana *(Da Tang xiyou-ji* 10 [Beal: II, 195]), a region identified with the East of Bihar and the West of Bengal. From there, Jainism spread into Orissa (Kaliṅga). An inscription by king Khāravela of Kaliṅga, dating around the 1st century BC, shows that Jainism was already honoured in the court. The king had numerous sleeping quarters hollowed out of the rock on Mount Udayagiri for Jain ascetics. Once again, Xuanzang furnishes eloquent details from the 7th century. At that time, the Buddhist pilgrim noted that Nirgranthas were in a majority in Orissa *(Da Tang xiyou-ji* 10 [Beal: II, 208]). The presence of Jainism in Orissa was still considerable in the 16th century.

12. THE SCHISM IN JAINISM

THE GREAT DROUGHT

The very first centuries in the history of the monastic community are truly mysterious. We have lists of masters and we know some of the deeds associated with dynasties, but we still find ourselves within the realm of legend admixed with the historical record.

Just as in most Indie traditions, Jainism has been articulated by a chain of masters, known in India as *paramparā.* Spiritual authority does not reside in any Church or clerical hierarchy, but rather in a lineage that goes back to the *tīrthaṅkara.* The task of orally transmitting the Jina's teachings followed a path that tradition sums up as follows. From the spoken word of Gautama and Sudharman, the teachings were passed on to Jambūsvāmin. These latter three are termed omniscient *(kevalins)* because they attained liberation in their own lifetime. From Jambū the teachings passed on down through four generations of masters until reaching Bhadrabāhu (4th-3rd centuries BC)—seventh in the line of succession from Mahāvīra. The leaders of these generations received the title of "awakened ones versed in the complete teachings" *(śruta-kevalins).*

According to the Digambara persuasion, Bhadrabāhu was the last *śruta-ke-valin,* one who possessed the mastery of all the teachings preached by Mahāvīra (Pūrvas, Aṅgas). This is an important historic and doctrinal issue, because under his leadership the seeds of division first made their appearance.

There is some consensus in that Bhadrabāhu was the master of Candragup-ta, the first emperor of the Maury a dynasty. A persistent Digambara tradition tells that Candragupta ended up renouncing the throne and retiring with Bhadrabāhu to the sanctuary of Shravanabelgola, in the Deccan. Legend has it that they both undertook the sacred fasting unto death *(sallekhanā).* It is possible, just as Jain tendencies maintain, that as a result of a long drought and famine (perhaps by a degree of political chaos as well) the community was forced to split into two large groups. Recall, that renunciants lived off the charity of lay persons. In cases of food shortage they would be the first ones to suffer, in which case it makes sense to assume that they opted to minimise the impact and one group migrated to the Deccan (approximately Maharashtra, Karnataka, and Andhra Pradesh) looking for new forms of subsistence. Bhadrabāhu led the group that went South. The group which stayed in the North was left in the hands of his disciple Sthūlabhadra.

In Bhadrabāhu's absence, Sthūlabhadra convened a council or assembly of masters in Pāṭaliputra, the Mauryan capital. This must have been around 300 BC, although experts question the historical evidence for this meeting. The object of this council was to organise the orally transmitted teachings. Sthūlabhadra collected together all the material into eleven Bodies (Angas), but left the 12th, the most important one, unfinished. This would have contained 14 Ancient teachings (Pūrvas), the direct teachings of Mahāvīra and Pārśva. According to some sources, some emissaries were sent to seek out Bhadrabāhu, but they only managed to obtain fragments of the Pūrvas. In Hemacandra's opinion *(Pariśista-parvan* 9.55-113), Bhadrabāhu wanted to transmit part of the teachings personally. Having transmitted ten of the fourteen Pūrvas, noticing that Sthūlabhadra used the knowledge for magical purposes, refused to teach him the four remaining Pūrvas. At all events, it is clear that Bhadrabāhu was not present at the council. We know that a few centuries later, this 12th *aṅga* which contained the fourteen Pūrvas disappeared forever. It was known as the *Dṛṣṭivāda.* In Jainism, then, it is recognised that its tradition, scripturally speaking, contains substantial gaps. The fact is that without Pūrvas there can be no possible liberation.

TWO APPROACHES

From then on, two tendencies within Jainism went on evolving in parallel and taking root in local subcultures. The southern tendency, which was detectably more strict in its practices, ended up feeling shocked by the northern group's lack of rigour. Not only did they not accept the authority of the eleven Aṅgas and of the incomplete *Dṛṣṭivāda* from the council of Pāṭaliputra, but they also vigorously opposed a practice that they considered highly improper: the use of clothes by the ascetics.

It is probable that there would have always been a certain conflict with respect to the issue of nudity. Let us remember that tradition says that Pārśva did not insist on it with his followers, and Mahāvīra, even if he himself imposed it, would relax this rule during the monsoon period. In fact some passages of the *Ācārāṅga-sūtra* (1.6.3.1-2) presuppose nudity, while various places in the *Uttarādhyayana* (2.12) imply the use of clothes. Most likely, the separation came about gradually. Perhaps the stories about the drought emerged at a later date to help explain the divergences, but in any case there are no reasons to doubt the truth of the matter—as it already appears in the *Āvaśyaka-cūrṇi.* We have no knowledge of any sudden break at any given moment or place, but we do know about eight minor splits or schisms *(nihnavas).*

Śvetāmbara tradition affirms that, before his enlightenment, Mahāvíra had to face a first threat of schism, brought about by his son-in-law Jamāli. The attempt was not successful. In the following centuries there were various different heresies or deviations, none of which prospered. Although we might doubt about the historical actuality of these stories, all this indicates that there was tension within the community.

The real *de facto* split took three or four centuries to become openly recognised. In fact, almost everybody accepts that on returning from Deccan, Bhadrabāhu (who went naked) led the entire order for some years. He was followed by Sthūlabhadra (who wore clothes). The next master Mahāgiri again opted for nudity. In all probability, the Jain ascetics of this period are the famous gymnosophists that Alexander the Great's troops came across on their campaign in India. If this is true, complete nakedness would have been an established fact by around 320 BC. The next *pontifex* was Suhastin (3rd century BC), the emperor Samprati's tutor. Under his leadership, the order's numbers increased considerably, but the leaders who came after were scarcely able to maintain unity. All these "second generation" masters (by this time only partially versed in the teachings) are known by the honorific title of "elders" *(sthaviras)*. Finally, around the year 80 CE, the great division came to pass. The Jain community split into two large tendencies or persuasions, two traditions or spiritual families, all that is included in the Sanskrit term *saṃpradāya:* Śvetāmbara and Digambara Jainism. The names make explicit reference to their first and main point of discrepancy: *wearing clothes* as against *nudity.* Those dressed in white or "white-clad" *(śvetāmbaras)* must have been in the majority in the North [see FIG. 12], and those who went unclad or "sky-clad" *(digambaras),* in the South [see FIG. 11]. Each tradition has its own explanation of the split.

THE BHOṬIKAS

According to Śvetāmbaras, halfway through the 1st century, the respected master Vajrasena was responsible for the community. It is said that, encouraged by a despicable self-initiated monk named Śivabhūti (in reality an arrogant warrior who must have done no more than stay one night in a retreat) Vajrasena formed the Bhoṭika heretic sect, with the aim of re-establishing the—by now-impracticable path of the *jinas (jinakalpa).* In time, the Bhoṭikas became the unclothed Digambaras.

THE ARDHAPHĀLAKAS

Of course, Digambaras have a different version of the matter. One of the explanations for how the deplorable practices of the Śvetāmbaras came to be institutionalised is told by Harisena (10th century). He says that during the famine of the times of Bhadrabāhu certain monks in the northwest were incapable of subsisting via the Digambara method of asking for food—standing with the palms extended, limited to only one meal a day, in only one place. Their lay followers persuaded them to use shallow begging bowls to collect food from different houses—the Śvetāmbara method. One night, a naked monk while on his begging round called at a pregnant woman's house. His stark nakedness frightened her to such an extent that it brought on a miscarriage. In view of such a tragedy, Hariṣena recounts that the lay people proclaimed:

> "O Sages, as long as this drought lasts you cannot practice your vows [of nudity and eating from one's joined palms] properly Therefore for the duration of this calamity you should visit the households at night covering yourself with a piece of cloth *[ardhaphālaka]* held in your left arm and the begging bowl in the right. You may undertake the necessary expiation when normal times return" (cited in Jaini 1991:44).

The fact is that these monks maintained these lax customs, and in time they became known as "those who wear a partial piece of cloth" *(ardhaphālakas),* meaning partially dressed, partially naked. According to Digambaras, these Ardhaphālakas in due course bécame the Śvetāmbaras. At the same time, the Digambaras, remained in the Deccan, led by Viśākha, a direct disciple of Bhadrabāhu, strictly keeping to the rule of nakedness.

THE SCHISM

However, the truth is that the aforementioned Ardhaphālakas occupied an intermediate stage between what would later be the two great Digambara and Śvetāmbara tendencies. We have evidence in Mathura of *jinas* depicted carrying one piece of cloth in their left hand, just as the Ardhaphālakas were supposed to have done. These Ardhaphālakas would almost certainly have been the predecessors of yet a third distinct group, the Yāpanīya [see pages 226-228], which continued to go naked but, for reasons unknown, used a cloth in the Ardhaphālaka style when they were in public (Jaini 2000: 297-312).

Philological and historical research has shown that none of these versions are very old. Experts say the *de facto* division would have taken centuries in coming about, at least until the council of Vallabhī (5th century), which was an exclusively Śvetāmbara event. In fact, no text before the 3rd century mentions the name *digambara* or *śvetāmbara.* The first clothed statue of a *tīrthaṅkara,* an unmistakable manifestation of Śvetāmbara Jainism, is a Ṛṣabha from Mathura, which also goes back to the 5th century. It is only from this date on that a schism in Jainism can be said to exist.

This was expected. When Jainism went on expanding, the means of communication between the renunciant groups became more problematic. As there has never been a Jain Church, or not even a central authority that controls practices or dogmas, there would possibly have been flexibility with respect to certain issues. The combinations of different factors and sensibilities ended up crystallising into a series of differences.

Although Digambaras and Śvetāmbaras have turned their backs on each other for centuries (especially, at a monastic level, where the followers of both tendencies did not recognise their religious rivals as genuine ascetics), their dogmatic differences have not been all that great, in retrospect. Moreover, when it comes to refuting rival viewpoints, it is surprising to find that their methods and arguments are similar, if not identical. This issue deserves further consideration. In Christian tradition, all divisions, sectarian disputes, and divergence have arisen from doctrinal discrepancy, but in India matters do not necessarily work like that. Doctrinal issues are usually subordinate to ritual and ascetic practices. In other words, the differences between Śvetāmbaras and Digambaras centre as much or more on manners of practice than dogma, properly speaking.

THE ISSUE OF NAKEDNESS

There is unanimity on one issue. Digambaras and Śvetāmbaras accept the fact that Mahāvīra was a naked ascetic *(acelaka Śramaṇa).* The same goes for the *gaṇadharas* and of the earliest followers up until Jambū. That is why monks of the earliest generations were referred to as *jina*-like *(jinakalpins).* The main characteristic of the path of *the jinas (jinakalpa)* was its reclusive nature. That is to say, the monks were naked anchorites with or without disciples, but they were not obliged to follow monastic rules or to involve themselves in worldly affairs, such as preaching the doctrine. Both tendencies agree that the path of the *jinakalpins* came to an end with Jambū, the last person to attain liberation in this world. Since then, the only way possible for humanity has been the path of the elders *(sthavirakalpa),* the most advisable way in a period of spiritual decline. Following monastic rules and obedience to the masters now becomes compulsory. One of the duties during these times is to propagate the teachings and initiate disciples. Up to this point all are agreed, but it is from here on that divergences arise.

The first discrepancy, and by far the most visible and important one, concerns nudity in religious life. This is an aspect with enormous practical repercussions.

THE DIGAMBARA POSITION

According to Digambaras, there is no reason not to follow the model of nudity as it was preached by *the jinakalpins... and* the *sthavirakalpins.* They accept that we find ourselves a mid the Sorrowful Age and that now there are no omniscient sages on the face of the Earth who live the life of anchorites as they did, but that does not imply that they should abandon nudity. For Digambaras, nudism is a *sine qua non* condition to attain liberation. Accordingly, the representations of *tīrthaṅkaras* in Digambara temples do not wear clothes [see FIGS. 1,32].

The background for this would be the renunciation of wealth and possessions *(aparigraha),* even rags. With the exemptions of a little brush with which the ascetic sweeps his path clear of diminutive creatures and a water bowl for his personal hygiene, the Digambara ascetic does not possess anything. Nudity has become the hallmark *(liṅga)* of the Digambara mendicant lifestyle. It is obvious that Digambaras sought to follow in the footsteps of Mahāvīra and his examples. The Jina himself had declared that the lack of clothes brought one closer to Jain precepts *(Ācārāṅga-sūtra* 1.6.2.3). What is more, the ascetic who lives naked is he who permanently shows that he is free of temptation from women.

The first author to show that a controversy on these lines existed was the Digambara mystic Kundakunda (2nd century). This is how he put it, as quoted by one of his commentators:

> "In the path of he Jina [i.e., in the Jaina mendicant order], the acceptable ascetic requisites are said to be the emblem consisting of the physical form in which one was bom, namely, total nudity" (in Jaini 1991: 146).

For Kundakunda, one becomes a Nirgrantha on renouncing all types of inner and outer attachment. The naked monk transcends even the smallest sign of pride-even in his clothes—and of shame—wearing clothes implies residual sexual desire, expressed through the concept of shame *(lajjā).* Obviously, nakedness does not necessarily imply the overcoming of desire, but wearing clothes does always indicate the lingering presence of desire.

The case is that Digambaras have always dressed in "air", at least up until the arrival of the Muslims in India, around the 11th century. When the Islamic authorities forbade nudism, Digambaras had no choice but to accept certain exemptions with due expiation.

THE ŚVETĀMBARA POSITION

The first in counteracting Kundakunda's arguments was the Śvetāmbara master Jinabhadra (6th century). In his *Viśeṣāvaśyaka-bhāṣya* he put up a spirited defence of wearing clothes and the ascetics' begging bowls.

It is quite feasible that Mahāvīra did not impose nakedness on his mendicants, perhaps in deference to Pārśva. There is no doubt that there was some relaxation of this rule during the rainy season, and that is what the most "liberal" Śvetāmbara thinking defends. Such thinkers accept that the path of nudism of the *jinas* was a superior way to reach liberation, but consider it to be totally impractical in modern times. To follow the path of the *sthavirakalpins,* the use of clothes is necessary. Certainly, it avoids scandalising anyone. Thus, Śvetāmbaras are suspicious of Digambara nudity and these days consider this practice to be in appropriate.

As the community went on leaving Mahāvīra and the *jinakalpins* behind in time, and the sensation of participating in the Sorrowful Age took hold of its members, Śvetāmbaras did not even feel the need to eliminate the scriptural references to nakedness. This justification is very similar to the practices known as *kalivarjya* in Brāhmaṇical texts, i.e., those practices that were once legitimate but were disallowed in times of degeneration *(kali-yuga)*. As time went on, Śvetāmbaras became more radical in their outlook, eventually saying that wearing clothes was an integral part of religious life.

THE SPIRITUAL LIBERATION OF WOMEN

The next point of discordance has to do with the spiritual progress of women. The debate centres specifically on the possibility or not of women attaining liberation *(strīmokṣa)*. The issue has been an important point of disagreement between Digambaras and Śvetāmbaras over the centuries and has produced dealings and commentaries which are unique of their kind.

THE DIGAMBARA POSITION

Digambaras maintain that liberation in this life is impossible for women. They go on to say that a woman *tīrthaṅkara* (Malli) never existed, that Mahāvīra was never married and his embryo was not transferred to the womb of Trisalā, his mother.

Commenting on the true nature of renunciation, Kundakunda warns:

> "[A nun] eats ony one meal a day and wears a single piece of cloth...
>
> According to the Teaching of the Jina, a person wearing clothes cannot attain *mokṣa*... The path of *mokṣa* consists of nudity; all other paths are wrong paths.
>
> Women have no purity of mind; they are by nature fickle-minded. They have menstrual flows. [Therefore] there is no meditation for them free from anxiety" (in Jaini 1991:35).

With these words, Kundakunda rules out any possibility of liberation for a soul incarnated in the body of a woman. The reason is clearly connected with the issue of nudity. As they cannot go naked, nuns cannot have the rank of a full mendicant and, therefore, cannot aspire to liberation in their present life. They are at the same level as any Śvetāmbara.

However, Kundakunda also insists on the biological aspect. He affirms that women do not possess a pristine diamantine body or the necessary capacity of concentration for reaching the highest levels of meditation that lead to liberation. Moreover, as it is said in his *Pravacanasāra* (224.12), their bodies are inhabited by millions of microscopic beings, which they inevitably hurt. Although not everybody agrees in attributing these ideas to Kundakunda (Dundas 1992: 242), it is clear that this has been the classical Digambara position.

So, just as women's volubility impedes them from the highest goal, their weakness also impedes them, unlike men, from descending to the seventh hell.

Indeed, both Jain tendencies accept that women cannot be reborn in the lowest of hells. According to Digambara Jainism there is a certain correlation between these two extremes, as to be able to reach these destinations one requires the same intensity of thought and action. Just as there is a positive *dhyā-na,a* pure meditation *(śukladhyāna* [see pages 499-501]) that leads to liberation, there also exists a negative *dhyāna,* what is known as cruel meditation *(raudrad-hyāna* [see page 499]), which automatically sends one to the seventh hell. Therefore, according to Prabhācandra (10th century) the incapacity of women to descend to the seventh hell is proof of their incapacity to reach the Siddha-loka (Jaini 1991: 120-123). This impediment in developing the most extraordinary states is the reason why, according to Digambaras, there are no women *tīrthaṅkaras* or *cakravartins.*

To reinforce their positions and respond to the criticism from Śvetāmbaras, authors such as Jayasena (10th century) fiercely criticised female anatomy. Misogyny is exaggerated when describing the feminine body as being plagued with millions of minute beings, which perish, for example, in menstruation or by the incessant erotic appetite of women. Sexually speaking, in India women have been considered extremely voracious (Fohr 2006: 159). Because of their very condition, they are an invitation to desire and a species of assassin who will inevitably bring the poor male who comes into contact with them face to face with one hell or another. Just as Padmanabh Jaini (1991: 14) has commented, menstrual cycles are a constant reminder to women that they are sexually desirable. This awareness produces shame and dependence on clothes. Moreover, it makes them fear sexual harassment. For the Digambara thinker Guṇabhadra (9th century), women embodied the direst of provocations:

> "They wrongly call cobras to be poisonous by sight, when it has been clearly seen that by half a glance of women the world is wholly burning. When thou hast turned away from them, they roam about thee in anger. The only poison is women. Do not therefore approach them" *(Ātmānuśāsana* 126).

Admittedly, nowhere do Digambara scriptures deny liberation for women. Moreover, the most sacred Digambara text states clearly that women can attain all levels of spiritual progression and liberation *(Satkhaṇḍāgama-sūtra* 1.92-93; cited in Jaini 1991: 110). How, then, does this square with the traditional Digambara position? The monk Vīrasena (9th century) in his commentary to these passages provides answer:

> "The word *maṇusiṇī* [woman] in the *sūtra* means a man who is characterised as psychologically female" (cited in Jaini 1991: 110).

This issue, which might seems laughable these days, has spawned hundreds of pages of syntactic studies and controversy between Śvetāmbaras and Digambaras.

The interesting thing is that it is conceded that a male with homosexual tendencies would be able to attain liberation whereas a woman would not.

To sum up, the Digambara position establishes that women are inferior in all these respects to men. Although they accept that women can be graced with purity, morality and self-control (Jaini 1991: 176), and may be called nobles *(āryikās),* which is the title conceded to their ascetics, to reach the *summum bonum* they would simply have to be reborn as males.

THE YĀPANĪYA-ŚVETĀMBARA POSITION

The first thinker to counter the Digambara argument was not a Śvetāmbara, nor even Jinabhadra, the fervent defender of ascetics wearing clothes. It was Śākaṭāyana (9th century), a monk who belonged to the Yāpanīya persuasion, a sect in between the Digambara and Śvetāmbara tendencies. Śākatāyana devoted a whole piece, *Strīnirvāṇa-prakaraṇa,* to this topic. Right at the beginning of his exposition he affirms that:

> "There is *nirvāṇa* for women, because, like men, they are fully endowed with the causes [that bring about that condition]. For the cause of *nirvāṇa* is the Three Jewels [see chapter 30], and this is not incompatible with womanhood" *(Strīnirvāṇa-prakaraṇa* 2).

Only right vision, knowledge, and conduct can be the cause of liberation, and the Three Jewels are equally as possible and perfectible in men as in women. This not only concords with the maxim of the philosopher Umāsvāti (accepted both by Digambaras and Śvetāmbaras) that the Three Jewels form the path that leads to liberation *(Tattvārtha-sūtra* 1.1), and that nowhere in the scriptures does it say that women cannot attain *mokṣa (Strīnirvāṇa-prakaraṇa* 49), but in fact the state of the perfect one or liberated one is neither male or female *(Strīnirvāṇa-prakaraṇa* 26).

Availing themselves of Yāpanīya reasoning without completely rejecting the misogynous Digambara line of argument, Śvetāmbaras consider women capable of attaining liberation and following the same spiritual progression as men. Perhaps what must have happened, as Josephine Reynell (1991: 41) has shrewdly observed, was that Śvetāmbaras were perceptive enough to recognise the importance of women in the transmission and maintenance of their religion. Women play a fundamental role in the reproduction of the community [see pages 321-322], but ancient texts like the *Uttarādhyayana-sūtra* (36.52-53) already accepted the spiritual liberation of women:

> "Ten hermaphrodites reach, at the same time, perfection, twenty women, one hundred and eight men; four householders, ten heterodox, and one hundred and eight orthodox monks".

Moreover, as we have already seen, Śvetāmbaras maintain that the 19th *tīrthaṅkara,* Malli, was a woman, and they also consider that the first person in this cosmic cycle to reach liberation was Marudevī, Ṛṣabha's mother. The 17th century authority Meghavijaya exclaims: how is it possible that the noble mother of the *jina,* she who even the gods come to worship for her purity and compassion, who as queen brings incomparable happiness in bearing the *jina,* should not, as sublime as she was, be worthy of *mokṣa* (cited in Jaini 1991: 185).

For Śvetāmbaras there is no relationship whatsoever between the impossibility of being so intensely sinful as to be reborn in the seventh hell and the possibility of attaining liberation. When all said and done, this shows the goodness of women, who generally speaking have a less violent nature than men, as demonstrated by their little inclination towards weapons. Furthermore, countering Digambara reasoning that one cannot find women who are versed in *mantras* and scriptures, the master Guṇaratna (14th-15th centuries) argues that this line of argument goes against the omniscients who preferred to remain silent and not preach, and even so attained *mokṣa* (cited in Jaini 1991: 155). They accept that the female body teems with microscopic beings, but consider that the latter's deaths are not brought about intentionally, and so do not constitute an obstacle to women's progress.

That does not mean to say that there is equality in practical terms, as nuns (whether Digambaras or Śvetāmbaras) are subordinate to a male master. We shall be looking at this in the next chapter. The Śvetāmbara position in doctrinal and practical terms is identical to that of Buddhists. There is nothing that impedes women from attaining *nirvāṇa,* but in what refers to religious life and clerical organisation their position is clearly disfavourabled. Just as Padmanabh Jaini (1991:23) has observed, neither Buddhists nor Śvetāmbaras have seen any contradiction at this level, as women's position within the religious community simply reflected their social position.

As nakedness plays no part in Śvetāmbara practice, the nakedness issue does not arise. For Śvetāmbaras, clothes are, like the little brush or the water dish, props to be used along the spiritual path and in no way can be considered as possessions *(parigraha)* (Jaini 1991: 185). True non-attachment necessarily comes from within. Non-attachment does not refer to material things themselves but to the mental attachment to them. For that reason, Megahavijaya states:

> "The women under dispute [i.e., the nuns] are worthy of attaining *mokṣa* in that very life;
>
> because they are capable of undertaking specific kinds of austerities and the minor vows *[aṇuvratas]* of the layperson.
>
> Whosoever is so [capable] is similar to the other, namely the male human being, who is admitted to be capable of attaining *mokṣa*" (in Jaini 1991: 185).

* * *

It is quite possible that these differences derive from the social implications that an order of naked women would necessarily have. Of all the statues of the *jinas,* there is only one known representation of Malli with breasts and long hair, and no Śvetāmbara temple represents her as such. Turning to the most ancient Digambara texts, we have already seen that they affirmed that nuns as well as monks could attain liberation. It was probably the social impossibility of feminine nudity which lead to Digambara attitudes being so radical. However, none of the Digambara texts explicitly prohibit women from taking the vow of nudity. Neither do they specify why an order of unclad women is not allowed. And this proves to be a vital issue, since nakedness was in the Digambaras' case deemed indispensable for attaining *nirvāṇa.* What then? Surely, the reason was the idea of female nudity in public. Except for some rare instances of Śaiva *yoginīs* this has been and still is unacceptable in Indian society. These days it is a question of public decency; in olden times it was a question of order. According to Digambaras, a naked woman would incite the loss of control in others, and would end up being raped sooner or later, which shows the difficulty involved in a woman's taking the ascetic path. This position is confirmed by Brāhmaṇical texts like the *Artha-śāstra,* the *Kāma-sūtra* or the *Manu-smṛti* (Jamison 2006: 209). Since there cannot be two ascetic paths, women would have to wear clothes but generate enough spiritual worth to able to be reborn as naked males and aspire to liberation. These days, even Digambara nuns themselves accept that the female body impedes them from seriously advancing along the spiritual path and need to reborn as males, as N. Shāntā (1985: 644) has demonstrated in his superb work. For Śvetāmbaras, the only women who cannot join the order are those who are pregnant. Apart from this detail, there is nothing against the full and complete asceticism, enlightenment and liberation of women.

It is important to point out, however, that what we have here are paradig-matically dogmatic issues. Where traditions are unanimous in accepting that no one since Jambūsvāmin would be able to attain liberation on this earth in this present era, the question of women's spiritual liberation becomes essentially theoretical. Just as Shāntā (1985: 640) has shown, we should be clear that the Digambara exclusion from liberation is only temporary, since all those, male or female, who lead a correct ascetic way of life would attain *mokṣa* in a future life.

THE NATURE OF THE *JINA*

The third difference between both tendencies has to do with their conceptions of the nature of the *jina.* We have already had the occasion to touch upon some of the viewpoints.

For Digambaras, such a being is not involved in worldly affairs, nor does his organism maintain its normal bodily functions. In the moment of reaching omniscience, the body of the *kevalin* undergoes miraculous changes. His gross body goes through a metamorphosis, transforming into an utterly pure body. The impure fluids (urine, semen, excretion, mucus, etc.) are transformed into a lactose substance. The omniscient one now does not speak, eat, defecate, sleep, etc., since he has transcended all basic instincts (Jai-ni 2000: 293-294). He teaches through magical, divine sound.

Śvetāmbaras, with their consistently more human approach to the Jina, consider that these beings, while being sublime, pursue the normal human activities.

OTHER DIFFERENCES

A fourth point of dissension has much to do with the sacred texts. Although not all Śvetāmbara groups have the same body of scriptures, there is unanimity in accepting the first canon compiled in Pāṭaliputra, which would have contained portions of the original teachings of Mahāvīra. In the council of Vallabhī (5th century), when the transmitted material was written down, the Śvetāmbara community became clearly aware of their peculiarity. Perhaps this fact played a greater role in the final schism than the issue of nudity. Digambaras, for their part, firmly maintain that the old texts were all lost forever. We will dedicate chapter 22 in its entirety to Jain texts and scriptures.

Lastly, there are some differences with regards to procedures and utensils employed by ascetics. Digambaras do not have a begging bowl, they receive food in the palms of their hands and only eat once a day. Apart from clothes, Śvetāmbaras carry a bowl and can have two or three meals a day. We shall be looking at monastic etiquette in more detail later on [see pages 438-443].

Apart from these, and a few other minor details, generally speaking their practices are the same.

13. THE ASCETIC COMMUNITY

INITIATION

Jainism makes it very clear, especially in its more ancient formulations, that in aspiring to emancipation one must follow the path of the male or female ascetics *(sādhus, sādhvīs)* who have renounced the world. Although in theory it is possible for a householder to attain liberation, as in the case of king Bharata, or even for a non-Jain (Stevenson 1915: 170-171), one would have had had at all events the perfect saintliness of a Jain renunciant. The path can prove to be extremely arduous if one does not join the Jain order. Invariably, that means initiation *(dīkṣā)* first as a novice, later as an ascetic, and directing all one's acts and thoughts to the goal of liberation *(nirvāṇa, mokṣa).* As this goal is not likely to be reached by the end of this lifetime, at least one can lay the foundations to reach it in another future one, maybe on another island in the Middle World.

The first thing a candidate must do is make a petition of initiation to a master *(ācārya)* or a female spiritual preceptor *(guruṇī).* The name, which is applied to initiation *(dīkṣā),* was already used in the context of Vedic ritual. It described the preliminary purification practices (fasting, meditation, and continence) of the one who would carry out the sacrifice as well as that person's state of purity, ready to offer sacrifices. As Jan Gonda (1965: 337) said, with *dīkṣā* one obtained a new birth and a higher state of existence. Not surprisingly, then, renunciant orders not only adopted the name, but also some of the features of Vedic *dīkṣā.* Nevertheless, in this chapter we shall be leaving aside the historic account and concentrating on the present functioning of the renunciant community.

Who can be initiated into monastic Jainism? The rules for admission are very similar for Śvetāmbaras and Digambaras. They are also comparable to those of Buddhism. Candidates must be more than eight years old. They must not be ex-convicts. Also, people with physical or mental disabilities are not admitted either, nor are pregnant women or women with small children. A master or mistress of the ascetic community must approve the candidature, which similarly needs family consent. The local lay community (which finances the ceremony) must also be consulted. In principle, the order is open to all castes, although people from very low castes are not likely to be accepted among Digambaras in the Deccan.

There are various reasons for renunciation and initiation. It could be an intense spiritual calling, the example of someone in the family, the attraction of the monastic community, the need to escape from a difficult economic situation, advice from a spiritual preceptor, an unbearable social or family situation, and so forth. Some texts even admit that there are those whose desire initiation might be due to feelings of hate, illness, or to lack of respect. It is clear that the initial motives may not always be spiritual. However, N. Shāntā (1985: 448) mentions statistics on the motives for which one hundred women decided to undergo initiation and the figures speak for themselves: 59% for entirely spiritual reasons; 11% out of a desire to increase their knowledge with a spiritual aim; 10% out of the desire to serve the community; 3% to avoid marriage; and 17% to find a refuge in society. At all events, Paul Dundas (1991: 132) points out, what is significant for the tradition is effectively what is done *after* becoming an ascetic.

Sociologically speaking, the majority of ascetics come from existing Jain families for whom *sādhus* and *sādhvīs* have a special significance and authority. Many belong to merchant or artisan castes. Most ascetics are of rural origin, which is odd, bearing in mind that the Jain community is the most urbanised in all India. Nevertheless, not an insignificant number of ascetics come from non-Jain families.

Technically, full initiation *(mahā-dīkṣā)* must be preceded by a period of lesser renunciation or initiation *(bhagavatī-dīkṣā).* During the novitiate, which lasts from a few weeks to a few months, the candidate shares in the way of life of the ascetics, except as regards meals, where she or he will continue to eat with laypersons. Those who stay at this level and do not opt for complete initiation are, for example, the Digambara *kṣullakas* (fern, *kṣullikās)* or *ailakas,* who wear some articles of clothing and who are considered as being something like semi-ascetics or very advanced laity.

From the very first day, the novice is under the tutorship of a master, who will begin to instruct them in some of the Prakrit languages in which the sacred texts are written and perhaps also in Sanskrit. In effect, during the apprenticeship these studies have the nature of a trial period. It is the determination of the candidate that is evaluated. Depending on the order, some important *sūtra,* usually short and clear such as the *Daśavaikālika,* will be taught. Full initiation into the order follows this period. However, tradition bestows much more importance on the first ceremony than on the second one. We shall thus concentrate on the minor initiation.

The admission rite can vary depending on the different tendency or sub-school. Nevertheless, the basic scheme is reasonably similar in all cases.

Somewhat contrary to the spirit of renunciation, in the week before initiation the candidate personally invites and entertains members of the family— decked out in her or his best clothes. Equally, the neighbourhood invites the novice to eat. The model is identical to marriage ceremonies. The candidate usually fasts the day before the initiation. The auspicious day, previously determined by an astrologer, comes at last and they go to the chosen place agreed with the local lay community.

In many cases, the candidate is transported with all pomp and ceremony on horseback or on an elephant to the temple or retreat [see FIGS .13,14]. The male novice wears his best clothes while female novices have their hair loose and wear all their jewellery and maybe even the sari they used on their wedding day. While the crowd advances, sweets and coins are thrown which the poor who accompany the procession hasten to catch. With this gesture, they emulate the year before the initiation of Mahāvīra, in which he distributed his wealth amongst the subjects of his kingdom. Obviously, the elephant emulates the palanquin in which Mahāvīra was carried by Indra himself. From a sociological point of view, the paraphernalia and pomp of these initiations serve to give the group a clear sense of power and influence (Singhi 1991:150-151). For Śvetāmbaras, the initiation ceremony of an ascetic is a major transcendental event and a formidable expense. In some cases, the family or caste priest (usually a Brāhmaṇa of lesser rank) is asked to paint auspicious signs on the novice, in a similar fashion to the way *jinas* are decorated in the temples. Female novices usually have their hands and feet adorned with henna, again in an identical way to weddings.

Initiations are always performed before an image of a *tīrthaṅkara,* or in a temple *(mandira),* or marquee *(maṇḍapa)* specially erected for this unique occasion.

The actual ritual is very simple. Novices recite a *sūtra* or *bhakti* (which is the name given to certain Digambara hymns) and prostrate themselves in the classical way before their master. They then address the public and ask for general forgiveness. The ceremony maintains the ancient custom of painfully pulling out the novice's hair in five handfuls *(keśa-loca),* although in some cases they shave their head leaving five tufts to be gently pulled out [see FIG. 15]. This practice is identical for men and women, and is not found in any other re-nunciant religion in India (except in the ancient order of the Ājīvikas) and most certainly is intended to test the candidate's resolve and dedication. Buddhists also symbolise renunciation by shaving their head, but the pulling out from the roots perfectly illustrates the difference between monastic Jainism and Buddhism. These rites are a clear parallel to adulthood rites in many cultures— those, more particularly, that include an ordeal. From that day on, the ascetics do not grow their hair longer than "a cow's hair". This means shaving every 15 days (except during the rainy season) or every six months for female ascetics.

Following that, the novice asks his family's permission to go ahead with the initiation. Among Digambaras, it is the master who approaches the members of the family and other ascetics with the question: "Can she or he be allowed to take the initiation?" The crowd gives its assent. At that moment, the master has the ascetic repeat the vow of equanimity (*sāmāyika)* for life [see FIG. 16]. The aspirants are then admitted into the order. Initiations usually end with the *namaskāra-mantra,* the most sacred of Jain litanies [see below], and devotional chants.

The initiation of renunciation also implies giving up one's lay name and, consequently, any socio-spiritual class *(varṇa)* or caste *(jāti)* previously held. The ascetic's name would probably follow that of the master's lineage (finishing in *-vijaya, -kīrti, -candra, -nandi,* etc.), thus establishing graphically the continuity of the lineage. Only in the Śvetāmbara sub-order of the Sthānakavāsīs, do they retain the lay name. Apart from just a few items, which we shall mention below, from this day on the initiate will not possess anything for the rest of their life.

MONASTIC ORGANISATION

As we have seen, the whole of the Jain religious community is termed an assembly (*saṃgha),* a term which is also used in Buddhism. In the same way, as the latter, Jains in the broadest sense include the lay community, thereby expressly accepting the intimate relationship between both sides of the *saṃgha.* Here, we shall concentrate on the ascetic side.

Although the ideal of the solitary ascetic is still highly esteemed, for reasons of safety and order the religious community has since ancient times subdivided into distinct units or groups. In the first degree, there are the companies *(gaṇas)* usually made up of three ascetics, who stay together all the time. The itinerant unit is also known as family *(parivāra, kula).* The exception is found among Digambaras who, being so few in numbers, find it hard to form ascetic groups and find it necessary to join up with *kṣullakas, ailakas* or *brahmacārins,* i.e., advanced lay people. At the same time, companies and families affiliate themselves to different sub-orders (*gacchas, saṃghas)* of Śvetāmbara and Digambara Jainism. However, it is organised, the life of a Jain ascetic is one of permanent contact with their masters and companions. There is little space for privacy and solitude. The ties of solidarity among ascetics are usually very pronounced.

From the first day of the initiation the candidate is called a saint, embodier of goodness (*sādhu,* fern, *sādhvī)* or silent one *(muni),* which are the modern equivalent for the old names *nirgrantha* (fern. *nirgranthī)* or *Śramaṇa* (fern. *śramanī).* Traditionally, the novice's master is called *upādhyāya,* a preceptor whose main job consists in teaching the texts of the order. These days there are very few ascetics with this title. Other ranks in disuse are those of elder (*sthavira),* reader (*vācaka)* or company leader (*gaṇadhara, gaṇin).* Among Śvetāmbaras, a title of respect for masters or learned monks is that of *sūri.* Without a doubt, the rank, which occupies the preeminent place, is that of spiritual guide or master (*ācārya),* a title which is also known in Hinduism and Buddhism. It is he who supervises the admission and tutorship of the novice. Usually, the *ācārya* is one of the elder members of the community and the head of a spiritual lineage or company. As it is also generally he who explains the deep meaning of the texts and teachings imparted by the *upādhyāya,* he needs to be someone who is well versed in the doctrine and of maximum spiritual purity. In fact, the master is qualified to make his own interpretation of the scriptures and to choose his successor. For groups of nuns the male *ācārya* designates a female spiritual guide *(guruṇī)* to represent him.

This organisation centred around a master favours the division of the community into different lineages. Every time an *ācārya* or *sūri* has undertaken a reinterpretation of tradition, a new suborder or subdivision is produced within the two main tendencies, Śvetāmbara and Digambara [see chapter 19].

The *ācārya* is also responsible for listening to the ascetics' confessions, and for recommending ways of expiating reprehensible conduct. The rules for deference and modes of address for each member of the community are well stipulated, and carried out to the letter. Prostration before the master, especially during confessions, is compulsory. An object known as "representation of the master" *(sthāpanācārya),* a small stool or tripod made of sandalwood, provides a good example of the importance of the *ācārya.* When the monk places it before himself while praying or to studying, it symbolises his spiritual guide and, indirectly of the tradition that goes back to the *tīrthaṅkara.* This device is unique to the Śvetāmbaras.

Every time a new *ācārya* is chosen in a group, it is a very important event celebrated by the community as a whole, as much by laity as by ascetics. It is equivalent on a monastic scale to the succession to the throne.

Ascetics can choose the *ācārya* or *guruṇī* they wish to guide them. In fact, the candidates make the express petition for initiation to one or other specific master. Once the trial period is over and she or he receives full initiation, they technically go on to be responsible to the master or mistress and not on any central authority. Owing to their itinerant lifestyle, ascetics may take quite a long time in meeting up with the *ācārya* again. Nevertheless, the link between master and disciple remains very strong.

Although the renunciant is always subject to his master, when a *sādhu* or *sādhvī* has gathered a following of disciples (usually when they have reached a certain age and prestige) they can travel with the disciples as their preceptor *(guru)* and live quite independently from the original *ācārya.*

As can be seen, the monastic *saṃgha* is very different from a Church. This feature is typical of South Asian religions, where instead of great religious institutions we find lineages of masters *(guru-paramparā)* or small spiritual refuges *(āśramas)* where the relation between master and disciple *(guru-śisya)* exists.

Peter Flügel's study (2006: 362) on the demographic trends in Jain monas-ticism has shown that the total number of Jain mendicants has increased from 9,222 in 1987 to 11,737 in 1999; an overall growth of almost 27%. Given that the Jains had one of the lowest relative growths of all Indian religions, the divergent growth rates of the mendicants and the lay population indicate an increasing popularity of monastic life. Flügel aptly concludes that, apparently, what we call westernisation and modernisation have not contributed to a decline, but to an increase in the popularity of monasticism among Jains.

THE ORDER OF *SĀDHVĪS*

Śvetāmbara female ascetics are usually given the name of "saints" *(sādhvīs),* the Digambara ones "nobles" *(āryikās),* even if occasionally other names are used.

The female ascetics live apart from the monks in retreats, under the orders of a sort of mother superior *(pravartinī, gaṇinī).* In turn, different groups of *sādhvīs* directed by various superiors from the same order are responsible to an elderly and respected female ascetic *(guruṇī, sādhvī pramukhā),* who is in turn under the control of a male *ācārya.* The role of spiritual master always falls to the *ācārya,* who undertakes the formal initiations of the ascetics, listens to their confessions, resolves the doubts that arise in their studies, directs their itinerant routes and decides the time and place of their settled periods during the rainy season. The relation between *sādhus* and *sādhvīs* replicates the Indian patriarchal pattern where the woman changes to belong to the husband's family and lineage. However, as the *ācārya* will take a different route on his next journey, it could be a very long time, even quite a few years, before the group of nuns meet up with their *ācārya* again. As a result, female ascetics' true relationship is with their *guruṇī.*

Although female Śvetāmbara ascetics are considered to be spiritually equal to males, the *sādhvīs* follow stricter rules than the *sādhus* do, again a reflection of the ultimately patriarchal nature of Indian society and indeed most of religions. It is virtually impossible for a female ascetic to reach the level of *ācārya,* as it is stipulated in texts that they can only become one after 60 years of being initiated—a male ascetic, after only five *(Vyavahāra-sūtra* 7.19-20; cited in Shāntā 1985: 417)—a figure which in any case seems purely theoretical. In all this, we can find a parallel with Buddhism, which in the same way prescribes a series of stricter rules of conduct for nuns, and they are also subject to a male preceptor. Among Digambaras the misogynous strain is more pronounced [see pages 186-187]. Ostracism is particularly felt during the nun's menstruation. Women are prohibited from studying sacred texts while having their periods (considered in India as being very polluting); nor at that time can they enter into temples or take part in any prayers or chants. The nuns, especially Digambara *āryikās,* remain in total silence and reclusion. According to N. Shāntā (1985: 668) *āryikās* and *sādhvīs* both deplore this type of ostracism.

Nevertheless, these asymmetries in temporal power are usually diluted in practice, essentially because the number of female ascetics is triple that of males [see Table 2], a constant factor that seems to have held true throughout the entire history of Jainism. Viewed from within, the discrimination is less marked than it appears. The female ascetics are de facto organised into a parallel and independent system. Only on rare occasions does a group of nuns come across a group of monks—although these days Digambara monks and nuns travel together quite often. Many Śvetāmbara nuns administer vows to lay people, bless them, conduct their ceremonies and preach to them. The texts may say what they like but the *sādhvīs* have a well-deserved autonomy. As the field research of Sherry Fohr (2006: 167) shows, most of the Śvetāmbara nuns do not consider themselves inferior to monks in status or spiritual abilities. Mary Whitney Kelting (2001: 41) arrives at the same conclusion: the actual degree of subordination is far less than the texts suggest. The greater rigidity of the rules is considered a way of safeguarding the nuns' chastity and protecting them. In fact, Lawrence Babb's work on the neo-Hindu Brahmā-Kumarī movement has shown that the life of the female Indian renunciant has a great potential to transform gender relations. For Babb (cited in Laidlaw 1995: 58), the Brahmā-Kumarī movement is an indigenous form of Indian feminism. As can be seen, women also dominate the practice of Jainism in quantitative and qualitative terms at lay level. Despite the misogynist strains of thought in Jain texts—in which women are portrayed as temptresses—most of the nuns interviewed by Sherry Fohr (2006: 170) believed differently: if anyone is more inclined toward sexual activity or misconduct, according to them, it is men.

Perhaps, the most prestigious nuns would be those from the Kharatara-Gaccha Śvetāmbara order, whom one can see preaching and teaching in public with total authority and ease. According to N. Shāntā (1985: 431-432), Sthānakavāsī *sādhvīs* have a more liberal and progressive approach to study. The Terāpanthīs, while being a very strict order, today have a high level of education. By contrast, the Tapā-Gaccha female ascetics [see FIG. 23], the most important Śvetāmbara sub-order of them all, still live in a very unfavourable environment for women's emancipation. Although Digambara nuns [see FIG. 24] are considered an

TABLE 2: Census of Jain ascetics (1999)

Order/Suborder	*sādhus* *munis*	*sādhvls* *āryikās*	Total	
Śvetāmbara Mūrtipūjaka	1,489	5,354	6,843	5,568 Tapā-Gaccha (1996) 252 Añcala-Gaccha(1996) 224 Kharatara-Gac. (1996) 329 Others (1996)
Śvetāmbara Sthānakavāsī	533	2,690	3,223	
Śvetāmbara Terāpanthī	154	557	711	
Digambara	610	350	960	
TOTAL	2,786	8,951	11,737	

inferior class (technically they are only advanced lay women), from the lay Jains' point of view they are as respected and honoured as the Śvetāmbaras. It is clear that the more liberal position of the Śvetāmbaras in terms of women's emancipation has a lot to do with the disproportionate number of Śvetāmbara *sādhvls,* given that there are even fewer Digambara *āryikās* than there are monks. It is precisely amongst the Digambaras that we find a higher proportion of women joining the order after being widowed. But as Sherry Fohr (2006: 174) has shown, it has also been the monastic rules and the strict gender separation—not as stringent in the less organised Digambara sect—which have enabled female renunciation to be considered safe and respectable according to Indian canons.

THE FIVE GREAT VOWS

Some time after the lesser initiation *(bhagavatī-dīkṣā),* the novice takes the major initiation *(mahā-dīkṣā).* In contrast to the pomp and festive atmosphere of the first initiation, this renewal and confirmation of the rank of the renunciant is much more austere. The candidates would have fasted for three days before this. If in the lesser initiation she or he took the vow of equanimity for life, now they perform the swearing of the five great vows *(mahāvratas)* which similarly cannot be broken.

The day that the novice takes the five great vows, she or he goes out to seek alms for the first time. Out of tradition, Śvetāmbaras first go to their family home. Nevertheless, the parents can cede this most highly valued right to wealthy people in the community who are known to pay huge sums of money to have the honour of giving the recently initiated ascetic their first donation of food. The layperson who has the honour of providing it is considered to acquire a fabulous religious merit. This gesture symbolically re-enacts the first occasion on which the renunciant Ṛṣabha, who went on to be the first *jina,* received alms suitable for a Jain saint, from the hands of a layperson. This link between both sections of the Jain community is renewed daily when the monks go out to beg.

THE VOW OF NON-VIOLENCE

The first great vow states:

> "I renounce all killing of living beings, whether subtile or gross, whether movable or immovable. Nor shall I myself kill living beings [nor cause others to do it, nor consent to it]. As long as I live, I confess and blame, repent and exempt myself of these sins, in the thrice [past, present or future] threefold way, in mind, speech, and body" *(Ācārāṅga-sūtra* 2.15.i.1).

In a very strict way, bordering on the obsessive, ascetics must be especially careful to keep this first vow, that of *ahiṃ sā.* Everything revolves around ways to avoid inadvertently hurting living creatures, to the greatest extent possible. If the layperson worries about harming creatures, which have various senses, ascetics must take into account the innumerable beings with only one sense *(ek-endriyas).* It is the ascetic who understands, like Mahāvīra, that these forms are graced with life, that these *jīvas* incarnated in the lowest forms of existence suffer the same as all the others. Where there is sentience and suffering, there is no justification for refusing to take that suffering into consideration. On taking their solemn vow in its total form, ascetics are bound to walk barefoot, and not use any mechanised transport, nor dig the soil so as not to destroy bodies in the earth. They promise not to blow on any flame or extinguish any fire, to protect the beings in fire. They will drink filtered water and will abstain from bathing, swimming, or walking in the rain, to show respect for the lives in water. And they vow not to fan themselves and—some of them—to wear a cloth mask over their mouth out of deference to the beings in the air. Regarding vegetation, ascetics will even avoid walking on grass or touching any kind of plant.

One needs to grasp the effort all this entails. The ascetic's attention is permanently focused on keeping to the way of non-violence. On cultivating nonviolence one is cultivating non-hate, non-hurt, non-harm, non-aggression, and more; in other words, one purifies oneself, halting the inflow of *karma.*

Jainism has been criticised for being contradictory in placing so much attention on respecting the tiniest of living creatures, while on the other hand ignoring the serious problems of society and the scourges of humanity (hunger, illness, war). This, of course, blithely ignores the fact that Jains are responsible for a large number of charitable institutions [see pages 445-446]. Moreover, Jains insist that the solution to the problems needs to take place within each person. Only with internal purification can one bring about social transformation, and it is to this end that ascetics consecrate their lives. At the same time, ascetics forge an absolute identification with all beings through their behaviour. An ascetic is:

> "He who treats living beings as self
> And views them with equanimity...
> Escapes he the bondage of evil deeds.
> Knowledge first and then Compassion"
> *(Daśavaikālika-sūtra* 4.23.9-10).

All lives are *interchangeable,* and the most difficult challenge is to extend nonviolent behaviour to the tiniest of beings, which one can only achieve by taking asceticism to its most rigorous limits. It is not a case of being sensitive to the situation of these beings, but considering them as equal, with radical and absolute equanimity. It is out of knowledge and wisdom that compassion *(dayā)* and respect will spring. This attitude of mind, spirit and action, needs to be communicated, to an extent emulating the *tīrthaṅkaras,* in such a way that the ascetic is devoted to teaching others the sacred doctrine and the path to salvation.

THE VOW OF TRUTHFULNESS

The second great vow states:

> "I renounce all vices of lying speech [arising] from anger or greed or fear or mirth. I shall neither myself speak lies, nor cause others to speak lies, nor consent to the speaking of lies by others. As long as I live [*ditto* as in the first vow]..." *(Ācārāṅga-sūtra* 2.15.ii.1).

With the second great vow the ascetic abstains from all lies, and at the same time is committed to telling the truth *(satya)* always. The ascetic must cultivate moderation, benevolence, gentleness, respect and overcome vanity.

THE VOW OF ABSTENTION FROM STEALING

The third great vow states:

> "I renounce all taking of anything not given, either in a village or a town or a wood, either of little or much, of small or great, of living or lifeless things. I shall neither take myself what is not given, nor cause others to take it, nor consent to their taking it. As long as I live *[ditto* as in the first vow]..." *(Ācārāṅga-sūtra* 2.15.iii.l).

The third great vow concerns not stealing *(asteya),* and means purification from covetousness and avarice, inherent in all intentions to steal. Of course, this also implies non-violence, as all undue appropriation involves some kind of violence. At its most profound, it is affirming that one possesses nothing and there is no external object worth owning.

THE VOW OF CHASTITY

The fourth great vow states:

> "I renounce all sexual pleasures, either with gods or men or animals. I shall not give way to sensuality. As long as I live *[ditto* as in other vows]..." *(Ācārāṅga -sūtra* 2.15.iv.l*)*.

The fourth vow is that of chastity. From the monastic point of view, the sexual act is paradigmatic of passion and desire, and therefore is strictly forbidden. Obviously, the vow goes further than abstaining from copulation *(maithuna-virati)* and includes abstaining from listening to provocative works, contemplating the female body (one must remember that the texts were written by men) and so forth. One consequence of this vow is that the *sādhus* and *sādhvīs* dress in the simplest and most modest way. None wear jewellery or perfumes. To avoid any temptation—or danger—*sādhvīs* always go around in groups, even when they go to confess before the *ācārya.* For many of them, celibacy was the most important of their vows (Fohr 2006: 162).

THE VOW OF NON-POSSESSION

The fifth great vow states:

> "I renounce to all attachments, whether little or much, small or great, living or lifeless; neither shall I myself form such attachments, nor cause others to do so, nor consent to their doing. As long as I live [*ditto* as in the first vow]..." *(Ācārāṅga-sūtra* 2.15.v.1).

On cultivating the vow of non-possession *(aparigraha),* plainly the most important vow after that of non-violence, the ascetic combats greed and selfishness, which are the prime causes of violence in the world. From the moment she or he is initiated into the order they will only "possess" the objects they were given the day of *dīkṣā.* Let us go over them.

One of the very few companions on the ascetic's journey and one which permanently symbolises his dedication to non-violence is the whisk broom *(rajoharaṇa, piccikā),* one of the distinctive signs of Jainism. Depending on the order, the brush is made of wool or fallen peacock feathers. It is designed so that nothing, not even damp, sticks to it. Ascetics use this brush constantly, before sitting, walking or lying down to sleep. The aim is always to remove any living beings that would inadvertently be squashed, stepped upon or injured by the ascetic's actions.

The ascetics of the Śvetāmbara Sthānakavāsī and Terāpanthī sub-orders also have a cotton cloth *(mukhapaṭṭikā, muhpaṭṭi)* which they wear as a mouth mask (permanently) so as not to harm invisible air creatures. Other orders only use it on special occasions. Quite a few ascetics carry a piece of cloth which they use to filter their drinking water. As for clothes *(śvetavastra),* they consist of a simple white cloth and a woollen shawl for the winter. *Sādhvīs* wear a long skirt or a sari, a blouse and a veil to cover their head and shoulders.

Another of the few objects ascetics carry is a bowl, which serves for asking for alms *(pātra,* among Śvetāmbaras) or for containing water for hygienic reasons *(kamaṇḍalu,* among Digambaras). The *sādhus* and *sādhvīs* of certain Śvetāmbara orders usually carry a long wooden stick *(daṇḍa).* Apart from being a distinctive sign it serves for moving objects out of the way and for gently driving away any dangerous reptile or insect that may cross their path. Ascetics are allowed to wear graduated spectacles, a wristwatch and there is no objection to having prayer beads *(mālās)* to accompany recitations and murmuring of *mantras.* They may also own some books *(pothī)* containing the texts of their studies, which they keep in a woven bag. Sometimes they carry images of saints or famous masters. Śvetāmbara *ācāryas* can have a little table for preaching *(sthāpanācārya).*

Apart from these utensils (the majority of which are only used by Śvetāmbaras) ascetics have nothing else. Not even shoes or sandals. And in any case, it is stressed that ascetics *do not own* any of these objects. They are aids donated by lay persons for their spiritual practice.

Obviously, the vow of non-possession is linked to the vow of non-stealing, but it goes further than the lack of possession of material objects. Ascetics must literally dispossess themselves of their notion of "I", of self which is the agent capable of coveting and possessing. Only in the state of absolute poverty, abandoning all possessions and identification with one's "me", one's self, can one purify the soul.

* * *

The great vows together make up a practice of internal purification. Consequently, the ascetic will cultivate a series of dispositions *(bhāvanās, brahma-vi-hāras)* in daily life, also well known in Buddhism *(Majjhima-nikāya* 1.39.13-16): loving benevolence *(maitrī)* towards other beings; delight *(pramoda)* at being alongside other advanced beings on the path; sympathy and compassion *(karunā)* for those who suffer, along with a desire to help them; indifference and calmness *(mādhyastha)* towards those who insult *dharma* (Hemacandra, *Yoga-śāstra* 4.117-122). These instructions serve to cement proper understanding of each vow.

THE LIFE OF ASCETICS

The rules that govern the life of ascetics may well go back to Mahāvīra, even though not linked to episodes in his life (just as occurs in the Buddhist monastic code). Generally, they are classified into such groups as ways to ask for alms, manners of speech, ways of entering into people's houses, places to study, recommendations on how to relieve one's needs, etc. The *Uttarādhyayana-sūtra* (26.12) instigates ascetics to dedicate the first quarter of their day to study *(svādhyāya),* the second to meditation *(dhyāna),* the third to making their begging round *(bhikṣā),* and the fourth again to studying. Nevertheless, in practice this schedule has ended up as a mere theoretical model. Not only does it not make reference to the errant way of life, but also hardly touches upon the interaction with the lay community.

AN ASCETIC'S DAY

A more realistic schedule would be the following: the ascetic rises very early," at first light. The first thing he or she does is recite in a murmur *(japa)* and in Prakrit the *mantra* of salutation to the five Supreme Beings *(pañca-na maskāra-mantra)*:

"Obeisance to the *Arhats [ṇamo arahamtāṇaṃ],*
Obeisance to the Liberated Ones *[ṇamo siddhāṇaṃ],*
Obeisance to the Religious Masters *[ṇamo āyariyāṇaṃ],*

> Obeisance to the Religious Instructors *[ṇamo uvajjhāyāṇaṃ]*,
> Obeisance to all Saints in the world *[ṇamo loe savva-sāhūṇaṃ]" (Kalpa-sū tra, Jina-caritra* 1).

This is Jainism's best known and most sacred chant [see pages 475-476], repeated in hundreds of texts, on an infinity of occasions. Afterwards, the ascetic will meditate.

Next, they will make a general confession *(pratikramaṇa)* regarding possible overnight transgressions of the vow of *ahiṃsā.* Then, they will undertake the inspection *(pratilekhanā)* of clothes and utensils. This compulsory activity is carried out two or three times a day. In all cases it is designed to remove with the greatest care any life form that may have ended up in their clothes, books, bowls, blankets or brushes. The inspection also occurs when ascetics relieve their needs. Not only does all this seek to avoid killing some minuscule being, but also it serves to maintain the ascetic in a vigilant spirit, of concentration on a single object *(ekāgratā).*

In theory, ascetics do not clean their teeth, as activities of that sort are regarded as being excessively worldly and, additionally, imply the destruction of lives. In practice Śvetāmbara *sādhus* and *sādhvīs* tend to be quite cleanly and clean their teeth with their fingers after every meal. Unlike Hindu *sādhus,* no Jain ascetics smear their body with ashes, wear adornment or paint sectarian marks on their forehead.

The best times of the day for meditation *(dhyāna)* are at sunrise or before retiring for the night. The habitual place for meditating is the temple where monks congregate to see the *jinas (darśana).* Ascetics never give any offering of flowers, incense, or rice, typical of lay folk, nor do they wear special clothes for the ritual. They simply meditate *(bhāva-pūjā)* on the qualities of the *jinas,* on the situation of bondage, or on the possible types of rebirth. Sthā-nakavāsī or Terāpanthī ascetics, who do not worship images, carry out inner worship in their monastic retreat.

The rules on asking for food *(gocarī, āhāra-viddhi)* are most meticulous. Which is understandable, food being directly linked to the connection between soul and body, that is to say, bondage to this world. Hence, the reason that fasting becomes such a habitual practice among ascetics and lay people. Usually, making the rounds to seek food takes place around 10 o'clock. On their return, ascetics will again confess to any possible negligence which they may have been guilty of in their coming and going. Just as in the early morning confession, it is really more of a general repentance *(pratikramaṇa)* than a confession of specific sins. We expand on this aspect further on [see pages 453-455]. Digambara ascetics eat only once a day; Śvetāmbaras eat twice (the second time always being before sunset). The round is banned at times of heavy rain, mist, or strong winds, when going about could cause the death to a number of beings of only one sense.

A considerable part of the day (especially during the sedentary period in the rainy season) is spent studying sacred texts, the languages in which they are written (Prakrit languages, Sanskrit, modern Indian languages) or other systems' doctrines. This represents one of the most effective ways of conserving Sūtras at the same time as being a meditation practice. The instructor is not normally the *ācārya,* who is more of a supervisor, but a *guru* or *guruṇī.* There are those who have the opportunity to study with a scholar *(paṇḍita).* Some orders have study centres for ascetics. Another common activity, also during the rainy season, is the instruction of laity or receiving visitors.

Ascetics spend the night in retreats *(upāśrayas)* usually found adjacent to temples. Before retiring, they make another general confession, like the one at dawn. They usually meditate before going to sleep which is normally around ten o'clock.

A LIFE IN PERPETUAL PILGRIMAGE

In keeping with a model followed by India's renunciants for thousands of years, religious spend their time in pilgrimage, always on foot and unshod [see Figs. 11,12]. These days, in an over-populated, noisy, impassable, and half-industrialised country, the life of a pilgrim is considerably harder than before, when the Sūtras that regulate the forms of pilgrimage were composed. The journey between two places is called *vihāra,* a term which Buddhism would later use as a name for their monasteries.

The life of a pilgrim reflects his or her own internal pilgrimage. Of course, this itinerant lifestyle has the object of freeing oneself from attachment. It is an activity of maximum self-control. Many ascetics even use their brushes when they are walking, a precaution to avoid accidentally killing the most diminutive creatures that cross their path. Itinerant life allows ascetics to interact with communities of laypersons—and spread Jainism. Ancient texts advise and approve of ascetics learning languages and dialects of the regions they visited. When ascetics are approaching a locality, where there is a significant lay community, dozens of lay people frequently come out to escort them in procession to the retreat where they will spend the night.

Normally, masters or ascetic elders set the itineraries. They always have end points such as a centre of pilgrimage, a famous library, or a temple where lay people would conduct important rituals, or could simply be a route through different communities to maintain links with laity. They could also go toward where they could find their *ācārya,* with whom they could deepen their understanding of the meaning of the texts and teachings. Nevertheless, crossing the great "black ocean" *(kālā-pānī)* is forbidden, which is why Jainism has been confined to India and, until the 20th century, no ascetic had ventured out of South Asia. In practice, quite a few renunciants tend to stay in their favourite areas, and during the course of ageing, they reduce their itineraries within a progressively smaller local areas.

THE SEDENTARY PERIOD

The exception to this wandering lifestyle takes place during the rainy season or monsoon (from mid-June until the beginning of October) when ascetics are allowed to congregate in villages or cities with their preceptors. This retreat during the rains is called *caturmāsa.* Although this practice is habitual among other renunciant groups in India, in Jainism it is directly linked to *ahiṃsā.* The Sutras say that in the moment when seeds germinate and innumerable of little animals colonise the path, ascetics must, in the knowledge of this circumstance, refrain from their pilgrimage *(Ācārāṅga-sātra* 2.3.1.1). During this period mendicant rounds are modified.

The sedentary period of the monsoons is a time of stability. It favours study and interaction with the laity. Ascetics can attend personal talks, conferences, and public or private courses. During this period, fasting is continuous. It is also in this period when the most committed lay people come to record or collect ascetics' texts, which will be one day published. The climax to the *caturmāsa* comes about with the extremely important festivals of Paryusana (for Śvetām-baras) or of Daśalakṣaṇa-parvan (for Digambaras). We shall be describing these festivals at greater length in chapter 28.

THE RETREAT *(UPĀŚ RAYA)*

The retreat for ascetics is called *upāśraya,* which literally means "refuge". Ancient texts also use the understated term "bed" *(śayyā),* with which the transitory aspect of the retreat remains clear [see FIG. 20]. Digambaras do not even have retreats, but stay in temples or rooms belonging to lay Jains which they simply call "abodes" *(vasatikāsthāna).*

The *upāśraya* does not really resemble what we understand as a monastery, even though it is a possible translation, and certainly during medieval times monasteries *(maṭhas)* were set up where monks settled. But the situation in present times has changed. Following ancient models, ascetics stay in these retreats from a few days up to a few weeks. Only during the rainy season can they spend their nights in the same place (although not necessarily at the same retreat) for three or four months. Except for a few cots there is no furniture or decoration. There may be mats for sitting on, some books and alms bowls.

The retreat belongs to the local community and is maintained by the laity. Apart from the ascetics' cells, it frequently also has a large room which lay people use as a fasting hall or meditation room, or a place for receiving religious instruction from ascetics. In this way, the retreat becomes a shelter for ascetics and at the same time a community centre for the local lay association, open to everyone at all times of day. Many are situated next to a temple and, on occasion, they form part of a larger complex, which could include a library, hostel, school, etc.

If the locality where ascetics have to spend the night has no retreat they can stay at a lay house, at a hostel for pilgrims, at a Hindu *āśrama,* at the home of someone who is not a Jain (subject to such person being vegetarian and of good repute), or in abandoned houses or failing that out in the open.

Although these retreats belong to the local lay communities and therefore are designed and prepared to receive ascetics of the specific order to which they are associated, ascetics from other orders are generally well received.

RULES

Texts are full of lists detailing disrespectful conduct *(āśātanā)* (Tatia and Kumar 1981: 27-30), rules on expulsion *(sāmācārī)* (Tatia and Kumar 1981: 5-10), types of monks with distorted behaviour *(śabala)* (Tatia and Kumar 1981: 14-20), etc., which regulate monastic organisation. Being the maximum authority on scriptures, which are the source of authority for the monastic community, it is the *ācārya* who administers and represents authority. Normally after every quarter day, confessions *(ālocanā)* are made in relation to the preceding quarter. The formula used urges the ascetics to reprove themselves and to do so before the master *(pratikramaṇa)*. After confessing and repenting comes the expiation *(prāyaścitta)*. Redemption carries with it various types of penance (usually fasting or some kind of abstinence) well described in texts relating to ascetic conduct such as the Śvetāmbara Cheda-sūtras or the Digambara *Prāyaścitta-grantha*. Not all texts coincide. It is quite clear that they are the product of different theoreticians who at no time felt the need for these issues to be harmonised among the different orders. Expiation can also include temporary isolation, a symbolic reduction in years of ascetic life and even a new initiation. Normally expulsions (with or without the possibility of readmission) are not so much for specific offences committed as for qualitative deviances—ill-will, frivolity, homosexuality (Schubring 1934: 284).

INTERACTION WITH LAITY

It has been oft repeated that the institution of renunciation is a way of denying the world (Schweitzer 1935: 74). It can be certainly so for renunciants who isolate themselves in jungles or in the mountains. However Jain ascetics maintain a strong link with society. Given their condition of itinerants, they pertain to the local community in which they find themselves on their route. Although an ascetic renounces the world, she or he takes on a function within society, and their authority is proportional to their exemplary conduct and wisdom.

Given that monks and nuns do not possess anything, they completely depend on the faithful's material contributions, which in Jain terms is known as giving *(dāna)*, dealt with in greater depth in chapter 28. Lay people offer daily food, shelter, clothes, medicine, etc. They build temples, retreats, fasting halls, and they maintain all these institutions with their donations. In return ascetics give them spiritual instruction and the no less important spiritual worth *(puṇya)*.

Ascetics are those men and women who, for the layperson, truly embody the principles of Jainism. Their authority is not derived from any temporal power, nor from their participation in the liturgies, but from universal principles that manifest themselves through non-violence, non-attachment, sincerity, composure, serenity, study, mindfulness, chastity, self-control and the search for liberation.

Ascetics supervise the vows and fasts of the laity. They take their confessions and they can even have influence over political positions. The relationship between ascetics and laity tends to be quite enduring. Since ascetics also represent the lineage of the masters from whom they derive, many lay people consider them to be their religious preceptors *(gurus).* They are the repositories of the knowledge of tradition and the ones who have perpetuated the texts.

It is important to stress the continuity that exists between the lives of lay people and those of the ascetics. The ethical code (consisting of the five vows) is the same for both, the only difference being that the former only follow them partially, while ascetics adhere strictly. A spiritually advanced layperson can, behave like a monk. These days, for example, it is quite common for ascetics to travel from one place to another accompanied by lay people [see FIG. 44]. In fact, the arrival of a well-known and charismatic group of renunciants is one of the great occasions for the local Jain population to feel united and have a sharper self-perception as "Jain". The life of an ascetic is an extension of the mindful head of a lay household and as a result the feeling of unity among all the members of the community is very strong. It can even be the case, more frequently than may appear from reading Jain literature, that the lay community exercise a degree of control over monks (Stevenson 1915:211). The laity permanently keep an eye on the activities of *sādhus* and *sādhvīs.* They are concerned that any variation in the canons might lead to a disintegration of Jain *dharma,* and so, as N. Shāntā (1985: 685) has said, quite often outsiders are more conservative than insiders.

As has been mentioned, the closeness between both sections of the *saṃgha* is very evident during the rainy season, when ascetics are invited by local communities to stay in their retreats. There are almost daily religious talks *(pravacanas).* Some are improvised chats with small groups of laypersons who come and go. Others are formal sermons which, in the case of a reputed renunciant, are held in special marquees to accommodate a large audience. The usual topics are non-violence, renunciation of bad acts, inner peace, goodness, detachment, purity of intention, victory over passion and simplicity (Shāntā 1985: 551). The sermons are generally clear and didactic, usually in the local languagfe or in Hindi. In addition, ascetics personally instruct all those who come to see them. Normally they are available in the evening. At this time of the year, and especially during the Paryuṣaṇa festival, many confession rites and fasts take place under the guidance of ascetics.

Part VI

The Development of Jainism

As we move forward in time, the history of India becomes progressively more intelligible. Archaeology and epigraphy provide valuable information. But not that much. If we compare the documentation that we have on India with that of other areas of the world (China, Europe, and the Near East) the information available on South Asia is unexpectedly opaque. Almost comparable with more ancient periods.

Jain historical narratives in this more Sorrowful Age have altered slightly. The time of the *tīrthaṅkaras* and the sublime beings has long passed, so that the Universal Story takes on a more historical tone. Of course, these later narratives are still not concerned with "historical facts" as such—in any case, elusive as ever—but rather ordering them according to their relevance and significance for the community: lineages of ascetics, schisms, migrations, biographies of the exemplary masters, and so on. We have seen this with the account of the drought and the subsequent schism in Jainism.

In this section of the book, we shall attempt to do the same as the Jain chroniclers: make the present more comprehensible. But we shall focus on the question from a different angle. Instead of tracing the monastic lineages of the different sub-currents and schools, which would be the accepted way, we shall follow events from a geographic point of view—a simpler, more didactic procedure.

If until now, we have confined ourselves to Northern India, to the great region of the River Ganges, in this Part we shall be looking at developments in four great geographical blocks, (see FIGS. 18,19). In the first place [chapter 14], there is the central area, which takes in most of the states of Uttar Pradesh and Madhya Pradesh. This region lies close to the lower and middle reaches of the great river, where historically speaking Jainism first appeared. Then, (chapter 15), we shift our attention to the Deccan plateaus, comprising principally the southern part of Maharashtra state, the state of Karnataka and most of Andhra Pradesh. After that (chapter 16) we shall be studying the South of India, which comprises the states of Tamil Nadu and Kerala. Lastly, (chapter 17) we touch on the important North West area of India: Rajasthan, Gujarat, Northern of Maharashtrá, and Western Madhya Pradesh. While the principalities and kingdoms of antiquity were not the same as the modern divisions and state boundaries, for the sake of clarity we shall take the modern divisions as ours for the duration of the journey here undertaken.

The penetration of Jains into this area occurred between the 2nd century BC and the 11th century CE. From the 15th and 16th centuries onward, Jainism began to stagnate. At the beginning of the 15th century, the religion had the same geographic boundaries and social patterning as now. For historical reasons, the Deccan region and the South were and still are, basically Digambara, while the Centre and North West have both groups, even though the Śvetāmbaras are more numerous.

Adhering to this script, we shall be looking at both historical approaches based on facts and, to a lesser extent, at the way the community itself has viewed its own history. It would be frankly absurd to attempt to provide a purely chronological account. I prefer to follow a particular thematic thread to be able to understand its dynamics. This will allow us to consider in some detail one of the persistent stereotypes that have clung to this tradition: the idea that Jainism is static, conservative, changeless and unoriginal. Contrary to what one might think, and what the community itself often reflects, no tradition is static; it is an evolving accumulation that gathers up and encapsulates elements of its history. It constantly draws on other ways of understanding the world. This historical and geographical review will enable us to discover in greater depth the *dynamics* of Jainism and understand the Jainism of today.

In fact, it is not possible to speak of the dynamics of a religion separately from socio-political history or an overview of the literature, art or anything else. All histories form a part of one and the same process or history of a society. For that reason, we will concentrate particularly on the interaction of the Jain religion with Others, and especially on its contribution to fields such as literature, ritual and politics. In this way, we can insert the tradition into a wider framework and see the true scope and attainment of Jainism in the construction of Indian civilisation.

14. JAINISM IN CENTRAL INDIA

FANNING OUT FROM THE GANGES

At least by the 3rd and 2nd centuries, before the Common Era, Jainism had spread beyond the limits of the Gangetic Valley. What is to some extent surprising and not fully explained even today, is that as it spread to other parts of the continent, the area that saw the birth of the religion began to run dry of Jain elements. Perhaps this had to do with the installing of the Śūṅga dynasty (2nd-1st centuries BC) initiated by a Brāhmaṇa general who brought the Maurya dynasty to a close. The Śūṅga monarchs openly proclaimed themselves to be pro-Brāhmaṇic, and while it is not certain that there were persecutions as such, many Jains must have preferred to move out of an environment that was increasingly hostile to them. Clearly, other basic economic and political factors must have also played their part.

Although Jainism never completely disappeared from the region where Mahāvīra preached, in part thanks to the sacredness of some of the most important sites, it is a fact that around the 8th century the middle and lower Ganges was emptying of Jain elements. Buddhism, on the other hand became so established in Bihar that the very name of this modern state was taken from the word used by Buddhists to refer to their monasteries *(vihāras)*. Today, the Jains of Bihar and Bengal are the descendants of waves of immigrants who moved into the area from the West from the 18th century onwards

Nonetheless, it was from this point onwards that Jainism begins its golden age. The period that goes from the 5th to the 12th centuries is the high-point in its splendour. It is then that the Jain community proceeded to endow the lay community with its signs of identity.

THE JAINISM OF MATHURA

Thanks to its privileged situation as a centre of communications, from the 4th to the 3rd centuries BC onward, the city of Mathura, in the South of Uttar Pradesh, developed conspicuously as an economic and social centre. We know that not long after the city became a prominent cultural centre, it was not for nothing that this city was already a sacred place in remotest antiquity. There are Buddhist and Jain legends—and not as mythical as might seem at first sight–to the effect that the Buddha, Pārśva and Mahāvīra all visited the city. It was surely there, a place that was always a centre for the worship of Kṛṣṇa, that the Jains began to "Jainise" the tales of Kṛṣṇa, and to connect them with those told about the *tīrthaṅkara* Nemi. It also corresponds with the origins of Vaiṣṇavism.

Thanks to certain inscriptions, we know that around the 1st century CE there were in Mathura no end (84) of Jain orders *(gaṇas),* schools *(gacchas)* branches *(śākhās)* and families *(kulas)* deriving from different Śvetāmbara lineages. The documents speak of two types of teachers: the ordinary ones, or readers (*vācakas)*—indicating that there were written texts on Jainism at that time—and the heads of schools *(gaṇins).*

At the Kaṅkālī Ṭīlā site, archaeologists have found a Jain *stūpa* and two temples dating from the 2nd century BC to the 2nd century CE. Professor Umakant Shah (1955: 64) has identified the *stūpa* as dating from the time of Pārśva, thanks to an inscription that says it was built by the gods *(devanirmita)',* that is, it was so ancient that no one, even at that time, remembered who had built it. Although it might not be that ancient, the existence of a *stūpa* in itself presupposes the existence of an organised lay community, at a surprisingly early date. Given their vows of non-attachment, ascetics are not allowed to build temples, nor retreats, nor monasteries, nor buildings of any kind. Strictly speaking, they should not agree to others doing it either, since the building of any structure will entail the unwitting destruction of an immense number of beings *(Uttarādhyayana-sūtra* 35.8-9). All Jain buildings prior to this date were simple caves, conditioned to be able to receive ascetics [see Fig. 20]. So the existence of the *stūpa* and the temples clearly point to vigorous lay worship, which would necessarily have to have the backing of the ascetic community.

THE JAINISM OF THE LAY PEOPLE

This ushers in a whole series of queries about the history of Jainism. Although for a long time now we have known that Jainism and Buddhism were two differentiated religious movements, in actual practice many scholars have continued to view Jainism from a Buddhist point of view. They assume that the Jain faith developed *parallel to* Buddhism, with similar development and avatars. Speaking on popular devotional worship of the Buddha or the Jina, Herman Jacobi (1884: I, xxi) maintained that these religious expressions had nothing to do with the *original* Jainism or Buddhism. They would have developed, he argued, among the lay community when India regarded devotion *(bhakti)* as the supreme path to salvation. Influenced by the irresistible force of this popular religiosity, Buddhism and Jainism had little choice but to adopt these forms of worship. While it is true that the Buddhists and the Jains *first* constructed their monastic communities and *then* the organised lay communities subsequently appeared, the integration of the latter was very different in the two instances. Buddhist monks opted for taking control of the temples and *stūpas* and still today carry out rituals for the lay community. This had its doctrinal justification, since Mahāyāna Buddhism accepted the fact that the laity could achieve liberation, but this did not happen in the case of Jainism, and happened only to a lesser extent in Theravāda Buddhism. Only towards the 8th or 9th centuries did it come to be accepted that lay Jains could attain liberation, and even in this case only those who, as it were, devoutly replicated monastic life in a lay context. Consequently, Jain ascetics, while having no objection to lay worship, did *not* and still do *not* involve themselves in it. The interaction between Jainism and the lay community did not happen during worship. It is important to realise this to be able to grasp the seemingly disparity between the otherworldliness of the religious (focussed on liberation) and the, let us say, "popular" attitudes of the lay Jain community, centred on gaining merit.

Unlike Buddhism, then, there were in Mathura lay followers who had taken control of certain forms of devotional worship of the *jinas.* Inscriptions have shown that these devotees were merchants, traders, jewellers, dancers, bards, craftsmen, and the headmen of small villages. That is to say, the more or less wealthy class who still today support this tradition. Sonya Quintanilla (2004: 187-206) has linked the devotional lay Jainism of Mathura to the Ardhaphāla-ka sect, which seem to have particularly favored image worship.

Where did this worship originate? What did it have to do with liberation? How does it relate to modern worship?

WORSHIP OF THE YAKṢAS AND CAITYAS

Present day Jain worship *(pūjā)* [see chapter 27] is heavily influenced by Hindu tradition, but, as with Hindu *pūjā,* it is entirely possible that it stems from pre-Hindu and pre-Jain practices. Most likely, it originates in the very ancient worship of marvellous beings *(yakṣas).* This ritual culture has never been the exclusive cultural province of any religion in particular, but is common to the Indian people. Both Brāhmaṇic and Śramaṇic traditions had to assimilate it, whether more or less conscious of the fact. Interestingly, *yakṣas* and *yakṣīs* were remarkably prominent and important to the local population of Mathura during the 2nd century BC and 2nd century CE period.

Originally, the term *yakṣa* meant divinity *(deva, devatā).* As Ananda Coomaraswamy (1928: 1, 36-37) has observed, all Indian deities, even the Buddha, have on some occasion been referred to as *yakṣas.* Even today, Jains use the terms *yakṣa* and *devatā* interchangeably, to refer to the protective deities of the *jinas.*

Certain *yakṣas* served as tutelary deities of the city *(grāmadevatā, kulade-vatā)* and were invoked to protect it. Others had the power to confer fertility and cure sickness. But there were others that were malevolent. In addition to having a tree associated with them, some of these genies or nymphs had a little shrine known as a *caitya.* Coomaraswamy (1928: I, 18) reminds us that the word *caitya,* besides meaning funerary mound in the classic sense, often simply means a sacred tree with its altar. Normally, these *caityas* were sited on the outskirts of the village; in a cave, on a hill, or by a river. Thus, these *yakṣas* and other associated supernatural beings *(nāgas, gandharvas, devas),* were protective spirits who watched over the territory, the clan or the village. Travellers, including Śramaṇas like Mahāvīra or the Buddha, would pass the night next to such sacred trees or in the little shrines dedicated to the *yakṣas.* Neither Mahāvīra nor the Buddha were fearful of confronting these spirits and it is said that they submitted them to their respective movements. For Paul Dundas (2003: 135), there is little doubt that acommodating these spirits, "converting" them, as it were, and thus their devotees, was a necessary strategy for proselytising religions like Jainism and Buddhism. Jain texts like the *Anuttaraupapātika-daśāh* describe the well-known shrine to the *yakṣa* Pūrṇabhadra, near Campā, the *yakṣa* protector of the city and the clans of the region. Significantly, it is said to be there that Mahāvīra gave his first sermon. It can not be accidental that so many of Mahāvīra's sermons took place (or better, are depicted as taking place) at these shrines associated with *yakṣas.* The *sūtra* describes the shrine of Pūrnabhadra as rich, famous, ancient, with sunshades, bells, banners, visited by musicians, story-tellers, dancers and wrestlers (Coomaraswamy 1928:1, 19-20). The ritual invariably included prostration before an image, the singing of hymns, offerings of flowers, incense, and items of clothes or food. In other words, *yakṣa* worship was similar if not identical to what is known today in India under the generic term of *pūjā* (Coomaraswamy 1928: I, 27-28). The emergence and growth of this cult, consistently devotional as it was in nature, is well attested for the first centuries before the Common Era in Hinduism, Buddhism, and Jainism alike. It was in fact a general tendency. Obviously, with the incorporation of these popular deities with their firm following, Jainism was able to become more attractive to a large section of the population. It can even be said, that the spread of Jainism involved an *alliance* with the cultic sites of *yakṣas* and *yakṣinis* (Dun-das 2003: 135-136). Nonetheless, the Jain scriptures do not often mention them, and the ancient Jain images depicting them are few.

Subsequently, the *caitya* was replaced by the *stūpa,* a more complex mound that guarded the relics of the Jaina saints *(arhat-caitya).* However, in contrast to Buddhism, which developed widespread *stūpa* worship, Jains did not really take this very far. We know of no worship of relics of the *jinas* comparable to worship of the relics of *buddhas* and masters in Buddhism. It is possible that this was a difference that was deliberated cultivated to distance Jains from other religious groups.

THE ANCIENT ICONOGRAPHY

In terms of iconography, Mathura already exhibits many of the motifs that would subsequently be normative in Jainism. In certain panels the *jina* occupies a central position, whether represented anthromorphically or figuratively, in which case he is usually symbolised by a miniature *stūpa,* a wheel of the law *(dharma-cakra)* which embodies his teachings or some footprints *(pādukās)* that represent his liberated image and character. These three symbols are pan-Indian, as we also find them for example in ancient Buddhist iconography. There are depictions of trees *(vrkṣas),* under which their sages attained enlightenment. Additionally, columns *(dhvajas)* or pillars *(mānastambhas)* associated with the *jinas* have been found, perhaps reminiscent of the Vedic altars, and the so-called eight auspicious symbols *(aṣṭamahgalas),* which became immensely popular in sculptures and friezes [see Fig. 17]. These are symbols whose origin and meaning are lost in the distant past.

We cannot be exactly sure when adoration of images of the *jinas* and their *yakṣa* attendants first began. According to Śvetāmbara tradition, a sculpture dating as far back as Mahāvīra's time was carved out of sandalwood showing the prince Vardhamāṇa practicing asceticism in his palace, a year before undergoing his initiation. The Jina portrayed in this mode is known as Jīvantasvāmin, an iconographic motif that was frequent in the medieval period. It is comparable to the Buddhist idea of *bodhisattva* as "he who is on the path of buddha-hood". Thus, in the words of Maruti Tiwari (1995: 15), the Jīvantasvāmin would be a *jinasattva.* However, all references to these primordial Jīvantasvāmins belong to a late period, not earlier than the 6th century, and few experts will go as far as to vouch for the tradition.

It is not unlikely that ancient liturgy began to centre on living ascetics teachers *(guru-vandana),* as it is practiced even today [see pages 451-453], and later became image-oriented (Dundas 2006: 385). The first apparently Jain figure is a torso found in Lohanipur, in Bihar, probably dating from the 3rd or 2nd century BC. A terracotta figure from Ayodhya has also been documented for the 3rd century BC. The earliest identifiable depictions of *tīrthaṅkaras* are some seated figures of Ṛṣabha from Mathura (2nd century BC). Worship of the *tīrthaṅkara* Ṛṣabha is also documented in the 1st century BC in the inscriptions of the king Khāravela of Kaliṅga in Orissa. It is said that Khāravela stole the statue of Ṛṣabha from a Nanda king, so we might take it that worship of the *tīrthaṅkaras* was already established during the Nanda dynasty (5th-4th centuries BC). However, more conclusive evidence is needed to confirm this.

During the centuries that followed, the region of Mathura was ruled by the Śāka and Kuṣāṇa dynasties (lst-4th centuries), originating from central Asia. This fact favoured the non-Brāhmaṇic traditions. Brāhmaṇism has always tended to identify itself with Indianness, and accordingly "foreign" dynasties have usually sided with non-Brāhmaṇic religious traditions. However, the Śāka and Kuṣāṇa dynasties were considerably cosmopolitan and Hinduism also flourished. In fact, according to the eminent art historian Pratapaditya Pal (1994: 16), we can consider Mathura to be the birthplace of the iconography of the three religions of India.

THE RELIGION OF THE TEMPLES

From Mathura, Jainism and Jain art spread out through the whole of central India. If Kuṣāṇa art represents the true beginning of Jain art, the Gupta period (4th-6th centuries) is that of its consolidation and culmination, although there scarcely remain any traces of Jain Gupta art today. With the Guptas, the sculptural and architectural canons of Indian art became perfectly codified. The period from the beginning of the Gupta Empire and the more serious incursions of Islam (12th century) is known as the *Indie* (Hindu-Buddhist-Jain) period of Indian civilisation (Larson 1995: 75). This was one of the most important periods of transformation of Indian traditions, a dynamic fed by two processes: religious rivalry and the development of loving devotion *(bhakti)*.

RELIGIOUS RIVALRY

The Buddhist and Jain threat was a constant in the history of medieval Brāhmaṇism. It formed the backdrop in front of which endless streams of changes and reorientations of the Hindu tradition took place. Counteracting to the enlightenment of the Buddha and the *jinas,* the orthodox Brāhmaṇas put forward the infallibility of the Veda. In front of the anthropomorphic image of the Jina or the Buddha they had that of God *(īśvara).* In answer to the monasteries of Jain and Buddhist renunciants, Śaṅkara placed the monastic centres *(mathas)* and his order of Daśanāmi renunciants. Mādhyamika Buddhist thought was attacked by the Vedānta and the Jain *anekāntavāda* was attacked by the Mīmāṃsā. In answer to the *jinas* of Jainism with their freedom from attachment and the compassionate *bodhisattvas* of Buddhism there arose Śaiva, Vaiṣṇava, and Śākta devotionalism, and the list goes on.

In some cases, the competitive strive for hegemony was healthy. Philosophically speaking, for example, the existence of imposing rivals encouraged and motivated philosophical discourse, taking it to its greatest levels of profundity and subtley. What emerged was an Indie philosophical synthesis which brought together Hinduism, Jainism and Buddhism. In other aspects the challenge produced more negative results. The effect that the universalism of the Jains and the Buddhists had on Brāhmaṇism was a more dogged exclusive outlook. Employing the most acid irony the Brāhmaṇas noted the fact that there were so many converts to Jainism and Buddhism among such degenerate and immoral individuals as the untouchables (Caṇḍālas) and the barbarians (Mlecchas), this being proof enough of their falsity. The Brāhmaṇas spurned all "otherness", from the social ritual of the Mlecchas and Caṇḍālas, to rival philosophies, which they considered some kind of partial or aberrant version of Hinduism, generally from Vedānta Advaita.

These reorientations are not to be seen simply as the reactions of the Brāhmaṇas. Rather, they are an assimilation of Brāhmaṇic and Śramaṇic (Jain and Buddhist) elements along with popular and regional ones, with Hinduism acting as the vehicle. A good instance of this is the classic Advaita Vedānta taught by Gauḍapāda and Śaṅkara, who owe so much to the Upaniṣads as to the dialectic methods of Mādhyamika Buddhism. As David Loy (1988: 200) has said, the disputes between Advaitins and Mādhyamikas seem to be more like family squabbles between brothers than confrontations between religions. This religious rivalry, then, is less a case of rivalry between "religions" as such, more an accommodation to diversity and an astonishing interaction between countless currents and layers of civilisation.

THE EMERGENCE OF THE TEMPLES

From the 4th and 5th centuries onward, the geography of India began to be populated by temples *(mandiras)* commissioned by the royal families and, in the case of Jain temples, also by wealthy lay worshippers. It is probable that there had always been small shrines (like the *caityas* consecrated to the *yakṣas),* the sort that even today are to be found everywhere in rural India. Slowly, the *caityas* dedicated to the *yakṣas* began to evolve into the temples dedicated to the *tīrthaṅkara* or the *buddha* or the *īśvara.* In this process, it seems that the initial impetus came from the Buddhists who were building splendid *stūpas* even before the Common Era. The Jains were not far behind them, as the archaeological site at Mathura shows, dating as it does from the 2nd century BC. The Jains had a special predilection for mountain tops, which they covered with sanctuaries, shrines, and temples, in some cases forming large sacred complexes.

None of the oldest scriptures mention either *tīrthaṅkara* adoration or the sacred assembly *(samavarasaṇa),* the model for Jain worship. But little by little they begin to appear. Vimala Sūri's *Padma-carita* (3rd-4th centuries) provides very good descriptions of the worship of the eight substances, which is still a typical practice among Jains [see pages 420-423], the consecrating of a picture of the Jina, the building and restoration of temples, the general worship in all villages, cities or mountains, and even worship in the homes of devout Jains (Kulkarni 1952: 86). Interestingly, as time weert on, there began scriptural references to divine beings who came to the aid of humans. Brāhmī (Sarasvatī) the goddess of wisdom, very soon became a part of the Jain pantheon. The mythology of the 63 sublime beings began to be formalised. At the same time, the descriptions of the sacred assembly waxed more and more excellent and mythical. In other words, as we leave the last *jina* further and further back in the past, his teachings and his person take on a more universal impact. This was an evolution comparable to what happened with the Buddhist *stūpa,* which went from being a mere standing stone to being a representation of the Buddha, the *dharma* and the entire cosmos. Similarly, the sacred assembly came to represent the world with the radiant Jina in its centre, with his teaching and followers all around [see Fig. 6], so that the *tīrthaṅkara* does not just stand for transcendence of the world but, as Ken Folkert (1993: 152) says, he *establishes it.*

Devotional worship was continually gaining ground and becoming pre-eminent among Indian religious practices. In the 7th century, the philosopher Jaṭāsiṁhanandi praised the religious merit achieved by building temples, images and worshipping. For Jaṭāsiṁhanandi *(Varāṅga-carita* 22.33; cited in Singh 1975: 25-26) *Jina* worship was indispensable for lay Jains to achieve final liberation.

THE PARTICIPATION OF THE MONARCHIES

An important point in the development of Indie traditions was the participation of royalty in the construction of these temples. For some time previously, kings had begun to refuse Vedic sacrifice as a form of sanctioning their authority and government. Most kings from Aśoka onwards (3rd century BC) until Harsa (7th century CE) tended to legitimise their rule by favouring all religious groups and financing the building of temples. It can be said that the Gupta period was the birthplace of the "religion of temple worship". This religious form came to eclipse all others.

By building temples of Viṣṇu, Śiva, the Devī, the Buddha, or the Jina, the medieval kings *literally* brought these gods, supreme beings, and perfect ones onto their territory. The king played the part of earthly regent for the divine beings and financed their worship. He maintained his position as the leader of the sacrifice, but replaced Vedic ritual with the temple of the Lord.

For the kings of the time, financing the construction of a temple and engraving their name as the benefactor not only indicated that they were devotees *(bhaktas)* of the Lord of that temple, but to an extent, they shared in the attributes of the deity, and being protected by the same. This point is important since it tended to put the *jinas* at a disadvantage compared with Hindu gods. *The jinas,* as we shall see, are absentee lords who dwell in the Abode of the Liberated Souls, and do not intervene in this world. Though they could construct the *centre of the cosmos,* their charisma in the kings' eyes would be always be less than that of the ever-participating gods and goddesses of Hinduism. It is hardly stretching it to say that the tandem formed by temple Hinduism and Hindu devotionalism came about as the complete reformulation of Hinduism in the face of the challenge posed by Buddhism and Jainism. These latter traditions did not accept the existence of socio-spiritual classes so that they would be highly attractive to the ritually lower classes. Only a form of Hinduim that was open to everyone could survive. This was none other than devotional Hinduism, since God, as seen in the *Bhagavad-gītā* [see page 169], makes no distinctions between caste or gender. The sovereigns who built for the benefit of notably more approachable and popular gods, would be equally venerated and supported both by the lower castes and by members of the more influential castes. Accordingly, the emergence of the temple religion was especially beneficial to Hinduism, or more exactly—at the risk of complicating things—for the *gods of India.* This is because many Indian gods (not necessarily Hindu gods) began to be connected with the *jinas,* normally as a guardian spirit *(yakṣas, yakṣīs, śāsanadevatās).* From the 5th century onwards, the notion of a pair of guardian spirits associated with each of *the jinas,* became firmly established. This was also the time when the characteristic emblems *(lāñchanas)* of the *jinas* were fixed. In other words, the Gupta period saw the codification of the entire Jain pantheon. The twenty-four *jinas* with their escort of *yakṣas* and *yakṣīs,* together with deities such as Sarasvatī, Lakṣmī, Ambikā, Kṛṣṇa, Balarāma, Rāma, Bāhubali, and other sublime beings *(śalākāpuruṣas),* found their perfect place in the Jainism of the Gupta period. Thanks to this process of reorientation, Jainism was still able to compete for centuries with the consummately attractive Hindu devotionalism.

JAINISM IN MADHYA PRADESH AND MAHARASHTRA

In the days of the emperor Samprati, Jainism took hold in Malva (Avanti), specifically in Ujjain (Ujjayinī), an important cultural, ritual, and economic centre in central India. Numerous Jain stories and legends are linked to this region and city. Not very far away is Vidīśā (Daśārṇa), which was also a well-known Buddhist centre and one of the first places where statues of the *jinas* were venerated.

As we have said, the Śāka and Kuṣāṇa dynasties were more than willing to support Jainism. With the advent of the great Gupta dynasty, the religion of the Nirgranthas continued to prosper, especially in central India. In the small village of Lalitapura, nowadays on the boundary between Madhya Pradesh and Uttar Pradesh, there are more than thirty Digambara temples. The complex, known as Deogarh, contains a myriad of representations of *yakṣīs* like Ambikā and Cakreśvarī, or goddesses like the regent of wisdom, Sarasvatī. Another artistic and cultural centre of the first order is Gwalior which boasts the greatest concentration of Jain images in all India.

Jainism suffered a bleak reversal with arrival on the scene of Mihirakula, the king of the Huns *(hūṇas*—the xiong-nu?), putting an end to the Gupta empire at the close of the 5th century. The Jains look upon him as a terrible enemy of their religion. They recount that the king decreed that any lay person who gave food to the ascetics would be fined. This contrasts with the great emperor Harṣa (7th century), who succeeded in re-establishing a vast empire in the North. In a sense, Harṣa sought to emulate Aśoka. By family tradition, he was linked with Śaivism; his father had been a devotee of Sūrya; his brothers and sisters were attracted by Theravāda Buddhism; he personally embraced Mahāyāna. Logically, in his kingdom all forms of worship were encouraged.

Let us make our way into the interior. In a remote area of the North of Madhya

Pradesh is to be found the fabulous complex of Khajuraho, built during the short-lasting Candella dynasty (10th-11th centuries). Some 30 temples there are Hindu, consecrated in most cases to Śiva and Viṣṇu. Half a dozen of the temples are Jain. Of especial interest are the ones devoted to Ṛṣabha and Pārśva and the one known as Ghaṇṭāi, owing to the bells *(ghaṇṭās)* sculpted on its pillars. Apart from their beauty, the temples of Khajuraho are world famous for the fabulous and blatantly erotic sculptures on the temple fronts. The architecture and sculpture of the Jain temples are no less fabulous and erotic than those of the Hindu temples. At first sight, it would seem a violation of the ascetic principles of Jainism, which would not conceive of any Jain god or godess in the throes of amorous passion. Clearly, what we have here is an expression of pan-Indian Tantrism, a particularly powerful ritual and artistic expression between the 9th and 11th centuries. Although the erotic figures of the Jain temples are possibly a little less "obscene" than their Hindu counterparts—and possibly two of the Jain temples at Khajuraho, had been formerly Hindu temples (Hege-wald 2006: 412-413)—from the Tantric standpoint this contradiction has its own logic. As a general rule, Indian temples represent the world of sensual experience on the outside of the building. Hence the baroque and erotic nature of some exteriors. In Khajuraho there are a multitude of gods, goddesses, celestial musicians *(gandharvas),* nymphs *(apsarās)* and fairies *(vidyādharas)* portrayed in exuberant expression of vitality and sensuality. They represent the way of life in the Upper World, the blissful universe of the gods, but this is an imperfect state of happiness, not to be compared with the serenity of the *jina* that dwells in the central chapel. If the outside of the temple is sensuous, logically enough the interior will be austere, dark, cold even. Once the devotee passes through the walls into the temple and approaches the image at the centre, the florid decoration decreases. A similar transition is expected to occur within the devotee.

A similar perfection is to be found in Maharashtra, in the little-visited Digambara temple of Ellora, dedicated to Pārśva. Furthermore, it is the only temple of the well over thirty in the complex (Hindu or Buddhist in the main) in which worship is still carried out. Mention needs to be made of the not too distant Mount Mangitungi, and Mount Muktagiri, the mountain of pearls.

15. JAINISM IN THE DECCAN REGION

MIGRATION TO THE DECCAN REGION

A recurring Jain tradition tells of how the emperor Maurya Samprati, encouraged by his master Suhastin, established Jainism in ignoble (non Aryan) lands he had conquered, sending ascetics to spread the true *dharma* (Hemacandra, *Pariśiṣṭa-parvam* 11.83-102). In other words, the emperor made himself responsible for the "civilisation" of southern India. Paul Dundas (1992: 99) believes that this tradition is an age-old reminder of a gradual infiltration of groups of mendicants into the South. These wandering monks would have acted as transmitters of prestigious northern culture, which included Jainism, in the Deccan and southern India, where there had been little contact with the Aryan ethos in the first centuries before and after our Era. Similar legends can be found in Buddhism and Brāhmaṇism.*

There was already confirmation of "a forest lineage" that was made up of proverbially austere ascetics in the heart of the Deccan (southern Maharashtra and Karnataka) in the 4th century. Possibly the allusions are to the Mūla-Saṃgha, which at a later date would become known as Digambara Jainism. There is constant reference to this group in the 5th and 6th centuries, along with a multitude of other Digambara sub-groups, consolidated on geographic patterns or the lineages of reputed masters. These days, the predominant trend in the Deccan region continues to be Digambara. The Śvetāmbaras one finds in the South or in the Deccan region all come from recent migrations.

THE GAṄGAS: THE FIRST JAIN DYNASTY

Very early on there was a truly Jain dynasty established at Karnataka: the Gaṅga dynasty. The champion of the kingdom was Siṃhanandi, a Digambara ascetic. It is said that this master helped king Konguṇivamia ascend to the throne in the

* For example, the story of Mahinda and Saṅghamittā, Aśoka's sons, sent to spread Buddhism in Ceylon or the story of the seer *(ṛṣi)* Agastya, who introduced Brāhmaṇism into the South.

middle of the 3rd century, although all references to the ascetic belong to the later years of the dynasty (9th-10th centuries). It is told that as a sign of his abdication from Buddhism and conversion to Jainism, the king had a pillar (possibly one of the Aśoka pillars) destroyed. The involvement of an ascetic in a political matter such as the establishment of a dynasty is infrequent in the history of Jainism. Because of their religious vows, no ascetic should get involved in such mundane matters. Whether or not the story of Siṃhanandi is actually true, the act was never condemned and no reproach was expressed either by the lay or ascetic communities.

It is documented that at the end of the 4th century the Gaṅga king Mādhava II donated a whole town for the use and enjoyment of the ascetics from Mūla-Saṃgha. The following Gaṅga kings were all devout Jains and for seven centuries made their capital into one of the most important Jain centres in history. The dynasty remained solid until the 11th century and it extended to Belgaum (bordering on Maharashtra), the Coorg country (bordering on Kerala), and Tanjore (in Tamil Nadu). Many wealthy lay people followed the monarchs' example and had temples, retreats and hostels built throughout the region. Merchant participation in the donations is evident from the 10th century, when commerce in the Deccan region and southern India increased owing to new contacts in the Arab and Chinese worlds.

SEDENTARY ASCETICS

All this shows the ambivalence of tradition in the view of the necessity for patronage, on one hand, and the vow of non-possession *(aparigraha)* on the other. Great thinkers like Kundakunda or Vaṭṭakera, both being from the first century CE, clearly oppose the idea of ascetics abandoning their itinerant lifestyle to dwell in permanent retreats or monasteries. What an ascetic had to do was to wander without stopping (except during the monsoons) spending the night in caves or in houses of lay persons of irreprochable conduct. The truth is that at the end of the 4th century, we begin to find more and more groups of ascetics staying in permanent retreats and living a sedentary life. The model of the ascetic's life was changing. The number and importance of solitary ascetics gradually decreased.

As with Buddhist retreats, the small Jain *upāśrayas* turned into large monasteries of an almost feudal nature. Settlements of numerous of ascetics and royal donations favoured the possession and exploitation of substantial economic resources. Monasteries owned farmland and were engaged in the elaboration of agricultural productes, free of state taxes and red tape. The largest ones were not only places of worship *(mandiras),* for congregations of ascetics *(upāśrayas),* and sources of wealth, but also became centres for learning and charity houses, incorporating schools *(gurukulas),* libraries *(grantha-bhaṇḍāras)* and hostels *(dharma-śālās).* Jain charity houses *(dāna-śālās)* were pioneers in distributing food among poor people and giving shelter to the needed. This also favoured relations between the lay and ascetic communities. Epigraphs have revealed that great *ācāryas* like Vīradeva, Pūjyapāda, Jinasena or Guṇabhadra became chaplains of Gaṅga nobles.

SHRAVANABELGOLA

The spiritual centre of Digambara Jainism of the Deccan region has always been Shravanabelgola, not far from Mysore, in Karnataka. The village extends alongside a pond at the foot of two prominent peaks: the small mountain (Candragiri, Cikkabeṭṭa) and the big mountain (Indragiri, Doḍḍabeṭṭa). The whole area is replete with temples, statues and pillars from different periods. Hundreds of inscriptions relate to the sacred death by voluntary starving *(sallekhanā)* on these two mountains, emulating the legendary end of king Maurya Candragupta and his master Bhadrabāhu [see page 180]. In the 7th and 8th centuries alone, we know of some sixty cases of *sallekhanā,* not only among monks and nuns but also among pious laymen and laywomen (Singh 1975: 163-166).

In the 10th century, general Cāmuṇḍarāya, a high-ranking officer of the Gaṅga kings had the famous statue of Bāhubali or Gomateśvara made [see FIG. 8]. The statue at Shravanabelgola is a three-dimensional masterpiece; freestanding from the rock it was sculpted from. It is said that statue was modelled on the venerable master Jinasena [see forward]. Since the end of the 14th century, a spectacular congregation has periodically taken place at this sanctuary [see pages 433-434].

The fact that a military person like Cāmuṇḍarāya would openly support Jainism, the religion of non-violence par excellence, apparently must not have seemed incongruous to the community. There is a logical explanation. Jainism, especially Digambara Jainism, encourages heroic individualism and illustrates the cultivation of self-perfection with martial and warlike metaphors. It is no coincidence that chivalrous and aristocratic circles in southern India and the Deccan should be drawn towards such a tradition. According to Burton Stein (cited in Dundas 1991: 175), Jainism endowed warriors and aristocrats with noble rank and respectability *(ārya*—from the North) avoiding the necessity of becoming involved with the agricultural culture of the period, then associated with devotional Hinduism. On the other hand, this would give Jainism the status not of a heretical sect but rather of that of a crucial ideological element at a time of great changes in southern India. Nor is it surprising either that general Cāmundarāya himself, author of a Jain *Purāṇa* of the same name, should have had temples built dedicated to the ever powerful gods Viṣṇu or Śiva. Following the example of most Indian politicians, a convinced Jain such as Cāmuṇḍarāya did not forget to maintain a healthy eclecticism. It is true that governors would have endowed Jainism with respectability, but it is also true that the existence of a substantial lay community (with considerable economic clout) would oblige the incorporation of Jain elements.

Since then, Shravanabelgola has remained the most important ritual centre in the Deccan region and the South. Cāmuṇḍarāya founded a monastery in 982, the successive heads of which claim to be descendants of Cāmuṇḍarāya's *guru,* the celebrated philosopher Nemicandra Siddhāntacakravartin.

Bāhubali, despite never being a *tīrthaṅkara,* has received special worship in Karnataka. Imitating the sanctuary of Shravanabelgola, other monarchs had gigantic statues of Bāhubali erected. The images of Karkala (15th century) and Venur (17th century) being of particular interest.

THE YĀPANĪYAS

Owing to a range of different factors, Digambara Jainism from Karnataka was exceptionally liberal. For one thing we have to insist on the participation of ascetics in the construction of the political, economical and social scene, an issue that would somewhat allow them to relax their initial rigidity. Pelaxation of ascetic ideals from the North enabled Jain *dharma* to take root among the population. However, liberalism in the Deccan region had much to do with the implantation of one particular tendency: Yāpanīya Jainism.

The origin of this variant is obscure. It possibly emerged as a development out of the Ardhaphālakas [see pages 182-183], those partially naked and partially dressed. From there they also acquired the name of Gopya-Saṃgha, the community that "waits [for better times]", referring to the drought that brought about this practice. Later on, these Ardhaphālakas would immigrate to the Deccan and finally drop the practice, making themselves indistinguishable from Digambaras.

Yāpanīya Jainism prospered for a thousand years. Around the 5th and 6th centuries, they had their centre in Halsi (Palāśika) and afterwards extended towards Aihole and Kolhapur. We know they were very active setting up images of the *jinas* and building temples in the North of Karnataka, thanks to inscriptions that have been found. They would later spread throughout the rest of Karnataka, Andhra Pradesh and extend toward Tamil Nadu. The lay community became quite powerful.

Curiously enough, these mysterious Yāpanīyas were neither totally Digambaras nor totally Śvetāmbaras. The ascetics went naked, an unmistakable mark of Digambara Jainism, and their images are portrayed in this way. They did not recognise the loss of the sacred scriptures: their scriptures were those of Śvetāmbaras. Other points of view held by them were also clearly similar to the Śvetāmbaras. For instance, they considered that those achieving omniscience would continue to take food and they recognised the possibility of women achieving liberation (although they did not think that the *jina* Malli was a woman). In fact, the first author to counter the Digambara opinions against women achieving liberation was the Yāpanīya Sākaṭāyana [see page 188]. While ascetics went about naked, for Yāpanīyas a minimal amount of clothing was allowed. For instance, a *sādhu* or a *sādhvī* suffering from an illness could use bandages or clothing. Here, we find a difference between them and Śvetāmbaras, as it is obvious that this explanation does not justify the permanent use of clothing. The truth is that neither Śvetāmbaras nor Digambaras considered them one of their own. Although their name appears among the Digambara *saṃghas,* the latter refer to them as being pseudo-Jains *(jainābhāsas).* According to Padmanabha Jaini (1991: 43), the Yāpanīyas represented an ancient ecumenical movement that tried to combine features of the naked *(acelaka)* and clothed *(sucelaka)* factions of Jainism. But Jaini observes that, as has so often happened in India, they were rejected by both and reduced to being just another sect.

Among other contributions, the Yāpanīyas took considerable pains to encourage the worship of the gods, which attained very appreciable proportions in medieval Karnataka [see below]. Possibly, they were also the initiators of the institution of the priesthood *(bhaṭṭārakas),* which was to become a characteristic feature of Jainism in the South and the Deccan. By the 14th or 15th centuries, however, they had been completely assimilated by Digambaras.

JAIN TANTRISM IN KARNATAKA

Jinasena in his *Ādi-Purāṇa* (1.21.231; cited in Singh 1975: 33) refers to the recitation of the most sacred of Jain litany, the *namaskāra-mantra,* being condensed into forms of 16, eight, six and five letters. Moreover, these can be condensed down to the one powerful syllable *(bīja) Oṃ.* Jinasena claims that its murmured repetition confers the most beneficial effects, even liberation. Texts describe in detail all forms of worship, from the installation of images to the forms of daily worship at home or in a temple. In all cases we come across the recitation of chants *(mantras),* murmuring *(japas),* circumvalations *(pradakṣiṇās)* (Jaṭāsiṁhanandi, *Varāṅga-carita* 23.57; cited in Singh 1975: 41), symbolic gestures *(mudrās),* the use of mystic diagrams *(yantras),* etc. This is pure Tantric ritualism, and as we shall see when we come to talk about worship, these features fitted well among all forms of Jainism, but it was probably the Yāpanīya-saṃgha and the Drāviḍa-saṃgha groups that which mostly contributed to their evolution.

Among Jains in Karnataka, some deities who accompanied the *jinas* became especially popular. For example, the goddesses Padmāvatī (Lakṣmī), Kūṣmāṇḍinī (Ambikā) and Jvālāmālinī. In origin, these were all ancient *yakṣiṇīs* who had no separate existence apart from the *tīrthaṅkaras.* Around the 11th or 12th centuries, they began to be worshipped as divinities independently from the *jinas.* They were considered as great possessors of mystical powers and some Tantric-style texts, such as the *Jvālinī-kalpa* by Indranandi, were centred on the subtleties of their worship. Following the general directives of Tantric esotericism, the *Bhairava-Padmāvatī-kalpa* (2.2-4; cited in Singh 1975: 59) recommends the use of the syllables *hrāṁ, hrīṁ, hruṁ, hrauṁ,* and *hraḥ* to purify head, face, heart, stomach and legs respectively.

THE RĀṢṬRAKŪṬA DYNASTY

Other dynasties in the Deccan region also tolerated and protected Jainism. The Rāṣṭrakūṭa dynasty (8th-12th centuries) was of particular importance. Initially, it was based in Morkhand and later moving to Malkhed, near Hyderabad. The most eminent of Jain monarchs in the Deccan region was the Rāṣṭrakūṭa Amoghavarṣa (reigned 815-877) who marked the turning point and high point of Jainism in Karnataka and Maharashtra. Thanks to him, numerous temples and sanctuaries were built. It is said that the king abdicated and became an ascetic and even wrote a Jain treatise.

ROYALTY ACCORDING TO THE *ĀDI-PURĀṆA*

Amoghavarṣa's spiritual preceptor was the master Jinasena (9th century), author of the *Ādi-Purāṇa,* the most important Digambara work relating the Universal History. The continuation to this chronicle, the *Uttara-Purāṇa,* was written by his pupil Guṇabhadra (9th century), who also had a Rāṣṭrakūṭa king as a patron (and it was finally completed by a third hand). Jinasena concentrated on the life story of the first *jina* Ṛṣabha and his sons Bharata and Bāhubali, while Guṇabhadra concerned himself with the rest of the sublime beings of Jain mythology. Taken together, these two texts form the *Mahā-Purāṇa,* not only one of the most important works dealing with Jain mythology, but also one of the best doctrinal expositions, and an exquisite example of Sanskrit literature.

The *Purāṇa* was undoubtedly written to be read in the kings court and contains many teaching points. Jinasena was a member of a monastic group, possibly originating in the North, but which had become inextricably linked to Shravanabelgola. According to his own testimony, this lineage traces back to Ṛṣabha, who recited the *Ādi-Purāṇa* to his son Bharata. The text was transmitted down through the ages until it came to the *gaṇadhara* Gautama who in turn recited it to king Śreṇika of Magadha. Just as Ṛṣabha instructed his son Bharata, and Gautama instructed Śreṇika—who, recall, is to become the future *jina*—Jinasena recited it to Amoghavarṣa, and in doing so he instructed him in the behaviour befitting a Jain ruler. In fact, the *Ādi-Purāṇa* presents us with the first model of royalty à la Jain, an issue which would later on be developed by Somadeva and put into practice by the Śvetāmbaras in Gujarat [see pages 244-246].

In Jinasena's opinion, the institution of royalty (while being necessary) is ambiguous. In spite of his greatness, Bharata's conquest still remains as an inter-saṃsāric issue, and thus an infinitely inferior victory to that of Ṛṣabha or Bāhubali. It was these omniscient beings who were victorious in the real battle. For Jinasena, Ṛṣabha is the real king. He had not just conquered India, but all three worlds. Bharata's inferiority is clearly illustrated in the chapters telling of his conflict with Bāhubali, just before becoming the great *cakravartin.* It will be recalled that Bharata challenged Bāhubali motivated by greed, and cheated in the battle, but the king's inferiority does not detract from his grandeur here on Earth. On becoming a *cakravartin,* Bharata encouraged his vassals to protect the Jain community and free their counties from bad influence of Brāhmaṇism. He fasts and worships before going into battle, he reduces taxes in newly conquered lands: he remains ever calm, but at the same time he is full of energy, he even holds sway over barbarians and foreigners who live beyond the pale of *karma* and *dharma.*

For Jinasena, the warriors and nobles (Kṣatriyas) were instated by Ṛṣabha to protect different sections of society. In the first place, the religious community; which means that king should accumulate material prosperity *(artha)* to benefit the deserving without going against *dharma.* This notion is pan-Indian. Secondly, royalty must protect the true doctrine, that is to say, Jainism. Third, royalty must protect the *jīva.* That is to say, at a given moment the monarch will have to renounce the world and practice asceticism, in sharp contrast to the Brāhmaṇical model. Fourth, royalty must protect its subjects; and the best way to do this is be surrounded by loyal ministers and a faithful army. The main function of protecting one's subjects is defending the kingdom from scribal barbarians *(akṣaram-leccha)*—in other words, Brāhmaṇas who venerate the Veda and proudly boast of their scriptural knowledge.

THE JAIN CONTRIBUTION TO THE KANNADIGA CULTURE

One positive aspect of the development of Jain monasticism was the notable increase in production and transmission of scriptural texts. Instead of spending their time in pilgrimage, ascetics would devote time to the study and copying of texts. Ram Singh (1975: 108) affirms that the appearance of epic-lyrical *(kāvya)* and purāṇic *(Purāṇa)* literature, along with the development of regional languages, can be attributed to ascetics and Jain preceptors who lived in monasteries.

All of the first works we have knowledge of written in Kannada language are by Jains. Śivakoṭyācārya (8th century), author of the *Voddha-ārādhana,* was a devout Jain. Jain ascetics monopolised Kannada literature up until the 11th and 12th centuries.

One must not forget the contributions (in Kannada, Sanskrit, or Prakrit languages) to Jain philosophy or to Indian knowledge in general. Pūjyapāda, the grammar master and commentator (5th-6th centuries), was native of Karnataka and was the preceptor of the Gaṅga king Durvinīta. Besides his lucid defence of spiritual liberation in women, the before mentioned Yāpanīya Śākaṭāyana (9th century) is regarded as the leading Jain grammarian. Another memorable author was Yogīndudeva (6th century) a writer of excellent mystic treatises. Among the didactic texts of particular importance there is the *Varāṅga-carita* by Jaṭāsiṁhanandi (7th century) and the *Yaśastilaka-campū* by Somedeva Sūri (10th century), a Sanskrit text of superb literary quality, considered to be one of the high points in epic narrative. Later on, with Amitagati (10th-11th centuries), didactic works were enriched by his encyclopaedic *Subhāṣita-ratnasaṁdoha.* Two important authors writing on the Digambara Universal History must not be forgotten: the above mentioned Jinasena and Guṇabhadra, not to mention Raviśena (7th-8th centuries) who wrote one of the Jaina Rāmāyaṇas. Lastly, there is the philosopher Nemicandra (10th century), general Cāmuṇḍarāya's preceptor, much loved by Digambaras, to whom they gave the title of "Emperor of the doctrine" (Siddhāntacakravartin). The Tantric contribution comes mainly from Indranandi (10th century).

The Jain contribution at the time of forming cultural, political and social signs of identity in Karnataka was enormous.

THE DECLINE OF JAINISM IN THE DECCAN

With the disappearance of the Rāṣṭrakūṭa dynasty, Jainism began to decline in the Deccan. The last monarch in this dynasty, Indra, tried to retrieve the empire, and when unsuccessful he retired to Shravanabelgola, where just like so many other pious Jains he opted for the voluntary death through one last and definitive fast.

However, Jainism still had its occasional flushes of brilliance under some monarchs of the Cālukya, Kalaṣa, and Hoysala dynasties. It is related that the origin of the latter traces back to a Digambara ascetic who had to undertake an act of violence in self-defence. Whether that were so, we do know that various Hoysala rulers were committed Jains, and showed benevolence towards Jainism, even if in the last few centuries of the dynasty there was a clear swing in favour of Vaiṣṇavism. Today, we are still able to contemplate the beautiful Jain temple in the ancient Hoysala capital of Halebid [see Fig. 32]. With the fall of the dynasty, the region came under the rule of the clearly Brāhmaṇic-orientated Vijayanagara Empire.

What factors might explain the decadence and stagnation of Digambara Jainism in Karnataka and southern Maharashtra? Three linked socireligious reasons played their part.

The first factor was the arrival on the scene of the "heroic followers of Śiva" movement (Vīraśaiva), a very special type of devotional Śaivism, founded by Basava (1106-1167). TheVīraśaivas were very active proselytes and knew how to connect with the devotional vein of a large section of the population in the area of Karnataka. Since the 12th century, they have not stopped expanding and they have also managed to keep their independence from Brāhmaṇism,* taking

* These days, inevitably Vīraśaivas to constitute a caste apart, denominated the *liṅgāyata,* basically centred on the area of Mysore. It is the caste with most members (some 6 million) and in many places the dominant one. They have their own priests, known as Jaṅgamas. Similarly, they have their order of strictly celibate renunciants, the Viraktas.

over from the Jains in this respect. We know of rather drastic persecutions of ascetics and attacks on Jain properties by fanatic Vīraśaivas. Theologically speaking, they were astute in their attacks on the Jain concept of the *tīrthaṅkara.*

Second, a fully codified Vaiṣṇavism from Rāmānuja (11th-12th centuries), the Śrīvaiṣṇava movement and philosophy. Thus, the greatest of Hoysala kings, Biṭṭideva (reigned 1106-1141), was converted to Vaiṣṇavism (changing his name to Viṣṇuvardhana) and the remainder of the dynasty followed in his footsteps, even if his own wife continued as a devout Jain. This swing in dynastic preferences took power away from the community.

If the Vīraśaivas replaced Jains as being the most prominent religious group independent from the Brāhmaṇas, Jain monasticism was overtaken by the only monastic movement within Hinduism: that of the Daśanāmis, devotees of the philosopher Śaṅkara (8th-9th centuries). This third factor steered the monastic tradition in the South towards Vedānta and Hinduism. We know that the major monastery at Shringeri in Karnataka, one of the four main Śaṅkarian "seats" and supposedly founded by a direct disciples of Śaṅkara, was in fact Jain up until the 14th century. Philosophically speaking, nor was the Brāhmaṇic—almost Vedic Restoration—to be underestimated, exemplified by one of India's main philosophers: the Mīmaṃsāka Kumārila. With the advent of Śaṅkara and Kumārila, Jainism came to be regarded as being clearly heterododox *(nāstika).*

The Digambara community continued to wane. Many of their members were converted to Vaiṣṇavism, or joined the Vīraśaivas. Their strong economic power dwindled appreciably, an already much felt reality in the 14th century. However, thanks to centuries of institutional support, the Kannadiga and Maharashtri communities could face the gloomy future with a degree of solvency. Due to their specific weight they succeeded in retaining a substantial amount of power within the Vijayanagara Empire. Inevitably, the community developed a tendency to concealment and closing of ranks. Since then, they have clearly been on the defensive and their interest in proselytising has been minimal.

Their lowest ebb would be reached in the 19th century: the ascetic community had almost entirely disappeared. Indeed, at the end of the century we have news of the existence of only one lone Digambara ascetic in the whole of southern India. This being Siddhasāgara (1828-1903) who had to initiate himself by shedding his clothes before an image of a *tīrthaṅkara.* A very similar case was that of Śāntisāgara (1873-1955) [see page 275]. Owing to their efforts, these days the fully initiated Digambara community comprises more than a hundred members.

Similarly, lay community in northern Karnataka and southern Maharashtra (at the present time, one of the regions in India with the highest densities of Jains) had practically lost all its signs of identity. Since the passing of their glorious days the process of absorbing Hindu ideas and practices had been unstoppable. At the end of the 19th century a group of distinguished lay people organised themselves and founded the southern Indian Jain Association (Dakṣina

Bharata Jain Sabhā), a reformist organisation that has had notable success. Without the active participation of this committed lay association, it is more than likely that the Digambara Jainism of the Deccan region would have dissolved within the immense Hindu melting pot. Jainism would then have been reduced to a simple caste. Thanks to their involvement, it has recovered, or rather has created, a community with a strong personality. These days, Jains constitute a minority among the Kannadigas and Maharashtris but a much-respected minority.

ANDHRA PRADESH

Culturally speaking, the area where Telegu is spoken in Andhra Pradesh has always been very close culturally to the Kannadiga culture of Karnataka and the Maratha culture of Maharashtra. This was an important region for the transmission of Jainism from Orissa.

During the very first centuries of the Common Era the Āndhra dynasty, with its capital in Pratiṣṭhāna, not far from present day Haidarabad, was openly in favour of Śramaṇic movements. Although most Āndhra regents aligned themselves with Buddhism, various monarchs supported Jainism. Tradition tells how the king Śātavāhana Hāla came to write an anthology of verses in Prakrit (von Glasenapp 1925: 60). Under the powerful Āndhra kings Maharastri-Jaina, a Prakrit language used by Śvetāmbara Jains in Maharashtra, came to be developed. This was a direct predecessor of modern day Maharashtri.

Around the 2nd century, Kundakunda, one of the most brilliant thinkers in the history of Jainism, lived between Andhra and southern Karnataka. His monastic name was Padmanandi, while Kundakunda came possibly from his birthplace, in Andhra Pradesh. He was the author of some of the most important doctrinal treatises and hymn collections in Jainism. Kundakunda is so revered among Digambaras that his name is on a par with that of Mahāvīra and Gautama and above Bhadrabāhu and Viśākha, the "founders", so to speak, of the lineage. According to the Digambaras, one of Kundakunda's disciples, perhaps not an immediate one but from the same lineage—Umāsvāti—was the greatest philosopher Jainism has produced.

Jainism was well rooted in Andhra Pradesh until the 8th and 9th centuries competing with Buddhism. The coastal cities of Vishakapatnam and Nellore have revealed various Jain sites and temples. Over the centuries these traditions gave way before the advent of devotional Hinduism and the incoming Islam; the latter made Haidarabad its headquarters in the Deccan.

16. JAINISM IN THE SOUTH

THE TAMIL DIGAMBARAS

In the far South of the continent, in the country *(nāṭu)* where Tamil is spoken, Digambara Jainism also knew moments of splendour. Although the present Jain community of Tamil Nadu and Kerala is small, its historical weight is important and memorable.

We know of caves and shelters where ascetics lived at very early dates (3rd-2nd centuries BC [see Fig. 20]), especially in the districts of Arcot, Trichy, Maturai and Tirunelveli. In all probability, these pioneer *sādhus* reached Tamil country via the Orissa/Andhra coastal corridor. Succesive waves arrived coming through the Deccan. Epigraphy shows considerable popular support, especially among the merchant and ruling classes. Possibly, the peak of Jain splendour in Tamil Nadu was reached with the Kalabhara kings (3rd-4th centuries), a dynasty originating from the North of India and very prone to favouring Śramaṇic movements. Little by little, Jains became scattered throughout the South, finally reaching Kanya Kumari and jumping to the Island of Ceylon. According to the Sinhalese chronicle *Mahāvaṁśa,* Jainism arrived in Sri Lanka in the 5th century BC—which is somewhat surprising. This evidence cannot be ruled out, given that Étienne Lamotte (1958: 374) speaks of a Nirgrantha retreat to the North of Anurādhāpura built in the 4th century BC, a retreat that, after it was demolished, became the foundation of the very famous Buddhist monastery of Abhayagirivihāra (Lamotte 1958: 405-406).

The nucleus of southern Digambara Jainism was formed by the Drāviḍa-Saṃgha, a lineage founded by Vajranandin (6th-7th centuries). The latter was a disciple of the great commentator Pūjyapāda. This community brought about a considerable softening of certain dietary prohibitions. A clearly local "tone" pervaded all Tamil Digambara forms and practices.

By the mid 7th century, the Chinese pilgrim Xuanzang *(Da Tang xiyou-ji* 10 [Beal: II, 227-231)]) already noted the presence of many Jains in the Tamil kingdoms of Drāviḍa, Cōla and Malakūṭa. On the outskirts of the sacred Kañchipuram, in a suburb today known popularly as the Jina-Kañchi, some of the most beautiful Jain temples were built. The members of the community enjoyed an outstanding economic position and cultural role, and it is even suspected that king Pallava Mahendravarman̲ I practised Jainism.

In the eyes of the Tamil elite, both Jainism and Buddhism represented prestigious, noble *(ārya),* and respectable cultures, from the North. This paralleled what happened in Karnataka and Maharashtra.

The turning point came when the holy Appar (6th-7th centuries), a former Jain ascetic, persuaded king Mahendravarman̲ I to be converted to Śaivism. Little by little, the country of the Tamils changed from being an eminently Śramaṇic land to being the bastion of Śaiva and Vaiṣṇava devotional worship. The process was slow, but unstoppable. Many of the present day Vaiṣṇava and Śaiva sacred places are sited on what were Jain monasteries or Buddhist centres of worship. Although neither the Pallava kings of Kañchi, nor the Cōl̲as of Tanjavur nor the Cēral of Vañci (possibly, in Kerala) persecuted Jainism, the South became progressively empty of Jain elements. By the 14th and 15th centuries the Drāviḍa or Mathurā assemblies had disappeared completely.

THE CONSTRUCTION OF TAMIL IDENTITY

Providing a brief study of the disappearance of Jainism in the South of India could throw considerable light on the different factors in play in that religion, its interaction with Hinduism and its role in the construction of Tamil identity. As we have already seen, the main cause for the retreat of Jainism in the South was the gradual rise of the theist devotional groups. From the hymns of the Śaiva saints (the Nāyan̲ārs) and of their Vaiṣṇava counterparts (the Āl̲ārs), it is clear that the adversary of Tamil devotionalism was the Buddhism/Jain tandem. The Jains came to be considered as outsiders vis-à-vis Tamil culture (Sivaraman 1987: 156); a culture that started to redefine itself under the umbrella of devotionalism, clearly located within the Hindu-Brāhmaṇical current, and clearly at the expense of the Śramaṇic movements. The saints Appar (6th-7th centuries) among other devotees of Śiva, and Tirumaṅkai (8th century) and Campantar (6th-7th centuries), among other followers of Viṣṇu, made fun of the daily practices of the "heretical" Jain monks, who did not even speak good Tamil or Sanskrit but used a garbled Prakrit dialect. This negative portrayal of the Jains was an important part of the process of definition and consolidation of Tamil devotional worship. There are 1,001 stories of confrontation, which always and inevitably ended in the glorious victory of the followers of Śiva over the ascetics and Jain doctrine. It could be said that from the 9th-10th centuries onward a sort of cultural and ideological alliance was formed between the peasant population in the South (Vellāla) and the Brāhmaṇa élite with a view to bring an end to the nobles' patronage of the heretic groups and to promote the religion of love *(bhakti).* One of the strategies used by the Pallava, for example, was to give land tax-free for Brāhmaṇas (*brahmadeyas*), so that closer ties were formed between the local culture and Brāhmaṇical culture and a cultural homogeity could be achieved. This policy was increased under the Cōḻa, who, while maintaining a policy of general religious tolerance, ended up consolidating Hindu hegemony.

Among the Tamil Brāhmaṇas, there were different orientations. Some remained faithful to the old sacrifices and were versed in the Veda. Others had developed a sophisticated liturgy explicated by new scriptures (Āgamas), and centred on the ritual dedicated to Śiva or Viṣṇu. Gradually, the temples consecrated to these gods began to be found scattered throughout the southern landscape, and it was this type of Hinduism that best expressed the Sanskrit-Tamil synthesis. The āgamic cult *(pūjā)* finally replaced Vedic sacrifice *(yajña)*. But considerable care was taken to legitimise this worship, so to ensure its being well rooted in the Vedic-Brāhmaṇical culture. Accordingly, it will be understood why the followers of Śiva regularised the relationship between Vedic *mantras* and the Śaiva *mantra (Oṃ, namaḥ śivāya),* which Campantar states is the essence of the four Vedas *(Tēvāram* 3.307.1).

The devotional religion of the Tamil country was distinctive in its very sensual, often erotic, aesthetics, and its exaltation of the personal and ecstatic experience of God. This, of course, was at first glance at least, far-removed from the austere and dispassionate religion of the Jains. Thus proclaimed Campantar *(Tēvāram* 1.69 [Peterson 1989: 170]):

> "Do not listen to the words of the mad Jain monks
> who carry mats, and pluck their hair,
> and eat their food standing.
> Love and worship the spouse
> of Umā of the full breasts,
> the Lord [Śiva] who dwells in the shrine of Aṇṇāmalai,
> whose slopes shelters packs of lions".

Both Appar and Campantar reflect to perfection the way in which southern Indians viewed an atheist and ascetic religion. Appar came to regret his lost years as a Jain ascetic and would denounce his old faith as the greatest of his sins *(Tēvāram* 4.39.1-4). It is said that the saint had Jain temples destroyed in Kuddalor and sanctuaries devoted to Śiva built in their place.

Having said all that, the observations made here need to be qualified. The big "but" in all this is that it sets up an artificial and misleading dichotomy between ascetic Jainism and devotional Hinduism.

The conventional narrative expressed by Hinduism—favoured by the Śaiva saints over the centuries down to today—says that the triumph of Hinduism in Tamil country represents a reaction reaffirming the joyful, positive, non-exclusive, and essentially Tamil way, versus the dead weight of joyless Jain and Buddhist puritanism, conservatism and negation of the world, with its anti-social and renunciant values, foreign to Tamil culture. Nevertheless, we have reason enough to question such a radical overview. The inscriptions reveal much more osmosis and borrowings than the saints would care to admit. The process in which Jainism declined as Śaivism was in ascendency, must have been a long one (at least six or seven centuries) and a complex one.

We know, for example, that the appearance of Śaiva temples associated with monasteries *(maṭhas),* specialising not only in ritual or education but also involved in local politics or economy, derived from the model of the Jain monasteries. We know that participation of Jain *sādhus* and *sādhvīs* as spiritual guides and social workers was very intense and brought them very close to the population. We are aware, too, that Tamil Jainism was very open to having women act as teachers and even as objects of veneration. In no sense did the *sādhvīs* occupy a secondary place in society. Not only was Tamil Jainism more open than Hinduism, it went even further than what was permitted by Jain textual tradition. The women ascetic-teachers (Tamil: *kurattiyār)* were set over numerous of people: *sādhvīs,* novices and lay pupils. Some, certainly, were in their turn disciples of masters *(ācāryas, bhaṭṭārakas),* but others were *guruṇīs* in their own right or headed monastery-schools. This phenomenon is unique to Tamil Jainism. It points to local forms of Jainism over and above adhesion to the Śvetāmbara or Digambara persuasions. Probably, they were nominally Digambara, but let us remember that there were in the South intermediate groups, like the liberal Yāpanīyas. Religious affiliation has not always been clear-cut in India. Nor indeed have the boundaries between religions. We know that the Tamil Jains had their own lineages, led a sedentary life, focused on the worship of images and had little to do with monastic communities. In other words, they had more in common with the Hindu women (and men) of Tamil Nadu than with the pan-Indian Jain ascetics.

A somewhat similar thing happened with southern Śaivism. Śaiva-Siddhānta, the type of Śaivism that predominates in Tamil Nadu, has many points in common with Jainism. Śiva worship shares considerable similarity with worship of the *jinas* [see pages 410-411]. Their soteriological thought is surprisingly similar: both envisage a plurality of spiritual and immaterial monads *(jīva, āt-man),* whose predominant characteristic is consciousness *(cetaṛiā, caitanya)*; these are monads that are trapped by action *(karma),* seen as having material form rather than just being a latent psychological force. Śiva worshippers seek to identify themselves with Śiva, but in no sense do they seek union or fusion as they do in other Hindu schools. Instead, like the Jains, they speak of the separation and autonomy *(kaivalya)* of the liberated one. Perhaps it was the presence of so many similarities between Jainism and Śaivism that obliged the Śaiva saints to emphasise the differences. The religions of India are very permeable, with doctrines that are always ready to include, adopt, or borrow new ideas. Tamil devotionalism drew not only on Vedism and orthodox Brāhmaṇism but also on Jainism, Buddhism, and on the Yoga of Patañjali, Sāṃkhya, Pāñcarātra,

Pāśupata as well as local traditions. The resultant synthesis was a new religious way of worship that was enormously attractive. Accordingly, the poems of the saints, rather than contrasting two *ethos,* masterfully illustrate the hermeneutic arguments used by followers of the religion of love *(bhaktas)* to combat the heretics *(pāṣaṇḍas).*

In the end, the Cōḻa (10th-11th centuries) linked once and for all royal worship with local Śaivism, by favouring the setting up of a canon of texts, values and rituals. As Indira V. Peterson (1989: 183) has put it, this process resulted in the ossification of cultural and nationalist religion, which sought to exclude the Jains as a symbol of all that was alien to Tamil religious and social values. Since then, Jains have played no significant role in public or political life.

JAINISM AND TAMIL LITERATURE

Throughout its long history of interaction with the different Indian populations, Jainism has continually made valuable contributions. Possibly, the most eloquent example is the part it played in the development of the Tamil language. Even though, politically speaking, Jainism was never powerful in Tamil Nadu, from the cultural point of view it played a leading role. A review of this aspect will illustrate to perfection just how integrated into Tamil culture Jainism at one time was.

The first grammar of this language, the *Tolkāppiyam,* was written by a Jain ascetic from Kerala, possibly around the 4th century. In fact, the *Tolkāppiyam* is considerably more than a grammar. It is a veritable work on rhetoric, with sections devoted to phonology, morphology and semantics. Here, we already have the two bases of Tamil poetics (Caṅkam): the inner realm, represented by love *(akam),* and the outer realm, represented by war *(puṟam).* Many centuries later, the Jain ascetic Pavaṇanti (12th century) was to compose the *Naṉṉūl,* the official grammar of Tamil, and Amitacākar (10th- 11th centuries), wrote the *Yāpparuṅkalam,* the basic work on Tamil prosody.

Similarly, the most notable Tamil texts on ethics produced between the 1st and 5th centuries were all written by Jains. The much venerated *Tirukkuṟal,* ascribed to Tiruvaḷḷuvar (3rd century), while not properly speaking a Jain text (Gros 1992: 18), reveals an author very influenced by the doctrine of non-violence. Very much in line with Tamil tastes, we find nothing similar to the radical asceticism of the North. Instead the work praises family life and human relationships. Given that the *Tirukkuṟal* avoids any reference to any particular dogma, it is not surprising that Jains, Buddhists, Śaivas, and Vaiṣṇavas all lay claim to it. As in so many cases of this kind, rather than adhering to any particular faith, Tiruvaḷḷuvar expresses the eclectic South Asian spirit.

Of the five long poems *(kāppiyam)* of classic Tamil literature, three were composed by Jains and two by Buddhists.

THE *CILAPPATIKĀRAM*

The most acclaimed of these national poems is the *Cilappatikāram.* It was composed by Iḷankō Aṭikaḷ (5th century), a prince of Kerala (Cēral) that renounced the throne and became a Jain ascetic (*aṭikaḷ).*

Quite possibly, stories and popular tales had circulated for centuries, recited by bards, before being brought together by Iḷankō. The result was an astounding superb work of synchretism. It presents a fascinating mosaic of stories from the oral tradition, Jain doctrine (above all relating to *karma, ahiṃsā* and *nirvāṇa),* pan-Indian mythology, snippets on migrations and invasions, as well as portrayals of cultural and social life in Tamil country. Everything is narrated in the classical syle of the Tamil poetic tradition (Caṅkam), with incursions from the Sanskrit literary tradition. The poem consists of three books, which take the names of the three Tamil capitals, Cōḻa, Pāṇṭiya and Cāral. If the feeling that pervades the first book is erotic (*akam),* and the tone of the last is heroic *(puṟam),* the author adds a new category, the mythical *(Purāṇam),* which dominates the middle book. The classic categories of Tamil poetics is woven in masterly fashion into the epic.

Unlike other epic poems *(Mahābhārata, Rāmāyaṇa, The Iliad, Epic of Gilgamesh,* and so forth) the protagonist of the story is no hero, nor a divine being. The central figure is a woman: Kaṇṇaki. Furthermore, the story does not revolve around a great battle. No, consistent with the Jain tone of the poem, the theme of non-violence pervades the plot. The latter is as follows.

Kaṇṇaki and her husband, the merchant Kōvalaṉ, live a leisurely life in the marvellous city of Pukār, the capital of the kingdom of Cōḻa, on the Koromandel coast. From certain references it can be deduced that Kaṇṇaki and Kōvalaṉ are Jain lay people *(Cilappatikāram* 10.59-62). After falling in love with a courtesan, Kōvalaṉ commits adultery and squanders his fortune. Suspecting that the courtesan is unfaithful to him, Kōvalaṉ goes back to his virtuous wife and together they decide to rebuild their life in Madurai, capital of the realm of Pāṇṭiya. The only thing they possess are their ankle bangles *(cilampus)* from Kaṇṇaki. On the journey, they are joined by Kavunti, a Jain ascetic who travels with them to the gates of the city. While the story has unfolded until now in one of the classical settings of Tamil literature, the sea, the crossing to Madurai represents the wild untamed regions. In Madurai Kōvalaṉ is cheated by the perfidious goldsmith of the kingdom and is accused of having stolen the so-far untraced bangles of the queen of Madurai. Kōvalaṉ is summarily and unjustly executed by the king. Overcome by grief, the newly widowed Kaṇṇaki seeks to demonstrate her husband's innocence showing her bangle, twin to the other. From this point, the sweetly devoted wife (similar in role and characteristics to the Sītā of Rāmāyaṇa) changes to become someone with a remarkably strong character. Her harangue to the king is eloquent; she does not wish vengeance, but instead she wants to remove, from the throne a monarch who has violated the first duty of any ruler: that of protecting his subjects. The king recognises his fault and dies, clearly as a consequence of the action. Soon after-wards the queen also dies. The formerly docile Kaṇṇaki becomes the very personification of wrath, the terrible and fiery side of many of the goddesses of India. Tearing a breast from her body, Kaṇṇaki sets fire to the city and razes it to the ground. The goddess Maturāpati, the guardian of the city, consoles her with an instructive story concerning her husband's *karma* in a former life. In a previous existence, Kōvala<u>n</u> had broken his vow of non-violence and killed an innocent merchant, hence his unjust death in this life. In a few weeks, the goddess explains, Kaṇṇaki will be united with her husband in heaven. Kaṇṇaki leaves the city and goes to the kingdom of Kerala (Cēral), where her death will take place. The inhabitants of Kerala see her ascend to the heavens in the mountains (another habitual setting in Tamil literature) and the bards narrate to the king what had happened in Madurai. The king of Kerala is Cenkuttuvan, said to be the author's brother. Cenkuṭṭuva<u>n</u> decides that Kaṇṇaki should be worshipped as the goddess Patti<u>n</u>i and for that reason decides to carry out an expedition to the Himalayas to obtain the rock out of which her statue will be carved. On the journey, Cenkuṭṭuva<u>n</u> defeats the armies of the North and proclaims himself cultural unifier of the three Tamil kingdoms, thus creating the Tamil nation *(Tami<u>l</u>akam)*. In this way, the king shares in the power of the Great Goddess, institutionalises her worship and proclaims himself universal monarch *(cakravartin),* one who enjoys the goddess's protection and is enthroned by means of the Vedic sacrifice of *rājasūya.* With the apotheosis of Kaṇṇaki as the goddess Patti<u>n</u>i, translator R. Parthasarathy (1993: 9) notes, the sacred nature of the *Cilappatikāram* is established. This is not a descent of the divinity (as in the Hindu epics) but rather an ascent of the human, a feature that fits better with the Śramanic tone of the work.

For our purposes the most interesting aspect of the epic is the female ascetic Kavunti. It is not surprising that her intervention as a spiritual guide takes place in the wilderness. Having come across the ascetic in her cave, the couple are given a cogently explained lesson on the greatness of Jain *dharma* and the inexorable nature of *karma.* In fact, the Jain notion of *karma* pervades the whole narration. Taking with her only her alms bowl and her whisk broom, murmuring sacred *mantras* as she goes, Kavunti offers to act as their guide for the journey. After several days of travelling they arrive in Shrirangam (today the headquarters of one of the most influential Vaiṣṇava groups in all India) where they meet a Jain sage *(cāraṇa).* The sage treats them to an instructive talk on human objectives clearly subordinated to the highest aim of all: enlightenment and liberation. Travelling onward, they meet a Brāhmaṇa who harangues them on the excellences of the cave at Viṣṇu and the benefits of the books (the Vedas), which praise it. Surprisingly, the holy woman replies without hesitation, in a lucid and direct way:

> "Oh brahman, versed
> In the four Vedas, who is committed to making us

Know the truth! We have no wish
To enter the cavern [of Viṣṇu]. The text composed
By Indra who lives for untold ages
Is clearly seen in our scriptures. Don't you look for
All that was done [*karma*] in past births
In the present one? Is there anything precious [liberaton]
That cannot be achieved by those who protect life *[ahiṃsā]*
On the earth and are unfailing in truth [*satya]*? Go,
Seek to worship the feet of the god [Viṣṇu]
You love. As befits us we too
Have a long way to go" *(Cilappatikāram* 11.182-194).

Kavunti's firm and serene manner is a faithful reflection of the Tamil female ascetic of the time. She lives according to *dharma,* she knows the Jain scriptures and shows a good knowledge of the Brāhmaṇical scriptures. Her speech is supremely poetic and, despite being a woman, she has no hesitation in replying with clarity to a Brāhmaṇa.

Despite the markedly Jain *ethos,* Iḷaṅkō's narrative portrays mutual understanding between the different Śramaṇic and Brāhmaṇic groups. The Tamil religious situation of the times was evidently typified by a high degree of eclecticism, which Iḷaṅkō was able to reflect. In speaking of the temples of Pukār, mention is made of those of Skandha (Murukaṉ), Indra, Sūrya, the Nirgrantha temples, and those of the goddess Śāstā (Cāttan), *(Cilappatikāram* 9.12-22). The honouring of Śiva, Viṣṇu, Kṛṣṇa, and Balarāma is celebrated, which shows how far the sanskritising of the Tamil lands had gone, as well as containing the references to Vedic sacrifices and ideals. Not to mention the goddess Kaṇṇaki/Pattiṉi (still worshipped today in Sri Lanka and Kerala) who is none other than the Great Goddess of Hinduism, but seemingly with a heterodox Jain-Buddhist origin. The author is not, by any means an apologist for Jainism. He not only provides a good, reliable vision of the Hindu world, but he mentions without any resentment the doctrines of the Buddha and the Ājīvikas.

THE *CĪVAKACINTĀMAṆI*

Another fascinating example of the immersion in Tamil civilisation is to be found in the *Cīvakacintāmaṇi.* This is the second of the great epics in the Tamil language, written by the Digambara ascetic Muni Tiruttakkatēvar (9th- 10th centuries). Taking as its point of departure a nucleus of oral literature, the work has been continually rewritten and transformed. This second epic, which is located mid way between the picaresque and the mystical, tells of the viscitudes of the hero Cīvakaṉ.

A pecularity of this epic is its openly obscene tone, and the very explicit erotic descriptions it contains. The author justifies this in the following way. As a member of the academy of poetry in Madurai, his colleagues accuse him of ineptitude when it comes to writing Treatises of Love. By way of reply, Tiruttakkatévar writes the *Cīvakacintāmaṇi,* which tells of the eight wives of Cīvakaṉ. But, how can a *sādhu* from an ultra-ascetic tradition like that of the Digambaras write such a text?

For James Ryan (1998: 69), this masterpiece of erotic love was not written to glorify it. When Jains write of the world of phenomena from a practical point of view, they do not spare details concerning the conjugal life of the lay protagonists. What Tiruttakkatēvar did was to use the Tamil genre of love poetry *(akam)* for his own purposes. If the devotional poets used the *akam* genre to glorify the love of the devotee for Śiva or Viṣṇu, the Jain ascetic used the imagery of the *akam* to turn sexuality against itself. At every turn, Tiruttakkatévar shows the danger of incontinence and sexuality. At the same time, he could be glorified as one of the great poets of the great and ancient Tamil tradition (Caṅkam). Counterpointing and interrelating sexual impulse and the rejection of the world, royalty and asceticism, marriage and renunciation. Tiruttakkatēvar succeeded in integrating the metaphysics and values of North India and the exquisite aesthetics of the South.

Cases like the *Cīvakacintāmaṇi* show to what extent Jainism has been intricately interlinked with Indian civilisation and the lands to which Jainism extended. The stereotype of a Jainism isolated in its austerity, disconnected from the major currents of Hindu cultures, cannot be sustained. It was precisely the introduction of the ascetic and monastic orders, such as the Buddhists and Jains that became one of the paths, via which the Dravidian South began to become more Aryan or more hybrid. In this respect, the role played by Jain ascetics and lay persons was of key importance.

17. JAINISM IN THE NORTH-WEST

THE EXPANSION IN GUJARAT

Indologists say that the Gupta period (4th-6th centuries), one of the most glorious in Indian history, is the period when Brāhmapism was re-established and the definitive foundation stone of classical Hinduism laid down; the time when Brāhmaṇical ideology allied itself intimately with royalty (Flood 1996:52). The Hindu Purāṇas with their ironic and mocking descriptions of Buddhist and Jaina heretics, seem to confirm the resurgence of Brāhmaṇism (Matchett 2001: 17-18). And it is a fact that during this period many Jain groups migrated westward from centres such as Mathura or Ujjain. However, there is no record of persecution, and the disrespectful tone of the Purāṇas reflects the classical prejudice of the Brāhmaṇas rather than the true feeling of the society. In fact, during the Gupta period Jainism was firmly established in central India. What happened is that some groups responded to the new political and religious situation by moving to the area of Saurashtra, in Gujarat, where the prosperous kingdom of the Maitrakas of Vallabhī offered succulent commercial opportunities. We know that the region of Kathiawar had, since ancient times, been an important commercial enclave. Centuries earlier the emperor Samprati had opened up the region to ascetics, so that the region would have been declared noble *(ārya).*

Although the Jain community in Gujarat was initially made up of Svetām-baras and Digambaras in more or less the same proportion, it is a fact that around the 4th and 5th centuries the Śvetāmbara line had come to be the majority. Many Digambaras had followed the migratory path that led them to the Deccan and the far South.

In a short span of time, Saurashtra became the nerve centre of Jainism in the northern and western parts of the continent. Proof of this is that in the middle of the 5th century a great Śvetāmbara council was held in Vallabhī. The outcome of this council was the scriptural compilation of the main Śvetāmbara orders, known by the name of Siddhānta [see pages 336-340].

The lapse of time between the Council of Valabhī (5th century) until the Vāghelā dynasty (13th century) can be considered to be the Golden Age of Śvetāmbara Jainism in Gujarat. Vallabhī developed into an impressive centre for studies, full of monasteries that emulated great Buddhist complexes. Apart from the study of Jain principles as such, the monks gave classes in history, grammar, mathematics, medicine, astronomy, even Buddhist and Brāhmaṇical philosophy—including the study of the Veda.

Owing to the presence of Jainism over so many centuries, some of the most important centres for Jain pilgrimages are found in this state: Girnar, Shatrunjaya and Taranga mountains. Furthermore, Gujarat is the most vegetarian state in the whole of India. The desert region of Kutch (Kaccha), a forgotten region that borders the Sindh region of Pakistan, has the highest density of Jains on the continent [see TABLE 4]. The Jain contribution to the Gujarati language is almost as great as that to Kannada or Tamil. The first two works in old Gujarati, the *Bharateśvara-Bāhubali-ghora* by Vajrasena (7th century) and the extensive version of Śāḷibhadra (12th century) both have as their main theme the mythical battle between Bharata and Bāhubali.

GUJARAT AND THE JAIN NOTION OF ROYALTY

Generally, the Jain lay community has always been critical of ascetics who are involved in politics. This is a tendency which has been maintained over the past 600 years, ever since the last Jain kingdom disappeared from India. Since then Jains have seen political leaders as potentially hostile. Thanks to their influential position as traders, industrialists and bankers, the community has always had connections with political power but have seldom become involved in politics. However, we know that in pre-Islamic India, Jains came to formulate rather elaborate notions of royalty and political management. The first attempt at applying their notion, that we know of, occurred with the Gaṅga dynasty in the Deccan region [see pages 223-224]. But the great exercise in putting a Jain model of royalty into practice took place in Gujarat, between the 9th and 12th centuries, during different dynasties. The high point came with Kumārapāla (12th century), whom the texts unanimously portray as being a great Jain ruler. Although the Jain notion of royalty shares many points in common with the Brāhmaṇical model, it was with Kumārapāla that the differences were also made evident. Just as John Cort's excellent work shows (1998: 87-96), the trail that leads to Kumārapāla was a gradual one. For centuries, the advance towards a Jain kingdom was achieved little by little. Let us see how this occurred.

The first king who showed Jain influence in his model of government was Vanarāja Cāvaḍā (8th century). He was crowned according to an old and solemn rite of Vedic origin. The unusual thing was that the preceptor who led the service was a Jain *ācārya* and not a Brāhmaṇa. What is more, he ordained the king with a sacred powder called *yāskṣepa,* typical of Śvetāmbaras. These two elements are very significant. It transpires that the king was crowned with the charisma bestowed by the powder from a Jain ascetic and not by water typically used by Vaiṣṇavas or Śaivas. It is said that Vanarāja was a devotee of the Jain master Śīlaguṇa Sūri and that he financed the building of a temple dedicated to Pārśva. Nonetheless, Jain texts still portray him as being an eminently Śaiva king.

THE SOLAṄKĪ DYNASTY

In the mid 10th century, king Mūlarāja founded the Solaṅkī dynasty (also called Caulukya) in the very heart of Saurashtra. He established his capital in Patan, considered in its day as one of the most beautiful cities in the whole of South Asia. He was consecrated by means of another classical solemn Vedic rite, the *vājapeya.* Although a devotee of Śiva (he was the great promoter who had the extremely important Śaiva temple built at Somnath), Jain texts describe him as being a very tolerant king. In all likelihood, Mūlarāja could not do without the substantial Jain community, and therefore he financed the construction of Digambara and Śvetāmbara temples. A perfect example of the power of the prosperous Jain community of merchants is to be found in the person of the layman Vimala. During the reign of Bhīma (reigned 1022-1064), Vimala financed the building of some of the most fascinating temples in India on the sacred Mount Abu.

Jayasiṃha Siddharāja (reigned 1094-1143) was another Śaiva king from the Solaṅkī dynasty who openly supported Jainism and had several temples built. Unlike Mūlarāja, this monarch was closely involved with Jain ascetics. It is said that he organised the famous Patan debate, where the Śvetāmbara monk Vādideva Sūri overcame the Digambara ascetic Kumudacandra. Vādideva's victory would establish the Śvetāmbara doctrine as the "official" Jainism in Gujarat to this very day. This event shows very active participation in a matter that was internal to the ascetic community.

Jayasiṃha Siddharāja died without leaving an heir. The throne passed to a distant nephew called Kumārapāla (reigned 1143-1175). Here, we come to the king who would create the Jain kingdom "par excellence" in India. But before we start, we have to introduce an outstanding personality.

During Jayasiṃha's days a wise man appeared on the scene, crucial in the growth of Gujarati Jainism. We refer to Hemacandra, the brilliant court scribe (1089-1172). In fact, his first work, a Sanskrit and Prakrit grammar, was called *Siddhahema* ("written for Siddha[rāja] by Hema[candra]"). It was the first piece in Sanskrit in swaying away from the traditions of Brāhmaṇic scholars. He also wrote poems, prose, metrics and lexicology.

The rise of Kumārapāla was mainly due to the combined efforts of Hemacandra and a Jain minister. In his *Triṣaṣṭiśalākapuruṣa-caritra* Hemacandra relates that Mahāvīra prophesised to king Śreṇika of the close ties between king Kumārapāla and the ascetic Hemacandra. Therefore, there would be a replica of his relationship with the king of Magadha 1,500 years in the future, even though this were at the height of the Sorrowful Age. It is said that the *ācārya* converted the prince who took the vows of a Jain layman.

By petition of the monarch, Hemacandra was commissioned to write new works on philosophy, mythology, history, political science and meditation.

Although, perhaps Hemacandra lacked the originality of a Haribhadra or the profound mysticism of a Kundakunda, he surpassed all in erudition and breadth of knowledge. No doubt owing to his participation in politics the main parts of his biography are well known. Hemacandra is maybe with the exception of Yaśovijaya (17th century), the last of the giants of Jainism. The Śvetāmbara tradition in Gujarat is possibly the most vigorous and self-confident of all Jain communities in India. Much is owed to Hemacandra, whom they fervently called Omniscient One of the Age of Kali (Kalikālasarvajña).

ROYALTY ACCORDING TO HEMACANDRA

The traditional Indian argument about royalty always bases itself on the concept of the *cakravartin,* he who is put on the throne by the charisma of priests and ascetics, virtuously making use of his political-military power and impeccable morality, conquers the four cardinal points and unites the six parts of India. All Indian religious traditions incorporate the notion of this great man *(mahāpuruṣa),* who would conquer India in the name of the Lord of the Cosmos *(īśvara,* Buddha, Jina). Although Jains share this notion and in their Universal History we can always find 12 *cakravartins* for each cosmic cycle, their scholars always clearly distinguish between the conqueror of the world and the insuperable otherworldly spiritual conqueror. We come across this in the story of Bharata and Bāhubali and with Jinasena's notion of royalty [see pages 228-229]. However the ideal proposed by Hemacandra in his *Laghvarhannīti-śāstra* sought to unite both concepts. The figure of Bharata is an obvious example. In fact, Bharata's mother also had 14 auspicious dreams, an unmistakable sign that a *cakravartin* is somebody of extraordinary nature and who in John Cort's words (1998: 98) has an ontological potential similar to that of a *jina.* Before embarking on the conquest of neighbouring kingdoms, Bharata would go through the *posadhopavāsa-vrata,* a fast that would put any Jain layman at the same level as an ascetic. Hence, Cort comes to the conclusion that Bharata had to firstly assume the renunciant state since it was the power derived from renunciation that enabled him to conquer the world (Cort 1998: 99). His immersion in the ascetic's traditional values is what differentiates the Jaina *cakravartin* from his Brāhmaṇical counterparts.

KUMĀRĀPALA'S REIGN

Kumārapāla put Hemacandra's ideas into practice. He had temples built galore; he prohibited the sacrifice of animals, betting, the consumption of meat and alcohol. Butchers had to abandon their profession whil being compensated for doing so. Brāhmaṇas had to substitute sacrificing animals for offerings of vegetables. All these Jain features contrasted with the classical image of the Indian *rāja* a great deal, a character who is invariably known as being carnivorous, who drinks liquor, hunts, is a great warrior, and has a harem to satisfy his sexual desire. Apart from all this Kumārapāla's personal behaviour was an example for his fellows. His reign built up to the peak of Jainism in northern India. The legend goes on to say that the king committed euthanasia by means of a final and definitive fast, following the example of his master who had fasted unto death a few years earlier. According to their own notion of history, a Jain kingdom would never be seen in Bharata-varṣa again.

Even in his fervent Jainism Kumārapāla was friendly to other religions and he maintained Śaivism as the state religion. Although his reign was undoubtedly the first and only example of a truly Jain kingdom in history—with permission of the Gaṇga dynasty—and it is clear that his interest in Jainism was authentic, it should be noted that, taking the classic line of Indian political practice, Kumārapāla also supported Śaivism. We owe to him, the restoration of the Śaiva temple at Somnath.

After the unrest caused by Muslim invasions, Śaivas regained power. The hostility towards Jains of some Śaiva Brāhmaṇas, especially during the reign of Ajayapāla (12th century), Kumārapāla's nephew, marked the decline of Śvetāmbaras in the North West. Later the Muslim forces would thoroughly dismantle and erode the Jain position [see below].

NON-VIOLENCE AND PACIFISM

To sum up, Kumārapāla tried to reproduce the Jain ideal of royalty He achieved it spreading the typical value of *ahiṃsā.* However, neither Kumārapāla nor Hemacandra urged pacifism. *Ahiṃsā* is not the same thing as pacifism. Let us reflect on this matter in greater detail, being to my mind a crucial point.

As we already know, the Hindu conception of state and royalty [see pages 87-89] has its classic example in the *Artha-śāstra* by Kautilya (1st century). This Brāhmaṇa versed in the art of politics has been traditionally identified with Cāṇakya, the councillor who helped Candragupta Maurya (4th-3rd centuries BC) to form the first great Indian Empire, and which Jains claim as their own. Although the connection is improbable, the Jain notion of state (which is said to go back to the times of Ṛsabha and Bharata), is perfectly in tune with the *Artha-śāstra.*

Now in fact, nowhere in the *Artha-śāstra* is it said that peace is preferable to war. In Kauṭilya's opinion the nature and vocation of the king, his *raison d'être,* is conquest. When it comes to governing, the monarch has to defend his kingdom from enemies (internal or external) and there is no room for childish sentiment. Indian politics have always been characterised by a pragmatism and machiavel-lianism of the first order. In all this, Jains do not differ in the least from Brāh-manical experts. Therefore, one must not confuse *ahiṃsā* with pacifism; neither is one to think that Jainism has always been maintained within the non-violent merchant classes. Jain literature is not pacifist in the modern sense of the word, and Gandhi's pacifism à la Jain can be attributed just as much to Tolstoy or Christianity.

As protests and campaigns in defence of non-violence—which are occasionally aggressive—show Jains are not truly pacifists. Recall that neither Hemacandra nor Siṃhanandi impeded the establishment of monarchies, nor were Jain generals ever condemned. Metaphors of conquest and heroism are a constant. What Jainism prohibits outright is blatantly aggressive war. Intentional violence and the issue of self-defence tend to be avoided. Some texts go as far as to consider aggression in self-defence as being a form of violence. Whereas others, following Somadeva Sūri, include a dictum allowing it as a last resort (Jaini 1979: 313-314). Although they warn that those who act in such a fashion are considerably lengthening their path through *saṃsāra,* it is plain to see that Jainism only insists on total and complete non-violence in the case of ascetics. It is true that Jainism has never espoused ideals such as the idea that death on the battlefield is almost equal to martyrdom—on the contrary, it tends to think that death accompained by hatred and violence can never be salutary (Jaini 2004: 57). Remember that in the Jain Rāmāyaṇas the good *vāsudeva* Lakṣmaṇa goes to the same hell as does the wicked Rāvaṇa, whom he killed for a "right cause" (Jaini 2004: 60). But the fact is that there is virtually no Jain text that dwells on the ethical implications of war. In India, whether it be in the Jain or Hindu tradition, violence is accepted, paradoxically but precisely, if it serves to defend non-violence. If what is involved is protecting the community (which enables and exemplifies the release from *saṃsāra)* it is not considered *hiṃsā.* A good example of this dual-moralism is the existence of the warrior ascetic Nāgās (Śaivas or Vaiṣṇavas) who resort to violence to protect *sādhus* and renunciants devoted to non-violence (Bouillier 1993: 213-243). The classic archetype of such dialectics resides in the king or warrior, one who protects non-violent Brāhmaṇas or ascetics while upholding social order. How can this ideal coherently be reconciled with the king's duties, which imply war, punishment, or violence?

The *Bhagavad-gītā* provides us with the ideal solution, where it urges the carrying out of one's own duties *(svadharma).* In the case of monarchy, royal *dharma* implies violence *(hiṃsā)* or punishment *(daṇḍa),* always and only when the subject is free of selfish desire, unattached to the consequences of his actions. The king's duty is to defend the kingdom's and its subject's prosperity, in such a way that, according to Somadeva Sūri, war is justifiable *(Nītivākyāmṛta* 30.5). It is true that Somadeva insists on the fact that weapons are not as efficient as wisdom; weapons are fallible; but useful and necessary. Therefore Kumārapāla would necessarily have been guided by the *ahiṃsā* principle at a personal level, especially with the Kṣatriyas' typical activities (hunting, animal combats, drinking, etc.). But he was forced to use a certain amount of violence when dealing with government issues.

For Jains, the king represented something like the perfect layman. He occupies the throne of Indra, king of gods. But, in no sense is he an emanation of divinity, a perception that Śaivas and Vaiṣṇavas tend to have. The Jain *cakravartin* is on the path to liberation, he is a sublime being, but not a divine one. Without a doubt he would become a *deva,* but in his worldly function he would basically act as the chief of the Jain congregation *(saṃgha).* For this reason, in the light of threats or attacks against the community, Jain leaders, whether kings or laypersons, would have taken measures to counteract violence.

JAIN-MUSLIM RELATIONSHIP

The expansion of Islam, on account of its rapidity, is undoubtedly one of the most surprising phenomena in the history of religions. In the middle of the 8th century there was already news of Muslims in the Sindh region (today in southern Pakistan). At the end of the same century, Turkish-Afghan Muslim invaders reached as far as Vallabhī, the cultural and political capital of western India, destroying it. For the Śvetāmbaras and in fact, for the whole of northern India, this incident marked the entrance of the Muslim world onto the scene.

Nevertheless, the true Muslim "conquest" of India was to come about some centuries later. This is a key point to be able to understand the complexity of the encounter between Indian and Islamic civilisations. For, as Gerald Larson (1995: 103-104) indicated, it was not the original Arab race that overran the Indian continent, but the Abbasides phase, and more specifically its eastern extension in the Turkish-Afghan state of Ghazni. This means that by then, Islam was an extremely complex and cosmopolitan civilisation. Islamic law had absorbed a kaleidoscope of elements such as ritual, legislation and Hebrew scriptures. Neo-platonic and Greek philosophy, as well as ideas adopted from Christian escatology, had come to form part of Islamic mysticism. Greek science was studied. Byzantine and Sassanid art, architecture and ritual had been assimilated by the Ummayyads and Abbasides, the same being true for the plethora of political ideas and forms of administration. Central-Asian, Afghan, Egyptian, Zoroastrian, Manichean and other components had been brought together and merged. Thus, when Maḥmūd of Ghazni and Mu'izzudīn Muḥammad of Ghuri embarked on their campaigns, this was not yet another of the countless invasions that northern India had received over the centuries, however, rough it may have been. This was the entrance on to the scene of quite a civilisation, as rich and potent as Indian civilisation itself.

In 1026, Maḥmūd devastated Punjab and put down at the edge of a sword the cities of Kanauj, Mathura, and Somnath. A century and a half later, the very same kingdom of Ghazni succumbed to the sword of another Central Asian general, Muḥammad of Ghuri, who also turned his gaze on India. The Sultan vanquished a Rājput confederation and the whole of northern India fell into the hands of the Muslims. The Delhi Sultanate (1206-1526) ended up being formed, and this governed over the course of various dynasties and, engulfing different minor Sultanates, would control all northern India, until the arrival of the very powerful Moghul Empire.

The relations between Jains and Muslims varied depending on the predatory instincts of each governor. For example, at the end of the 13th century and the beginning of the 14th, the symbolically important temples on mount Sha-trunjaya were destroyed. The following Muslim governor at Gujarat hastened to restore them, and even helped the community financially. It is evident that many leaders had plainly noticed the economic importance of the Jain minority and preferred not to mix religious issues with political and economic interests. Not all governors proved to be so pragmatic. Many temples and sacred sites in northern India disappeared or were converted into mosques. Atrocities committed by unscrupulous Muslim generals in Gujarat, Delhi or Rajasthan are still remembered to this day. As far as Jains were concerned, this type of sporadic aggression became accepted as a natural state of affairs in the Sorrowful Age.

All this did not prevent the building of Jain sanctuaries at different times. In the 13th century the Vāghelā kings (successors to the Solaṅkī dynasty) supported numerous Jainist enterprises. Among others, they promoted constructions on Mount Abu, in Girnar and in Shatrunjaya. Behind all this, we consistently find the determination and devotion of two brothers, Vastupāla and Tejapāla, ministers of the Vāghelā court.

With the establishment of the Moghul Empire (1526-1707) the greatest India had known since Aśoka, relations again became uneven. We know that different Śvetāmbara schools gravitated around the court of the powerful Moghuls. The great emperor Akbar (16th-17th centuries), who had a library full of Jain manuscripts, maintained strong links with the head of the Tapā-Gaccha, *ācārya* Hīravijaya Sūri (1527-1595). Along with dozens of other ascetics, Hīravijaya spent two years at court teaching the emperor the principles of Jainism.* He succeeded in persuading the emperor to ban hunting, to let caged animals free, and to abolish the sacrifice of animals during the celebrations of the Jain festival of Paryuṣaṇa. His disciple Śānticandra urged him to moderate the taxing of those of his subjects who had not been converted to Islam. In the same way, Jinacan-dra Sūri convinced him to protect Jain temples from the depredations of certain unscrupulous governors. The sacred mountains of the Jains were declared of cultural interest. However, Akbar's "Aśokian" tolerance contrasted with the harshness of other leaders. Jehangīr, his own son, guided by a maximally confused religious policy, showed at a times great ill-will towards the Kharatara

* Akbar had moved the capital of the Empire to Fatehpur Sikri, near to the tomb of a Chistī *ṣūfi* saint, where he built a house of worship not only for different types of Muslims (Sunni, Shi'ia or *ṣūfī* Muslims), but also for all Hindu movements (whether Vaiṣṇava or Śaiva), Jains, Sikhs, Christians (Orthodox, Jesuits) Parsi-Zoroastrians, Jews and even materialists. It is said that he installed a "religion of God" *(dīn-i-ilāhi)* in his court. In reality, one could think of it as more of a ministry of ecumenical dialogue—or even a state religion—than a new syncretic religion.

Gaccha, in those days the most influential of Śyetāmbara Jainism's sub-schools. While governor of Gujarat, Aurangzīb, who was later to be the last great Moghul emperor, had a great temple, dedicated to Pārśva, demolished and a mosque built in its place. These continual demonstrations of unfriendliness shown by Muslim authority—which we do not have to confuse with the general Muslim population—seriously damaged the Jain community. In the same way that devotional Hindu groups fought against Jainism in the Deccan region and the South, in the North, Muslim authorities went on a crusade against the atheist, infidel, and idolatrous Jains.

JAINISM IN RAJASTHAN

The arid zone in what is the present day state of Rajasthan has been one of the historic strongholds of Jainism. Traditionally, Rajasthani Jainism has been linked to that of central India and Gujarat. This region was the birthplace of countless developments and memorable personalities. One of the most enlightened of such figures that India has ever produced was the philosopher Haribhadra (8th century), who spent most of his life in Rajasthan and Gujarat. A Brāhmaṇa scholar by family tradition, Haribhadra ended up being converted to Jainism thanks to Yākinī Mahattarā, an ascetic nun. Later on, Haribhadra would praise and exalt her as his spiritual mother (cited in Shāntā 1985: 182). Owing to his immense erudition and his vast knowledge of rival philosophic systems, Haribhadra moulded Jainism into a sufficiently wide ranging system to be able to compete with Brāhmaṇical and Buddhist traditions. Although it is plain to see that the purpose in his synthesis of other systems was to subordinate them in some way to Jainism, his just and conciliatory exposition was nevertheless astounding, and pre-dated by centuries the typical neo-Hindu positions of the 19th century [see pages 359-361].

It was also in this region where, at the beginning of the 13th century, Jagaccandra Sūri founded what is today the most important school within Jainism: the Tapā-Gaccha. It is in Rajasthan, that the Terāpanthī, another important order, saw the light and where at present it has its headquarters. The Kharatara-Gaccha also has widespread influence in Rajasthan. So it is not at all surprising that proportionally speaking, Rajasthan is one of the most Jain states in India [seepage 304].

Since the Muslim invasions began, northern India has never known another Jain or Hindu kingdom of any calibre. That did not stop some of the small principalities (vassals, firstly of the Moghuls and later the British) from supporting the religion of Mahāvīra. Such is the case for the *rāṇās* of Mewar. The Jains sought links with the state, with the explicit intention of gaining the state support for their business actvivities, while the state depended on the resources of the Jains, especially during warfare periods (Kapur 2002: 118-119). This region still continues to be a focal point for Jainism. Thanks to the initiative of minor Mahārājas, they were able to build complexes such as those in Ranakpur (Ra-jasthan) or Gwalior (Madhya Pradesh), being impressive for their stateliness even today. The temple dedicated to Ādinātha in Ranakpur, built during the 14th and 15th centuries is considered to be one of the masterpieces of Jain architecture [see FIG. 10]. The ground plan of the temple is a perfect replica of the sacred assembly *(samavarasaṇa).*

All this shows that in Western India, especially in Rajasthan and Gujarat, the key social and political pairing was not the Brāhmaṇa-Kṣatriya (as in the classical model of *varṇas)* but the Rājput-trader, with Brāhmaṇas playing an im-portat but less central role (Babb 2004: 54).

MOUNT ABU

The spiritual centre of Rajasthan is the mountain of Arbuda, more widely known as Mount Abu, close to the present day border with Gujarat. It is also a sacred mountain for Hindus. In a little grove in the massif known as Dilwara are to be found what are possibly the great masterpieces of Jain architecture and sculpture [see FIG. 47]. For many people, these treasures represent the peak in Indian art. Particularly fine are two exquisitely majestic temples. One is the temple dedicated to Ādinātha (Ṛṣabha) built in the 11th century, under the aegis of the Jain minister Vimala. The other is the no less majestic Lūṇa Vasahī (13th century) consecrated to Nemi, which was erected with the generosity of the twins Vastupāla and Tejapāla, officers in the Vāghelā dynasty in Gujarat.

Part VII
Jain Orders

Throughout its long history, Jainism has remained quite faithful to certain fundamental principles. If we take into account the time that has elapsed, we shall see that, doctrinally speaking, the tradition has proved pretty stable. In this respect the schism between Śvetāmbara and Digambara divisions is scarcely detectable. But alongside this conservatism we find a counterposed spirit of renewal. Inevitably, the clash with Hindu and Muslim theism (a double process that put an end to the glorious period of Jainism) contributed to feed a series of reform movements which, in the end, provided a revitalising force rippling through the Jain religion.

Generally speaking, the Jain "reforms" constituted an attempt to reinstate the original doctrines and eliminate practices that were seen as a straying from the path. It was always a case of getting back to the "true Jainism" of the times of Mahāvīra and breaking with the ascetic lineages that had "gone astray"; reaffirming, for example, the primacy of non-violence above all other considerations; eliminating practices (for example the worship of images); incorporating symbols (the cloth mask for ascetics); and making the body of scriptures available to laity (Dundas 1992: 210). As such, the reforms were inspired by a "fundamentalist" resurgence, an interest in getting back to the "original Jainism" of the ancient scriptures. It is clear, however, that there is no one "true Jainism", nor even clear indications of what Mahāvīra preached. Perhaps owing to this impossibility, the anti-sectarian vision of the reformers ending up producing the opposite effect: the successive divisions of Jainism in the new orders and sub-schools. While there exists a clear sensation of brotherhood between all Jains, it is a fact that the sectarian spirit has dominated many Jain groups. This is reinforced by the tendency to subordinate questions of doctrine to ritual and the authority of "spiritual transmission". As a consequence, the tradition bristles with lineages of masters *(paṭṭāvalīs),* orders *(saṃpradāyas),* companies *(gaṇas),* schools and sub-orders *(gacchas, saṃghas),* families *(kulas)* and branches *(śākhās),* with relations between them often being less than perfect. The true framework within which Jainism has expressed itself has been these small units.

We shall be devoting this Part to the study of these reforms and the most important orders and figures in Jainism, from the post-Gupta period (6th century) until now. Chapter 18 will describe the framework within which these reforms are to be viewed. Chapter 19 provides a review of the micro-historical features of these quintessential orders and personalities. With these two chapters, the historical section of this volume will be complete.

18. POST-GUPTA JAINISM

BHAṬṬĀRAKAS AND *CAITYAVĀSĪS*

The appearance of the first reform movements is closely linked to the complex situation in which the tradition found itself between the 9th and 13th centuries. The backdrop to this was not just the advance of Islam or Hinduism. It also had to do with the unstoppable emergence of monastic institutions, which had become centres of power and sedentary organisation, at the expense of the ideal of the solitary, wandering ascetic.

All this had its *raison d'être.* Until the very first centuries of the Common Era, ascetics spent the greater part of the year wandering along the dusty byways of the country and only for the four months of the monsoon did they gather together in monastic shelters excavated out of the rock. This irrespective of whether the ascetic groups were formed by solitary individuals or small groups. The point is that the lay community was generous with the renunciants. This material generosity *(dāna)* translated into the construction of a myriad of temples *(caityas, mandiras)* and, from the 5th century onward, in retreats for ascetics *(upāśrayas)* and monasteries *(maṭhas)* attached to temples. With the passage of time, the community of ascetics accommodated to the ways of the lay people, adopting a sedentary way of life no different from that of the householders [see pages 224-225]. In summary, the demands of the large community altered many of the premises of old Jainism. That does not mean that it was merely the needs of the lay community that forced the change to sedentary patterns. I think the ascetics were more inclined to monasticism than is generally thought. In any case, the sedentary ascetic would come to be a sign of the decadence of the Sorrowful Age, but accepted as an unfortunate solution for corrupt times. Nonetheless, I agree with Kendall Folkert (1993: 172) in that more than "decadence" as such, monasticism could be regarded as an innovation. Thanks to monasticism, the ties between the lay community and the ascetics became closer. This helped the ideal of the *sādhu* to remain alive in the community.

THE *BHAṬṬĀRAKAS*

It was in this climate that the institution of the scholar *(bhaṭṭāraka)* appeared in the heart of Digambara Jainism—*bhaṭṭāraka* being a pan-Indian title of respect used equally to honour the *jinas,* learned Brāhmaṇas and even Śaiva ascetics. Originally, the Jain *bhaṭṭāraka* was the religious preceptor of a group of naked ascetics who lived in a monastery *(maṭha).* This role must have originated during the 7th and 8th.centuries. This institution increased notably in importance during the difficult times of the Islamic penetration. At this time, for example, the Muslim rulers caused such vital questions as religious nudity to be at stake. Some *bhaṭṭārakas* proclaimed pragmatically that ascetics could wear clothing when they left the monastery enclosures. In other words, in the face of the real threat posed to the continuation of the order, the community turned to the *bhaṭṭāraka* for guidance. The fact is that as the middle ages wore on, Digambara Jainism became progressively disassociated from the ideals of the naked, nomadic ascetics and gravitated toward the *bhaṭṭārakas.* Since they were not initiated renunciants, the *bhaṭṭārakas* possessed their seats of power *(pīṭhas)* where they led a pompous sedentary life, not very different from the *Śaṅkarācāryas* and other heads of monastic Hindu orders (von Glasenapp 1925: 80), whose tendency to ostentation is sometimes striking.

The principal function of the *bhaṭṭāraka* was—and still is—the administration of the monastery, the temple, and the other dependent institutions: schools, libraries, lands or hostels [see Fig. 21]. Their mission was and is religious, as well as social and political. They have the power to mediate in disputes over religious property. They supervise the vows of the laity and supervise many domestic ceremonies (births, marriages, funerals, etc.). At the same time, they act as physicians, astrologers, preceptors, and confessors. Although *bhaṭṭārakas* do not possess disciples, probably because of the scarcity of Digambara *ācāryas,* they act as spiritual directors. They are in charge of consecrating temples and images. Frequently they preach to the community and organise pilgrimages. For all these reasons, perhaps the best translation for *bhaṭṭāraka* would be "cleric".

In the Deccan region each major Jain caste had, and still has, its own *bhaṭṭāraka,* who could mediate in caste litigation. What was crucial; these *bhaṭṭārakas* represented the local communities or the corresponding caste when dealing with the Musim *nawābs* or the Hindu *mahārājas.* It is said that in the medieval period there were sixty-three *bhaṭṭāraka* "seats". Today there are only eleven: six in Karnataka, three in the Maharashtra, two in Tamil Nadu and one in Rajasthan.

THE *CAITYAVĀSĪS*

Among the Śvetāmbaras, the counterpart to the *bhaṭṭāraka* were the monks who received the title of *caityavāsī* ord *yati.* As their name indicates, they represented the—semi-initiated—ascetics who dwelt *(vāsa)* in temples *(caityas).* They did not shave their heads, used sandals, and were allowed to travel by means of transport. Like the Digambara *bhaṭṭārakas,* they acted as clergy in the temple rituals and offered their services as specialists in medicine or esoteric science.

The emergence of the *caityavāsīs* is linked to texts relating to monastic rules, the Chedasūtras and their commentaries. This literature had allowed for a series of exceptions to the rules of conduct of the mendicant ascetics which paved the way for sedentary asceticism. Just as in the case of *bhaṭṭārakas,* they made the temples their places of power and they gathered around them a goodly number of followers, controlling the temple/monastery. Here, we see the same dichotomy between the ideal of a hermit-like asceticism and an asceticism which seeks to interact with society. If, as in Digambara Jainism, the image of the solitary ascetic in the forest was maintained as the most authentic ideal, the chronicles show that this model was becoming the exception.

In the year 1017, there was already forming in the region of Saurashtra, in Gujarat, a reforming group headed by ascetics who challenged the power of the *caityavāsīs* and its monastic form of Jainism. They called themselves "dwellers in the forest" (Vanavāsins) and even though they were not especially successful, they sowed the seed for other reforms to take place. The "followers of the correct method" (Viddhimārgīs) were more successful, and in 1024 they succeeding in overcoming the *caityavāsīs* in a debate organised in Patan. Their followers nicknamed them the "fierce ones" *(kharataras),* hence their present-day name: Kharatara-Gaccha [see pages 265-267].

We know that over the course of various centuries there were numerous debates between these two positions. For the reformers, the dwellers in temples constituted a clear deviation from the life of the mendicant devoid of possessions. Furthermore, they accused the latter of spending the money donated by the laity in sumptuous temple rituals. For their part, the *caityavāsīs* argued that if it had not been for their institutions, Jainism would have disappeared.

Even though the temple dwellers were attacked on various different fronts, they maintained part of their influence. Just like the *bhaṭṭārakas* of the Deccan region, these *caityavāsīs* were crucial to the relations between the community and the ruling Muslims or Rājputs. Today, there are just a dozen *yatis* left and their properties have passed into the hands of lay organisations, which administer the temple accounts and control its capital.

THE CHALLENGE OF MONASTICISM

The ties between the ascetic community and the lay community had created the conditions for the existence of this series of non-begging *quasi*-ascetics. And as *bhaṭṭārakas* and *caityavāsīs* argue with some justification, without stable influences like them, it is more than probable that Jainism would not have survived. Even though they may have moved away from the traditional rigour, in general *yatis* and *bhaṭṭāraka* have been, and still are, extremely cultured people. Thanks to them, many collections of manuscripts have been preserved. It is with the advent of the *bhaṭṭārakas* and *caityavāsīs* of the post-Gupta period (7th century onwards) that one can really speak of a Jain *monasticism,* similar to that of the Buddhists, and different from traditional *asceticism.*

Although the expansion of the monastic rules to accommodate the sedentary life has been viewed as a dangerous deviation from the ancient practices, the fact is that the ascetic ideal stayed alive. The basic principles of Jainism were conserved at the same time that the monastic rules were expanded to adjust to the needs of different types of ascetics. Instead of interpreting the message of the *tīrthaṅkaras* in a rigid, fixed and immutable way, the Śvetāmbara tradition set out a series of areas and basic themes to follow and left the evaluation of the rules to the free and unbridled choice of the masters.

However, it is also evident that this type of religiosity could represent a lax and occasionally corrupt form of Jainism. It is said that in the mid 16th century, the itinerant and austere way of life of former days was a mere lingering memory. Many *yatis* and clerics had not only abandoned the pilgrim life, but slept in comfortable beds, dined sumptuously, had no scruples about accepting money, and may even have broken the vow of chastity on occasions. These individuals and this type of Jainism encouraged many reformist movements that we shall be looking at in the next chapter. Given the present day number of Digambara *bhaṭṭārakas* and Śvetāmbara *yatis,* reforms went quite surprisingly far.

THE SUBDIVISIONS OF THE COMMUNITY

Such tensions were not new. Since early times Śvetāmbara and Digambara Jainism had known moments of dissent. Like in all tradition, based on monastic initiations and transmission of spiritual lineages, there is here a tendency to fragmentation. Normally, the bifurcation of the lineage would take place when the charismatic master decided to reinstate ascetic rigour in response to a certain laxity in the community. Although not as tumultuous as the Buddhist tradition, the Jain tradition has been quite tortuous. We have already commented that in Mathura there were said to be umpteen different orders [see page 214] and we have seen that Jainism in Gujarat, Karnataka or Tamil Nadu gravitated around different *saṃghas* or *gacchas.*

It was these schools *(gacchas* in Śvetāmbara Jainism and *saṃghas* in Digambara Jainism) that really and truly articulated the tradition. Although the term "company" *(gaṇa)* did not disappear, the terms *gaccha* or *saṃgha* largely replaced the ancient nomenclature. Nowadays, the schools are divided in turn after the manner of the Indian castes, with their own sub-castes *(samudāyas),* lineages *(gotras)* and families *(kulas, parivāras).* More than feeling they are Śvetāmbara or Digambara, Jains feel spiritually bound to one school or order in particular.

THE IMPORTANCE OF THE *GACCHA*

Originally, the *gaccha* represented a group of ascetics grouped around a master *(ācārya, sūri).* Gradually, they came to include also lay men and women who supported them. Accordingly, when we speak of a *gaccha* we may refer to the restricted meaning of sub-school of renunciants or to the wider sense of lay community which follows and supports a sub-school of renunciants.

Each *gaccha* or current has its own religious buildings, its ascetic leaders, its own sacred places and festivals. People congregate around the *gaccha,* as an independent entity. It is the *gaccha* that organises the.pilgrimages; it is with fellow members of one's *gaccha* that one fasts; it is the *gaccha* that provides the meal bringing the fast to an end. It is the *gaccha,* lastly, which provides the marks of identity and structures the life of the local community. Although nominally the temples, retreats or the rest of the religious institutions pertain to one tradition of renunciants or another, they really belong to the lay community. The temple, for example, is controlled by an organisation of lay persons from different families, normally known as assembly *(sabhā)* or local community *(saṃgha),* one of whose tasks is to manage the finances and the maintenance of the temple. The lay organisation decides when renovation needs to be conducted, which officials have to be recruited for the maintenance, or for the liturgy, when and how funds need to be raised (to pay for the buildings, festivals, fasts), when and how to invite an ascetic to reside in the village during the rainy season, when a new image has to be consecrated, how to organise a pilgrimage, and so on. All the responsibility and cost of the organisation of the order devolves on the lay community. Unlike in Buddhism, Jains monks have never been owners of the religious institutions or the adjacent lands—recall that the *bhaṭṭārakas* and *caityavāsīs* are not initiated ascetics.

In a city, there can be various .different temples and retreats for ascetics belonging to different *gacchas,* and for different assemblies. On the walls of the retreat or the temple, there will be written the region *(kṣetra),* the lineage *(gotra),* the caste *(jāti)* and the sub-order *(gaccha)* to which it belongs. The temple acts as the local community centre. Adjacent to the temples one typically finds sited the retreats *(upāśrayas),* libraries *(grantha-bhaṇḍāras),* fasting rooms *(poṣadha -śālās),* assembly rooms *(dharma-śālās)* for the big ceremonies, and even a kitchen that the lay community can use for weddings and other secular events. These institutions also depend on the lay assembly.

THE SECTARIAN SPIRIT

Nowadays, there are reasonably good relations between the different Jain orders, yet the fact is that historically, Jainism has typically suffered from splits and schisms. Rivalry between groups has been marked at times and during the last two thousand years has not ceased to cause differences to be magnified. For the medieval thinker, Śrutasāgara (cited in Dundas 1991: 170), all those who did belong to the Mūla-Saṃgha Digambara group simply were not Jains.

Regarding the split at the highest level (that of the major division between Śvetāmbaras and Digambaras), the situation is still more tense. Digam-baras and Śvetāmbaras have made a point of having their festivals fall on different days. The disputes over who owns the places of pilgimage have been, and still are, acrimonious. Perhaps the prototypical instance has been the appropriation by the Śvetāmbaras of Mount Girnar, at one time an important Digambara sanctuary. This is simply the best-known example of the more than a hundred law suits currently in process over the ownership of the sacred places. There have been occasions, as in the conflict over Bahubali Mountain in Kolhapur, at the beginning of the 1980s, when the confrontations have taken on shades of "communalism", a term that Indians give to religious conflicts that are fed by political factions, castes and their interests including Mafias of different stripes.

Each and every order has its own history, lineage and ways of understanding tradition. If we count the minor subdivisions we are talking of more than one hundred *gacchas.* We shall be looking at these orders in the next chapter. But first, there is something we should think about. Let us take another look at history.

THE SURVIVAL OF JAINISM

Gradually, the inroads of Islam began to undermine, increasingly, the strength of Jainism in the North, especially during the tumultuous 12th and 13th centuries. In the South, the turning point came with the Cōḻa monarchs, and their fervent devotion to Śiva, and with the followers of Viṣṇu at the close of the Hoy sala dynasty. The combined result of these two and their fight against "atheism", at times to the point of dogged intransigence, was the prolonged but constant retreat of the Jain community. Many temples in the North were turned into mosques, while in the South just as many were turned into Hindu temples.

From the soteriological point of view, India was turning its back on the austerity and gritty effort of Jaina *yoga.* The *Bhagavad-gītā* or the *Bhāgavata-purāna* and their exaltation of loving surrender *(bhakti)* was set up as a fabulous counter to Jain asceticism. In some respects, the *Gītā* was the Hindu answer to the Śramaṇic movements. For that reason, it is Kṛṣṇa, an *avatāra,* who instructs the Kṣatriya Arjuna in the *yoga* of action *(karma-yoga)*— in a new way of approaching action as a sacrifice *(yājña)* offered to Kṛṣṇa. Vedic ritual thus becomes transpersonal action. Here we have, yet again, a new practice which is ratified by the Brāhmaṇical tradition through the adoption of the language of sacrifice. For the *Gītā, yoga* is neither action *(pravṛtti)* nor inaction *(nivṛtti),* but awareness in action *(karmasu-kauśalam),* action with understanding. The true yogi is one who sets aside all attachment and allows his soul to *participate* in the world, because the world is the Lord's creation. It is for this reason that so many devotional groups base themselves in one way or another on the major guidelines given in the *Bhagavad-gītā.* While many Jain masters today like to compare the *Gītā* with the teachings of Mahāvīra, the devotional *ethos* of the latter, seeking to participate in this world, differs from the traditional Jain position. Let us not forget that the *Gītā* is an integrating synthesis of Vaiṣṇava devotion. Nevertheless, like so many of Indian scriptures, the *Gītā* cannot be easily labelled or pigeon-holed. Although devotional worship and theism are praised in that work, it also assimilates the orthodox and gnostic currents, among which we could include Jainism. Its exposition is surprisingly syncretic and eclectic. The doctrine of awareness in one's action, for example, is shared completely by Jainism. If the action is conducted devoid of intentions, in a state of detachment concerning the results *(phala-tṛṣṇa-vairāgya),* it becomes non-action, which is the Jain ideal. In disassociating itself from the old Brāhmaṇism and stressing the personal relationship with the divine, the *Gītā* shares and promotes the same experiential mood as the Śramaṇic movements. To an extent, the Hindu devotional groups are the heirs of Śramaṇic spirituality. Not only do they share the "individualist" feel but they are similarly free of most of the Brāhmaṇical taboos relating to the purity of the socio-spiritual classes or castes. Having said that, what is important, is that historically India opted for *bhakti, love* and transpersonal *surrender* to the Divinity as *the* way, and the attraction of the Jain ascetic gradually waned.

However, Jainism did not disappear, and of the old Śramaṇic movements it is the only one that has survived on Indian soil. Ājīvaka did not survive beyond the 13th century, Buddhism in India did not see out the 15th century. While there are Buddhist communities in India, these are either isolated groups in the trans-Himalayan borderlands (and geographically, culturally and linguistically connected to Tibet) or they are groups of Dalits converts who have opted for Buddhism seeking a new social and political status. Buddhism transformed "Indianness" into something that could be exported, and as Alan Watts (n/d: 47) put it, Buddhism is arguably the greatest contribution India has made to civilisation. If Buddhism retains a mere symbolic presence in its country of origin, Buddhists in China, Japan, Thailand, Sri Lanka, Korea, Tibet, Burma and a long list of other countries, look to India as the spiritual homeland. Very much in the Brāhmaṇical style, Buddhism knew very well how to adapt to the most diverse of contexts. It used the notable idea of skill in means *(upāya-kauśalya),* the void as an infinite adaptation to the the believer's condition or consciousness, in all types of cultures and peoples. Scholars have asked, how is it that the malleability of Mahāyāna did not work in the country of its origin?* and how, on the other hand, has a small community like the Jains been able to survive down to today when Buddhism was not able to do so? We have seen that the Jain religion

* Or it worked too well, to the point that Buddhism ended up integrating itself into the heart of Hinduism. External similarities (Mahāyāna devotional worship, Tantric rites, non-dualist philosophy) could well have led Hindus finally to not differentiate between the two religions. The well-known tendency of Hinduism to include instead of attacking must have acted in concert. For the ordinary run-of-the-mill devotee it mattered little whether Buddhism might have repudiated the Veda—virtually forgotten by everybody; what mattered was that Buddhism led to the same objective of emancipation as Hinduism, and it could well be that Buddha was that odd *avatāra* of Viṣṇu as some Brāhmaṇas were astutely suggesting.

was supported by some monarchies; but then so was Buddhism. We have commented that Jainism has a universal message; but this is true of Buddhism too. We therefore, have to look for additional factors.

First, the influential position of the lay community has to be considered. A great number of money lenders, traders, industrialists, jewellers, politicians and scribes belonged to the Jaina community. Thanks to their economic, cultural and social weight [see pages 305-307] the community succeeded in gaining the respect even of otherwise hostile rulers.

Second, it has to be recognised that there has been a degree of compromise with Hinduism, at least after the penetration of Islam in the North. After all, despite historical rivalries, in the eyes of many Hindus, Jainism is a "sister" religion. Sinclair Stevenson (1915: 19) maintained that Jainism had "taken refuge" or camouflaged itself within Hinduism such that to the Moslem conquerors they appeared like an undifferentiated group within Hinduism. Jainism admittedly did adopt a strategy of compromise in ritual areas (in worship, mythology, sacraments, social structure), although the result in turn was duly "jainised". Jainism adjusted to the local customs and allowed, in certain cases, mixed marriages with Hindus [see page 300].

Third, the cohesion of the community needs to be emphasised; a community which in this case showed itself to be more cohesive and organised than its Buddhist counterparts. According to Arthur Basham (1954: 292), Jain ascetics held the lay members of the order in high regard. It is clear that the members of the lay community were not considered as mere friends and patrons of the ascetic order, as seems to have been the case with post-Gupta Buddhism.* Although Buddhist monks depended on the lay community for their sustenance (just as the Jain ascetics did) the lay community in this case did not exercise control over the Buddhist monasteries. It is significant that the greater part of the immense body of Buddhist scriptures has to do with philosophical matters. In contrast, the Jain masters devoted an astonishing amount of their efforts to the discipline of the lay Jains in a series of texts known as the Śrāvakācāras [see pages 343-344 and 474]. While Buddhist monks concentrated in large monastic complexes (Nālandā, Vikramaśīla, Vallabhī or Odantapuri, for example) far-removed from the secular life (and indeed easily identified by unscrupulous Muslim warriors) the Jain ascetics "went back" to the little retreats next to the

* In other Buddhist countries (Thailand, Burma, Sri Lanka, for example), the bonds between the lay and monastic communities have been much more solid. In South East Asia it is customary for adolescents to spend two or three months of the rainy season in the local monastery. They are provisionally initiated into the order, such that the links (already close enough, given the Buddhist monks' participation in the rites, education and healthcare in the community) become much stronger throughout life. This could not have been the case in post-Gupta India, which would explain a certain distance that then existed between monks and laity.

temples, in direct contact as always with the lay people. The Jain reformers who avoided the monasteries turned out to be decisive. The itinerant life of the ascetic, going from retreat to retreat, in daily contact with lay persons to collect food, would explain the great links between the two sections of the Jain community. This interaction is found in the bosom of the small orders. As a result, the fragmentation of the tradition—which *a priori* might seem an impediment—has brought about much closer and more compact ties between communities, and this played a crucial part in Jainism's continuing survival on Indian soil.

19. JAIN SCHOOLS AND ORDERS

MŪRTIPŪJAKA

The main stream in Śvetāmbara Jainism is known as Mūrtipūjaka. It is numerically the largest group of all, both in terms of ascetics and of lay followers. Just as its name suggests, it is characterised by its practice of worshipping *(pūjā)* images *(mūrti),* which are representations of the *jinas* and deities of Jainism. The followers are also known as "those of the way of temples" (Mandirmārgīs), But the Mūrtipūjaka is not a homogeneous order. It is made up of various sub-schools *(gacchas)* that simply share the feature of worshipping images.

Even though in the past there were several Mūrtipūjaka *gacchas,* all of which claimed to represent authentic Jainism and traced back their lineage to the great Sudharman via Vajrasvāmin (1st century), only half a dozen or so have survived up to the present day, and only three currently have initiated ascetics: the Kharatara-Gaccha, the Tapā-Gaccha and the Añcala-Gaccha. The first two deserving special attention.

KHARATARA-GACCHA

The Kharatara-Gaccha emerged in Gujarat under the guidance of an ascetic called Vardhamāṇa (11th century). Some say that Vardhamāṇa was disturbed by his master's laxity respecting the doctrine. Others state that he was not used to dwelling in a monastery as a *caityavāsī.* The truth is that this obscure figure started a new monastic lineage called "path of the correct method" (Vidhi-Mārga).

Apart from this foundational event, the main event for which the *gaccha* is remembered, is the debate between the fiery scholar Jineśvara, and the *caityavśsī* monk Sūra. The controversy took place in Patan in 1024. The chronicles that tell the story of the *gaccha* spare us no details of Jineśvara's great victory.

Jineśvara was able to demonstrate to the monarch who was acting as judge to the affair, that just as texts such as the *Daśavaikālika-sūtra* indicated, ascetics could not live in places specially designed for their use (Granoff 1990: 177), nor could they accept food from kings *(Daśavaikālika-sūtra* 3.3), use thrones or beg food in large groups. (Granoff 1990: 176-178). The king, who was an impartial and just man, was completely convinced by Jineśvara's arguments.

The tough, biting language that Jineśvara employed led everyone to call the group "particularly fierce" *(kharatara).* The old name was forgotten.

The *sūri* who succeeded Jineśvara was Jinavallabha. It is said that upon reading the *Daśavaikālika-sūtra* he became aware of more deviations in the doctrine and ascetic practices. Since then, the *Daśavaikālika* has become the most venerated *sūtra* in Śvetāmbara Jainism and the Kharatara sub-order has gone to great efforts in codifying a written canon. In its lists, there are always 45 texts, considered by some experts—somewhat erroneously [see pages 334-336]—as being the "canon" of Jainism. The distinctive hallmark of the Kharatara-Gaccha has been their reference to scriptural authority when organising their ascetic life and when condemning their arch-rivals, the *caityavāsīs.*

Śvetāmbara tradition has thrived upon hagiographic portrayals of their charismatic masters. More than intellectual achievement, it is the magical powers *(siddhis),* along with mastery in spells and sacred litanies *(mantras),* that make them stand out; as it is with such powers that ascetics could protect the community and exalt Jainism. Kharatara-gacchins have been particularly inclined to such stories, in which four masters receive the title of *dādāguru,* roughly translatable as "grandfather master". Thanks to the power obtained through *tapas,* chastity and *mantras,* these masters were able to overcome the malignant forces that tormented people. In the same way as Jesus Christ in Christianity, the *dādāgurus* performed their miracles to attract new followers to the Jain path. It is said that when correctly propitiated they can beneficially intervene in human affairs [see pages 428-429].

The first of these *dādāgurus* was Jinadatta (1075-1154), successor to Jinavallabha and probably the most beloved of all the *sūris* from the Kharatara-Gaccha. His hagiography is the perfect example of the master who instigates lay piety, who stands up for Jainism in numerous debates, who exalts the Jain religion by the consecration of temples, images and initiation of ascetics and gains innumerable converts—a worldly profile, which does not emerge in his personal autobiography (Granoff 1992: 65-66). Due to his miracles and his knowledge of *mantras,* Jinadatta Sūri gained the title of "spiritual leader of our age" *(yu-gapradhāna).* When he died, his soul reincarnated as a divine being. It is said that when his life in the Upper World comes to an end he will be reborn on the continent of Videha, where he will achieve liberation under the guidance of *tīrthaṅkara* Sīmaṅdhara who is preaching there.

The second *dādāguru* was Jinacandra Sūri (1140-1166) successor to the before mentioned and popularly known as Maṇidhārī [see Fig. 39]. Just like Jinadatta, Manidhārī spread Jainism, consecrated temples, images and deployed his incredible miraculous powers in benefit of Jainism. The third *dādāguru* was Ji-nakuśala Sūri (1280-1332). The fourth and last *dādāguru* was Jinacandra Sūri II (1537-1612), who managed to achieve a degree of friendship with the Muslim authorities. For that reason, he is sometimes referred to as the "influencer of the emperor Akbar" *(akbar pratibodhak),* and that, in fact, is how he is distinguished from his namesake predecessor. Owing to the mediation of Akbar, many Jain centres of pilgrimage were protected. Although there is not a great deal of certainty as to whether or under what circumstances Akbar actually invited him to his court, the hagiographies speak of several miraculous happenings during his stay there.

The order was firmly established in Gujarat, Sindh, Madhya Pradesh, Delhi, Bengal, and especially so in Rajasthan. These days the Kharatara-Gaccha carries much less weight than in former times, and it finds itself in a rather languid situation [see TABLE 2], but its contribution to Jainism, especially in forming the idea of a "canon" was decisive. Given the increasing popularity of the worship of the *dādāgurus,* the order remains strong in Rajasthan.

This order has also attracted a greater amount of female ascetics, who have always been very well considered. Two of these stand out, Puṇya Jīvana Jyoti (1858-1920) and Sādhvī Vicakṣaṇa Śrī (1912-1980), this last being one of the order's most beloved superiors *(pravartinīs).* The story of Vicakṣaṇa provides us with a unique case, as immediately after her death, the community began to "canonise" her and she became the first *sādhvī* to be formally "beatified". Thousands of devotees have her as their *guruṇi,* and tens of thousands of Jains attended the consecration of her image in Jaipur.

TAPĀ-GACCHA

The main Mūrtipūjaka *gaccha* is the Tapā-Gaccha, the largest and most influential sub-order in Jainism. It was founded in 1228 in Rajasthan, when Jagac-candra Sūri left another apparently excessively permissive order. The name *tapā* obviously derives from *tapas* (asceticism), practice which Jagaccandra devoted himself to with great diligence. As in the case of the founder of the Kharatara-Gaccha, the picture we have of Jagaccandra is also very shadowy. And as with Vardhamāṇa, this obscure figure serves as a foundation for his school.

The key figure of the Tapā-Gaccha was the monk Dharmasāgara (16th century). He was a writer with an unusually controversial style. In his work, *Pravacana-parīkṣā,* he attacks the Digambaras harshly, and is especially aggressive with the Kharatara-Gaccha. The dispute centred on the sectarian affiliation of Abhayadeva Sūri (11th century), author of famous commentaries on Śvetām-bara scriptures and claimed by both *gacchas.* The disputes between the Kharataras and the Tapā-gacchins would continue later over the ownership of the sacred Mount Shatrunjaya, in Gujarat.

Hīravijaya (1526-1595), one of its members, represented the Jains in the court of the emperor Akbar [see page 249]. Another outstanding Tapā-gacchin master and thinker was Yaśovijaya (1624-1688), a philosopher and reformer venerated even today. Never since the days of Hemacandra had there been such a prolific Jain intellectual, with such a wide range of knowledge. He defended the worshipping of images, a practice which also other Jain groups brought under attack [see below]. At the same time, Yaśovijaya was a key figure in steering the ascetic path towards the ancient parameters of austerity. He strongly attacked *yatis* and *caityavāsīs*.

The great push forward of the Tapā-Gaccha came after a frankly bad period (18th-19th centuries), when the totality of ascetics had dropped to 25 *sādhus,* with not even one *ācārya.* The lineage was reactivated thanks to the participation of the lay community, that for a time took it upon itself to designate its own masters. The expansion gathered force in Gujarat, especially in Saurashtra and Kutch. In just over a century and a half, the number of Tapā-gacchins ascetics has grown from a mere dozen or so, to over 5,000, constituting more than half of all Jain ascetics [see Table 2].

The most important modern reformer was the mendicant Vijayānanda Sūri (1837-1896), better known as Ātmārāmjī. Initially Ātmārāmjī hovered around Sthānakavāsī Jainism [see below], a reputed iconoclastic group. After meticulously studying texts, he came to the firm conclusion that image worship was an acceptable practice, and so he was initiated again but this time in the Tapā-Gaccha sub-school. Ātmārāmjī came into contact with Western scholars, whom he helped considerably. In 1893 he was invited to the famous World Parliament of Religions in Chicago. Because of his ascetic vows of refraining from using any means of mechanical transport—and thus not able to cross the dark waters of the ocean—he could not attend the conference. A layman by the name of Vircand Gāndhī went in his place, and after his success in Chicago he taught Jainism in the United States and the United Kingdom [see page 325].

Various 20th century masters, all of whom have been models of saintliness and scholarship, have been providential in maintaining the sub-order: Vijaya Dharma Sūri (1866-1922) [see Fig. 29], Buddhisāgara Sūri (1874-1925), Vijaya Vallabha Sūri (1870-1954) [see Fig. 25], Ānandasāgara Sūri (1875-1950) and Muni Puṇyavijaya (1895-1971). Among contemporary *ācāryas,* Bhadraṅkar Vijaya (1903-1980) stands out as one of the most brilliant Jain thinkers in the 20th century. Another leader with enormous charisma has been Muni Jambūvijaya (1922-2009) [see Fig. 27], author of a number of critical editions of Jain texts.

STHĀNAKAVĀSĪ

LOṄKĀ-SAṂPRADĀYA

In the middle of the 15th century, an unusual character appeared among the Śvetāmbaras at Ahmedabad, in those days an Islamic stronghold, that fiercely opposed the worshipping the images of *tīrthaṅkaras.* We refer to the layman Loṅkā Śāha (1420-1475).

Even if the Sthānakavāsīs do not trace their lineage back to Loṅkā, they consider him as being the inspiration for their reformation. Tradition states that Loṅkā was a rich Gujarati merchant very well situated within the community.

Owing to his mastery in penmanship, he was entrusted to copy the whole canon for a venerable ascetic. On comparing scriptures with the behaviour of ascetics around him, Loṅkā was disturbed by the number of divergences from the original teachings. He came to the conclusion that temples, with all the riches and the worship of images which they fomented, were not backed up by the scriptures. Tradition had become corrupted; worshipping images of the *jinas* in temples was harmful. Out of all the texts Loṅkā recognised the authority of thirty-two. It is told that he received some kind of monastic initiation and became leader of a reformist group.

In reality, this narration of Loṅkā's life is fruit of 19th century biographies written by Sthānakavāsīs. Present-day experts admit they do not know the reasons Loṅkā had for accepting only certain texts, and rejecting the worship of images. According to some, he was no more than a poor scribe with little knowledge of Prakrit languages. According to Dalsukh Malvania, he opted for his iconoclastic attitude not directly because of Islamic influence as Shantaram Deo (1955: 440) thought, but precisely as a means of defence in face of the destruction visited on temples by the Muslims (Dundas 1992: 212-213). Almost no one accepts that he might have become a *sādhu,* even if it is evident that he left his life as a householder to become some kind of mendicant.

From a strictly scriptural point of view, Loṅkā had enough doctrinal support for rejecting the worship of images. There is no mention of image worship in ancient texts and all scriptures stated that the construction of buildings leads to loss of lives. It is not necessary to invoke the anti-iconic attitude of Islam or a pragmatic answer before Islamic onslaughts to understand Loṅkā's position (Dundas 1992: 213). Everything seems to indicate that the worship of images had already been a controversial issue for centuries. Basically, what Loṅkā did was to raise texts that did not mention the worshipping of images to the highest category.

The fact is that once the layman Bhāna self-initiated himself in 1467, Loṅkā's group was able to advance with the authority of a spiritual master. The group prospered due to the support of a Jain minister in Gujarat. The hagiographies of the Tapā-gacchins, their rival worshippers of images, tell that a century after the death of Loṅkā, his followers went back to worshipping images. These days, the Loṅkā-Saṃpradāya (or Lumpāka) forms a minority sub-order and does not even have initiated ascetics.

STHĀNAKAVĀSĪ

Toward the end of the 17th century, Lavajī, a layman who belonged to Loṅkā's group and Vīrajī of Surat, the son of a powerful nobleman, together with a merchant by the name of Dharmasiṃha, broke away from the Loṅkā-Gaccha. Almost certainly, Lavajī was initiated as a *yati,* although there is some confussion over the issue. The fact is that he was unhappy with the discipline of the Loṅkā-Gaccha and opted for returning to the code stipulated by the

Daśavaikālika-sūtra. They were joined by three ascetics. The small group went to live in ordinary houses *(sthānakas),* hence their name: "house dwellers" (Sthānakavāsīs), in contradistinction to temple dwellers who worshipped images. Logically, the Sthānakavāsīs conduct a strictly mental worship *(bhavapūjā),* a worship without images. According to the Sthānakavāsīs, *jinas* could not be venerated as if they were deities. The gods enjoyed (more than anyone else) the pleasures of the Upper World, whereas the *tīrthaṅkaras* had severed contacts of all kinds with the world. One could not offer them fruit, flowers or anything of that sort, nor would doing so liberate one from *karma.* From the point of view of the Sthānakavāsīs, the worship of icons is a pernicious distortion, motivated by the selfish interests of priests and *yatis,* who took advantage of the good faith and piety of lay people. In the footsteps of Loṅkā, they discarded texts that mentioned worshipping images. A large number of Loṅkā-gacchins joined them. The sub-school firmly established itself in Gujarat and Rajasthan.

Lavajī was also responsible for the introduction of the most eloquently distinctive symbol of the Sthānakavāsīs: the cloth or gauze mask *(muhpaṭṭi)* with which ascetics permanently cover their mouth to avoid harming the tiniest life-forms. This is their symbol of their dedication to non-violence. Much has been said about the effect of this reform but the truth is that its introduction was no novelty. It could hardly be so in a group bent on restoring the "originar" forms of Jainism. The *Uttarādhyayana-sūtra* (26.23-27) already mentions the mask as part of the ascetic's kit; its use is mentioned by Haribhadra (8th century); and European travellers in the 16th and 17th centuries speak of it as a distinctive sign of Jains. As the travellers so rightly observed, even the Mūrtipūjaka ascetics wore it (when praying and on the occasion of certain festivals). Additionally, lay people would be seen using it in certain specific rituals. Paul Dun-das (1992: 217) has noticed that the truly controversial innovation of Lavajī's leadership was the wearing of the mask *permanently* by ascetics. The Sthānakavāsī ascetic has to wear the *muhpaṭṭi* at all times, and throughout life. Another distinctive feature of the Sthānakavāsīs is that they keep their original lay names.

The reforms of the Sthānakavāsīs had a substantial effect upon other groups, even Digambaras. This went beyond the boundaries of Jainism, being as it was a predecessor of many Indian iconoclastic movements, prior to Sikhism. The Āryasamāj neo-Hindu movement itself, constituted in 1875, owes part of its strength to the Sthānakavāsīs' anti-iconic attitude influencing its founding member, Dayānanda Sarasvatī (Farquhar 1914: 104).

The number of Sthānakavāsīs ascetics at the present time is second to that of the Tapā-gacchins. Their influence is very great. Their strict and puritan posture has been helpful in redirecting ascetics' behaviour back to traditional austere parameters. The Sthānakavāsīs' devotion to the ideals of non-violence and compassion is recognised by all. They are strong in a vast area of the Northwest: Gujarat, Rajasthan, Punjab, Madhya Pradesh and Maharashtra.

Obviously, with the lay community deprived of ritual in temples (always a key point in their sense of identity) the connection between ascetics and common folk had to develop along other lines. On one hand, lay worship has been able to mould itself along similar lines to that of ascetics [see pages 451-453], on the other, in insisting on rigorous asceticism it has led the lay community to live the monastic ideal at a more intense level than other groups. Although they are technically speaking Śvetāmbaras, perhaps their non-iconic worship makes them more different from the Śvetāmbaras than the latter differ from many Digambaras.

In the contemporary scene, the monk Sushil Kumar Muni (1924-1994) became well-known as the leading promoter of scholarly dialogue and mediator in communal disputes. He has been considered one of the most important masters of meditation that Jainism has produced. He went as far as to break the ascetic vow to be able to leave his country and preach the doctrine of *ahiṃsā* far afield.

TERĀPANTHĪ

A Sthānakavāsī split took place in the 18th century. In the semi-desert region of Marwar, Ācārya Bhikhana (1726-1803), better known as Ācārya Bhikṣu, founded the Terāpanthī order. Perhaps because this is a young group, the chronicles of this order are unusually exact and offer quite an amount of information on the life, religious context, teachings and reforms made by Ācārya Bhikṣu.

At the age of 25 years, Bhikṣu was initiated as a Sthānakavāsī ascetic, but soon afterwards he began to question the behaviour of his companions, who were accustomed to begging for food from the same families (something which according to the monastic code should be avoided whenever possible) and being in the habit of living the sheltered, sedentary life of their "residencies". In 1759, he broke away from the order and left the *sthānaka* together with some other ascetics. For some time, the little community found themselves in a very precarious situation, immersed in a hostile medium. They lived in caves and their practice included extended fasting along with periods of ascetic rigour. These features continue to be characteristic of the order.

Bhikṣu preached intensively for more than forty years in the regions of Marwar and Mewar. Gradually, what was once only a small group of dissidents developed into a full-blown and respected order. At the time of his death, there were over a hundred *sādhus* and *sādhvls.*

He had an original interpretation of Jainism. From Bhikṣu's point of view the background to *ahiṃsā* was neither compassion nor the gaining of worthiness, but self-discipline based on a clear understanding of the spiritual nature of all living beings. For example, in his day, it was a common practice for the Sthānakavāsīs to buy live animals from the slaughterhouse to later on set them free. Bhikṣu thought that this practice—which still has not completely disappeared—

was limited to the ethic sphere, a method of gaining spiritual worthiness. Going beyond this ethic level, however, Bhikṣu stressed the purely religious transcendental sphere. There is no way for an ascetic to buy worthiness: hence the severe nature of the Terāpanthī path. The ascetic's duty consists in cultivating *ahiṃsā,* bringing about their own spiritual evolution; worthiness cannot be bought. The movement based itself also on the doctrine of total non-intervention for any living being, since helping an animal to avoid death was to take responsibility for any violence this animal might commit in the future. Moreover, assistance can never be given unselfishly, and so giving aid works against the compassionate—but attached—ascetic or devotee. In the same way, the Jain axiom that accepts the killing of an inferior being (a tree for example) in order to aid the progress of superior beings (the construction of buildings for humans), was not, and could not, be justified. In Ācārya Bhikṣu's eyes, all living beings were strictly equal.

The Terāpanthīs, given their Sthānakavāsī origin, share quite a few things in common with them. Just like the Sthānakavāsīs, they insist on wearing the gauze mask permanently, they firmly reject the worship of images, and they praise practically the same texts. However, their ascetics lodge in rooms provided by lay people.

Bhikṣu organised his group into one single company *(gaṇa),* leading their lives according to an extremely severe code of conduct, with one supreme leader who would always bear the title of *ācārya,* and who would always be named during his predecessor's lifetime. His insistence on the *ācārya* being the focal point (responsible for all initiations, administrating discipline and naming his own successor), has given the community enormous cohesion, even if this did impede mobility. Even these days, the proclamation of Bhikṣu's last rules are still celebrated at the grand festival of Maryādā, when the community meet to discuss internal affairs and problems. The task of expanding the order and imposing the definitive form of the monastic code fell to the fourth *ācārya* Jaya (19th century), to whom we owe the detailed chronicle of Bhikṣu's life, a document which gives the Terāpanthī order a clear notion of its past.

This order has remained mainly confined to Rajasthan, with the cities of Bikaner, Jodhpur and Udaipur as its main centres. Most of Bhikṣu's followers are from the Osavāla-vīsa caste, the one to which he himself belonged.

AṆUVRATA AND *PREKṢĀ-DHYĀNA*

Among contemporary developments of the Terāpanthī group, it is worth mentioning a movement known as the "little vow" (Aṇuvrata), which was begun in 1949 by the ninth *ācārya*, Tulasi (1914-1997) [see FIG. 31], the most important *ācārya* after Bhikṣu and Jaya. He was initiated at the age of eleven; when he was twenty-two he became the youngest *ācārya* Jainism has ever known.

The Aṇuvrata involves twelve religious vows. They range from the classical *ahiṃsā,* environmental prescriptions, non-discrimination toward fellow human beings, the practice of religious tolerance, developing control over one's senses, living life free of addictions, etc. Every Anuvratin seeks to universalise these ideals of self-control (Tulasi n/d: 4), social peace and harmony, transcending religious boundaries. The ideals of Aṇuvratins run parallel to those of the Gandhian movement, while being somewhat less political in orientation. Their object is to encourage people to adopt a way of life that leads to a less violent, more frugal, united, peaceful, and unattached world.

With the Aṇuvrata, Tulasi managed to restore the traditional ascetic spirit and at the same time raise the Terāpanthī to a higher level of social commitment. Even if they have had scant influence on the often corrupt political life in India, their purpose has been faithful to and consistent with the scholarly and universal model of Jainism proposed by Bhikṣu.

The tenth *ācārya* and spiritual heir to Tulasi is the ascetic monk Mahāprajñā (born 1920 [See Figs. 30, 31]), a great revitaliser of Jain meditation, which had been all but forgotten by its own tradition. The type of meditation encouraged by Mahāprajñā is a synthesis of ancient Jain meditative practices, Buddhist *vipaśyanā* meditation (Pali: *vipassanā)* and some elements from modern science. Its name being *prekṣā-dhyāna,* which according to its creator-promoter, is a system of meditation engaging one's mind fully in the perception of subtle internal and innate phenomena of consciousness (Mahāprajñā 1994: 1). Its purpose is to purify the mental states. It is a compulsory practice for ascetics and members of the Aṇuvrata movement. It is not unusual to find ascetics from other orders joining in with *prekṣā-dhyāna* sessions.

Another innovation coming from the modern Terāpanthī, is the dispensation allowing some of their ascetics to travel overseas. These—somehow lower—ascetics, known as *samans,* are also allowed to travel by mechanised transport, in addition to being able to accept food, especially prepared for them.

In Ladnun, near to Tulasi's birthplace, the order has opened its only permanent and fixed centre (where all ascetics flock annually): the Jain Vishva Bharati. The centre is situated in the midst of an unusually green and fertile location in the middle of the Rajasthan desert. There one can find schools, libraries, ayurvedic hospitals, meditation retreats and hostels.

Owing to these types of reform, the Terāpanthīs have been able to make themselves known quite well internationally as a "modern" movement, and as representatives of Jainism in its totality. In fact, half of all websites with a Jain commitment belong to the Terāpanthī order.

DIGAMBARA SCHOOLS

If the Śvetāmbara story is one of rivalry between *gacchas,* the Digambara story is one of rivalry between *saṃghas,* although in general, there seems to have been less of this than on the Śvetāmbara side.

The largest Digambara *saṃgha* in antiquity was the Mūla-Saṃgha, the true embryo of all Digambara Jainism. Historically, however, there were other communities of importance. One of these, was the Kāṣṭha-Saṃgha, founded near Delhi by Loha (1st century BC), the leader of a group of ascetics who stayed in the North during the Great Famine. It is said that this Loha was in Agar (Agaro-hā), and converted the king and his warriors (Rājputs), and out of this conversion came the Jain caste of the Agaravālas. Although this *saṃgha* still today possesses lay followers, there are no initiated ascetics. Another school was the Gopya or Yāpanīya-Saṃgha, which began life in the 2nd century and eventually disappeared a thousand years later. A third extinct *saṃgha* was the Drāviḍa-Saṃgha, typical of Tamil Nadu. Yet another was the Mathurā-Saṃgha, possibly founded around the 10th century. The differences between these communities come down to details like the type of whisk broom used by ascetics or have to do with dietary restrictions. Although these points may seem slight to us today, not to say laughable, we know, that these issues have loomed large in India. Only one of these communities, the Mūla-Saṃgha, has survived. In theory, the five subdivisions of Digambara belong to it.

BĪSAPANTHĪ

The "twentieths" (Bīsapanthīs, Viśvapanthīs) consider the *bhaṭṭārakas* to be their spiritual preceptors. They trace their origin back to Vasantakīrti (12th-13th centuries), one of the *bhaṭṭārakas* who pragmatically opted to wear clothes when nakedness was forbidden by the Muslim authorities of North India. One of the characteristics of the Bīsapanthī cult is the wafting of little lamps *(āratī)* before the image of the *jina,* the offering of flowers, fruit, milk and sweets *(prasāda).* They worship the guardians of the temples *(kṣetrapālas)* and lesser gods.

Bīsapanthī is the largest Digambara subdivision in northern and central India. They are found in Rajasthan, Gujarat and Maharashtra.

TERAHAPANTHĪ

The "thirteenths" (Terahapanthīs) on the other hand, also known as the Terāpanthīs (not connected with the Śvetāmbaras of the same name) worship the images in a very plain rite in which only inert substances are used: spices, coconuts, incense and rice. They do not carry out *āratī* or worship temple guardians. They came into being at the beginning of the 17th century in opposition to the "liberalism" of the *bhaṭṭārakas* and Bīsapanthīs. They were inspired to a considerable extent by the mystic writings of Banārasīdāsa [see below]. Today they form the other major Digambara subdivision in Rajasthan, Uttar Pradesh, Maharashtra and Madhya Pradesh.

The opposition between these two Digambara groups is such that they do not visit each other's temples.

TĀRAṆAPANTHĪ

The Tāraṇapanthīs took their name from Tāraṇa Svāmī (1448-1495), a charismatic master who lived in central India. This reformer was opposed to the worship of images. As a substitute, he recommended a ritual centred on the fourteen sacred scriptures that he had written and compiled himself. These texts are kept in their religious buildings, which are known as *caityālayas.* Tāraṇa was influenced by Kundakunda and other authors in the Digambara's mystical tradition, where there is scant reference—if any—to image-worship (Cort 2006: 272). They are found mostly in Madhya Pradesh. The famous master Osho (1931-1990) was born as a Jain, in a family of followers of the Tāraṇa-Panth (Cort 2006: 293-297).

TOTĀPANTHĪ AND GUMĀNAPANTHĪ

The last two Digambara sub-sects are very minor. The Totāpanthī number a few thousand followers and the Gumānapanthī, founded in the 18th century by Gumāna Rāma, enjoyed a certain splendour around the end of that century, but are now much depleted.

* * *

Within the Digambara ascetic tradition the biggest upheaval in modern times was brought about by the monk Śāntisāgara (1873-1955), who was a native of Karnataka. As a young man, Śāntisāgara devoted his life to going on pilgrimage to the sacred places and observing the lesser ascetic vows. He took the vow of an *ailaka,* one degree before being initiated as a Digambara *sādhu,* but he was obliged to do this before an effigy of the *jina* Nemi, as there was no master who could initiate him. Years later he completed his initiation, quite possibly with a *bhaṭṭāraka* officiating.

Like many contemporary Digambaras, Śāntisāgara was interested in Kun-dakunda's mysticism. Thanks to his efforts a good part of the impressive material of the Mudabidri library in Karnataka was made available to the general public. The title of *ācārya* was bestowed upon him by popular acclaim. Apart from his teachings, he was valued above all for his charisma and his sincere as-cetism [see FIG. 28]. From that time forth, he devoted himself to revitalising the Digambara ascetic tradition, giving it back its signs of identity. He fasted to death on mount Kunthalagiri.

Virtually all fully initiated Digambara ascetics at the present time trace their lineage back to Śāntisāgara. Outstanding monks in this tradition are Vidyānan-daji Mahārāj [see FIG. 43] and Samantabhadra [see FIG. 45].

CHARISMATIC LEADERS

Starting in the 13th century we begin to find thinkers, reformers and leaders other than ascetics—lay Jains on the lines of Loṅkā Śāha. A pioneer was the great Digambara philosopher and scholar Āśādhara (8th century). Other cases of enlightened laity were the brothers Vastupāla and Tejapāla, ministers under the Vāghelā regime.

BANĀRASĪDĀSA

There is little doubt that the most acclaimed lay Jain writer of all was the brilliant poet Banārasīdāsa (1586-1643), a member of the important Śrīmālī caste of Agra. By family tradition, he should have been drawn to one of the Śvetāmbara *gacchas,* but the fact is that his youthful years were hardly "spiritual". Unusually, for a member of a merchant caste, he combined his amours with his study. With the passing of the years, Banārasīdāsa began to adopt the customs of an ideal layman: *tīrthaṅkara* worship, meditation, and the classical dietary restrictions. In 1623 he joined with a group of neo-Digambara traders in Agra known as the Adhyātma. The members of this group were interested in realising the soul within *(adhyātma),* following the mystic teachings of Kundakunda. Banārasīdāsa himself became the translator of Kundakunda's works into Hindi. It was in this setting that Banārasīdāsa underwent a remarkable change, a spiritual transformation, which led him to act in a way that excited comment. He went as far as to break his vows and was pilloried by the merchant community. The brunt of Banārasīdāsa's criticism was aimed at the *bhaṭṭārakas* and the excessive ritual of the temples. For Banārasīdāsa, true worship was to be found within. Nonetheless, a reading of Nemicandra—and his model of spiritual ascension in fourteen steps [see pages 470-473]—provided him with a framework in which he could accept even the most "exoteric" and ritualistic religion as a preliminary part of spiritual progress (Banārasīdāsa, *Ardhakathānaka* 631-634).

His major work is a sort of autobiography known as the *Ardhakathānaka.* In addition, he wrote poetry in Hindi. His poem *Samayasāra-nāṭaka* dramatises the battle that the heroe *(*the *jīva)* has to enter into debate to vanquish the villain *(karma).* His most eminent follower was Paṇḍit Ṭoḍarmal of Jaipur. Though the Adhyātma group did not survive for more than a century, the positions taken by them would later be adopted by the Digambara Terahapanthi order.

Banārasīdāsa exemplified to perfection the ideal of the lay worshipper who, once freed from the trammels of the ascetic community, took it upon himself to choose his own path to spiritual progess.* For all the scriptures written by ascetics

* Banārasīdāsa can be situated in the broad tradition known as *sant-saṃpradāya.* This was a tradition of devotional saint-poets from different religious traditions (Hinduism, Jainism, Sikhism), castes (predominantly low ones), and regions (where Hindi, Punjabi and Marathi

might say otherwise, it is obvious that there has always been—today more clearly than ever—a lay current or tradition that has gone far beyond the role of being merely a material support for ascetic monks and nuns. Banārasīdāsa represents this model which the ascetics have scarcely had a hand in.

RĀJACANDRA

In direct line of descent from Banārasīdāsa we have someone who is, in his turn, the most acclaimed lay writer of modern times: Śrīmad Rājacandra (1867-1901), also known as Raychand [see FIG. 26]. He was born in Gujarat, in the bosom of a Sthānakavāsī family on his mother's side and Hindu Vaiṣnava on his father's side. He moved to Bombay where he became a reputed jeweller. It was there that he wrote his major work, the *Ātmasiddhi,* a short poem in which he sums up his interpretation of Jainism for these days of the Sorrowful Age.

For Rājacandra, Jainism had gone downhill because of the sectarian rivalry and its excessive dependence upon the rites. He declared himself to be openly against institutionalised renunciation—or the "religion of the muzzle" as he called it. Although he condemned the idea that the worhip of effigies or the use of mouth masks (muzzles) might lead to salvation, he accepted that these practices could help one make spiritual progress. He proposed a universally valid model, based on a virtuous life, and above all on meditation on the soul. Following Kundakunda, Rājacandra maintained that the soul is eternal and capable of liberation. Emancipation comes when one sees that the only thing that really is, is the *jīva.*

Toward the end of his life he led a life that converged on monastic ideals. He died young, perhaps, as Paul Dundas (1992: 226) suspects, through the effects of his continual fasting. An *āśrama* has been built in his honour in Idar, in Gujarat, and thousands of Jains flock there, holding him to be the greatest saint of our age. His lay status and his teachings of veneration of the *guru* as a means to attain self-realisation (not liberation) have an strong appeal for lay persons (Salter 2006: 259). There are those who say that he attained omniscience (supposed to be impossible from the point of view of traditional doctrine) and there are those who consider him to be the 25th *tīrthaṅkara,* Rājacandra is recognised for his influence on the young Gandhi, who deserves a special mention in this section.

are spoken). They lived between the 13th and 18th centuries. Among Marathi *sants* we have Jñāneśvar (13th century) and Tukārāma (17th century), followers of Vithobā. Among the Hindi and Punjabi *sants,* a more heterogeneous group, we have Kabīr (15th-16th centuries), Nānak (15th-16th centuries—the first Sikh Guru), and Dādu (16th century). What they had in common was their praise of a Formless God *(nirguṇa-brahman)* and a substantially anticlerical attitude.

GANDHI

The contribution made by Mohandas Karamchand Gandhi (1869-1948) in the construction of an independent Indian state, first as an opponent to British colonialism, and subsequently, for developing ideologies for the future Indian nation, is known by all. His words and his figure exemplify to perfection one of the classical political languages of India: the language of "saintliness". The men who speak this language usually choose asceticism and other renunciatory values, and although they tend to be on the sidelines, they have been very present in public life and in the spirit of the political class, as a kind of reference point (Jaffrelot 1998: 85). This is the political transposition of the Brāhmaṇic values of renunciation, purity, non-violence, chastity and asceticism. These are values which, are all just as equally rooted in Jainism. His contradictions apart, Gandhi was the renunciant in statecraft or the ascetic statesman, and precisely because he embodied ascetic values he was also considered a spiritual leader, a great soul *(mahātma).*

A member by birth of the Moḍh Vāṇiyā caste [see pages 307-308], Gandhi grew up imbued by the values and manners of the devotionalism of the Vāniyās of Kathiawar, in Gujarat. This was a fundamentally Vaiṣṇava religiosity with powerful Jain, Islamic and neo-Hindu influences of the 19th century. He studied law in England and there he came to know the Theosophists' English version of the *Bhagavad-gītā,* and the reading of this left a deep impression on him. In England he also became familiar with Christianity, the rationalism of the Illustration and 19th century liberalism. He worked for twenty years as a lawyer in South Africa, where he began to put his ideas in practice.

Politically, Gandhian non-violence translates into civil disobedience and non-cooperation. It is a type of heroic practice, like that of the *tīrthaṅkara,* which demands supreme self-control. Gandhism goes deeper than simply political action. It is a religious thought, rooted in the very life of the *mahātma,* with not a little input from Jainism.

The connection between Gandhi and Rājacandra began around 1884, when he was a lawyer who still had not returned to India. When he returned, the young Gandhi took Rājacandra as his main master. The *mahātma* was always to recognise his debt to Rājacandra:

> "I have met many religious leader or teacher. I have tried to meet the heads of various faiths, and I must say that no one else has ever made on me the impression that Raychandbhai did" (Gandhi 1927: 89).

The basic message that he received from Rājacandra was that religion *(dharma)* was the process by which the individual soul *(jīva, ātman)* gradually becomes emancipated from its material bonds *(karma)* to be able to achieve liberation (*mokṣa*). Deeply immersed in the Jain doctrine of the plurality of philosophical standpoints *(anekāntavāda* [see pages 358-363]), Rājacandra provided him with the hermeneutic tools to sustain the religious "tolerance" typical of Gandhism. For the *mahātma,* Hinduism was a sort of *metareligion* that took in the different theist expressions of India (Śaivism, Vaiṣṇavism), as well as Buddhism and Jainism. This pan-Indian spiritual substratum provided a vehicle for the Indian state-civilisation. On many occasions, Gandhi confessed that it was thanks to Jain philosophy that he had succeeded in establishing the unity of all religions:

> "I am an anekāntavādi... It is implicit in Vedānta philosophy, while in Jain philosophy it is explicitly stated" (cited in Jordens 1987: 8).

The tolerance that he sought to impart was in fact the expression of the three pillars upon which he anchored his philosophy: non-violence *(ahiṃsā),* truth *(satya)* and continence *(brahmacarya).* Christopher Key Chappie (2000: 143) adds the rider that the foundations of the Gandhian resistance movement, that is, the determination to embody truth *(satyāgraha)* and active non-violence *(ahiṃsā),* come directly out of the first two Jain vows. Nonetheless, Gandhi also based his notion of non-violence on a somewhat personal reading of the *Bhagavad-gītā,* to which he added Christian viewpoints, perhaps without being altogether conscious of doing so. At all events, Gandhi infused politics with these values of renunciation, or, to put it another way, of universal *dharma* based on such values. This ideal was evident in his own person, and this archetype, for India, is much more powerful and legitimate than any claim to ethnic, linguistic, geographic or historical unity.

Thanks to the universal nature of his message, Gandhian non-violence has been taken up by those with a clear debt to *mahātma:* Martin Luther King in the United States, Nelson Mandela in South Africa, and Aung San Suu Kyi in Burma. Thus, it was thanks to Gandhi that the characteristic feature of Jainism as a whole, *ahiṃsā,* passed beyond the frontiers of Asia and became known—in its Gandhian form, that is true—to the entire world. Indirectly, Gandhi has been the greatest propagator of the values of Jainism in the present age.

KANJISVĀMĪ-PANTH

The Digambara group that most is growing in importance and numbers in the 20th and 21 st centuries is the Kanjisvāmī-Panth, founded by the neo-Digambara Kanji Svāmī (1889-1980), a native of Gujarat.

Kanji was first initiated as a Sthānakavāsī ascetic. Everything pointed to his having a promising career as a Śvetāmbara until, in 1921, he discovered the mystical writings of Kundakunda. He went on to study the writings of other Digambaras like Ṭoḍarmal and Rājacandra, and he became convinced that the authentic Jainism was the Digambara kind. For years, he remained nominally a Sthānakavāsī ascetic. This spiritual crisis was resolved in 1934, when he symbolically did away with his muzzle and proclaimed himself to be a Digambara layman.

Kanji never wrote. For him, Kundakunda had already said all that could be said on Jaina mysticism. Consequentially, Kanji's message was focused exclusively on the *jīva,* the only thing that was eternal and unconditioned. All the rituals and practices directed to acquire merit were relegated to the mundane, and thus were irrelevant to spiritual progress. Although Kanji did not reject worship of the images of the *jinas,* as lay Jains advanced spiritually they should, he maintained, leave these practices behind and concentrate on meditating on the *jīva.* Even the value of *ahiṃsā* was secondary to contemplation of the soul.

Kanji never chose to be initiated as a Digambara monk, although he remained celibate throughout his life. In 1937 he founded the Digambara Svād-hyāya Mandir, in Songadh (Gujarat), and this became the headquarters and most sacred place of the Kanjisvāmī-Panth. His attitude toward ascetics was somewhat ambiguous. Although formally affiliated to Digambara Jainism (basically because it "recognises" Digambara monks and nuns) the order does not have its own ascetics. Following Banārasīdāsa, Kanji's followers have remained basically a lay movement, directed by lay scholars *(paṇḍitas)* who give sermons and run study groups. It also possesses quasi-nuns known as *brahmacāriṇīs.* The current head of the group is Campābahen Matājī (born 1924).

The Kanjisvāmī-Panth is Jainism's most proselytising sect and possibly the one that is making most headway at the present time. When spreading the word, Kanjisvāmī, like other neo-Hindu groups, has to some extent set aside the methods of traditional India and opted for the missionary tactics brought by the Protestants. Kanji himself travelled to Kenya to spread his teachings. Thanks to the very large sums of money received from the faithful, many educational activities are organised and books and booklets published. The order is presided over by a governing board with a president elected every five years. Its direct style, less tied to monasticism, but impregnated with Kundakunda's mysticism, renders it attractive for numerous lay seekers. Furthermore, it is equally seductive for many Jains in Africa and Europe, who have always been less associated with the monastic interpretation of the tradition [see pages 323-325].

JAINISM AND MODERNITY

The 19th and 20th centuries saw the reaction to the convulsion caused by the inrush of European ideas. The phenomenon is pan-Indian and is to be found in Hinduism just as it is in Jainism, Islam, Sikhism and even Zoroastrianism.

Jains were quickly aware that the encounter with the Europeans was not just another instance of foreign domination. What they were witness to was nothing less than the clash between the Western notion of "modernity" and the Indian notion of "tradition". The new waves of thought, new technology, the new social values and the expansion of education—in English—threatened many of the values, customs and practices of the Indian people. Once military solutions were ruled out (at the end of the 18th century, the beginning of the 19th and the Indian Rebellion of 1857-1858) there remained solutions that can be put under three headings: 1) open "acceptance" or adherence to all that was new, including Western-style secularism or British-style liberalism and democracy; 2) an intransigent "orthodoxy" or traditionalism, although with the assimilation of certain attitudes; 3) a solution consisting of "synthesis" or ductile reformism that resulted in neo-Hinduism and neo-Jainism. The label "neo-Jainism", certainly, is a carrying over into the Jain context of the phenomenon known as "neo-Hinduism": the adaptation of the Hindu tradition to the new trends effected by reformers and philosophers as heterogeneous as Rammohan Roy, Vivekananda, Sri Aurobindo, Gandhi and Sarvepalli Radhakrishnan. Nonetheless, the label is useful for our purposes and serves to show the parallels that there were between the different streams of thought and communities in India when it came to adapting to this new challenge.

The distinction between these different types of response has nothing to do with doctrines and teachings—rather it has to do with relationships vis-à-vis the tradition and the degree of receptivity toward that which was new. In no sense was neo-Jainism a head-on break with tradition, and traditionalism is an out-and-out defence of the same. It is not always possible to draw a clear line between the two sets of attitudes, given that traditionalism assimilated new things and adopted new attitudes and neo-Jainism and neo-Hinduism have always sought to anchor themselves in the tradition.

Within Jainism, the attitude that mainly interests us here is neo-Jainism, which is what has most successfully penetrated the community. The Jains were pioneers in many of the reforms that went forward in the India of the 19th and 20th centuries.

UNRESTRICTED ACCESS TO THE TEMPLES

One of the first movements of reform emerged among the Digambaras at the beginning of the 20th century. It styled itself the "Right to Worship Movement" (Dasā Pūjādhikāra Āndolana). Many Jain castes are subdivided into *dasā* and *vīsa* factions, the subgroup which allowed widows to remarry and the ones which do not. The former, the *dasā* faction, is considered inferior to the latter, since it permits a practice which is considered "low" according to Indian criteria on purity. We shall be speaking of Jain castes in the next chapter. The thing to grasp here is that *dasā* Digambaras were not allowed worship in the temples. The movement, sought to do away with this discrimination. A clear egalitarian sense in the Western style is detectable here, but notice that it is a sense which at all events is accessible to the tradition, since classical Jainism possesses, by Indian standards, an openly egalitarian outlook. The upshot was that the issue was brought before the courts, which found in favour of custom, that is to say, maintaining the exclusivity of worship for the *visas.* As a result, many Digambaras went over to the Śvetāmbara side. In the twenties, the Akhil Bhāratiya Jain Pariṣad of Delhi brought up the matter again, and this time with notable success. Ever since then *daśās* have every right to worship in Digambara temples and have even built some.

THE INITIATION OF CHILDREN

Among the Śvetāmbaras of Bombay and Gujarat, a forceful movement came into being opposing the initiation of children into the order. The practice of initiating children of seven or eight years of age was common, even though it went against the Jain norm that those who enter the order should do so consciously, knowing the implication of adopting asceticism as a way of life. This cause was well defended by the Jain Yūvak Saṅgha of Bombay. Although the practice has not disappeared completely, Vilas Sangave (1991: 237) has described the powerful impact the campaign and the legislation had on the community.

Important also was the part played by the Digambaras of the Dakṣina Bharata Jain Sabhā in this same issue. The Sthānakavāsīs have agreed that under age candidates for initiation should undertake a period of 5 years of study of Jain doctrine.

JAIN PUBLICATIONS

Reaction to the work of Western scholars of Sanskrit and Indian studies supposed a turning point for Jainism. The pioneer work by Weber, Jacobi, and Bühler could not have seen the light without the inestimable help of masters (like Muni Puṇyavijaya or Vijaya Dharma Sūri) or committed laity (like Jagmander-lal Jaini). Many manuscripts were jealously guarded in fabulous libraries that these *sūris* opened up to the outside world for the first time. One immediate consequence of the contact with Indologists was a renewed interest in history and philosophy, and above all, the sacred scriptures. Thanks to this surge, the greater part of the labour of gathering, editing, and publishing the classical works was carried out by the Jains themselves. The second spin-off was the appearance on the scene of newspapers, gazettes and journals dedicated to delving into the tradition, in order to promote Jain points of view. Most of the editions used the vernacular languages, although a considerable part was published in English.

There appeared within the tradition a group of scholars and experts who were opposed to this modernising trend. This was organised around the motto "Movement Opposing the Printing of Scriptures" (Śāstra-mudraṇa Virodhi Āndolana). These scholars took the traditional view that the scriptures had to be read in manuscript form and, more importantly, had to remain inaccessible to the uninitiated. Notwithstanding, the reaction was not sufficiently powerful to halt this trend.

Within the academic world, the Jains have themselves become the best promoters of Jainology. True to their proverbial love for books they have set up a multitude of centres for research and study. Among contemporary scholars we should mention A.N. Upadhye, H.L. Jain, D. Malvania, K.K. Dixit, and N. Ta-tia; a number of these have gravitated toward the emblematic L.D. Institute of Indology of Ahmedabad.

THE WEIGHT OF RATIONALISM

One challenge that had to be met was seeing the Jain tradition taken apart in the light of academic, scientific and rational research which on occasions put in doubt many of the centuries-old beliefs. I am not referring here to the criticism originated by the missionaries, preachers and historians (which were ably answered by associations like the Bhāratavarṣīya Digambara Jaina Mahāsabhā) but rather to the often friendly and approving approach of authors like H. Jacobi and A. Guérinot. Perhaps we cannot talk here of neo-Jainism in the same way that we can neo-Hinduism, but it is clear that Jainism has undergone a quiet but thoroughgoing process, a restructuring in the direction of modernisation and rational, scientific approaches. Hence movements like the Aṇuvrata, hence the recovery of Jain mysticism and meditation, not to mention phenomena like Kan-jisvāmī. As a result, the Jain intellectual elite is making terrific efforts to bring their traditional view of the cosmos in synch with the postulates of modern science. Given the materialist, mechanicist, and atheist ethos of the Jain tradition, there are areas of considerable similarities. However, given its dependence on the Universal History (its cycles, multiple worlds, biology, sublime beings, miracles,) the task is not always that simple.

JAIN ATTITUDES TOWARDS THE ENVIRONMENT

Many of the "reforms" promulgated by Jain associations have to do with the environment, vegetarianism and the treatment of animals. As Harold Coward (cited in Wiley 2002: 47) puts it, to harm any aspect of nature—be it air, water, plants, or animals—is tantamount to harming oneself. There is, a clear environmental ethic within Indian thought (perhaps not sufficiently understood and applied).

The austerity favoured by classical Jainism might seem excessive in the eyes of contemporary modern society. Nonetheless, it is plain that reducing consumption and the possession of goods to the minimum would do much to reduce the harm done to the environment. It is not that ascetics recommend that all laypersons cut down to the minimum observed by the renunciants, far from it, but there is no doubt that the example of frugal living, lack of possessions and non-attachment shown by the ascetics has had a formidable effect on the ways and perceptions of the lay community.

Note, however, that the "ecological" attitude of monastic Jainism differs greatly from modern environmental activism. Traditional monastic Jainism is literally other-worldly (soteriological path), and the concern of protecting others' lives is really a by-product of the self-purification practice. The truth is that

Jains have rarely understood *ahiṃsā* as involving them in pacifist groups or movements to minimise violence in society (Cort 2002: 81). Moreover, as John Cort (2002: 65-66) has shown, environmentalism is a new episteme, arisen out of the scientific and intellectual challenges of the past decades, hence the modern Jain environmental ethic is at best nascent and largely unconscious. The fact is that it is emerging, especially among overseas Jains. This new consciousness reflects, as Anne Vallely (2002: 193) has seen, a shift in ethical orientation away from a traditional liberation-centric ethos to a sociocentric or "ecological" ethos. In the "Green Jainism" of the diaspora asceticism is being de-emphasised and non-violence ceases to be linked to a renunciatory world view. But although we are witnessing a different understanding of concepts such as "nature", *"ahiṃsā"* or "suffering", the deep respect that Jains have traditionally professed for the natural world already distinguished Jainism as potentially the most ecofriendly of all religious traditions (Chappie 2002b: 128). It is not a suprise that Satish Kumar, one of the most important enviromentalist thinkers of our times, had been an ascetic Jain.

Part VIII
Society

Religions are social facts. Of course, they are *not just* social facts (consider mysticism for example), but that does not invalidate the functional aspect of religiousness. Society and religion together make an indissoluble whole (and nowhere more so than in the Indian world) in perpetual agitation and cross-fertilisation, while neither of these two notions can be reduced to the other. It is above all in this Part where the historical and Indological discourses have to come to terms with the sociological ones. Immersing ourselves in the social magma of the Jain community within the South Asian context, we are better able to understand the Jainism of today and this community's particular signs of identity. To look more deeply into Jainism necessarily means entering into the fascinating universe of Indian anthropology.

The first thing that springs to mind is that the Jains do not form an easily identifiable group, with well defined edges. The Jain community is porous and diffuse, and does not form an entity that is isolated from the rest of Indian society. It is not differentiated through its adhesion to certain practices and beliefs. The community is not even very united amongst itself. Immersed as it has been in an eminently Hindu ocean, it has steadily taken on signs of identity typical of Hindu or modern India. In fact, their scriptures do not proscribe any adhesion to anything secular, or anything other than what could be considered soteriological. As Somadeva Sūri states:

> "All *laukika* [worldly] norms are valid for us Jains provided they are not in contradiction with our *samyaktva* and our *vratas* [our doctrines and our religious practices]" *(Upāsakādhyayana* 36.480; cited in Lath 1991: 28).

Hence many of the regional or pan-Indian cultural features are also found among the Jains. This adaptation to local customs, norms, and expressions has contributed in a decisive way to the survival of the ancient Śramaṇic way down to our days. Solidly rooted in the local culture, Jainism is as typically Indian as Hinduism.

A more problematic issue, *a priori,* is that of adaptation the sociospiritual classes *(varṇas)* and castes *(jātis)* of India, given the dependence of the former on the Brāhmaṇical values. Caste society is a very complex phenomenon that needs to be studied with some considerable care. To properly address the issue, we need to undergo [in chapter 20] a brief immersion in Brāhmaṇical ideology.

From there go on to look at the way in which Jainism has adapted itself to the predominant, mainstream pattern. Lastly, we look at the Jain castes as such. Subsequently, in the following chapter [chapter 21] we look at the situation and position of the Jain community today, its relationship with its surrounding environment, as well as the way in which the community sees itself. We also consider the role and position of women within Jain society, a key aspect in the consolidation and transmission of Jainism. There will also be a short section on the interesting phenomenon of Jainism overseas.

20. THE JAIN CASTES

THE SOCIO-SPIRITUAL CLASSES *(VARṆAS)*

Before proceeding to answer the question with which we began this part (how does Jainism fit in with the Indian society?) we first need to review, at least briefly, some of the features of India's peculiar caste system.

We already know that ancient Vedic ideology conceived four—or five-large social classes *(varṇas),* each one with a precise spiritual rank. The order of the hierarchy from top to bottom is the known: Brāhmaṇas, Kṣatriyas, Vaiśyas and Śūdras. To this can be added—but more often ignored—the *avarna* people, the "Untouchables".* They are those who fall beneath the "purity line".

It is said in one of the famous Vedic hymns *(Ṛg-veda* 10.90.12-13) that the different classes had originated from the dismembering of the original Cosmic Being, the Puruṣa or Prajāpati. Therefore, the establishment of these clearly hierarchical classes along with their specific functions, was work of the Creator. Maintaining this microcosmic order *(dharma)* meant maintaining harmony with the macrocosmic order *(dharma, rta).* Just as the Vedic sacrifices emulated and even constituted the ordering of the universe, respect for social order reflected the rhythm of the cosmos. Even after the concept of the Vedic Purusa was left aside, the Brāhmaṇas of classical and modern Hinduism have maintained the same model (with even more strictness, if possible), simply substituting the demiurge for the highest new gods: Brahmā, Viṣṇu, or Śiva.

A crucial notion from Brāhmaṇic ideology is that the duty and law that holds up society *(dharma* in its restrained sense) is not universal. Certainly, there is a patronymic *dharma,* clearly that of the Brāhmaṇas, but right conduct *(dharma)* is something specific *(sva)* to one's social class *(varṇa).* According to the *Manu-smṛti* (1.88-91), the particular *dharmas* relating to each of the four great social

* Educated Indians place them under the heading of "Scheduled Classes" or "Backward Classes", although the latter term includes not only the Untouchables but also a large number of castes traditionally considered Śūdras. Following a 16th century Gujarati saint, Gandhi called them "children of God" (Harijans), although today many former Untouchables prefer to call themselves "oppressed" (Dalits).

divisions are: the teaching and study of the Veda for the Brāhmaṇas, the protection of society for the Kṣatriyas, agriculture and commerce for the Vaiśyas and service to others for the Śūdras. This has to tie in with the stage in life *(āśrama)* in which each person finds himself: student of the Veda, householder, hermit or renunciant. One also must take into account family *(kula)* and country *(deśa)*. In other words, *dharma* is not the same for everyone. There is not a universal morality, at least in the society of the Corrupt Age *(kali-yuga)*. Each individual's behaviour must reflect their social-spiritual class, age, gender, family, regional tradition, stage in life, occupation, etc. Taken as a whole it will give shape to each person's own *dharma (svadharma)*. And so important is it to comply with one's *svadharma* that:

> "It is better [to discharge] one's own [appointed] duty incompletely than to perform completely that of another; for he who lives according to the law of another [caste] is instantly excluded from his own" *(Manu-smṛti* 10.97).

Men must follow the *dharma* proper to men and not that of women. A Brāhmaṇa cannot behave like a Śūdra; or a city dweller like a farmer... Why should people have to be guided by a universal pattern? Brāhmaṇic perception of the society is intrinsically unequal. Each person is different. This refers just as much the body and psyche as to spiritual capacity. No one is born by chance into a given spiritual class, but as a consequence of the law of *karma*. Those from a high rank have a luminous *(sattva)* body, mind, and spirit, so they are naturally inclined to engage in spiritual occupations. By birth, Brāhmaṇas are qualified *(adhikāra)* for the study and transmission of the Veda and the carrying out of traditional rites. This is their *svadharma*. On the other hand, from the Brāhmaṇic point of view, for an Untouchable to enter into a sacred place or listen to the Veda is against the order of things; is adharmic.

The Law Treatises (Dharma-śāstras) did not spare us the least detail in describing duties, rites, prohibitions and recommendations for each of these classes, especially the ones concerning the authors themselves: the Brāhmaṇas. Nothing was left to free will. The correct studies, type of diet, the most convenient partner for marriage, ritual obligations, down to the most basic details— such as how to rinse out one's mouth after eating and which way to look when sneezing. Guy Sorman (2000: 88) says that the Brāhmaṇas' meticulously defined and structured society of classes would be the "Indian solution" to how to organise a society without a state. There is something true in what he says. However, Mahāvīra, like most Śramaṇas, did not accept the Brāhmaṇas' theological explanations. Or at least, he took very little notice of them. Neither the Brāhmaṇas, nor the sacred tradition on which they based themselves and the sacrifices which emulated the creative act of the Puruṣa—none of these were legitimate according to the Jains. Any conception of society in which any of these elements applied would be questioned by Jainism.

THE CASTES *(JĀTIS)*

Nevertheless, Jainism could not turn its back on the social reality of India. The fabric of Indian society is not made up of these four or five classes but by some thousands of endogamic units, which the Portuguese of the 16th century called *castas.* This term probably translates the Sanskrit word *jāti,* which—among many other things—literally means "birth" (Monier-Williams 1898: 418).

Jāti is the first and most evident feature of caste. One is born into a particular caste for being son or daughter of parents who are from the same or very similar caste. One's caste is for life: it is inherited. Caste is being born *(jāti)* into a certain sub-segment of society. As a rule, members of a same caste have recognisable surnames and can usually trace their origin back to the same human or divine ancestor. These ancestors and protectors of the caste are regularly propitiated. Therefore, the caste's principal rule is *endogamy:* marriage between members of the same caste, although in northern India there is a certain tendency toward hypergamy [see below].

The second point to take into account is the *traditional occupation* of each caste. There are castes of carpenters, scribes, farmers, priests, barbers, scavengers, moneylenders, etc. Thus, if the first aspect causes separation, the second tends to reconnect them, as within society all professions and trades are obliged to co-operate amongst themselves. The traditional occupation of a caste has been loosened quite a bit in the last century, and maybe less than a third of the Indian population today maintains the traditional occupation of their caste. Even if it is now possible to be from a blacksmith caste and devote oneself to agriculture or to the sale of rickshaws, that does not mean that one does not continue to be a "blacksmith", having been born into a blacksmith's family.

The third point has to do with certain *cultural customs.* Members of the same caste worship the same deities, and take part in the same festivals, follow the same specific rites according to certain rules, they dress in a characteristic fashion, they usually have particular diets, sometimes they support predictable religious orders and may even speak their own dialect.

Perhaps the aspect which best defines caste limits, apart from marriage rules, would be *eating habits.* Members of a caste only share food cooked and served by someone from the same caste, or slightly inferior or superior. Diet is equally a primordial barometer. Food taboos (belonging to each caste) and rules of commensality, govern the relations among castes.

Usually, every caste has a local organisation *(pañcāyata)* that sets rules and penalises behaviour in the community. But in reality everybody "sees to it" that order is respected, as everyone knows everyone else's birth-line. Castes are not camouflaged. The *pañcāyata* of a dominant caste (usually the most numerous and the one which controls the land) tend to become the judge in inter-caste disputes. This peculiarity explains the proverbial mistrust the Indian people have for their governors, and their predilection for more autarchic systems of government as well as their ability in differentiating between justice and equality—unlike Westerners, who all too often confuse them (Sorman 2000: 151).

In summary, a caste is a homogeneous unit with a very strong sense of "ethnic group", "community", "clan", and even of "family". In actual fact, the Indian state governs over not only "citizens" but also "communities", of which there are estimated some five thousand. There are castes numbering hundreds of individuals contained in little counties, whereas others are immense, reaching up to tens of millions of people, spread out through various states. In the case of the latter, there are subdivisions of first, second, third, and even fourth degree. These subdivisions, usually called sub-castes, form up the real endogamic units. In other words, the castes that are not segmented, form the *jāti.* In the ones that are, the endogamic unit, *the jāti,* is the sub-caste.

It has been mainly through the castes that the Indian civilisation has been able to simultaneously encapsulate the thousands of linguistic, cultural, and ethnic communities, which make it up. It is also here where the eclectic—rather than proselyte—character of Indian spirituality and the lack of a unifying theology enters on the scene. Hence we have a civilisation we could hardly call monolithic, it is polymorphic and is able to contain all the cultural, economical and technological levels conceivable. Owing to the voluntary impermeability of different communities, they have been able to conserve their identity, and at the same time interact with others. Only in India can someone dress how they want, eat what they want, pray to whomever they want without anyone bothering them. It is important to evaluate the caste society not only in terms of social injustice. Caste helps to preserve different identities, it gives security and shelter to its members, and it provides a certain degree of protection against outside influence. But castes are not included informally. The preferred model for society in India has been hierarchical. This is where Brāhmaṇical ideology and the political aspect of caste interferes and intervenes.

CASTE AND CLASS

The crux of the matter is establishing what relation there is between these thousands of castes and the four social-spiritual classes that the Brāhmaṇic treatises talk about. Because according to the Brāhmaṇical views on the issue—and let us remember that the Brāhmaṇas stand for authority in all senses—the *jāti* must be backed up by the *varṇa,* which is the transcendental order prescribed in the Veda. The four classes work as a type of pan-Indian scheme. The traditional Brāhmaṇical explanation says that the *jātis* arise from mixed marriages between members of different *varṇas (Manu-smrti* 10.5-56). Hence, the castes of carpenters, sculptors or that of the Caṇḍālas respectively derive from the union of a Śūdra man with a Vaiśya, Kṣatriya, and Brāhmaṇa woman. Obviously, this answer is a device to explain the damnable confusion in the order of classes that prevail in these times of *kali-yuga,* but it does not help us to work out the equivalence between caste and class. Historians reject the theory of inter-*varna* marriage as an explanation for the evolution of the *jātis* (Kolenda 1978: 35).

Some have seen shades of racism in all this. Since *varṇa* literally means "colour", the traditional society of *varṇas* would then be something like a Brāhmaṇical apartheid, and the castes would represent—at least in their origin—a range of different ethnic groups. Those of a fair complexion would be the nobles (Āryas), those with dark skin, servants and slaves (Dāsas), and so on. However, a racial reading of the issue turns out to be reductionist. It is not that the Indian society does not take race or ethnicity into account, but, as Thomas Trautmann (1997: 210-211) has said, it is far from obvious that *varṇa* means skin colour. The colour, which the Brāhmaṇic treatises refers to, is in the first place symbolic. It has to be with interior purity and spiritual quality.

According to Louis Dumont (1979: 69-85), the hierarchy of classes and castes has the ideology of purity/impurity as its basis. According to McKim Marriott (1968: 103-114), hierarchy refers to the relation of dependence and transactions that are established among castes. According to Nicholas Dirks (1990: 59), the king (i.e., power) was the central ordering factor in the social organisation of caste. The truth seems to be a combination of all. When putting into order the hierarchy of the caste (that is, transpose it onto the hierarchy of the *varṇas),* factors such as economic power, land ownership, the relation of dependence and the Brāhmaṇical criteria on purity come on the scene. It would otherwise be inconceivable that a Rājput, who is invariably carnivorous, warrior, drinker, and hunter (highly impure parameters according to Brāhmaṇic criteria) would be considered a noble Kṣatriya.

Owing to the need for finding correspondences, there is a certain confusion, even in India, between caste *(jāti),* lineage *(gotra)* and class *(varṇa).* Many Indians often talk about *the jātis* in the language of the *varṇas* (Dumont 1979: 101). A great degree of Western misunderstandings about Indian society are also due to the fact that European languages tend to use the same word *caste* to translate indifferently *varṇa* and *jāti.* Nevertheless, I consider it being indispensable to differentiate the notions and for that reason, I translate *varṇa* as "class" *and jāti* as "caste" or "sub-caste". As will have been gathered, neither the classes nor the castes are exactly what in modernity is referred to as "social classes", a question that has to do primarily with economic criteria, and which also exist in India as the discordant third element in the picture.

HIERARCHY AND MOBILITY

Owing to the need to be fitted into the social-spiritual classes, to some extent all the thousands of castes are put into an order of hierarchy; hence the clear notion of superior and inferior—or central and peripheral castes. Of course, individuals can try to camouflage themselves within a superior caste than their own by birth, in a conscious or unconscious way. For example, emigrating to another place, a city where they have new occupation opportunities, is a way to improve their rank—if they are successful. But for those who do not emigrate it is virtually impossible to change their caste status. They would have to drastically modify their eating habits, their speech and expressions, occupation, the deities they worship, their way of dressing, their name and surname, and the most important factor of all being that the possibilities of choice of marriage partner would be practically nil.

Things being as they are, the hierarchy in their extremes are more or less clear. In India no one questions the fact that Sanskrit scholars (Paṇḍitas), are high ranking Brāhmaṇas, however, poor they are, nor does anyone doubt that scavengers (Bhangīs) are untouchables, even though they may be successful businessmen. Nonetheless, the issue is not so evident or clear-cut at the broad intermediate levels. Here the correlation is sometimes extremely forced. The fact is if *individuals* cannot improve their rank, the *castes* or *sub-castes* as blocks can. Things could go as follows.

At a given moment, a group or part of a group renounces practices which are considered degrading and impure from a Brāhmaṇical point of view, adjust their rites to the Sanskrit tradition of the Brāhmaṇas, they become vegetarian, forbid widows from remarrying, adopt new vows and purifying restrictions that will enhance their rank, begin to avoid mixing with people considered to be particularly impure and even modify the name of the caste. Possibly, the turning point comes about when they can ask for a substantial dowry for an eligible groom. The fact is they would at this point, after various generations, lay claim a higher rank to the one they are—or were—accorded by others. Generally, the change in rank succeeds if there has simultaneously been an economic improvement and more active political participation in part of the group (Srinivas 1996: 88). In other words, the group will rise if apart from adjusting to Brāhmaṇical canons in terms of purity, they adjust to the social-economic canons in terms of dominance. Curiously, the "blessing" is endowed by Brāhmaṇas priests, usually when they accept to conduct the rites of the group in question. From this moment onwards, the members of this group will go on to be considered Kṣatriyas, for example, instead of Śūdras, and its members will wear the distinctive "sacred thread" of those from a higher class. The other sections from the group that, in the words of the sociologist M.N. Srinivas, did not Sanskritise—or Rajpu-tize—their customs, would be considered ritually lower. A new sub-caste or caste would be born. As Srinivas's work has shown (1996: 73-101), this process of fragmentation has been constant in Indian society.

Furthermore, there are strong regional differences. Studying the powerful merchant castes of Gujarat, John Cort (2004: 100-102) has seen that when castes interact, the principle of separation is stronger than that of hierarchy. Owing to all these factors, instead of a single hierarchy we should be prepared to see— with Dipankar Gupta (2000: 80)—the caste system as being composed of multiple and contending hierarchies.

The cliché of a pitiless, immobile and stagnant society comes just as much from the model offered by the Brāhmaṇic Dharma-śāstras (only concerned in justifying the Brāhmaṇas superiority and not reliable when it comes to reflecting society as a whole), as from the colonial perception. One cannot ignore the fact that thanks to it Europeans could justify their imperial politics and its vaunted moral superiority. As a matter of fact, some scholars think that caste, as we know it today, is not an unchanged survival of ancient India, but basically the product of an historical encounter between India and the colonial rule (Dirks 2001: 5). As Susan Bayly (1999: 96) aptly says, even at the dawn of the 19th century, the boundaries between 'pure' and 'impure', 'caste' and 'tribe', even Hindu and Muslim, were still flexible and less defined in everyday life than was later to be the case. It is not that the British invented caste, but that the census of the population that the British carried out (among many other things), achieved an ossification and a pernicious factionalism in Indian society (Pániker 2005: 366-370). It was only in the 19th century that caste became a reality for numerous Indians (Bayly 1999: 232). It is the modern state, which requires delimited and rigid categories to be able to govern it from a distance; and, in India, the category that was susceptible to being measured, defined and petrified was "caste". This strategy, along with the admittedly static perception of Indian higher classes, has given us a fuzzy picture of Indian society.

THE JAIN POSITION

ACCEPTANCE OF CASTE

The important thing to retain in all this explanation of castes and classes is that Jainism does not eliminate castes. Or better said, like Buddhists, they deny that "birth" has anything to do with rank, or that the *jāti* has to be situated within a hierarchy. On the other hand, they do not deny that there are a series of social molecules (castes) with a functional value. That is to say, they accept the social reality of thousands of castes but not the theological explanation of the four social-spiritual classes—the idea of "universal castes" (Halbfass 1991: 353)—and the hierarchy according to people's purity and birth. In many places in Jain texts, the notion that purity and spiritual level is inherited from birth is explicitly disapproved (J. Jain 1947: 185). But aside for this issue, all Jain castes share the structural features of the rest of Indian castes.

Normally, this is justified by saying that, immersed in the Hindu Ocean, it is inevitable that such a thing happens. Many Jains see it this way, and it is partly true, except that one would have to speak about an Indian Ocean rather than Hindu one. Everything seems to indicate that the Indian social structure, even if it has been reinforced and legitimised by the Brāhmaṇical theology of the *varṇas,* is a social phenomenon which predated Hinduism. From Georges Dumézil we know that the system of *varṇas* is an old Indo-European pattern involving a functional threefold division of society (Eliade 1976: I, 208)—also found among the Celts, Iranians, Hittites, Latins and Osetians (Dumézil 1968: 1, 9-27)—that was superimposed on an aboriginal system of *jātis,* possibly originating in the Indus civilisation (Kolenda 1978: 24-29). Put another way, caste is a structure rooted in Indian society that goes far beyond that of belonging or not to Hinduism. The system of castes we find among the Jains (or among Christians, Sikhs and even Muslims in India) is a basically social institution.

INTERMISSION OF BRĀHMAṆICAL IDEOLOGY

However, the matter gets complicated, as there are clear indications of Brāhmaṇical theology in Jain castes and texts. Although it is possible that in the first generations of Jainism there were no differences in class or caste, as the Jain population grew (in number, time, space and power) influential Brāhmaṇical ideology began to infiltrate their society.

The honour of institutionalising social-spiritual classes in the style of the Brāhmaṇas goes to a large extent to the Digambara master Jinasena (9th century). As we already know, his *ādi-Purāṇa* tells the story of the first *tīrthaṅkara* Ṛṣabha. In a sense, Jinasena made Ṛṣabha out to be a kind of Purusa or Brahmā god. He explicitly called him the Primordial Male *(ādi-Purāṇa* 34; in Strohl 1990: 220), which is the literal meaning of the Puruṣa concept. Although the *tīrthaṅkara* did not create the universe—he is, however, called the organiser of the world and lord of the animate and the inanimate *(ādi-Purāṇa* 34; in Strohl 1990: 220)—he did create human society and civilisation, which in terms of what we are dealing with here, comes to the same thing. Ṛṣabha, it turns out, embodied attributes identical to the Brāhmaṇical gods. Jinasena went as far as to state that apart from teaching all the arts and sciences, Ṛṣabha established the division of the social-spiritual castes and classes deriving them from different parts of his body *(ādi-Purāṇa* 16.243; cited in Singh 1975: 74). However, this division did not reflect cosmic order, as it did for the Brāhmaṇas, but a form of social and political organisation. The sacrifice's creative energy is clearly rejected (Babb 2004: 150-151). Hence the clerical class was not created in first place. Once Ṛṣabha achieved omniscience, it was his son Bharata who definitively established the order of castes and created the class of the Brāhmaṇas. Jain Brāhmaṇas?

The mythical explanation that Jinasena gives is a little naive, but it is worth commenting on. It tells that the emperor Bharata planned a type of trial or examination on the *ahiṃsā* inviting everybody to the palace. Bharata noticed that not all the laypersons were the same. Those who entered through the gate without care and trod on the garden were considered an inferior rank. Those who refrained from entering until they were provided with a path that did not imply the destruction of lives were considered "twice born" (*dvi-jas),* which is the term given by Brāhmaṇas to members of the three superior social-spiritual classes. Jinasena called them Deva-brāhmaṇas. Almost certainly, the only thing Jinasena did was to provide justification for a social phenomenon that already existed. It is possible that these Jain Brāhmaṇas appeared as a result of the virtuous conduct of a group of laypersons. That is how Hemacandra (12th century) presents the issue *(Triṣaṣṭiśalākapuruṣa-caritra* 1.155.343-346; cited in Laidlaw 1995: 111), possibly following the *Āvaśyaka-cūrṇi.* According to this text, there was a group of simple and pious people, the Sāvagas, who every time they saw someone killing a living being, detained them by shouting "do not kill" *(māhaṇa),* for which they went on to be called Māhanas, which is the Prakrit form of the Sanskrit Brāhmaṇa (J. Jain 1947: 186).

Most probably, as Padmanabh Jaini (1979: 291) suggests, the appearance of a Jaina-brāhmaṇa class would have had to do with the conversion of members of Brāhmaṇas castes to Jainism. From the earliest days of Jainism, several individuals from the Hindu clerical class came to form part of the Jain community (recall the eleven *gaṇadharas).* In religious terms, what Brāhmaṇas being converted to Jainism meant is that they renounced Vedic ritual and the rank that rites could offer them. In social terms—even biological ones—Brāhmaṇas remained the same: pure and luminous people. This adaptation is complex, as we find that this Jain who cannot be a Brāhmaṇa, simultaneously is one, and thanks to this the Jain community can have a superior level of laymen at the same time as rejecting the attributed supremacy granted to the Brāhmaṇas class/caste.

It is in the Deccan region, at the heart of the Digambara community, where we find this inherent caste of Jaina-brāhmaṇas or Upādhyāyas, with very similar characteristics to their Hindu counterparts. They maintain that they are the real Brāhmaṇas, descendants of Bharata and not the renegade Hindu priests, apostates who have fallen from the authentic spiritual path. They took on the task of studying and preserving the genuine Veda and organising religious ceremonies. With the gradual decline of virtue, many Brāhmaṇas strayed from the teachings of the *tīrthaṅkaras.* Regrettably, these days the majority of Brāhmaṇas in Bharata-varṣa follow erroneous practices and beliefs—Vedism/Hinduism. Although there are few Jaina-brāhmaṇas, what is important is that Jains have ended up having the identical notion of hierarchy as the Hindus—although on accepting food which is offered them, as a part of their temple worship, the Jaina-brāhmaṇas cannot be considered any purer than common devotees. On this question, note that there are numerous Digambara stories (Hariṣeṇa, *Bṛhatkathākośa* 31; cited in Warder 1972: VI, 237) about the consequences of associating with lower class people; and the initiation of an Untouchable into the order of Digambara ascetics would be strange indeed.

Let us recall now, that when in ancient texts Jain authors talk about Untouchables converted to Jainism, as in the case of Harikeśa [see pages 173-175], it is not stated that the social hierarchy was unjust or detestable. What they do insist on is that birth into a high level rank does not necessarily provide one with a high spiritual level nor vice versa. Remember: One becomes a Śramaṇa by equanimity, a Brāhmaṇa by chastity... The rhetoric is effective, but in no way does it constitute a repudiation of the class system; no more than, as James Laidlaw illustrates with a fine analogy (1995: 113), saying that one can recognise a gentleman by his manners and accomplishments rather than by his pedigree.

Jinasena was not the only one to write about this issue. The explanation which Somadeva Sūri (10th century) provides is rational rather than mythical. At the beginning of this Part of the book, we stated that, as Somadeva conceived it, the *dharma* of laymen was dual. On one hand, it was composed of a series of worldly activities *(laukika)* that is, social customs, laws, regulations, institutions, etc. On the other, a supra-worldly path *(pāralaukika),* which is the real path that leads to liberation. Both are acceptable *dharmas* as long as the first does not interfere with the second:

> "For the [Jain] householder there are two *dharmas, laukika* and *pāralaukika.* The basis of *laukika dharma* is *loka,* the social world as it is. The basis of *pāralaukika dharma* is he Jain canon" *(Upāsakādhyayana* 36.476; cited in Lath 1991: 27).

Mukund Lath (1991: 27) has pointed out the similarities of this form of reasoning to the Western categories of "secular" and "religious". Thanks to this hermeneutic tool, Somadeva could justify the existence of *jātis* by birth within the Jain community. What harm could it do to a Jain, Somadeva asked himself, to adjust to social and juridical practices, as long as they did not contradict religious vows and the right vision that the sacred texts teach? After saying this, Somadeva goes on to describe the correct marriage code for the laypersons, and the first rule is that Jains must wed someone from their own caste.

This has given many Jains a double sense of identity. On the one hand, they belong to one or another caste. On the other hand, they have their identity as Jains. Somadeva saw that it was impossible to eliminate the feeling of belonging to the caste. So, to allow the second identity, being a Jain, he formulated the idea of the notion of two *dharmas.*

JAIN CASTES

It is usually said that there are 84 Jain castes—a symbolic number; the truth is that the real figure, apart from being undoubtedly higher, is unknown (Sangave 1959: 103-131). On one hand, we have castes which are made up exclusively of Jains. On the other, we have something resembling Jain sections of widespread pan-Indian castes. In this case, we usually have to do with merchant castes (Baniās, Mahājanas) where, it happens, some of their members are Jains. As such, they form a separate sub-caste. Within the large Agaravāla caste, for example, we find Hindus Sikhs, Muslims and Jains.

In general, Jain castes take on the name of their origin, which endows them with a great sense of having "roots. The Śrimālīs say they originate from Bhīnmāl (Śrimāla); the Osavālas believe they come from Osian; the Agaravālas from Agar (Agroha). As some groups came to specialise in different occupations, they also took on the names of their professions.

Many northwestern castes are also sub-divided by a higher stratum *(vīsa, bar)* and a lower one *(dasā, lohar)*. At the same time, every caste can be divided into sub-castes or endogamic segments, which normally arise through conflicts or emigration. Every known sub-caste has its own myth of origin (kept by castes of genealogists), its tutelary deity *(kuladevatā)* and even a chronicle *(Purāṇa)* which relates its history. Diet or marriage rules can vary from one sub-caste to another. Usually, the members of a *jāti* use the same kind of clothes, pattern designs, decoration and even colours. Simply, the ones who are well off use a cloth or a furniture of better quality. Each caste has its own council *(pañcāyata)* that watches over their fellow members and their keeping to the customs. Although it has the power to excommunicate, expulsions are very rare. The influence of the *pañcāyatas* has declined considerably these days.

Since a large part of the community dedicates itself to some kind of business or commerce, sociologically speaking, the vast majority of Jain castes are included within the pan-Indian category of Vaiśyas (the merchant class). In fact, many merchant classes (Hindus or Jainas) share very similar origin myths (Babb 1999: 246). Even though, in theory, Jains fall beyond the Brāhmaṇical *dharma* (and could be considered as mere Untouchables) they *really* belong to the higher levels of the Indian society. With their obsession for vegetarianism, non-violence and vows of austerity, Jain castes adjust magnificently to the criterion of purity—they consider themselves equal and, in some parts of India, above the Brāhmaṇas. We must also add their decisive economic weight to this.

MARRIAGE RULES

Since Jainism has hardly offered any indications about its marriage rules (rites, divorce, polygamy, the buying and selling of wives, dowry), the regulations for these matters are laid down by the caste, and the caste always follows traditional local customs. In the vast majority of cases marriage ties are pacts between families, arranged and decided by the progenitors.

The patriarchal structure of Indian society disapproves of a man marrying a woman of higher caste than himself *(pratiloma* marriage), but it does accept hipergamy: marriages where the man is of higher caste than the woman *(anulo-ma* marriage). However, the most frequent marriage is isogamic (within the caste), although ties between members of the most important castes (Śrīmālīs and Osavālas) happens often.* On the other hand, marriage between a Śrīmālī or

* Although Śrīmālīs and Osavālas have their own temples and retreats, administered by the respective castes, they rarely worship separately and habitually visit each others' temples. This fact, reinforced by their similar socio-economic situation, shows that there is a certain homologation between the two castes, hence intermarriage across the two is not condemned, although it tends to be much rarer (Cort 2004: 86-87).

Osavāla with a member of another Jain caste is strongly condemned. Moreover the marriages between the *visa* and *dasā* sections of a same caste are frowned upon. The great exception to the rule comes with the joining in matrimony of Jain and Hindu factions of the same caste, at first sight, a surprising act. Since the marriage partners belong to the same group of merchant castes (Baniās) and there is a similarity in their customs, it is considered to be a workable marriage. It is striking that the marriage between a Dasā-śrīmālī and a Visā-śrīmālī is—or was until recently—shunned upon, whereas one between a Dasā-śrīmālī-srāvaka (Jain) and a Dasā-śrīmālī-mesari (Hindu) is tolerated. That shows that the ties of caste can be stronger than religious ones. Relations between Agaravāla Jains and Agaravāla non-Jains are also closer than that between Agaravāla Jains and Khaṇḍelavāla Jains, despite the fact that both belong to the Digambara sect (Babb 2004: 192). Marriage can also strengthen commercial links and allow entrance into other markets (Reynell 1991:47). When a family officially announces an advantageous wedding, its prestige and credibility increases.

In general, marriages between members of economically unequal standing are not encouraged. In the North, marriage is prohibited for individuals who belong to the same lineage *(gotra),* to avoid union between blood relatives. In the Deccan and the South they follow the Dravidian custom, where marriage between cross-cousins is traditional. Some *pañcāyatas* have tried to provide regulations when it comes to the question of dowries (without much success) and have tried to stop the use of ivory bracelets (which involve violence) at wedding ceremonies.

The *gacchas* and *saṃghas* play a very small part in marriage rules. That does not mean to say they are irrelevant in caste matters. Belonging to a certain *saṃgha* or *gaccha* endows one with an identity just as vital as that of the caste. There are some castes, that of the Paravāras in Madhya Pradesh, for instance, in which *all* its members are followers of a Jain sub-order, in this case the Digambara Tāraṇapanthī. Nevertheless, the normal thing is for different sections of a caste to be affiliated to different religious orders.

SOUTHERN CASTES

The main castes in the South and the Deccan region (Madhya Pradesh, Andhra Pradesh, Maharashtra, Chhattisgarh, Karnataka and Tamil Nadu) would be:

That of the Caturthas, who devote themselves to agriculture. The Pañcamas, distributed among different trades and commerce. The Śetavālas, very powerful in Maharashtra. The same goes for the Humbadas. Then there are the Sādaras, a merchant caste in Tamil Nadu. The Jaina-brāhmaṇas or Upādhyāyas, the hereditary caste of Jain priests, without an equivalent in the North. Sometimes these Upādhyāyas are recruited from the largest castes, the Caturthas and the Pañcamas.

The vast majority of Jain castes in the Deccan region are Digambara and do not make any distinctions between sub-groups that allow women to remarry *(dasā)* and those who do not *(visā)*. Unlike with the castes in the North, in the Deccan there are relatively poor Jain communities. The *ahiṃsā* doctrine has not stopped some Jains devoting themselves to agriculture, a very unusual thing in the North. They have religious heads *(svāmīs, bhaṭṭārakas)* with the power to arbitrate in caste matters.

NORTHERN CASTES

The main castes in the North (Rajasthan, Gujarat, Uttar Pradesh, Madhya Pradesh, Delhi and Bihar) would be:

That of the Osavālas, of Rājput origin and mainly Śvetāmbara, although they have Vaiṣṇava sections; well situated in commerce and very strong in Rajasthan. The Śrīmālīs, which is basically Śvetāmbara and very influential in Gujarat. The Poravāḍas, with Hindu and Jain sections. The Agaravālas, basically Vaiṣṇava Hindus, but with important Digambara sections. The Khaṇḍelavālas, who have become bankers and wealthy businessmen, strong in Rajasthan and exclusively Digambaras. The Humbaḍas, with Digambara and Śvetāmbara sections, centred in Rajasthan. The Paravāras, numerous in Madhya Pradesh and Uttar Pradesh, mainly Digambaras.

THE CASTE SOCIETY TODAY

Many Jains say that caste should not be given importance. It is not only a Jain argument, it is common among most middle class urban Indians, the representative segment of Jainism. However, one thing is modernising rhetoric and the other reality.

Although the contemporary urban society has put some of the traditional features of caste into check (commensality, maintenance of traditional occupations, inter-caste relations through the *jajmāni* system, caste councils) one should not take for granted that its weight and influence is any less. More than a *structure,* the caste is a very adaptive *dynamic force,* in such a way that it is capable of adjusting to an endless amount of contexts. It has been doing it for many centuries. Pauline Kolenda (1978: 151-155) has noted that due to mobility and diversification of occupations, to a certain degree the dynamics of cooperation and interdependence between castes has been broken, and on the other hand one becomes aware of an increase in competition between certain combinations of castes. In other words, if the principle of hierarchy—driven by a ritual language based on the concept of *varṇa*—has somewhat relaxed, that of division and difference—based on *the jātis*—has become more pronounced. The interesting thing is that at the same time as this variation arises, the feeling of solidarity within the caste remains intact. There are *castes* but perhaps not a caste *system.*

As many sociologists have observed, what happens is that the caste becomes more camouflaged and becomes substantialised. It transforms into a group in competition with the rest. In Louis Dumont's words (1979: 280), substantiali-sation is a process that marks the passing from a universe where emphasis is put on interdependence, to a universe of self-sufficient, essentially identical impenetrable blocks in competition. Externally, the caste is criticised or played down, but its ideology has been internalised. It is as if a component of "class" and "class struggle" were introduced. What arises is what the Indians call "community", a label referring to an interest group that becomes a lobby, a pressure group. The caste takes on form and becoming a community it carries with it awareness of social and religious class to the point of having an ethnicist tone. In short, it contains all the necessary elements for modern ideological conflicts (Barnett 1975: 159). This is complex, but it has its explanation.

Marc Galanter's work (cited in Larson 1995: 223) has shown that there are four ways of conceiving castes: (1) a sacred vision of caste, the old model of hierarchy based on purity and ritual interchange, still very powerful in rural India; (2) a sectarian view of caste, when a religious community—such as Vīraśaiva in Karnataka [see pages 230-231]—becomes a self-contained unit (it becomes the Liṅgayāt caste); (3) an associative view of caste, where large groups form associations to further certain interests (normally cultural and political); and (4) an organic view of caste; where large low-ranking castes group together to form a front out of common interest—take for example the so-called Other Backward Classes, who have obtained a degree of positive discrimination on the lines of that possessed by the Scheduled Castes and Scheduled Tribes. Interestingly, the Indian Constitution itself, while abolishing the sacred aspect of caste, accepts other aspects. The hierarchical and mythical view of traditional Brāhmaṇism is rejected but the pluri-ethnical, casteoriented view of society is accepted to further secularisation and equality. This is something that, as Gerald Larson has observed (1995: 226), is simply a modern, de-mythologised transposition of one of the key concepts of Indian civilisation: *dharma.*

Despite the fact that Indian society has within it all the ingredients for a social explosion (an infinite number of peoples and languages, social inequality, caste hierarchies, religious divisions) confrontation is rare, much less frequent than the press (Indian or Western) would have us believe. While not denying the fact of interreligious clashes, domestic violence and friction between castes, an honest balance shows that contrary to what is often projected, communal violence is not the norm (Varma 2005: 8). If we add to the above-mentioned factors the situation of general poverty and widespread illliteracy, and a figure of more than a billion inhabitants, it is a miracle that confrontations are not more frequent. Beyond its evident abusive aspects, the caste society is a complex and subtle solution legitimising difference and diversity. And this is something that Indians are loath to let go.

21. JAINISM IN SOCIETY

JAIN PROSELYTISM

Jain teachings, truth, doctrine, its path, all concepts encapsulated in the all-purpose term *dharma,* represent the first attempt to *universalise* an Indian way of spiritual progression. The most ancient Jain text says, in an absolutely natural fashion, that the Jina's teachings should be imparted to all forms of living creatures in the cosmos *(Acārāṅga-sātra* 1.6.5.3). Adopting this identity simply means adhering to certain beliefs, practices and a Jain way of living. It can become "official" through reciting the *namaskāra-mantra* [see pages 475-476], but in reality it is not necessary. Although at an ascetic level, there is clearly an initiation into the order, a layperson is not converted. He or she chooses it, or does not. The formalities in conversion are superfluous. Whilst being universal-ist, the Jain religion is not proselytising. Its missionary instinct has been mild, as it shares the Indian sensibility in that it is unnecessary to make of someone what he is not (Panikkar 1994: 37). Indian civilisation has always detested proselytism. At most, it uses "inclusion", that is the integration and appropriation of values and practices from other religions, but it is suspicious of conversion. Proof of this is that after more than 800 years of Muslim and Christian presence, the two most aggressive religions in the world in this regard, the results have been frustrating. In 1947, the year of Partition, in South Asia only 24% of the population was Muslim and less than 2% Christian.

Jain attitudes are coherent with what Michael Carrithers (cited in Dundas 2003: 127) has characterised as the "spiritual cosmopolitanism" of the religious life in India. Religious identities in South Asia are malleable and have not the hard and fixed exclusivity found in other areas. There is nothing strange or reprehensible in a Jain layperson occasionally worshipping Hindu deities. As Paul Dundas (2003: 127) has shown, this does not betoken abandonment of Jainism and conversion to Hinduism.

Although in its early period it promoted certain missionary activity, and chronicles give an exaggerated account of spectacular conversions, the truth is that Jainism has never had numerous followers. It has never sought converts to the same degree as Buddhism has and much less in the commissary way of monotheisms. In Jain texts the nearest term to "converted" might be the Sanskrit *pratibodhita,* that Dundas (2003: 128) translates as "awakened". Except in rare cases—all being recent—Jain orders have not established exceptions in their rules to favour missionary activities. In fact, according to the *Sūtrakṛtāṅga* (2.2.58), missionary activities do not have the objective of converting non-believers but rather the purification of ascetics. As a result, up until the 14th century, Jainism was confined within the borders of South Asia. Except in medieval times when the Chinese pilgrim Xuanzang (7th century) tells of naked ascetics in Kapisa, Central Asia *(Da Tang xiyou-ji* 7 [Beal: 1,55-56]), and save for the doubtful legend of two disciples of Haribhadra being murdered in Tibet (von Glasenapp 1925: 351), Jainism has remained on Indian soil. Although some mild missionary activity existed in the past, these days Jains are not oriented in converting non-Jains, but rather in trying to promote in society their values of non-violence or vegetarianism.

JAINISM TODAY

Currently the number of Jains is estimated at around 4.2 million, which represents approximately 0.4% of the population of India according to the 2001 census [see TABLE 3]. Out of these 4.2 million, almost two thirds would be Svetām-baras and a little more than a third would be Digambaras. The former are concentrated in the Northwest. These days the major part of the Digambara population is found in West and central India.

It is possible that this figure may be on the low side, as in the Indian government's population statistics many Jains may have declared themselves as being Hindus. The dividing line between both traditions can be ambiguous. In any case, we should not be far wrong in saying that the total amount cannot be much more than 4.5 million, even if some authors state that the figure is around 7 million (Jaini 1994: xxv). These divergences throw into relief the cautious approach one must take when talking about religious affiliations in India. The figures only serve to give an idea of the phenomenon we are dealing with, but they must in no way be accorded statistical validity.

Proportionally speaking, the state with the highest density of Jains (2001 data) would seem to be Maharashtra with 1.34%, followed by Rajasthan with 1.15%, Delhi with 1.11%, and Gujarat with 1.03%. Going by districts (1991 data), the first would be Kutch, in Gujarat, with 4.58% [see TABLE 4]. There are hardly any Jains in Bihar where Jainism originated and where some of their most sacred centres of pilgrimage can be found.

From these figures, it can be deduced that wherever there is a Jain community, they are always in a minority [see FIG. 22]. This is a key point to recall. Indeed, the proportion of Jains within the Indian Union continues to be on the decrease in relation to other communities.

TABLE 3: Jain population census in India (2001)

Maharashtra	1,301,843
Rajasthan	650,493
Madhya Pradesh	545,446
Gujarat	525,305
Karnataka	412,659
Uttar Pradesh	207,111
Delhi	155,122
Tamil Nadu	83,359
Haryana	57,167
Chhattisgarh	56,103
West Bengal	55,223
Other states	175,222
TOTAL INDIA	4,225,053

TABLE 4: Districts with a high density of Jains (1991)

Kutch (Gujarat)	4.58%
Kolhapur (Maharashtra)	4.16%
Belgaum (Karnataka)	4.11%
Mumbai (Maharashtra)	3.56%
Sangli (Maharashtra)	3.34%
Udaipur (Rajasthan)	3.07%
Sagar (Madhya Pradesh)	2.92%
Ahmedabad (Gujarat)	2.79%
Ratlam (Madhya Pradesh)	2.66%
Jalor (Rajasthan)	2.54%

THE JAIN POSITION WITHIN INDIAN SOCIETY

Despite its small size, the Jain community is disproportionately influential in Indian society. Its economic weight has been and still is enormous. Jains are very well placed within urban professions such as in commerce, industry, the jewellery business, government, banking, money lending, law, publishing, and communication media. They stand out as being skilful intermediaries for all kinds of agricultural and manufactured goods throughout the whole of western India. It suffices it to say that the market in semi-precious stones in Jaipur, quantitatively speaking the largest in the world, is substantially controlled by Jains. For five centuries, the ports of Surat and Bombay (Mumbai) have been at their service enabling them to export goods to the Persian Gulf, Europe, China, and Southeast Asia. It has been calculated—probably with a certain degree of exaggeration— that at the end of the 19th century half of the total volume of trade in India passed through Jain hands (J. Jaini 1916:73). This commerce was anchored in the sophisticated indigenous banking system, that had already begun to evolve in the 16th century independently from Europe's. The Portuguese Tomé Pires (cited in Frank 1998: 214) advised that "those of our people who want to be clerks and factors ought to go... and learn" from the Gujarati merchants because there "the business of trade is a science in itself. In this issue Jains would have had a substantial hand (Laidlaw 1995: 87-88). Later on, the arrival of the Pax Britannica and the improvement in communications, only served to strengthen the position of the commercial classes. However, at the risk of stating the obvious, it is as well to make it clear that not all Jains are merchants nor are they all rich and powerful.

It is interesting that in no place in Jain texts, not even in the ascetics' sermons, does the idea come across that becoming rich or acquiring wealth should be something negative in itself. If anything, quite the opposite. The idea comes across that prosperity *(artha)* is the result of good *karma.* Only voluntary poverty—that of the renunciant—is regarded as being a virtuous attribute. This is a general feature in Indian religiousness as a whole. In contrast to the Abrahamic religions, money is not the root of all evil. The prosperous Indian merchant is considered to be a social benefit, and his family an embodiment of success. Indeed, wealth is identified with a goddess: Lakṣmī. Ratnaśekhara Sūri (15th century) (cited in Dundas 2002; 104-105) could not be more clear:

> "The omniscient Jina states that purity of business activity is the basis of *dharma*... There is nothing which does not succeed through economic activity *[artha].*"

What is specifically frowned upon is the desire to be rich and the ignorant enjoyment coming from the possession of things. For this reason, Max Weber defined Jainism as being a variety of puritan asceticism almost Protestant in its nature; a Puritanism which could have been evolved into an endogenous capitalist bourgeoisie, were it not for ritual prohibitions—for instance, on travelling—and the traditionalism of the caste system in the Indian world (Weber 1921: II, 210-211). However, the situation is more complex. In many aspects Jainism is far removed from the Puritanism that Weber ascribes to it, and the supposed ritual taboos only affect ascetics. Jain merchants have always travelled. These days, a good part of their conversation consists of recounting the difficulties they have in finding vegetarian food when travelling abroad. James Laidlaw (1995: 362-363) correctly says that Jainism includes asceticism, austerity and detachment at the same time as material and economic interest almost in the manner of a pendulum, bringing together apparently contradictory ideals in a uniquely Jain fashion. We shall go more deeply into this in chapter 28.

In principle, the mass movement towards trade could be consequence of the *ahiṃsā* doctrine, which induces Jains to take up professions that involve the minimum possible violence towards other living beings. In addition, the specificity of their ethics, which include austerity, responsibility, self-confidence and personal effort, has proved an excellent framework for commercial activity. Nevertheless, there are also reasons to think that other factors (social and economic) have contributed a great deal to the formation of this commercial bent. And as a result, a practitioner of Jainism may have a much clearer feeling of being a merchant than being a Jaina. This issue merits wider scrutiny, as it will provide an expanded view of the intricate world of Indian sociology.

JAINS AS MAHĀJANAS

The majority of Jain castes correspond to the pan-Indian Vaiśya class. Then again, few people speak in terms of *varṇa;* only educated people who want to demonstrate their familiarity with Brāhmaṇical values. Therefore, these merchants are more frequently known by the generic term of Baniā or Vāṇiyā, which literally means "merchant". Baniā is not a caste name but a generic term (such as Brāhmaṇa or Dalit) which is quite often used to describe merchant castes. In the same way, as the term "Jew" has been used in Europe, it is not unusual for the term Baniā to be used in a derogatory fashion. There is a Rajasthani proverb that says: "the mango, the lemon, and the Baniya—they only yield when they are pressed hard by the neck" (Laidlaw 1995: 103). Given this negative stereotype many merchants prefer the honorific term "great person" *(mahājana)* or the alternative one *seṭh,* from the Sanskrit for "chief" *(śreṣṭhi).*

Half of the Mahājanas in the Northwest of India are Vaiṣṇava Hindus (the majority Puṣṭimārgī followers of Vallabha). The other half is Jain (mainly Śvetāmbara). There is also a small proportion of Muslims. Quite a few Mahājanas originate from the Rajasthani region of Marwar. During the colonial period many emigrated with notable success to large cities. Calcutta (Kolkata), which was the capital of British India, became an important commercial centre for Marwaris. Almost all of the commercial castes in Gujarat claim Marwari origin, and these Gujaratis were also responsible for a good part of the growth of Bombay (Mumbai) in the 19th and 20th centuries. As a result, the terms Baniā, Mahājana, and Marwari (Mārvārī) have practically gone on—somehow mistakenly—to be synonyms throughout the whole of India.

The fact is that these traders as a group share similarities in diet (vegetarian) language (Marwaṛi), customs (dress) and occupation (merchants) which may endow them with a greater sense of identity and solidarity than that of belonging to Vaiṣṇavism or Jainism. Before being followers of one or another religion, these people consider themselves to be Mahājanas. (Although it is also true that their particular caste identity can be more salient that their social identity as traders.)

Marwari, for instance, is a dialect of Rajasthani with its own alphabet. It is the language and writing used in their accountancy. Thanks to their skill in pronunciation, a specialised vocabulary, and differentiated alphabet, Mahājanas can make themselves totally unintelligible to everyone else. It is widely known that they secretly use their dialectal form in business transactions. Some people attribute strange powers, not always wholly benign, to their accounting ledgers.

Most Mahājanas wear classical clothing consisting of a spotless white shirt *(kurtā)* and kilt *(dhoti)*. Such dress, also associated with the independence movement and with Gandhi's personal austerity, carries connotations in India of high ritual status. In the matter of diet, too, they clearly stand out from the rest. All Jain and Vaiṣṇava Mahājanas are strictly vegetarian. On special days, they also avoid certain vegetables, such as garlic, onions and tomatoes. All these taboos come regulated by the *ahiṃsā* doctrine, one that all Mahājanas have in common.

For these reasons, a Jain Mahājana would certainly have much more in common with a Vaiṣṇava Mahājana than, let us say for example, with a Digambar-ra Jain from the South. Hence the cross-marriages between those communities. Moreover, there are associations of Mahājana castes that include Jains and Vaiṣṇavas. Many of their religious activities are similar, especially the idea of gaining worthiness with the practice of generosity *(dāna)* and public service *(sevā)*. Christine Cottam Ellis (1991: 104) has shown that for Mahājanas doing business is *dharma* in itself; their religious duty at the same time as their source of worthiness. If a business fails, then without a doubt this is due to lack of faith or some unworthy deed, something which can only be put right by generosity or public service, usually leading to the participation in committees and associations of a social or religious nature. The goddess Laksmī (patron saint of commerce) is present on all Mahājanas' domestic altars. The shops of Mahājanas also have images of Lakṣmī and Gaṇeśa (Hindus also have one of Viṣṇu, while Jains add Mahāvīra) to whom prayers are offered every morning. Both groups participate in festivals such as Dasaharā and Dīvālī. Michael Carrithers and Caroline Humphrey (1991: 291) have pointed out that with the emergence of Gandhism, inspired to a good degree by Jain ideals and Mahājana culture (being from this background himself) this lifestyle was reinforced and legitimised.

For example, as far as Jain Mahājanas from Rajasthan are concerned, only temple committees are specifically Jain institutions. Therefore, the label "Jain" is just one of the labels a merchant from Rajasthan, who happens to be Jain, can use. Social identity can fluctuate. A person can emphasise belonging to the *Mahājana* category, or to the specific caste into which he or she was born (for instance, *Osavāla)* or indeed lineage, language, occupation, region, and so on, or again may rather emphasise Jain sentiments and proclaim *Jaina* identity, but in no way would such a person need be a Jain at the expense of other identities.

JAINS AND RĀJPUTS

Although in the northern and western India everybody identifies Jains with Baniās and Vaiśyas, if we were to ask them about their roots, they would invariably say that, even though these days they are known as Baniās or Mahājanas, their ancestors were Rājputs—the warrior and aristocratic castes from Rajasthan and other areas of North India; the Kṣatriyas par excellence. How can it be that nonviolent people who mainly devote themselves to commerce boast about coming from a warrior origin? The question is of great interest.

A large degree of Jain identity is based upon the rules stemming from *ahiṃsā*. Out of their insistence on non-harm Jains are the most vegetarian and abstemious people on the planet. Their professions and trades are controlled by the ethics of non-violence. Hunting is unthinkable for them. Because of the *ahimsā,* they go so far as to finance dispensaries for birds, cows, and even insects and they are capable of rescuing animals from slaughterhouses. The Rājput identity stands for almost the complete opposite. Rājputs are carnivorous. Alcohol forms an essential part of their hospitality. Being warriors and kings, they are reputed hunters and the martial arts are well known to them. In spite of all this, Jain Khandelavālas pride themselves on descending from the *rājā* of Khaṇḍelā. The Srimālīs aver that they trace their origins to the Kṣatriyas from the city of Bhīnmāl (Srimāla). The Agaravālas declare that they are of a Rājput origin; as do the Poravāḍas, and the Osavālas claim their lineage to Rājput clans from the city of Osian. How does one explain all this? Following Lawrence Babb's excellent study on the Osavālas, I shall try to shed some light on the matter.

Osian (Osiyān) is a sleepy half-forgotten place in the desert of Thar. Although there are no longer practically any Osavālas living in Osian, they still consider the temple of Mahāvīra (8th century—the oldest in western India) to be their "mother temple". The other emblematic temple in the city is that of the goddess Saciyā Mātā.

In addition to worshipping the *tīrthaṅkaras* and their accompanying deities, Jains also venerate the goddesses who have protected their families and clans. This trait is a pan-Indian one. Once or twice a year, marking the half-yearly festival of Navarātri, Jain families give praise to the gods of their lineage *(kulade-vatās).* The guardian goddess for most of the *Osavāla jātis* is Saciyā Mātā. Many Osavālas send their sons to the temple of Saciyā Mātā to undergo their tonsure ceremony, and some go to study at the school adjacent to the temple of Mahāvīra. But our interest right now is in the goddess—or, better put, what concerns us is the goddess's "conversion". Because what is significant about this issue is that Saciyā Mātā was a goddess worshipped by the Rājputs, and when she was converted to Jainism, so were the warlike Rājputs.

Osavālas' legend tells us that during the reign of the *rājā* Upaldeva, there was in Osian a temple dedicated to Cāmuṇḍā, one of the most ferocious goddesses in India, associated with the terrible forms of Durgā, which is the generic name usually assumed by India's great goddess (Mahādevī). Durgā in her furious form is Cāmuṇḍā; more precisely, she is the "destroyer of the buffalo demon" (Mahiṣāsuramardinī), who held all the gods at bay. During the festival of Navarātri, it was a custom until very recently, to sacrifice goats and buffaloes in honour of the goddess. Therefore Cāmuṇḍā's nature is identical to that of the Rājputs, who are warriors and carnivores. It is thus consistent that she was the guardian goddess of the king's lineage. Owing to her power *(śakti)* the goddess can protect families, aid warriors on the battlefield, and, through the figure of the king—who is her main devotee—act as custodian of the kingdom. Sacrificing a buffalo during Navarātri is a way of legitimising the king's government.

The legend continues with a Jain master named Ratnaprabha Sūri, who was the instrument to put an end to the bloodthirsty sacrifices in reverence to the goddess. In their place, he introduced the offering of sweets. Obviously, the angry Cāmuṇḍā, presented with such an insult, induced an illness in one of the ascetic's eyes, but Ratnaprabha bore the pain and illness with such composure and stoicism that the goddess grew afraid of him. She apologised and accepted that there would be no more sacrifices in the temple. From then on, she became known as Saccī Devī, from where her present name is derived.

Lawrence Babb (1996: 155) describes other versions of the story of Saciyā Mātā. The truth is that the legend of the Osavālas' origin is not one tale alone but a medley of different stories. In every case we find a bloodthirsty, carnivorous goddess who is pacified by the miraculous intervention of a Jain ascetic, and a king who is converted to Jainism. The legends of the Kharatara-Gaccha that are linked to Osavāla clans never cease to tell of kings having hard times because of incurable illnesses, snake bites, demons attacking people, Muslims destroying temples and hardships on the battlefield. At a crucial moment the Rājput king is miraculously aided by a powerful *ācārya.* The intervention of the ascetic puts an end to the crisis in question and precipitates the conversion of the king and his subjects.

The crucial issue in the conversion of Rājputs lies in the conversion—or rather the pacifying—of the goddess. On becoming vegetarian, she goes on to be the protector of the temple of Mahāvīra and the king's descendants, the latter having been converted by the ascetic. When the Rājputs become Jains, the act of sacrifice in honour of the goddess disappears. Babb (1996:157) states that now Saciyā is a vegetarian Durgā, acceptable to the Osavālas. This is also a typical phenomenon for many Vaiṣṇava groups, which have made ferocious, bloodthirsty goddesses docile, and have adjusted their values (Clémentin-Ojha 1993: 141-154). After her pacification comes her conversion, but how can one be converted without going against the ideal of *ahiṃsā?* Catherine Clémentin-Ojha (1993: 147) shows us that the conversion comes about via the *integration* of the goddess,* the sacred places and the temples associated with her.

All this reveals her complexity. Usually her bloodthirsty, aggressive forms

* Although the goddess has been pacified, she does not lose her terrible and violent side, hence, her capacity to protect the community remains intact. Although, on being initiated she has taken the vow *of ahiṃsā,* she can resort to violence when it concerns the community who embody transcendence.

are identified with her unmarried status—or where her marriage takes second place. It is said that these types of goddesses have a hot "ritual temperature". On the other hand, the more benevolent and pacific manifestations are linked to the married goddess. They are said to be colder. Lindsey Harlan's work (cited in Babb 1996: 158) provides us with the notion that the Rājputs consider that the goddess of lineage possesses both facets. Men believe she protects the kingdom and the clan. For women, she is the protector of the home. The unmarried, independent, warrior goddess is linked to the "masculine" facet; the cold and pacific married goddess to the "feminine". The interesting thing is that in the worship of the goddess of the lineage in her domestic manifestation, which is a realm primarily associated with women, fasting replaces blood sacrifice as the central ritual motif. Thus, in a certain sense, the Jain appeasement of the goddess simply represents the supremacy of the domestic and feminine aspect that the goddess *already had* for Rājput women. In the Navarātri, not only do the Osavālas no longer offer animal sacrifices, but the main ritual has become fasting.

From the time of the conversion onwards, the Rājput king proceeds to worship the guardian goddess according to Jain precepts, he abstains from drinking alcohol and eating meat and he refrains from hunting or using weaponry. The Rājput has been transformed and along with him the rest of the community. A new Osavāla clan, or a new Jain caste which was once a warrior clan, has been born.*

Just as Babb (1996: 169) has illustrated, the Osavālas and the Śrīmālīs see themselves as being those who in the wake of Jain ascetic influence, renounced the violent ways of warlike kings and averted sacrificial violence. This is something perfectly congruous with tradition; after all, did not the *tīrthaṅkaras* came from a Kṣatriya background? All of them renounced their military and monarchic careers to take the path of asceticism and *ahiṃsā.* In the transformation from Rājput/*tīrthaṅkara* to Jain/ascetic, the laypeople has a model of how groups could convert to Jainism (Babb 1996: 169). However, asceticism cannot be taken too far as, in contrast to the renunciant, the Jain lay person must maintain him or herself in the world and perpetuate the community. Jains are presented with two possibilities, one being to take the path of asceticism for life (as *sād-hus* and *sādhvis* do) or temporarily take part in ascetic practices which their life allows them [see chapters 29 and 30]. This is the lay Jain's path. Although they cannot form a community of ascetics, Babb (1996: 170) indicates that they can be an ancient warrior community who respect and give praise to ascetics. This is how the mythology of the Osavāla origin represents the Osavāla identity.

* Lawrence Babb (2004: 13) has found striking parallels between these Jain narratives and the caste origin myths of many Hindu trader castes of Rajasthan: the story of how martial violence is rejected and warlike Rājputs are transformed into vegetarian and non-violent traders.

INTERACTION WITH OTHERS

For centuries, Jains have had to compete with Buddhists and Hindus to gain support from nobility. Except in isolated cases, the struggle between different religious groups has not been of the same bloody nature as that occurring between Hindus and Muslims in the last 150 years. However, this image of religious harmony and absolute tolerance in pre-Islamic India contrasting with the confrontation and conflict of post-Islamic times is not quite exact. Hymns of Tamil poets [see page 235] leave no room for doubt about serious rivalry with Buddhists and Jains, of the intentional destruction of images of the Buddha and the forced exile of Jain ascetics. The *Periya-Purāṇam* by Cēkkiḻar (7th century), the text which narrates the lives of Śiva and the 73 Nāyaṉār saints (note the appropriation of Jainism's number of sublime men) even tells of thousands of ascetics walled into the great temple of Mīnākṣī (Mīṉāṭci) in Madurai, for having pronounced Śiva's name in vain (Hudson 1989: 396), although the accuracy of the account is not at all clear (Peterson 1989: 273). It is perhaps nothing more than a legend illustrating the triumph of Śaivism over Jain asceticism.

Having said that, rather than the rivalry, it is the constant *interaction* between different religious groups, which needs to be emphasised. This interaction has been to a great extent possible due to the propensity of Indian tradition for adapting to and include elements from neighbouring traditions. Jainism is not an isolated reality detached from the Indian framework.

It is plain to see that for centuries the clearest notion of the Other for the Jain community was constituted by Buddhism. Satires concerning the positions taken by the Other are a constant in both traditions [see page 158]. One could say, with the exception of the Jain Haribhadra, one of the broader and sharper minded in Indian Philosophy, who went as far as to concede that the Buddhist *bodhisattva* was comparable to the *tīrthaṅkara (Yoga-bindu* 271.4; cited in von Glasenapp 1925: 504), that the monastic communities of both traditions purposely turned their backs on each other. Nevertheless, as we could see in chapter 7, the similarities between the two religions are enormous, and naturally so, given their common Śramaṇical origin.

From the 11th century onwards, the place of Buddhism was taken over by Śaiva Hindus, especially by the Pāśupata-śaivas (in Gujarat), the Vīraśaivas (in Karnataka), and the Śaiva-siddhāntins (in Tamil Nadu). If the monastic forms of Buddhism had a strong influence on Jain monasticism in the primal centuries, it is clear that the Śaivite forms of worship and ritual also deeply left their mark on Jainism. Conversely. Śaiva festivals in Bengal imposed themselves upon others that were Jain in origin (Sarkar 1917: 141), and many medieval images of Śiva as lord of the *yogins* are modelled on images of the *jinas.* Although Jain and Śaiva stories tell of rivalry, it would also be true to say that both communities prospered simultaneously. We know of many kings who were followers of Śiva and yet supported Jain ascetics and Jaina kings who helped Śaiva poets. More-over,

Jainism adopted a whole series of common terms from Śaivism, probably as a way of making it attractive to the followers of Śiva, but also owing to the multiple meanings of Sanskrit expressions. Hence, for Jains the word *śiva* itself means "liberation"; the *liṅga* ceases to be the phallic symbol of the god and changes into the distinctive ascetic emblems (brush, begging bowl, or nudity); *paśupati,* an epithet of Śiva, means the Jina, as is *mahādeva.* Two of the most compact Śaiva movements, the Śaiva-Siddhānta and the Vīraśaiva, were responsible for the decline of Jainism, but not without first taking on many of its practices and doctrines.

The Jain community was also subjected to Islamic influences and interacted with the Moghul court [see pages 248-250]. The concept of indecent activities inside temples *(āśātanās)* has more in common with the Islamic notion of the "sacredness" of buildings *(barakh)* than the traditional Jain attitude (Williams 1963: xxiii). We know that Jain bankers and magnates provided the Moghuls with hefty loans. Nonetheless, Islam definitely represents the most hostile opposition, the Other in the sense of "opposite". In the Śvetāmbara micro-history of Rajasthan, Gujarat, Uttar Pradesh and the Punjab, the Muslims have stood out as being destroyers of temples and the Jinas' images.

These days, the place of the "friendly" Other is occupied by the Vaiṣṇavas, especially the Puṣṭimārgīs followers of Vallabha, with whom the Jains from the North have traditionally maintained good relations and have allowed mixed marriages. According to David Lorenzen (1972: 39), although the Vaiṣṇavas took over from Jains in popularity, it was not without first adopting some of their practices, especially vegetarianism, rejecting all forms of violence and repugnance for the ecstatic style of ritual sometimes employed by some Śaivas. It is not an exaggeration to say that the Jain Baniās and Mahājanas have contributed just as much as, if not more than Brāhmaṇas, to set high class Hindus' signs of identity. Globalisation and modernisation are definitely the most important challenges that the community has to face these days. The fact is more palpable for Jains, with 70% of their population dwelling in urban areas as against 24% for Hindus and 35% for Muslims (Bose 1997: 5). It is well known that the impact of social and cultural changes is always felt more in cities than in rural areas. Given their role in society as merchants, bankers, and industrialists, Jains are well endowed with experience and resources in this respect. According to John Cort (1998: 7), the community was one of the first to interact with Europeans. Once British dominion became established Jains were also pioneers in responding to the discourses of missionaries and of modernity.

JAINISM AND HINDUISM

As a result of all these interactions, borrowings and osmosis, these days Jainism is quite close to Hinduism. More than that, in sociological terms, the differences between them are practically non-existent. Both communities are so intertwined that some Hindus consider Jainism to be just another sect or subdivision of their own tradition, and moreover, some Jains accept the label of being *Hindūs* in the most inclusive sense. There are some nominally Jain communities in Rajasthan and Karnataka whose knowledge of Jainism is rather limited and whose religious practices are more like those of Hindus than the traditional Jain ones. It is a commonplace characteristic in South Asia, where there are more than a few communities in this peripheral position. This is enhanced by the ambiguity of the Indian constitution: when using the term *Hindū* it includes Hindus, Buddhists, Sikhs, and Jains. This is a good example of the classic association Hinduism = Indianness; Hindu = Indian. In the same way, Indian legislation (which does not have a uniform civil code), has oscillated intermittently between the inclusion or non-inclusion of Jainism in the jurisdiction of Indian law, with periods of certain recognition of specific practices.

With the increasing politicisation of religion in India, many Jains have been drawn towards the Hindu nationalist ideas of the BJP (Bharatiya Janata Party), without giving much thought, it should be said, to the consequences deriving from such action. However, it would be wrong to consider the BJP as a "fundamentalist" party, which is the label accorded to it by the media in the West. The fact that many Jains are drawn towards it and are welcomed demonstrates this point. Moreover, since there is no Hindu dogma as such, and members of the BJP do not interpret Indian identity in dogmatic terms, one cannot accuse it of being "fundamentalist". A better way of describing it would be "nationalist" or "traditionalist and "bourgeois". The BJP is the party that represents the more or less urbanised upper classes and the growing Indian middle classes. So, it is not surprising that the Jain response to the nationalist threat would be to subsume itself—for want of a better expression—within the same groups that the BJP represents. Given their Baniā status (it is worth remembering the negative connotations of the term) and their heterodoxy, the Jains are potential "outsiders". They have invariably tended towards immersion as a form of self-defence.

Living in such an "Hinduised" medium, many Jain practices have been brought ever closer to Hindu ways. It is relevant that in many Śvetāmbara temples members of Hindu castes are employed as temple workers [see page 423]. Moreover, Jains usually use Brāhmaṇas for their domestic religious ceremonies. As a result of this literal "Brāhmaṇisation" one can detect clear feelings of caste hierarchy *(vīsa* and *dasā* sections, commensuality taboos, notions of purity). Likewise, Jains participate in the majority of Hindu festivals, for instance the Dīvālī and the Holī festivals, their forms of worship are very similar, many Jains frequent Viṣṇu temples, Jain ascetics perform roles very similar to Hindu *sādhus* and *gurus,* they have adopted esoteric Tantric rites, and some of the social customs and behaviour patterns of Hindus. As Gérald Larson (1994: 58) sums up, when one visits an Indian, at first sight one cannot tell if he is Hindu or Jain. Lawrence Babb (2004: 144) points that when a group adopts Jainism, this transformation is not characterised as ceasing to be 'Hindu'. Consequently, there is a certain relative uncertainty concerning Jain identity. One can understand that in a population census some Jains include themselves in the category of *Hindūs,* voluntarily or involuntarily. If we add to this the centuries of mixed marriages with Vaiṣṇavas, the scene becomes rather complex. In fact, one can be a Jain while without ceasing to be an Indian, and here lies the nub of the issue.

JAIN IDENTITY

Religious communities in South Asia resist the sort of labelling that the monotheistic religions generally use to define boundaries. I agree with Paul Dundas (1991: 186) in that, if we can escape these restrictions, perhaps we would discover that in the end categories such as "Hinduism" and "Jainism" dissolve in a continuum that can only be described as "South Asian". Hindus and Jains belong to a religious and social reality that I would dare to call "Indic", but this is already another issue (Pániker 2005: 71-74).

However, it is true that Jains see themselves as being a religious group, different from Hinduism. This is just as or even more important than what we perceive as observers. Moreover, the other communities (Hindu, Muslim, Sikh, etc.) regard them as being one single collective, even if on many occasions it is due more to economic criteria rather than religious ones. If Jains participate in many Hindu festivals, it is significant that the same thing does not happen the other way around. So it would be a mistake to come to the conclusion that there is no notion of "Jainism", no way of life, no world view, nor even a Jain culture. This is an important issue, because if Jainism were to become indistinguishable from the surrounding ocean it would cease to exist as a differentiated entity. This is something of which Jainism has always been aware.

Dundas (1991: 185) himself has pointed out that even if Jainism contains all the significant components of Hinduism (the Purāṇas, the Law books, social ethics, similar rituals, *mantras,* deities, ascetic emblems, rules on diet, etc.) the big difference for Jainism is the fact that Ṛṣabha promulgated all these elements according to the principles of non-violence. That is to say, both the practices they have taken on from their neighbours, as well as those that are common to all Indians, have a plainly Jain touch. For instance, Jain fasting has different connotations to the Hindu equivalent. This we shall see. The sacred cord, which many Jains wear in like fashion to upper class Brāhmaṇas and Hindus, refers back to the principle of non-violence. And while there has been borrowing between different traditions, Jainism has always looked to bringing its own signs to the fore in opposition to the Other. This attitude has usually been expressed in a strongly anti-Brāhmaṇic fashion. The issue can be traced back to the most ancient texts and was very palpable during the post-Gupta period, in spite of Hinduising interference in tradition.

Jains know that they have their own temples, meditation halls, ascetic retreats, places for pilgrimage and places for cremation specifically different from their Hindu counterparts. This matrix formed by ascetics, temples, liturgies, rites and laity that make up the Jain way of life, has been able to reproduce itself over a span of more than 2,000 years, conferring on its participants a sense of belonging to a community *(saṃgha)* beyond sectarian or caste divisions. 'Jainness', writes Lawrence Babb (2004: 175), is a quality that is transmitted in the form of teachings and initiation, not by physical descent. Thus, Jain groups are those castes that custody Jain mendicants.

Doctrinally speaking, Jains share a much more coherent, tidy metaphysics and cosmology than the astonishing doctrinal anarchy that prevails in what has been called Hinduism. There is a widespread notion that Jainism is characterised by abandonment *(tyāga),* meaning the sacrifice of worldly pleasures, in contrast to Hindus, who are characterised in terms of pleasure *(bhoga),* which is attachment to the things in this world.

There is a specifically Jain lifestyle that is independent and coherent, however much it fluctuates and interpenetrates the world that surrounds it. Jainism is not a ghetto nor a closed entity, but it is not an isomorphic collective lost in the ocean of Hinduism either.

All these interactions and oppositions have ended up moulding the Jain community and Jainism as a religion. One last example will serve to illustrate the enormous complexity of this issue, and submerge us in the thousands of microcosms which exist within Indian society.

JAINISM AND TRIBAL INDIA

There can be found in specific rural temples in the Northwest of the continent a fascinating religious interaction between Jains and tribal groups, especially the Bhīls (Humphrey 1991: 201-225), a tribe speaking an Indo-European language. A study by Caroline Humphrey looks at four famous Jain temples in Rajasthan and their relation with the Bhīls. Each temple annually organises a very popular procession *(mela)* among the Rajasthani farmers, which Jains and non-Jains attend. It is an interesting occurrence, as in towns non-Jains rarely visit the temples of *the jinas.* But in the case of rural temples—where the Jain population is not precisely very dense—tribal groups regularly frequent them. Significantly, these are the most celebrated and splendid temples in the community.

Let us pay a visit to the village of Rishabhdeo, situated to the South of Udaipur. Half the population is Jain, and the other half Hindu. 95% of the Jains are followers of the Bīsapanthī Digambara order and only 5% are Śvetāmbaras. As in other instances, the two communities have been in dispute over the ownership of the Kesaria-ji, the famous temple in Rishabhdeo. After an official judgement, it was determined that Digambaras would worship in the morning and the Śvetāmbaras in the evening. Apart from the central image of the *tīrthaṅkara,* there are images of Hindu and Bhīl deities. Interestingly, when the Bhīls visit the temple they ignore all the Jain motifs—with the exception of the central image—and they concentrate on their *bhomias.* The *bhomias* represent protective divinities, always associated with the land and the soil. Many are in a process of "Sanskritisation", i.e., in the process of assimilation to a great pan-Indian divinity. In this part of India, the tribal divinities assimilate themselves to the terrible forms of Śiva, such as Bhairava, Bhairon and Bharu [see FIG. 36]. While these forms of Śiva can be represented anthropomorphically, most *bhomias* are still very abstract. Some are just simply stones, while others are rocks covered with a gold leaf or silver paper.

Why do the Bhīls have such an interest in Jain temples? The explanation reveals complex relationships. Behind most images in temples, there is a long story, a story which describes the miraculous powers of the icon in question. The legend of a poor farmer—in this case a Bhīl—who is digging a hole next to a tree and finds an image which has been buried for hundreds of years, is one of the classics. Although after being found it is taken to a temple, the actual place where it was located will forever remain sacred and the descendants of the discoverer will have ritual privileges.

Caroline Humphrey (1991: 209) has observed that Bhīls believe in the power derived from "seeing" *(darśana)* the miraculous image of the *tīrthaṅkara.* This contradicts the Jain idea that no *jina* is able to or would want to intercede in the affairs of their devotees. We shall be going over this in detail in chapter 27. Only the protective divinities in Jain temples are able consider devotees' petitions, but the Bhīls ignore this issue. They are not Jains, after all. Here, an obvious question arises: why do Jains open up their temples and allow their gods to intervene for the benefit of others? On the one hand there are strong economic reasons. Owing precisely to the fact that these localities are in rural areas, the temples act as bazaars for the tribal population in the district. These fairs always take place when and where there is no other important market. Therefore, Jains have an economic interest in the matter. A typical profession among Jains is that of moneylender *(sahukar).* Loans from Jain moneylenders are still preferred in rural India in many cases to bank loans, for several reasons: they have the advantage of staying open most of the day. They provide a very quick service, they do not require bureaucratic paperwork, and there are fewer questions asked than in banks (Jones 1991:128). Bhīls are habitual clients of the Jains. Moreover they buy many everyday items from Jain shops in the bazaars. This "interested" tolerance of the Jains is, despite appearances, clearly not at all sectarian. Not only do Bhīls benefit from the use of the temple, but they also have access to hospitals, hostels, orphanages, and schools, which the Jains open as part of their religious service *(sevā),* and donation *(dāna)* to society.

But relations between the two communities are rife with resentment and misunderstanding.Bhīls are extremely hostile toward Baniās. Hindu folklore has always tainted Jaina-Baniās as *exploiters, strangers* and *un-Hindu.* There are tribal political movements (for example the one formed by Anup Das) with particularly anti-Jain ideology. Tribesmen consider Jains to be mean people who will always try to cheat in commerce and gain excessive profit. There have been cases where ascetics have been attacked and beaten. In certain impoverished circles the Jain *sādhus* are seen as "magicians" capable of stopping the rain with their powerful *mantras*. With the aid of their magicians, Jain merchants can sell grain at a higher price. Jains consider Bhīls to be rude, uncouth people who tend towards robbery, even murder, and who are moreover inclined to drink alcohol and eat meat. That said, there is no confrontation in the style of Muslims and Hindus. The dichotomy is more economic than religious. As Jains find themselves in a strong financial position, others tend to see them as being exploiters.

One could advance the argument that if the Bhīls worship the *tīrthaṅkaras* in the temples it means that they recognise a certain spiritual power in the Jains. Moreover, many will attend from time to time the sermons given by Jain ascetics, maybe join in some of their fasts and will refrain from using garlic and onion while there are renunciants in their village, to be able to offer them "pure" food. However, the truth is that Bhīls are not in the least ascetic or well behaved in their attitude when inside the temple, and during the fairs many of their dances can be savagely ecstatic.

Many Jains think that the Bhīls must consider the statue of Mahāvīra to be one of their *bhomias,* due to the fact that the image had been dug up, and the *bhomia* is the protector of the land. Therefore, the Bhīls happily ignore any religious demarcation or boundary. The strange thing is that, as Caroline Humphrey (1991: 219) has observed, what is allowed during the fairs at the rural temples would certainly not be allowed at normal Jain temples. Not only is there no resentment, but the ritual explicitly recognises the role of non-Jains who discovered the buried image. This explains how the temples happen to contain the non-iconic images of the *bhomias.* In reality, these *bhomias* do not differ too much from the protective divinities *(kṣetrapālas, śāsana-devatās)* that can be found in all Jain temples, and that were at one time *yakṣas* and *yakṣīs.* Thus, what Jains are doing is to open up their tradition to popular beliefs and practices; something they have not ceased to do over the past two thousand years. This process creates complex links.

From the Jain point of view, there is a great difference between their form of worship *(pūjā)* and the tribesmen's vision *(darśana),* or their peaceful processions and the wild ecstatic tribal dances, or between their magnificent temple and the humble corner where the Bhīl found the image, or between their otherworldly *tīrthaṅkara* and the *bhomias* or tribal *bhairavas.* Thanks to this assimilation-and-distinction, Jains attract tribesmen to their religion, at the same time as they create an obvious hierarchy. What is not so clear, as Caroline Humphrey (1991: 222) suspects, is whether non-Jains recognise these differences under the same set of values as Jains. This dual process of attraction/hierarchisation is reinforced by the economic ties and the position of spiritual power held by the temple owners.

All this becomes much more significant when we compare it with the antagonism that there is between Digambaras and Śvetāmbaras when addressing their disputes. Owing to their sectarian differences, the temple at Kesaria-ji has to accommodate two types of worship everyday. In the morning Digambaras give praise to naked statues, whereas in the evening Śvetāmbaras do likewise before clothed images. This gives rise to an unusual incongruence. It cannot be accepted that a Jina can be both Digambara and Śvetāmbara at the same time, but on the other hand the fact that others see him as a strange *bhomia* is tolerated. It is here that Jains become aware of their own identity. They are not worried about Bhīls calling Mahāvīra and Ṛṣabha by the names of their own divinities and thinking about *jinas* in their own manner, because they are *non-Jains.* Not being Jains they have no sectarian attributes, and therefore are free to do and think as they please, but once they accept the Jain path, the smallest detail can lead to discord and confrontation, just as has happened so many times with Digambaras and Śvetāmbaras.

JAINISM AND GENDER

Gender is a vital issue if we want to look more deeply into the anthropology of India. In the case of Jainism it is an essential consideration, given that the importance of women in the configuration, reproduction and transmission of Jainism is of much greater value than could be deduced from a merely textual or iconographic study.

Generally speaking, the situation of Jain women does not differ from the rest of women in India. It is true that Jains have a high female literacy rate (90.6% while in India as a whole it was only 47% in 2001). As a rule, Jain society maintains the same patriarchal pattern as in the whole of South Asia. The interests of the family are put before any kind of individual interest. The ideal family in South Asia is patrilineal; inheritance and ascendency is only contemplated through a male lineage. It is also patrifocal; males from all families inherit their paternal homes and bring their wives to live there with them. Authority rests with the men whereas the family honour resides in part on the purity of the women. To control women's sexuality, the traditional family relies on institutions such as women's seclusion *(pardā;* Anglo-Indian: *purdah)* typical of northern India, and arranged marriages (Seymour 1999: 8), commonplace in the entire continent. Since it is women who are in transit from one family to another and it is they who bring new generations into the world, they have the potential to upset the system if their sexuality is not controlled. An Indian girl is educated to be an obedient, hard-working, self-sacrificing, home-loving woman. In the North, from the age of puberty it is customary for the young woman to refrain from appearing in public, and when she does she wears a veil. The socialisation of the adolescent girl is determined by a very specific goal: that on her wedding day she should be able to leave home and family, the place of her childhood and youth, and enter into a new world, that of her husband, where she knows nobody and will have to compete with other women. This transition can be quite traumatic, as the newcomer—probably a young woman of eighteen or twenty—enters into her new family through the "back door" (especially if her dowry is not what was expected). She hardly has any kind of relationship with her husband, whom she knows very little, and acts as a "servant" to her sisters-in-law and mother-in-law; she dedicates her time to looking after her sisters-in-law's children as well as cooking and cleaning the house. In fact, she spends most of her time in the company of the other women in the extended family, with whom she will be close, and susceptible to having problems. Perhaps, this is the reason why the young Indian woman is so unarguably mature—compared to men.

The day in which she gives birth to her first baby her position in the family considerably improves. The concept of "mother" is much more important than that of "wife" in the patriarchal society. Moreover, in the first few years of marriage, the husband-wife relationship is rather tenuous. It is not unusual for them to sleep in separate rooms and not address each other by their first names. As Susan Seymour (1999: 8) says, emotional intimacy evolves gradually and should not be expressed too openly. Romantic love is regarded with suspicion (though it is extolled in the cinema and literature) because it is excessively individualist, too dependent on attachment and passion which, on the whole, are very dubious emotions for South Asian spirituality.

Until the day she gives birth, the new wife is nothing more than a sister-in-law to all the women in the family. Once she is "mother" her sphere of responsibility and influence grows. That has nothing to do with work or personal emancipation. In traditional India, it is frowned upon for women to work—except in very poor families. In fact, the more upper class the family, the more taboos there are in this regard. From the moment an Indian woman becomes a mother, she is in charge of her own home and she considers herself *fulfilled* and considers that her housework complements her husband's role and responsibility—essentially economic. She is the cornerstone on which her home and family's happiness is based. In India, it is the family and not the individual which is the true foundation of society. A woman who keeps her home pure (i.e., who cooks the approved foods, attends the temple frequently, undertakes occasional fasting, takes care of her own as well as her daughters' chastity and mixes very little with "impure" individuals) is the root to all success both as a source of personal worthiness and in social esteem. From their own point of view, Indian women do not see themselves as being oppressed as some may do from a Western viewpoint. In Werner Menski's opinion (1991: 50), Indian women have not been as subjugated as some texts (Indian and Western) would have us believe.

Of course, we are talking about traditional Indian families, usually based on the extended (joint) household model. In a more modern context, for instance, institutionalised reclusion of women has been relaxed, as has the idea of the impurity of menstruation and the practice of under-age marriages. In addition, women with formal qualifications are now more valued. In fact, Jain scriptures have always been in favour of women's education, and proof of that is the fact that

Jain women are more highly educated than Muslim or Hindu women. Since modern urban families are more nuclear, the whole universe of relations (with other women, communally brought up children, mothers-in-law) tends to cool. Indian women are more like Western women in this context. Given that Indian girls' adolescence has been prolonged, these days they have closer ties with their brothers and sisters, and they can go into higher education. They reach marriage more mature, cultured and independent. They almost certainly have a closer relationship with their husbands. On the other hand, they may feel more lonely. If things do not go so well economically they tend to miss the security of the extended family—which is almost a commonwealth. In spite of all this, many of the features of the joint family are kept up: the pattern is still patrifocal and patrilocal, marriages are still arranged, the idea of the purity of the home is kept alive.

WOMEN AND RELIGION

The model Jain woman would get up at dawn and meditate in front of the family altar for the prescribed 48 minutes. Before every religious act—which would include the task of cooking—she would have a "purifying" bath. The aim always is to maintain the purity of the home, in Brāhmaṇic style—in some cases even more exaggerated. In fact, purifying practices extend across all religious barriers; they belong more to the ideology of high castes than specifically to Hinduism or Jainism. Pious women go to the temple daily. During the monsoon season they attend the sermons of male or female ascetics every evening. For the rest of the year, they try to get to listen to ascetics who are passing through their district. Many women practise the rite of confession every day. The rest invariably confess at the festival of Paryuṣaṇa. These are the women who usually undertake collective fasting [see pages 455-458]. If that were not enough, women are the ones who set the rules for and are in control of the kitchen area, a key place for all religious forms in India. There is great number of food taboos they will have to be aware of and learn about, especially during fasting days and the monsoon season. Jain women generally follow the rule of not eating after the Sun has set [see page 484]. As their diet is (invariably vegetarian, but with greater or lesser emphasis on *ahiṃsā)* so will the family's social status and devoutness be seen.

The men appear to be more centred on doing business and working to maintain the family, and less on religious practices. Their main activity consists of going to the temple daily—or weekly—usually only to "see" the Jina rather than take part in the more elaborate worship. Very few practise meditation and the vast majority reserve their confession for the festival of Paryuṣaṇa. Their food taboos are similarly less strict (owing to the dictates of business relations) and fasting is again confined to Paryuṣaṇa. Obviously this less active participation does not detract in the least from the man's sense of identity as a Jain. The only religious activity in which men shine is the act of generosity [see pages 443-445].

All in all, Jain women are considerably more active in religious issues than men. In this, they do not differ a great deal from Hindus, also more participative and attentive than men—except for retired ones. For Jain women religion stands out as a symbol of their reputation and their morality. By her example the mother or householder's wife shows her moral purity to her children and to the entire family. Women take advantage of fasting, confession, and collective sermons to mix with and talk to other women from the same caste or religious order. This happens particularly in parts of India where reclusion is practised, which restricts their liberty of movement. It is at these religious gatherings where they can gather information about possible future brides or bridegrooms for their children. Although the actual responsibility for initiating and conducting the business of marriage terms is left to the men, women have enormous influence when it comes to choosing a candidate. Therefore, women are not only directly responsible for lineage and family reputation, but also for the very reproduction of their religious *gaccha.* This is reinforced by the importance of mothers in the upbringing and religious instruction of their children. It is one of their tasks to take the children to the temple (usually from the age of 4 or 5) for them to learn the names of the *tīrthaṅkaras* and the recital of sacred *mantras.* They also tell them tales and stories from their tradition. Girls learn the more complex recitations needed for fasting and meditation ceremonies. They learn from the pious *satīs* how to combine what is considered meritorious conduct in one context *(mokṣa-mārga)* with what it is in another context (*pativratā* or right behaviour of women) (Kelting 2009: 171).* In devout families, every adolescent ready for marriage will undergo periodical fasting in order to ensure a good marriage. Through fasting girls prove they have control over their appetite and impulses. As boys grow up, they will drift away from their mother and enter into their father's world and take their place in the family business, but they will never forget that they owe their Jain sense of identity initially and essentially to their mother.

JAINISM OVERSEAS

Let us take a leap across the "black ocean". To the data in TABLE 3, there need to be added some 100,000 or 150,000 Jains living outside India. These figures are solely an approximation.

Uprooted as a result of the needs of the British Raj' in the 19th and early 20th centuries, several Gujaratis emigrated to East Africa. Among them, there were a considerable number of Jains. Being good Baniās, they skilfully

* Note that in the Jain context, a *satī* is the epitome of the virtuous wife and is not linked to the Hindu rite of a woman dying with her deceased husband. In fact, some Jain *satīs* have never been married, and most end becoming nuns (Kelting 2009: 110).

slipped into commerce and administration. Yet, in terms of reproducing their culture, Jains living abroad have a disadvantage: they have no ascetics. Therefore, one of the first things every community goes about is building a temple where they can house an image, which has been consecrated beforehand in India by an *ācārya.* The first Jain temple to be built outside South Asia was completed in Nairobi, Kenya, in 1926. African Jains kept up their identity traits basically as a way to perpetuate their links with their homeland and their traditional lifestyle. They have skimpy knowledge of the philosophy and ethic values from which their festivals and rituals were derived. Although vegetarianism is a common rule at home, a major part of African Jains eat meat when they go out. Distance and the passage of time took its toll.

As a result of hostile political, regimes, many Indo-Africans emigrated to the United Kingdom in the 60's and 70's. Between 20,000 and 25,000 Jains live in the U.K., and most of them come from three African countries: Uganda, Kenya, and Tanzania. The great majority are of Gujarati origin, belonging to the large Śrīmālī and Osavāla castes. These days the major concentration of Jains in Europe can be found in the Midlands and the Greater London area. Most of them are Śvetāmbaras, followers of Mūrtipūjaka. In the United Kingdom they are known as the Dehrāvāsīs. There is also a small contingent of Sthānakavāsīs.

For many Jains overseas, their religion is no more than another aspect of their social identity, possibly not even the most important. Some are well off, like the prosperous community of diamond merchants in Holland and Belgium. The vast majority are small merchants like the shopkeepers of Leicester. Rather than Jains, many feel themselves to be Gujaratis or members of a caste, or Indians, or simply immigrants, but at the same time, there have been efforts to establish an international Jain community and an inclusive religious identity across caste and sectarian lines. Anne Vallely (2002:196) mentions the Jain Society of Toronto, founded in the early eighties, which houses a temple that is used jointly by Śvetāmbara Dehrāvāsīs (idol worshipping), Śvetāmbara Sthānakavāsīs (non-idol worshipping) and Digambaras.

Of course, with the adaptation to other cultures and contexts, changes have taken place in the ways of Jains overseas. This is something quite palpable in Jainism in the U.K. and U.S.A. For example, for a great number of North American Jains sect and caste are no longer significant markers of identity. Intermarriage is common between sects and with Hindus. Perhaps the only non-negotiable characteristic of being Jain is vegetarianism (Vallely 2002: 204).

The first major difference in these Western countries with respect to India is that there are no *sādhus* or *sādhvīs,* since they cannot travel abroad owing to the vows they have taken. Recently, some Terāpanthīs have been given dispensation from these types of restrictions. Similarly, the master Sushil Kumar founded a Sthānakavāsī *āśrama* in New Jersey. But overall, the dearth or total absence of ascetics is clearly felt. To fill this need, respected leaders from lay associations act as figures of authority and take on some of the roles which ascetics have in India.

Just as in the case of other immigrant communities with their own identity traits, Jains in America and Europe question to what extent they should adapt to Western lifestyles, and what role their religion has to play in this process. The different positions with regard to these questions could be summed up in terms of three tendencies that, according to Marcus Banks (1991: 248-257), we could call "orthodox", "heterodox" and "neo-orthodox", even if Jains might probably refer to the first category as "old-fashioned", to the second as "traditional", "simple" or "uncultured", and "modern" or "scientific" for the third. Although we are talking about Jainism overseas, and especially their adaptation to the Anglo-Saxon world, one should not ignore the fact that these issues have a certain boomerang effect, which, with certain modifications, could give us the key to understanding what a more modern or westernised Jainism is actually like in various Indian urban areas.

Generally speaking, the orthodox tendency is women's and older men's territory. The reason can possibly be found in the fact that these two groups have more time available to comply with rituals and are more sheltered from external influence. Since this position has to do with adherence to specific rituals, its correct description would be "orthopraxis" rather than "orthodoxy" (Banks 1991:248).

The main feature of the "heterodox" position, possibly constituting the majority, is their belief in a Supreme God. From the viewpoint of many European Jains, the *tīrthaṅkaras* are a manifestation of a divine principle and are endowed with the capacity to intervene in worldly affairs. Such a notion, clearly heterodox in the eyes of traditional Jainism, turns Western Jainism into another form of theism. Some, who are more influenced by Vedānta philosophy, talk about a divine principle above and beyond the *tīrthaṅkaras,* a sort of "Absolute" *(brahman)* that creates and controls deities and *jinas.* The belief in God implies a substantial change in the religion's aim. The goal is no longer liberation *(mokṣa),* but to please God through devotion *(bhakti).* As a result, British Jains have no problem with worshipping in Hindu, Sikh, or Christian temples. Likewise, it is quite common to find Hindu deities in their homes, and also Hindu practices have gone on to form part of their religious expression. One thus finds a certain amalgamation with the other Indian spiritual traditions.

Neo-orthodoxy is a different tendency, perhaps closer to what we would call the New Age trends of modern spirituality. From this point of view, Jainism is no longer a system for achieving liberation *(mokṣa)* but a science for the individual "here-and-now". This neo-orthodoxy has played down certain aspects of Jainism—those that do not fit in with a rational vision of the world. On the other hand, however, it has sought to provide scientific support for its ideals such as vegetarianism, non-violence, meditation and belief in self-perfection. For example, diet restrictions are looked upon from a purely medical standpoint. Meditation and austerity bring about mental peace, etc. For the neo-orthodox, monastic Jainism is overly strict and obsolete. The neo-orthodox tendency is more aware of its deviation, and is also more proselytising. It is inspired by the layman Rājacandra [see page 287] and on the ex-ascetic Chitrabhanu [see below]. As Marcus Banks (1991: 253) has observed, those in India who take this neo-orthodox position also cite Rājacandra and Kanji Svāmī [see pages 279-280] as their sources.

JAINISM IN THE WEST

Unlike Buddhism and Hinduism, there is hardly a Jainism for Westerners. It is worth reminding ourselves here that to maintain his vows, Ātmārāmjī was not able attend the famous World Parliament of Religions in Chicago and in his place went the layman Vircand Gāndhī, who, after his success in Chicago went on to teach Jainism in the U.S.A. and the U.K. Vircand managed to form a small community of followers, on which his Gāndhī Philosophical Society was based. He was the first Jain to become a master for Westerners.

Vircand has not been the only one. Chitrabhanu, a much loved figure in North American neo-orthodoxy, is a Śvetāmbara ex-ascetic who left the order and married one of his women disciples. He lives with one foot in India and another in the U.S.A., where he has established a Jain Meditation Centre. His teachings are pretty eclectic, perhaps closer to masters such as Osho—who himself was brought up in a Jain family—even though he has not developed any great following as a *guru.* As can be found with other somewhat controversial masters, Chitrabhanu is not well regarded in India, where desertion from ascetic practice for marriage has always been a motive for reproof.

Part IX
Texts

Jainism does not say that its scriptures are of divine origin (as is claimed for the Bible and the Qu'rān) or of non-human authorship (such as the Veda). Jainism clearly emphasises that their texts, and as an extension, their religion, are of completely human origin. Jain teachings are fruit of the wisdom of those who reached enlightenment and the many masters who achieved self-control. Jain texts came from spiritual experience.

Obviously, these texts teach the truth *(satya),* and in this sense they are just as eternal, undying and doctrinal as the rest of sacred texts in the world. Moreover, since they relate the experiences and teachings of the *jinas,* there can be no error in them. However, unlike revealed texts, for Jains this truth has not manifested in abstract words *(logos, vāc),* but is rooted in the knowledge and conduct of their omniscient victors *(jinas),* ancient leaders *(gaṇadharas, sthaviras)* and masters *(ācāryas)* of the community. Authority does not reside so much in the scriptures themselves, as in the lineages of the masters who transmitted these teachings. Anyone who opens to this same truth can add their grain of sand to the Jain texts. The doctrines and teachings they contain are relevant from the moment they encourage the transformation of consciousness and behaviour.

However, somewhat in a contradictory fashion—and without doubt because of the influence of Brāhmaṇic resentment of the Veda falling into impure hands—historically speaking there has been distrust regarding the texts being read by unqualified people. Until the end of the 19th century, Jain texts were not only unknown in the world outside India, but Indians themselves were not familiar with them, and, which is even stranger, they were unfamiliar to the great majority of Jains as well. Thanks to the work of different lay associations and to the efforts of committed masters, the universe of Jain texts has been opened up to all levels of society. These days, most of them have been translated into Hindi, Gujarati, Marathi, and even English.

In this part, consisting solely of chapter 22, we access the vast body of scriptures from Digambara and Śvetāmbara Jainism. The exposition will serve, moreover, as a reflection on the notion of a "canon", a concept, which is rooted in Western mentality, but can lead to misunderstandings when speaking about the East.

22. JAIN SCRIPTURES

THE CANON

The enlightened ones, and the masters who followed in their path, have left an immense body of texts. Perhaps, it is their marked monastic tone that unites them. The majority are philosophical treatises, manuals for ascetics, didactic works and mythological expositions. Even pieces of a more worldly nature (narration, fables, legends, tales) are strongly imbued with ascetic values. This literature is known under different names. The more usual ones are Doctrine (Siddhānta), Tradition (Āgamas) and Exposition (Anuyoga).

LANGUAGES

The bulk of the texts are written in different varieties of Prakrit. The Prakrit languages being the common or natural tongue *(prākṛta-bhāṣā)* derived from Sanskrit, the refined and perfectly constructed language *(samskṛta-bhāsā),* in which the sacred texts of Hinduism (Veda, Itihāsas, Purāṇas, etc.) are written The relationship between the Prakrit and Sanskrit languages to an extent parallels the one between Romance languages and Latin. However, in the opinion of Jains, the Prakrit languages are at the same level as Sanskrit and not below it. They make up the authentic language of the wise and the gods; the matrix from which all languages emerged.

The oldest Śvetāmbara scriptures are written in a variety of Prakrit called Semi-Magadhi *(ardhamāgadhī),* possibly derived from a dialect once spoken in Magadha in age-old times. It is said that it was Mahāvīra's mother tongue, although there is no certainty about this. At all events, Semi-Magadhi ended up becoming a specifically Jain dialect. Around the 1st and 2nd centuries it was only understood by Jain ascetics. With the Śvetāmbara insistence on it being preserved, it became a clear sign of sectarian identification. Something similar happened in Theravāda Buddhism with the ossification of the ancient Prakrit called Pali *(pāli).* Other later Śvetāmbara texts are written in a form of language close to Maharashtri *(mahārāṣṭrī-jaina),* this too being exclusively Jain. In fact, the majority of Śvetāmbara texts use a hybrid form closer to Maharashtri-Jaina rather than to Semi-Magadhi, which shows that their writing was several centuries later than Mahāvīra's time. Digambara texts frequently recur to another form of Prakrit known as Shuraseni *(śaurasenī-jaina),* typically from the region of Mathura, once again specifically Jain. The use of the so-called "corrupt tongue" *(apabhramśa-bhāṣā—intermediate* between Prakrit and Modern Indian languages) and Sanskrit *(samskṛta-bhāṣā)* comes on the scene somewhat later on, being common among both tendencies during medieval times. The use of Sanskrit bestowed much greater prestige on Jainism among elite cults in post-Gupta India. The Digambara stream was mainly responsible for its use. Only the more modern texts are written in vernacular languages, such as Gujarati, Hindi, Tamil, and Kannada. As we already know, the Jain contribution in the development of vernacular languages has been enormous. From the 19th century onwards English has also been used.

THE TRANSMISSION OF THE TEACHINGS

The word *āgama* is the nearest Sanskrit equivalent to "scripture". It literally means anything handed down and fixed by tradition (Monier-Williams 1899: 129). The best translation, therefore, is probably "tradition" rather than "canon" or "canonical literature". Let us look into this.

Tradition states that every *tīrthaṅkara* proclaimed and preached 14 Ancient Texts (Pūrvas). Accordingly, the original teachings of Pārśva and Mahāvīra would be contained in their correspondent 14 Pūrvas. From what one can gather from allusions to these works, these Pūrvas would have included speculation over the nature of the cosmos, comment on the views of rival schools and fundamental questions of our karmic bondage. They would have also included material on astronomy and astrology. Sadly, no *pūrva* has reached our times. How can we explain this?

In Mahāvīra's times, if it were true that writing existed in India, it would possibly have been directed towards secular subjects. Indian religious tradition has always given prestige to oral tradition, while holding writing under suspicion. Thus, the Jina's teachings were passed on down to the followers orally. It was transmitted from master to disciple by means of classical mnemonic methods. The most habitual model during this period, common to Buddhism and Brāhmaṇism, was that of short rules or aphorisms (Sūtras). These aphorisms appropriately gathered together formed a sermon *(sūtra)* or chain of aphorisms *(sūtra).* It is clear that in deliberately composing their teachings in the form of Sūtras, Jains and Buddhists alike were not only imitating Brāhmaṇic experts, but they were also seeking to compete with them. Jain Sūtras are full of traces of this oral origin: chants, flourishes, and choruses. The purpose being to facilitate their memorising and make them rhetorically more powerful. For their part, Brāhmaṇic grammarians opted for synthesising the key points in very compressed phrases. Hence, the difference in style between the highly enigmatic and concise Brāhmaṇic Sūtras, and those of the Jains which are very repetitive.

In contrast to Brāhmaṇism, where the transmission of the Veda was, and still is, a ritual obligation for different Brāhmaṇic families, the whole Jain scriptural body was transmitted from renunciant to renunciant in their retreats or monasteries. Due to the non-attachment vows of ascetics, in olden times monks were not allowed to possess "books". Moreover, the mnemonic techniques were less elaborated than those of Brāhmaṇic scholars. Owing to these factors Jain transmissions suffered more breaks than did those of the Veda.

Tradition states that Gautama, Sudharman, and the other *gaṇadharas* took it upon themselves to systematise Mahāvīra's teachings. This material would have constituted the Ancient Texts (Pūrvas) and the extremely important Limbs (Aṅgas). The relationship between Pūrvas and Aṅgas is not entirely clear, but in principle the former predate the latter and have more authority. At all events, since the Aṅgas are a compilation of Mahāvīra's teachings just as they were heard by his direct disciples, their authority is very great.

The leaders that followed continued transmitting these Pūrvas and Aṅgas. It is said that the first recension of a "canon" occurred 160 or 170 years after the Jina's death, at the council of Pāṭaliputra, at the end of the 4th century and beginning of the 3rd century BC. Scholars put little stock in this. Śvetāmbara tradition insistently states that, apart from the eleven Aṅgas then compiled, there was also a twelfth *aṅga,* called *Dṛṣṭivāda,* which contained part of the Pūrvas material. It is recounted that Bhadrabāhu (4th-3rd centuries BC) would have been the last *pontifex* to know the fourteen Pūrvas by heart. In Pāṭaliputra his disciple Sthūlabhadra retained only a portion of these Pūrvas [see page 181]. This part came to constitute the famous *Dṛṣṭivāda.*

Gradually, the following generations lost the knowledge of the *Dṛṣṭivāda.* By 680 years (according to the Digambaras) or 1,000 years (according to Śvetāmbaras) after the *vīranirvāṇa,* nobody remembered the Ancient Texts anymore. The difference between Jainism and other traditions is that they accept there are scriptural gaps of great magnitude. This is understandably enough, if we remember the Jain idea that not long after the passing of Mahāvīra, the continent of Bharata entered into the Sorrowful Age. The loss of the Pūrvas was the result of the inevitable degeneration of things. And without Pūrvas there is no possible liberation.

Although Śvetāmbaras state that the eleven Aṅgas have fortunately survived down to our times, Digambaras—who have completely different scriptures—deny this. Not only does Digambara tradition state that the fourteen Pūrvas were lost, but it also considers the Śvetāmbara's eleven Aṅgas to be false. However, Digambara tradition has preserved the titles and summaries of sections from the "lost" Aṅgas, and if we compare their lists with those of the Śvetāmbaras we see that they are practically identical (von Glasenapp 1925: 121), so that the existence of teachings pre-dating any sectarian difference cannot be discounted. According to Paul Dundas (1992: 70), everything points to an original shared textual tradition, which gradually diverged.

How is it that tradition could not succeed in passing on such fundamentally important texts as the Pūrvas? Perhaps, they were so difficult that made people lose interest in this portion of the teachings, and all effort was concentrated on preserving the Aṅgas, or it could be, as Walter Schubring (1934: 76) thought, that tradition believed it convenient not to continue transmitting them, as they contained excessive references to rival tendencies.* Allusions that in the future, as in the *Ṛṣibhāṣita* [see pages 127-128], could be wrongly interpreted and lead ascetics astray, but this loss is not as tragic as it might seem. Both tendencies maintain that the spirit of the Pūrvas was not extinguished. The Aṅgas of the Śvetāmbaras refer to the Pūrvas again and again and one might come to the conclusion that they were even based on them. In fact both blocks or scriptural bodies were composed by the same hands: those of the *gaṇadharas.*

Let us restrict ourselves to the Śvetāmbara tradition, which has a notion closer to what is classically known as a canon. While there is considerable consensus over the Aṅgas, this is not so in the case of the so-called Subsidiary Limb (Aṅgabāhya). Effectively, running parallel to the transmission of the Aṅgas, which are said to go back to the *gaṇadharas,* other different masters added their texts and teachings along the way. This body of texts that makes up the Aṅgabāhya provides a sort of gigantic appendix to the Aṅgas. However the number and even the titles vary considerably depending on the list in question. To put it another different manner: the authority of the most important texts is recognised, it is the lesser ones that come under discussion, texts that in reality, are interchangeable.

It is said that, 830 years after Mahāvīra's *nirvāṇa,* around mid 4th century, two almost simultaneous councils were held in Mathura (under the supervision of Ārya Skandila) and in Vallabhī (under Nāgārjuna Sūri) with the identical purpose of establishing the recension of the texts. Sadly, Skandila and Nāgārjuna were never able to compare their compilations, such that the two different versions were transmitted parallely. Almost certainly to avoid more losses and to reconcile the different editions, around the middle of the 5th century, Devarddhi Kṣamāsramana organised a new council in Vallabhī. It was at this council where the *Dṛṣṭivāda* was officially declared "lost" by the Śvetāmbara tradition. At Vallabhī the whole body of teachings were written down on palm leaves. Out of interest, Devarddhi introduced variables such as "according to one version", and "Nāgārjuna's followers think". The prudent Devarddhi did not want to omit or add anything new.

In contrast to the first council at Pāṭaliputra, the historical reality of these three councils is accepted by all. It is quite clear that the transcription of the texts corresponds to a moment in time when the study of the scriptures had gained in prestige (possibly when monastic institutions had similarly grown) and when the threat of the total disappearance of the teachings was strongly felt. In the ascetic's

* In fact, the Indian term to denote a philosophical opponent is *pūrvapakṣa.*

rules on behaviour an exception was established in the vow of non-possession to allow for the preservation of the texts.

THE IDEA OF A CANON

For decades, one of the Western scholars' obsessions consisted of searching out the holy books of the East and their "Bibles" or "Canons". Their aim was to discover the cradle of each religion, something considerably in fashion in the 19th century, with their renewed interest in the origin and evolution of things. And in their praiseworthy enterprise, they emerge as having an erroneous notion of traditions founded on a "closed" scriptural body such as that of the Christian Bible. In the case of Jainism, it was Georg Bühler who established, at the end of 19th century, that their "canon" consisted of forty-five texts [see below]. For a century, nobody questioned Bühler's list, as no one doubted, seconding Max-Müller, that any religious tradition was based on a sacred scripture which at a given moment in its history had become fixed. The truth is that this fascination for "Bibles" or "Canons" is a projection of the Judeo-Christian tradition. Just as Kendall Folkert (1993: 61) has shown, it has been the Christian vision of its own Bible, and particularly from the protestant viewpoint, that has been the basic model, which has structured our representations of scripture, in the comparative study of religions. One of the main tasks of this great scholar of Jainism, was to show how the notion of a fixed Jain canon has been harmful to the understanding of their tradition. I think, as Folkert did, that it is mistaken to transfer Christian thought patterns to the Indian situation. In the Christian world, the Bible is that original source revealed by God, its religious value being irreducible and closed from all that which does not belong to it. To the Westerner, in other words, the Bible is canonical scripture in the sense that it acts as a vehicle for religious authority: it is an independent and absolutely closed book without any possibility of alteration, and the norm in all dogmatic religious issues.

In India things do not work like that. The scheme Pūrvas-Aṅgas-Aṅgabāhya shows a clear decreasing progression in the knowledge of Mahāvīra's words (Pūrvas), passing through what is directly derived from them (Aṅgas) to what is derived indirectly (Aṅgabāhya). Obviously, this does not correspond to the idea of a canon in the West (Folkert 1993: 48). The widespread idea that the body of forty-five scriptures was *fixed* at Vallabhī is inexact. At the above-mentioned council, Devarddhi Kṣamāśramaṇa undertook the labour of editing the transmitted Śvetāmbara material and having it transcribed, but in no way did he cause it to be a closed canon consisting of forty-five scriptures.

In India, venerated texts do not completely take the place of a doctrinal authority. It is more common for them to be used as a ritual guide. They are not necessarily "sacred" in the essentialist Christian sense, nor are they a closed canon that cannot change with the passing of time. In India, religious teachings can be plural, are always open to re-evaluation and commentary, and derive their significance from *oral* and *ritual* contexts. The mistake of many Indologists has been in projecting the notion of "canon" as a dogmatic religious authority on traditions that are mostly based on texts with ritual authority.

The Veda, for example, is not a "book". It acquires its full meaning when it is recited during ritual. In the eyes of a Hindu, the Veda has to be intoned to express its potency. It is more like a "missal" than the Bible. Indian texts do not only have a specific meaning, derived from their reading, but they are something that should be used. Jains do not read their venerated texts just as someone would read a book. In general, they use compendiums and "missal" collections which are given the generic name Pratikramaṇa-sūtras. Hence they mix extracts from ancient texts, chants and hymns organised according to the acts of worship they form part of. The language used in these Sūtras is usually Prakrit, but transcribed with Gujarati or Hindi scripts in such a way they can be pronounced correctly. A series of commentaries in a vernacular language explain the content and give instructions. These texts, which do not appear on compiled "canonical" lists, constitute the way in which the vast majority of Jains perceive their scriptures.

Let us take a look at a classic instance. One of the most venerated texts among Śvetāmbaras is the *Kalpa-sūtra,* traditionally but wrongly attributed to Bhadrabāhu. Of all scriptures it is the one to have been most copied and usually comes accompanied by magnificent illustrations. At the important festival of Paryuṣaṇa, the Śvetāmbara lay worshippers collectively recite it with immense devotion [see page 430-431]. However, what is recited either has very little to do with the original Prakrit text, or is Vinayavijaya's (17th century) commentary in Sanskrit, or the translation to Gujarati. A fundamental part of the event, accompanying the recitation, consists in publicly showing the illustrations from the pages of the manuscript. Thus, just as John Cort (1992: 179) has appreciated, within the Śvetāmbara perception of the nature and content of this text, we come across different ways of understanding it. It could be presented in the form of th matrix text in Prakrit (simply known as the *Bārasā-sūtra)',* or as the Prakrit text along with its commentary in Sanskrit plus its translations into vernacular languages (the *Kalpa-sūtra)* and even as the stories that appear in the illustrations, which is not a bad way for adepts to understand the tradition. In summary, the text is an object of devotion in itself and must be inserted in its devotional and ritual context at the festival of Paryuṣaṇa. If we cannot grasp this link between the written, the oral and the ritual, our perception of Jain texts will be mistaken. Therefore the very widespread idea that there are 45 Jain scriptures (11 Aṅgas and 34 Aṅgabāhyas) forming the Jain canon, is totally inadequate. At most, it represents a general approximation to a canon for the Śvetāmbara sub-order of the Kharatara-Gaccha. It is true that the 45 texts have been the dominating factor in the general vision of the Śvetāmbara tradition, but in no wise does this represent the way in which all Śvetāmbaras understand their tradition. Some lists speak of 40, others 50 and even 84 texts. The Sthānakavāsīs and the Terāpanthīs have their own list of

32, and this is not to mention the Digambaras, who undoubtedly as a piece of their strategy of differentiation from Śvetāmbaras, maintain that all ancient scriptures were lost. To all this, one must add the numerous alterations, omissions and modifications they have undergone. In the 11th century, the commentator Abhayadeva frankly admitted that it was difficult to explicate the texts, as they were full of gaps and incoherences. Many traditions had been lost and there were different versions of the same text (J. Jain 1972: 48). The typically unsystematic form of Indian texts, their contradictions and disconnections, betray the fact that many hands have played a part in their elaboration. In all, it is something that has not bothered Indians very much, so that for example the Śvetāmbara tradition never bothered to eliminate passages that mentioned rules about going naked from their texts.

Having cleared that up, we can now approach venerated texts somewhat somewhat less impeded by clichés. If we can take the "canonical" strait jacket off Jain scriptures we shall be in a position to appreciate and judge them much better

THE SIDDHĀNTA

In spite of the losses, Śvetāmbara Jainism insists that the major part of the compiled material in the first council at Pāṭaliputra was successfully transmitted down to the one at Vallabhī. These large portions constitute the Principal Limb (Anga) and the Subsidiary Limb (Angabāhya), in turn making up the scriptural body known by the generic title of Doctrine (Siddhānta).

AṄGAS

Although the Siddhānta was "published" nearly a 1,000 years after the death of Mahāvīra, there is no doubt that this contains extremely ancient portions, especially in the section of the eleven Aṅgas. Colette Caillat (1970: 158) mentions a study founded on metric criteria which considers that certain portions of the Aṅgas are earlier than the 4th and 3rd centuries BC. More than one paragraph could be a direct echo of the very words of Mahāvīra himself. Generations and generations of ascetics would have transmitted the Aṅgas, incorporating new teachings and adapting their form to the linguistic changes that would have taken place in Prakrit languages.

The first *aṅga* is one of the most venerated of all. It is called *Ācārāṅga-sūtra* because it largely concerns the behaviour *(ācāra)* of ascetics. It also contains the least mythical of Mahāvīra's biographies. The first part of the *sūtra* (forming the *Ācārāṅga-sūtra 1*), and especially the passages in verse that have to do with the doctrine of non-violence, possibly constitute the most ancient portions of all Jain texts.

The second *aṅga,* called *Sūtrakṛtāṅga,* is another of the oldest texts, especially the first portion, the *Sūtrakṛtāṅga I.* Apart from general teachings of the doctrine, it includes interesting descriptions of rival schools' positions. Just as in the case of Buddhist Sūtras which have similar content the object here was to instruct ascetics in erroneous beliefs and know how to refute them.

The third *aṅga* is the *Sthānāṅga-sātra,* a kind of encyclopaedia that treats mythology, cosmology, practice and doctrine. The fourth, the *Samavāya-sātra,* is similar. Both texts take on a formula dear to Indians since ancient times: grouping things according to their number (three jewels, four types of birth, seven fundamental principles). This method (identical to the *Aṅguttara-nikāya* of Buddhism) was designed for advanced students of the doctrine.

The fifth *aṅga,* the longest in the Siddhānta, is the *Vyākhyā-prajñāpti,* held in such veneration that it usually bears the title of the Sublime Sermon (*Bhaga-vati-sūtra).* It deals with the whole range of interests in Jainism: philosophy, cosmology, epistemology, history, anatomy and practice. In Moritz Winter-nitz's opinion (1907: II, 426-427), some sermons take on the tone and style of Mahāvīra himself. The *sūtra* also offers us a vivid description of his life and his relation with the *gaṇadharas.*

A good part of the remaining Aṅgas consist in expositions of the doctrine and rules of conduct, some of which are clearly directed at laypersons, constituting evidence of their later writing and composition. They are full of the life stories of *tīrthaṅkaras,* biographies of exemplary saints, even material, which can scarcely be considered Jain. Many chapters are intended for people who have not been versed in the subtleties of the doctrine, much in the fashion of the Hindu's, Itihāsas and Purāṇas, or the Buddhist's Jātakas and Avadānas. For example, stories of the *tīrthaṅkara* Malli are found in the sixth *aṅga,* the *Jñātṛ-dharmakathāḥ.* Some of the biographies of model laymen and the social life in the period of Mahāvīra are found in the seventh *aṅga,* the *Upāsaka-daśāh,* that outlines the already classic model of the various states of a layperson's spiritual progression and religious vows. The mythology of Nemi and Kṛṣṇa is related in the eighth *aṅga,* the *Antakṛddaśāḥ.* The ninth, the *Aṇuttaraupapātika-daśāh,* discourses on the penitential conduct of ascetics, and the most elevated divine rebirths. The 10th, the *Praśnavyākaraṇa,* centres on the major religious vows, and the way in which *karma* contaminates the soul, and reveals a much later style. The 11th *aṅga,* the *Vipakaśruta* tells stories about people in the light of the theory of *karma.*

UPĀNGAS

The first collection of texts in the Aṅgabāhya is given the generic name of Relating to the Aṅgas (Upāṅga). In theory, it is a prolongation of the Aṅgas, but its correspondence is purely theoretical.

The themes of the twelve Upāṅgas are extremely varied. They talk about ontology, astrology, monastic discipline, ethics, mythology, and more or less legendary topics. Many are made up of very similar stories (notably the *Nirayāvalikā,* the *Kalpāvataṃsikā* or the *Puṣpacūlā).* Invariably, they talk about a man who at a given moment, renounces the world to become a Jain monk, studies the sacred texts, practices asceticism, fasts unto death and finally achieves liberation or the highest heaven. Some *Upāṅgas* (the *Vṛṣṇidaśā* for example) are interesting to historians and scholars of religion as they speak of very ancient Brāhmaṇic and Śramaṇic groups of renunciants and the lives of ancient kings. Others, such as the *Jīvabhigama,* consists of long lists of classifications of different types of living beings, the places in the cosmos where they reside, heavenly bodies and constellations, etc. A special mention must be given to the fourth *upāṅga,* known as the *Prajnāpaṇā-sūtra,* which is said to contain the essence of the lost *anga,* the *Dṛṣṭivāda.* This is one of the few scriptures for whom we know the author. It was written by the ascetic Ārya Śyāma (1st century), identified with the saint Kālakācārya. It contains more philosophical material than most other texts of the Siddhānta. For cosmographical and cosmolog-ical references, the *Jambūdvīpa-prajñāpti* is a valuable source; it also expands to quite an extent on the life of Ṛṣabha. The most interesting *upānga* in terms of literary value is the *Rājapraśnīya.*

PRAKĪRṆAKA-SŪTRAS

The collection known as the Miscellany (Prakīrṇaka) contains ten texts on different topics: psychology, hymns to the *jinas,* astrology, monastic ritual, forms of renunciation and mythology. The *Taṇḍulavaicārika* deals with medicine and anatomy. The *Bhāktaparijñā* enlarges on voluntary death. Within the category of *prakīrṇaka* were added brief texts of diverse content which would have achieved a certain degree of authority.

CHEDA-SŪTRAS

The six Cheda-sūtras revolve around the discipline of ascetics. They would more or less correspond to the Vinaya of Buddhism. Two of these Cheda-sūtras are attributed to the great Bhadrabāhu. One that is worth a special mention is his *Bṛhatkalpa,* one of the fundamental pieces on monastic discipline. The *Ācāradaśāḥ* is even more famous. Chapter eight is centred on monastic life during the monsoon season (the *Sāmācāri)* to which appendices have been added about the life of Mahāvīra and other *jinas* (the *Jina-caritra)* plus lists of his first disciples (the *Sthavirāvalī),* all these making up the famous *Kalpa-sūtra,* which is recited at the festival of Paryuṣaṇa and during confessional ceremonies. It is confused with the *Bṛhatkalpa,* as sometimes it is attributed to Bhadrabāhu. Other Cheda-sūtras are the *Vyavahāra-sātra,* the *Niśītha,* and the *Mahāniśītha.* There is unanimity in considering that the sixth *cheda-sūtra* ceased to be transmitted centuries ago and has been lost. In its place, the *Jītakalpa* is usually included, composed at a later date by the monk Jinabhadra (7th century).

MŪLA-SŪTRAS

The next section in the Aṅgabāhya is the one devoted to the four Basic Sūtras (Mūla-sūtras).

One of the most relevant of these Sūtras is the *Daśavaikālika,* ascribed to Ārya Śayyambhava (Jambūsvāmin's grandson). This collection consists of ten chapters (based on the old Pūrvas) along with two appendices in the form of homilies aimed at an ascetic. It deals with the most important questions of the tradition, especially the rules of behaviour for ascetics. This is another of the most ancient texts and it has a special value for schools such as the Kharatara-Gaccha and the Sthānakavāsī.

Another *mūla-sūtra* is the *Piṇḍa-niryukti,* somehow mysteriously attributed to Bhadrabāhu. It centres on details of the way in which ascetics should go about begging and how they feed themselves.

The most beloved of all Mūla-sūtras is the *Uttarādhyayana,* one of the most important texts in the Siddhānta, and which is said to contain the last words of the Jina. It is an excellent anthology of Jainism, containing the work of various different authors, arid parts of it are extremely old. Moritz Winternitz (1907: II, 448) has described this as a combination of aphorisms, ballads, dialogues and parables in the form of ascetic poetry from ancient India. It resembles the Buddhist *Dhammapada* or the *Suttanipāta,* and also the famous *Śanti-parva* from the *Mahābhārata.*

Finally, the *Āvaśyaka-sūtra,* another text of an encyclopaedic nature and highly valued in the ascetic community. Essentially, it covers the six compulsory ritual actions *(āvaśyakas)* at monastic retreats [see pages 493-495]: cultivating equanimity, worshipping the *tīrthaṅkaras,* repentance and confession, homage to the masters, and abandonment of the body. Along with a multitude of tales, parables, myths, and allegories, there are *mantras* that must be recited at these practices. This is another of the ancient texts from Śvetāmbara recensions. The added literature that accompanies these compulsory duties is enormous [see below]. In fact, traditional Jain classification divides the Aṅgabāhya into texts that are and are not associated with the six ritual practices.

CŪLIKĀ-SŪTRAS

The last sub section is composed of two independent texts of a hermeneutic nature: the *Nāndī-sūtra,* attributed to Devarddhi (5th century), and the *Anuyo-gadvāra*, composed by a master by the name of Ārya Rakṣita (1st century). They both deal with all that which ascetics should know, in a rather encyclopaedic fashion and placed in an epistemological context. Both of them provide interesting descriptions of heretic doctrines. In the *Nāndi,* there is a long list of masters of ancient times.

* * *

In this way, the Siddhānta or "canon" of the Kharatara-Gacchins comes to an end. The Sthānakavāsīs and the Terāpanthīs have their own lists containing thirty-two texts. Although they accept the eleven Aṅgas and the twelve Upāṅgas, they do not recognise the validity of many scriptures in the Siddhānta. Since the sacred texts are not immovable, it is unnecessary that the Sthānakavāsīs "reject" previous canonical material, simply they have a certain freedom in selecting and putting limits on transmitted material.

COMMENTARIES

One of the particularities in Indian traditions is the tendency to write commentaries on its relevant texts. In quite a few cases, the *sūtra* is difficult to grasp without their help.

Already before the Siddhānta was published at Vallabhī, some of the most ancient texts had acquired commentaries. Chronologically speaking, the first are those known as Concise Explications (Niryuktis). Most are written in Jaina-Maharashtri. They usually involve short verses that aided memorisation of the *sūtra.* Some were included in the Siddhānta, such as the *Piṇḍa-niryukti,* but when it comes down to it the Niryuktis can be just as cryptic as the Sūtras if they are not extensively interpreted afterwards. The next exegetic layer consists of the Commentaries (Bhāsyas), also mostly in Jaina-Maharashtri. Following on, we find a kind of recension called the Dispersions (Cūrnis), which are in a mixture of Sanskrit and Prakrit. They correspond to the period when Sanskrit began to take over from Prakrit, that is to say around the 6th and 7th centuries, even if a few could be dated back to an earlier time. Finally, we have the Explications (Vṛttis, Ṭīkās), written in Sanskrit. The initiator of this period of commentaries in Sanskrit was Haribhadra (8th century), who it is said even wrote Ṭīkās on non-Jain texts. Other notable commentators were Śīlāṅka (9th century) , Devendra Sūri (11th century), Abhayadeva (11th century), Malayagiri (13th century) and Vinayavijaya (17th century).

Out of all the texts, the *Āvaśyaka-sūtra* is the one which has attracted the highest number of commentaries, glosses and explications. A vast body of texts revolve around this *sūtra.* The commentaries made profuse use of popular tales and legends to illustrate and elucidate important concepts. It has been thanks to these commentaries that many narrative and story tale gems from ancient India have come down to our times. It is clear that we are halfway between oral tradition, which provides more freedom to the narrator, and the much less flexible written form. The added literature in the *Āvaśyaka* is so important that the original *sūtra* is totally displaced by the most ancient commentary, the *Āvaśyaka-niryukti,* dating back to the 1st century. A multitude of sub-commentaries and explications have been added to this text, without which the meaning would be incomprehensible and of no use (Balbir 1990: 70).

THE ANUYOGA

As mentioned, Digambaras do not accept the authority of Śvetāmbara texts. Although they do share the majority of the dogmatic declarations in the Siddhān-ta, they consider that the language and form of these texts are not authentic. They state that the Aṅgas and a part of the Aṅgabāhyas are mere substitutes for material that has been lost, bearing the same titles of older material. In general, experts have not taken the Digambara perception of scriptural tradition into account and it is not at all strange that their texts are seen as a "secondary canon" (Winternitz 1907: II, 455). Doubtless, this would have to do with their rather more enigmatic position with respect to the idea of a "canon", which is even further away from Western presuppositions.

According to the Digambara Yatirṣabha *(Tiloyapaṇṇattī* 4.1476-1490; cited in Jain 1947: 39-40), after Mahāvira, only Gautama, Sudharman and Jambū had absolute knowledge of the teachings. The following masters up until Bhadrabāhu still knew the fourteen Pūrvas. The later generations only retained the 11 Aṅgas and 10 Pūrvas. Later, only the 11 Aṅgas were remembered. At the beginning of the Common Era, only the *Ācāranga* was left. Seven centuries after the death of the Jina, nobody could pride themselves on knowing his teachings perfectly.

For some, this vision is the true reflection of the scriptural losses as the ascetic communities were expanding geographically. According to others, it consistuted the Digambara reaction to the Śvetāmbara manipulation of texts, a position, which ended up being a strategy to put distance between them and the Śvetāmbaras. Perhaps, it can be taken as simply transposition of the idea of the gradual degeneration of *dharma.* And one cannot disregard K.K. Dixit's opinion. In the views of this great scholar, at the beginning of the Common Era, both traditions had compiled a body of texts which would have made the study of the old Aṅgas unnecessary. All important rituals, doctrines, history and ethics would have been gathered into treatise such as the *Anuyogadvāra,* the *Nandi-sūtra,* the *Āvaśyaka-niryukti* or the *Tattvārta-sātra* and their commentaries (for the Śvetāmbaras), and the *Saṭkhaṇḍāgama,* the *Kaṣāyaprābhṛta, the Mūlācāra* or again the *Tattvārta-sūtra* and their commentaries (for the Digambaras). The notable difference would have come about after the schism, when the Śvetām-bara stream felt the need to preserve ancient material, whereas the Digambara stream did not (Dixit 1971:79). This would explain the surprising doctrinal unity, in spite of the disparity in the texts venerateded (Folkert 1993: 51).

As a consequence, Digambaras have their own scriptural body and they recognise that their material comes, almost in its totality, from masters born generations after Mahāvira, most of whom originated from the Deccan and southern India. This does not detract in any way from the sacredness of their texts since the Indian viewpoint on what makes up a body of scripture *(āgama)* includes all texts of a certain antiquity, which have been preached by some illustrious master. If the texts embody teachings of the highest level, they are also considered to be sacred and infallible.

THE DIGAMBARA ĀGAMA

The Digambaras maintain that the *Dṛṣṭivāda* did not completely vanish. They think that the second and fifth *pūrva* of the *Dṛṣṭivāda,* centred on the theory of transmigration, could have been transmitted from master to disciple. In face of the threat of losing these teachings forever, the ascetic Dharasena (2nd century) passed them on to his disciples Puspadanta (2nd-3rd centuries) and Bhūtabali (2nd-3rd centuries) on Mount Girnar. They transcribed them onto palm leaves. The result was the *Ṣaṭkhaṇḍāgama,* quite plausibly the first *written* text in the Jain tradition. It is a difficult work, compiled in an aphoristic form, which almost exclusively deal with the doctrine of *karma.* Based on the same sources that drew on the *Dṛṣṭivāda,* anotner ascetic by the name of Guṇabhadra (3rd century) compiled a treatise known as the *Kaṣāyaprābhṛta.* These two texts, written in a variety of Shauraseni-Prakrit, come closest to being a Digambara version of what we would understand as a "canonical text", as they go directly back to the "word" of Mahāvīra. It is common to call them major Āga-mas. Both were widely commented on by Vīrasena (9th century) and Jinasena (9th century) being a great source of inspiration in the works of great Digambara philosophers. The collection of the two texts and their commentaries is extremely voluminous.

The rest of Digambara scriptures are in one way or another "post-canonical". They consist of an enormous block of texts that have received various generic titles, perhaps the most usual of which is Exposition (Anuyoga).

The Śvetāmbaras also compiled their own Anuyoga, enlarging upon the oldest material from the Siddhānta. If we were to unite both Anuyogas, we should obtain an incredible amount of material, possibly the most important collection of non-Vedic literature that has ever existed in India. Even though with this classification—which I take from Padmanabhi Jaini (1979: 78-87)—Digambara and Śvetāmbara material is mixed, the truth is that aside the differences already mentioned in chapter 12, their spirit is very similar and their teachings are practically identical. Since the Anuyogas are divided into four great categories, sometimes they are traditionally referred to as the "four Vedas" of the Jains.

PRATHAMĀNUYOGA

The first category or class of texts is given the name of First Exposition *(Prathamānuyoga),* that is to say, history. In general, it concerns the biographies of the *jinas* and other legendary beings: that is, the material which the Universal Story is composed of. These biographies have always been popular among laypersons. One of the first texts in this category, dating before the Digam-bara/Śvetāmbara split (Kulkarni 1952: 63-68), is the *Padma-carita* by Vimala Sūri (3rd-4th centuries). It is the first of the Jain *Rāmayāṇas* [see pages 471 -472].

Among the Digambara's own texts properly speaking, those that stand out are the *Adi-Purāṇa* by Jinasena (9th century) and the *Uttara-Purāṇa,* a continuation of the former, composed by his disciple Guṇabhadra (9th century). Both Purāṇas make up what is called the *Mahāpurāṇa,* which we have already discussed in chapters 4 and 15. The *Padma-Purāṇa* by Raviśena (7th-8th centuries), the most important Digambara recension of the *Rāmāyaṇa,* also falls into this category. Another Jinasena (8th century) wrote the *Harivaṃśa-Purāṇa,* a Digambara version of the *Mahābhārata.*

Among the Śvetāmbaras, the most important text on history is the well known *Triṣaṣṭiśalākāpuruṣa-caritra* by the great Hemacandra (12th century). This author also wrote an important document about the ancient history of the Śvetāmbaras, the *Sthavirāvalī-caritra,* perhaps better known as the Appendix *(Pariśiṣṭa-parvan)* as it could be considered a prolongation of the previously mentioned one. The text is partially based on a biography of Jambū, the *Jambū-carita* by Gunapāla (8th-9th centuries). Out of all Śvetāmbara biographies, possibly the most popular would be the *Pārśvanātha-carita* by Bhāvadeva Sūri (8th century).

KARAṆĀNUYOGA

The second category of treatises is given the name of Exposition on Technical Questions *(Karaṇānuyoga*); that is, cosmography. It basically consists of texts on astronomy, astrology and cosmology. The *Trilokasāra* by Nemicandra (10th-11th centuries) and the *Jambūdvīpa-prajñāpti* by Amitagati (10th-11th centuries) stand out from the rest.

CARAṆĀNUYOGA

The third category goes under the name of the Exposition on Discipline *(Caraṇānuyoga)',* that is to say, ethics. Parts of these texts are aimed at renun-ciants, but a not inconsiderable portion is directed towards laypersons.

One of the most important Digambara texts on the discipline of renunciants, possible the main one, is the *Mālācāra* by Vaṭṭakera (2nd century). Quite highly regarded, is the *Bhagavati-ārādhanā* by Śivārya (2nd century). Two basic works on the behaviour of renunciants are attributed to the notable Kun-dakunda (2nd century): the *Pravacanasāra* and the *Niyamasāra.* Their rules are virtually "canonical" to the Digambaras, even more so than those collected in the venerated *Ṣaṭkhaṇḍāgama,* a text which it seems soon became restricted to a tiny elite group of highly educated monks.

The manuals that concern lay discipline are called the Śrāvakācāras, of which the Digambara tradition has preserved quite a few. The oldest one is the *Ratnakaraṇḍa-śrāvakācāra* by Samantabhadra (5th century), a keen Tamil thinker. Somadeva Sūri (10th century) wrote the sensational *Upāsakādhyayana,* a manual for laypersons inserted in his religious novel *Yaśastilaka-campū.* There is one *śrāvakācāra,* the *Sagāra-dharmāmṛta,* written by a layman by the name of Āsādhara (13th century). Among the Śvetāmbara Śrāvakācāras, the most well-known are the *Śrāvaka-prajñāpti* (5th century), traditionally but incorrectly attributed to Umāsvāti (Williams 1963: 2-4), the *Dharma-bindu* by Haribhadra (8th century) and the *Yoga-śāstra* by Hemacandra (7th century), especially intended to instruct the king on how to lead a perfect life as a layman. In this text, Hemacandra provides a thorough treatment of the classic Jain methods of contemplation. Although the manuals for renunciants and laypersons mainly concentrate on ascetic and liturgical practices, there are others that deal with *yoga* and meditation. Undoubtedly, the work of Kundakunda, the *Samayasāra,* is the most important piece on such subjects. The *Tattvānuśāsana* by Rāmasena (10th century) has a more practical approach. The above-mentioned Haribhadra compiled various treatises on *yoga (Yoga-bindu, Yogadṛṣṭi-samuccaya)* and devised a model for understanding *yoga* in the light of Jain asceticism [see page 473].

The Kathākośas are anthologies of didactic stories that serve to explain all types of issues related to ethics, monastic practice, transmigration mechanisms and mythology. They move back and forth between narrative literature and oral tradition. Helmut von Glasenapp (1925: 136) has observed that Jains have recensions of practically all Indian fairy tales and fables. Unlike purely religious texts, this more secular type of literature has captivated many Western experts. For the traditon, it has been vitally important in propagating religious notions, as much among ascetics as laypersons.

A special mention must be given to the *Ārādhanā*; a collection containing 150 stories passed down by Śvetāmbaras and Digambaras alike, which shows its antiquity. Additionally the *Bṛhatkathā* is another source of numerous stories, the majority having king Śreṇika as their protagonist. In the 10th century, the Digam-bara Hariṣeṇa recompiled them in his *Bṛhatkathākośa.* Most of this stories with a lesson were intended to be recited in private meetings and in temples. The *Kālakācārya-kathānaka* is usually recited at the festival of Paryusana.

In addition, religious novels (Dharmakathās) have been important in the popularisation of Jainism. Those by Pādalipta Sūri (5th century), Haribhadra (8th century) and Siddharṣi (10th century) are excellent.

DRAVYĀNUYOGA

The last category of texts in the Anuyoga, has much to do with substances *(dravyas)* of which the cosmos is composed. For that reason, this type is called the Exposition on Substances *(Dravyānuyoga),* meaning, philosophy.

Unquestionably, the *Tattvārthādhigama-sūtra,* abbreviated as *Tattvārtha-sūtra,* is the most important text within this category. It was compiled by Umāsvāti (3rd-4th centuries), a magnificent philosopher from South India. We will come back to this thinker and his presentation of his *sūtra,* recognised and accepted by both Digambaras and Śvetāmbaras, in the next chapter. The famous Digambara commentaries on the *Tattvārtha,* by Pūjyapāda Devanandi (5th-6th century), Samantabhadra (5th century) and Akalaṅka (8th century), form part of the *Dravyānuyoga.*

Siddhasena Divākara (5th century), likewise claimed by both streams of Jainism, was one of the fathers of Jain logic. His main works are the *Sanmati-sūtra* and the *Dvatriṃśikā.* The famous *Nyāyāvatāra,* for long ascribed to Siddhasena Divāraka seems to be the work of a certain Siddhasena Mahāmati (8th century).

The works by Kundakunda mentioned in the previous section could also be classified as *Dravyānuyoga,* as, apart from dealing with monastic conduct, he concentrates at length on philosophical issues. Equal emphasis should be placed on his *Pañcāstikāyasāra,* the *Sātraprābhṛta* and the *Darśanaprābhrta.* Some experts maintain that the philosophical differences perceived in books attributed to Kundakunda are so great that it is hard to believe they were works by the same author (Johnson 1995: 231).

Samantabhadra (5th century), author of the *Aptamīmāṃsā,* along with his commentators Akalaṅka (8th century) and Vidyānanda (9th century), form part of the traditional *Dravyānuyoga.* Another important philosophical tract is the *Dravya-saṃgraha* by the Digambara Nemicandra Siddhāntacakravartin (10th century), considered to be general Cāmuṇḍarāya's master. This is one of the most accessible and concise philosophical compendiums in Jainism. His *Gommaṭasāra* is more technical and encyclopaedic.

Among the Śvetāmbara philosophical scriptures, those written by the prolific Haribhadra (8th century) stand out. Given his knowledge of Brāhmaṇism he was a fierce opponent of Hindu and Buddhist doctrines. He covered a colossal range of subjects. He wrote novels, satires, doxographies, treatises on logic, ritual, ethics, *yoga,* aesthetics, manuals for laypersons, etc. Moreover, He was the first Indian philosopher to write a doxography in Sanskrit and the only Jain to write commentaries on non-Jain texts. R. Williams (1963: 4-8) thinks that to undertake such a range of activities and posses such a spectrum of knowledge, there must have been two authors of the same name. This thesis has not provoked any kind of reaction from Indian Jains.

One type of literature that also could be included in this category of scriptures is that of Poetic Hymns (Stotras) praising the *jinas* and their teachings. This hymnology, used very much in the act worship, has served to propagate and diffuse philosophic teachings and concepts. Some of the most beloved ones are the *Śobhana-stuti* by Śobhana (10th century), the *Upasargahara* by Hemacandra, the *Svayambhūstotra* by Samantabhadra, and the *Bhaktāmara-stotra* by Mānatuṅga (6th century), cherished by Śvetāmbara and Digambaras alike. Among the latter mentioned, the hymns by Kundakunda are much venerated and form the basis of the Digambara's daily liturgical ritual.

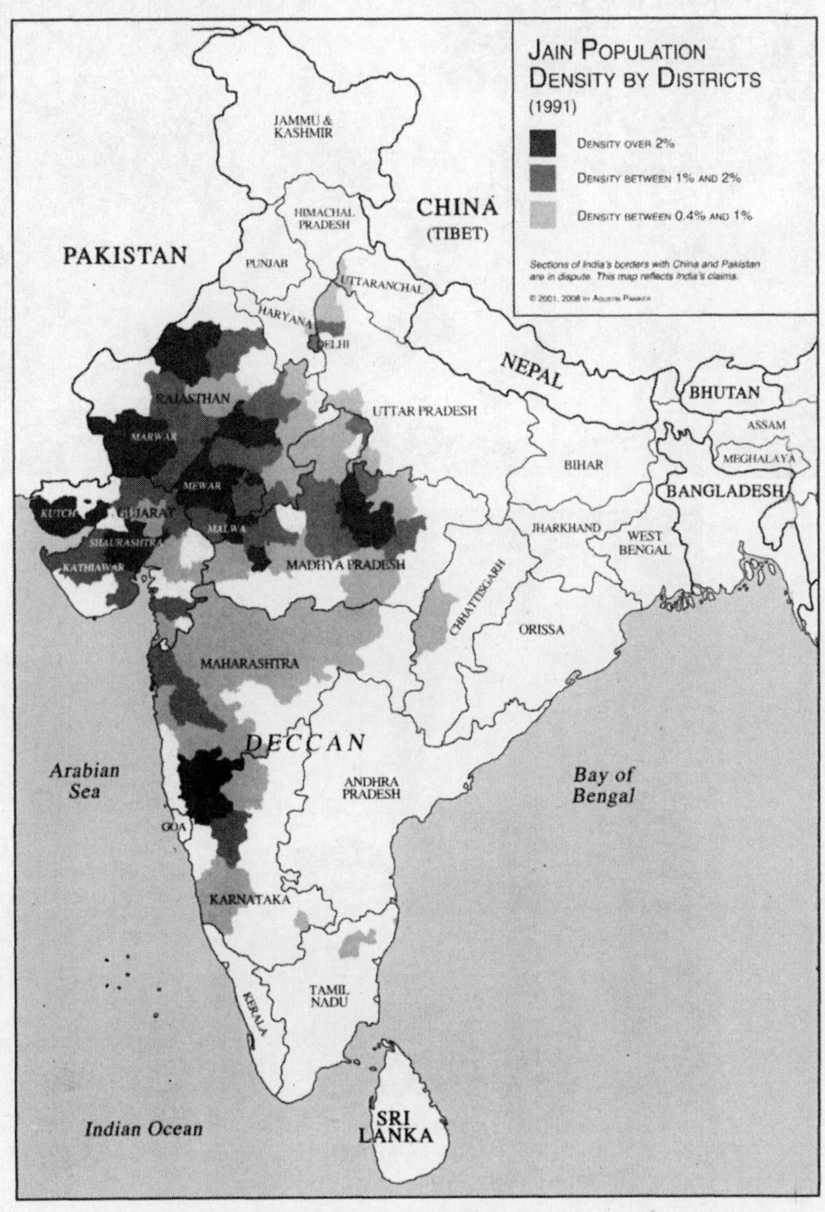

FIGURE 22: Jain population density by districts. (Source: Agustīn Pániker.)

FIGURE 23: Two Śvetāmbara nuns of the Tapā-Gaccha order and their superior in the retreat at Śri Ātma Vallabha Sanskriti Mandira, Delhi. In the background, a photograph of Śri Mrgavati. (Photograph: Agustín Péniker.)

FIGURE 24: A Digambara superior supervises the novices' study. Ramtek, Maharashtra. (Photograph: Kurt Titze. Courtesy of Motilal Banarsidass publishers.)

FIGURE 25 Bust of the great tapā-gacchin *ācārya* Vijaya Vallabha Sūri, in the Śrī Ātma Vallabha Saṅskṛiti Mandira, on the outskirts of Delhi. (Photograph: Agustín Pániker.)

FIGURE 26: Rājacandra Rājīvbhāī.

FIGURE 27: Muni Jambūvijaya, renowned master and scholar. (Photograph: Kurt Titze. Courtesy of Motilal Banarsidass publishers.)

FIGURE 28: The great reviver of the Digambara tradition, Ācārya Śāntisāgara, in the middle of the back row, surrounded by ascetics and *ailakas.* The photograph was taken around 1934. (Courtesy of Motilal Banarsidass publishers.)

FIGURE 29: Vijaya Dharma Sūri. (Courtesy of Motilal Banarsidass publishers.)

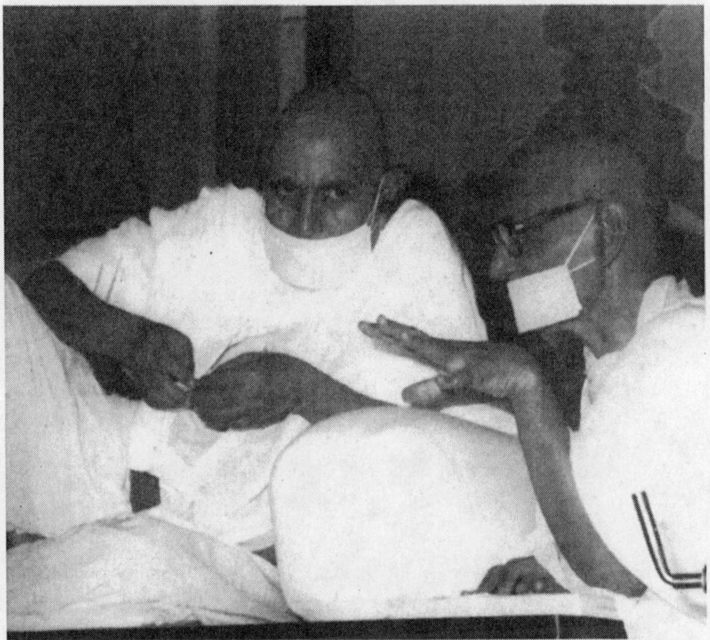

Figure 30: The 10th terāpanthī *ācārya* Yuvācārya Mahāprajñā in Ladnun, 1994. (Photograph: Kurt Titze. Courtesy of Motilal Banarsidass publishers.)

Figure 31: The 9th terāpanthī *ācārya* Tulasi and his successor, Yuvācārya Mahāprajñā.

FIGURE 32: *tīrthaṅkara* in the posture of abandonment of the body *(kāyotsarga)*. Temple at Halebid, Karnataka, 12th-13th centuries. (Photograph: Agustín Pániker.)

FIGURE 33: The first *tīrthaṅkara* Ṛṣabha seated in the lotus position *(padmāsana)*. Temple dedicated to Mahāvīra, Osian, Rajasthan, 8th century. (Photograph: Agustín Pániker.)

FIGURE 34: *Jinas'* escorts. Jaisalmer, Rajasthan.
(Photograph: Marcelo Di Pietro & Agustín Pániker.)

FIGURE: 35: A group of devotees carrying out ritual bathing *(abhiṣeka)* of a miniature replica of the statue of the *jina* to be seen at the altar in the background. With them, in the foreground, is a priest *(pūjaka)*. Śāntinātha Temple, Delhi. (Photograph: Agustín Pániker.)

FIGURE 36: Worship of the village's tutelary divinity *(grāmadevatā)* or guardian of the locality *(kṣetrapāla)* Bharu, in Amber, Rajasthan. (Photograph: Agustín Pániker.)

FIGURE 37: Women praying to the *jina* after taking rice grains and shaping them into *svāstikas,* the three points that symbolise the Three Jewels, the Half Moon and the liberated soul. Śāntinātha Temple, Delhi. (Photograph: Agustín Pániker.)

FIGURE 38: A lay Jain, dressed to play the part of Indra, bathes the statue of *the jina* in a classic *snātra-pūjā.* (Photograph: Caroline Humphrey. Courtesy of Caroline Humphrey.)

FIGURE 39: Image of the *dādāguru* Jinacandra Sūri Maṇidhārī in a temple in Jaipur, Rajasthan. (Photograph: Lawrence Babb. Courtesy of Lawrence Babb.)

FIGURE 40: One of the peaks of Sameṭa Śikhara, in Bihar, the place of pilgrimage of choice for many Jains. Here, twenty *tīrthaṅkaras* reached *nirvāṇa.* (Photograph: Kurt Titze. Courtesy of Motilal Banarsidass publishers.)

FIGURE 41: View of the complex of temples devoted to Nemi (15th century), on the sacred mountain of Girnar, Gujarat. (Photograph: Agustín Pániker.)

FIGURE 42: A Digambara monk on his round. He performs a gesture to ask for food which the faithful know well.
(Photograph: Kurt Titze. Courtesy of Motilal Banarsidass publishers.)

FIGURE 43: The Digambara ascetic Vidyānandaji Mahārāj exhorting an audience in Kolhapur, Maharashtra.
(Photograph: Michael Carrithers. Courtesy of Cambridge University Press.)

FIGURE 44: The Digambara ascetic Vidyānandaji Mahārāj *en route (vihāra),* accompanied by lay devotees, at Bahubali, near Kolhapur, Maharashtra.
(Photograph: Michael Carrithers. Courtesy of Cambridge University Press.)

FIGURE 45: In August 1988 the multitude carried the body of the *ācārya* Samanthabhadra-in yogic posture —to the place of cremation.
(Photograph: Sanmati Publication. Courtesy of Motilal Banarsidass publishers.)

FIGURE 46: Śvetāmbara image of the *tīrthaṅkara* Nemi. Rajasthan, 12th century. National Museum, New Delhi. (Courtesy of the National Museum.)

FIGURE 47: Marble of Neminātha, the 22nd *tīrthaṅkara* of Jainism. Mount Abu, Rajasthan, 12th century. Freer Gallery of Art & Arthur M. Sackler Gallery, Smithsonian Institution, Washington.

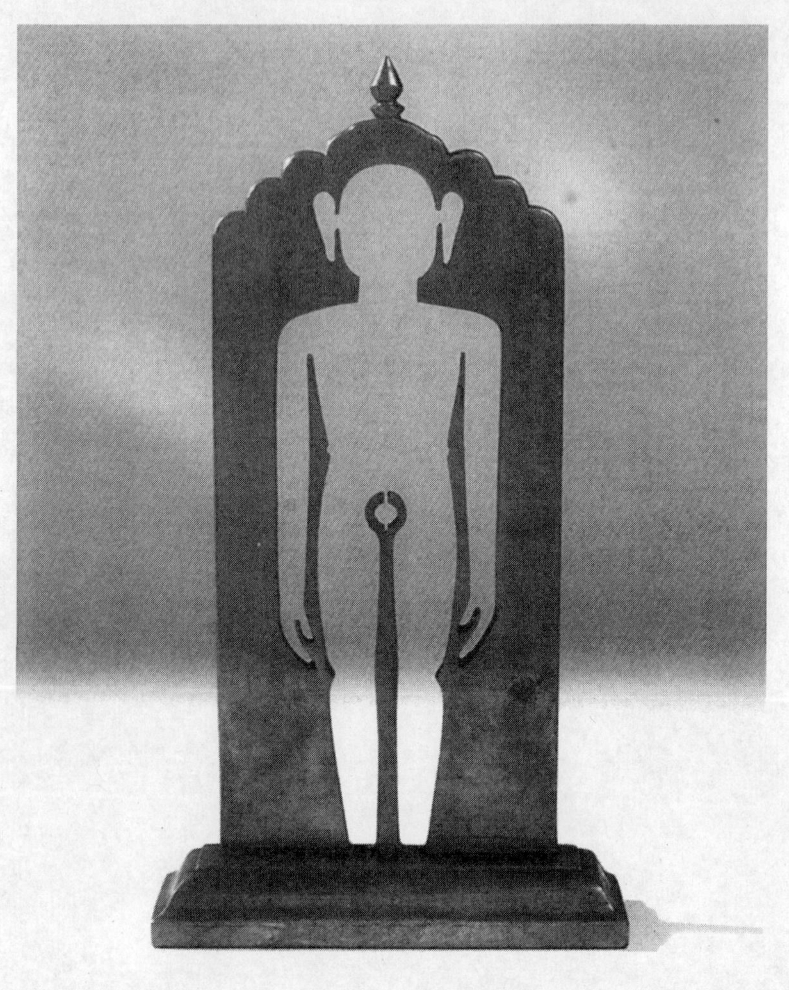

FIGURE 48: *Siddhapratimā-yantra. Jina* represented as a liberated soul. Metal. Rajasthan, 19th century.

Part X
Philosophy

On questions of external practice, the sectarian differences between Digambaras and Śvetāmbaras have been acute. One even gets the impression that there has not been much interest in reconciliation. On the other hand, their uniformity in terms of doctrine is quite stunning. Not even the fierce debates over the body of scriptures have been cause for doctrinal disunion.

Perhaps due to the acute sense of loyalty to the teachings, or their position of being less numerous than other religions in India, the main doctrines of Jainism have remained relatively unchanged over the centuries.

A good part of this coherency has much to do with the work and prestige of Umāsvāti (3rd-4th centuries). It is no exaggeration to say that this incisive thinker laid the basis for all classical Jain philosophy. The fact alone that his *Tattvārtha -sūtra* received more than twenty commentaries, shows this.

If we compare Jainism with its Buddhist sister religion, we find nothing similar to a Great Vehicle (Mahāyāna) or Tantric Buddhism (Vajrayā-na). Had Jainism been a dominant religion in the South, a Digambara Mahāyāna would quite probably have arisen, as R. Williams (1963: xix) suggests. As this was not the case, Jain philosophy has remained reasonably similar for Digambaras and Śvetāmbaras alike. This does not mean there have been no internal philosophical debates or innovations. On the contrary: Jain philosophy has been characterised by its great subtlety. We shall see it.

One stumbling block when it comes to dealing with Jain or for that matter, Indian philosophy in general, lies in the word "philosophy". The term, as it is understood in the West, is inappropriate for traditional Indian thinkers, for at least three reasons.

First, the so-called Indian "philosophies" consist more in streams of thought rather than in constructions worked out by an isolated wise person. Indian philosophy emerges within the context of a tradition of scriptures, principles, and established ideas. Hence, the eminently exegetic character of its works. Every recognised Indian school of philosophy begins with a major *sūtra* that brings together and interprets the teachings of the tradition. The thinkers that come after will comment on and explain the *sūtra.* In the Vedānta, for example, the *sūtra* of central importance is the *Brahmā-sūtra* by Bādarāyaṇa; in the Yoga philosophy it is Patañjali's *Yoga-sūtra*; and in Buddhism, possibly the *Abhidharma-kośa* by Vasubandhu. For Jain the *sūtra* that provided the cornerstone was the *Tattvārtha-sūtra* by Umāsvāti. As in every philosophic *sūtra,* the aphorisms in the *Tattvārtha-sūtra* are most concise and brief, much more than what one finds in the Aṅgas. It is in these texts that the term *sūtra* acquires its true nature as a condensed rule. Which is one reason why the majority of philosophical treatises need commentaries, sub-commentaries, glossaries and even self-commentaries. Without such exegesis the aphorisms are not likely to be understood. This link to tradition differs a great deal from the Western philosophical norm. Most Indian philosophers never say they innovate—even when they do so—but rather refer back to ancient knowledge passed down from the *ṛṣis* and *jinas* of more virtuous ages than the present.

Second, Indian philosophies are never "pure theory", in the Greek sense. The practical and liberating perspective (soteriology) is never ever forgotten. Indian thinkers do not try to describe reality alone nor do they search for an abstract truth. They are trans-philosophers in the sense that if the truth does not lead to an emancipating practice, then it does not have much value. The *Uttarādhyayana-sūtra* (7.9-10) is wary of those that revel in words and intellectualism, but do not act or behave in compliance to their principles. In fact, one can detect a certain shift, over the course the history of Indian philosophy, from conceiving philosophy to be "the science of perception" *(darśana)* to the "science of liberation" *(mokṣa-vidyā)*. Jainism is very downright in this respect. If a metaphysical reflection cannot be used to explain the origin and end of suffering, then there is no need to go deeper into the subject. Philosophy, in a Jain context, leads to right vision *(samyak-darśana)* and right knowledge *(samyak-jñāna)* the basis for the right conduct *(samyak-cāritra)* that will lead us to liberation.

Finaally, Indian philosophical discourse is different from its Western counterpart. The Indian thinker first defines which means of knowledge are to be considered valid, *(pramāṇa)*. He then devotes a great deal of time and precision to defining the concepts that are used. Usually, the positions of the opponent *(pūrvapakṣa)* are referred to, before proceeding to refute them and duly present one's own. Thus, the Indian philosopher tends to be concerned with many more fields than usual in Western philosophy. The range of interest is enormous: ontology, epistemology, logic, metaphysics, linguistics, psychology, ethics, physiology, biology, aesthetic theory, scriptural exegesis, meditation, and much more.

One might well wonder if, after considering these aspects, it is still relevant to speak of Indian "philosophy". Given that Indian thinkers are linked to religious traditions and lineages, perhaps "theology" would be an alternative, but in fact that too would be inappropriate, given that many of these schools are utterly atheist and have nothing to do with a *theos*. In the dozen or more philosophical traditions in India, at least half (Cārvaka, Sāṃkhya, Buddhism, Jainism, Mīmāṃsā, and even Advaita Vedānta) are atheist, or trans-theist. For want of a better term, philosophy will serve, provided we bear in mind the considerations discussed here. Perhaps, the most practical solution would be to search for the term with the closest fit in Indian terminology. The task is certainly very complex, seeing that to subsume Indian religious-philosophical thought under one term, Raimon Panikkar (1997: 113-146) has put forward some 30 candidates. If pressed to chose, perhaps the most appropriate term would be one of the most recurrent in Sanskrit literature: *darśana,* literally, "point of view", "doctrine", "seeing", "contemplating", "apprehension" (Monier-Williams 1899: 470-471). This, according to Wilhelm Halbfass (1988: 267-268), is the term most favoured by Jains.

Over the course of the three chapters of this Part, we shall be covering the basic points of Jain philosophy. In chapter 23, we look at epistemology, the nature of reality, and the refined Jain logic. In chapter 24, we go into two basic branches of Jain metaphysics: the spiritual *(jīva)* and the non-spiritual *(ajīva).* This topic complements the cosmological ideas presented in Part I. The purpose of Indian philosophy is practical, never merely speculative, as we have said. The point is to achieve the knowledge and vision that will enable us to understand the nature of the situation of alienation in which we find ourselves. Accordingly, after considering the nature of soul and matter, we look into the complex analysis of the state of bondage of human beings, and this will be the subject of chapter 25. We will consider *karma* and its mysterious mechanisms, a crucially important issue in understanding Jain philosophy and soteriology.

23. THE NATURE OF REALITY

A SHORT HISTORY OF JAIN PHILOSOPHY

The Jain contribution to Indian philosophy has been enormous, and certainly much greater than might seem at first sight. Although its philosophical viewpoint or *darśana* has not created the same interest as the Advaita Vedānta or Mādhyamaka Buddhism, and we do not have to do with universally recognised figures such as Śaṅkara and Nāgārjuna, the finesse expressed by some of their philosophers has little reason to envy these giants.

Once again, we must take into account when referring to philosophers, that the separation between philosophy and theology in Europe is not transferable to South Asia. In India, those who are given the name of master (*guru, ācārya)* are spiritual preceptors and masters in philosophy at the same time; they are both saints and thinkers. The truth is not only communicable, but must also be realisable. Therefore, one must speak about "philosopher-theologians", enlightened saints who are also consummate scholars.

Historically speaking, the first phase in Jain philosophy is what experts term the Āgamic period (Dixit 1971:12). This concerns a body of teachings spanning from the *Acārāṅga I* (4th century BC) up until the recension of the council of Vallabhī (5th century). The most representative texts are the *Sūtrakṛtāṅga,* the *Uttarādhyāyana-sūtra,* the *Prajñāpanā-sūtra,* the *Nāndī-sūtra,* the *Anuyogad-vara* and the *Vyākhyā-prajñāpti.* All these form part of the Siddhānta. One could also include the post-canonical *Āvaśyaka-niryukti* plus the Digambara *Ṣaṭkhaṇḍāgama.*

This entire corpus contains an immense quantity of philosophical material; but it is very inconsistent and there is a lack of systematisation, which is relatively common with orally transmitted prose. The task of systematising Jain philosophical teachings from a solid philosophical point of view *(darśana)* fell to Umāsvāti, otherwise known as Umāsvāmin, considered one of the greatest philosophers India has ever produced. It was he who gathered together this 800 or 900-year-old philosophic doctrinal inheritance together. He must have lived around the 3rd century (Vidyabhusana 1978:168), although there are some who propose a later date (Shastri 1989: 12). His Brāhmaṇical origin afforded him great familiarity with rival philosophic systems and also with Sanskrit. His main work, the *Tattvārtha-sūtra,* was the first Jain book to be written in the sacred language. On compiling the *Tattvārtha* aphoristically in Sanskrit, Umāsvāti followed Brāhmaṇic models and brought the Jains out of their narrow circles, and made them competitive (Schubring 1934: 59).

As a good Indian philosopher, Umāsvāti dealt with everything ranging from epistemology, logic, psychology, cosmology, ethics, ontology to mythology. The *Tattvārtha-sūtra* is still one of the best manuals on Jain doctrine and is still read in Jain homes and temples. One curious thing is that Umāsvāti is equally recognised by Śvetāmbaras and Digambaras alike, since his work must have been written prior to the sectarian split up, and thus the *sūtra* received different commentaries from within each tradition. On the Digambara side, the most important are the *Sarvārtha-siddhi* by Pūjyapāda Devanandi (5th-6th centuries), the *Tattvārtharāja-vārtika* by Akalaṅka (8th century) and the *Tattvārthaśloka-vārtika* by Vidyānanda (9th century). The *sūtra* and these commentaries form the major part of the texts that ascetics read during their training and studies. The most acclaimed Śvetāmbara commentaries are by Sid-dhasena Gaṇin (8th century) plus the *Sva -bhāṣya,* attributed to Umāsvāti himself, although this is questionable. Given that all Jains accept Umāsvāti's thinking, one could say the *Tattvārtha-sūtra* represents the essence of Jain philosophy.

After Umāsvāti's contribution, Jain *darśana* became considerably more sophisticated. The next stage could be called the period of logic (Dixit 1971: 88). The first giant of this period was Siddhasena Divākara (5th century) also recognised by both Śvetāmbaras and Digambaras—could he have been a Yāpanīya? (Jain and Upadhye 1971: 8). Kundakunda (2nd century) stands out on the Digambara side: while pre-dating Siddhasena and Umāsvāti, he can be considered to be another of the initiators of the logic period. After him came Samantab-hadra (5th century) with his phenomenal *Aptamimāṃsā.* The golden age of Digambara philosophy began with him, a period which also included the penetrating thought of Akalaṅka (8th century) and Vidyānanda (9th century) of whom it is said he antagonised the Vedāntin Śaṅkara as well as the Mīmāṃsāka Kumārila, the two most prestigious philosophers of their times. Professor K.K. Dixit (1971:148) has no doubt in hailing his works, namely the *Tattvārthaśloka-vārtika* (which is a commentary on Umāsvāti), and the *Aṣṭasahasrī* (a commentary on Akalaṅka) as being the greatest achievement in Jain philosophical speculation. The last Digambara philosophers of importance were Nemicandra (10th century) and Prabhācandra (10th century). Among Śvetāmbaras, the philosophical work devolved upon Mallavādin (5th-6th centuries), author of the *Naya-cakra,* and Jinabhadra Gaṇi (6th century) who wrote the *Viśeṣāvaśyaka-bhāṣya.* After that comes the prolific Haribhadra (8th century). From the 10th century onward, Digambara philosophy went into clear decline and it was the Śvetāmbara tendency, which up until that time had been following in their wake, took over the initiative. At this point, a commentator named Abhayadeva (11th century) enters on the scene, who drew on the Digambara philosophical heritage along with Merutuṅga (14th century).

In general, Jain and Hindu philosophy concluded their most creative phase around the 13th century, at the time when the kingdoms of northern and central India collapsed before the Islamic generals, coinciding with the virtual disappearance of Buddhism from Indian soil.

With the lack of an imposing rival such as Buddhism, and the lethargy into which Brāhmaṇic tradition then sank, the need for the sophistication of philosophy, sharp thought and speculation clearly diminished. However, two more giants in philosophy were to emerge in the Jain tradition. These were the chronologically late (but excellent) Yaśovijaya (17th century), who was a great commentator on Haribhadra and a keen connoisseur of rival philosophies, and Vinayavijay a (17th century) son of the famous Tejapāla, and compiler of the encyclopaedic *Lokaprakāśa.* In this period, classical philosophies such as Buddhism, Sāṃkhya and Mīmāṃsā were either in decline or had completely disappeared, and the rivals to take into account were the Vedāntins of the Śaṅkara tradition and the Navya-Nyāya school of logic.

This all too brief history of philosophy does not do justice to the immense power of Jain intellectual tradition, which Indian society has always accorded great prestige. In fact, the use of Sanskrit from the 3rd-4th centuries onward points to a significant fact. In Sanskrit, Jains could express themselves in the language of the Brāhmaṇas and Mahāyāna masters and overcome them. But there was more. Additionally, its use indicates that Jainism was transforming Jain teachings, once purely soteriological, into an authentic religious and cultural tradition. If the Jains wished to be universal or "civilisational" they had to resort to the *lingua franca* in South Asia. Accordingly, the Digambara sage Pūjyapāda Devanandin (5th-6th centuries), the Yāpanīya scholar Sākaṭāyana (9th century) and the Śvetāmbara Hemacandra all wrote Sanskrit grammars. The Jain treatises of medieval times began to deal with subjects such as musical theory (Pārsvadeva), politics (Hemacandra, Somadeva Sūri), natural sciences (Sānti Sūri), mathematics (Mahāvira), medicine (Pūjyapāda), as well as Tantric esoterism, aesthetic theory, *yoga,* architecture, astrology, etc., but approaching them from an Indo-Jaina perspective. All this, without mentioning the tremendous output in Jain literature, in the form of poetic narration, epics, poetry, tales, and fables.

EPISTEMOLOGY

The key question in Indian thinking is: what is reality *(sat)*? What is the nature of that which exists *(sat)?* All philosophies or *darśanas* have devoted considerable effort to answer this ultimate question. This is a vital issue, we repeat, not for the love of Truth and Reason, but because philosopher searches for liberating metaphysical knowledge *(jñāna, prajñā, buddhi).* The sage looks to force the way to another level of existence, to transcend the human condition, and to accomplish this he needs to be aware of his own condition, along with the nature of that which surrounds him.

Normally, before directly answering the question, Indian philosophers tend to comment upon and evaluate the different modes of valid knowledge *(pramāṇa)* and determine which of them they consider to be correct for the liberating knowledge. This is a doubly important point in Jainism. Being a non-theistic system, Jains cannot fall back on faith and on divine grace. As Padman-abh Jaini (1979: 89) has observed, Jains are obliged to rely on their own initiative and effort, both in their worldly matters and their path to liberation. For that reason, they need a philosophical system that does not demand blind faith and at the same time adjusts to their everyday life experience. In the last analysis, it is true that authority rests on the fact that Jainism was preached by a chain of 24 omniscient beings who perceived all metaphysical, ontological, ethic and cosmological categories, and in this Jainism would prove to be as dogmatic and non-verifiable as any theistic religion. Erich Frauwallner (1953: II, 213) had already noted that since the *jinas* were omniscient, their doctrines could not be modified. That would explain why posterior philosophical speculation would have preserved so many archaic features. Moreover, since their tradition considered that after Jambūsvāmin, no one else had achieved *kevala-jñāna,* this provided an irrefutable argument in the face of their Hindu and Buddhist counterparts' accusation that nobody had ever bumped into an omniscient in the street. However, beyond such doctrinal and hermeneutic squabbles, tradition has also insisted with surprising frequency that their teachings should square with reality, explain the nature of things and be defensible through use of reason.

Accordingly, before going on to explain what the nature of existence is, one needs to define what the nature and characteristics of knowledge are. The question would be: what type of knowledge is valid for the apprehension of reality?

Knowledge *(jñāna)* is not valuable in itself, but it is so to the extent that it allows us to discriminate between good and bad, to perceive what can help us on the path to emancipation and what cannot. In other words, its interest does not lie so much in the manner in which we perceive the world, but how knowledge can help us grow spiritually. Knowledge always has soteriological ends; hence the appreciation of knowledge of the ultimate metaphysical realities, which will enable us to achieve liberation. On the other hand, not too much value is accorded to the knowledge of "names" and "forms", which is the way Hindus describe this phenomenal world. This premise, which is common to all gnostic systems in India (Buddhism, Vedānta, Sāṃkhya, etc.) should always be borne in mind.

The first thing that Jain philosophers agree on is that knowledge reveals our own soul as the subject that knows, and the world as the object that is known

(Siddhasena Mahāmati, *Nyāya-avatāra* 1). Their position in opposition to other Indian schools, is that of total realism. There is a knower subject and there is a known object. Obviously, this knowledge can be correct or distorted. But when it is cleansed by personal purification or the teaching of a master, consciousness reveals the nature of reality. Thus in fact of maximum importance in the achievement of *nirvāṇa.* Because perfect knowledge is self-revealing—and this is where Jains differs from Nyāya and Mīmāṃsā philosophies. But we shall return to this below. For now we concentrate on knowledge of the exterior world.

In general, Jain philosophy *(Uttarādhyayana-sūtra* 33.4) recognises five types of valid knowledge *(pramāṇa):* (1) ordinary knowledge gained through one's senses, experience and personal thought *(mati-jñāna);* which includes memory, induction, analogy, recognition; everything which is based on sensory perception and deductive reasoning; (2) knowledge derived from reason and words *(śruta-jñāna);* which is knowledge achieved through words, numbers, signs, symbols and so on—here is where the important knowledge acquired from the study of scriptures and sacred sermons comes in; (3) limited supernatural knowledge *(avadhi-jñāna)* such as clairvoyance, typical of very advanced ascetics and divine beings; (4) knowledge of other people's thoughts *(mahaḥparyāya-jñāna),* meaning telepathy—which is no longer obtainable these days;.and (5) absolute knowledge or omniscience *(kevala-jnāna);* meaning infinite awareness of all substances along with their qualities and modifications; only accessible to omniscient beings- who are gone from among us in this day and age.

Of these five types of knowledge, the first two are what Indians call "mediated", "indirect" or "acquired" knowledge *(parokṣa),* that is to say knowledge complemented by memory and the senses. This type of knowledge can be valid *(jñāna)* or erroneous *(ajñāna).* Being valid, from the Jain point of view means effective in practical terms. Correct "mediated knowledge" is that which enables one to do good and avoid wrongdoing. Hence, until the correct knowledge—of Jain truths—is obtained one will linger in the realm of unknowing.

The three other types of knowledge belong to the category termed "immediate", "direct" and "innate" knowledge *(pratyakṣa).* This type is direct apprehension of the object, where the sensorial apparatus has no function. As the soul's own nature is *knowledge,* it needs no external assistance to know. Immediate knowledge is therefore something like pure intuition. With the aid of clairvoyant knowledge *(avadhi-jñāna),* Indra knew of the birth of the *jina* Mahāvira in Jambūdvīpa *(Kalpa-sūtra, Jina-caritra* 15). With the aid of telepathy *(mahaḥparyāya-jñāna)* Mahāvīra was aware of all beings' thoughts *(Ācārāṅga-sūtra* 2.15.23). The most pristine kind of immediate knowledge is the one termed *kevala-jñāna* or "unique". It is perfect knowledge in all respects: complete, absolute, unique and omniscient. Whoever possesses *kevala-jñāna* is a perfect being *(siddha),* someone who can know the self in its pure state, someone like the liberated while living *(jīvanmukta)* in Hinduism, or the saint *(arhat)* in Nikāya Buddhism, and he who is "on the path of buddhahood" *(bodhisattva)* in Mahāyāna Buddhism. We know that Jambūsvāmin was the last human being to achieve this, here in this land of Bharata.

By making a distinction between the two categories of knowledge, Jain philosophy was prepared to open its doors even to idealism, but in its essence Jain epistemological viewpoint is distinctive in its marked *realism.*

THE NATURE OF REALITY

The reality of what there is here within and what out there actually exists, it is authentic. But let us return to the initial question: What is existence? What is reality *(sat)*? From the Jain point of view, what exists is formed by a series of substances *(dravyas).* "Substance" in Jain metaphysics is the substratum underlying everything. Jainism sees the terms substance *(dravya),* existence *(sat)* and reality *(tattva)* as being synonyms. Umāsvāti *(Tattvārtha-sātra* 5.29) uses them interchangeably.

These substances or realities can be divided into two independent categories: the animate or spiritual substance *(jīva),* and the non-animate or non-spiritual substance *(ajīva).* Non-animate substances can be further sub-divided into five additional ones: matter, space, time, movement and rest. In the next chapter we shall go into these in more detail, now it is only necessary to give an overview, and it is generally agreed that what exists can be divided into the animate and the non-animate *(Vyākhyā-prajñāpti* 25.2 [855b]). Jainism takes it that these two substances *jīva* and *ajīva* are eternal and exist by virtue of their own nature *(svabhāva).* That is to say, reality is essentially *permanent.* Jain thought simultaneously postulates that these substances constitute the substratum of their own qualities *(guṇas)* and modifications *(paryāyas).* These qualities and modes allow us to differentiate one particular thing from another. Which means that at a modal level reality is *impermanent.* Gautama asks Mahāvīra about the permanence or impermanence of the soul. The Jina answers:

> "Beings in general [*jīvas*] are eternal from the material point of view *[dravya],* not eternal in respect to their conditions *[paryāya]" (Vyākhyā-prajñāpti* 7.2 [299b]).

In short, there is an essential basic or underlying substance which possesses series of qualities that are constantly undergoing modification. There is no substance without qualities, and no qualities without substance. The Universe is eternal but not static. The universal exists but so does the particular. The cosmos is constantly changing owing to the origination *(utpāda),* destruction *(vināśa)* and permanence *(dhrauvya)* of the qualities and modifications of these substances *(Tattvārtha-sātra* 5.29).

In terms of Indian philosophy, this concept of reality, which postulates simultaneous permanence and impermanence, is termed identity-and-difference *(bhedābheda).* One given thing is partially identical to its qualities because each quality or each mode forms a part of it, but these are not the thing. An atom is a portion of matter, which has its own self-created and indestructible nature by virtue of the force of permanence, but its qualities of colour, smell, taste, texture, can be modified incessantly owing to its origination and destruction. The atom is materially eternal but modally impermanent *(Vyākhyā-prajñāpti* 14.4 [640a]). Another typical example of Indian philosophy is that of the pot and the clay. Some only see the substantial unity between both objects. Since the pot previously existed in the clay, the truth is, according to some, that there is no modification whatsoever. Others, on the other hand, see the pot as a modification of its original state. There is no pot or clay but only transformation. As Jains see it, the concepts of "unity" and "transformation" (of the pot) are nothing more than abstractions.

THE DOCTRINE OF NON-ABSOLUTISM

Since there are stacks of different qualities and their modifications are virtually numberless (originating from an infinite past and extending into an equally infinite future) no one can completely grasp what exists. There are too many variables. We can only choose one angle of vision, and this will always be partial and relative. Whatever judgement we formulate is incomplete, owing to our condition of bondage to this world. It can be valid for worldly activities but in no sense can it embrace the enormous complexity of reality. At a given moment, one may perceive the unity *(ekatva)* of a substance or the multiplicity *(anekatva)* of its modifications, but not both at the same time. Only omniscient beings can simultaneously capture the permanent and temporal in reality.

This complexity of what exists, being at the same time unity and multiplicity, eternity and change, permanence and impermanence is expressed by the famous Jain doctrine of non-absolutism *(anekāntavāda).* Professor Ka-padia (cited in Desai 1983: 6) explains the meaning of the term as a whole as: "not" *(an-)* "one" *(eka)* "side, end" *(anta)* and "statement, exposition" *(vāda),* which he takes to mean "many-sided exposition". Perhaps a simpler gloss would be that of the philosophy of relativity or multilaterality. However, you may wish to gloss it, on the subject of that which is, the *anekāntika* (the person who recognises multiple aspects of reality) cannot make absolute affirmations. One and the same thing can, according to the *anekāntavāda,* be simultaneously characterised by contradictory features. Affirmations can be true from one standpoint, but only from within the framework of certain conditions and limitations. With the aid of this doctrine of non-absolutism, Jain philosophers can integrate opposing points of view, which inevitably crop up in the minds of those who are trapped in this world.

This goes way back. In the *Vyākhyā-prajñāpti* (2.1 [112a]), Mahāvīra had already used a perspectivist method to convert the Brāhmaṇa Skhandaka Katyāyāna. With the advent of Kundakuṇda, the method became sophisticated when he proposed a model with two levels of truth. Umāsvāti developed it further to be able to reconcile the contradictory judgements of the tradition. The first philosopher to give a solid viewpoint on the subject was Samantabhadra in his famous *Āptamimāṃsā,* which would later be commented on by Akalaṅka and Vidyānanda.

THE EXAMINATION OF OTHER SYSTEMS

A clear outcome of the doctrine of non-absolutism is that the truth can be reached through different approaches. This view, which is incidentally very Indian, is taken to its limit in Jainism. Obviously Jains do not go back on their convictions; quite the contrary. Thanks to *anekāntavāda* they consider themselves able to reach a level of impartiality empowering them to evaluate other systems and subordinate them to their own. Thus the *anekāntavāda* is an efficient tool with which to defend traditional positions. In other words, even with its doctrinally tolerant spirit, the Jain posture does not lead to total relativism.

Just as in the other Indian philosophical systems, Jains have devoted considerable time and effort to studying, exploring, and criticising opposing postures, those that for them are heterodox *(nāstikas).* Like the others, their knowledge of rival philosophies is at least very acceptable, if not more. The *Sūtrakṛtāṅga* (2.2.79) had already explored and criticised many rival doctrines in the light of Jainism. Siddhasena Divākara (5th century) did the same by questioning rival points of view when affirmed in an absolute fashion. For this great master of logic, the Sāṃkhya philosophy was a case of eternalist absolutism *(dravyāstikaya-naya),* Buddhist philosophy was one of temporal absolutism (*paryāyāstikaya-naya)* and the Vaiśeṣika philosophy a mechanical juxtaposition of both. The task of examining contemporary thought patterns fell to the lucid Mallavādin (5th-6th centuries). His *Nayacakra* was the first of India's doxographies. He studied 17 philosophical systems, including the doctrines of the Upaniṣads, the Sāṃkhya, the Vaiśeṣika, the grammarian Bhartrhari and the Buddhist master of logic Diṅnāga. Similarly, Jinabhadra Gaṇi (6th century) used the episode of the "conversion" of the eleven *gaṇadharas* to criticise eleven rival systems. Mahāvīra convinces his disciples by arguing against eleven non-Jain positions, which ends up with them being converted. The first doxography written in Sanskrit was also Jain. It was the *Ṣaḍdarśana-samuccaya* by Haribhadra (8th century), which considered the doctrines of Buddhism, Nyāya, Sāṃkhya, Jainism, Vaiśeṣika, Mīmāṃsā and Lokāyata. Haribhadra's compendium is by far the most important and is quoted by all. Following on from Haribhadra, among others we have Śīlāṅka (9th century), Malliṣeṇa (13th century), Rājaśekhara (14th century) and Merutuṅga (14th century).

Jainism has taken the typically Indian "inclusivist" approach, which means accepting a slice of the truth from other systems, but subordinating this to an inferior position within one's own order of truth. For instance, according to Haribhadra, the Other is right but only partly so. There is no need to reject, simply subordinate. Thus the Buddha taught the doctrine of impermanence to strengthen one's sense of non-attachment, but not from a real point of view *(Śāstravārtā-samuccaya* 6.51-53; cited in Nyāyavijayajī 1952: 421). The Vedānta proposed non-dualism, not as a representation of reality, but to help human beings reach the state of equanimity *(Śāstravārtā-samuccaya* 8.8; cited in Nyāyavijayajī 1952: 422). This hermeneutic astuteness is, precisely, very typical of the Vedānta philosophy (i.e., Mādhava, *Sarvadarśana-saṅgraha).* Even when thinkers such as Haribhadra or Yaśovijaya admit that followers of other faiths may have had the enlightenment experience of all genuine holy ascetics, they are actually implying that such individuals (Patañjali being the classical example) follow a code of behaviour approved in both their own path and that of the Jains (Dundas 2004: 133-134). They are Jainas without knowing it.

However, to be fair to Jainism, we must underline the fact that of all Indian philosophies, theirs is the one which shows most impartiality toward other systems. As Wilhelm Halbfass (1988: 266) points out, the Jain's interest in doxography has not only consisted in criticising their rivals' points of view, but also in putting them all into some kind of systematic order, and indeed recognising their very existence. In a notably conciliatory and modern tone, Haribhadra says:

> "I did not choose Mahāvīra as my friend
> And [the Hindu sage] Kapila my enemy and others like him;
> Listen to him only and follow him,
> Whose teachings reveal genuine truth"
> *(Lokatattva-nirṇaya* 1.38; cited in von Glasenapp 1925: 338).

Anticipating a basic position in 19th and 20th centuries' neo-Hinduism, Haribhadra affirms:

> "The ultimate truth transcending all states of the worldly existence and called *nirvāṇa* is essentially and necessarily one even if it be designated by different names" *(Yogadṛṣṭi-samuccaya* 129-130; cited in Dundas 1992: 196).

This is the recognition that the extinction *(nirvāṇa)* of Buddhism, the liberation *(mukti)* of the Vedānta, the solitude *(kaivalya)* of the Sāṃkhya and the emancipation *(mokṣa)* of Jainism, are *quasi* identical terms that simply "name" the ultimate goal in Indian soteriology. Haribhadra attempted to minimise the differences between the concept of God *(īśvara),* nature *(prakṛti),* void *(śunya),* non-duality *(advaita),* etc. Moreover he saw no objection to considering God as the creator (an untenable position as far as Jainism is concerned) for the benefit of devotion *(Sāstravārtā-samuccaya* 3.10-14; cited in Nyāyavijayajī 1952: 419-420). Nonetheless, this line of thought must not be taken too far, when considering thinkers such as Haribhadra. His criticism of other points of view did not lead him to embrace a *philosophia perennis.*

To a certain extent, it was due to this labour of comprehension, explication, inclusion, and co-ordination of the other systems, that Jains developed their acute Anekāntika perspectivism. The culmination of this work is to be found in the *Syādvāda-mañjari* of Mallisena (13th century). The philosopher's conclusion is that every system, when its position is taken to its absolute term, becomes erroneous. All other philosophies and theologies invariably reduce their vision of existence *(sat)* to one single aspect *(ekānta).*

BETWEEN BEING AND IMPERMANENCE

While in the very first centuries of the period of logic, Buddhists were the rivals to contend with—most notably Dharmakīrti (7th century)—with the passage of time, Jain philosophers found themselves more and more in confrontation with scholars of Vedānta. These two philosophies are always a target of the astute *anekāntika.*

Vedānta philosophy maintains that being *(sat)* or existence, which they call absolute *(brahman),* is unitary *(eka)* and non-dual *(advaita).* That which is absolute is eternal and does not modify or change. Any suggestion of multiplicity is illusion *(māyā);* it belongs to the world of phenomena.

According to the Jains, the Vedānta represents an extreme vision, that of eternalism *(nityavāda).* For the *anekāntika,* the Vedāntins only perceive the substantial aspect of existence and forget or ignore its modal aspect, but substance is inseparable from production, maintenance and destruction. It is criticised in the *Sūtrakṛtāṅga* (2.6.48 and 51) as such:

> "[If there were but one Soul common to all beings] they could not be known [from another], nor could they experience different lots...
>
> You have, in your mind, made equal both those who lead a blameable life, and those who in this world practise right conduct. Friend, you are deluded".

Therefore, Vedāntins are not capable of showing the way to liberation, as they are not able to explain the nature of our state of bondage, nor can they differentiate between worthy and unworthy conduct.

Buddhism denies the reality of all substance *(dravya)* and only accepts what are modifications. For a Buddhist, existence never ceases to change. Given that there is no substance and only impermanence *(anitya),* Jains consider that Buddhists cannot explain in logically valid way the state of bondage or liberation. This is how Haribhadra explains it:

> "If the one in *saṃsāra* is nonexistent
> Or is in fact only here a moment at a time,
> Then a liberated one is not liberated!"
> *(Yogadṛṣṭi-samuccaya* 205; cited in Chappie 1998: 26).

Who is it that enjoys the bliss of liberation? Merutuṅga asks himself *(Ṣaḍdarśana-nirṇaya* [Folkert 1993: 386]). If there is nothing trapped nothing can be liberated. From the Jain point of view, the Buddhist position represents the other extreme, that of annihilationism *(ucchedavāda).*

Jainism takes up a position between Vedāntic and Buddhist extremes. Not everything is pure permanence, Being *(brahman),* sameness, as Vedāntins claim, nor is everything impermanent *(anitya),* voidness *(śūnyatā),* difference, as Bauddhas would have it.* For Jainism, both postures bear some truth—from their own conceptual schemes—and therefore, we do not have the right to absolutely condemn them. This is *anekānta.* The opposite being *ekānta,* an absolute, narrow, one-sided, and dogmatic judgement.

IMPLICATIONS OF THE *ANEKĀNTAVĀDA*

The correct position is neither that of absolutism nor annihilationism, or of any other variable, but it is the multiplicity of methods of analysis and synthesis. This is what the doctrine of non-absolutism *(anekāntavāda)* consists of. This position, a strong feature in Jainism, has altogether very interesting implications. The mood of the *anekāntavāda* can prove an efficient antidote for all types of dogmatism, at the same time as being a valuable hermeneutic support to be able to pass judgement on all the other positions. The implicit dogmatic flexibility in the *anekāntavāda* can be a totally efficient tool in intercultural dialogue. There we have Haribhadra's eloquent example.

Jains like to say that this non-extremism is the logical conclusion of the doctrine of non-violence. *Ahiṃsā* is the practice of respect, control and austerity. Accordingly, the Jain philosophical mood has to be equally respectful, conciliatory, and broad-minded. In this respect, the *anekāntavāda* states that if one rigidly defends a certain point of view, one ends up being violent. At the other extreme, if one refrains from adopting a point of view one becomes aimless, lacks a sense of identity and lamely accepts others' aggressive points of view. Both extremes violate the principles of *ahiṃsā.* The Jain position concerning

* The Buddha adopted a similar position, in considering extreme both the position that things have self as that they do not. However, the general Buddhist position has been fundamentally non-substantialist *(anātman),* which is what Jains have in mind when they criticise Buddhists.

Others' philosophies combine tolerance with fidelity to their own cosmological and ethical position. This has to be seen as a sort intellectual *ahiṃsā,* as A.B Dhruva was fond of saying (cited in Folkert 1993: 224). Respect for all forms of life has its metaphysical counterpart: neither plurality nor unity are dislocated (Mookerjee 1944: 272). Perhaps this vision is a little idealistic, since as will immediately be seen, Jain logic is used to refute rival tendencies, rather than explain the multiplicity of opinions, but as John Koller (2002: 20) has argued, *anekāntavāda* philosophy provides an ontological basis for the principle of nonviolence. Moreover, this is the way in which the tradition actually sees itself. These days, Jains do not regard the Other as being in the wrong, it is simply that their point of view is incomplete. This has led many Jains in the 20th and 21st centuries to argue for a degree of composure and respect for all the religions in the world. Taking their inspiration from Haribhadra or the perennialism of neo-Hinduism, others have tended towards the notion that all religions are essentially the same and the different paths all lead to the same goal.

JAIN LOGIC

It has repeatedly been said that the concept of Reason is foreign to India. Certainly in the way the Hellenic and Western world understand it. It hardly appears in the history of Indian philosophy, but that does not mean we should rush to say the Indian mind is dogmatic or irrational. The world of Indian logic (Nyāya, Vedānta, Buddhism, or Jainism) is made up of a "rational" complexity and subtlety that very often one will be hard put to find in the West.

Since their beginnings, Jain philosophers have felt that appealing for virtuous conduct would not be viable unless their doctrines could be logically defended. Apart from the different positions taken by Vedāntins and Bauddhas, they were faced by no more and no less than the highest level of Brāhmaṇic orthodoxy, being the philosophic tradition of the Mīmāṃsā. The latter skilfully backed up the infallible authority and eternal composition of the Veda, as having not been written by any human hand. For this powerful Brāhmaṇic tendency, the statements made by Jainas, Buddhists, Yogis and Vedāntins concerning omniscient beings who preached about the path to salvation, thus aiming above *dharma* and the Veda, were simply fallacious. As Olle Qvarnström (2006: 96) has seen, the debate over whether or not a man was capable of omniscience or having a direct experience of *dharma* parallels in some measure the perceived threat of Christian and Sufi mystics by those who administered the Word of God in the Bible and the Qur'ān. The supposed transcendental experience of yogis was, in the eyes of the Mīmāṃsāka Kumārila *(Śloka-vārtika* 2.132), totally subjective, meaningless and of no use at all.

Within this tense dialectic and intellectual atmosphere, some of the most brilliant philosophical steams of thought that history has known, came into being.

The controversies among thinkers were not restricted to the written word, they were also expressed in public in oral debates, through which rhetorical and logical arguments evolved in a marvellous fashion. Of course, Indian logic is not only a way to strengthen arguments, it is a way to eliminate ignorance, acquire wisdom concerning what is beneficial—in achieving liberation—and of adopting it. Abstract logic, detached from transpersonal experience is a blind and useless tool, and it is from this perspective that we have to seek to understand Jainism's original contribution to logic.

The first thinker to logically establish the omniscience of the *jinas* was the father of Jain logic, Siddhasena Divākara (5th century). The methods of Samantabhadra, Akalaṅka, Mallavādin and Hemacandra are also notable. According to K.K. Dixit (1971: 111), Siddhasena and the other Jain masters of logic conceived their methods, not so much to explain the existence of other points of view, but to demonstrate the reductionism in them all. Jain logic interacted with the Brāhmaṇic philosophical system, Nyāya, born of the art of controversy, and the system which most boldly dedicated itself to it. As a result, the most important contribution from Jainism to Indian philosophy concerns logic.

NAYAVĀDA

The first great Jain creation in this field is the so-called doctrine of standpoints *(nayavāda).* This method, possibly the work of the great Śvetāmbara philosopher Mallavādin (5th-6th centuries), represents a logical systematisation of the doctrine of non-absolutism. An analytical tool to channel knowledge through the prism of non-absolutism.

All Jain logical methods entail the view that reality is multiple and relative, due to the infinity of qualities and modifications that it features, for which all asseveration has non-absolute value. The argument is for unwavering perspec-tivism. However, despite the fact that everything can have a general and particular aspect, these aspects do not exist separately. The pronouncements of Vedāntins and Buddhists are partial expressions of the truth *(nayas). Naya* is knowledge of a thing in its relationships, in its context. Hence, the Vedāntins speak from the standpoint of substance *(dravya-naya),* whilst Buddhists speak from that of its modifications *(paryāya-naya).* One standpoint as much as the other, one *naya* as much as the other, are incomplete in terms of independent judgements. Nothing stated about a thing can be absolutely true at all times and in all circumstances.

Recalling a classic example (Dasgupta 1922:1,176-178), we can affirm that the substance we have in our hands "is a book", as it seems to us that its qualities and characteristics do not have a separate existence apart from that of the substance we call "book". We can separately perceive its qualities and come to the conclusion that without the qualities of form, colour, and texture, there is no book. The variable points of view can be counted in their hundreds, given the impressive complexity of existence. To opt for the point of view of the substance or its modes, we are dealing with just two of the multiple *nayas* one can choose from.

Jain philosophy considers seven *nayas* to be the most representative ones. The most standard classification states that, to describe reality we can opt for: (1) The standpoint of common sense *(naigama-naya)* in which no differences are observed between general and specific qualities of an object; or for (2) the practical standpoint *(vyavahāra-naya),* in which one considers the object in its practical experience and its specific qualities; or for (3) the general standpoint *(saṃgraha-naya),* in which one only takes into account the object's general properties; or for (4) the manifest standpoint *(ṛjusūtra-naya),* where one only considers the present; or we can take linguistic standpoints, such as (5) the verbal standpoint *(śabda-naya)* in which the relation between word and object and its conventional meaning is considered; or for (6) the meaning of something *(evambhūta-naya),* where only the conformity of the word with the function of the object is considered, and lastly (7) the etymological standpoint *(samabhirūḍha-naya).*

Each *naya* represents a possible standpoint. Each one is correct within its own sphere. Therefore, the error of absolutism is in establishing that only one possible *naya* is true. For instance, the Vaiśeṣikas and Nāiyayikas are only concerned with the point of view of common sense *(naigama-naya);* materialists and Vijñañavādin Buddhists, the practical point of view *(vyavahāra-naya);* the Vedāntins, the general point of view *(saṇgraha-naya);* Theravādin Buddhists, the here-and-now point of view *(ṛjusūtra-naya)*. From the moment an asseveration becomes absolute and excludes the rest, it is erroneous—let alone when the *nayas* are used incorrectly. A judgement can only be completely valid if it pervades all these perspectives and points of view in their multiple forms *(anekatva).* Only when the object is considered from all these perspectives, can the point of view be valid. This is in accordance with the Āgamic position, that is to say: Jainism.

In reference to the six philosophical systems in Brāhmaṇism (Sāṃkhya, Yoga, Nyāya, Vaiśeṣika, Vedānta and Mīmāṃsā) Jain logic refers to the old, perhaps Buddhist, parable of the king who shows an elephant to six people blind from birth. Each of these philosophies is like one of the blind men touching the animal. One will say the animal is like a tube (the trunk) another, like a fan (the ear) another, like a column (a leg), another like rope (the tail), etc. *(Udāna* 6.4; cited in Winternitz 1907: II 85). Each will try to describe the animal from their limited and partial appreciation of the part, from their own standpoint *(naya).* They are in error with this vision *(darśana),* when they elevate what is a partial appreciation, a limited point of view, to an absolute truth. Every truth is limited to the conditions and chosen point of view, therefore, it is incomplete. Jainism considers the Hindu schools of philosophy contain a partial truth, but when they are considered independently and when they try to explain it as a whole, they become false doctrines. Or, as John Koller (2002: 22) puts, the *nayavāda* is a method of partially conceding the opponent's thesis to avert his argument, while at the same time persuading him to consider the other side of the case.

We must emphasise that the seven *nayas* are but seven abstractions of an incalculable number of possible *nayas,* as Siddhasena Divākara stated *(Sanmati-sūtra* 3.47; cited in Dixit 1971: 111). More generally, Kundakunda had already opted for establishing two *nayas* or points of view. The formulation of these two points of view is extremely ancient, as it is mentioned in the *Vyākhyā-prajñāpti* (18.6 [748a]). On the one hand, we have the conventional viewpoint *(vyavahāra-naya),* the way of seeing things in accordance with their differences, forms, modes and through which we can perceive them with our senses and intellect. On the other hand, we have the absolute viewpoint *(niścaya-naya),* the superior perspective which directly grasps the essence of things, in their selfness, without differences. Kundakunda often refers to the *niścaya-naya* as *paramārtha-naya,* the standpoint of superior reality. Going on from the *vyavahāra,* through analysis one can progressively cease to conceptualise, abandon what is empirical and, like the sages, come to see things in the light of the *niscaya-nayā.* In fact, Kundakunda gravitated towards positions similar to those of Advaita Vedānta and Mādhyamaka Buddhism which in a very similar way assumed these two same points of view: conventional reality *(vyavahāra)* and superior reality *(paramārthika).* More in the traditional vein, Jinabhadra Gaṇi *(Viśeṣāvaśyaka-bhāṣya* 72; cited in Dixit 1971: 126) affirmed that *nayas* contradicted each other solely because of false doctrines, but Jain doctrine understands and deals with all of the *nayas,* and thus, is free of error. Certainly, the need to preserve doctrines and traditional practices played a great part in the development of the *anekāntavāda* and the *nayavāda,* as well as allowing for plurality of Jain points of view.

In summary, reality reveals itself in different ways, depending on our level of awareness and according to how we opt for considering specific conditions. What can be true from one point of view, can be untrue from another. This cardinal appreciation from Jainism precedes, by quite a few centuries, Hegel's dialectics, which contain certain parallelism to the Jains (Dixit 1971: 168-171).

SYĀDVĀDA

The doctrine of standpoints *(nayavāda)* is a logical endnote to the doctrine of non-absolutism *(anekāntavāda).* In reality, what Jains do when saying that one can only speak about the unity or the modality of existence is to recognise the limitations of speech and intellect. To overcome this they use a logical method which is called "the doctrine of qualified asseverations" *(syādvāda),* sometimes translated "the perhaps doctrine", as it derives from the word *syāt* meaning "perhaps".

According to this logic, an asseveration *(naya)* is only corect when it is qualified by the indeclinable notions "perhaps", "in a certain sense", "in context" *(syāt)* and "in fact", "certainly" *(eva).* This qualification recognises the limitations of our points of view, and opens up reality to a plurality of dimensions. In the absence of such, we would fall into the fallacy of absolutism and reductionism.

When the Vedāntins state that "the soul is eternal" they fall into the error of not qualifying the statement. This is where the "perhaps", "in a certain sense" and "in fact" come on the scene. Rather than making such an affirmation, they should say "perhaps, in a certain sense *(syāt)*—opting for substance and not its modes—the soul is in fact *(eva)* eternal", and only then would it be valid. Only when we qualify the statement with these two tools will it make any sense, and more importantly, will it leave room for other statements. Which means one recognises that reality is being observed from the prism of a point of view *(naya),* opting to see the permanent substance of things. By the same formula, the next thing to state would be "perhaps, in a certain sense—opting for the modes and not the substance—in fact it is not eternal". The word *syāt* encapsulates, then, the conditions that qualify a given statement. *Syāt* means "seen under certain conditions". Unquestionably, the *syādvāda* represents a valuable effort to include or embrace other doctrines. For Amṛtacandra *(Laghutattva-sphoṭa* 476), even false doctrines can lead to supreme reality, if they are qualified by the term *syāt,* capable of destroying the venom in their absolutism.

In the spirit of non-absolutism, *syādvāda* leads to the famous seven fold application of the *syāt,* known as "the system of the seven parallelogisms" *(saptabhaṅgi-naya).* In Jain logic reality is not reduced to just two syllogisms: to be or not to be; or the four Hindu and Buddhist variables. The subject is much more complex.

The seven syllogisms state that something considered from a certain point of view—from that of its own existence, its situation in time, its location in space, or its own particular state of being:— (1) "in a certain sense, in fact, exists" *(syād asti eva),* but one can also say; (2) "in a certain sense, in fact it does not exist" *(syād nāsti eva),* because it can be observed from another point of view. These first two syllogisms are the fundamental ones, those that make the *syādvāda,* a synonym for *anekāntavāda* (Nyāyavijayajī 1952: 341). Combining both in a *sequence,* we have: (3) "in one sense, in fact, it exists, and in another—the future, for example—it does not" *(syād asti-nāsti eva).* If one wants to express a paradoxical simultaneity, then we have: (4) "in a certain sense, in fact, it is inexpressible" *(syād avaktavyaḥ eva).*

Jains can assume the standpoint of Vedānta (the thing exists), or that of Buddhism (it does not exist), or the holistic standpoint (it exists but it did not or will not), or the apofatic (which can only propose its being indescribable, as how can something be and not be at the same time?) This, without needing to reduce any of these to the ultimate truth. It is the perception that words do not express all reality. As John Koller rightly argues (2004: 96), the fourth statement, the inexpressible, is from the Jain point of view the most important, as it is intended to reconcile what might appear to be exclusive, or contradictory, opposites, but which are, for the *anekāntika,* merely partial, one-sided statements. Now combining *simultaneously* this indescribability with the existence, the non existence, and the existence and non-existence in sequence, we obtain the remaining three syllogisms: (5) "in a certain sense, in fact, it exists but it is indescribable" *(syād asti avaktavyah eva);* (6) "in a certain sense, in fact, it does not exist and it is indescribable" *(syād asti avaktavyaḥ eva);* and (7) "in a certain sense, in fact, it exists and [in another, future time] it does not exist and it is indescribable" *(syād asti-nāsti avaktavyaḥ eva).*

The relationship between *nayavāda,* which is analytical in its approach, and *syādvāda,* which is synthetic, can be resumed in the following fashion: for each judgement of agreement on any and every *naya,* there are up to seven alternatives according to the *syādvāda.* Naturally, Jain philosophers do not qualify each and every statements they make with the *syādvāda,* but this does not detract from the power of the Jain philosophical method.

We are dealing with a way of expressing the enormous complexity of the nature of reality and the provisional character of all affirmations: each proposition stops us from affirming or refusing anything in an absolute manner. Or as Sarvepalli Radhakrishnan (1923: I, 302) interpreted it, all propositions are true, but only under certain conditions, hypothetically. The validity of an affirmation is always partial and provisional.

This ductile way of thinking allows Jains to accept seemingly opposing positions. Just as Christopher Chappie (1993: 93) has shown, the attack on science as perceived by Creationists, for example, could have been mitigated or avoided by using a "grammar" like that of the *syādvāda,* which would allow us to say, "from a certain perspective, the world appears to be very ancient, and to have included many life forms. However, from the perspective of human suffering, this story can be read another way". Something similar is conducted every day by millions of Jains, reconciling traditional cosmology with science [see pages 38-39]. The multiplicity of existence allows the taking of different paths towards the highest goal. This fits in perfectly with the pluralist nature of Jainism. All paths can be valid... in a certain sense *(syāt).*

This method, highly original as it is, can be traced back to the oldest writings. Herman Jacobi (1884: n, xxvii-xxviii) pointed that the position taken by the *syādvāda* is not far removed from the doctrine of non-knowledge *(ajñāvāda)* of the sceptics, one of the Śramaṇical groups in antiquity [see pages 116-117]. For Edward Conze (1951: 141-142) they were the naked philosophers in India, which he identified with the Digambaras, who gave Pyrrho of Elis (4th century BC) many key notions for the evolution of sceptical philosophy in Greece. And Noble Ross Reat (1996: 37-38) has also observed a similarity to Buddhist quadruple negation *(catuṣkoṭi).* This would seem to confirm that there was mutual influence and cooperation between different movements. However, it would not be until the genius Samantabhadra came along with his *Āptamīmāṃsā* that the method of the seven paralogisms *(sapta-bhaṅgi-naya)* would be used for the first time, in its classical formulation.

ANEKĀNTAVĀDA AGAINST JAINISM

Anekāntavāda, nayavāda, syādvāda form an original conglomeration of Jain thinking. These methods must have emerged fiercely in the arduous philosophical debates with Buddhists and Brāhmaṇas throughout the "golden mille-nium" of Indian philosophy. Just as H. von Glasenapp (1958: 312-313) and M. Hiriyanna (1945: 69) pointed out, the doctrine of non-absolutism can also have been used against itself: if all our knowledge of reality is relative, the Jain view must be also relative. Certainly, Jain affirmations, even when they are perfectly qualified when advancing the point of view *(naya)* upon which they base themselves, and even when they are perfectly formulated owing to the "perhaps, in a certain sense, in fact" *(syāt, eva),* cannot be considered absolute. Jainism concedes this limitation, but it has a quadruple antidote.

On the one hand, the focus of non-absolutism, the seven points of view and seven syllogisms do not present themselves as another philosophical vision, since they do not claim to represent reality, but only seek to overcome the limitations of inadequate knowledge. In fact, non-absolutism is similar to the radical deconstruction of the philosophy and common sense put forth by the Mādhyamika Nāgārjuna. Instead of saying that things are devoid of a nature of their own *(śūnyatā),* as Nāgārjuna would do, the *anekāntika* says that things are of a non-absolute nature. Just as Professor Bimal Matilal (1999: 3) has observed, the traditional Buddhist position is to reject extremes (of Self and no-Self, of eternalism and annihilationism) in order to remain on the "middle way". Jains, on the other hand opt for accepting all the variables, with qualifications. When making all the variables relative and refraining from raising any of them to the rank of the whole truth, the *anekāntika* underlines the insufficient, unsatisfactory and dualist nature of philosophy. And, in aiming towards totality, including contradictory viewpoints, "the Jain point of view" ceases to be a point of view.

Second, if it is true that every syllogism is a partial truth, all seven at once get nearer to the whole truth, and they do so not because they represent reality as it really is, but because; (1) they help one out of the dialectic jam, and help one towards what is truly real: *nirvāṇa;* and (2) plurality is, as B.K. Matilal (1985: 314-319) says, the nature of reality. Consequently, Jain pluralism is not only intellectual, but also metaphysical [see next chapter]. It is reality itself—and not just how we perceive it—that is many-sided. Herein lies the strength of *anekāntavāda* and its divergence from purely relativistic approaches (Vallely 2004: 109). Thanks to this, Jains are better prepared than absolutists—whether monists or even non-dualists—for true dialogue. Absolutists inevitably tend to downgrade the rival point of view, as a mistaken vision of the only possible point of view—theirs. Typical cases are the Advaita Vedānta, Vaiṣṇava theism and Islamic and Catholic monotheism. On the other hand, pluralist philosophers (such as Jains, Sāṃkhyites and Yogis) are more ready and receptive to listening, accepting and even exploring the Other's points of view (Chappie 1996: 127). If reality is many-sided, it reveals itself in manyfold ways.

Thirdly, Jains do not argue for perspectivism of a radical kind—which would simply lead to scepticism. Contrary to what its critics imply, epistemo-logical respect for others is not relativism. It does not mean conceding that all arguments and all views are equal (Koller 2004: 89). The philosophy remains faithful to its ethics, cosmology and practice. It possesses the certainty and conviction of Jain truth, which does not impede positive appraisal of the other points of view. In other words, Jainism combines perspectivism with an apologist approach. It avoids fundamentalism yet possesses commonly agreed convictions on appropriate conduct and cosmology. This brings it to situate itself on the middle path: expanded to include and accept other points of view, the *anekāntika* can stay in the middle without rejecting them. Jainism clearly encourages openness to other thought.

The matter does not end here. Its philosophy always implies that the omniscient *jina* is one who is able to *see* the proverbial elephant, who is able to take in the seven syllogisms or multiple points of view, without the paradox blowing his mind. As Siddhasena Mahāmati (8th century) says:

> "Objects... possess many different characteristics, and may be taken from different standpoints. They are understood in their entire characters by omniscience alone" *(Nyāya-avatāra* 29).

All truths are partial because they originate from a particular standpoint, with the exception of omniscient knowledge. The *kevalin* is one who possesses the infinite wisdom that can coexist with any point of view. Accordingly, radical perspectivism fades before the light of the vision and understanding of *kevala-jñāna.* Only the Jain *tīrthaṅkara* can show the true path.

24. METAPHYSICS

JAIN DUALISM

The plurality of Jain approaches *(anekāntavāda)* do not lead to scepticism or idealism, but rather to non-absolutism. Simply, the real world is subject to changes so that it has to be viewed from different angles, but however, we may want to look at it, there are a series of substances *(dravyas)* or principles (*tattvas)* accepted by Jain philosophy and which the tradition maintains were apprehended by Mahāvīra on reaching full enlightenment [see page 143].

The first two basic principles postulate the existence of the animate *(jīva)* and the inanimate *(ajīva)*. In its distinction between a spiritual substance and a non-spiritual one, the Jain system is, metaphysically speaking, strictly dualist. In turn, inanimate substance can be divided into four or five "extended" entities *(astikāyas) (Uttarādhyayana-sūtra* 28.7): space, matter, movement, and repose. Digambaras add a fifth entity, time. The study of these basic substances will occupy us throughout the whole of this chapter.

In contrast to other Indian philosophies, with the formulation of these principles, Jainism once again evidences its realism. Without *jīva* and *ajīva,* either the world would not exist, or it would collapse into oneness, or it could not be perceived or known, all of these being possibilities inconsistent for Jainism. What is more, without a proper understanding of these principles, there cannot be correct knowledge *(samyak-jñāna)* of the Jain path, and the fact is that no other society has placed such a high a value on metaphysical knowledge as India has. This is not surprising when we consider that the very problem of suffering is the result of ignorance, of lack of knowledge of the true spiritual nature of reality. Consequently, among the range of Indian religions, Jainism is one of the traditions that has put most emphasis on the need for its members to know the true nature of things. There is unanimous agreement that the correct knowledge of *the jīva* and the *ajīva* is, as T.U. Mehta (1993: 119) has said, a requirement *sine qua non* for all understanding.

THE REALITY OF THE SOUL *(JĪVA)*

The first and most important of the principles of Jainism postulates the reality of the soul *(jīva).* We have already touched on this concept on repeated occasions, but now is the moment to give the matter careful study.

As Hermann Jacobi (1884:1,3) remarked, it is possible that Jains arrived at their concept of *jīva* through the study of nature. The word *jīva* literally means "living being", "principle of life" (Monier-Williams 1899: 422), and from here they derive the concept of soul. Given that the soul is the vehicle or carrier of life, it is called "life" *(jīva).* Likewise, given that it is animate, a living being is called *jīva* (Schubring 1934: 152). Life and soul are synonymous terms. The soul is an active principle of life, it is vitality, and hence, according to M. Hiriyanna (1945: 60), it would be more correct to translate jīva by animate. This is a completely common sense vision and is animist or hilozoist in its outlook. Remember that the Jain conception of "animate" includes elements that are apparently as inert as drops of water or specks of dust. Over time, the concept of *jīva* shifted slightly until Jains no longer associated it so much with lives, with its biological and material implications, as with the consciousness of the animate, with an immaterial essence whose characteristic feature is *knowledge.* The implicit sense of *jīva,* therefore, is that of soul or spirit.*

If we afirm that Jainism is eminently realist as a system and that it is eminently compatible with common sense, how can it postulate the reality of something as intangible as the soul?

When Mahāvīra instructed Gautama for the first time he warned him that the existence of the soul is difficult to prove by the established means of knowledge *(pramāṇas):* that is, by inference, direct perception, with the aid of scriptural authority or through comparison, but difficult does not mean that the soul is hypothetical. The reality of the soul can be proved through the experience of being *aware of oneself,* since consciousness cannot be detached from an individual (Jinabhadra Gaṇi, *Viśeṣāvaśyaka-bhāṣya* 1652-1653 *[Gaṇadhara-vāda* 104-105]). And this is direct perception. Consciousness is proof of the existence of an agent. And this is an inference. In a style reminiscent of the Upaniṣads, a very ancient sentence in the scripture says:

"The Self is the knower [or experiencer], and the knower is the Self. That through

* Spirit would be preferred to soul given the Christian connotations attaching to the latter concept in the West. Although soul is closer, etymologically speaking, to the Sanskrit *ātman,* it is said of the soul in the Christian context that it is capable of understanding, wanting and feeling and informing the human body, which does not square with Jain notions. Spirit, on the other hand, is both a natural vigour and an immaterial essence, an idea which better fits with that of *jīva.* The problem with spirit is in its association with lesser numinous beings or genii; hence I have given priority to soul, which is also the most extended translation of *jīva.*

> which one knows, is the Self. With regard to this [to know] it [the Self] is established" *(Ācārāṅga-sūtra* 1.5.5.5).

Even the doubt about the existence of the soul shows that there is an agent that doubts, as the celebrated Jinabhadra Gaṇi observes *(Viśeṣāvaśyaka-bhāṣya* 1557 *[Gaṇadhara-vāda* 9]). This subject, which is behind all activity of the being, is the soul, the spirit, the self or the animate. This is something, which even the Vedas over and beyond their plurality of teachings, do not cease to repeat, and this is scriptural authority.

The jīva is a subtle individual and independent substance. We do not have to do here with a Supreme Being *(ātman, brahman),* as is proposed by Vedān-ta philosophy, but rather an individual spiritual monad *(jivātman),* as maintained by the German philosopher Leibniz. All living beings have their soul. The cosmos is full of *jīvas.* Here, Jainism is close to Sāṃkhya and Yoga philosophies, which similarly speak of a multitude of souls *(puruṣas).* For Jains, there are as many *jīvas* as beings. Criticising Vedānta monism, Jinabhadra Gaṇi affirms *(Viśeṣāvaśyaka -bhāsya* 1582 *[Gaṇadhara-vāda 34]):*

> "In the world, there are different souls... on account of the difference in their characteristics, etc. For, if they were [only] one, there will be non-existence of *sukha* [happiness], *duḥkha* [misery], *bandha* [bondage] and *mokṣa* [emancipation]".

This point is important. It underscores the solitude of existence and the individuality of the path. Hence, one must not take it that Jainism postulates "individualism" of a narcissistic type. No, this individual soul is not the ego (although it may have constructed one) or is here to dominate the world. Rather, inserted within a cosmology and cosmography that relate it to the other forms of existence, it is here to pave the way of perfection. A path which, via non-violence and austerity, will lead to the unconditioned, which really is the transcendence of individuality. Without this spiritual substance, the whole world, and the search for perfection and liberation would not make sense.

Broadly speaking, *jīvas* can be put into two major classifications: the liberated ones *(mukta)* and the corporeal *(saṃsārin, bandha) (Tattvārtha-sūtra* 2.10). Obviously, liberated *jīvas* dwell in the confines of empty space, without any type of relation with the material world. They lead a life of pristine existence and possess infinite knowledge, energy, perception and bliss. The liberated soul, simply, is the *jīva* in its perfect or pure state. It is a different story with the cor-porealised or those "bound" to this world. We already looked at this in chapter 3, but now we need to clarify several things concerning all *jīvas.*

In the first place, all *jīvas*, liberated or otherwise, are *essentially identical.* There is no difference between the soul of a *jina* and that of a grub. The first is pure, faceless and the second is marred, but its purity can be restored. The

Daśavaikālika-sūtra (10.5) has it that, despite appearances to the contrary, the ascetic is one who realises that all varieties of *jīva* are essentially equal to oneself. This is of cardinal importance, since the success of non-violence—as the Paṇḍit Sukhalaji (1962: 31) reminds us—is not possible if a sensitivity towards the suffering of others, as if they were our own, is not acquired. In this sense, there is nothing unique in human incarnation, nothing that entitle human beings to a superior status. Second, *all jīvas* lived in the past, are alive now, and will live in the future. That is to say, *the jīva* is eternal, not-born and immortal. For Jainism, life or death are simply modifications of *the jīva.* Hence it can be deduced that the number of spiritual monads is always constant. Third, *the jīva* is immaterial. Not being material, it is invisible. Fourth, *the jīva* has the potential for consciousness, knowledge, perception, energy and happiness. Lastly, it can be said that it is the sole agent responsible for all its actions *(kartā)* and is the receptor of the fruits of such action *(Uttarādhyayana-sūtra* 20.37).

Here, Jainism departs from Sāṃkhya. For the latter system, matter *(prakṛti)* can change or transform itself but soul *(puruṣa)* cannot be. Brāhmaṇical philosophies have always considered that what is eternal cannot change. However Jains believe that all reality is eternal—insofar as it is substance *(dravya)*— but is subject to change—insofar as it is mode *(paryāya).* For classical Jainism, soul can transform without this disturbing its own nature. The bondage of the soul is not an illusion. The relationship between *jīva* and body is complex, since it is not easy to explain why the immaterial soul has to suffer the results of actions carried out by the material body [see pages 388-390]. In any case, *the jīva* acts, and in doing so becomes impregnated with a kind of subtle karmic matter, which will provide it with the body in which it lodges (or in which it will subsequently find lodging in the future rebirth), the type of knowledge it possesses, the duration of its present corporeal life, and so forth.

No god or God controls these spiritual monads. Each soul has forged its own course. Jainism is resolutely individualistic, pluralistic, and voluntaristic.

A curious feature of Jainism is that it holds that the *jīva* has dimensions. Each monad contains a countless number of infinitesimal spatial units *(pradeśas).* It lodges in the body that houses it like a lamp illuminating a closed room. This adaptation does not imply any change in the conception of the spirit, but rather in its qualities. Whether the body in question is that of an insect or one as big as the cosmos itself, the number of these units remains intact. This position is unique to Jainism and differs from the Sāṃkhyan notion of the *puruṣa,* which pervades the whole universe *(vibhu).* With this notion, Jainism underlines the independence of the consciousness and avoids the problems that the similarly pluralistic Sāṃkhya has to contend with (Loy 1988: 205 and 276).

THE QUALITIES OF THE SOUL

Jains talk of the numerous qualities of the *jīva.* It is said that it possesses, for example, the quality of eternal life, or that of sublime conduct, or that of total amorphousness. All *jīvas* have these, although some have them so darkened or "infected" that they can scarcely be glimpsed. All the qualities of *the jīva's* own nature *(svabhāva)* can be reduced to three: the soul is consciousness *(caitanya),* bliss *(sukha)* and energy *(virya).** These three qualities are the abilities that *siddhas* possess in their plenitude.

Consciousness *(caitanya, cetanā)* is the primordial quality of the soul, its distinctive feature par excellence *(Tattvārtha-sūtra* 2.8). Thanks to consciousness the soul can be the agent, the knower. Consciousness is always active and it is this activity which reveals both the nature of objects that are known and the nature of the soul. In other words, when knowing any object, by the mere act of knowing, the soul simultaneously knows itself. Normally, one speaks of two types of consciousness: perception *(darśana),* which is the first-hand apprehension of things, and knowledge *(jñāna),* which is the apprehension of what is known. In the last chapter we already made mention of the five types of knowledge. In its perfect state *the jīva* is *pure jñāna* and pure *darśana.* Precisely, two of the Three Jewels or Pilars of Jainism make explicit reference to right vision or perception *(samyak-darśana)* and right knowledge *(samyak-jñāna).* It is simply that the passions and emotions stop the consciousness of *the jīva* from manifesting itself freely and fully.

Bliss or happiness *(sukha)* is another of the spirit's qualities, although normally the term is used descriptively, to denote the liberated soul. By its very nature, soul is pure bliss, because it possesses the third jewel of right conduct *(samyak-cāritra)* but, as a result of corrupt actions, it generates karmic matter which renders it imperfect.

It is said the animate also possess a force or energy *(vīrya)* which impels it to perceive or know. One possesses consciousness to the extent that the infinite energy of the soul manifests itself. As is the case with bliss, our state of attachment clogs the energy. Passions cause an energetic vibration *(yoga)* that bring about the unfortunate association of the *karmas* with the soul. We shall be looking at this in the next chapter.

THE IMMANENT DIVINE

This understanding of the *jīva* enables Jainism to differentiate itself from the atheist persuasions of a materialist type. Since the *jīva* in its pure state is perfect, it would not be far wrong to describe it as "divine essence", a divine principle present in all beings. But then this divinity lacks theology and anthropomorphic

* It is tempting to seek an equivalence with the three characteristics that Hindus attribute to the soul *(ātman).* Of course, from the Vedāntic point of view the soul is unqualifiable *(nirguṇa)* but to describe it in some way usually recourse is made to the well-known *saccidānanda.* The soul with attributes *(saguṇa-brahman)* is being *(sat),* consciousness *(citta)* and bliss *(ānanda).*

features, and only takes on this guise when Jains meditate on totally liberated *jīvas,* that is, the *jinas.* Today, many Jains go as far as to refer to the the completely liberated soul (Nyāyavijayajī 1952: 31) or the totality of these *jīvas* in their pure state as "God" (Nahar and Ghosh 1917: 263-264). This is akin to the *īśvara* concept of Yoga philosophy, and indeed could be seen as a form of defence against being downgraded as "atheists" by the theists. Although Jainism rejects the existence of God as creator or preserver of the cosmos, it does not deny the absolute divinity of all living beings. How else could one describe the soul, which is infinite consciousness, infinite bliss and infinite energy, other than divine? Not for nothing, one of the words used to describe the soul in its liberated and pure form is supreme soul *(paramātman).* Unlike the materialist, who take the body and soul to be identical, Jains insist on the absolute independence of soul, though confined within the bounds of the body in order to act.

The Jain religion is atheist only in the sense that it denies the existence of a creator and all possibility of divine intervention in the affairs of men and women. Taking a position similar to those found in Hinduism, Jainism is firm in its affirmation that we all possess the divine, the unconditioned, or whatever we may like to call it, in our innermost selves. As Geoffrey Parrinder (1976: 50) puts it, Jain mysticism is, like that of Yoga, a mysticism of the soul, not of God. The goal of true spiritual progress is not "out there", it is not an external object with which to unite or rejoin, but rather is found within oneself. What is more, the *jīva* is the only thing that can truly be called One-self. This idea owes much to the works of Kundakunda (2nd century), the best exponent of Digambara mysticism. For Kundakunda *(Samayasāra* 144), the *jīva* is the only ultimate category, which gives the measure of things. For that reason he calls it supreme *(paramārtha)* or realised soul *(samayasāra).*

According to Kundakunda, every *jīva* is in fact already liberated. It is simply that it has lost its awareness of its own nature, of its *divinity.* The rest of the cosmos, i.e., the magma of *ajīva,* only has a provisional and transactional value. For that reason it is called mundane *(vyavahāra).* In Kundakunda's writings, this model of two levels of truth or reality, known also in Mādhyamaka Buddhism and Advaita Vedānta, found one of its first expositions. Kundakunda's interest here was in showing that the true nature of the *jīva* can have no connection of any sort with karmic matter:

> "Absolutely pure, having the nature of perception and knowledge, always non-corporeal, I am indeed unique. Hence not even an atom of alien things whatsoever [whether living or non-living] is related to me as mine" *(Samayasāra* 38).

The *jīva* is not, properly speaking, bound to the material, rather, as the *Samayasāra* (278-279) has it, it only appears so because of impurities such as attachment. The *jīva,* freed from identification with bodily, mental and verbal actions, is the omniscient, the *kevalin,* the knower of itself. This is *nirvāṇa,* the absorption and full realisation of the soul. As a result, Kundakunda succeeds in doing away with classical Jain dualism, which is limited to the mundane sphere. This position approaching non-dualism notably influenced Haribhadra. We shall be returning to this at the end of the book.

THE REALITY OF THE NON-SOUL *(AJĪVA)*

The second basic principle of Jainism postulates the reality of the inanimate *(ajīva).* For Jainism, all that is not soul or life, is the inanimate. The spiritual is as real as the non-spiritual. In Jain philosophy, there is no room, at least in theory, for the doctrine of cosmic illusion *(māyā),* which considers that all that is not soul is no more than an illusory superimposition covering what is soul. Although Kundakunda is one step away from this conclusion, he decides not to take that step. Jainism, on the contrary, has always accepted the reality of the material world. Nevertheless, while it is real, the world that we perceive is still a creation of ignorance. Once the soul is realised, the infinite forms of the cosmos will fade away, since they will be transcended by the omniscience of the *kevalin.*

If the *jīva* is all that has life, *ajīva* is all that does not possess life. If *jīva* is the animate and the spiritual, *ajīva* is the inanimate and the material. If *jīva* is characterised by counsciousness, energy, and bliss the *ajīva* is characterised by non-awareness; yet it is that which can be touched, smelt, seen, or tasted. The *ajīva* provides the medium and the mechanisms by means of which *the jīva* functions and acts. All beings, other than the liberated, ar made of *jīva* and *ajīva.*

The *ajīva* consists of the "five extended substances" *(pañcāstikāyas)* or simply substances *(dravyas):* space *(ākāśa),* means of movement *(dharma),* and of rest *(adharma),* time *(kāla),* and matter *(pudgala).*

SPACE

Space *(ākāśa)* is that which is occupied by the substances; that is to say, the world *(loka)* which we have already looked at in chapter 2, but space is also that which is not occupied, that is, the non-world *(aloka).* In the latter, there is no substance. Only *ākāśa* exists in its totality and eternity, given that neither the means of movement *(dharma)* or repose *(adharma)* can act [see below]. Although one space is equivalent to the manifested world, and the other is a transcosmic abyss and is completely empty, in reality there is only one infinite space. Given that it is infinite, it is composed of an infinite number of spatial units *(pradeśas).*

Between the minute *pradeśa* and the immense "string" *(rajju)* many spatial measures are postulated which it is not necessary to name here.

MEDIA OF MOVEMENT AND REST

Space in itself is not the pre-condition for movement of things to occur, or rather it is not the *only* one. If things were to depend on space alone, there would be movement, but not a cosmos but chaos would come about. For there to be a *kosmos,* not a nonsense, some supports are needed, some laws which govern movement and repose. These are *dharma* and *adharma.*

Here, a brief clarification is in order. The concept *dharma* is one of the most polyvalent in Indian spirituality. The word can mean religious law or duty, which is the sense in which it is generally used by orthodox Brāhmaṇas, especially in their Treatises on Duty (Dharma-śāstras). By extension, in Hinduism, *dharma* means virtue or merit, and *adharma* lack of virtue, or demerit. It can also mean religion, seen as an ensemble of duties, practices and doctrines promulgated by the spiritual masters. This is the sense that it has when we talk of Jaina *dharma* (Jainism) or the *dharma* put forward by the Buddha (Buddhism). It also has a more cosmological sense, which has to do with the ordered flow of the cosmos which the Vedic poets called *ṛta* [see page 24]. It is this ultimate notion, which Jain thinkers refer to indirectly when they speak of *dharma* and *adharma* in their technical, philosophical sense. It could be that these entities emerge as a result of cosmographic debates on the nature of the non-world *(aloka).* If nothing can exist there, whether spiritual monads or matter, or time, this means that in the *loka,* on the other hand, there is a governing order which enables things to exist, move and cease moving.

Dharma and *adharma* are the cosmic principles that form the substrate for all that can move. They do not occupy a particular space, but rather, like the other, interpenetrate the whole of the universe. As Nemicandra *(Dravya-saṃgraha* 17-18) says, they act on the souls and on matter, one in the manner of the water that allows the fish to move, and the other like the shade that invites the traveller to rest. *Dharma* or *adharma* do not make anything move or cease to move, but if anything has to move or to stop, this cannot be done without the presence of these fulcra and the conditions of space and time. *Dharma* and *adharma* interpenetrate with space and time, and the triad forms the conditions that sustain all things. This meaning of the term *dharma,* is unique to Jainism. It has no parallel in any other Indian system of thought, although we may detect some Vaiśeṣika influence.

TIME

Time *(kāla)* is an eternal continuity, or better, it is a process of persistence; hence the fact that it is often represented as a wheel *(cakra).* Time is the instrumental cause by virtue of which changes can take place. It does not in itself generate change but rather, like space, is only its efficient cause, the factor that enables substances to exist and at the same time operate their innumerable transformation. It is the eternal flow which, when associated with substance, is also affected by its modifications, but time does not act on the cosmos as whole. There are parts of the cosmos that have no time, such as the non-world.

The smallest unit of time is termed the "instant" *(samaya).* Each instant forms the present. The word in turn refers to what we could call points of time (Nemicandra, *Dravya-saṃgraha:* 22), seen almost in a material way. Thanks to this formulation, the Digambaras consider time as substance *(dravya),* a position which the Śvetāmbaras do not share. If *kāla* is eternal or everlasting time, without beginning or end, *samaya* is a discrete portion.

Countless *samayas* form a *nimiśa,* which is the micro-time taken for a person to blink. From this, to the unspeakably large *sāgaropama,* numerous of quantities of time are postulated.

MATTER

The inanimate is formed, finally, by matter *(pudgala)* which is the physical basis of the world. It is the most important component of the inanimate, since it is the only substance that has form, and in the last analysis, it is what we explicitly see, taste, smell and touch of the world. All that is not space or time, the means of rest and movement or the *jīvas,* consists of matter.

The Jain concept of matter is atomistic. According to N.N. Bhattacharyya (1976: 140), Jains were probably the first thinkers in India to formulate the theory of the atom, and this theory states, first that there is an infinite number of material and indivisible atoms *(paramāṇus, aṇus).* Second place, it says that matter is eternal substance. Or rather, matter, seen from the point of view of substance, is in fact eternal. But its qualities are not. Or rather, matter seen from the point of view of modalities, is not in fact eternal. Each atom possesses the quality of colour *(varṇa),* smell *(gandha),* taste *(rasa)* and texture *(sparśa).* These qualities undergo endless transformation.

Atoms have no extension in space. Each occupies a unique infinitesimal point *(pradeśa),* and is therefore imperceptible. It is so irreducibly small that in reality it is without form *(amūrta),* while being the basis for all forms. The senses can only perceive matter when atoms come together, forming agregates *(skandhas)* or molecules. These atomic "fusions" only occur between atoms of different types thanks to their cohesive force. The laws and means that govern such fusion or linkage are those of *dharma, adharma,* space, and time.

Not all such aggregates can be perceived. Some are so subtle and intangible that they are beyond the reach of our senses. However, the *skandhas* or aggregates of atoms can join together to form still larger entities. It is at this point that we can perceive matter. All that we perceive is a *skandha* or a collection of *skandhas.* One particular aggregate of atoms is what produces the effect of fire, another the effect of air, and what is more important, the molecules of material make up the body in which the *jīva* lodges. As Umāsvāti *(Tattvārtha-sātra* 5.19) says, *pudgala* is the material cause of the body, speech, mind, and breathing. Accordingly, matter is of enormous importance, since it is literally what associates or links with the *jīvas*, and modifies its nature. We could even ask ourselves, along with Wilhelm Halbfass (2000: 72), if there is any particle of matter which has no connection, direct or indirect, with a *jīva.*

The union between the body and the spirit is the product of action, of *karma,* as we shall see in a moment, but we should comment here that even *karma* is considered to be matter-like *(pudgalika).* but it is a matter so subtle that we cannot perceive it with our senses.

PARALLELISMS

This substantialist conception of the inanimate, along with the insistence on the reality of change, both in the animate and inanimate realms, make Jainism a philosophy of change *(pariṇāmavāda).* All that exists is modified unceasingly. Jainism's atomistic vision of the material world, while close to Vaiśeṣika, is also surprisingly similar to the theory of atoms in Greek thought, for example as expounded by Leucipus or Democritus. This substantialist trend of thought in Jainism goes hand in hand with a markedly "scientific" tone, much more so than in other philosophies. This fact has led professor K.V. Mardia (1990: 101-110) to make an interesting comparison between modern science and Jainism—albeit somewhat detached from its practical and mythical context.

Since Jains maintain that the soul exists and is affected by its acts, Jain doctrine also falls into the category of what in India is known as the doctrine of action *(kriyāvāda);* that is, that the soul (which exists) is joined to a material body (which also exists) by means of its acts. The Vaiśeṣika also takes this view. The opposing thesis, that the soul does not exist (Buddhism, materialism) or is not altered by its acts (Vedānta, Sāṃkhya, Yoga) is known as the doctrine of non action *(akriyāvāda).* Many of these schools, for example, Vedānta and Yogācāra Buddhism, teach that the phenomenal world of action is illusory *(māyā),* a position which contrasts with Jain realism.

Out of all the philosophical systems in India, the ones that come closest to Jainism are undoubtedly Sāṃkhya and Yoga. It is feasible that Sāṃkhya was a peripheral Brāhmaṇic, or even Śramaṇic, development in origin—one that finally merged with the enormous Vedic/Hindu stream. Both Sāṃkhya and Jainism speak of infinite matter *(prakṛti* for Sāṃkhya, *ajīva* for Jainism) opposed to an infinity of monads *(puruṣas and jīvas* respectively). The two systems take it that matter is able to change or evolve and their position on *karma* and *saṃsāra* seems to stem from a vision of the world which incorporates common sense elements (Schubring 1934: 14-15). It is more than likely that Jainism drew on ancient Sāṃkhya to defend its atheism. Note, that Sāṃkhya and Jain theories of knowledge are very similar. According to N.N. Bhattacharyya (1976: 187), the Jain concept of *mokṣa* and the Buddhist concept of *nirvāṇa* appear to have derived in the first place from the Sāṃkhyan idea of liberation *(apavarga, mukti).*

However, it could have been the other way round (Zimmer 1951: 281). For Sāṃkhya, the cause of bondage is ignorance. Liberation is obtained through correct knowledge of reality, and this knowledge is based on discrimination *(vive-ka, Sāṃkhya)* between soul *(puruṣa)* and non-soul *(prakṛti)*. A formula, which any Jain would accept. In all, given the Jain emphasis on psycho-physical self-realisation, it may be that the Yoga system of Patañjali (who accepts many of Sāṃkhya's philosophical premises) constitutes the *darśana* closest to Jainism.

Seemingly, the Indian philosophical system furthest from Jainism is Vedāntism. Their cosmologies, their logical methods, their epistemology and their ways to approach liberation are all quite considerably different. The great Vedāntin Śaṅkara (8th-9th centuries) devoted considerable space to criticising the fundamental principles of Jainiṣm *(Brahma-sūtra-bhāṣya* 2.2.33-36), immediately after attacking Buddhist positions. However, the differences between Vedānta and Jainism are very much softened or sweetened if we compare the work of Kundakunda with that of Śaṅkara. Kundakunda's theory of the two levels of realities is closer to Śaṅkara's view than that of Nāgārjuna (Johnson 1995: 95-96), and his conclusions clearly anticipate the concept of non-duality *(advai-ta)* typical of the Vedānta of both Gauḍapāda and Śaṅkara. Some even suggest that Śaṅkara inherited these notions from the Jain tradition (Chakravarti 1950: 77). What is more, when Kundakunda says that the *jīva* is pure consciousness, tasteless, formless, odourless, is non-manifest, soundless, beyond the spectrum of any characteristic and with no decipherable configuration *(Pravacanasāra* 173), this could perfectly easily be a description of the Vedāntic *ātman-brah-man* (Johnson 1995: 125-126). And the Jain goal of liberated isolation *(kaivalya)* coincides fully with the non-dual experience of the Advaita Vedānta or of Yoga in separating pure consciousness from objects.

25. KARMIC BONDAGE

THE DOCTRINE OF *KARMA*

Again and again, from beginningless time, the *jīvas* return to this world. Why? What drives the eternal wheel? What is the cause of *saṃsāra?* All of these serious questions have the same answer: because of action (*karma).* The *jīvas* materialise and return to this world because of the acts they have committed, which have an effect on them. *Karma* is the link between the *jīva* and the *ajīva; karma* is the cause of *saṃsāra.*

THE LAW OF *KARMA*

In Vedic times, Brāhmaṇas conceived *karma* basically as a *sacrificial act* along with its results. It was said that sacrifice summoned a power *(brahman, apūrva)* that could produce a favourable effect on the person who made the sacrifice. The act of sacrifice and its consequence was termed *karma.* Mahāvīra, like other Śramaṇas, understood that *all action,* and not only the ritual, yielded its fruit. More than this, *karma* was every action and every *intention.* Given that the causing action along with the crystallised effect are both called *karma,* in the broad sense of the word, *karma* is that law of cause-and-effect, responsible for continuity. This discovery was tremendous. It would establish the inexorability of an impersonal law, and the urgency of dominating one's actions, given that it is the fruit of action that drags the soul down and obliges it to transmigrate. In a certain sense, *karma,* conditioned life, is the same as *saṃsāra.*

This was not an entirely new concept. The sages of the Upaniṣads were already working on it. Historically speaking, the first reference to *karma* in its classical meaning "any action" (not only ritual ones) that would lead to retribution, occurred in the well-known *Bṛhadāraṇyaka-upaniṣad* (3.2.13), a Vedic teaching transmitted sometime between the 9th and 8th centuries BC. These were the times of the most ancient Upaniṣads, and the origins of the Śramaṇic movements. It is possible, certainly, that the seeds of this concept were not exclusively Vedic. For some authors it would not be totally amiss to think of proto-Jainism as the "discoverer" or inventor of the Indian doctrine of *karma,* as it must have been conceived as a counterweight to the doctrines of the creation of the universe. According to David Kalupahana (1986: 244) the idea of *karma* as volitional or intentional is pre-Buddhist and possibly Jain. The fact is that no other Indian system of thought has been concerned as much as Jainism has with the mechanism of our state of bondage. Alain Daniélou (1985: 124-125) attributes the very idea of transmigration to the Jains. The fact that the old Buddhist texts *(Majjhima-nikāya* 1.93) tried to debunk the Jaina theories of *karma-saṃsāra* proves that they were already central and well established. However, as in the case of renunciation [see pages 107-109] and non-violence [see page 151], the opposition between a Śramaṇic and a Brāhmaṇic-Vedic spirituality should not be taken too far. As Herman Tull (1989: 31-41) has equally shown, the classical notion of *karma* can be perfectly well derived from the Vedic sacrificial concept. The important thing is not the paternity of the insight but its explanation and its implications.

Karma governs the cycle of transmigration and the millions of possible rebirths as an impersonal force. This autonomy that *karma* has (shared also by Buddhists, Sāṃkhyites and Mīmāṃsākas) gives Jainism a solid argument against the notion of a God as the creator. Moreover, Jinasena subsumes various basic and ultimate concepts of Hinduism under the heading of *karma:*

> "Law, Creator, Dispenser, Destiny, previous *karmas* and the Lord are different names *of karma"* (Jinasena, *Ādi-Purāṇa* 4.36; cited in Krishan 1997: 44).

No external agent can interfere in this law of retribution. Joseph Campbell (1962: II, 264) said that, given the centrality of *karma,* Jainism is a mechanicist religion. For Jainism, anthropomorphic theisms are unsatisfactory and denote a dubious arbitrariness. Max Weber (1922: 416-417) wrote that the most formally perfect solution to the problem of theodicy we owe to the doctrine of *karma* from India. Wilhelm Halbfass (1991: 298) was of similar opinion. All living creatures are responsible for their own situation in the world of *saṃsāra,* because the particularity of the law, as we know, is that *karma* seeks retribution automatically and mechanically. The *Sūtrakṛtāṅga* (1.12.11) is very explicit on this:

> "Misery is produced by one's own works, not by those of somebody else [viz. fate, creator, etc.]".

Only a precise understanding of how these mechanics work can provide the means to detain the infinite cycle of the *saṃsāra. Nirvāṇa* is definitively freeing oneself from *saṃsāra,* freeing oneself from the cycle of existences imposed by *karma.* In other words, *nirvāṇa* is freedom from *karma.*

GENERAL FEATURES

As we have outlined, the Jain conception of *karma* is quite similar to other Indian systems. In Jainism, Vedānta, Buddhism or Yoga, every action *(karma, kriyā,yoga)* leaves a series of traces, colours, or latent potentialities *(saṃskāras, leśyās, bījas, vāsanās)* in the subtle physiology of the agent *(karta)* that sometime or another will mature *(phala, vipāka)* into the form of a new life. These latent aspects are responsible for a multitude of features in the new existence.

This could lead to a strict determinism, of the Ājīvaka style, if it were not that all systems consider that a good part of our actions can alter karmic predisposition. What is done can be undone. Action along with knowledge can be emancipating. One can purify the karmic imprint, through asceticism, ritual, meditation and devotion. The cards are dealt but the player is free to combine them as she or he wishes and is able to throw away unwanted cards.

While *karma* is strictly individual (not even gods or *bodhisattvas* can intervene, as happens in Hinduism and Buddhism), contemporary Jainism accepts collective, social and even national *karma.* The improvement of society depends on the improvement of its individuals, as Muni Nyāyavijayajī (1952: 313) says.

Of course, *karma* is not the only explication Indians turn to, to describe individuals' events and experiences. Apart from *karma,* planetary conjunctions also come into play, and are of cardinal importance when articulating the vitally important concepts of auspicious moments *(śubha, maṅgala)* and inauspicious moments *(aśubha),* the acts of evil spirits, witchcraft, and even the evil eye. Some of these explanations blatantly contradict one another, but that does not really bother Indians very much. On the other hand, karmic astrologers will take it upon themselves to show the harmony between the stars and *karma,* even to the point of reading *karma* through planetary conjunctions and their relations. Christopher Fuller (1992: 250) has shown that the theory of *karma* enjoys a lesser reputation among popular tradition (as it tends to legitimise certain individuals within the social-religious elite), but in the end, it is the most solid, scripturally valid and it permits the reconciliation of apparently incoherent incompatible hypotheses.

MERIT AND DEMERIT

Obviously, not all actions have the same value or extent. There are worthy actions *(puṇya)* and unworthy *(pāpa)* actions. Giving water to someone who is thirsty is a worthy action, the same goes for speaking kindly, giving food to ascetics and shelter to the needy. Killing life is something unworthy, the same as hating, lying and stealing. The archetype of worthy action is non-violence (compassion, respect, generosity, and caring). That of unworthy action is violence (hate, greed, aggressiveness). Jain treatises never cease to number the types of actions and their effect according to karmic law. Being born as a human is already in itself a reward for worthiness. Beauty, strength and happiness are consequences of worthiness. The highest retribution is to be reborn as a divine being.

All this has very strong implications for individuals. With good actions one is building up one's general merit that will lead to an elevated rebirth, whereas with evil deeds one is conditioned to lower rebirths. Hence the highly ethic component in Jainism and Indian religions. Among laypersons it is merit and demerit, or worthiness and unworthiness, which counts, as with this one is forging ones future existence. To that layperson, who has trust in Jainism, knowledge of its fundamental principals, is charitable with *sources of merit* (for example ascetics) and who is guided by the Three Jewels, such a person is promised, after enjoying the heavens of Indra for various aeons, and after being newly reborn as a human being, endowed with all types of virtues, that he or she will achieve liberation in eight human lifespans *(Praśamarati-prakaraṇa* 302-308).

The formulation of worthy and unworthy actions (an unknown formulation in ancient Jainism) only makes sense when a great body of laypersons come together to form part of the community. This fact is inevitably and coherently linked to an extensive mythology and cosmology replete with heavens and hells. In Jainism, the labour of introducing these concepts is also owed to Umāsvāti, who made the path of spiritual progression equally compatible with the activity of laypeople. For many such, their religion is at bottom a question of generating "good *karma"* and securing a good rebirth. The parallelism with Buddhism and Hinduism is very clear.

In fact, it should be noted that for the majority of Indians the value placed on the law of *karma* does not reside as much in its rational explication of diversity, as in its ethic and, to a lesser extent, soteriologic value. What is more, almost nobody bothers to look too deeply into the mechanisms and implications of the subject. It is an aprioristic axiom, and one of the fundamental points of reference of the tradition in its totality (not a mere philosopher's speculation). There is no attempt to prove whether the "law" can or cannot be empirically demonstrated. It is taken for granted.

Thus, *karma* does not claim to be the only source of explanation for our situation, nor is it merely a solution for theodicy. Turning to other agents (witchcraft, planetary conjunctions, and so forth), shows that in people's eyes, *karma* is not the only rational explication, but a point of reference (being the most approved and accepted by the masters) relating to a superior moral and cosmic *or-der.* From the layperson's point of view, what matters is not knowing why we are trapped, but in determining how to act, how to do good deeds. It has nothing to do with cataloguing our past lives, as some New Age spiritual practices tend; this would be considered a distraction, a waste of time and precious energy (Chapple 1990: 258). *Karma* rewards worthy action with the purification of the soul from evil and attachment. By cultivating appropriate behaviour, the effects of past actions can be mitigated and eventually eliminated. For this reason, some treatises formally included worthy action *(puṇya)* and unworthy action *(pāpa)* as two more of the fundamental principles in Jainism *(tattvas)* *(Uttarādhyayana-sūtra* 28.14).

Once the ethic impact of the doctrine on people has become clear, what we are interested in pointing out in this chapter are the karmic mechanics according to Jain theoreticians: their explanation to the situation of bondage.

The first thing that one gathers is that whether the amount of merit or demerit is lesser or greater, *all* action leads to rebirth. Merit does not lead to liberation, but to a better rebirth. This is how Kundakunda explains it:

> "A shackle made of gold is as good as one made of iron for the purpose of chaining a man. Similarly *karma* whether god or bad equally binds the *jīva*" (*Samayasāra* 146).

Although with worthy action one is presented with a brighter future, virtuous behaviour alone can never lead to liberation. I must make clear that rather than go into the moral implication of action now, what interests us here is its metaphysical aspect. Here is where Jainism is insistent in stating that all intentional action will bear its fruit, which will make us return to the *saṃsāra.* It is clear that the doctrine of *karma,* rather than explaining the situation of people, and more than offering a pattern of behaviour, was formulated to deconstruct the mundane. The formulation of a law of causal dependence makes no sense without the proclaiming of an escape route from the swarm of causes and effects, without the proclamation of the possibility of *realisation* of the unconditioned state *(nirvāṇa, mokṣd).* So, we should hardly be surprised to see that the idea came about through circles of renunciants, Brāhmaṇic and Śramaṇic alike, whose objective was to escape from the contingency, causality and what is temporary. Nor is it by chance that the first mention of *karma* would take the form of a secret doctrine that the sage Yājñavalkya revealed to his student in the depths of the forest.

THE INFLOW OF *KARMA*

These ideas are shared by other Indian soteriologies, but if Hindus consider *karma* to be a transcendental and invisible power that accompanies the agent's coarse and subtle levels, as a moral substrate, Jains are the only ones to state that this power is *matter* in the literal sense. In Hinduism and Buddhism *karma* is without form *(amūrta).* In Jainism *karma* has a specific form. For this reason, they call it karmic matter *(kārmaṇa-pudgala).* Since it is made up of material atoms, *karma* is another component of the *ajīva,* the non-spiritual. All this has not to be taken metaphorically. The fact is as follows.

In Jainism, karmic matter moves around freely throughout the entire universe, as if it were interstellar dust. This fine dust is indifferent and it only becomes a precise type of *karma* when it interacts with a spiritual monad. When the soul acts, the surrounding karmic particles automatically infiltrate. This is what is called inflow *(āśrava).*

Thus, *karma* not only has a moral dimension, but also a physical implication. *Karma* is the committed action and *karma* is the matter that adheres to the agent. The two meanings of the word are inseparable. What was once karmic dust is now converted into *karma,* a physical substance, adhering to the soul.

It is said that when undifferentiated karmic matter adheres to the soul, it produces a vibration *(yoga)* with the spirit's energetic quality. This *yoga* allows the inflow of *karma.* Umāsvāti *(Tattvārtha-sātra* 6.1-2) resumes the classical approach:

> "The operation of the body, speech and mind is action *[yoga].*
>
> The threefold action is he case of the inflow *[āśrava] of karma".*

The concept of inflow or *āsrava* is one of the most important concepts in Jainism. It forms, nothing more and nothing less than the third fundamental or basic principle *(tattva),* coming after the reality of the *jīva* and the *ajīva.* Inflow is like the hole through which the karmic liquid or dust penetrates: like a magnet for the karmic dust drifting about the universe, or as Jain masters like to say, the *jīva* seems like a vessel in distress with countless breeches that let in karmic water, and these have to be sealed by correct spiritual practice. On penetrating into the soul, the subtle matter resulting from action becomes a specific type of *karma* (according to the nature of the action). Once it has adhered to the soul, *karma* is separated into a particular number of particles *(karma-prakṛtis),* each one having a different effect on the *jīva.* We shall soon take a look into this.

UNINTENTIONAL ACTION

We should stress that such vibrations of energy in the soul relate to the activities undertaken by the individual using their body, speech and thought. This is fundamental. Action is not only physical: it can also be dialectic or mental. In the final analysis, it is volitional.

If in a given action it is not only the deed itself that counts, but also the associated thought and intention (to the point that it is the intention that is considered to be *karma)* the issue presents us with a problem. What happens with actions caused by mistake, unintentionally? Mahāvīra's answer, and that of ancient Jainism as a whole, is clear: even if they are unintentional, unworthy actions continue to be such *(Sūtrakṛtāṅga* 2.4.2-3). No action escapes the law of *karma.* The absence of unworthy intention does not absolve. A text such as the *Dasavaikālika -sūtra* (4.1) insists that careless action whether intentional or not, leads the soul to bondage. Perhaps, the intensity and duration of *karma* might be less, but not for this reason does it cease to "pollute" the soul. However, this position needed to be modified if Jainism wanted to prosper, not only among laypersons, but even among renunciants. So later, philosophers were not so tough on this issue. The *Vyākhyā-prajñāpti* (3.3 [182b]) comments that involuntary unworthy actions on the part of ascetics during their spiritual labours are liberated in the shortest possible amount of time and, therefore have no effect. Finally, with Kundakunda's help we get closer to the classical position:

> "If a subtle living organism is crushed or killed with he contact of the feet in movement of an ascetic who is careful in his walking towards his destiny, the scripture does not hold him liable even for a slight bondage as a consequence of that" *(Pravacanasāra* 217.1-2).

Emphasis is put on the inner state *(bhāva)* in which action is carried out and not the physical deed in itself. Therefore, ascetics who maintain their internal purity, externally reflected by adhesion to monastic rules, are free of all violence and its effects.

In the centuries that span from Mahāvīra to Kundakunda, Jainism underwent change in the same direction as Buddhism (possibly in the lead): the karmic quality of an act is decided by the intention and internal state that accompanies it, and not by the deed in itself. Ancient Jainism is close to the ideal of a superhuman ascetic absolutely detached from the world and concentrated on the permanent care and control of their actions, but such a model could not be very popular and would always depend on factors, circumstances and accidents beyond the ascetic's control. It is Kundakunda who takes the definitive step in stating that, once ascetics *realise* their own spiritual nature, they cannot then be subject to bondage, since they are only knowledge *(jñāna) (Pravacanasāra* 159-160). As we shall see later on, the implications of Kun-dakunda's positions go deeper than may seem at first sight.

THE SOURCES OF *KARMA*

What are the sources of these *karmas*? Every action? One in particular? Properly speaking, the dust infiltrates as a result of any and every action, whatever it is. However, in the *Tattvārtha-sūtra* Umāsvāti distinguishes between acts accompanied by passion *(kaṣāya),* which produce karmic inflow, and acts free of passion. In the latter case, while there is karmic inflow, the resulting *karma* has no effect on the cycle of transmigration. This is one of Umāsvāti's innovations.

The philosopher mentions five types of activity, five "doors" which favour the entrance of karmic matter into the soul *(Tattvārtha-sātra* 8.1). The first is false belief *(mithyātva),* which means the belief in mistaken doctrines. The second is the lack of self-discipline *(avirati),* which must be interpreted as the attachment to worldly things: food, sexual pleasure, jewellery and other material objects. The more indulgent one is with these objects the more karmic matter infiltrates and sticks to the *jīva.* The third is laxity *(pramāda),* which is moral weakness and lack of attention. Violent action is that which is in reality committed through negligence and carelessness. Hence the meticulous care of ascetics when walking, talking, attending to the call of nature. The fourth type of activity, and without a doubt the one which carries the most weight, consists of the passionate activities *(kaṣāyas)* themselves. In Umāsvāti's opinion, passion holds the key to bondage. The term *kaṣāya* literally means "bond" (that which *bonds* or ties the *jīva* to this world), with the implicit meaning of passion.

It is the equivalent of the *kleśas* in Buddhism and Hinduism. By passions Jains understand all types of desire *(rāga)* and hate *(dveṣa),* usually expressed in the form of four very strong passionate activities: anger *(krodha),* pride *(māna),* deceit *(māyā)* and greed *(lobha) (Dasavaikālika-sūtra* 8.37). Passionate activity is nothing other than the expression of the sensation of an "I", an ego, an agent who desires, who depends on things, the very root of ignorance. Hence, the importance of dominating it. Passion is so cardinal an issue that Umāsvāti redefines violence *(hiṃsā)* as the destruction of life through passion *(Tattvārtha-sūtra* 7.8). The fifth activity through which karmic material is infiltrated is the above-mentioned mental, corporal or verbal activity or union *(yoga)* with worldly objects. If *yoga* is the true "door", passion, false beliefs, laxity and indiscipline are attitudes which allow the particles of cosmic dust to adhere to and bind the soul. A spirit characterised by these activities is like a sticky body to which the corresponding karmic material will inevitably adhere. Only arduous asceticism is able to burn it and to dry its stickiness.

Umāsvāti's task of systematising brought about a change in the notion of *karma.* All ancient Jainism's emphasis on physical, external action is redirected within. From Umāsvāti's standpoint, it is the volitional load of passion which binds us. This is a new development, because although it is true that dispassionate, non-violent action is the action of ascetics par excellence, if what really counts is the state of mind, intention and lack of passion, then being a layperson becomes less problematic. The doctrine is better adjusted to the needs of lay Jains, who can go about their activities without these necessarily implying violence and passion. For William Johnson (1995: 87), the importance of the *kaṣāya* doctrine of Umāsvāti lies in the way it provides an adequate framework for the layperson's daily behaviour. That is, it consolidates a rational framework so that ascetic and lay paths can justify themselves without mutually disqualifying each other.

However, the materialist conception of *karma* presents us with a problem which is difficult to solve. Kundakunda *(Pravacanasāra* 173) asks: how can something immaterial, such as the *jīva,* interact with something material such as *karma?* A similar problem arises in Sāṃkhya philosophy. The only answer is that such an association can be inferred from the real experience of bondage in which we find ourselves (Jaini 1979: 114), and because thousands of omniscients have proclaimed it as such. However, Kundakunda looks at it from another angle; and he comes to the conclusion that there is an external material *karma (dravya-karma)* and an internal immaterial *karma (bhāva-karma),* a modification in the consciousness of the *jīva.* Through certain attitudes *(bhāvas)* the *jīva* "invites" the material *karma* to infiltrate. The key to bondage is in the internal state of the *jīva.* It is the *jīva* that in the last analysis creates the *saṃsāra* through its impure, negative states and levels of consciousness *(bhāvas, upayoga).* According to the conventional point of view *(vyavahāra-naya),* the *jīva* is the cause that produces and modifies karmic matter; whereas from the higher point of view *(niścaya-naya),* the *jīva* is the agent, who produces modifications and transformations in its own consciousness *(Pravacanasāra* 184). From the higher plane, there is no contact between the *jīva* and *karma,* simply *karma* infiltrates into the same place as that occupied by the *jīva.* In sum, the *jīva* is pure consciousness and cannot transform matter, but it is conceded that the empirical, impure *jīva* is capable of modifying its consciousness under the influence of karmic matter. This new understanding has important implications in soteriology [see pages 505-510].

THE BONDAGE OF THE SOUL

Once passionate activities—or relevant mental states if we follow Kun-dakunda—have produced karmic inflow *(āśrava),* they irremissibly tie *(bandha)* the *jīva* down, like ballast that stops hot-air balloons from floating upwards. This condition of bondage of the *jīva* is *bandha.* Because of its ultra-light nature, following the law of its own lack of gravity, the *jīva* has a tendency to rise. Unfortunately, all the spirit's purity becomes literally contaminated by the karmic matter it has accumulated, due to the ignorance and nescience that impels it to act egotistically and passionately. The result is a small portion of eternity, *the jīva,* imprisoned in a material web. The Jain's goal is to cut free from these limitations caused by matter in such a way that the *jīva* is aligned with its nature of potential omniscience. While the soul is not freed, it is inevitably bound to the laws of birth and death, pleasure and pain. The bondage *(bandha)* of the soul to matter constitutes the fourth fundamental principal *(tattva)* proclaimed by Jainism. As can be seen, *āśrava* and *bandha,* inflow and bondage, are inextricably linked.

Once it has ripened, like fruit, *karma* is extinguished *(nirjarā)* and reverts back to its state of undifferentiated cosmic dust until the time when more passionate activity released from another living being congeals it once again and it associated with another soul. As the *Sarvārthasiddhi* (275; cited in Jaini 1979: 113), the most important commentary on the *Tattvārtha-sūtra,* has it:

> "The soul has successively taken in and cast off every particle of [karmic] matter in the universe".

It will be seen that the whole Jain soteriological edifice has to do with how to stop more *karma* infiltrating into the soul and how to dispel what is already accumulated, but we shall be discussing the way out of this dilemma later [see chapter 32]. For the moment, we will stay with the mechanism of *karma.*

SUBTLE PHYSIOLOGY

How does *karma* adhere to the soul? How can it produce its effect in later lives? Where does this extremely fine matter reside? To answer these questions one must tackle the subtle physiology of beings. Here is the true connection between the soul and matter.

Jains believe that all living beings are made up of different superimposed bodies. In general five are spoken of.

On the one hand, we have the ordinary physical body *(audārika-śarīra),* determined by a particular type of *karma* that regulates its constitution, size, sex, etc.

Then, there is the transformation or metamorphic body *(vaikriyā-śarīra).* This body, made up of very fine matter, can change in size, which explains the "miraculous" nature of certain beings. This body only exists among divine beings, hell beings, certain animals and spiritually advanced human beings.

Then, there is the so-called transference body *(āhāraka-śarlra),* which allows the soul to act at "a distance" from the physical body. It is a subtle body only recreated for a few moments by very advanced ascetics, which enables them to astral-journey to consult with omniscient beings about difficult points in teachings, while their material bodies remain in their original position.

The fourth possible body is the energy body *(taijasa-śarira),* composed of igneous matter. It is responsible for the vital temperature of beings. Among other things, it is also used to digest food.

Finally, we have the subtle body which is fundamental to understanding the mechanism of transmigration: the karmic body *(kārmaṇa-śarīra),* made up of the totality of karmic matter associated to the soul. This body stores *karma* and is the vehicle which will accompany the soul on its transmigration. It is continually transforming as every action leaves its impression there. As the *ācārya* Mahāprajñā (1998: 189) says, is like an enormous computer that register each vibration and gives out in course of time the consequences thereof.

Each one of these five bodies is more subtle than its predecessor but at the same time denser (made up of more particles). All unliberated souls possess the fourth and fifth bodies, with which they have been associated since time immemorial *(Tattvārtha-sūtra* 2.42). In addition, they may have one or two of the other bodies.

The idea of a material body, which envelops other energetic and subtle bodies, also exists in the Vedānta philosophy, although formulated in a different way. This is the famous theory of the five sheaths *(kośas),* already mentioned in writings as ancient as the *Taittirīya-upaniṣad* (2.2-5).

COLOURS

Another very graphical way to illustrate the inflow of karmic matter into the "room" occupied and illuminated by the "flame" of the soul, is the theory of colours (*leśyās)* or the spiritual colouration of the *jīva.*

For Jains, activity tints matter and soul as if it were a dye. That is, infiltrating *karma* is dyed the colour corresponding to the nature of the activity committed, and the soul will take on this colour. Accordingly, the colour of the soul indicates its level of bondage to the world, its level of spiritual purity. The

Uttarādhyayana-sūtra (34.1-9) mentions six colours. The souls that are in transit through infernal existences are black, blue or grey. Souls of lesser animals can also be yellow. Those of divine beings are yellow, pink or white. Human beings' souls can be any of the shades or shadows (von Glasenapp 1925: 210-211). This theory is similar to that of auras and halos, and it is almost identical to the Ājīvikas' theory of human classes *(abhijātis)* [see page 118]. What we have here is possibly the predecessor to the sophisticated Sāṃkhyan theory of qualities *(guṇas)* of existence: luminosity *(sattva),* energy *(rajas)* and darkness *(tamas).* The link between the *leśyā* and the *guṇa* theories could be find in Patañjali *(Yoga-sūtra* 4.7).

A beautiful parable tells of six men approaching a mango tree laden with fruit. All six were hungry and wished to eat, but to climb up the tree would mean harming the multiple life forms which inhabited it. One of the men (the one with the black shade), suggested cutting the tree down. The second one (coloured purple), conceived the plan of cutting down only the thick branches. The third (grey-tinted) only the thin branches. The fourth (orange) the little twigs. The fifth (pink) just the fruit. The sixth (white in colour) only the ripe mangoes which had already fallen to the ground. The parable anticipates modern ecology by many centuries, in the light of the Jain theory of *ahiṃsā.* Each man in the fable represents a particular spiritual state or level, from the lowest to the highest. Consequently, each one is tinted with the relevant *leśyā.* Omniscient beings—who by the way are able to perceive the auras of others—have a white *leśyā;* but liberated ones *(siddhas)* no longer have any *leśyā* at all.

VARIETIES OF *KARMA*

Starting with Umāsvāti, Kundakunda and Nemicandra, numerous of Jain scholars have been concerned with explaining the mechanism of *karma* and its varieties. Later on, a series of highly technical treatises, the *Karmagranthas,* were devoted to meticulously classifying and expounding on the different varieties of activity and their inevitable consequence. They constitute, in turn, a distinctive characteristic of Jain philosophy. Thanks to these treatises the Jain theory of *karma* is much more elaborated and systematised than its Hindu and Buddhist counterparts. In Śvetāmbara Jainism, the *Pañca-saṃgraha* by Candra Rsi and the *Karmagrantha* by Devendra Sūri (13th-14th centuries) are the most important treatises. In Digambara Jainism, the greater part of their teachings on *karma* is found in their venerated *Saṭkhaṇḍāgama* and *Kaṣāyaprābhṛt.*

The classifications of *karma* are important to Jains because it is here that they can be informed about which activity leads to and implies what consequence. However one should not take the lists too literally, for fear of falling into the determinism that Jainism has always abominated. Strict determinism would eliminate the whole Jain soteriologic edifice at a stroke. According to Jainism, *karma* establishes the conditions and possibilities in the life of an individual, but it is not responsible for every event and plan of action of any given individual.

Normally, the *Karmagranthas* take into consideration four aspects of *karma,* or four ways of considering human bondage—which is the relevant one, so-teriologically speaking. First, it can be considered in terms of the intensity *(anubhava)* with which the karmic material is tied to the soul. Second, it can be handled according to the number of particles *(pradeśas)* which have adhered to it. Obviously, the amount of infiltrated karmic matter depends on the intensity of the activity and (an important point, this) it would also depend on the mental state at the time of its assimilation. The more intense the action or passion the more compacted would the infiltrated karmic matter be. Thirdly, the *Karmagranthas* consider the time *(sthiti)* taken for the matter to have an effect on the soul, and the duration of such effects. Certain karmic particles can bear fruit straight away, within 48 minutes, and last for a split second, while others can hold themselves latent for extremely long periods, almost as long as a cosmic cycle even, but at a given moment they will bring about their consequence. Lastly, scholars consider the nature *(prakṛti)* of each type of *karma,* Here we shall not consider the first three aspects but instead focus on the different types or natures of *karma,* which is the most significant consideration when seeking to understand the subject.

When karmic matter comes into contact or association with the soul it transforms into two types of *karma.* On the one hand, we have destructive *karmas (ghātiyās)* or that which has a negative effect on the qualities in the soul. On the other hand, we have neutral *karmas (aghātiyās)* responsible for certain conditions in transmigration. These two categories of *karma* each subdivide into four types.

Within the destructive *karmas* we have: (1) *karmas* which darkens or obscures perception *(darśanāvaraṇīya);* (2) that which darkens or obscures knowledge *(jñānāvaraṇīya)*; (3) that which darkens or obscures energy *(vīryāntarāya);* and (4) that which pollutes happiness *(mohanīya).* Within the neutral *karmas* we have: (5) that which determines body type, *(nāma)*; (6) that which decides one's social or family situation *(gotra);* (7) that which concerns pain and pleasure in worldly experience *(vedanīya);* and (8) that which decides one's life span *(āyus).*

In a meticulous and indeed somewhat tedious way, the *Karmagranthas* offer all manner of technical explanations about the details of the absorption of *karma.* When a *karma* particle is absorbed by the *jīva* and lodged in the karmic body it divides automatically and in specific proportions, into each of the eight varieties of *karma.* According to karmic calculation, the major part of *karma* will go to those that concern pain and pleasure in worldly experience *(vedanīya),* and the least part to what decides life span *(āyus),* and *karma* can be divided up yet again into 148 sub-varieties of each of the eight types. Karmic accountancy is likely to prove confusing to readers if we concentrate too much to the 148 sub-varieties, so here let us be more concise and dwell on the eight main types of *karma.*

DESTRUCTIVE *KARMAS*

The first type of *karma* clouds the spirit's capacity for perception and vision *(darsanāvaraṇiya).* It particularly acts upon the sensorial and empirical types of perception *(mati-jñāna),* along with articulated perception *(śruta-jñāna).*

The second variety of *karma (jñānāvaraṇiya)* complements the preceding one, clouding over the other three forms of knowledge and awareness as conceived by Jains. It acts upon limited supernatural knowledge *(avadhi-jñāna),* telepathy *(manaḥparyaya-jñāna)* and the ultimate, superior knowledge *(kevala-jñāna).*

These two varieties of destructive *karma* have much to do with the way of understanding the world. People affected by these two types of *karma* (and we all are, to a greater or lesser extent affected) have their perception and knowledge completely obfuscated. They would be absolutely heterodox or could hardly come to have faith in Jainism. It will take an arduous task of introspection, which in Jainism is called right vision *(samyak-darśana),* to open up one's eyes and destroy these varieties of *karma.*

The third type of *karma* is illustratively called the obstacle *(antarāya)* of the soul's energy *(vīrya),* which weakens it. Alteration of the quality of the spirit's energy produces a vibration *(yoga),* which in its turn will attract more karmic material. Generally, this *karma* manifests as a brake on our giving, or an incapacity to obtain or enjoy things, over and over again.

The fourth type of negative *karmas* is the most important and most difficult to conquer or overcome. These *karmas* contaminate the spirit's happiness to such a degree that it finds itself affected by the greatest confusion and the deepest of passions. The whole structure of karmic bondage is based on these "deceptive" *karmas (mohanīya),* as their destruction allows for the elimination of all other varieties of *karma.*

Within this category, there are *karmas* similar to the *darsanāvaraṇiya-karmas* which impede knowledge of the true religion inherent to every *jīva* as a natural course (von Glasenapp 1915: 8). A soul infected by this type of *karma* has the particularity of seeing things as different from what they really are (Jaini 1979: 118). Eternalists and annihilationists are a good example of this. There are also sceptics and nihilists; and the misguided people who believe in the sacrifice of animals or who believe in a God who provides and punishes.

Another type of *karma,* which enters into this category, and possibly the most important of all, is that which obstructs behaviour. *Karmas* of this type generate passion and desire in human beings—and are naturally produced by passionate activity and attachment. Sixteen types of passion *(kaṣāyas)* are mentioned, including those cited earlier: anger, pride, deceit, and greed. Other lesser types, which come under this category, are sensual pleasure, having no sensual pleasure, laughter, sadness, fear, sexual appetite, etc. This *karma* has a direct influence on the type of future rebirth [see later].

Even when someone manages to overcome these forms of *karma,* there are still more, which cloud over one's positive tendencies towards renouncement and austerity. The subtlest passionate forms induce one to apathy and lack of willpower, which are in truth other forms of attachment. The *karmas,* which bring about this are among the most difficult to overcome. In fact, no other *karma* can be eliminated, while these *karmas* that cloud over the soul's happiness remain active.

NEUTRAL *KARMAS*

We shall now look at the first of the neutral varieties of *karma.* What are known as *nāma-karmas* are responsible for many aspects of the body in a new rebirth. Obviously, their function depends on the presence and quantity of negative *karmas,* so that they act in a more mechanical way to construct the new destiny. Influenced by this, the *nāma-karmas* will determine the soul's destiny *(gati)*—as divine being, human, animal or infernal being, and its birth within one of these destinies (as an elephant, a celestial musician, a tuft of moss, etc.), with a physical body along with its specific features of size, form, gender, constitution, etc., apart from the characteristics of the other subtle bodies. The *Kar-magranthas* speak of 93 sub-divisions of this type of *karma,* some of them very curious—such as the one that causes the body above the navel to be beautiful, and the *karma* that endows honour and glory, and the one that makes a person unfriendly or the one that causes the *jīva*, once its body is dead, to go to its correct destination. The most important sub-variety is the *karma* that will form the body of the *tīrthaṅkara,* an extremely rare *nāma-karma,* which is linked to a multitude of exceptional circumstances in previous lives.

The sixth type of *karma* will determine the likelihood of birth in a family of noble or otherwise lineage, along with physical strength, splendour, saintliness, wisdom and all their opposites.

The *vedanīya-karmas* are responsible for the feelings of happiness or un-happiness and the feelings of pain and pleasure in the face of the circumstances of life. With animals and creatures from the infernal regions, disagreeable feelings are predominant. In gods—and to a lesser extent human beings—agreeable feelings predominate.

Lastly, the *āyus-karma* will define the life span of they *jīva* in its next reincarnation. Strictly speaking, it will define a certain quantity of life (Schubring 1934: 185), as we are talking about material particles and not about a lapse in time. One good thing to say about the *āyus-karma* is that unlike the other types *oī karma* it sticks to the soul in the last third of a person's life and is never carried over to other existences (Stevenson 1915: 181). The implication is clear. Through good behaviour at the end of their lifetime, Jains can partly define the *karma* of life span in their next life. However, the doctrine tends to be somewhat fatalist, as it implies that the life span of this life is determined in the last phases of the previous one. Just as in other Indian religions, Jainism considers that the mental and spiritual state at the moment of death is particularly important [see page 488].

INCARNATION

At the moment of physical death, the *karmas* adhering to the soul will have defined to a large extent the conditions in a future incarnation. No one can predict what these will be, since karmic arithmetic is inscrutable and unfathomable, but we do know its mechanisms, and the computation of quality, quantity, duration and intensity of the eight (or 148) types of *karma,* is inscribed perfectly in the karmic body and the energy body, as if it were a genetic code. During the infinitesimal fraction of time in which the soul leaves the physical body, it is only tied to these two subtle bodies. It is said that as the last portion of one's life span *(āyus)* is extinguished, the weightless *jīva* flies at incredible speed until the heaviness, density and gravity of millions of *karmas* brings it down into a new incarnation. And, as Walther Schubring (1934: 195) puts it, in summary, it enters into the new life as a whole, real and independent, on its own responsibility and through its own *karma,* by force of good, evil and mixed deeds.

Given that Jains do not suscribe the notion that the soul pervades de whole cosmos *(vibhu),* they have described the movement of the *jīva* in the moment of transmigration *(Tattvārtha-sūtra* 2.26-30). This instantaneous moment (no more than four *samayas)* between one existence and another, has spared Jains all manner of speculation, all too common among Buddhists and Hindus, over what happens to the transmigrating entity in the stage *between* one incarnation and the next. Similarly, no type of mortuary rite on the lines of a funeral (*antyeṣṭi)* and the offerings to the departed *(śrāddhas)* typical of Hindus, is necessary to facilitate the journey. The *Sūtrakṛtāṅga* (2.3.21) has it that the *jīva* which is lodged in the correct womb and, feed on the nenses of the mother and the semen of the father, gradually increasing and attaining to the proper dimensions of a foetus, they come forth the womb. Here once again Jainism is different from Hinduism and Buddhism. For the latter systems the problem of transmigration (our earthly bondage) is fundamentally epistemic. The problem is ignorance *(avidyā)* of our true reality or essence. For classical Jainism, bondage to the world is, *in addition,* ontological in nature. *Karma* is a physical burden adhering to the soul, a corporeal prison. *jīvas* are living entities with bodies because they have acted, spoken, desired or thought. They have weighed themselves down with matter, and according to their acts, their rebirth will be of one sort or another. An organism is no more than the external manifestation, formed by a number of material and subtle superimposed layers, of a whole series of desires, attachments, emotions, intentions or thoughts from previous lives.

Part XI

Practice

In the West, the words "belief or "faith" are usually taken to be synonymous with "religion". One is asked, "do you believe in God?" Depending on the reply, one is catalogued as a believer, an atheist or an ineffable agnostic. In India, things work somewhat differently. Few people adhere only *nominally* to a religious tradition. A Jain is not just that son or daughter of parents belonging to a Jain caste, and/or one who believes in the truths of Jainism. Above all, Jains are those who follow guidelines and recommendations which distinguish them; they are those who *practice* Jainism. Beliefs and affiliations go along with the practice. Like most Indian traditions, Jainism constitutes more an orthopraxis than an orthodoxy (Staal 1975: 173). Speaking of Hinduism and of Indian religiosity in general, Frits Staal (1990: 389) provides a very graphic example: a Hindu could be a theist, a pantheist, an atheist, a communist and believe whatever he likes, but what makes him into a Hindu are the ritual practices that he carries out and the rules to which he adheres; in short, what he (or she) *does.* What Jains do, Jain orthopraxis, forms the contents of this Part. Bearing that in mind, I can state that this is the most important section of the whole book.

Although there are differences between Digambaras and Śvetāmbaras in terms of ritual recommendations and the way these are performed, conceptually a single ensemble of Jain guidelines can be defined. Anyone who follows them can be considered, *de facto,* a Jain—although, I repeat, such considerations are not attached too much importance in South Asia. I have grouped them in the following ten points:

(1) worship of the *tīrthaṅkaras (deva-pūjā);* (2) festivals and celebration of holy days *(utsava);* (3) pilgrimages *(yātrā);* (4) generosity *(dāna);* (5) rites of passage *(saṁskāras);* (6) homage to the masters *(guru-upāsti, vandana);* (7) confessions *(pratikramaṇa);* (8) fasts *(pratyākhyāna, tapas);* (9) study *(svādhyāya);* and (10) meditation *(sāmāyika).*

Many of these recommendations, quite fully followed by most Jains, are clearly interconnected and tend to be carried out simultaneously. For example, when lay Jains go to venerate a master, they may also carry out ritual confession, or the other way round, when they practice meditation or embark on a fast, the ritual requires homage to the master.

Ascetics perform many of these practices (fasting, meditation, confession, etc.), which are considered obligatory for them *(āvaśyakas)*. However, given that their orientation is somewhat different, and given that some practices (generosity, rites of passage, festivals) do not apply to them we shall concentrate here basically on lay religious practice. Without at any point losing sight of the ascetic ideals, since several of these practices establish the primordial core of Jainism: the interrelation and exchange between lay and ascetics.

What do lay Jains seek in carrying out these practices? Basically they aspire to acquire religious merit *(puṇya)*. By marking up a good karmic score they are paving the way to a future existence in one of the heavens *(deva-loka)* or in a Land of Bliss *(bhogabhūmi),* although all this might contradict the ascetic ideal of the destruction of all *karma,* which is the only way to reach liberation. It is as though the ideal of lay Jainism takes them away from the otherworldly goal of liberation *(mokṣa),* as if they were unable to assimilate it into their every day lives. Are there two Jainisms, as we asked in the Introduction?

Having reached this point it would be useful to pause and think about this. There is a tendency to think of the ascetic Jainism of the monks as the true orthopraxis, and the Jainism of the laity as a lesser and more popular form of religiosity. A Jainism of the "small tradition" as the anthropologists would say. This perception—which by the way is identical to perceptions held of Buddhism (Swearer 1995: 5-7)—is due in part to the fact that the experts never understood how an ascetic path, one that was purely soteriological, could become a religion in the broadest and most conventional sense. Only a sort of concession to popular spirituality, necessarily with influences from the Hindu environment could seemingly explain such a fact. This would resolve, what is more, the apparent discord between monastic practices and goals and the activities and goals of the lay community.

There is no question that there is influence from the surrounding Hindu culture and there have been concessions to popular needs. In fact, the total exclusion of ascetics from most lay rituals (cult of the *jinas*, rites of passage, etc.) has helped greatly to harmonise practices with those of the surrounding environment. Yet an explanation framed *solely* in these terms would seem one-sided. The dividing between monastic and lay practices is not as obvious as at first seems. The practices of lay worshippers are not concessions to the plebs. A meticulous study of religious practices reveals that ascetic models have penetrated their practices. They are not, certainly, practices preparatory to renunciation, as ascetics would be pleased to say,* but are practices adapted to the Indian environment of which they also form part and are constantly fed by ascetic values pertaining to Jainism.

* The same is true of the Brāhmaṇical scheme of life stages *(āśramas)* and aims in life *(puruṣārthas)* which lead finally to renunciation *(saṃnyāsa)* and the search for liberation *(mokṣa)*. It is clear that Indians do not feel about their practices in as an ideal a way as their religious leaders would like.

The model of spiritual progress, which we shall look at in the last Part [see chapter 31] takes it that there are all sorts of continuities between lay and monastic practice, and the treatises that concentrate on the discipline of lay Jains, the Śrāvakācāras, indicate a path of purification for lay persons which is identical to that followed by ascetics, if somewhat softened. Of course, it is not completely clear to what extent the recommendations in these treatises—written almost all of them by medieval ascetics—have been and still are followed by lay Jains, but their general influence on the tenor of the community and on many of its practices is plain to see.

Accommodation to the surroundings, similarly, did not occur indiscriminately. Recall Somadeva, the master who postulated a dual or two-fold *dharma* for lay people: firstly, mundane practices *(laukika);* above that, the other-worldly path *(pāralaukika)* leading to liberation. Although Somadeva did accept local customs and laws, he condemned many of the practices of Hinduism: Sun worship, the Vedic ritual of conjunction *(saṃdhyā),* the sacredness of cows, tree worship, funerary offerings *(śrāddhas),* bathing in rivers to achieve merit, Somadeva and other masters were unflaggingly against the position and the nature of certain Hindu divinities.

Thanks to such efforts, the "popular Jainism" of the lay community has remained pretty well linked to the "otherworldly Jainism" of the ascetics. During the rainy season, when the ascetics settle down temporarily, relations between the two groups become very close. This connexion serves as a counterbalance to the complete exclusion on the other hand of the ascetics from lay religious ritual, and it serves to both preserve the monastic tradition and to imbue lay practice with ascetic values. For these reasons it would be reductionism to set up a division between the authentic Jainism as practised by monks and nuns, and a light brand of Jainism amongst the laity. As Padmanabh Jaini (1991: 188) has so graphically expressed it, the lay community live a kind of amphibian life, with one foot on the mundane path of making money and gaining merit, and the other, a little more diffident, set on the path to *nirvāṇa.*

I agree with Kendall Folkert (1993: 10) in that it would be fair to classify the practices of Jainism in two essential types. First those practices (monastic and lay) basically shaped by the ascetic ideal, and second, those practices (mainly lay) that are less directly linked to asceticism. Many of these practices, especially the first (fasts, meditations, confessions) not only generate spiritual worth *(puṇya),* but imply the extinction *(nirjarā)* of karmic matter, a question that, as we shall see in the last Part, is crucial for progress toward liberation. Accordingly, lay practice, provided they have been carried out in a state of austerity and sincerity, involve much additional soteriological value. Thanks to such, the ascetic values of Jainism can be incorporated into the this-worldly lives of the lay Jains. When laypeople begin meditation, fasting, or go to confession, they see themselves as strivers *(Śramaṇas)* or bondless ones *(nirgranthas),* burning *karma* by means of spiritual ardour *(tapas).* For many

Jains, if heaven or *nirvāṇa* awaits them after an exemplary life, that is not the point.

The most extended external and visible religious practice of the Jain religion is *jina* worship. Although Jainism has remained somewhat more distanced than Hinduism from the classical way of devotion *(bhakti-mārga),* it would be a mistake to consider it as a religion exclusively for superhumans seeking enlightenment. The *sādhus* and *sādhvīs* are a fundamental pillar of the community, and express to perfection the Jain ideal, but they are a minority, and for most laymen and women, devotional worship is essential. The latter is a religious area that is basically managed by them, and therefore beyond the control of monks and nuns and is less impregnated with ascetic values. This practice may not be the most relevant, but it is the most visible and is furthermore followed by millions of Jains. In addition, it is one of the practices that has endowed the lay community with a more pronounced sense of identity, since it possesses an enviable richness in its symbols.

Given that worship is intimately linked to the institutions, art, mythology, iconography, and even ontology, we shall be looking at these issues in the following chapter [26]. Conducting brief iconographic study we shall see that, despite its faithfulness to certain firm philosophical principles, Jainism has also gone through many complex changes in terms of ritual, symbology, and the pantheon of goddesses and gods. Subsequently, we shall move on to consider the forms of worship themselves [27].

In the following chapter, [28], we shall touch on other practices that are habitual among lay people. These are practices that, like *jina* worship, are less rooted in monastic ideals. Here, we find activities as important as pilgrimages, participation in festivals and the practice of generosity. Even so, thanks to these auspicious activities the links or bonds between lay and monastic communities are greatly strengthened. Perhaps ascetic ideals are less evident, but it is clear that through these, interaction between all members of the community as a whole is harmoniously intensified.

Finally, [chapter 29] we look at the most ascetic practice. For Jains, the most significant of religious activities perhaps is fasting. As this tends to be private, or when conducted communally, is generally performed in special settings, it is unlikely that the casual visitor will notice it. But fasting constitutes one of the clearest distinguishing features of Jainism. Along with confession, it is the activity that is perhaps most imbued with ascetic values, but it is not the only one. The veneration of the masters, meditation and study are equally integrated into the ascetic framework. Those who are most attentive to these practices are those who, in addition to garnering religious merit, adhere more closely to the ascetic ideals of the extinction of *karma* and most clearly are aiming at *nirvāṇa.*

26. JAIN ICONOGRAPHY

BRIEF OVERVIEW OF JAIN ART

Devotion to the *jinas* is a subject with many ramifications in art, in mythology, in social behaviour, and even in Jain philosophy. Before proceeding to look at worship proper, we need to dip into these fields.

First, we need to see that Jain "art" is not, and has never been "Art", in the sense that creativity has been perceived in the West from the 18th century onwards. Whether in sculpture, literature, dance, music, painting, theatre or poetry, what the Indian artist seeks to do is to create a state *(bhāva)* or aesthetic emotion *(rasa)* in the reader, the devotee or the beholder, such that the aesthetic sentiment elevates both of them and enables one to transcend any mundane or egocentric emotion. For that reason, Indian artists *(śilpin, kavi)* are invariably anonymous. They are not interested in being original or innovative, and do not even pursue their own ideal of beauty. Beauty consists in respecting the canons *(śāstras),* in being faithful to the iconography—which does not preclude innovation—and evoking the appropriate aesthetic taste *(bhāva, rasa)* in the connoisseur.* We do not have to do here with the isolated genius of the Romantic tradition of the West. At no point is there any mention of the artist as having special sensitivity or talent. The Indian artist is, if you like, the genius focussed on emulating the original creative act, an agent of liberation, and accordingly it is not unusual for them to be called adepts *(sādhaka)* or yogis *(yogin).* In the words of Chantal Maillard (1999: 14-15), Indian art is a *yoga,* a path for the development of self-awareness. Accordingly, Jain creative expression is inseparable from the Universal History, ritual, the practice of generosity, or the ideals of tradition. In this chapter, we shall try to piece all this together.

As far as possible, veneration for the *jina* and Jainism should translate into material generosity *(dāna)* to help in the construction and restoration of temples and images or for the consecration of statues to be honourable. The disproportionately

* Classical aesthetic theory speaks of nine flavours *(rasas):* erotic sentiment *(śṛṅgāra),* comic sentiment *(hāsya),* pathetic sentiment *(karuṇā),* furious sentiment *(krodha),* odious sentiment *(vibhatsā),* heroic sentiment *(vīrya),* terrible sentiment *(bhayānaka),* marvellous sentiment *(adbhuta)* and lastly, quiescent sentiment *(śānta).*

high number of Jain temples and images to be found throughout India is due to the prestige, the merit and the nobility associated with those who financed and carried out the construction of a *jina's* effigy or temple.

THE IMAGE OF THE *JINA*

The epicentre of Jain worship is the image, icon, or effigy *(mūrti)* of the *tīrthaṅkara.* Stylistically speaking, Jain sculpture follows virtually the same canons as Hindu or Buddhist art in India. The rules concerning symmetry, proportions of bodily limbs or the symbols (curly hair, large ears, nose like the beak of the *garuḍa* bird, the *svastika,* Moon, Sun and a shell in the hands.) are perfectly detailed in the treatises. The images share many of the distinctive marks *(lāñcharias)* and gestures of the hands *(mudrās)* of Indian sculpture. In fact, some statues of the Buddha in the classical lotus posture are still taken to be images of the *jinas,* and vice versa. The motif of the Buddha protected by the snake Mucalinda is practically indistinguishable from that of Pārśva.

The preferred iconography is that of the *jina* in meditation [see FIGS. 33, 47] seated in the lotus posture *(padmāsana)* surrounded by auspicious signs. The scene could represent the sacred assembly *(samavarasaṇa)* of the *jina* preaching his first sermon to the gods, humans and animals, or perhaps the last before attaining *nirvāṇa.* In addition, there are a good number of images that show the *tīrthaṅkara* on the posture of abandonment of the body *(kāyotsarga),* that is, standing and motionless, with arms hanging down [see FIGS. 1, 10, 32, 46]. This constitutes one of the classical postures for the practice of ascetism *(tapas)* and a distinctive feature of Jain iconography. These two iconographic postures are the *only* ones allowed. Obviously, in the murals and bas reliefs there abound representations of the five auspicious moments of any *jina's* life, and the tales of the tradition, such as the battle between Bāhubali and Bharata, earlier existences of Pārśva, Mahāvīra and Śāntinātha, Nemi's "wedding", but even in these cases—as also in the pamphlets, comics, or illustrations of manuscripts—from the moment when the *jina* has attained omniscience, only the *kāyotsarga* or the *padmāsana* postures are possible. Things go on around him, but he remains impassive, seated or standing. As James Laidlaw (1995: 249) has pointed out, there is great reluctance to think that the *jina* might do anything.

Once the image has been sculpted by the artist, it should be consecrated *(pratiṣṭhā)* by a master or *guru* at an astrologically favourable moment. Some images are also famous for their sacredness attributed to supernatural origins [see page 318].

Owing to the emphasis on non-violence, the aesthetic flavour *(rasa)* most appreciated by the Jains is that of serenity, quiescence and peace *(śānta).* And according to the Kashmiri philosopher Abhinavagupta (11th century), arising as it does from mental calm the *śānta-rasa* is the state of peace out of which all *rasas* come. It is that level of consciousness in which all emotional states appear in their true nature: transitory (Maillard and Pujol 1999: 92). In all refined Jain art we will find nothing similar to the explosion of strength and motion of Hindu art. The vitality (the multiple heads and arms, symbol of divinity and energy) typical of Hindu images, is deliberately ignored. The inactivity and quietude of *the jinas* better reflect the ideal of this tradition. The non-attachment of the *jina* is such that he would not act or come for the benefit of anyone. In time, the Buddha came to be represented in other different iconographies *(abhaya-mudrā, varada-mudrā,)* that show his preoccupation and infinite compassion for the people of this world. That is unthinkable for a *jina.*

The body of the *tīrthaṅkara* is a mine of symbologies and parallels. All bodies are the consequence of the *karmas* of previous existences. It follows on logically that the *tīrthaṅkara* resides in a perfectly robust anatomy of unsurpassed purity—but without a trace of muscles—with diamantine bones and a skin that cannot be broken [see FIGS. 46]. He never gets dirty or sweats, nor does his hair or nails grow. This notion is important to capturing the reach of Jain asceticism. The mortification of the body (in the manner of certain Śaiva ascetics) is not well thought of in Jainism. Jain *tapas,* is based on the principle of privation, and not mortification. To liberate the soul, the *jina* does not destroy his body. So important is the idea that the *tīrthaṅkara*'s body is perfect, that many debates and disagreements between Digambaras and Śvetāmbaras have had to do with the *jina's* corporeal necessities. As noted, the *tīrthaṅkara's* body has the auspicious marks that all sublime beings have and, as they advance towards omniscience, other marks or signs come to join these. The body, in short, is the mirror of the soul, and is represented thus in the iconography. The image of the *jina* houses a veritable ontology.

The effigies of the *tīrthaṅkaras* may vary according to religious group, the order or the region. Śvetāmbara images possess prominent glass eyes, with a fixed and somewhat icy gaze [see FIGS. 33, 34]. The idea is that the devotee or worshipper should *see* the *jina* preaching to the holy assembly and should see that the *jina observes* everyone. Their statues are also usually adorned with jewels and vestments [see FIGS. 10, 33]. The eyes of Digambara *jinas* always look inwards, since the *tīrthaṅkara* does not return the gaze of the devotee (Brand 1995: 74). Out of the entire range of Indian art, the Digambara Jains alone represent their saints totally naked. [see FIGS. 1, 32]. Hence, the Digambaraa preference for representations of the *jinas* in standing position, the only way in which their nudity can be clearly seen. In the case of sitting *jinas*, when the genitals cannot be detected, it is not unusual for there to be conflicts between Śvetāmbaras and Digambaras over the affiliation of the statue. As Heinrich Zimmer (1935: 84) perceived, this nudity is of an arid sublimity. The Jain artist reflects the complete anonymity of those who became liberated. The naked state expresses the complete lack of ties: the purity of one who has honed away all imperfection.

Given that all liberated souls are qualitatively identical there are no external signs that might distinguish one *jina* from another. The exceptions are Pārśva and Supārśva, who are always protected by a seven-, nine-, or 1,000-headed snake *(nāga),* which rears up above the figure of the *jina.* In some cases, Ṛṣabha is represented with long hair. Aside from a doubtful statue of a naked *yoginī,* which some have identified with Malli, not even the Śvetāmbaras represent the female *tīrthaṅkara* Malli with a woman's body. This has undoubtedly to do with the emphasis put on the notion that all *tīrthaṅkara* is, as it were, identical, replicable, interchangable. At a deeper level, it relates to the idea that liberated beings lose all sexual attributes. It is true that the *jinas* are represented with male bodies (solely in the case of the Digambaras) but even so their genitals are almost those of a child, and *jinas* are never portrayed ityphalic. India has always valued the androgynous that is beyond any characterisation.

Apart from these exceptions, the remaining *jinas* can only be identified by their emblems *(lāñcharias,* [see TABIE 1]) carved into the base of their pedestal, or the name that appears on the wall behind. This fact reflects to perfection the identically pristine nature of all liberated souls, and in this too, Jain iconography clearly departs from Hindu iconography.

Although the *jinas* are not adorned (in the case of the Digambara figures) or hardly so (Śvetāmbara figures),* it is quite usual to include in the work the eight accompanying symbols that are always close to all *tīrthaṅkaras:* a halo, throne, three parasols, *aśoka* tree, some flowers, drum, celestial music, and fan. It is said that these objects were created by the gods to show their veneration for the *jinas.* Another series of auspicious symbols *(maṅgalikas),* normally in this case too numbering eight, and which form part of a rich and very ancient symbolism, are engraved into the door jambs, in the effigy itself or in portable chapels [see FIG. 17]: the *svastika,* a floral symbol *(śrīvatsa)* on the chest [see FIG. 46], a pitcher *(kalaśa),* the throne on which the *jina* is seated *(bhadrāsana),* the *nadyāvarta* symbol, powder horn *(Vardhamāṇa),* couple of fishes *(matsya-yugma)* and mirror *(darpaṇa).* These symbols are present in all Jain temples and the majority of Jain homes. The Digambara version would substitute one or two of these by a parasol, a fan, a water pot or a fly switch.

Other important iconographic motifs are the wheel of the liberated ones *(siddha-cakra),* the footprints of the liberated *jina (pādukās),* a lectern which symbolically represents the master *(sthāpanācārya)* and certain mystic diagrams *(yantras)* which include syllables of power such as *Oṃ* or *Hrīṁ.*

Beside the *tīrthaṅkara,* Jain temples have images of the community's deities

* Notwithstanding, in *ritual* contexts, the ornamentation of Śvetāmbara images can be exuberant. In contrast to what we find in a museum, in Śvetāmbara temples the images are often profusely covered with garlands of flowers and gold leaf. It should be borne in mind that, as Ananda Coomaraswamy (cited in Cort 2007: 173) showed, the adornment of an image completes it and confers that which is essential to its validity. Hence John Cort (2007: 173) deduces that the Śvetāmbara use of ornamentation highlights the *jina* as monarch, whereas the naked and austere Digambara *jina* celebrates renunciation and asceticism.

or saints. These include the 11 *gaṇadharas,* with Gautama in first place. Unlike the *jinas,* however, the saints and spiritual leaders are often represented with the gauze mouth mask and the whisk broom of the renunciants, symbols of *ahiṃsā,* but also symbols of the renunciant tradition. In this way, they are represented more as transmitters than as leaders or "ford makers". In some figures, Gautama is depicted with his hand raised, in a gesture of "fear not" *(abhayamudrā)* typical of Buddhism. Gautama's compassionate and benevolent nature, very visible in festivals such as Dīvālī, his awakened or enlightened nature *(buddha),* not to mention his name, possess disturbing similarities with Gautama Siddhārtha the Buddha. Some Jains in Rajasthan have no hesitation in referring to Gautama simply as Buddha (Laidlaw 1995: 259).

Other popular figures are those of the lineage to which the temple belongs. This is the case with the *dādāgurus* of the Kharatara-Gaccha [see FIG. 39]. In addition to holding the whisk broom and the mask, the saints and masters of orders often also carry a sacred book. Given that the *gaṇadharas* heard the doctrine from the *jina,* they do not need help in textual form. But the masters of later times did need to rely on holy scriptures.

PAINTING

Special mention should be made of Jain painting, especially the illustrated manuscripts of western India, an art that reached its zenith between the 16th and 18th centuries. The illustrations of the lives of the *jinas* are always accompanied by mythological scenes and very elaborate symbology. They are simple in tone, almost naïf, colourful, attractive, but never seductive. Their mission is to help the reader's concentration or indeed explain graphically the main events in the lives of the *jinas* for those who could not read.

The frescoes of some caves and temples are just as notable. Of particular note are the Pudukottai frescoes in Tamil Nadu, which date from the 7th century, and those in certain caves in Orissa, which are even earlier.

THE TEMPLE

Of all Jain institutions, the most important is that of the temple *(mandira, caitya).* The lay community has devoted a considerable part of its wealth in construction and maintenance of temples. With vanishingly few exceptions, all local communities *(saṃghas),* however small, have one or more temples in the vicinity. Close to the temples, there will usually be the retreats for ascetics *(upāśrayas)** and other religious buildings.

Historically, the appearance of temples must have occurred around the 2nd

* Groups like the Sthānakavāsī or the Terāpanthī do not have temples, and so go to the retreats to carry out their religious rites. The equally iconoclastic Digambara Tāraṇapanthī use locals known as *caityālayas* where they venerate the books of Tāraṇa Svāmī.

and 1st centuries BC, when there is the attestation of a temple in Mathura [see page 214]. All the religious constructions dating from before this time are simple retreats for ascetics.

Architecturally, Jain temples follow the usual Indian patterns. They generally consist of an open space *(maṇḍapa)* in which there is a closed parlour *(sabhā-maṇḍapa)* containing the chapel *(garbhagṛha),* which houses the main image *(mūlanāyaka).* These areas are generally surrounded by a balustrade containing images of the other *tīrthaṅkaras,* deities and saints of the community. Normally, the structure as a whole is covered by a series of domes. The architectural and sculptural complex of any Jain temple taken as a whole can be considered a replica of the sacred assembly *(samavarasaṇa* [see FIG. 6]) so that the ornamentation of many of them can be incredibly elaborate and refined. Some of them are based on the same architectural floor plan as the sacred assembly *maṇḍala.*

Today, Jain temples are still outstanding for their beauty and perfect state of conservation. There are no better kept temples in India than those of the Jains. The efforts made by the community to renovate them and restore them are more than well-known all over India. In fact, most images in Jain temples were destroyed by Muslim or Śaiva depredation. Given that Jains do not permit mutilated statues within the shrine, statues and images have been constantly restored or replaced. Almost none of the Jain temples these days contains their original image.

In Gujarat, the most notable complexes are those in the sacred Shatrunjaya and Girnar mountains or those of the city of Ahmedabad. In Rajastahan, the outstanding examples are the complexes in Dilwara (Abu), the temple of Osian, and those of Ranakpur and Jaisalmer. In central India, there are the superb complexes of the Khajuraho and Gwalior, both in Madhya Pradesh. In the Deccan region, the best examples are those of Shravanabelgola, Mudabidri and Belgaum, in Karnataka, and of Muktagiri in Maharashtra.

THE "DIVINITY" OF THE *JINAS*

We now turn to forms of worship *(pūjā).* Anyone who has watched or taken part in a ritual in a Jain temple will have noticed the similarity with Hindu worship. Certainly, scholars may have detected distinctive features, but at first sight, the address, veneration and devotion, which is accorded to the *jinas* does not differ too much from that directed by Hindus to their gods, but the *jinas* are not gods. Not gods, but could it be that the worshippers take them as such? Is there perhaps a contradiction between the official atheism of Jain philosophy and the feeling and expression of the lay worship? Let us explore the question, vital as they are for understanding Jainism as it is practised in India.

From the lay perspective, the *tīrthaṅkaras* certainly evince certain similarities with the gods of the Hindu pantheon. For the lay worshippers, the *jinas* are like veritable deities *(devas)* and it is for that reason that the ritual veneration of the *jinas* is known as "worship of the divinity" *(deva-pūjā)*. Frequently, the *jina* is addressed as Supreme Lord *(parameśvara)* or Lord *(bhagavān),* titles that are also conceded to the Hindu gods, but these *jina-devas* are not gods. For Hemacandra *(Yoga-śāstra* 2.4), the term *deva* denotes an omniscient being who has described things as they really are, who has conquered the passions, and is venerated by the entire universe. That is a true *deva.* Not only that, but the Hindu gods, addicted to weapons, war, women, music, dance, rosaries, and other sectarian signs, cannot be considered, from the Jaina point of view, true divinities. The Jain literature does not pull punches in its, often very satirical, criticism of the supposed Lords of the universe. Śiva was a frequent target, sometimes depicted as a Jain ascetic fallen into disgrace, if not in more severe terms. The attitude towards Viṣṇu was more ambivalent, clearly enough because of Jainism's close links with the Vaiṣṇavas.

The Jain god *(deva)* is quite different from the Lord *(īśvara)* of Hinduism. Jains would never confuse their *tīrthaṅkaras* with any deity. So, what do we make of that?

Jains, basically, worship ascetics. This is a fundamental feature of the religion. The more ascetic the venerated being, the more worthy that being is of veneration. Paradoxically, the more ascetic he is, the more inaccessible he becomes, being more removed from this world. And so the more venerated he is, the less he responds. The *tīrthaṅkara,* who exemplifies asceticism taken to its ultimate conclusion, is then *inaccessible* for the worshipper. This is truly important.

Despita the affective link with the *jinas,* Jains know—at least in theory—that the *tīrthaṅkara* not only has no mission in the creation and preservation of the world, but having attained liberation, is a being who dwells in the confines of the non-world and can no longer intervene in the affairs of the cosmos. He cannot listen to their petitions; he cannot help them. Rather, he is aware of the devotees (since he is endowed with omniscience) but cannot answer them, for he has taken renunciation to its logical conclusion: he has broken off all links with the worlds of the cosmos. His help consists solely in the message he bequeathed the universe. It may be that he is called god, or it could be that in accordance with the modern Mūrtipūjakas like Ātmārāmjī, the totality of the souls who reside at the highest level of the cosmos are collectively called God (Cort 1995: 599), but this will always be an absentee "god", an absolutely transpersonal "lord". As Padmanabh Jaini (1979: 194) has put it, the *jinas* are venerated as a particular mode of the soul, as the ideal that the worshipper aspires to attain. The icon is used as an aid to visualisation, as a meditative support that will strengthen the correct vision. This logic underlying worship is typically Indian. For Hindus, anyone who meditatively fuses their thought with an object (whether a *guru,* a point of the body, a *tīrthaṅkara,* a god, etc.) will experience a profound change in their nature, and may end up becoming identified with the object meditated upon. The *deva* is, simply, the realisation of the *jīva* in the human being. It is the divinity or the omniscience within oneself that the *tīrthaṅkara* represents.

Even if the *jina* comes to occupy a central place, like that of the gods of Hinduism, and originates a plethora of fervent hymns, he will never be like the chosen deity *(iṣṭadevatā)* of Hinduism, with whom one can enjoy an intimate and personal relationship. For example, the goal of certain Vaiṣṇavas in North India, known as Puṣṭimārgīs (with whom Jains have close links) is to enter into a personal relationship of dependence with Kṛṣṇa. It is said that Kṛṣṇa is present in the image that represents him. In their relationship with Kṛṣṇa, Puṣṭimārgī worshippers can adopt various emotional attitudes *(bhāvas).* The most highly valued is the maternal attitude *(vātsalya)* (Barz 1976: 88). Devotees identify themselves with Yaśodā, the adoptive mother of Kṛṣṇa. In maternal spirit, they make offerings of food (highly esteemed by Puṣṭimārgīs, but taken a dim view of by Jains), which are called "bliss" *(bhoga).* Through the bliss they produce, Kṛṣṇa transforms them into "grace" *(prasāda).* The item of food, lovingly proffered by the believer, is divinely transformed by Kṛṣṇa, who in turn feeds the devotee with grace divine. The Kṛṣṇa devotee partakes of this food right there in the temple. None of this is feasible in Jainism because the deity, the *jina,* does not possess this transactional component that Kṛṣṇa or Viṣṇu have. *Jinas* are absolutely autonomous entities who do not respond to petitions, as we have said. John Cort (1998: 9) has rightly defined the *jina* as the exemplary Other, as an otherness without any presence. In this respect, Jain worship differs from that of Hinduism and is closer to Buddhist models. Like the *jina,* the Buddha attained *nirvāṇa* and is no longer present in this world. The offerings made to the Buddha, at least in South Asia (Sri Lanka, India) simply express reverence to the Buddha and his teachings. As in Jainism, there no transaction between the Buddha and the Theravādin devotee.

Having said that, this "absence" should not be taken too far or misinterpreted. On the one hand, this absence can be as rich and stimulating to the worshipper as any presence. On the other hand, in Indian spiritual language, the Jain layperson considers the *tīrthaṅkara* to be something like the great ancestor, he who showed the path in ancient times. It is said that the *tīrthaṅkaras* left behind them a kind of metaphysical echo of the goodness generated by their presence that continues to reverberate in the cosmos and which can be mobilised by means of the relevant rituals (Babb 1996: 7).

While the intentions behind Jain worship are not the same as those found for the most part in Hinduism, as Lawrence Babb's studies show (1998: 154-156), they share structural features with the Śaiva-Siddhānta worship of South India. We already looked at this in chapter 16. At the risk of being repetitive, it would be useful to recall some of the basic issues. For the Śaiva worshippers of the South, it is not a case of seeking union with Śiva, who remains an autonomous entity, but rather of becoming *a śiva,* with the same powers and qualities. As with *the jinas,* Śiva is an ascetic, a yogi free from attachments to this world and, as such, does not establish transactions with the devotee. It is true that, like the Kṛṣṇa of the Puṣṭimārgīs, it is thought that Śiva descends and enters into the *liṅga,* which serves as the physical vehicle for his presence. But the deity has scant if any transaction with the worshipper. What this is about rather is the purification of the soul *(ātmaśuddhi)* such that the devotee permanently takes on Śiva nature. This is very similar to what we find in Jain worship where the devotees seek to emulate the *jinas* rather than seek union with them or interact with them. In many aspects, it would seem as if Śaiva ritual culture were Jainism in a "Hindu" guise (Babb 1998: 155). As in Jainism, the food offerings to Śiva are not consumed by the worshippers. They are given to a ferocious deity known as Caṇḍa, who acts as guardian of the temple. These considerations have led Babb (1998: 156-157) to rethink ritual divisions in India, not in terms of Hindu and non-Hindu, but of traditions that emphasise transaction and those which do not, or only in attenuated form. While in terms of soteriology and doctrine, Jainism might be considerably different from the many and varied forms of Hinduism, ritually speaking its differences from forms like Śaiva-Siddhānta are much slighter. On the ritual level, borderlines are diffuse in India.

THE JAIN PANTHEON

People cannot direct their petitions and intercessory prayers to the *jinas,* but men and women all around the world have always prayed asking for prosperity, health, descendants, liberation, and Jains are no exception. So, who can answer the prayers of the devout Jain? There is not god who could answer the Jains, but there are *the jinas's* escorts *(sāmānikas),* the protecting deities *(śāsanadevatās),* the gatekeepers of the temple *(dvarapālas)* or of the temple territory *(kṣetrapālas).* Given that these gods and demigods dwell in the heavens and not in the Abode of he Liberated Souls, they are able to listen to the devotees [see FIG. 34].

Although many of these supernatural beings are not actually of Jain origin, and many masters were against their invocation [see below] around the 9th and 10th centuries it was decided to make their worship legitimate. The best solution was to unite them with the *jinas.* The importance of these gods, goddesses, and spirits in the religion of the people must not be underestimated. In fact, the *tīrthaṅkara* most loved and with the most temples dedicated to him, Pārśva, owes much of his popularity to the association with his protective deities, the *nāga* Dharaṇendra and the *yakṣī* Padmāvatī (Jaini 1991: 194-195). The representation of the *nāga* protecting a sitting Pārśva and Padmāvatī covering him with a parasol-since being a female she could not touch a male ascetic-appear in some caves at Ajanta dating from as early as the 9th century. Like old-time *yakṣas* and *nāgas* they have kept up their function as protectors. Protecting the *jinas* as they do at difficult or calamitous moments, it is natural that they should be invoked in worship as intercessors.

These divinities are all benevolent and capable of receiving and granting the petitions of the faithful. It is said that the divinities hearken to the call of the devotees *(bhakta)* and, full of compassion, go to their aid because they recognise their spirit of devotion *(bhakti)* not towards them but towards the *tīrthaṅkaras.* In any case, they do not fulfil any soteriological function. In the realm of art and the Jain conception of things, they come to play the same role as the *bodhisattvas* in Buddhism, although their worship is always subordinated to that of the *tīrthaṅkaras* and is rarely independent from them. In the elaboration of this pantheon and iconography of escorting gods and goddesses, the influences of Śaivism is detectable. It constitutes an influx of mundane values and, following up an observation by Paul Dundas (1992: 182), in its incorporation and association with the *jinas* a desire can be discerned on the part of Jainism to make certain concessions to the mundane aspirations of the lay followers.

THE GODDESSES

Very many of these divinities are goddesses and common to the Hindu pantheon. Indeed it is the goddesses and not the gods who in reality look after the devotees. In the Jain context, they are commonly called *yakṣis* or *yakṣiṇīs,* that is, angelic or numinous manifestations. Unlike many Hindu goddesses, the Jain ones are vegetarian, are unmarried and champion the values of non-violence and containment. Many act as protector goddesses of the family lineages *(kuladevatā)* of the Jain castes.

One of the most important is Cakreśvarī. She is the *yakṣi* who protects Ṛṣabha. It is said that she can confer prosperity and even liberation (?) from the earthly prison. Ambikā (or Rudrāṇī) is Nemi's protector or *śāsanadevatā.* She is especially popular among the Śvetāmbaras of Gujarat. In fact, mount Girnar, which has always been associated with the *jina* Nemi, was and is venerated by the Śāktas as a place sacred to the goddess Ambājī. Although there is actually nothing linking Ambikā to Nemi, Jains had no difficulty in making her Nemi's guardian goddess. In all probability, the most venerated of all the Jain goddesses was and is Padmāvatī, whom we mentioned above. She is also known as Lakṣmi or Śrī (Viṣṇu's consort in Hinduism). She is the patron of trade, fortune and beauty. The goddess is the object of enormous veneration [see page 433] because she protects areas of human activity that are vital for Jain traders.

The acceptance of certain of these goddesses was such that they even supplanted the *jina.* This was what happened in the medieval cult of Jvālāmālinī or of Padmāvatī, a cult energetically condemned by the masters.

Another venerated goddesses is Brahmī, the patron of wisdom, known in Hindu India as Sarasvatī . Other protector goddesses of wisdom are the 16 *vidyādevatās.* Like Hindu women, Jain women turn to "hot" goddesses (Śītalā, Māriyammāṉ, Manasā, Ṣaṣṭhī.) in the case of illness, or when epidemics strike. Not infrequently, they hire the services of a Brāhmaṇa, but the most normal thing is for the women to take special vows *(vratas)* to placate or appease the goddesses. At the same time, there exists a whole mythology and popular cult of the "little mothers" *(mātṛkās),* renowned for their magical powers, for their control of the flows of nature, for their physical strength and their horrid appearance, but in whom the maternal instinct is very strong. When their procreative powers are alluded to, they are frequently enumerated in groups of seven. They represent, possibly, the most elemental and yet most universal level of religiosity. No Indian religion or sect has succeeded in monopolising them. Thus, they are beyond Hinduism (Vaiṣṇavism, Śaivism, Śāktism, Jainism, or any other *-ism).*

THE GODS

Apart from the *nāga* Dharaṇendra, few masculine escorts or guardian spirits are as important as the goddesses. The gods seem to be nothing more than a "shadow" of the goddesses, in the words of Walther Schubring (1934: 16), but there are other powerful intercessors. Accordingly, Jains have the counterpart of the village deity *(grāmadevatā)* typical of the Hindus, which protects the settlement or the temple from calamities—and in which case receives the name of *kṣetrapāla.* Precisely the most popular "gods" are nearly all local protectors or guardians. Given that the *jina* has withdrawn into himself, he cannot have the function of protector. This mission is reserved for fierce guardians who need to be especially propitiated. Some of these are associated with tribal groups, and not necessarily Jain, but whose power has been completely linked with the image of a *jina.* This is the case of certain divine spirits of the earth *(bhomias), bhairus,* or *bhairavas* [see FIG. 36]. The Bhairava of Nakora in Rajasthan is famous, and considered extremely powerful. Many Jains who go on pilgrimage to Nakora offer liberal sums of money to have the privilege of carrying out the rites for Bhairava. The quantities are much greater than those paid to officiate in the worship of Pārśva, to whom the temple is actually dedicated. Another powerful deity in Rajasthan is Ghaṇṭā Karṇa Mahāvīra (not to be confused with the *jina* Mahāvīra) similar to the Hindu Hanumān.

It is common to see Jains worshipping some deity that, in principle, would be exclusively Hindu (Skanda, Hanumān, or Śiva). From the 9th century onward, we even find a certain assimilation of the god Gaṇeśa with Gautama, Mahāvīra's favourite disciple. Both are the central figures of two of the most loved of Jain festivals [see pages 432-433]. The Vedic pantheon, on the other hand, is practically absent from Jainism. Agni, Vāyu, Soma, or Varuṇa play some part in the mythology, but are clearly secondary. The only exception to this is the great Indra (Śakra) and the worship of the sixty-four *indras* (among Śvetāmbaras) or the one hundred *indras* (among Digambaras).

The veneration of constellations and planets, strengthened by the great interest Indians have in astrology/astronomy, is also to be found among Jains. If the power of the planets has textual support, the practice of worship of demigods such as malignant spirits *(bhūtas)* or ghosts of dead women, typical of grassroots India, is less favoured by the ascetics. A whole series of practices—which Jains themselves recognise as lesser—are associated with the placating of these potentially malevolent agents. The use of *mantras,* amulets and mystical diagrams is called for. Indeed, Jains have a reputation in India for being particularly well-up on magic (von Glasenapp 1925: 449), and the interpretation of dreams, a theme which is clearly rooted in the Jain Universal History. At all events, referring to the protagonism of goddesses, gods, spirits, and lesser genies, Somadeva, once again, is, clear:

> "Whoever treats as equals to the Jina, the Lord of the three worlds, and these demi-gods of the lower worlds, and worships them equally, surely is heading downward [toward purgatory]. These deities were conceived in the holy scripture purely for the sake of guarding the teachings of the Jina. Therefore, these demi-gods should not be honoured beyond their proper share in oblations by Jainas who hold the right view" (Somadeva Sūri, *Upāsakādhyayana* 697; cited in Jaini 1991: 197).

Of course, they did not pay too much attention to Somadeva.

LOVING DEVOTION *(BHAKṬI)*

It is clear that in the incorporation of these divine and semi-divine beings, an important part was played by the development of Hindu-inspired loving devotion *(bhakti).* The need to adapt the epics and popular stories was equally decisive. The *Mahābhārata, Rāmāyaṇa,* and oldest Hindu Purāṇas are all plainly earlier that the Jain Purāṇas and Caritas, and their influence is evident, but that does not mean we should conclude that Jainism is subordinate, or see it as a mere strategy for survival in an essentially Hindu environment. The Jainising tactics are never gratuitous. As Richard Davis (1998: 218) has shown, the incorporation of Hindu gods can equally be seen as a representation of a specifically Jain "scale of forms". In this Jain vision of the cosmos, for example, the Hindu gods and goddesses simply act as protectors, a clearly lower rank than a *tīrthaṅkara.* Rather than Hinduisation, then, what we have here is a hierarchical appropriation, something quite classical in Indian religiosity. For this reason, medieval Jain masters entered into combat with the Vedic and Purāṇic gods, striking hard. Somadeva criticises the three great Hindu deities with considerable scorn:

"Brahmā has his mind obsessed with Tilottamā, the nymph,
And Hari [Viṣṇu], the Lord of Lakṣmī, is attached to her;
Śambhu [Śiva] is half-man and half-woman,
Look at these authorities on salvation!
Vasudeva is his father, and Devakī his mother,
He [Kṛṣṇa] himself engaged in royal duties;
Yet Hari [Viṣṇu/Kṛṣṇa] is called a god!
He dances naked and kills brahmans at will,
Destruction of the three worlds is his sport!
Yet Śiva is said to be a god!
One whose conduct is no better than that of a householder,
One whose conduct is inferior even to that of an ordinary mendicant,
If such a one be a god,
Surely, there would be no dearth of gods!"
(Somadeva Sūri, *Upāsakādhyayana* 62-93; cited in Jaini 1991: 190).

Despite the enormous social and emotional pressure that devotional Hinduism must have exercised, there is no Śiva-worship or Viṣṇu-worship in Jainism. Both appear in the mythology, admittedly, but they play no role in nor have any capacity in helping the devotee to attain liberation. The notion of divine grace *(prasāda),* of cardinal importance in devotional Hinduism, is conspicuous for its absence in Jainism. I agree with Padmanabh Jaini (1991: 196) in that the incorporation of protector gods must have helped precisely to prevent the influence of Vaiṣṇava or Śaiva *bhakti* among lay Jains. In any case, devotional worship shows no signs of being a degradation or deviation of a "genuine" Jainism, or of an "original" Jainism, since such considerations are not too applicable to South Asia. At all events, Mahāvīra would never have been born correctly, nor would have set off on the path of renunciation without the aid of Indra and the other gods.

Jain devotional worship is not then a Hindu intrusion into the Jain religion. It would seem more appropriate to think that, certain intentional borrowings apart, Jainism has simply drawn on the same common substrate sources and in the same way as Hinduism has. Like the latter, Jainism has reflected the changes that have come about in Indian religious expression—and there is need to avoid the all too frequent mistake of equating "Indian culture" with "Hindu culture", however much the Brāhmaṇas have encouraged us to think that. All Indian religious traditions (Hinduism, Buddhism, Jainism, Sikhism, and even the "imported" religions such as Islam, Christianity, and Zoroastrism) share an Indian religious culture where divine figures, religious practices, and rituals can be incorporated, reformulated or resurrected in any of the traditions.

The religion of devotion (*bhakti)* appears *simultaneously* in Hinduism, Buddhism, and Jainism, around the 2nd and 1st centuries BC, or perhaps a little earlier. And there are a number of reasons to think that Buddhism and Jainism, with their reverence for certain spiritually realised men, exercised considerable influence over the first Hindu devotional groups (Bhāgavata, Pāśupata, Pāñcarātra) (Larson 1995: 74). Worship of the gods among Jains is attested in Mathura in the 1st century BC. Balarāma—one of the sublime figures of Jain mythology—had already become a popular deity among the Jains of Mathura only a few centuries afterward, that is before he achieved such enormous popularity among Hindus as a result of the adventures of Kṛṣṇa. The same could be said of the 16 *mahāvidyās,* Jain Tantric goddesses that correspond to the 10 figures with the same name in Hinduism (Pal 1995: 25). Let us not jump, therefore, to the conclusion that Jainism imported all its mythology from Hinduism. Jainism is not as cold or as austere as it is made out to be, but at the same time it has not forgotten certain doctrines deeply rooted in the tradition.

WAVES OF TANTRICISM

In the same way, from the 6th century, Jainism was affected by the influx of Tantricism which swept the whole of South Asia. Tantra is a very complex phenomenon that we cannot go into here. For simplicity's sake, let us say that it is a mystic ethos that gelled to an equal extent in the various different Indian religions. The exchanges and the osmosis between all the different schools and religions was constant. Recall that some of its characteristic features began to appear in the Jainism of the Gupta era [see page 216] or during the Gaṅga dinasty [see page 227]. The Tantric forms of worship included the repetition of litanies, circumvalations, visualisations of the gods in different parts of the body, mystic diagrams on the ground and the food offerings. A series of ascetics took it upon themselves to devise new rites, new formulas and new litanies, with the result that a new type of clergy emerge, the *yatis* and *bhaṭṭārakas,* with a similar rank to the abbots *(mahants)* of the Hindu institutions. Present-day worship *(pūjā),* whether Jain or Hindu, has its roots in this period and this religious expression. The development of a science of *mantras* and the speculations over the nature of sacred sound in the Tantric esoteric style, while not going to the extremes of the Brāhmaṇic grammarians or the Kashmir Śaivism, has been notable in Jainism. The same could be said of the science of mystic diagrams. In certain celebrations the *siddhacakra-yantra* is still used. This is a complex *maṇḍala* of extremely high value for Jains [see page 434]. In all respects, Jainism has contributed in outstanding fashion to Tantric art, to its iconography and to certain Tantric practices.

Obviously, the transgressing and trans-social behaviour of Tantra, along with its "left-wing" ritual practices (sacred sex, intoxicating drink, and so forth) found no echo in Jainism. Normally, these practices are inserted in a non-dualist outlook (Vajrayāna Buddhism, Trika Śaivism, Kula Śaivism) but never so in a pluralist vision like that of Jainism. Since it lacked this fundamental ingredient (fusion of the mundane with the otherworldly) no technique of the *haṭha-yoga* or *kuṇḍalinī-yoga* type has prospered in Jainism. Padmanabh Jaini (1979:

254) thinks that the Jain attitude of disdain toward more esoteric forms of *yoga* or ritual perhaps stems from the recurrent tradition that Gośāla tried to pulverise Mahāvīra with his esoteric-spiritual ardour.

At the same time, the popularity of the Goddess (Devī), which achieved huge proportions all over India, became a part of Jainism in the form of worship of goddesses and *yakṣiṇīs* such as the above-mentioned Padmāvatī, Cakreśvarī or Ambikā. Many authors have seen in this a return to the very ancient "cult of the Mother", which has always been one of the main forms of devotion among the aboriginal populations of India (Eliade 1975: 152). Perhaps, things are not so simple (Inden 1990: 117-130). Anyway, there may have been some interesting changes in this process; like that of the local goddess of Osian, in Rajasthan, which we know from her conversion to Jainism [see pages 310-311]. Interestingly, even today in the temple of the goddess of Osian, Hindus worship her as Durgā and the Jains as Saciyā. The "Mother", the local goddess, can be identified with any of the groups who venerate her. It is really admirable that a goddess as bloodthirsty as Durgā could "be converted" to becoming such an upholder of non-violence as Saciyā and the family deity *(kuladevatā)* of one of the most important Jain castes, but such things are frequent in India. The goddess is right for a ritual that is neither Hindu nor Jain, but simply Indian or South Asian.

27. WORSHIP *(PŪJĀ)*

FORMS OF WORSHIP

In India, the key word to define religious worship is *pūjā.* This is a ritual expression that impregnates all Indian religions. Summarising, the essence of *pūjā* involves *honouring* the deity or omniscient being, represented by an icon, with acts of symbolic hospitality, but this pattern can take on countless variants and meanings.

Jains can conduct their worship when and wherever they want; at home, at the temple, on a mountain, daily, weekly, or just occasionally. *Pūjā* is a strictly personal matter. No scripture or person forces one to perform it, even if some texts do occasionally recommend it.*

Although people often go to the temple early in the day, early morning worship is usually performed at home, before a small domestic altar where there would be a material representation of one or *more jinas* in the form of a statue, photograph, or illustration. Whether at home or in the temple, everyone does exactly what he or she wants. There is no one single Jain form of worship. It can vary depending on the religious order, place, whether it coincides with a festival or special commemoration and/or according to the time of day. In the last analysis, it depends on the devotee's freewill, as worship is an eminently individual matter—even if it can be conducted communally—and each devotee has her or his own personal interpretation of its meaning. In major temples, it is common to go at the established times well known by everyone. In this case, depending on the temple and sub-order, the presence of some kind of clerical specialist may be needed. But even then, the variable forms of worship are unlimited. For this reason, for a good part of the day, there seems to be nothing happening in a Jain temple. Someone enters and then later someone else; they pray, sing, perform;

* As we already know, from the 13th and 14th centuries onwards some Jain groups stopped worshipping images. The idea was to purge Jainism of temple practices and to redirect the practice of worship towards meditation. As a substitute they divulge in the chanting of sacred psalms and meditating at home or in their retreat. However, Sthānakavāsīs and Terāpanthīs are nonetheless minority groups, so that for the majority of Jains the worship of images remains one of their primordial religious activities.

some are there for five minutes others for three hours. Although there are quite standardised *pūjās,* very often we get the impression that there is room for spontaneity and improvisation.

Worship is always directed towards the five supreme ones; completely omniscient and perfect beings *(siddhas),* omniscient beings who showed the path *(tīrthaṅkaras),* and the three degrees or levels of ascetics *(ācāryas, upādhyāyas, sādhus).* Deities associated with the *tīrthaṅkaras,* symbolic objects, and even sacred places can also be venerated. Naturally, the *tīrthaṅkaras* are the deserving ones par excellence, as they revealed the path in benefit of the whole world. Therefore, veneration of the *jina* is the most extended form of worship, and is also what dominates this chapter. Worship can be indifferently directed to any of the 24 *tīrthaṅkaras* or all 24 at the same time. The most popular ones are, in order: Pārśva, Ṛṣabha, Nemi, Mahāvīra, and Śantinātha. It is not unusual among some groups to give praise to *tīrthaṅkaras* who belong to other continents, such as Śīmaṅdhara, who these days preaches in Videha. Among omniscient beings that were not *tīrthaṅkaras,* Bāhubali, Gautama, and the other *gaṇadharas* are frequently worshipped.

Most Jain schools differentiate between two superimposed levels of worship: (1) the adoration of external objects *(dravya),* whether images of the *jinas* or saints and masters of the community; and (2) internal adoration *(bhāva),* which concerns the state of the worshipper's soul. In reality, the subject is more complex, but here there is no need to enter into finer points. If the external form of worship of material objects is the form performed by laypersons, mendicant monks and nuns are only allowed mental worship. But even if their interior worship is serene and virtually silent, it is nonetheless fervent. The majority of ascetics recite a type of highly devotional hymnology. They never consider the layperson's worship of physical objects to be a lesser or corrupt form of worship—as some texts from medieval times seem to suggest. On the other hand, they encourage laypersons to accompany their image worship with mental worship. Inner peace and devotion to the virtues of the *jina* are primordial when it comes to the effectiveness of external praise; not in vain most commentators consider *pūjā* as a form of meditation *(sāmāyika).* All laypersons recognise the importance of interior spiritual disposition. The murmured recitation of the name of the object of worship *(nāma-japa)* is a good way to practice inner worship, since the *jina*'s name invokes the ideal of the liberated soul. There are also different *mantras* consistently recited by all. In general, these are variations of the *pañca-namaskāra.* Another expression of internal devotion is in the prostration before an image of the *jina.*

The simplest form of worship is the so-called "vision", "sight" *(darśana)* or contemplation of the image. It is the commonest form of worship in temples and can be undertaken at any time of the day. The devotee enters, prays, "sees" the image and then leaves.

A slightly more complex variant is one which is denominated "temple veneration" *(caityavandana).* Apart from seeing and praying, the devotee circles the image three times and undergoes a series of precise gestures. There are no offerings nor is there any direct contact with the image. For these reasons, the *caityavandana* is also the type of *pūjā* that ascetics perform. As a consequence, this act of worship is the one that is considered "compulsory" in ritual texts.

While *darśana* and *caityavandana* are the simplest and most frequently practised forms of worship, there are other more elaborate ones, richer in symbolism, that are worth being studied in more detail.

THE EIGHTFOLD WORSHIP

One of the most patronymic *pūjās,* and possibly the most institutionalised and most practised of them all, is the one known as "ceremony of the eight substances" or "eightfold worship" *(aṣṭaprakāri-pūjā).* It is a typical form of worship among all Mūrtipūjāka Śvetāmbaras, and similar to that of many of Digambara groups. It takes its name from the eight different types of offerings that are given. Lay worshippers may bring them from their home or purchase them at the temple. It is an individual rite, but it is not unusual for groups of devotees to gather together regularly to perform it collectively. There is no reciting or reading from texts, even if some individuals may sing hymns. Some people perform this act of worship daily in its entirety; others only partially.

It is traditional to perform this *pūjā* in the morning. The man will wear his finest *dhotī* and the woman her wedding sari. Taking a ritual bath previously is indispensable, as devotees have to be at their maximum state of purity to be able to touch the images. For the same reason, there is a prohibition on wearing clothing made of leather, considered not only to be impure and contrary to *ahiṃsā,* but also excessively worldly. An interesting point is that since bathing is prohibited to ascetics owing to their vow of *ahiṃsā,* in a certain sense they are in a condition of impurity, which actually precludes them from touching the images. Obviously, no one would dream of mentioning or criticising this paradoxical impurity of renunciants. Impurity only concerns the substance *(dravya)* and not the inner state *(bhāva).* But as James Laidlaw (1995: 271-274) has detected, this may well be the ultimate explanation why ascetics cannot worship material images.

On entering the sacred precinct some devotees may put on the classical cloth muzzle to show their devotion to non-violence and not accidentally spit some impurity over the image. Others would simply pronounce the word "abandonment" *(nisahī),* which denotes the passing from the profane world to the sacred world, or to give a more Jain analogy, passing from being a householder to being a temporary renunciant.

Worship usually begins with the vision (*darśana)* of the icon. As mentioned above, prostration before the main image of the *jina* and the reciting of the *namaskāra-mantra* is frequently carried out. These are considered to be symbols of humility and reverence towards the ideals that the image embodies. Afterwards, it is habitual to circle the statue three times, as in *caityavandana.* Thus, the *pūjā* of the eight substances contains within it the two other simpler ones. This is typical in Indic ritual culture. Rites and forms of worship may be abbreviated, overlapped and nested in larger rituals (Staal 1990: 101-102).

Following this, the devotee enters into the central shrine. This is where the use of the eight classic components in this act of worship begins.

The first thing is sprinkling or worship with water *(snāpana, abhiṣeka).* The devotee symbolically bathes the *jina* by pouring a little water over the main image, or in the case of this not being possible, over a small replica which is found outside the *sanctum sanctorum* [see FIG. 35]. While this act is performed, the faithful visualise themselves as being Indra (Śakra) giving the newly born *jina* his first ritual bath on the summit of Mount Meru. This is also typical of other *pūjās,* as we shall see.

Once the image has been dried, the devotee or priest who is in charge of conducting the service will anoint certain parts of the statue with a little paste made from sandalwood. This second stage is termed worship with sandalwood *(kesara-pūjā).*

Afterwards, the name of the *tīrthaṅkara* to whom the service is directed is invoked and there is an offering of flowers *(puṣpa-pūjā).* The flowers have to be beautiful and fresh. Here, there seems to be a slight contradiction in terms of the doctrine of *ahiṃsā.* The somewhat forced justification of some interpreters of tradition is that the flowers are bought from the temple gardener (who is usually the priest) knowing that if they did not, the flowers would end up going to Hindu bloody sacrifices and *pūjās.*

These three acts of worship take place inside the inner shrine. In all three cases there is physical contact with the image or its replica. This highlights the difference between Jain and Hindu *pūjā,* since in temples dedicated to Rāma, Śiva and other Hindu divinities, devotees can never approach so close to the image, and the whole service is conducted by priests. In Jain temples, on the other hand, even foreigners can enter the *sanctum sanctorum.*

The next stage, the devotee goes to the main hall facing the image. As there is no need for physical contact—and hence there is no need for the high state of purity needed in the first three—many Jains only participate in this part of the worship.

The fourth component of the *pūjā* is worship with incense *(dhūp-pūjā),* in which the devotee waves incense sticks towards the image. The fifth consists of worship with camphor lamps *(dīpak-pūjā),* a similar operation to the previous one, which is usually performed in the centre of the hall. Afterwards, the devotee sits on the floor in front of a low table, where the sixth, seventh and eighth acts of worship are carried out.

The sixth component is worship with rice *(akṣat-pūjā).* On the table, the devotee forms the sign of the *svastika* with grains of rice, a symbol which is both an auspicious emblem and symbol of *saṃsāra.* Immediately above she or he draws three dots with small handfuls of rice, which is a symbol of the Three Jewels of Jainism, the path which will allow one to put an end to the flow of reincarnations. Above that, she or he draws a crescent Moon and a dot. These obviously symbolise the World of the Perfect Ones and the liberated soul [see FIG. 37]. This whole act is very illustrative of the fact that the purpose of worship is not to obtain benefit or any kind of grace from the *jina.* Rather it is to show that the ultimate goal sought is emancipation. All these symbols form part of the official emblem of Jainism [see FIG. C], which was adopted a few decades ago. This is surely the most distinctive part of Jain *pūjā,* having no parallel in Hinduism.

The seventh component is the offering of food *(naivedya-pūjā).* The devotee places some sweets on the *svastika* that she or he has created with grains of rice. A coin or two may also be included. In the eighth part, the follower also places some fruit together with the grains of rice which represents liberated souls. This is adoration with fruit *(phal-pūjā).*

Once this part is over, the custom is to recite the names of all the twenty-four *tīrthaṅkaras* or sing the "Hymn of the 24 *Jinas" (caturviṃśatistava).* Afterwards, the worshipper murmurs the words "abandonment" *(nisahī)* and, silently go through mental adoration, an internal contemplation *(bhāva-pūjā)* of the *tīrthaṅkara.*

The materials used in the eightfold worship are left behind and the caretakers of the temple collect them later.

THE MEANING OF THE SUBSTANCES

Each one of the offerings in the eightfold worship has its own meaning, even if not everybody interprets them in the same way. For example, in the opinion of the philosopher Haribhadra, the eight substances correspond to the five vows, plus devotion to one's master, knowledge and austerity. For others, sandalwood may symbolise the calming of the passions, incense serves to eliminate the "bad odour" of attachment to the world and to "refreshing" the devotee. The lamp may be taken as illuminating or eradicating ignorance, etc. There is no "official" interpretation.

The underlying logic of the offering of food is particularly interesting. Unlike Hindu *pūjā,* the food is not given with the hope of receiving something in return, nor is it later distributed among devotees. Rather it is *abandoned* there as an external symbol of renunciation. An informant of Lawrence Babb (1996: 93), expressed it in this way: "Oh Lord, I have these things, but I really do not want them—I want to leave them". Food is the basis of corporal existence and, therefore, is a vital ingredient in bondage. In which case, the offering of food may be interpreted as a ritual renunciation. This is quite different to most Hindu *pūjās,* where the divinity is supposed to be fed, and in turn feeds the devotee with his grace *(prasāda),* symbolised by the food given back to the faithful by the Brāhmaṇas. In Jainism there is no *prasāda,* there is no reciprocity between the devotee and the object of devotion. As John Cort (1991: 220) sums up, the offerings in Jainism are not for the *jina,* but to the virtues of enlightenment, liberation, and dispassion symbolised by the image.

TEMPLE EMPLOYEES

Due to the inaccessible nature of the *jinas,* there is no need for a priest or go-between to conduct the worship. However, larger temples usually take on employees *(pūjakas;* Hindi: *pūjāris),* although these people are not conferred any sacred authority. Apart from carrying out some of the more complex services, the *pūjāris* take care of the temple, bathe the images daily and have them consecrated periodically.

At the Digambara temples in the Deccan, the *pūjāris* are always Jains from the Jaina-brāhmaṇa caste we have already met with [see pages 306-308], often referred to as Upādhyāyas. They conduct daily *pūjā,* special *pūjā* at festivals, consecrate new images and undertake various domestic services. The technical reason that these priests are needed is that, in tune with their surrounding Hindu environment, lay worshippers cannot touch the images of the *jinas.* In ceremonies in which they decorated, polished and bathed them, the presence of a ritual supervisor is required. In fact, in Digambara temples in northern India, lay worshippers are able to perform the whole ritual.

In Śvetāmbara precincts the care taker is nearly always a Hindu, normally from a caste which is specialised in this matter, such as the bards (Bārotas) or gardeners (Mālīs). However, it is not unusual to find caretakers who are said to be from the Hindu priest class (Brāhmaṇas) or the caste devoted to agriculture (Kuṇbīs). In any case, these "priests" have no spiritual role. They are representatives of the local *saṃgha,* and are paid for their work. As extra perk for their services, they can keep the offerings left by devotees. This is one of the reasons why care takers are never Jains. Another reason is that in India, on the contrary to what one might think, priests' status is quite low (as they have to subsist on donations from the faithful), so that few Jains would deign to perform these less than prestigious tasks.

The presence of Brāhmaṇas of any kind is almost certainly closely linked to guardian spirits and deities. Indeed, for prayers to reach these benevolent beings, well known by Hindus, one will indeed need the mantric knowledge of the Brāhmaṇas. Apart from these "employees", it is the faithful themselves who take charge of the acts of worship, even when there are Jaina-brāhmaṇas in the temple. They are their own priests.

Another thing worth mentioning with regard to the main *pūjās,* is the surprisingly lively devotional chanting. I concur with Kurt Titze (1998:242) in that in Jainism one must "see it" and read it. And in going to their temples and festivals, one can also "listen to" Jainism, an aspect of great importance in a population such as in India, which is essentially sound-orientated.

SNĀTRA-PŪJĀ AND *PAÑCA-KALYĀṆA*

Another of the most significant devotional services is the "worship of the five auspicious events" *(pañca-kalyāṇa-pūjā)* in the life of the *tīrthaṅkara.* It will be recalled that these are: conception, birth, renunciation, enlightenment and liberation. Each *pañca-kalyāṇa-pūjā* celebrates the five events of one *tīrthaṅkara* in particular. The most usual of these being Pārśva and Mahāvīra.

This act of worship is performed to commemorate joyful events, such as weddings, anniversaries, and to mark the New Year (Kelting 2001: 139). It always takes place when a new image of *ajina* is installed in a temple, or when it becomes necessary to consecrate anew one of the images already in place. Without this consecration, the statue would be an inert figure. After the ritual, it is a sacred object. As Lawrence Babb (1996:27) has observed, this suggests that the *kalyāṇas* of the *tīrthaṅkaras* have left a residue of welfare in the cosmos that can be focused upon the images and mobilised by rituals in the service of worshipers. The complete service can go on for several days.

The part of the ritual, which commemorates the conception, birth and first ritual bath of every *jina,* is celebrated fairly frequently in Śvetāmbara temples, and not only in connection with the *pañca-kalyāṇa.* When this stage in the act of worship is independently performed, it does not celebrate the events of any one *jina* in particular, but all *tīrthaṅkaras* in general. It then receives the name of *snātra -pūjā,* and usually concludes with a variant of the "eightfold worship" or with an apotheosis using camphor lamps *(ārātrika;* Hindi: *āratī).* When this ritual is inserted within *pañca-kalyāṇa,* it is simply the preliminary.

The whole event, especially the *snātra-pūjā* stage, gives the impression of a theatrical performance. The Jain who finances the ritual plays the role of the king of the gods, Indra (Śakra) and his wife plays the role of Indrāṇī, Indra's consort. It is not unusual for these devotees to wear crowns symbolising their divine identity [see Fig. 38]. Members of the family play the roles of the child's parents. The rest of the congregation becomes the chorus and the audience at the same time—a very active audience that follows the script well known by all. The hymns and chants are printed in manuals and ritual hymnals. It is the text that places the ritual in a specific narrative, that of Ṛṣabha, Śāntinātha, Pārśva, or Mahāvīra. On this occasion, a metal replica of the *tīrthaṅkara* is usually used.

SNĀTRA-PŪJĀ

The first auspicious event, the conception, is preceded by the story of the previous lives of the *jina* in question. The key reincarnation is the second to last one where the *jīva* who is going to be the future *tīrthaṅkara* acquires the necessary *tīrthaṅkara-nāma-karma.* After the recitation of the texts, the officiator of the act of worship anoints the *jina* with water and sandalwood paste. The participants draw *svastikas* with grains of rice on the tables. Next, the first auspicious event is re-enacted. Owing to his clairvoyant knowledge *(avadhi-jñāna)* Indra knows that a great birth is going to take place. At this moment, the participants circle the image of the *jina* and recite the hymn that Indra sang at the moment of the *jina's* conception. The woman who plays the role of the mother has the fourteen recurring dreams. The semi-goddeses *dikkumārīs* who fanned the mother and cleansed the birthplace of impurities are represented. Offerings of saffron-tinted rice and flowers are made. After the "birth", Indra takes the child in his arms and places him on a pedestal, symbolising Mount Meru, where the ritual bathing *(abhiṣeka)* of all *tīrthaṅkaras* took place. The participants dance. Emulating Indra they wash the *jina's* feet with water, as in the "eightfold worship". Afterwards, they bathe the image with milk, then one last time with water [see FIG. 38]. When the gods conducted the baptism of one who would once again preach the path to salvation, their happiness was immense. Like the gods, devotees shout *jay*! ("victory") and give a donation of gold coins. Indra places the baby back into the mother's care and departs towards Nandīśvara, the island inaccessible to human beings where the gods go to venerate eternal images of the *jinas*. Lawrence Babb (1996: 70) has shown that the story of the birth and first bath of the *tīrthaṅkaras* is the one which is most told in Jainism; it has the same importance as the nativity of Jesus for Christians. This concludes the *snātra-pūjā*.

REMAINING *KALYĀṆAS*

The act of worship may proceed with the celebration of the remaining auspicious moments in the lives of the *jinas*. In the next stage *of the pañca-kalyāṇa*, the image is adorned with all kinds of jewels. The moment previous to renunciation is acted out, when the young prince is told by the deities—represented by young members of the family or neighbourhood—that the time has come to renounce the world. The image is taken outside the town and the ornaments are removed. The consecration of the image is then performed in a similar way to the vow of renunciation or initiation *(dīkṣā) of the jina*.

When omniscience arrives, the festival reaches its climax. The image is formally installed in its permanent place: the *jina* sits in meditation in the centre of the temple, surrounded by emblematic figures from the community. Of course, this scene represents the last sacred assembly. The following scene is to celebrate the final act, the one concerning *nirvāṇa*. Probably, the last auspicious moment is the one which awakens the least interest, even if some groups celebrate it at the festival of Dīvālī. The image, definitively situated upon the pedestal, attains the status of *tīrthaṅkara*.

For financing the installation of the image, the patron and sponsor of the ritual would come to be called "leader of the community" *(saṃghapati)*, and be respected by all.

GODS AND DEVOTEES

Let us focus upon some aspects of this *pūjā*. As can be seen, the first part *(snātra-pūjā)* commemorates the arrival of the *tīrthaṅkara*, who would establish the path that leads to liberation. The second part clearly forms a relationship between the *tīrthaṅkara* and those who venerate him, and the crucial issue is that it is the gods who are the worshippers of the *tīrthaṅkaras,* an aspect which has only been properly emphasised by Lawrence Babb (1996: 77). As Babb has observed, the importance that divinities have in Jainism now becomes clear. The gods in the Jain pantheon are not merely marginal adornments or simply dispensers of miracles. They represent *Jainism's model worshipers* (Babb 1996:77). Hence the protective divinities such as Bhairava and Padmāvatī come to the aid of their human companions who express their devotion and faithfulness to the *jina.* The role of the gods is not to be the object of adoration (as in Hinduism), but archetypal models of what a devotee should be. The gods are lay Jains, observes Babb (1996: 79). This identification between worshipper and god is not exclusive to Jainism, as it can also be found in Vedic rituals. Brian Smith (1989: 104-105) has shown that, thanks to the preliminary rites, in Vedic ritualism, those who perform the sacrifice became a divinity, and reached heaven in their own lifetime.

In Jainism, deities clearly represent a way of ritual action. It is not the highest form, which is asceticism, but even though they are inherently non-ascetic, deities can *admire* and *support* ascetics, in addition to listening to their teachings (Babb 1998: 143). However, the reverse cannot occur. Ascetics cannot venerate gods, nor can they make offerings—other than mental ones—to the *jinas.* The key is that it is human beings who assume the role of the gods and worship the *jinas* and ascetics. Like them, if they remain vigilant, if they persevere in their faith and trust, then one day they may also be reborn as divinities, or better yet, one day they may come to practice asceticism, and become Jaina *sādhus* or *sādhvīs.*

THE PURPOSE OF *PŪJĀ*

Strictly speaking, *pūjā* is meditational. The *jina* does not intervene, but through devotion, auspicious karmic feeling rises in the devotee's soul. In a spirit of humility, he or she sings to the *jinas* as a form of gratitude for showing the path. This feeling of gratitude is enough to destroy negative *karmas* and at the same time generate worthy *karma (puṇya),* which will lead them to better rebirths. Or as John Cort (1995: 327) has shown, in venerating the superior qualities of a being who is more advanced on the path to liberation, one absorbs some of these qualities. The worshipper both eradicates accumulated *karma* and avoids attracting more *karma.* The *jina* does not respond, but in his presence the devotee experiences inner purification. It is not the *tīrthaṅkara* who confers spiritual merit. It is the worshipper who acquires it through contemplation, gestures and belief, a feeling of identity with something beyond this world; the sensation of being on the right path to liberation. This is where the "divine grace" of the *jinas* resides. The texts say that on contemplating the form of the dispassionate

Lord within the temple one's mind is automatically filled with the feeling of renunciation. *Pūjā,* if undertaken while in the right frame of mind, in the spirit of devotion and true love towards the Lord, is a first-class purifying agent.

Therefore, worshipping has high renunciative and ascetic value. Venerating the prototype of an ascetic, the *tīrthaṅkara,* is an act of asceticism. If worship brings merit *(puṇya)* or demerit *(pāpa),* this, from the point of view of the faithful devotee, has to be a secondary consideration. Not even the worship of Pārśva, who it is said is capable of intervening on behalf of devotees, contradicts the true intention of *pūjā.* A study of the worship of this popular *jina,* shows that it is the guardian spirits who are the agents that intervene in the matter. This is how Jinaprabha Sūri (14th century) saw it when he drew attention to the fact that the feat of the famous image of Pārśva at Śaṅkhapura, being capable of removing obstacles and endowing abundance, was thanks to the proximity of Dharaṇendra and Padmāvatī *(Vividhatīrthakalpa* 27). This is not pure theory, but something well understood by laypersons. No devotee thinks that merit comes from the *tīrthaṅkara,* but that it comes from the extraordinary power of the deities such as Padmāvatī, Cakreśvarī, Bhairava and Dharanendra.

Despite all this, it is clear that many Jains approach their *jinas* and deities in search of particular benefits and the accumulation of positive *karma.* This is something that Jains openly recognise, although with a vague feeling of guilt. They certainly would not ask the *tīrthaṅkara* for prosperity in business, but they would ask this of the Bhairava of Nakora, nor would they pray to a *jina* for a happy marriage, but they would pray to the goddess Lakṣmī for it. This puts the ascetic interpretation of worship into question. Also, the miracles that these beings are capable of performing run counter to the basic axiom that everything depends on *karma.* However, miracles are associated with *karma* in that they are unfailingly linked to good. Divinities, ascetics with supernatural powers and the escorts of the *jinas* performed miracles and can do so again while listening to the prayers of devotees, because they were performed in a *good cause.* Therefore, the incongruity or conflict with the law of *karma* is effectively non-existent in the eyes of a layperson. The problem that lays have is of another order. Just as James Laidlaw (1995: 78-79) has so perfectly illustrated, their religion urges them to renounce many aspects of the world which, according to the prevailing culture in which they live, are both practical and desirable. They should renounce their families, homes, businesses, caste, and sources of worldly help such as their prayers to powerful deities. The problem devotees have is that divine or miraculous intervention is not well considered.

This contradiction has led the worship with the eight substances *(dravya-pūjā)* to be somewhat devalued in comparison to internal worship *(bhāva-pūjā),* but no one can draw a clear dividing line. No one can say if ascetic practices aimed in their entirety at the destruction of *karmas* and not at producing good *karma* will obtain the desired result. Almost certainly, on giving donations one will gain merit, but when a donation is made in the spirit of non-attachment, it can in any case act as a purifying agent of the soul. The same can be said for non-violence, fasting, confessions... and *pūjā.* Only the events in the distant future will reveal whether one has succeeded in destroying *karma* or gaining merit (Laidlaw 1995: 28). Babb (1996: 100-101) has clearly emphasised the ambivalence there is between the ascetic tone favoured by tradition, which advocates the eradication of *karma,* on the one hand, and the vital necessities of people on the other. Even though Jains recognise that one must not attend acts of worship motivated by worldly interests, tradition itself endows one with legitimacy to do so.

WORSHIP OF THE *DĀDĀGURUS* AS A RITUAL SUBCULTURE

A good example of legitimisation of laypersons' aspirations and worldly desires is to be found in the worship of the *dādāgurus* or *gurudevas.* If we recall, the four *dādāgurus* (Jinadatta Sūri, Jinacandra Sūri Maṇidhārī, Jinakuśala Sūri and Jinacandra Sūri II) were masters endowed with miraculous powers, which they used in defence of Jainism and the community [see pages 266-267]. It is said that one can go to these masters to plead in favour of those in need, as their power is accessible thanks to a type of well institutionalised ritual. Among Kharatara-gacchins this kind of worship can be more prominent a ritual than that performed for the *tīrthaṅkaras.* As Lawrence Babb (1996: 127) has observed, the fact that many young people participate indicates that it is a flourishing ritual activity. It concerns a sectarian Kharatara-Gaccha ritual subculture that is regionally localised in Rajasthan. New temples are constantly springing up and new miracles are often reported.

The shrines specially dedicated to these *dādāgurus* are known as "gardens of the *dādā" (dādābārīs).* Normally, the masters are represented by their footprints *(pādukās),* although anthropomorphic images are becoming increasingly more common [see FIG. 39]. Similarly, many important temples have images of one or all four of them. It is possible that the worship of the *dādāgurus* stems from the worship of Gautama, recognised remover of obstacles among certain medieval Śvetāmbaras and still very popular. Unlike the *dādāgurus,* Gautama is a liberated soul, which makes his participation in worldly affairs theoretically impossible, and Gautama is not transactional. On the other hand, the four *dādāgurus,* who were all ascetics and masters who glorified Jainism, did not achieve liberation. Because of this the devotee can seek to activate the *dādāgurus's* compassion.

Although Jains would rather say that every *pūjā* is intended to ease one's mind and purify one's spirit, they are all aware that owing to their supernatural powers the *dādāgurus* can help devotees with material needs. Soteriology here yields in face of the obtention of miraculous benefits. It is not unusual for them to be compared to those antediluvian wish-fukfilling trees *(kalpavṛkṣas)* (Babb 1996: 126). Their asceticism has diverged from the path that leads to liberation and they are now associated with the miraculous power, so much so that it is not at all unusual to hear stories about ascetics and laypersons who meet with them "in person" or have visions of the *dādāgurus.* As Paul Dundas (1992: 122) has well appreciated, the similarity between them and Catholic saints and holy virgins is very clear.

Worship in itself can consist of simply "seeing" *(darśana)* the image of the *dādāguru.* This, of course, is always preceded by a gesture honouring the *tīrthaṅkaras.* More elaborate acts of worship require the chanting of certain texts, offering of incense, veneration of the footprints *(pādukās)* that represent the saint, as well as a variant, possibly, of the eightfold worship. In this case, on forming the symbols with rice one must not draw the crescent nor the dot, which represents the liberated soul. On special occasions, the ritual can be congregational.

In Babb's summary (1996: 134), the *dādāgurus* offer the possibility of pursuing worldly interests through a manner of worship that, since it is centred on them as ascetics, is consistent with tradition in insisting on the idea that asceticism constitutes the heart of the object of worship. In no sense, we have to interpret this ritual subculture as a form of Hinduism inserted into Jainism. Alternatively, when Jains worship the *tīrthaṅkaras* they come into contact with eternity. Devotees imitate the object of worship, the *tīrthaṅkara,* and, on doing so they focus upon the highest goal, liberation. But, at the same time they can adopt a royal identity, that of Indra or Indrāṇī, the gods whose object is to admire the *tīrthaṅkaras.* Thanks to that they will obtain religious merit. Although, they are without a doubt on the path to liberation, it is a longer path, a path that takes the way of happiness in this world. Since tradition tends to give prestige to the image of devotees as renunciants, there is a certain tension between the two identities. The conflict is resolved by *dādāguru* ritual culture. When Jains worship the *dādāgurus* they bring eternity into the world in which they live. Following Lawrence Babb's work (1996: 172), those who venerate the *dādāgurus* are the sons and daughters of those kings (Rājputs) who became Jains when powerful ascetics came to their aid [see pages 308-311]. Devotees are seekers after salvation who need worldly or material help. This act of worship is perfectly legitimatised in this way, given that the *dādāgurus* are members of a spiritual lineage which links them to the *tīrthaṅkaras.*

28. AUSPICIOUS PRACTICE

SACRED DAYS AND FESTIVALS

Sacred days and festivals *(utsavas)* in the religious calendar constitute a variety of devotional expression intimately linked to worship and the Universal History. The sacred calendar provides an opportunity to meet at local *saṃghas,* gain religious merit and display Jainism's signs of identity.

PARYUṢAṆA

The most emblematic Jain festival is Paryuṣaṇa, the "Period for Staying in one Place". The festival retains its original name and nature: the four months *(caturmāsa)* of the rainy season when ascetics are sedentary. These days, Paryuṣaṇa has gone from being a purely ascetic practice to becoming an eight-day communal experience, in which laypersons can live the ascetic ideal. It is mainly through the Paryuṣaṇa that ascetics and laypersons reinforce their mutual ties. Apart from this, it marks the beginning of the Jain calendar, the Jain New Year. The festival takes place in the months of August/September.

Every Jain family, over and beyond their habitual degree of religious participation, intensifies its religious observances during Paryuṣaṇa. *Pūjās* are more frequent and more elaborate. Temples are full. Some lay worshippers spend the eight days fasting, although most simply cut their habitual three meals a day down to one. The rest only observe the last day of total fasting. On this day, *saṃvatsarī,* laypersons temporally become ascetics. They attend the retreat closest to them and mix with ascetics to meditate, confess and fast.

The Paryuṣaṇa festival is considered to be so sacred that the Jain community asks the local authorities to stop all activity in slaughterhouses throughout the eight-day period. If necessary, the magnates in the community will pay the losses. Many Jains go back to their home village or city at this time to attend collective fasting, the ceremony of confession and the veneration of texts such as the *Kalpa-sūtra.*

Indeed, an integral part of the Śvetāmbara Paryuṣaṇa consists of listening to religious discussions *(vyākhyānas)* preferably concerning the *Kalpa-sūtra.* On the third day of the festival, it is customary to take a copy of this *sūtra* out on procession, from the ascetic's refuge to the house of the family that has financed and directed the event. The following days are marked by public recitations of the *sūtra* normally in the local language. As it was mentioned [see page 335], the recitation of this text forms part of an extensive series of ceremonies, which also include worship of images that illustrate fundamental moments in the life of the Jina. In the recitation of the episode of Mahāvīra's birth, for example, 14 silver images that represent Triśalā's 14 auspicious dreams are lowered down from the ceiling of the retreat onto a table. There they are praised, whilst corresponding passages from the *sūtra* are recited. Everybody throws rice and breaks open coconuts (a symbol of the auspicious) in a much more lively and festive atmosphere than one would imagine considering that this is an ascetic practice. On the last day *(saṃvatsarī),* ascetics only recite the text in Prakrit (the *Bārasā-sūtra)* as quickly as they can. For the three hours that the recitation lasts—a recitation which nobody is able to understand—pages of the *sūtra* are passed amongst the crowd, who perform a *pūjā* honouring the pages of the manuscript, with prostrations, bows and sprinkling of sandalwood paste. As James Laidlaw (1995: 281) has observed, there is nothing in the whole scene that could be described as listening to a text. In the evening, ascetics and lay Jains meet at the retreat for the annual service of confession *(pratikramaṇa).* This religious practice is an integral part of the festival, confessions are made to ascetics, to members of one's family, to friends and even to enemies—through the use of letters of repentance. For the great majority of Jains, the rite of confession is confined to *saṃvatsarī.*

Although the ascetic nature of the festival is beyond question, so too is the festive side. Women wear their best jewels and saris, which in itself proves a component of social exhibitionism. In fact, the *saṃvatsarī* coincides with a very colourful Hindu festival: Gaṇeśa-Catūrthi. This "coincidence" nevertheless represents a deft way of achieving immersion into the surrounding Hindu world. There is no connection between the god Gaṇeśa and the lives of the *tīrthaṅkaras,* nor is he known as a protector of Jainism, but the elephant god presides over the entrance of every Jain home or business. He is invoked in many Jain rites of passage and, significantly, in many of those things which Jainism says you should renounce: marriage, childbirth, new job, new house, or a business deal (Laidlaw 1995: 285). Therefore, after going through some days of austerity in the refuges and fasting halls, Jains join up with Hindus to joyfully celebrate the day of the benevolent Gaṇeśa.

The Digambara equivalent to Paryuṣaṇa is Daśalakṣaṇa-parvan, which lasts for 10 days and starts just when Paryuṣaṇa ends. In place of the *Kalpa-sūtra,* the *Tattvārtha-sūtra* is recited. The last day is also the most sacred, and is usually reserved for complete fasting and a special *pūjā.*

MAHĀVĪRA'S BIRTHDAYS

Of course, many festivals are intimately connected with the Universal History. The auspicious moments in the life of Mahāvīra are much celebrated events [see pages 424-425]. Between the months of March and April, both communities concurrently and fervently commemorate "Mahāvīra's Birth" (Mahāvīra-Jayantī). It is one of the very few events that all Jains *en bloc* take part in together, regardless of sectarian divisions. Owing to the concerted efforts of the whole Jain community, it is a national holiday in India. It is the only national festivity with an exclusively Jain meaning.

Another popular day is Vira-nirvāṇa or the "Anniversary of Mahāvīra's Death" [see below]. An exceptional occasion of showing the union of all Jains took place with the 2,500th anniversary of Mahāvīra's *nirvāṇa,* celebrated in 1975. Digambaras also celebrate Vīraśāsana-Jayantī, the anniversary of his first sermon.

DĪVALĪ

Like so many other Indian festivals, the "Festival of Lights" (Dīvāli, Dīpāvalī) is actually a cluster of festivals which lasts several days. It is usually celebrated at the end of October or the beginning of November, marking the end of the monsoon season and the beginning of the traditional Indian New Year. After Dīvāli, the auspicious semester in the calendar begins, the time in which marriages and initiations of ascetics take place.

Without a doubt, it is one of the pan-Indian festivals which is most deeply rooted in the population. However, the reasons for its celebration vary from one community to another. For the followers of Rāma, it represents the return of god Rāma from exile; for Kṛṣṇaism it celebrates the raising of Mount Govardhana by Kṛṣṇa; for Śvetāmbara Jainism it commemorates Mahāvīra's *nirvāṇa* and the *kevala-jñāna* of Gautama. According to the *Kalpa-sūtra (Jina-caritra* 128), on this day Mahāvīra achieved final liberation. Since the soul. which had illuminated the world had taken its leave, celestial beings and rulers decided to celebrate the sad occasion with lamps that emulated the light of the recently departed *jina.*

Usually, the *pūjā* offered to Mahāvīra (Vīra-nirvāṇa) is a public act, in which the community congregates and sings devotional hymns. A pilgrimage to Pava (the site of the *vira-nirvāṇa)* during Dīvāli, is extremely beneficial. Gautama's *kevala-jñāna* is usually celebrated immediately afterwards.

The festival celebrates the otherworldly and ascetic values of the omniscient beings of the past, and at the same time it affirms the values and interests in this world, perfectly reflected in the rite dedicated to Lakṣmī, performed by both Jains and Hindus alike. This is because Dīvāli has a special meaning for merchants (Mahājanas, Baniās), who, make up the bulk of the Jain community. It is interesting to note that Terāpanthī and Sthānakavāsī Jains, who do not worship the *tīrthaṅkaras,* join in worship of the goddess of prosperity.

A series of auspicious symbols (lamps, flowers, betel leaves, geometric designs, incense, camphor, and vermilion paste) are placed around the house, then are offered to the figures representing Lakṣmī and Gaṇeśa. An essential part of the ritual consists in blessing the account-books. The books are placed among the offerings along with silver coins plus items used in commerce (pencils, scales). An interesting thing is that the images of Lakṣmī and Gaṇeśa are placed next to those of Mahāvīra and Gautama. The whole affair seems to be somewhat syncretic, since Hindu and Jain elements are blended, and very different purposes are mixed. The heads of families paint auspicious signs on the books and mark symbolic objects of the family business with vermilion. Some families also draw Gautama, who in many aspects is the Jain equivalent of Gaṇeśa. Gautama, after all, is similarly pot-bellied (implying that the spiritual state is what really counts rather than the fasting) and similarly benevolent. In fact, Dīvālī is one of the few festivals at which Jains are not encouraged to fast (Laidlaw 1995: 368), although calls for this to happen are beginning to be heard (Dundas 1992: 186). On the contrary, there is a great variety of typical Dīvālī dishes and it is considered an ill omen to eat little or badly on this day. As shown by the central place, which the paunchy Gautama occupies, the message is obvious: a comfortable life in this world plus success in business and worldly affairs are not incompatible with progress along the path to liberation. Expressing this message perfectly, women show off their jewellery in honour of Lakṣmī. *Lakṣmī-pujā* consists of gently swinging camphor lamps in front of her image.

All this may give the impression that worshipping Lakṣmī and Gautama at Dīvālī is unseemingly materialistic. Nevertheless, for Mahājanas, their account-books constitute icons of the continuity and honour of the family (Laidlaw 1995: 374). Some have kept them for nearly 20 generations. All the family's business transactions and wealth are reflected in them, The books encapsulate a truth, which is intensely private (Laidlaw 1995: 375). It is not surprising that anti-Jain political movements [see pages 317-318] not only are wary of the magical powers of Jain *sādhus,* but wary too of the Baniās and their account-books.

VENERATION OF THE BOOKS

Digambaras take advantage of the Śruta-Pañcamī to venerate their sacred texts—always in the form of manuscripts—and clean them of dust and insects. It is said that this commemorates the moment in which Kundakunda initiated the writing of Digambara scriptures. Śvetāmbaras do exactly the same during the Jñāna-Pañcamī.

MAHĀMASTAKĀBHIṢEKA

For the Digambara community the ceremony of the "Anointing of the Head" (Mahāmastakābhiṣeka) is probably their most impressive festivity. It takes place at Shravanabelgola, in Karnataka, and only every 12 or 15 years, depending on astrological factors. It has been known to attract over half a million people—as in 1981, when it celebrated the 1,000 years of the statue's consecration—and in general stirs up collective devotional ecstasy like that found in Hindu *bhakti.* In the ceremony, well-to-do and respected members of the lay community pour milk, clarified butter, almonds, poppy seeds, liquid saffron and coins, from 1,008 large jars, over the head of saint Bāhubali's colossal statue [see FIG. 9]. As with other figures of beings of earlier marvellous periods, the statue is of enormous dimensions (rising up 17 metres in height). Bāhubali was for the Digambaras the first man to achieve *nirvāṇa* in this cosmic cycle, even before his father. Although Śvetāmbaras do not share this idea, they also attend the great festival. Even the *mahārāja* of Mysore has traditionally been linked to this great event.

SIDDHA-CAKRA

The Siddha-cakra is a festival which lasts for nine days and is celebrated twice a year. Daily *pūjās* are performed and a mystic diagram known as the *siddha-cakra,* which represents the five supreme ones and liberating agents, is venerated. It is so popular that many Jains carry it around and use it as a portable chapel.

OTHER SACRED DAYS

Quite a few sacred days in the calendar correspond to well-established traditional fasting periods, of which we will speak about in the next chapter. The community also participates in other pan-Indian festivals, such as Śītalā-sātama, Holī, Rakṣā-bandhana and Daśaharā, as a part of their social life. However, they try to avoid the ecstatic aspect of Hindu expression, and on occasions will try to Jainify the reason for the event. Just as Gaṇeśa-Catūrthi is linked to Gautama, Daśaharā is traditionally linked to royalty and is associated with Bharata. The Akṣayatṛtīyā is the moment when Ṛṣabha is praised. It commemorates both his initiation and the first time a layperson gave food to the first ascetic mendicant (the future *jina* Ṛṣabha) in this present cosmic cycle. At another level, it celebrates the merit and virtue that the lay community achieve owing to free, unselfish donations given to mendicants. Holī, on the other hand, is all but impossible to Jainify. Very much in the style of Western carnivals, it is the time when Indians invert their everyday social structure. Sexual and behaviour taboos are broken; the barriers between castes are momentarily cast aside. Everybody takes part in a binge in a rebellious spirit, which does not at all comply with Jain mood; in which case, the Jains who do participate in the festival do not do so as *Jains,* but as *Indians.*

PILGRIMAGES

Pilgrimages *(yātrās)* constitute a common practice in all Indian religions. They seem to have formed part of Indian religious expression since prehistoric times, but they have never been undertaken in so massively as in this present modern period. The key factor in their becoming popular is the improvement in communications.

Sacred places in India are known by the name "ford" *(tīrtha),* a word that is closely associated in Jainism with that of *tīrthaṅkara.* If the latter was the one who showed us how to cross the ford that leads from the worldly to the spiritual, *tīrtha* is, in Vilas Sangave's words (1959: 160), the place which shows to the way how to cross the ocean of *saṃsāra.* Unlike Hindus, many of whose *tīrthas* are effectively situated on the banks of rivers, Jains do not accord special holiness to closeness to water. Their predilection is clearly for mountaintops.

All Jain *tīrthas* are connected to the lives of the *tīrthaṅkaras* or saints and preceptors of the community. The origin of the *tīrtha* is usually described in some kind of legend that relates, for example, how an image which had been buried and forgotten for centuries was miraculously found. Thus, the sacred places of Jains are not linked either, as they are in Buddhism, to relics of the Buddha and other Buddhist saints.

In general, the vow to embark on a pilgrimage serves to gain religious merit, purify oneself, expiate bad *karma,* have a "sight" of the *jina* and, above all, to reinforce the correct vision in Jainism and not lose the objective of a spiritual life. The idea is that the pilgrim becomes a temporary renunciant, so that austere forms are advisable. Before setting off, one should purify oneself by fasting and meditating. While on route, one should eat once a day, sleep on the ground, remain celibate for the whole journey and, if possible, not effect any part of the journey in a motor vehicle. The pilgrimage can be conducted accompanied by one's family, in small groups or in large groups of devotees. In these cases the sense of asceticism/renunciation gives way to that of devotion/participation. Naturally, pilgrimage is much more powerful if it coincides with astrologically appropriate days or with some of the above-mentioned festivals.

On many occasions, wealthy members of the community finance large-scale pilgrimages to faraway places. They take responsibility of recruiting pilgrims (in former times, asking permission of the authorities), for paying the costs of transport, lodging and any services, which need to be organised. The event can be taken advantage of to erect an image. The patron acquires boundless merit and prestige among the community and is awarded with the title of *saṃghapati.* It is one of the clearest ways to gain prestige and practise generosity [see pages 443-445].

Pilgrimage structures much of the way of life and the itineraries of renunciants, who spend most of their time travelling from one place to another, according to the needs of the laity, following established routes of pilgrimage. It is not unusual for ascetics to undertake parts of their journeys accompanied by groups of laypersons [see Fig. 44], nor is it infrequent to find them joining large pilgrimages, as long as they are carried out on foot. Since Sthānakavāsīs and Terāpanthīs do not have places of pilgrimage, they consider their *sādhīs* and *sādhvis* themselves to be sacred spaces, and devotees undertake veritable pilgrimages to visit them. Similarly, for those who are unable to go on pilgrimages to faraway places, many local village temples have replicas substituting the great centres of pilgrimage.

Historically speaking, pilgrim itineraries to a considerable extent helped Jainism to spread throughout South Asia, and enabled far-flung communities to maintain links with large Jain centres. In this way, Jains have also reinforced the deeply rooted notion of "India" as a sacred land.

The list of Jain *tīrthas* is mind-bending [see Figs. 7, 18, 19]. Some are exclusively Jain, but many are also associated with pan-Indian and local Hinduism. Of course, the *tīrthas* are found in places where the major part of temples and images of Jainism are clustered. Generally, the sacred places in Gujarat and Rajasthan are these days claimed by the Śvetāmbaras, whereas the ones in Karnataka and Maharashtra belong to Digambaras. However, some places have not been exempt from dispute between the two *saṃpradāyas* [see below].

NIRVĀṆA-BHŪMIS

All the places where the 24 *tīrthaṅkaras* achieved *nirvāṇa (nirvāṇa-bhūmis)* are found on mountaintops. Naturally, the community populated all these peaks with shrines and small temples. The most sacred *nirvāṇa-bhūmi* is Sameṭa Śikhara, in Bihar [see Fig. 40], situated in the Parasnath (Pārśvanātha) Mountains. With the exception of Ṛṣabha, Vāsupūjya, Nemi, and Mahāvīra, all the remaining 20 *tīrthaṅkaras* reached their final liberation on the peaks of this mountain range. Digambaras and Śvetāmbaras have shared jurisdiction over this *tīrtha.*

Ṛṣabha and his ninety-nine children, including Bāhubali, achieved liberation on Mount Aṣṭāpada, better known as Kailash, these days situated in Tibet. Vāsupūjya did so in Campā, in Bihar, Nemi on Mount Girnar in Gujarat, Mahāvīra in Pava (Pāvāpurī), in the vicinity of Patna, nowadays the capital of the state of Bihar. On the site of the *nirvāṇa* at Pava there is a pool, in the centre of which there is an island, where the Temple of Water (Jalamandir) stands. It is said that the footprints in the rock show the exact place where Mahāvīra achieved *nirvāṇa.* Usually, the pilgrimage to Pava also includes a visit to the city of Rajgir, built upon the site of ancient Rājagṛha.

While Pava is administered by both *saṃpradāyas,* other sacred places have involved controversy. Such is the case with Mount Girnar, considered one of the five sacred mountains in Śvetāmbara Jainism, and from which Digambaras complain they were expelled. It is also a sacred mountain for followers of Śiva and the Devī.

TĪRTHA-KṢETRAS

Places where *arhats* and the great ascetics of the community attained enlightenment *(tīrtha-kṣetras)* are extremely sacred. Some examples are Mangitungi, in Maharashtra, Taranga, in Gujarat, and Gommatagiri, in Karnataka.

Among Śvetāmbaras, the Shatrunjaya Mountains, just outside the town of Palitana, in Gujarat, are especially esteemed. According to their legends, Puṇḍarika (son of Bharata and first *gaṇadhara* of Jainism), the heroes Rāma and Sītā, plus the five Pāṇḍava brothers, along with some hundreds of millions of *sādhus,* achieved their liberation there. The Universal History states that Ṛṣabha, Bharata, and Bāhubali visited the mountain. And it is said that Indra still frequents the spot (Jinaprabha Sūri, *Vividhatīrthakalpa* 1.96). Jinaprabha Sūri (14th century) describes how the *tīrtha* was raided and sacked by Muslims. According to this pilgrim, this did not stop even wild, savage animals dwelling free from sin, and devoting themselves to fasting and *tapas* under the place's nonviolent atmosphere (*Vividhatīrthakalpa* 1.42). On the other hand, birds of ill omen have never gather here at Shatrunjaya. At the end of the 16th century, the Tapā-gacchin head Hīravijaya Sūri carried out a mass pilgrimage and consecrated a temple to Ṛṣabha, financed by a rich merchant. Since then, the temples and sanctuaries have sprung up one after another in Shatrunjaya.

There are also *tīrthas* associated simply with monastic complexes and the corresponding temples. In this class of *tīrthas* we have Dilwara, in Mount Abu, Rajasthan. The complex at Abu is worth mentioning because of the perfection and beauty of the temples there, built between the 11th and 13th centuries.

ATIŚAYA-KṢETRAS

The spots where the *tīrthaṅkaras* preached and practised great austerities are also considered *tīrthas,* an example being Allahabad (Prayāga) in Uttar Praddesh, which is associated with Ṛṣabha's *tapas.* Places associated with the life of Mahāvīra are also venerated, such as Bhagalpur (Campā) and Rajgir (Rājagṛha), both in Bihar. Perhaps the most important place of pilgrimage in this category, would yet again be Girnar, where the *tīrthaṅkara* Nemi practised his penitence, taught the doctrine and achieved liberation [see Fig. 41]. For Digambaras, this honour falls to Shravanabelgola, in Karnataka, where the *pontifex* Bhadrabāhu fasted unto death and where the giant statue of Bāhubali is to be found [see Fig. 8]. Apart from participating in the great festival that takes place every 12 years, pilgrims are constantly arriving there to honour small temples that commemorate the hundreds of ascetics that undertook absolute fasting at this place.

OTHER *TĪRTHAS*

This last category of *tīrtha* includes the places where some of the auspicious moments in the lives of *jinas* occurred. For example, cities such as Benares (Vārāṇasī), in Uttar Pradesh, where Pārśva and Supārśva were born; and Besarh (Kundalapura), in Bihar, where Mahāvīra was born; or Ayodhya, the cradle of the first two *tīrthaṅkaras* and capital of the Bharata Empire. Those places where *jinas* renounced the world are also relevant *tīrthas.* Nevertheless, everything seems to indicate that neither Benares nor Ayodhya were Jain *tīrthas* from very ancient times. More likely, they represent appropriations of sacred pan-Indian places and in fact they have little relevance for Jains. On the other hand, there are some Hindu *tīrthas* which are claimed by Jains. This is the case with the important sanctuary at Pandharpur, in Maharashtra, dedicated to the god Viṭhobā (Kṛṣṇa) and which according to Jains was dedicated to Nemi before being taken over by Brāhmaṇas, or the one at Mallikarjuna in Shrishailam, in Andhra Pradesh, which it is said was dedicated to Malli (Sontheimer 1989: 324-325).

Finally, there are *tīrthas,* which are inaccessible to human beings, such as the island of Nandīśvara, a Land of Enjoyment, where deities go to give praise to the *jinas.*

GENEROSITY

An extremely valued religious activity among Jains is the practice of "giving" or "donation" *(dāna).* It also constitutes one of the main channels of interconnection between the lay and ascetic communities, and one of Jain society's distinguishing marks.

Generosity can take on different forms. One of these is the giving of the Jain religion, known as "the donation that eliminates fear" *(abhaya-dāna),* as Jainism is so great that it can eliminate any fear or worry. The highest form of this type of giving was the present given by the *tīrthaṅkaras* to humankind by preaching Jainism. The present-day variant is the one called the "donation of knowledge" *(jñāna-dāna),* in the form of sermons that ascetics give to laypersons.

The second form of generosity is the "donation of religion" *(supātra-dāna). tīrthaṅkara* worship is considered one form of donation to the religion, but it is especially the donation of food, clothes and begging bowls for renunciants (as well as, to a lesser degree, the financing of the construction of temples, images, pilgrimages, initiations, rituals,) which majority of Jains regard as a donation to religion. If the first one involves what ascetics *give* to laypersons, the second consists of what laypersons *donate* to ascetics. Here, we find ourselves in the very heart of the Jain religion: the interchange between renunciants and laypersons.

The third form is charity, toward any kind of living creature, a practice closer to the universal idea of compassion, and there are also conventional donations (giving to family relations, in business, giving of a daughter in marriage, etc.). Not to mention well-publicised donations that are intended as self-aggrandisement which nearly everybody criticises. Each of these types, in turn, is considered to be of lesser worth than the preceding one.

RITUAL GENEROSITY WITH FOOD

Out of all these forms of generosity, the one which we are most interested in is the donation to religion *(supātra-dāna)* that laypersons carry out; that is to say, the donations of food going to ascetics. Without this support, ascetics could not survive and the doctrine could not be transmitted. It is not surprising that texts put a great deal of emphasis on this point. This question, is well worth looking into.

In India, food transactions have a social and moral charge without equal anywhere in the world. One's diet reflects one's specific ritual rank or status. In any Indian village, observing who accepts what food from whom, one can establish a certain social-ritual hierarchy. According to the dominant ideology, the physical, psychic and spiritual constitution of every individual—in other words, their level of purity—is susceptible to disturbance from different channels. One of these channels, and almost certainly the main one, is that of cooked or uncooked food. Clothes, sexual fluids and even presents received are also dangerous channels. An orthodox Brāhmaṇa, for example, would take care to eat only vegetarian food, which had been prepared by another Brāhmaṇa, wearing only traditional cotton garments, strictly observing faithfulness in marriage and not accepting donations—even when many of them have to live on the degrading "payments" received from the congregation. Accepting food from someone always indicates that they are considered an equal, as one accepts their moral substance, contained in their food. most merchant castes, with Jains at the top of the list, are quite scrupulous when it comes to this matter. It would be difficult to find a Jain accepting food from someone who was not Jain or Brāhmaṇa. The strictest Jains would not even go to a restaurant and would rarely accept an invitation to dinner. Pious families would never buy prepared food. While they may be very conservative in this respect, and terribly afraid of being polluted, when sharing food with equals, Jains can be tremendously hospitable. It can be seen that giving food to ascetics is a much more complex and interesting matter than at first sight one would expect.

First, one must distinguish between being generous to an ordinary beggar and being generous to an ascetic mendicant. They are two very different things. Giving alms to a down-and-out is an act of charity. However, the donator does not receive any direct benefit from his or her good deed. It is considered that worldly people are not worthy receivers, as the giver does not gain any spiritual merit whatsoever. On the other hand, with renunciants *(saṃnyāsins,* Śramaṇas) and students of the Veda *(brahmacārins)* the opposite occurs. In fact, the verb which defines Śvetāmbara ascetics' going on their alms-round is *go-carī,* which means something like "eating like a cow" (Laidlaw 1995: 305), and never it is understood as "asking for charity" or "begging". In India, giving food to a saint *(sādhu)* constitutes one of the most powerful means of gaining religious merit *(puṇya).* Giving to ascetics takes one nearer to emancipation. The donor is surely conscious that it is the ascetics on their alms rounds *(atithi)* who confer, rather than receive favours. Therefore it is the donor who in effect "asks" the ascetic to allow him (or her) to "give" (food, clothing, medicine). The reward from this action toward a source of merit such as an ascetic is extremely positive, very likely to generate a favourable reincarnation. As we have already said. For a layperson, an elevated rebirth is just as important as the destruction of *karma* is for ascetics (Norman 1991: 36). Jinasena *(Ādi-Purāṇa* 38.270; cited in Singh 1975: 82) glorified the practice of "giving" as the most appropriate form of religious activity in these times and he considered it the most satisfactory way of spending one's fortune. Each of the 10 stories about exemplary laypersons from the *Upāsaka-daśāḥ* ends up mentioning the heaven which awaits the future *deva* owing to his exemplary conduct and their unstinting generosity towards ascetics. Therefore, when Hindu and Jain laypersons share their food with renunciants they are the first to express their gratitude. The giver, conscious of this beneficial interchange between both parties, as Pūjyapāda stated *(Sarvārtha-siddhi* 7.38; cited in Singh 1975: 84), will give food with a sense of deep devotion, happiness, trust and unselfishness. Obviously, the act of *dāna* does not secure any kind of merit if the donator is an aggressive, amoral or selfish person. The important thing is the spirit in which the transaction in undertaken.

The practice of generosity must comply with a particular etiquette; this means observing quite strict ritual guidelines, especially where the ascetic is concerned. Enlightened Śramaṇas, says the *Dasavaikālika-sūtra* (1.2-3), have to behave like bees, which take nectar from flower-buds gently, without harming them, or like cows that only feed on the blades of the grass and let the plant grow. This directive can be translated as the ascetic avoiding going to ask for alms at those houses (whether Hindu or Jain ones) where the food is not appropriate *(kalpanīya).* "Appropriate" here means strictly vegetarian and prepared according to specific rules. What this amounts to is the isolating of the ascetic from any violence that will inevitably occur in the preparation and cooking of food, but there is more: in the whole of South Asia, the quality of food depends to a great extent on the person who cooks it. This implies that the ascetic will be particularly attentive to the women's level of religiousness in the homes, as it is they who cook the food. He or she will only go to those homes where they are sure the women go on fasts quite often, attend religious sermons, avoid certain vegetables, and where at least one person does not eat after dusk—as the ascetics themselves do not. Although, ascetics do not have a social status, in a certain sense they are provisionally given the status of the purity of the home in question, for which reason the houses must be at their optimum level of purity. Texts abound with forms of begging and the reasons for which the ascetic can refuse food *(Daśavaikālika -sūtra* 6.1). The important thing when on their rounds, just as much as when eating, is maintaining a calm attitude and with mind unperturbed *(Daśavaikālika-sūtra* 6.1.2). Throughout the whole of their lives as renunciants, they will never eat even one meal of their own choice, nor eat one hot meal nor ever drink water that has not been filtered. It is recommended to be discreet, respect local customs, not distinguish between rich and poor homes, avoid bedrooms and go straight to the kitchen. Nor can they accept food made especially for them, not even if it was also made for other guests, Brāhmaṇas or beggars, just as the *Acārāṅga-sūtra* (2.1.1.12) states. The food, which laypersons give, even though it has to comply with rigorous standards of purity, must be what has been prepared for the household's own consumption. The ascetics arrive by surprise, so to speak, and will only accept the leftovers from the donor's meal, at least that is how it is depicted in texts. In practice, ascetics are less scrupulous, given that they cannot inspect the type of food and drink they are offered beforehand, and that it is usually faithful Jains that go to meet them. Nevertheless, laypersons will worry whether everything is in order. When the group of renunciants are sighted in the neighbourhood, there is frantic activity in the kitchens of the appropriate houses. All the utensils and floors are dried, as an ascetic would never accept food from a house that harboured *jīvas* on the floor. As James Laidlaw (1995: 322) has observed, where an ascetic accepts food from a given home, this means he or she recognises that the home follows the correct diet, similar to the ascetics themselves, and thus the family's prestige, honour and level of spiritual progress are perfectly reflected.

Śvetāmbara ascetics, who usually do their rounds in twos and threes, are received in the doorway, they are then greeted with deferential respect and are invited to enter. The entire operation takes place in the kitchen, which has undergone the proper last minute preparation. The ascetics inspect to see if there are any prohibited ingredients (potatoes, onions, garlic). Then, they question the mistress of the house on the acceptability of each dish. They continually ask not to be served any more, at which the mistress of the house invariably responds how little the ascetics have taken. When the ascetics decide they have had enough, they put the food in their own collecting bowl. They go through the same procedure in three or four more houses, and with their bowls full return to their retreats or to the residence where they are temporarily staying, to eat together with the rest of the ascetics. One underlying factor in the Śvetāmbara etiquette is that ascetics do not eat and drink in public. In their retreats, where there could be laypersons visiting, they always eat in a special room away from visitors' eyes and interest. Among Terāpanthīs, renunciants cannot even watch the *ācārya* eat (Laidlaw 1995: 313). Śvetāmbara ascetics eat seated and in company twice a day. The whole process is very similar to that of Buddhists monks.

The solitary Digambara ascetic, for his part, only make one visit a day and he does not carry a begging bowl. The ritual is significantly called "food liturgy" *(āhāra-vidhi)* and it is one of the purest expressions of the pledge of non-violence *(ahiṃsā),* non-possession *(aparigraha)* and asceticism (*tapas*). Given that ascetics of this type are few and far between, usually it is known beforehand in the neighbourhood if there is such an ascetic in the vicinity, and it is perfectly known what time his round begins. Householders or their wives will go out from the doorways of their homes to meet the lone ascetic to ask him to stop and accept their food. They will invariably find him standing in silence with the fingers of his right hand on his shoulder, a gesture, which indicates the intention to receive *dāna* [see FIG. 42]. Nevertheless, as with Śvetāmbaras, Digambara mendicants can refuse donations, as it is advised not to frequent the same house too often, especially those that are found close to their retreat. Ascetics do not forget the simile of the bees, which go from one flower to another. They would not only stop other families from gaining spiritual merit, but they could establish excessively close relationships with certain families, and this would be disastrous for the ascetics. Thus, Digambara ascetics do not really ask for anything, but respond to invitations. When *sādhus* or *āryikās* finally accept food, householders circle around them and proceed to wash their feet as a sign of respect; they declare the purity of their soul and of the food from their house. After reciting the *namaskāra-mantra,* they perform another act of reverence. It is allowed for *kṣullakas, ailakas* and *āryikās* (who are not ascetics technically) to be seated, but Digambara *sādhus* must always remain standing and receive food in the palms of their hands. For this reason they are also usually called *pāṇipātras,* "those who use their hands as a bowl". Ascetics do not enjoy the flavour of the food, as Vaṭṭakera says *(Mūlācāra* 816; cited in Dundas 1992: 152). They eat only to prolong their life dedicated to self-purification, study and the transmission of teachings. Until they have finished eating, they will remain silent. When they have finished they will murmur to themselves the promise not to eat or drink again until the next day. Afterwards, they may give the family a short sermon. As one can observe, the Digambara formula is in certain aspect the opposite to that of Śvetāmbaras. Ascetics come alone, they eat in the layperson's home and only once a day.

This operation as a whole encapsulates a multitude of Jain spiritual elements. The Digambara ascetic is circumambulated as if he was an image of the *tīrthaṅkara.* In fact among lay Digambaras it is a custom to worship them as in the *pūjās* performed in the temples. His attitude is that of the silent one *(muni),* the bondless one *(nirgrantha).* The logic, which lies behind this duly ritualised practice, is the interchange of food for merit and sermons, an act in which ascetics again are comparable to the *tīrthaṅkaras* who showed the path. In all this, we again find similarities to donations given to Buddhist monks in Thailand and Sri Lanka, who after receiving *dāna* perform ritual tasks. However, Jains never say they "give" anything to renunciants. If renunciants receive anything they would posses something, which would break their vow of non-possession. In fact, Śvetāmbaras mix together all the food from their collection, so that not only is the food less tasty, but any trace of individual donation is diluted. From the instant that it is placed in the dish, the food becomes *gocarī,* the same name given to the act of receiving food. Food donation forms part of a variety of religious and ritual expressions typical of South Asia. It can also be found in Hinduism. However, Lawrence Babb (1996: 61-62) has detected an important difference between Hinduism and Jainism. If Hindu renunciants (like Hindu divinities) receive food and *in return* give the leftovers back to laypersons in the form of divine grace *(prosāda)*, the leftovers from Jain ascetics (or the offerings to the *tīrthaṅkaras* at temples) are not returned. The transaction only goes in one direction: devotees to ascetics, or, as James Laidlaw (1995: 317) explains, givers offer their generous donation to a recipient who is very unwilling to receive it. From the renunciant's point of view, they obtain their food without anybody having "given" them anything. Here, we again come across the Jain maxim that those who are most worthy of donations or acts of worship are the ones who least want it, who are least attached. The more by surprise ascetics arrive, the less food they ask for, the more they praise the mistress of the house for giving less quantity, the less pleasure that is shown, the less gratitude expressed. In other words, the more they affirm their quality of non-attachment and renunciation, the more confirmed is the generosity (and in fact the spiritual worth) of the donors who offer their generosity.

RITUAL CHARITY, PRESTIGE AND RECOLLECTION

In addition to the restricted sense of donation of food, the practice of generosity with religion *(supātra-dāna)* can also and usually does involve donations of lodging, medicine, manuscripts, and, in the case of Śvetāmbaras, clothing. Likewise, another not insignificant portion of the practice of "giving" in the broad sense of the word is assistance given to religious institutions. This includes for example, the construction of images and fasting halls, having scriptures copied, financing pilgrimages, an issue worth looking into.

The ideal of spiritual practice for the great majority of Jain laypersons has been provided by the example of a series of distinguished community leaders *(saṃghapatis)*. This goes back to the monarchic tradition of having temples and fasting halls built, plus the donations of land. As merchant communities progressed, they took on this model and adjusted it to their secular situation. From the 16th and 17th centuries onward, instead of kings and ministers, we find pious magnates such as Śāntidās Jhāverī (17th century) or Vīrajī of Surat (17th century). Both were living when Europeans were operating in ports and cities such as Surat and Ahmedabad. Without the banker Śāntidās' participation and financial help, the British would never have been able to engage in any commercial activity on the West Coast of the continent. In his time, Sāntidās was considered one of the richest men in the world. He managed to convince the emperor Śāhjahān to give him land to build fasting halls and temples. He lent the rebel Murād Bakhsh large amounts of money that served to finance his rebellion against the Moghuls. The prince Murād donated the village of Palitana at the foot of the sacred mountain range of Shatrunjaya, for the use of Jain pilgrims (Rizvi 1987: 229). Once the rebellion had subsided, the emperor Aurangzīb was quick to pay Murād's loan back in case he himself had to ask Sāntidās for a loan in the future. Both belonging to Śvetāmbara *gacchas,* Śāntidās and Vīrajī's authority within their community was almost like that of an *ācārya.* The mechanism through which these barons radiated their model is typical of merchants (Mahājanas) in India, whether Jains or Hindus. The question is to gain reputation and prestige *(pratiṣṭhā).*

First, to gain reputation, one's conduct must be seen publicly to be exemplary. In the case of the Mahājanas, ethical piety involves keeping to a strictly vegetarian diet, always maintaining a temperate, balanced tone, not being unduly ostentatious, not getting involved in scandals, avoiding open involvement in politics, arranging marriages carefully and managing business with caution. On the other hand, part of their fortune should be channelled into religious donation *(dāna)* for example, consecrating images, financing a collective pilgrimage, paying for special *pūjās* or festivals, and paying for the initiation of ascetics or works of a philanthropic, charitable nature in general.

As recommended by the vows for lay Jains, [see page 482], it is not unusual for many followers to limit their earnings and belongings. If their fortune happens to exceed this self-imposed limit, they invariably redirect the surplus into *dāna.* Of course, this is the theory, but Jains have channelled'a not inconsiderable amount of money into their religious institutions, motivated by austerity and to gain reputation and prestige (*pratiṣṭhā).* If, as we shall see, fasting is women's main religious activity, generosity is men's practice par excellence. It is so important to them that there really is no need for them to take any vow to devote part of their earnings to charitable works.

In theory, donations should be made secretly, but in reality they have become more or less highly visible public acts. Usually, donations are required at festivals (such as Paryuṣaṇa) and some special sermons. There are practically no important religious ceremonies where there is no call for a donation. A couple of the organising committee members, microphone in hand, will encourage donations. Collections to finance consecrations of new images and to have the honour of giving food to recently initiated ascetics, can turn into authentic auctions among the well-off members in the community, with bids sometimes reaching astronomical figures. Although only a few people are in the bidding, the whole community attends. Spectators joke and make ironical remarks about who is going to bid, with what right. Everyone knows everyone else, and knows how each other's business is going. Every merchant worth the name, must win at least one of the collections, otherwise his prestige will suffer. The donators' names are clearly registered (in olden times this was inscribed on the flagstones in temples or on a plaque on the outside of religious buildings) and their prestige is thus perfectly established. Owing to this generous exhibitionism, benefactors in the community can avail themselves of credit, give the impression of having power, raise their social status and may be able to take advantage of the situation to arrange positive marriage alliances. The benefactor will be considered a patron of religion, community leader, someone to be compared to Indra (devotee of the *tīrthaṅkaras*), or of Śreyāṁsa (the first lay Jain to give food to

Ṛṣabha). Obviously, it is not only money that confers this status. As we have said, givers must show exemplary conduct, their houses must be models of—dietary—correctness, frequently visited by ascetics. To persuade ascetics that one's house is appropriate requires participation in religious events, nor is it unusual for a rich community leader who has, for example, earned the right to give the first food to a newly initiated ascetic (an act thought to provide a large amount of karmic merit), to turn the honour over to the ascetic's family. This act of renunciation, after paying up to tens of thousands of rupees, is considered extremely auspicious.

While, from the religious point of view, the practice of generosity serves to unite the people and give the community a strong sense of identity, from the social point of view it can divide the people as it tends to exaggerate the power and prestige of the successful.

BENEVOLENCE AND COMPASSION

Owing to this curious form of understanding non-attachment *(aparigraha)* and the value of social prestige *(pratiṣṭhā),* the lay community also maintain a series of institutions for the needy with the third type of generosity—charity. These donations are directed towards Jains and non-Jains alike and, in some cases, towards plants and animals.

On the one hand, magnates and assemblies finance schools for children and even adult women. Apart from normal secular teaching, from a very early age, love for all living creatures is instilled in the children. Michael Tobias (1991: 43) uses a very illustrative example from a school in Mumbai. In their daily meditation classes, the children are enjoined by the teacher to visualise their favourite animals and imagine ways of making them feel happy. In silence, every child begins the day concentrating for 48 minutes on this beautiful way of making every living creature happier.

On the other hand, there are the charity houses *(dāna-śālās)* open to every kind of person who needs help or shelter. Since the Jain concept of living creature *(jīva)* does not differentiate between human beings and animals, the community also has a series of veterinary homes or hospitals *(pāñjarāpoḷas)* for old and ailing animals. Homes for blind calves and old cows (abandoned to their fate after they cannot give any more milk) are quite numerous, and there are no large cities in Gujarat without one. This is the case also for buffaloes, camels, goats, monkeys, rats, chickens, parrots, doves, and other birds. These veterinary hospitals are also given donations by Vaiṣṇava Mahājanas. There are also institutions with special cells fitted for keeping insects. From the Jain point of view, animals have feelings. Just as in fables and tales, they have the potential to improve themselves. Offering protection to all living creatures is the social equivalent to offering protection (shelter) to monks or nuns. Of course, the community also finances free dispensaries and hospitals for the benefit of the whole of society. Quite a few have been opened by monks and nuns in depressed areas and they are kept up thanks to laypersons who live hundreds of kilometres away. On all these points, Jains are even ahead of the ever-charitable Christians, even if some of their institutions have not been sufficiently modernised. As Vilas Sangave (1959: 171) has pointed out, there is no humanitarian cause that does not receive help from Jains. During the drought in Gujarat in 1988, it was calculated that 60% of the voluntary organisations in the state were controlled by Jains, although Jains represented no more than 2% of the population of the affected area (Dundas 1992:170). And after the devastating earthquake that struck Kutch in 2001, it was again the Mahājanas who took the initiative. The austere and individual way of life of Jainism in no way underrates compassionate donations *(karuṇa-dāna, aṇukaṃpā)* to those in need.* On the contrary, the concept of *dāna* has taken on a much greater degree of intensity within Jainism than among Hindus. Although textual support is not really needed, Umāsvāti *(Tattvārtha-sūtra* 5.21) himself could not be clearer on this point:

> "Souls render service to one another".

While souls are individual spiritual monads, Jainism conceives the world as a network of totally interconnected beings. All forms of life are part of one same continuum. The individual souls do not live independently from each other. The situation that others are in is also the responsibility of every being, as all *jīvas* are responsible for the construction of the environment that all of us live in. Hence Muni Nyāyavijayajī (1952:140) states that service *(sevā)* is the best form of donation. The ethics of non-violence and benevolence are simultaneously directed inward and outward (Chappie 2002: xxxv). In the words of Hemacandra:

> "A [great layman] should use his wealth indiscriminately to assist all who are in misery or poverty, or who are blind, deaf, crippled, or sick, irrespective of whether [ideal] recipients or not" (cited in Jaini 2002: 146).

The classic criticism of the ideal of individual liberation as ultimately selfish, comes across as being frankly unfair. As Wilhelm Halbass (2000: 84) has seen, one needs to have a certain Eurocentric arrogance to deprive Jainism—and Indian thinking as a whole—of the concept of ethics. If the ultimate objective is, certainly, liberation, the path which one has to take to achieve it requires the development of an ethical attitude.

This shows that the cliché that India did not develop a concept of charity like that of Christians is false. One must also take into account that the Christian Church's charitable activities, undertaken with European tax payers' money in form of levied taxes, cannot be dissasociated from proselytism and missionary crusades.

RITES OF PASSAGE

Given their immersion in the Hindu social and ritual universe, with the passing of the centuries Jains began absorbing typically Hindu religious traits and practices which were conspicuous for their absence in ancient Jainism. The history of Jainism has been a constant tug of war between the perpetuation of perceived orthodoxy and interaction with Hindu society. Until the appearance of the *Ādi-purāṇa* by Jinasena, all Jain texts intended for laypersons outlined a path of interior purification clearly moulded by the ascetic ideal. From the apparition of the *Ādi-purāṇa* onward, however, rites of passage or sacraments *(saṁskāras)* are mentioned that mark important moments in our earthly pilgrimage and which have little to do with spiritual progress. All these rites were taken directly from Vedic/Hindu tradition and the language is definitely Brāhmaṇical. In the Jain context they are simply called "actions" *(kriyās).* To remind ourselves, the *Ādi-prāṇa* is the chronicle that "legitimised" a Jaina-brāhmaṇa class, so that it would not be surprising that the apparition of these rites were directly related to the ascendency of the Jaina-brāhmaṇas.

Adopting Hindu ceremonies must have seemed advantageous to a small community such as the Jains, especially to their more influential members. Hence, seen from the outside, their life would seem not to differ too much from that of Hindus. Moreover, they would avoid criticism from Brāhmaṇas, who while never having bothered too much about doctrinal issues, have traditionally been hostile towards "divergent" behaviour patterns, which in a Brāhmaṇical context means diverging from Brāhmaṇic ritual. As Padmanabh Jaini (1979:292) has put it, Jinasena's work can be best understood as a tool by which Jains would evidence apparent conformity with Hindu practices and yet somehow remain uniquely Jain.

The nature of these sacraments and ceremonies is strictly lay, as ascetics do not participate in them nor do they follow them. All Jain ascetic practice is directed towards liberation, so there is no room for these types of issues. But laypersons aspire to prosperous, auspicious, happy lives, so that any kind of ritual that can provide these ends is welcomed by the laity. It is said that these rites of passage generate religious merit, drive away evil spirits, protect individuals, purify, and help to form one's character and personality. The purpose of the sacraments is to punctuate the life cycle of the individual, from conception until death. In other words, until people have been ritually constructed *(saṃskāra),* they are not true social agents, a notion very much to Brāhmaṇical tastes. With the incorporation of these sacraments, Jainism put less emphasis on spiritual progress *(mārga, yoga)* and strengthened the idea of "religion" in the broader and more functional sense of the word. In the case of many of these life-cycle rituals, the services of

Brāhmaṇas or Jaina-brāhmaṇas are sought.

Digambaras took on the 16 typical Hindu sacraments and made them theirs and to this list they added quite a few more of their own, up to a total of fifty-three ceremonies. This process of Hinduisation initiated by Jinasena was extended by the contributions of Cāmuṇḍarāya and Āśādhara. For Śvetāmbaras, laypersons must go through the classic 16 sacraments described in their *Ācāra-dinakara,* written somewhat later than the *Ādi-purāṇa.* The amplification of this spectrum of religious practices culminated with Hemacandra.

PRENATAL AND INFANT CONSECRATIONS

Likely, the first consecration in the lives of Jains is the so-called "installation of the embryo" *(garbhādhāna),* a service which is celebrated previous to the moment of conception. The main intention of the service is to conceive a male child. Given the patrilineal and patrilocal nature of Indian society, males are the heirs to their family's properties and wealth.

In the months of pregnancy different rituals are celebrated—these days on the decline—with the intention of protecting the mother and foetus.

The birth ceremony *(jātakarman, priyodbhava)* is a naturally widely celebrated primordial sacrament. Usually, the birth takes place at the home of the mother's parents. The *guru* calls on the *jina* and also the goddess Ambikā to protect the new born baby, which receives its first ritual bath together with its mother. The presence of an astrologer is all but obligatory. On the third day, praise is given to the *jina,* at which the infant is present for the first time. In more "grass roots" homes, acts of worship of the "little mothers" *(mātṛkās)* and the goddess Ṣaṣṭhī are needed to placate their anger and protect the baby from Alness. In the more Sanskritised homes, a salutation to the Sun is included. Jain legal texts also describe the proceedings for adoption for those couples who cannot have their own biological descendants. Negotiations and rituals end with a birth ceremony *(jātakarman),* which makes the adoption official (von Glasenapp 1925: 462).

Infancy is full of consecrations of such things as the first time of leaving home *(bahiryāna),* first solid food *(annaprāśana)*, first haircut *(caula, cūḍākarma),* first ear piercing *(karṇavedha)* and the service celebrated on learning the alphabet *(lipisaṅkhāyana),* which is usually held at the age of five. Many of these rites have fallen into disuse.

The two most relevant consecrations during infancy are name-giving *(nā-makarma, nāmakaraṇa)* and initiation *(upanīti).* Both can also be found in Hinduism. The *nāmakarma* takes place 12 days after birth. Traditionally, the child's name is chosen at random, picking out of 1,008 epithets of the *jinas* and goddesses, but it is not uncommon for there to be an agreement between the astrologer, the *guru* and members of the family, with the starring role here being the oldest paternal aunt. The *upanīti (upanayama* in Hinduism) only concerns members of the upper social classes and used to happen when the male child was between seven and 12 years of age. These days, it is customary for it to happen the day before getting married. On this day, the preceptor performs an act of worship to the *jina* in front of the initiate's home, chants specific hymns and mutters the *pañca-namaskāra-mantra* three times into his ear. Also, the new initiates accept basic dietary restrictions *(mūlaguṇas),* which put them directly onto the first rung *(pratimā)* of spiritual progression [see pages 476-478]. At this point, the young person is "officially" initiated, a Jain, an adult, a twice-born *(dvi-ja)* able to wear the sacred cord of those in his condition. It should be stressed that this initiation, clearly Hindu in nature, is habitual in the South, but uncommon in the North. In former times, it was customary for the young man to go out to collect alms on this day and from then on to study basic knowledge with his preceptor for some years. Of course, the model here is the celibate student *(brahmacārin)* of Brāhmaṇism.

MARRIAGE

The next consecration would be that of marriage *(vaivāhikī),* definitely the most important one of all, especially for women. There are eight recognised traditional formulas for marriage in India *(Āśvalāyana-gṛhya-sūtra* 1.6), but only marriages known as *brāhma* and *prājāpatya* are encouraged. Just as in the rest of India, Jain marriages are pacts between two families agreed by the progenitors *(brāhma* style marriage) even though the joining together through love or own choice is tolerated—usually in modern urban settings. The choice must adjust itself to the rules of each caste, which are usually isogamous or hyper-ga-mous, even if some mixed marriage with Vaiṣṇavas is plausible [see page 300]. From the end of the 19th century onward, Jain reformers have been pushing very hard to abolish practices such as childhood marriages and the buying and selling of brides. Partly, thanks to the efforts of the Daksina Mahārāṣṭra Jain Sabhā, customs of this sort have ceased to exist within the Jain community and have considerably diminished in many other communities in India. Even though there has been a large amount of propaganda against dowries in Jain writings the truth is that this burden still exists within the community (and in an exaggerated way, as the phenomena is more serious the higher the standard of living), despite the campaigns against it, directed by reform movements. Divorce is accepted in certain circumstances and any desire to remarry on the part of widows must come to terms with local or caste customs (this only among the *dasā* section).

Astrologers arrange the date of the wedding and look into whether there are any planetary incompatibilities between the couple-to-be. The preparations are marked by rituals, most of which are not purely Jain. For example, it is very normal to perform an act of worship to the god Gaṇeśa (he who surmounts obstacles, always called upon when a new enterprise is begun) three days before the wedding.

The actual ceremony usually opens with an act of worship of an image of an omniscient being. The priest in charge of the ceremony (who is usually a

Brāhmaṇa) lights the three classic fires, which the bride and groom circle three times. When the groom takes the bride by the hand the marriage is ritually established.

OTHER RITES

From the religious point of view, the ceremony of taking vows *(yratāropa)* is relevant. It is one of the few sacraments that do not appear in Vedism/Hinduism. It is obvious that with its inclusion the community were looking for a way to integrate these "secular" services in a context of individual spiritual progress. We shall be looking at these vows in the next part [see chapter 31].

The funeral rite is the "last sacrament" *(antyasaṃskāra)* in the life of a layperson. The dead body is bathed and carefully decked out, then taken to the place of cremation. Three days after the incineration the ashes are usually scattered into the river. Then, normally lay Jains attend the retreat where renunciants spend the night to receive a sermon on the transitory nature of this world. The period of mourning is usually nine months, during which the widow will wear black, will not attend the temple and will follow a very simple diet. It is probable that from this day on she will devote herself earnestly to the contemplative and ascetic life. She will never more wear colourful saris, jewels, or the *bindi* on her forehead. Retired people and widowers will also involve themselves more in religious activities.

We do not find anything similar to the Hindu funeral *(antyeṣṭi)* or offerings to the deceased *(śrāddha),* nor is there a participation of Brāhmaṇas. These two rituals are essential for Hindus. In them they set out to transform the bodiless spirit *(preta)* of the dead person—thanks to offerings of rice from relatives and the participations of Brāhmaṇas—into a revered ancestor *(pitṛ)* (McGee 2004: 354). Obviously, the service not only contradicts Jain cosmology, but also challenges the Jain maxim that everyone forges his or her own destiny and rebirth. The omission of this service (except in certain strongly Hinduised families in the Deccan region) is clear proof that in spite of their assimilation to Hindu patterns, Jain orthodoxy is still alive. Nonetheless, the general tone of Jain rites of passage bears a clear similarity to Hindu *saṁskāras.*

29. THE PRACTICE OF ASCETICISM

HOMAGE TO THE MASTERS

Everything that comes under the heading of pilgrimage *(yātrā),* of worship in the temple *(pūjā)* and of festivals *(utsavas)* constitutes the bulk of devotional practice and veneration of the *jinas,* but there is a fourth expression of devotion: homage to the masters *(guru-upāsti).* Unlike the others, this is a religious act fit for both laypersons and ascetics alike, and one of those considered obligatory *(āvaśyakas)* for the latter. Thus, its purpose is not as much to gain good *karma* (at least in theory), than to eliminate *karma.* We shall begin with this practice in a chapter, which is devoted to the practices most deeply rooted in the ideal of asceticism. Obviously, there is no need to draw a hard and fast dividing line between the practices dealt with in the last two chapters and what we are about to consider now. Worshipping the *jinas,* pilgrimage and festivals might be more imbued with ascetic values than veneration towards the masters, fasting and meditation. Everything depends on one's mental disposition or state of mind *(bhāva),* but if the first mentioned are practices that can be taken as exclusively focusing on acquisition of good *karma,* with the second group it is more difficult to do so. This has been the subjective criterion I will use to separate auspicious practices from ascetic ones. Let us proceed now to looking at veneration of the masters.

With the passage of time, the lay community added the homage to ascetics who lived the ideal of non-attachment, non-violence, and pure conduct to their acts of worship of the *jinas.* It was a logical step. The usual *pūjā* is worship directed towards the ascetics par excellence, the *tīrthaṅkaras.* Logically, living ascetics, who take part in the sacradness of the *tīrthaṅkara,* are beings who are equally worthy of laypersons' worship. Renunciants symbolise, at least in attenuated fashion, perfect souls.

Given that ascetics are few and far between, local communities can go months without seeing one, and perhaps years without seeing a renowned *ācārya.* In the case of the extreme scarcity of Digambara ascetics, the function of preceptor *(guru)* may become the responsibility of spiritually advanced laypersons, the so-called *kṣullakas* and *ailakas,* or the female *āryikās.* These receive the same deference given to unclad monks. For those groups that do not perform acts of worship in temples (Sthānakavāsīs, Terāpanthīs) homage to the *guru* is given most importance.

The practice of veneration itself consists of, once again, the "vision" (*darśana)* and venerating of renunciants. There is little difference between this and simple *caityavandana pūjā* [see pages 419-420]. The ritual always includes prostration before the master along with the petition to be consecrated with a *mantra.* It can vary depending on the rank of the ascetic in question and on the occasion. In its full version, it provides a context for laypersons to make their confessions. The Śvetāmbara ritual of veneration includes the transaction with a sacred powder known as *vāskṣepa.* It is made of a mixture of sandalwood, saffron, and other substances, and is offered by laypersons to ascetics. The latter dusts powder over the devotee's head and neck. Upon receiving this, the lay worshipper touches the ascetic's feet—provided they are the same sex—and is again blessed with the *vāskṣepa* powder. The act means the assimilation of the teachings. From the laypersons' point of view, however, *vāskṣepa* has more miraculous connotations.

Jainism has managed to create a close link between large lay communities and small communities of renunciants. Ascetics have always been laypersons' spiritual masters *(gurus).* All committed Jains feel themselves to be pupils *(śiṣyas)* of an ascetic. Renuciants' main obligation to the lay community is instruction in the sacred doctrine [see FIG. 43]. It should be remembered that the sermons that ascetics preach to laypersons are considered to be the highest form of religious donation: the donation of knowledge *(jñāna-dāna)* For this reason, the concept of *upāsti* not only includes veneration of the masters, but also listening to ascetics' sermons. In such a way, the layperson becomes the genuine hearer *(upāsaka, śrāvaka).* On many occasions, the talks are recorded. Once at home, it is not unusual for devotees to circle the loudspeakers, as if the actual ascetic talking were present. In the lay community, the ascetics' physical or figurative presence is the best symbol of their identity.

This interconnection has done much to raise the level of accomplishment of renunciants. Laypersons know well how ascetics should behave and what is expected of them. Communities "watch" to see that no one strays from the right path. One important factor in the cohesion between these two groups is that ascetics have never involved themselves in the affairs of this world to any extent. There has never been a Jain Church. None of the ascetics question laypersons on their social and ethical behaviour. As Padmanabh Jaini (1979: 208) has well pointed out, the relationship between these two groups has never been tinged with fear or guilt.

Religious terminology in India concedes the *guru* another possible companion, besides the disciple *(śiṣya):* the devotee *(bhakta)* (Laidlaw 1995: 60). What is important for the *bhakta* is not so much the doctrinal orthodoxy of the teachings but rather the personal relationship with the ascetic. The *guru* is a direct manifestation of the divine or, in the case of Jains, the light of truth. It is the renunciant's personal quality that counts and not so much their teachings. It is in this sense that one has to interpret countless stories about miraculous powers of reputed ascetics or the popularity of the benevolent Gautama. For this reason, many Jains can go hundreds of miles (immediately before embarking on a new business venture or when arranging a marriage) on a pilgrimage to "look upon" the renunciant they have taken as a *guru.* The curious thing is that ascetics are unaware of the devotion they inspire, and paradoxically but logically, the more austere, non-attached they are, and the more they resemble the *jinas,* the more devotion they will inspire, and yet the colder and more distant will the relationship be with devotees. Indeed, as James Laidlaw (1995: 64) has pointed out, religious devotion can be seen, from another perspective, as positively irreligious.

CONFESSIONS

The practice of confession *(pratikramaṇa)* is one of the rites in which ascetic values are most clearly seen. Moreover it is one of the more ritualised practices, with little room for improvisation.

The rite of confession is usually a collective act held in ascetic retreats. However the participation of ascetics is not necessary. Normally, the confession takes place before their symbolic representation *(sthāpanācārya),* a small table engraved with auspicious signs (among Śvetāmbaras), but when there is a *sād-hu* or *sādhvl* present in the retreat, then he or she always takes part, in which case the homage to the masters usually includes the rite of confession.

Traditionally, five forms and moments are stipulated for confession: each morning, each evening, each night, every four months, and every year. Ascetics maintain them to the letter, as they form part of their six ritual obligations. Laypersons are less strict and usually restrict confession to once a year, on the occasion of the festival of Paryuṣaṇa and Daśalakṣaṇa-parvan. At this time, it is a tradition to write letters of reconciliation *(vijñaptis)* or visit acquaintances with the intention of apologising for something. Nevertheless, the number of Jains (especially women) who carry out group confessions daily or weekly is not inconsiderable. Moreover, they take advantage of the occasion to converse and interchange information about engagements, marriages, and deaths. Quite a fair proportion of women carry out the rite of confession daily at home, along with the practice of meditation. The rite includes the vow not to eat until an hour after sunrise on the following day. Thus, it also includes the practice of (nocturnal) fasting.

The rite itself contains three actions, which are repeated over and over again: inspection of one's body *(pratilekhanā),* veneration of the master *(guru-upāsti, vandana)* and abandonment of one's body *(kāyotsarga).* It is a clearly an ascetic pattern. The first action consists in gently cleaning the cushion where one is going to sit, and one's body, of any insect or small creature that may be present, brushing them aside with a handkerchief. The second stage is to carry out a series of prostrations before the master or a symbolic representation of such. The third entails keeping still while standing up, like the *tīrthaṅkara* or ascetic in meditation. The three acts are conducted consecutively at different moments during the rite. While they are undertaken, prescribed texts are read or recited. The aesthetics of *ahiṃsā* prevail during the whole ritual, but it all goes much deeper.

The heart of the ritual consists in reciting some rather odd lists of sins and transgressions. In James Laidlaw's view (1995: 211) this actually constitutes a good summary of Jain moral psychology and a demonstration of the characteristic tone of Jain ethical and religious discourse. The first list consists in enumerating all possible forms of violence *(hiṃsā).* It is declared that there are 8,400,000 life forms in the world, and that those confessing have no idea how many of these they have harmed. Here, in this first confession, Jains enumerate the thirteen possible types of reincarnation (700,000 earth *ekendriyas,* 700,000 water *ekendriyas*... 200,000 types of animals with four senses... 400,000 gods... up to 1,400,000 types of human beings). The second list entails enumerating eighteen types of major sins (violence, lying, stealing, greed, anger). That is, the evils that are combated with the five vows *(mahāvratas),* the passionate forms *(kaṣāyas)* that keep us in bondage to this world. The third list, an even longer one, is the enumeration of the possible transgressions of the twelve vows that pious laypersons may decide to take for life [see pages 478-479].

The rite of confession differs a great deal from Christian equivalents. Jains also have private confessions *(ālocana),* where specific sins are confessed to an ascetic who gives advice on pertinent expiation *(prāyaścittas),* but the *pratikramaṇa* is an expression of apology in general, rather than for any specific deed or misdeed. It does not, then, entail the confession consciously committed. As Laidlaw says(1995: 213), the ethics and the psychology of shame and guilt are bypased, because enumeration is focused upon all existing possible sins. Digambaras usually ask for forgiveness with an ancient and beautiful declaration, very representative of Jainism:

> "I forgive all living beings and poay that they all forgive me. I am friendly to all living beings and bear nobody ill-will" (Vaṭṭakera, *Mūlācāra* 2.8; cited in S. Jain 1989: 164).

An identical citation, included in the *Āvaśyaka-sūtra,* is also used by Śvetāmbaras at the time of the Paryuṣaṇa. Śvetāmbara tradition contains a perhaps even older formula much in the same way, as it establishes a dialogue between the ascetic and the layperson (which is recited by heart) in ancient Prakrit. The interchange clearly illustrates the type of relationship there is between both, since it includes the veneration of the master. They say:

> "I desire to worship you, kṣamāśramaṇa, with very intense concentration. (The guru: So be it.) You will have spent the whole day, fortunately, little disturbed. (The guru: Yes.) You are making spiritual progress. (The guru: Yes, and so are you.) You are unperturbed by your sense organs? (The guru: Yes.) I ask you pardon, kṣamāśramaṇa, for my daily transgressions. (The guru: I too ask pardon.) I must engage in pratikramaṇa [confession] to you, kṣamāśramaṇa, for any day-by-day lack of respect... anything done amiss through mind, speech, or body, through anger, pride, deceit, or greed, through false behavior and neglect of the sacred doctrine at any time; whatever offence may have been committed by me, forbearing monk, I confess and reprehend and repent of it and cast aside my past self *(Āvaśyaka-sūtra* 10; cited in Jaini 1979: 209).

These confessions always contain the line "through mind, speech, or body" or refer to sins "that one has committed, one has caused others to commit, or allowed others or encouraged others to commit", either consciously or unconsciously. In this way, the notion of an individual committing such and such a sin is transcended. Through confession Jains strengthen their idea that their soul is potentially the same as those of all others. Actually, there is no need even for a confessor. If there is a *sādhu, sādhvī* or their symbolic representation present, the "confessor" is nothing more than the image of the lineage that leads directly to the *tīrthaṅkaras,* and they cannot absolve anybody. So, the rite is a form of asceticism and concentration, a way to eliminate *karma.* Here, the heavens are not aimed at, and for that reason, the ritual requires the practice of abandonment of the body, and that it is followed by fasting. In a certain sense, going back to Laidlaw (1995: 215), the *praktikramana* is not so much a confession, in the manner the Christian tradition conceives it, as a reparation.

FASTING

If, to the casual observer, worshipping the *jinas* is the most visible religious practice in Jainism, possibly for Jains the following of specific restrictions *(pratyākhyāna)* and penitence *(tapas)* constitute the most meaningful forms of external practice. Invariably, these restrictions take on the form of fasting *(poṣadhopavāsa, uposatha, anaśana).* Again, this activity is common to laypersons and ascetics, for whom it is another of the ritual obligations. For the former, it is one of the activities in which they come to feel like real Śramaṇas, whose objective is to burn *karma* (not to acquire good *karma).* It is taken to such a point that most Jains consider fasting to be a superior form of spiritual practice, above worshipping in temples. For that reason, the most used term for fasting is *tapas.* The Jain custom of fasting is attested in the most ancient Buddhist texts *(Aṅguttara-nikāya* 1.204).

Given that food forms an essential part of the karmic prison, as it is responsible for the construction of our bodies, it is quite logical that Jainism has tended towards a certain attenuation of food intake as one of its most habitual ascetic practices, and in any case it is another way of differentiating oneself from the Brāhmaṇic *ethos* (in which food and eating are sacred matters). In Jainism, on the other hand, food has a rather poor reputation. Lawrence Babb (1996: 178) mentions a Jain friend in Ahmedabad who said, without a trace of irony, that one should eat with tears in one's eyes for creatures that had to die when one eats. Food is dangerous—and searching for food is the root cause of all violence in *saṃsāra;* it constitutes and symbolises the world of attachment in a concentrated way. Attenuation can even reach a total cessation, in a final fast, but we shall talk about this in chapter 31.

The vow of fasting can take a host of different forms. It can simply mean not eating or drinking until 48 minutes (one Indian hour) after the Sun has risen, as happens when the rite of confession is conducted. Or one can decide to fast for a few days, repeated annually for seven, 10 or 15 years. Tradition offers up to 40 forms of fasting. Devotees choose for themselves. It is very common to take the vow of partial or complete fasting on the occasion of the *parvan* days (thought to be very auspicious days, when the Moon is in its change of phase), or at specific festivals, or for personal reasons. Fasting is most frequent during the monsoon months, when ascetics are sedentary and there is more contact with the lay community. And so it often happens that laymen or women take the vow of fasting in the presence of an ascetic. The truth is that, as with confession, the benediction of, and supervision by, ascetics is not compulsory. One can take the vow privately (in front of an image of the *jina* or the representation of an ascetic), or joining up with a group that has the same intention. The important thing is to take the vow *(vrata)* with the declaration of intentions. To the contrary the vow would be unfruitful. In collective fasting, a patron from the community is needed to finance the ritual.

Many of these fasts are partial. James Laidlaw (1995: 216) has written that in Jainism fasting is frequently a form of eating. In these cases it usually means one very frugal meal a day. The important thing is that, whatever the instance, food is converted into religious activity, and since this has to do with not eating, this is also not doing. Non-action in Jain terms is the highest and surest form of eliminating *karma.* Fasting can provide religious merit (*puṇya),* without a doubt; but what is valued by the community is its potential for burning *karma,* which is where its soteriological value lies. For this to be the outcome, the mental attitude *(bhāva)* of non-attachment, composure, and purity is indispensable.

Fasting is also the external form which most differentiates Jains from their neighbours. While in Hinduism fasting does form part of its religious practice, and in fact the Sanskrit term *uposatha* denoted fasting that the Vedic Indians carried out before a sacrifice, in no way is the practice of fasting so extended, frequent or as prolonged as amongst Jains, nor does it have the same connotations. For example, Jain fasting commemorates the fast Ṛṣabha had to undergo on becoming the first renunciant of this cosmic cycle. People did not know how to give food to ascetics then, and they offered him jewels, treasures, and rich foods. Ṛṣabha had to go without eating for six months before, miraculously a layperson dreamed of seeing Jain monks in a past life—without a doubt in a previous cosmic cycle—and offered him the correct food in the appropriate manner. And Ṛṣabha was able to break his fast. In emulation of this gesture, one of the most common fasting periods in Jainism is prolonged for a whole year and combines one day of total fasting with one day of partial fasting. The fast comes to an end with the arrival of the festival of the Akṣayatṛtīyā. In this way, one takes part in the type of asceticism of more virtuous eras, thus emulating the superhuman efforts of the great heroes from the past. The goal of liberation lies behind the majority of Jain fasts. Lay Jains are very conscious that their fasting is the deepest and most faithful expression of the value of *tapas.*

A normal fast could be performed in the following fashion. After breakfast, duly purified laypersons will go along to the fasting hall of the community *(poṣadha-śālā),* which is usually found in the retreat. They stay there for a day and a half or two whole days, which is the typical lapse of time for many fasts. They sleep very little, they recite sacred *mantras* and read their scriptures. Although fasts are usually congregational, they induce silence and meditation. They seek to emulate the behaviour of ascetics. This aspect is perfectly reflected in the layperson's use of a feather whisk broom, cue of the very few utensils carried by ascetics, a symbol of their dedication to *ahiṃsā,* and which devotees will use to carefully dust the mat they plan to sit on. It is frequent for fasts to be accompanied by group prayers in the temple *(pūjā),* confessions to ascetics *(pratikramaṇa)* and listening to religious talks delivered by monks *(pravacanas).* Afterwards they will go home, give worship to the *jina,* give food to ascetics and break their fast. This participation by laypersons in the monastic ideal has greatly strengthened the ties between both communities.

Women particularly follow this practice with great earnestness. Fasting is a Jain women's best expression of purity, morality and chastity. As Josephine Reynell (1991: 64) has said, the photo album of their fasts comes out straight after their wedding album. Fasts serve to show that the lady is under control and has kept her womanly honour after marrying. Fasting during *purnimā* or full Moon is so habitual that in the case of many Jain women it is almost "compulsory". The same can be said for many fasts during festivals. There are quite a number of women for whom the fast called *Rohiṇī-tapas* (three days a month of total fasting), which is prolonged over a period of seven years and seven months, is the religious activity par excellence. It is practically impossible to find a Jain man or woman who does not have a degree of experience of fasting. In the case of women, the act gains more meaning when it is she who, without having had a bite to eat or a drop of water to drink, cooks, prepares and serves meals to the rest of the family who are not fasting. As Paul Dundas (1992:172) resumes, fasting is not a personal matter nor is it something imposed as punishment for bad conduct. Rather, taking a vow implies some kind of fasting is the most meaningful of a range of religious practices willingly adopted by women. Very often, the vow is suggested by an ascetic, testing the seriousness of her commitment, and by extension, of her family's in regard to the religion.

THE CRUSADE AGAINST THE BODY

From the Jain point of view, the body embodies the situation of bondage of human beings. This is something the scriptures never cease to remind us. All Jain ascetic practices, to a greater or lesser degree, have much to do with the privation of the body. But on looking deeper into ascetic practices, it can be seen that the principal of privation, rather than harming the body, tries to use it as an ally. Ascetics and laypersons when fasting use the body to control something much more evasive: the mind. The body is not the enemy; attachment and thoughts are. Jain fasting, even if it is spectacular, does not lead to self-destruction. Even the more ascetic Jainism of renunciants operates in the same way. It is true that for some people, suffering and pain (for example, illness) is welcomed. Such was the case when the Kharatara-gacchin saint Vicakṣaṇa Śri endured terminal cancer with impeccable stoicism, without the aid of medicines, but Vicakṣaṇa was not trying to harm her body, but was redefining the pain as voluntary asceticism.

In Jainism, there is another way of applying ascetic practice: subduing the body. Usually, those who take this radical path are strictly dualists: body and mind are antithetical principals, and only with a crusade against the body can the soul become aware of itself. Even though this radical position is a minority one, it has unquestionable influence in Jain imagery. Rājacandrạ gives us a perfect example of a Jain saint who uses asceticism to force the body to give in. Another notable figure in this respect, was the contemporary saint—in this case too, uninitiated— Amarcānda Nahar, who kept a vow of silence for twenty years, for ten years he ate without salt and for many more years he performed intermittent fasting. In the end he fasted unto death. For these people, their bodies were not an instrument of religious action, but the problem, the burden that had to be eliminated or transcended. The parallel with medieval Christian asceticism has been underlined, notably in the case of certain Christian nuns and female saints, controversially given the nickname of "holy anorexics". Notwithstanding, James Laidlaw (1995: 239-242) has also pointed out some differences—the first being gender, as the Jains who have followed this path have been men and indeed laymen. So comparisons must not be taken too far. As the iconographie study of the *jinas* suggests, one's body can be the reflection of one's spiritual qualities [see page 405]. This is the perception that the vast majority of Jains, laypersons and renunciants alike, subscribe to, so that the suggested dichotomy between body and spirit is rather attenuated. Laidlaw (1995: 393) concludes his outstanding work by saying that the opposite side of the coin to the anorexic saints is represented by such benevolent figures as the pot-bellied Gautama and the *dādāgurus*.

STUDY

Meditative study of scripture *(svādhyāya)* is another habitual practice among laypersons. Even though very few know the old languages (Semi-Magadhi, Sanskrit or Jaina-Maharashtri), the most important texts in Jainism are translated into vernacular languages.

Jains hold their manuscripts in very high regard. They are a symbol of the truth that encapsulate and represent the glorious link between them and their masters in the tradition. The attitude of the priesthood *(bhaṭṭārakas, yatis)* had much influence on the construction and maintenance of libraries *(grantha-bhaṇḍāras)*. Being responsible for religious institutions, they erected libraries where manuscripts donated by laypersons were stored. The libraries at Karanja, in Maharashtra, Mudabidri, in Karnataka, those at Bikaner and Jaisalmer in Rajasthan, and those at Patan, Cambay and Palitana in Gujarat, are formidable. The most important one, the one at Jaisalmer, was founded by the monk Jinabhadra in the middle of the 16th century to protect manuscripts, which were then threatened by Muslim zeal. However, the major part of the task of entrusting texts to be copied rested with the laity, who considered it to be extremely meritorious work. These days, lay associations finance nearly all libraries. The great care taken of sacred texts is reinforced and emphasised on the occasion of Śruta-Pañcamī and Jñāna-Pañcamī, when manuscripts are cleaned and dusted off and, if needed, new copies made. This has allowed that a great amount of the sacred literature has come down our times, in a very good state of preservation. In fact, the oldest Indian manuscripts that have been preserved are Jain texts dating back to the 10th and 11th centuries. Their value for the community as well as for the whole Indian civilisation is incalculable. Many of them are impeccably illustrated. Various reform movements, along with the labour of masters such as Muni Puṇyavijaya, enabled many such manuscripts come to light, to be translated into vernacular languages and printed on paper.

SCHOOLS

Within the community, there are different types of associations that dedicate themselves to study. Many are primary and secondary schools *(gurukulas),* such as the one inspired by the ascetic Mahāsatī Mohanadevī in Delhi, or the one built by Muni Samanthabhadra near Kolhapur, in Maharashtra. Quite a few free schools (the fruit and outcome of *dāna)* are intended to rescue Indian women from illiteracy. One noteworthy example is the *āśrama* at Sholapur, in Maharashtra, founded by Sumatibai Shah, a woman inspired by the ideals of Śāntisāgara and Gandhi.

Other schools *(pāṭha-śālās),* typical of the Tapā-gacchins, are restricted to the use of ascetics and laypersons who express their desire to go deeper into the knowledge of their religion. The Sthānakavāsīs have similar institutions called "seats of knowledge" *(yidyāpīṭhas).* The Terāpanthīs, who do not have retreats for ascetics, have in their large complex of Ladnun an imposing centre of learning called Śri Pāramārthika Śikṣaṇa Saṁsthā. The whole course takes seven years.

MEDITATION

The meditative tradition in Jainism has not been as strong as in Yoga and Buddhist streams, far from it. Although everybody recognises the importance of concentration *(dhyāna),* tradition has historically inclined towards asceticism *(tapas).* Except in groups such as the Terāpanthī and the Kanjisvāmī-Panth, there has been rather slight practice of Jain meditative *yoga.* In fact many Jains these days attend centres of *rāja-yoga* and Buddhist *vipaśyanā* meditation to fill in this vacuum. Even so, meditation is one of the most valued and prestigious practices in Jain tradition.

Padmanabh Jaini (1979: 221) sums up by saying that the practice of meditation *(sāmāyika)* is the way to integrate laypersons' religious activities within the yogic methods of the ascetic path. When meditating, laypersons become ascetics (and find themselves under the vow of *sāmāyika).* This was already stated by the great Vaṭṭakera:

> "Since through the performance of *sāmāyika* the layman becomes like a monk, for this reason it should be performed often" *(Mūlācāra* 533; cited in Dundas 1992: 149).

For most of people, this translates into types of concentration of a meditative/ devotional nature. This is practised daily for an Indian hour (48 minutes). It is quite common for laypersons to group together to perform it collectively. Women usually practice meditation at sunrise, at home.

The practice of meditation itself consists of various different recitations and hymns in honour and reverence to the *jinas.* Some people read the *Sāmāyika-sūtra,* others recite it off by heart, and the rest just murmur the *namaskāra-mantra.* The practice includes the vow of not harming things, intimately linked to the vow of *ahiṃsā* and the rite of confession. These recitations must be undertaken in the spirit of recollection, normally in the lotus position; otherwise, the *sāmāyika* would not have ascetic power. It is said that whoever perseveres with the restrictions and concentrations receives an inkling of the happiness and peace *(samyak-darśana)* of somebody who has overcome the *karmas* and passions that darken the taking the path of renunciation. We shall talk about meditation in more depth when we come to look at the ascetic path leading to *nirvāṇa* [see pages 497-501].

Part XII
Soteriology

Jainism has often been described as a deeply pessimistic philosophy and religion (Zimmer 1951: 227). For many, the Jain vision of the world is a nightmare without beginning or end. In fact, this imputation has been extended to the majority of Indian philosophies and ways of life. Since all ancient Indian religions were agreed that life is suffering, finitude and contingency *(duḥkha),* unavoidably so, given the mechanisms of *karma,* all seek an abstract otherworldly goal—liberation from this world *(mokṣa, nirvāṇa).* There is something in this. Nevertheless, such a criticism seems to me to be a rather perverse interpretation of the Indian scale of values.

The ultimate goal of Jainism is to restore the spirit or soul to its inherent state of purity in such a manner that it can achieve omniscience, which is its essential condition. However, we know that omniscience is out of reach in these far from virtuous times. No one after Jambūsvāmin has been able to attain enlightenment in this Sorrowful Age, in this land of Bharata. Did Jains always think so? No. The most ancient literature described a path that if it were followed to perfection and according to the precepts and instructions established by Mahāvīra, led unwaveringly to liberation in this lifetime. Gradually, this notion was modified. Vaṭṭakera (2nd century) established three human existences as requisites for liberation *(Mūlācāra* 97; cited in Dundas 1992: 129). As the ascetic community left the times of Mahāvīra and his disciples farther and farther behind, the feeling of impossibility of achieving salvation became more and more acute. Finally, they came to the classical assumption that enlightenment was simply unachievable in this Sorrowful Age. But this formulation did not rule out spiritual progress. Once the traditional objective became impossible, religious practice became aimed at not just extinguishing *karma,* but accumulating sufficient spiritual merit to ensure the continuation of a happy existence. With conscientious and exemplary conduct, the ascetic would be able to be reborn as a human being on another continent, perhaps the gigantic Videha, where there are *jinas* preaching to this day. There, with the *tīrthaṅkara* close at hand they would be sure to reach enlightenment, or the ascetic or model layperson could be reborn as a god, whose longevity is reckoned in aeons, and in a few existences could reappear on Bharata-varṣa when a future *jina* is on the scene. In any case, Indians are certain that one can put an end to the alienation *(duḥkha)* that characterises existence in the midst of *saṃsāra.* Contemporary Jainism strives to have the seed which will lead to liberation safely sown in this existence.

What is at issue here is to awake to the right vision *(samyak-darśana, samyaktva),* to the awakened state, and this is feasible. Indeed, the lack of the direct reward of liberation makes the Jain path truly transcendental. Is it not he or she on the path that leads beyond ego and the conditioned world—knowing that there is no liberation in this life—a veritable Nirgrantha? Activity without attachment towards a preconceived end is really activity that eludes *karma,* since there is no intention or agent, simply the act, and this emancipating activity is feasible, possible *here and now.*

Fortunately, Jainism does not postulate total karmic determinism nor an intractable pessimism. Instead of doing what karmic latency impels us to do, the individual with purity and understanding acts precisely to achieve freedom from any connection with his or her karmic past. The Jain path involves undoing what has been done. Action, as Jains see it, can be liberating. With virtuous conduct and clear understanding, the Jain begins to ascend the path which will lead to ultimate peace. As in other Indian systems, Jains have also laid out a map (a stairway with fourteen steps) which traces this spiritual progress *(yoga).* This provides us with the subject matter of the next chapter [30], beginning this final section, on soteriology.

If we deduce from the most ancient texts that only ascetics could attain liberation (and this seems to be the Digambara position, identical to that of Ther-avāda Buddhism), gradually it began to be seen that what is important is one's conduct and striving after purity. Accordingly, liberating practice is within the reach of anyone and everyone who has sown the seed of right vision, at least in theory. Indeed, according to Śvetāmbara Jainism, the first person to achieve liberation in this cosmic cycle, Marudevī, mother of the first *tīrthaṅkara,* was in no wise an ascetic. Furthermore, from the traditional point of view, there exists the possibility that non-Jains may attain the same objective. A text as early as the *Uttarādhyayana-sūtra* (36.50) leaves us in no doubt:

> "The perfect souls are those of women, men, hermaphrodites, of orthodox [Jains], heterodox [non-Jains], and householders".

And the *Sambodhaśaptati* has it that:

> "Be he a white-cotton-clad [Śvetāmbara] or a sky-clad [Digambara], a Buddhist or any other, he certainly attains liberation if he is equanimous and passionless" (cited in Nyāyavijayajī 1952: 150).

However, it would be wrong to say that lay Jains seek liberation. Emancipation from the wheel of lives and deaths is perhaps the final objective of the human condition, but not the purpose of *this life.* In fact, Lawrence Babb (1996: 24) comments that the topic of liberation is hardly ever mentioned in Jain homes. Not only is it seen as impossible, nowadays in this world, but far too remote a goal, one which in the eyes of the secular Jain invariably means embracing renunciation. Although there is extensive knowledge on the subject, liberation does not condition a layperson's religious life. What lay Jains aspire to, apart from social integration, is gaining enough religious merit *(puṇya)* to be able to secure a favourable rebirth, if possible as a divine being *(deva)*. In the Upper World, there are beautiful damsels *(apsarās),* celestial musicians *(gandhavaras)* and all manner of luxuries waiting for them. The charms of heaven are much more attractive than the abstract eternal bliss of *nirvāṇa.* On this subject, Jains do not differ too much from Hindus, Buddhists and the rest of us mortals, and this is something that, as K.R. Norman (1991: 38-39) pointed out, the Buddha just as much as Mahavīra clearly "authorised".

But at the same time, it would be wrong to think that lay Jains forget the goal of liberation. It could be that many of them have received little theological instruction (even the same could be said for ascetics), It is true that the idea of liberation in the present life seems strangely remote. It is a silent goal that presides over their lives, the fasting of the women, the donations made by the men, the confessions, the homage to the masters, the countless forms of worship and pilgrimages. All these have liberation as their final goal and purpose. It is clear, as it has been repeated on various occasions, that drawing a dividing line between monastic Jainism and lay Jainism, or between meritorious practices and those to attain liberation is, to say the least, somewhat forced.

For many laypersons, emancipating practices in pursuit of *nirvāṇa* are the practices that provide their life with its full meaning, and there is a clearly marked out and defined path, in some texts called Śrāvakācāras. Here we can find a model of behaviour consisting of twelve stages of spiritual progress *(pratimās),* totally in tune with the ascetic pattern. This is the appropriate conduct *(cāritra)* for those who have faith and correct understanding of Jainism, for those who have sown the seed of right vision *(samyak-darśana).* This lay path will totally occupy us in chapter 31.

Lastly [in chapter 32], we shall be looking at the supra-worldly path of ascetics; the way of interior purification that all Jains aspire to travel, if not in this life, as ascetics, then in some remote future life. For this is the path that leads to the beatitude of *nirvāṇa.* This is the path that Mahāvīra and the *tīrthaṅkaras* left to humanity, and this is the mystic-ascetic way that detains the wheel of the karmic prison.

30. JAIN *YOGA*

THE THREE JEWELS

As in all Indian traditions, Jainism is a path of spiritual progress *(yoga, mārga).* No Jain forgets that human existence is a unique and almost unrepeatable chance to advance spiritually. How is Jain *yoga* practised? What must Jains do progressively to ascend the ladder that will eventually take them to liberation?

In summary, Jainism provides us with three large blocks, three large areas of spiritual growth that have to articulate spiritual advance. They are so fundamental that tradition has called them the Three Jewels *(tri-ratna, rat-na-traya),* as we mentioned in the Introduction:

(1) right vision *(samyak-darśana),*
(2) right knowledge *(samyak-jñāna),*
(3) right conduct *(samyak-cāritra).*

Umāsvāti begins the *Tattvārtha-sūtra* (1.1) with the following aphorism:

> "The enlightened world-view, enlightened knowledge and enlightened conduct are the path to liberation".

The subject is therefore of prime importance.

The Three Jewels formulation is not that ancient; it was probably taking shape not long before Umāsvāti (3rd-4th centuries). This was a period in which Sāṃkhyite and Naiyāyika philosophers were arguing that only knowledge led to liberation. To this Buddhists added the ending of desire, and then Jains came saying that not only knowledge *(jñāna)* and conduct *(cāritra)* were needed, but also vision *(darśana).* Thus, the Three Jewels in Jainism are essentially different from the Three Jewels of Buddhism (the latter being the Buddha, his Teachings, and the Community). The Three Jewels in Jainism must be in harmony with each other, combine with each other, complement each other and be simultaneously applied, at all times. The *Uttarādhyayana-sūtra* (28.30) says:

> "Without [right] faith there is no [right] knowledge, without [right] knowledge there is no virtuous conduct, without virtues there is no deliverance, and without deliverance there is no perfection".

So, the Three Jewels cannot be separated. They constitute a single path, and lead both lay seekers and ascetics to liberation, Simply, what happens is that at a given moment lay Jains renounce their secular lives to become itinerant ascetics devoting themselves exclusively to achieving liberation. Although laypersons postpone this goal for themselves for some future incarnation, Jainism as a whole bases itself on the way of liberation and its attainment—sooner or later, on this continent or another. And that means cultivating the Three Jewels here and now.

RIGHT VISION

Of course, to set off on the path, one must begin with one or another of the jewels, and it is pretty unanimously accepted that without right vision (*samyak-darśana, samyag-dṛṣṭi, samyaktva)* there is no possibility of progress (Kundakunda, *Darśanaprābhṛta* 5.6; cited in S. Jain 1989: 163). It is not that right vision is more important than the other jewels: it is simply that without it, the others are most unlikely to prosper. The emphasis on the idea that one must first acquire correct vision is based on the typically Indian notion that the problem that we face is essentially one of ignorance. All Brāhmaṇic, Buddhist, and Jain schools coincide in that the state of alienation and suffering in which human beings labour under is due to their spiritual ignorance *(avidyā, aviveka, mithyātva*), to unawareness of the true nature of being. Eliminating ignorance is what is intended by right vision; it is the key that will open up the path to spiritual progress.

Darśana means, "to see". To see in the sense of penetrating into the most intimate depths of whatever one contemplates. So, it is not surprising that worshipping the image of the *tīrthaṅkara* is also called vision or sight (*darśana),* Similarly not surprising is the more restricted meaning it has of standpoint *(darśana)* or philosophy. In the context of the Three Jewels, right vision is generally understood as gnosis *(prajñā)* and faith *(śrāddhā).* In fact, these two apparently diverse meanings are interrelated. On the one hand, it consists in the correct way to see things, in understanding the true nature of the spirit and the rest of the Jain principles *(tattvas).* Usually, this takes the form of the firm conviction that the soul is different from the body. It has special qualities and, by means of spiritual discipline, can attain its essential nature—liberate itself, and, as Cāmuṇḍarāya *(Cāritrasāra* 2; cited in Williams 1963: 41) said, this conviction takes the form of a devotional attitude of faith or refuge in the *jinas,* the preceptor, the scriptures and doctrine.

In other words, right vision means firm conviction in Jainism. This implies instruction, study, devotion and confidence. It is true that many ascetics learn the Sūtras just because tradition insists on it and they are quite incapable of making a critical evaluation. However, it is equally true that without the conviction and belief in the truths expounded by Jainism, only with great difficulty could one set off on the path that leads to liberation. The Jain who believes in the seven (or nine) fundamental principles *(tattvas)* is a Jain endowed with right vision.

With right vision, an extraordinary quality of the soul is set in motion: the ability to liberate itself *(bhavyatva)*. This quality remains hidden in the unpolluted *jīva,* waiting to be activated. Certainly, not all beings have it [see page 57], since there are *some jīvas* who are not fitted for liberation *(abhavya),* but for the majority of beings the capacity for liberation can be activated, usually when they find themselves in a state of relative non-attachment, thanks to experiencing an encounter with *dharma* at a deep level—through meditation, instruction of a master, through an encounter with a *jina* or his image, recall of previous lives, understanding of scriptures, or as a natural process as a result of the weakness of the *darśanamohanīya-karmas*.

However, it comes about, right vision is like an illuminating flash. It can last for a fleeting instant *(pradeśa)* or an Indian hour *(muhārta),* but once it has occurred, an enormous amount karmic matter (that which obscures vision, naturally) becomes detached from the body. The yogi has a glimpse of perception free from any mental construction *(nirvikalpa),* the non-dual experience where there is no difference between the knower and the known. Whoever acquires correct vision reaches the fourth step of spiritual progress [see below]. True progress has begun. Such a person will never again stoop to the same levels of spiritual ignorance. It is said that with this enlightening vision, the soul obtains certain acquisitions *(labdhis)*. One has the sensation of infinite peace, an unprecedented energy which swiftly eliminates a great amount of *darśanāvaraṇīya-karmas,* or an infinite compassion for all living beings. From this moment onward, such individuals will change their way of life and will focus it upon otherworldly Jainism. Jain teachings will be unreservedly accepted, superstitious beliefs abandoned, an unselfish affection for others will be cultivated, taking shape of service *(sevā)* of the ascetic community. From now on, their attention will be focussed on the nature of the self *(svabhāva),* in such a way that psychi-emotional states such as hate, the lack of self-confidence or pride cease to be identified with the soul. It has been understood that it is not the agent that does anything, it is the agent that knows, that sees itself; the *witness.* It is only from this moment onward that life guided by *ahimsā* gains its complete and profound sense. The witness is totally identified with the rest of living beings. Its compassion is disassociated from feelings such as charity and pity, but based on correct vision of the spiritual substance of every being. Those who felt so strong a call to free the rest of tormented beings from the prison of *saṃsāra,* generate a peculiar *karma* that after several reincarnations will lead to the status of *tīrthaṅkara.*

RIGHT KNOWLEDGE

Whoever truly believes in Jainism will be in a position to understand the seven (or nine) fundamental truths *(tattvas)* of Jain philosophy: the reality of the soul, of inanimate matter, inflow of karmic matter, bondage of this *karma,* detention of this flow, rejection of *karma,* and liberation from all bondage. According to Nemicandra *(Dravya-saṃgraha* 42) this is right knowledge *(samyak-jñāna).* In brief, whereas right vision talks about belief and intuition, right knowledge speaks of grasping and knowing about reality, the key factors that play their part in our bondage to this world and in our liberation from it. In the final analysis, right knowledge can be summed up as discriminating or discerning between the animate *(jīva)* and the inanimate *(ajīva).* As such, the knowledge alluded to here concerns the nature of things and oneself. Of course, right knowledge implies the five forms of knowledge recognised by Jainism [see page 356]. Of particular importance here is scriptural knowledge *(śruta-jñāna),* since as Kundakunda sees it:

> "The Śramaṇa, who is lacking in the study of scriptures, does not know his self and the things other than his self; without knowing the objectivity how can the monk destroy the karmas?" *(Pravacanasāra* 233).

What one can gather from this is that deep understanding of Jain philosophy and doctrine is essential for spiritual progress:

RIGHT CONDUCT

Nonetheless, as all masters state, scriptural study and mere philosophic knowledge is not enough to enable one to progress spiritually. Right conduct *(samyak-cāritra)* consists of living and acting in accordance with the light thrown by the two previous jewels (J. Jaini 1916: 65). Right conduct (the practice of ascetic Jainism) is the path that will lead us to a worthy spiritual life and, eventually, to liberation. How can one describe this conduct? What type of behaviour is being talked about? That which has been generated dispassionately, guided by non-violence, by the purity of mind and heart that stems from asceticism and meditation. Beyond the inaction of primitive Jainism, correct conduct appeals to transpersonal action, to action free of all intention, since the yogi goes beyond any "self that can harbour desires and intentions. It is the action of non-action, of not-doing, like the Daoist *wei-wuwei* and action free from their results in the *Bhagavad-gītā.* This is the only conduct which can escape the consequence of *karma.*

THE LADDER OF FOURTEEN STEPS

Just as in other Indian systems, Jainism has described the map of spiritual growth that leads to *nirvāṇa* in great detail. Texts speak of 14 levels of spiritual progress *(guṇasthānas),* ranging from heresy and complete bondage to omniscience and complete independence. Except for the *Samavāya-sūtra* (26b; cited in Schubring 1934: 320), the ancient scriptures hardly mention these levels of progress. The first mention appears in the Digambara *Ṣaṭkhaṇḍāgama* (2nd century) and the doctrine has a privileged place in the *Karmagranthas*.

This map serves as a theoretical framework for all those ascetics and lay Jains who want to go beyond traditional or customary practices of mechanical repetition. Once a specific level is reached, laypersons might decide on the path of renunciation and dedicate themselves entirely to the cultivation of perfection. This model is a clear example of how there is no discontinuity between lay and ascetic practices. Of course, the levels are ideal and, as Helmut von Glasenapp (1925: 221) reminded us, their order is merely logical and not chronological. The steps are put into order according to the principal of ascending rising purity.

(1) The lowest step on the ladder concerns beings who find themselves in the sphere of false beliefs *(mithyātva, mithyādṛṣṭi):* total lack of orthodoxy. Here we have those suffering the effects of the powerful *karmas* that obscure vision *(darśanāvaraṇīya-karmas).* Their vision of reality is clouded. The result is complete ignorance of our true nature. Nevertheless, it is interesting to note that the falsity stage is considered to be a state of virtue *(guṇa).* The Jain explanation is quite encouraging. It is a virtuous state because in every *jīva* there is a minimal portion of knowledge, morality and right vision. If a *jīva* did not have these potential qualities it would not be a *jīva*. However, someone at this level might be one of those souls that are incapable of going in the direction of liberation, and such souls may remain on this step indefinitely. On the other hand, those who do have a soul capable of advancing *(bhavya)*, reside on this level for only a limited space of time. With a glimpse of right vision *(samyak-darśana),* thanks to which the *jīva* perceives its own nature for the first time, ignorance begins to vanish. With this formulation Jainism shows its intention of simultaneously embracing and transcending other spiritual and philosophical paths.

(2) Later, one goes on to distinguish between what is true and false. The soul has a vague intuition of right vision *(sāsvādana-samyak-dṛṣṭi),* but is still hesitant. This step usually only lasts for a short space of time.

(3) Doubts over the truth. The power of *karmas* that obscure vision *(darśanāvaraṇīya-karmas)* diminishes considerably, but is still very persistent. The candidate has an inkling of the nature of things, but yet hesitates. There is a mixture of truth and falsity *(samyak-mithyātva).* On many occasions, one is on this step only provisionally, as a result of falling from the fourth down to the first step.

(4) The fourth step is crucial. Here there is correct vision (made possible by the teachings of a *guru* or as a result of good previous *karma)* and the power of the *darśanāvaraṇīya-karmas* is very tenuous. It is the first step on the ascension

in the true sense. Such souls can discern between true and false, but because of their lack of self-control, it still cannot refrain from improper conduct. This is the level reached by those who have activated their capacity to achieve liberation, and have had the flash of right vision *(samyak-darśana).* It is true that the *darśanāvaraṇīya-karmas* eliminated by vision—of the true nature of the soul—may return to obscure it, but such influences have been weakened so much, that vision is now much easier and more constant. It is said that those who have correct vision no longer doubt the truth of Jainism, do not embrace any future desire, remain free of false beliefs (abandoning the worship of gods and demigods, masters from other traditions, superstitions), they tend to withdraw from public life, work to make other people feel more confident in their convictions, and lead the life of an ideal layperson (carrying out pilgrimages, having temples and images built, respecting sacred days, making donations). They cultivate unselfish love for liberation (which means helping the ascetics who seek it). Divine beings (and infernal beings!) can only reach as far as this level.

(5) The level of worthiness. Partial self-discipline is added to right vision. This is an important step, because as Sinclair Stevenson (1915:187) pointed out, up until now, faith and right vision have been the hub, but now the yogi realises the importance of conduct and follows the 12 vows typical of the conduct of laypersons [see pages 478-486]. The spirit of renunciation grows in the *jīva.* Laypersons who behave morally and have taken on the partial restrictions *(deśa-virati)* of the eleven states [see next chapter] enter in this category. This is also the level of Digambara female ascetics *(āryikās)* and the maximum that an animal can aspire to.

(6) The level of the first ascetic stage. This step is only possible for those who control even the slightest of passions; i.e., ascetics, those who have taken the path of total renunciation *(sarva-virati).* It is the state of full self-control with a degree of negligence, even though the motor force here is still inertia. This step is so high that if anyone died at this level they would be likely to be reborn as a human being with a clear tendency to be situated on the previous fifth level. This state lasts for a very brief period.

(7) The step of full control over passions without negligence *(apramatta-vi-rata).* Here the yogi can suppress passions or even eradicate them completely. In fact, the alternative of repression or eradication constitutes a disjunction. The candidate can carry on progressing in both directions, but only by taking the second one can he or she attain liberation. There is frequent oscillation, for example, between the sixth and seventh levels.

(8) This step is so high that they call it the level of complete self-moderation or unprecedented spiritual progress *(apūrva-karaṇa).* It is the first contact with bliss, once the yogi has been able to transform the quality of all karmic matter. Their meditative trances are intense and they become by turns absorbed in their *jīvas.* From here onwards, the ascetic's spiritual monad is coloured white only. It corresponds to the level reached by masters who have dominion over the

Three Jewels, even if there are some who think that these days no ascetic is capable of advancing beyond the sixth step. This demonstrates that the scheme of the fourteen steps of gradual progress is a purely theoretical tool.

(9) The delusion of pride is abolished. Karmic density in the individual con tinues to be on the decrease. The *jīva* gets purer and lighter. Such ascetics be comes asexual, and their libido is eliminated, even if they are beset by memo ries of their egoic past. They still have not completely eliminated traces of greed, meaning certain *karmas* that pollute the soul's bliss *(mohanīya-karmas).* Hence, this step is called the one of complete self-moderation with gentle volition *(anivṛtti-sāmparāya).*

(10) Complete elimination of greed *(sūkṣma-sāmparāya).* It is interesting to observe that the ascending ascetic first gets rid of sexual passion, hate and aggressive tendencies. Greed and avarice are the last egotistical residues to disappear. Notwithstanding, one must take into account that the majority of Jains come from merchant castes. Down to the slightest desire (to be able attain liberation, for example) must be repressed or eradicated.

(11) The turning point. Here, the ascetic must stand firm before avarice. For those who opted for the *repression* of passions, this is the highest state, for whatever has been repressed may sneak back. Hence, this is called the step of complete self-moderation with greed repressed *(upaśānta-kaṣāya).* The truth is, the path of repression will inevitably imply slipping back to lower levels. On the other hand, those who have opted for total *eradication* of passions can ascend to the next step. Whoever follows this path will find themselves in the first state of pure contemplation.

(12) Complete self-moderation with greed eradicated *(kṣīṇa-moha).* This is the liberation from all types of *karmas.* All *karmas* which pollute the soul *(mohanīya-karmas)* have been destroyed. The yogi extinguishes all links to the world: his or her light and energy repose unperturbed within the soul. Disassociation from all negative *karmas* is complete, so that there is no possible fall to a lower level. *The jīva* has become the omniscient witness *(kevalin).*

(13) On this level, the identification of the self in *yoga (sayoga kevalī),* also called active transcendence, takes place. *The jīva* becomes a worthy one *(arhat),* a perfect soul *(siddha)* in a human body. Whoever has attained this point and founded a community *(tīrtha)* to show the path, will go on to become a *tīrthaṅkara. The jīva* reaches all the corners of the universe. It knows everything and can do anything, even while still inside the body, but the body is not its home, it is simply a connection to this world, the fruit of neutral *karmas* that will not provoke any kind of rebirth. This is emancipation *(nirvāṇa),* as the yogi has been liberated from all negative karmic matter, the cause of bondage to this world. When they become aware that their hour has come, the *siddha* enters into a deep trance and, gradually, ceases to act. First, they quieten the activity of their minds, then that of speech and finally that of the body. All colouring *(leśyā)* disappears and they enter into the final order of virtue.

(14) Once liberated from the last karmic particle and absolute perfection is achieved in the most profound meditation, the *arhat* reaches the fourteenth level. This means self-identification outside *yoga (ayoga-kevalī)* or inactive transcendence. This is omniscience without qualities, isolation *(kaivalya)* which classical Yoga (Patañjali, *Yoga-sūtra* 4.34) or Sāṃkhya (Iśvarakṛṣṇa, *Sāṃkhya-kārikā* 68) also mentions. Here no one can remain in this earthly life. This final order of virtue lasts a very short time, as the *jīva* ascends like an arrow to the heights of the cosmos.

JAIN AND INDIAN *YOGA*

As mentioned before, this scheme of spiritual progress with fourteen steps *(guṇasthānas)* represents an authentic Jain *yoga.* I will come back to this in the last chapter in the book. What now is for commenting upon is the relationship between this kind of *yoga* and other Indian *yogas.*

The first Indian thinker to try to synthesise all Indian interpretations on *yoga,* in a rational and systematic way, was the great Śvetāmbara philosopher Haribhadra (8th century). In his works, *Yoga-bindu* and *Yogadṛṣṭi-samuccaya* Haribhadra made a comparative study between Jaina *yoga,* Patañjali classical *yoga* (Yoga), Tantric *yoga* (Kula), Buddhist *yoga* (Sarvāstivāda), Śākta *yoga* (Sākta) and Vedāntin *yoga* (Advaita). Thanks to him, Jains became interested in other systems and put less emphasis on the peculiarities of Jaina *yoga.*

Despite his liberal viewpoint, on laying down diverse points of view Haribhadra made it very clear that some paths were better than others (Chapple 1998: 16). For example, even when recognising the emancipating viewpoint of the Tantric *yogas,* Haribhadra harshly condemned them, especially with regard to their recommendations on behaviour, but then in a tone of reconciliation, Haribhadra admitted that, in the end, there were different paths and teachings to reach the same goal with the same intentions. In S.M. Desai's words (1983: 51), there were many practitioners and varied levels of consciousness using different vehicles—though some only appear to be yogic. Because of this, Haribhadra succeeded in comparing the famous eight limbs of Patañjali classical Yoga *(aṣṭaṅga-yoga)* with the 14 levels of spiritual progress of Jainism *(gunasthāṇas),* that he subsumed under the name of eight goddesses or eight types of understanding *(dṛṣṭis).* For Haribhadra, the practice of a universal *yoga* had to include murmured repetition *(japa),* reflection *(bhāvanā),* asceticism *(tapas)* and meditation *(dhyāna).* With the practice of this *yoga,* common to all systems, transcendental wisdom *(prajñā)* was generated; that wisdom which leads to—or rather *is*—liberation.

31. THE LAY PATH

THE PATH OF VOWS

The spiritual discipline for the vast majority of Jains is regulated by the practices pointed out in Part XI. But the Jain path does not stop there. There is unanimity in saying that a true Jain is one who, aided by right vision *(samyaktva),* embarks on the path of the 11 stages for laypersons *(śrāvaka-pratimās).* This is another fundamental way in which ascetic ideals mould the practice of the lay community.

Details of these stages can already be found in the Prakrit text *Upāsaka-daśāh,* with the religious vows *(vratas)* and infractions *(ariçāras),* but above all, there is one body of texts, the Srāvakācāras (of which forty are known in Sanskrit alone), which have most thoroughly and accurately set out to shape the ideal conduct of laypersons, the conduct which will be sure to place them on the path that leads to *nirvāṇa.* During the middle ages, the literature of the Srāvakācāras developed prodigiously, to a point where it rivalled in complexity and subtlety the Brāhmaṇic Dharma-śāstras. Among the Śvetāmbaras, perhaps the most emblematic would be the *Yoga-sāstra* by Hemacandra (12th century); in the case of the Digambaras, possibly it would be the *Upāsakādhyayana* by So-madeva Sūri (10th century). These texts are strongly infused with ascetic ideals but acknowledge the weight and the particularities of the lay community. The gradual replacement of the term "servant" *(upāsaka)* by "hearer" *(śrāvaka)* when referring to laypersons is illustrative of ascetics' change in attitude towards the laity. If the first term stresses maintenance of the ascetics (laypersons are those who serve food and give shelter) with the term "hearer", the focus is placed upon a less material link. The *śrāvaka* is not only one who *hears* the sermons of the ascetics, but is also a hearer because of his participation in the worship in the temples. From this point of view, the layperson fully participates in the sacred assembly *(samavarasaṇa)* which temple worship replicates.

Basically, the pre-concerted path in the Śrāvakācāras consists of a series of restrictions that take the form of a series of increasingly strict vows *(vratas).* These vows structure 11 stages *(pratimās)* of spiritual progress. These recommendations for morals and conduct are intended for laymen and laywomen who already understand the Jain teachings, and who are firmly anchored in right vision *(samyak-darśana)* and right knowledge *(samyak-jñāna).* The path of the eleven stages is none other than the application of right conduct *(samyak-cāritra)* within the lay sphere, and they who accomplish them will have reached the fifth level of virtue *(guṇasthāna)* on the ladder that leads to *nirvāṇa.*

Lay persons who set out upon the path of the eleven stages observe a lesser form of abstinence, known as partial restriction *(deśa-virati),* in contrast to the total restriction *(sarva-virati)* of the ascetics. In following these 11 steps, lay Jains would thus be prepared to eventually renounce the world. All Jain ethics contained in the texts are designed so that individuals can head towards liberation, which implies that at a given moment they will take the path of total abstinence. The latter is the true framework from where one can aspire to liberation. Nevertheless, this path for laity does not differ too much from that of the renunciant ascetics. In practice, the lay Jain who has followed these eleven stages, will have become a non-initiated ascetic. The stages of growth are simply a lay version of the monastic career. It must be said, along with Padmanabh Jaini (1979: 160), that Jain masters were realistic enough to understand that their religious institution could not survive without the active participation of a lay community that supported them, and so the "inferior" nature of these 11 lay stages—with respect to the ascetics' vows—has never been overly stressed. And as will be seen, this *yoga* for laity is in fact stricter than the practice of many monks and nuns of other religions around the world. Having said that, it must be pointed out that very few laypersons take these vows as a prelude to total renunciation. For the vast majority, the votive practices of the eleven stages overlap with the vows we have been looking at in the previous section: fasting, worshipping, meditation, study, pilgrimage, generosity, confession.

DARŚANA-PRATIMĀ

The first step on this path of progress is the stage of vision *(darśana-pratimā).* It comprises two religious observances intended to illuminate and strengthen right vision *(samyaktva).*

THE *PAÑCA -NAMASKĀRA-MANTRA*

The first one is devotional. It involves accepting the Jina as the ultimate divinity, the Āgamas as the valid scriptures, and the mendicant ascetics as the only masters. This statement of faith usually comes in the shape of a recitation of the most sacred litany in Jainism, the *pañca-namaskāra-mantra,* also called *pañcaparameṣṣhī-mantra.* Here it is again:

"Obeisance to the *Arhats,*
Obeisance to the Liberated Ones,

Obeisance to the Religious Guides,
Obeisance to the Religious Instructors,
Obeisance to all Saints in the world" *(Kalpa-sūtra, Jina-caritra* 1).

The five *(pañca)* referred to here are the supreme ones *(parameṣṭhins),* the five beings worthy of being worshipped: (1) those who expounded Jainism *(jinas, arhats);* (2) the perfect or liberated souls *(siddhas);* (3) the mendicant leaders *(ācāryas, bhikṣus);* (4) the preceptors *(ācāryas, upādhyāyas);* and (5) the ascetics *(sādhus, sādhvīs).* Not one actual name is mentioned. As Padmanabh Jaini (1979: 163) has written, Jain devotion is not directed toward a chosen deity, but toward an ideal: omniscience *(kevala-jñāna).* And the one who best represents this is the liberated in his own life who showed the path, the *jina* or *arhat.* For this reason, he is mentioned first. If the first two supreme ones represent omniscience, all five represent the ideal of asceticism and renunciation. In times such as ours, when there are no *tīrthaṅkaras,* the last three supreme ones are fundamental for teaching and propagating the Jain religion.

The *pañca-namaskāra-mantra* would certainly have been an auspicious litany in its origin, which transformed gradually into a form of benediction and expression of the power of Jainism. This *mantra* is recited orally or mentally in all important ceremonies, whether worshipping in temples, fasting or at the initiation of ascetics. Its recitation is the equivalent of declaring oneself a Jain and many devotees recite this litany upon rising every morning. But its auspicious nature and inherent power have not been forgotten. On the contrary. Jains coincide with Hindus and Buddhists in sharing the belief that all powerful *mantras* if recited and manipulated in the appropriate fashion and in the right context can be beneficial to the person who recites them. The *namaskāra* can expand or contract from 64 syllables down to its most concentrated expression in the syllable *Oṃ.* The *catuḥ-śaraṇa* or the *caturviṁśatistava* (the litany where the 24 names of the *jinas* are recited), are equally powerful *mantras.*

THE BASIC RESTRICTIONS *(MŪLAGUṆAS)*

The second religious observance of the *darśana-pratimā* is not devotional but rather ascetic in nature. It is one of the channels through which the ascetic ideal visibly penetrates into Jain homes. These are the basic restrictions *(mūlaguṇas).* They are compulsory for Digambaras. They are not strictly compulsory for Śvetāmbaras, but are kept in mind by practically the whole community.

The restrictions, all of a nutritional nature, are linked to the fundamental religious and ethical concept of Jainism: non-violence *(ahiṃsā).* The consumption of honey, five types of figs or alcohol are all prohibited. The reasons for not eating meat seem obvious in the context of the doctrine of *ahiṃsā.* Eating meat is a serious offence against compassion, and the same can be said for buying, selling, and cooking it. As Jain masters say, to eat meat would be to recognise vultures, wolves and tigers as *gurus,* and the truth is that no other community in the world puts so much pressure on its members to be vegetarian as the Jains do. It has been to a great extent thanks to Jainism that vegetarianism is practised all over India [see page 153] and slaughtering animals has been made illegal in several states.

From the Jain point of view, killing animals does not only imply suffering for other living beings, but carries a strong passionate charge *(kasāya)* for those who kill. The intention to cause harm or kill arises from hate and passion. Passion which, ineluctably chains us to the world of the *saṃsāra.* Therefore, in the end the violence is inflicted upon oneself, even when there is no harm done or any physical death. *Hiṃsā* exists where passion and hate are found, even when no being perishes. *Ahiṃsā* does not only mean abstinence from killing or cultivating non-violence, but implies a state of mind of non-attachment. Hence, the emancipating nature of the vegetarian diet. What we have here is not just a dietetic consideration, but first and foremost a form of inner purification. Whoever, through knowledge and compassion, respects other forms of life, shows a degree of spiritual progress (of purity, in Indian terminology) at a higher level than those who serves them up on his plate every day. Obviously, any form of nutrition constitutes to a greater or lesser extent an act of *hiṃsā.* Even Gandhi (cited in Chapple 1993: 55) accepted that no activity is possible without certain amount of violence. Thus, taking a pragmatic view, Jains have tried to minimise its impact and have worked out a kind of graduated scale regarding violence. The hierarchy comes ready marked out by classical taxonomies. Killing a plant, a static being with two senses, is a less serious act than killing an animal, a mobile creature with three, four and up to five senses; and killing an animal is less serious than killing a human. Consequently, a vegetarian diet is preferable to a carnivorous one; also within the vegetarian diet it is advisable to avoid certain types of fruit and vegetables, and so on and so forth. The principal that governs all this could be the observation made by Jagmanderlal Jaini (1916: 71): do not destroy life unless it is absolutely necessary to maintain a higher kind of life.

This explanation may not be totally convincing, for example, in explaining why Jains do not eat five types of figs, or honey, or drink alcohol. The matter goes as follows:

The most insignificant type of being in the universe is the strange *nigoda* [see pages 52-53]. It is thought that these microscopic creatures swarm where there are sweet products and fermentation in process. Inevitably the process of fermentation of alcohol leads to violence against these beings. Hence the prohibition in drinking alcohol, a substance, which to make things worse feeds evil passions and confuses the mind, and hence sweet honey is also prohibited, which furthermore is the product of laborious toil by thousands of bees. With calculated exaggeration, Hemacandra *(Yoga-śāstra* 3.37) goes so far as to say that those who feed on honey are worse than pariahs. Sweet plants and fleshy fruits also provide a niche for colonies of *nigodas.* Which explains why figs are out. A restriction, which also ties in with the veneration that all Indians profess for trees of the *ficus* family. These restrictions symbolise the scrupulous respect Jains have for even the most minor form of *jīva* and their intention to eliminate all violent and passionate activity, and the matter does not end there. Figs, alcohol, meat, and honey are all components of offerings that Hindus make to the spirits of their ancestors. So, the prohibition carries an implicit criticism of the Hindu *śrāddha* rite, adding a useful element of differentiation, doubtless necessary during the centuries of Jain expansion and proselytising.

* * *

Those who are initiated into the *mantras* (many Jain children do so at the *upanīti* sacrament or initiation [see pages 448-449]) and those who respect the restrictions of the *mūlaguṇas* can be considered a Jain in the broadest sense. It is true that this stage is observed by most of the Jain population more because of the weight of social convention than for authentic spiritual calling—rather in the same way that christenings and first communions are celebrated in the Catholic world. Jain practice, I repeat, is fundamentally centred on everyday worship and ceremonies at certain dates during the year. Nevertheless, with the observation of this first *pratimā* the following ten stages are clearly aimed at by Jains. As James Laidlaw (1995: 151-152) has succinctly and rightly remarked Jain asceticism is not so much a code of rules and prohibitions as an ascetic project: the development of ascetic persons.

VRATA-PRATIMĀ

The second stage of lay progress consists of a series of religious vows *(vratas)*. Accordingly, this level is called the stage of vows *(vrata-pratimā)*. It is the most important stage of all, and synthesises to perfection the ascetic behaviour of exemplary laypersons. The Srāvakācāras lavish the highest praise on the layperson who has resolved to carry out these vows. Emulating the ascetic path, with these vows one tries to limit to the maximum the inflow of karmic matter and to ensure that the inevitable bondage arising in a life-in-the-world is located within tolerable ascetic limits.

Only those who have taken refuge in the five supreme ones and stay firmly to the restrictions of the eight foods can proceed to this stage. From here onward, only a small portion of the community will continue, those who feel the spiritual call more powerfully but yet do not choose renunciation. Mostly, this concerns people of a certain age and again, the proportion of women is noticeably greater than men. The taking of vows constitutes a form of withdrawal from lay life, in words of James Laidlaw (1995: 174); but, contrary to what is stated in the scriptures, in real life they almost never constitute a preparation for life as a renouncer. Moreover, Laidlaw (1995:186) has observed that those who follow this pattern gain in respectability within the community and are usually very active in religious public life.

Ideally, the taking of vows *(vratāropa)* is considered the sacrament that follows that of marriage [see page 450]. The ritual can only be officiated by an ascetic and, unlike many *saṃskāras,* the language is clearly ascetic (and the use of Prakrit replaces Sanskrit). It is very common for the taking of vows to be done in collectively during a week of spiritual retreat. In these sessions, known as *upadhānas,* lay people live like ascetics (except the way the acquire their food). They spend the day praying in temples, meditating, making confessions, listening to talks given by monks or nuns, fasting. In addition it is quite usual to take the twelve vows simultaneously. After murmuring the appropriate *mantras,* the ascetic gives instructions concerning infractions that should be avoided and, in the case of their being broken, how to expiate them. Since the vows are irreversible, for life, the mistakes will be privately confessed in periodic rites of general confession *(pratikramaṇa)* or private confession *(ālocanā).*

(1) THE VOW OF NON-VIOLENCE

All texts and masters agree that the first vow of Jainism is not harming *(ahiṃsā)* any living being. Throughout the length of this book, *ahiṃsā* constitutes the hub of Jain conduct and ethics, the value that encapsulates in a summarised form the whole Jain religion. Thus *ahiṃsā* is not only the highest virtue of all, but in a certain sense it is the only virtue (Jaini 1979: 167). As Hemacandra says *(Yoga-sāstra* 2.31), if one does not abandon violence, any religious activity, no matter how worthy it may be, is unfruitful. Its practice is so extensive that there is no real need for actually vowing to follow many of the recommendations inherent to the vow of *ahiṃsā.* However, all those who have the desire to progress spiritually and guide their lives according to Jain *yoga* will need the presence of an ascetic to formally consecrate their vow not to cause harm to any living creature having two or more senses. From this moment on they must take great care not to intentionally kill any living creature that moves and, as Hemacandra advises *(Yoga-sāstra* 2.20), they will also avoid any unnecessary harm to any creatures that do not move. One of the most known and repeated Jain aphorisms has it that:

> "All living beings want to live
> And none is desirous of dying
> For this, knowing slaughter to be terrific,
> A *nirgrantha* avoids it" *(Daśavaikālika-sūtra* 6.10).

And therefore:

> "Desist I from all kinds of hurt

Caused to living beings
Be they minute or large
Mobile or without movement
Whoever may be living
Shall I not myself hurt
Nor order others to do so
Nor approve any so doing" *(Daśavaikālika-sūtra* 4.11).

Although this message is not exclusive to Jainism, this tradition has made it its heart. It is the virtue, which has most moulded and defined the lay and monastic cultures in the Jain community. This implies that the Jains who have taken this vow—and I repeat that virtually all Jains adhere to it, whether blessed by an ascetic—will have to seek professions that do not involve *intentional violence* towards other living beings. Neither hunting nor fishing is tolerated. Even though agriculture may also bring about the destruction of life, it is considered that the harm that it can cause is not intentional *(Vyākhyā-prajñāpti* 7.1 [288b]); thus, it is tolerated to a certain degree. It must be understood that lay Jains are required to avoid intentional violence, but not if it is accidental, occupational or part of protective acts. Here, a clearly realistic attitude is observed on behalf of ascetics, perhaps with lay influence, since the ultra-ascetic ideals of renunciants have not always coincided with those of the laity. Emphasis is put upon the purity of intention, in which case farmers are not violent if their souls are pure, and if they have no wrong intentions. In general, "respectable" forms of making a living are recommended, such as in handicrafts, government, writing, and science. As we know, the sector most encouraged, and which has occupied an influential part of the community, is commerce. But even in commerce certain limits must be respected. There must be no transaction with animal skins, alcohol, weapons.

The vow of *ahiṃsā* also implies abstaining from using animals in the name of science. By the same token it is not allowed for Jains to wear clothes that imply the torture of animals (leather, furs). This also extends to the decoration of their homes.

The *negative* nature of Jain formulations has been much insisted upon. However, all vows must also be seen inversely, in their positive sense. We saw that positive *ahiṃsā* [see pages 150-152] is active compassion *(karuṇa-dāna, abhaya-dāna)* towards all living beings. Although it is impossible to go through life without causing harm to other living creatures, Jains try to limit to a maximum the violence inflicted upon other *jīvas.* No other religious tradition in the world has put so much emphasis on this point such as Jainism has. It must be remembered that while other vows (not to lie or steal,) are common to many religions on the planet, the vow of *ahiṃsā* is unique to India and Buddhist countries in Asia.

Ascetics take this vow to its logical conclusion [see pages 199-200]. Unlike laity who avoid killing beings that have two or more senses, ascetics will also take great care not to cause harm to beings with only one sense.

(2) THE VOW OF SINCERITY

The second vow is the one concerning sincerity *(satya),* or, as it is usually referred to: abstaining from lying *(asatya).* What is lying? It is to deny what is, affirm what is not, or present something in a different form from what it really is. The underlying nature of all these is the same: all lies are volitional and are charged with passionate elements. Only those who have overcome anger, jealousy, frivolity, greed, can stay firm in veracity. Those who take this vow must be honourable in their profession and their business transactions. In fact, the lists of transgressions are very especially thought out with members of the merchant classes in mind.

Satya also implies avoiding undue use of language (insulting, aggressive or that which incites violence). Since the vow of *ahiṃsā* is primordial, Jains can avoid telling the truth if that truth could provoke the destruction of life. The typical case for this double bind is that of a hunter who enquires of a Jain in the middle of the forest, "which way did my prey go?" If the Jain responds truthfully, this is causing intentional violence. If a lie is resorted to, this is breaking the vow of veracity. Texts recommend silence, but also the prime importance of *ahiṃsā,* so a white lie would be conceivable.

(3) THE VOW OF HONESTY

Not stealing *(asteya)* is the third vow. More to the point, *asteya* means abstaining from that which has not been given *(adattādana),* and by "given" one must understand that which has been legitimately obtained (by legal transaction or inheritance). Whoever abides by this vow cannot even keep objects that others have lost or induce others to steal or adulterate products. As always, the point is to avoid passionate excess, in this case, greed and avarice.

(4) THE VOW OF CHASTITY

In the vow of chastity *(brahma-vrata),* the fourth vow, Jains abstain from all reproachable sexual activity. This vow implicitly contains a positive formulation: maximum fidelity to one's spouse; and another negative one: not to commit adultery. It can extend to reducing sexual activity at certain times of the day and of abstaining from it on the *parvan* days of the month, always with the couple's mutual consent. One must bear in mind that in India, chastity *(brahmacarya)* is something more than sexual abstinence; it represents sacred power and potential. Women on fasts are intimately linked to this issue. Thanks to these fasts, women cool ardour and neutralise their sexual desire, turning it into benign asexual strength. Although the idea of chastity and retention of semen are common in Christian Europe and Daoist China, in very few parts of the world is so much attention given to the subject as in India. All the same, sexuality has never been the "capital sin" in India that it represents in Christianity. If there is such a sin in Jainism, it is undoubtedly violence *(hiṃsā)*.

The vow contrasts with Hindu practice, which recommends precisely the opposite: sexual activity on the *parvan* days, as the conception of a child on such an auspicious day is all but a religious obligation.

(5) THE VOW OF NON-ATTACHMENT

The fifth is the vow of non-attachment regarding possession and acquisition of wealth *(aparigraha)*. It basically refers to voluntarily moderating, decreasing and limiting one's owning of land, grain, herds or flocks, jewellery, mansions, domestic service, luxurious clothing, and so on, every unnecessary item that society can offer us. The attachment to material objects does nothing more than reinforce the karmic bond and it is what chains us to the world of transmigration. A life guided by non-possession of wealth is also infinitely more benevolent to the environment than the headlong descent into consumerism of our times.

Nevertheless, the vow does not work as an antidote against the high standard of living of a large section of the Jain community. This can be explained. In the *Upāsaka-daśāḥ,* what the laity who take this vow really do is not increase their profits and fortune, and that is how the most communities interpret it. It does not mean getting rid of what one has, so much as voluntarily limiting one's goods and properties *(parigraha-parimāṇa)*. As it is not unusual for a Jain merchant to self-impose a specific limit on his equity and spend many years making donations not to break the vow of non-attachment. In a sense, the vow of *aparigraha* is understood as a near obligation to make religious and charitable donations.

Ascetics abandon all possession from the day of their renunciation. There is, certain divergence of interpretation between ascetics and laypersons over the meaning of this vow, something which does not occur with the previous four. Moreover, there is a surprising contrast between the objective of non-possession and the clear ostentation and lifestyle of many Jains, especially at festivals. The explanation is as simple as it is logical. If laity renounced their possessions, the ascetic community would have nothing on which to subsist. Without donations *(dāna)* there would be no Jainism and for there to be a donation there must be possessions. Hence, certain texts are lavish with their praise of donors, and praise to the uttermost the rewards deriving from donation. In addition, it must not be forgotten that donation—and in consequence, ostentation—is not only a way to gain religious merit, but also a way to gain social prominence and prestige within the community.

These first five vows are identical to vows taken by ascetics. The lay vows are called partial vows *(anuvratas),* as opposed to the great or major vows *(mahāvratas)* of the ascetics [see pages 199-203]. But in actual fact, the lay vows are simply toned-down versions of the *mahāvratas.* The only difference is one of degree.

The next three vows have the generic name of *guṇavratas.* They are amplifications and intensifications of the five basic vows.*

(6) THE VOW OF LIMITATION OF MOVEMENT

The sixth vow consists of limiting movements *(dig-vrata).* One voluntarily delimits geographical space (a small county, for example) and always stays within this radius of action. The idea is in not contributing to the propagation of violence, inherent to all action, outside this territory. The more areas and movements are reduced, the fewer lives are likely to perish. This vow is therefore, an extension of that of *ahiṃsā.*

(7) THE VOW OF LIMITATION OF ACTIVITIES

The next vow involves limiting the use of specific items and the practice of certain professions *(bhogopabhoga-parimāṇa-vrata).*

Whoever takes this vow explicitly rejects exercising undesirable professions. For example, those where plants are destroyed, mining, transport, digging wells, occupations which involve the use of fire, commerce with animals (or ivory, shells and other materials which are obtained by the death of some living creature) plus slavery. Significantly, many of these activities and professions are also forbidden for Brāhmaṇas in their books of laws *(Manu-smṛti* 10.81-94).

The limitations of specific items has much to do with diet, a subject with enormous religious overtones for Indians: meat, alcohol, honey, five types of figs already required by the *mūlaguṇas,* along with butter and ice (which brings about the destruction of life in water) as well as poison (which would kill organisms in stomachs!). And also the aphrodisiac aubergine (which provokes the tendency to sleep excessively). Special types of vegetables to avoid are those that are inhabited not by one *jīva* but multiple ones. Most of them are bulbous plants that grow beneath the soil: ginger, cardamom, garlic, bamboo, carrot, radish, curcumin, capers, tamarind, pomegranate, potato, and onion. Many strict Hindus do not eat leeks, garlic, mushrooms and onion either, since they grow in "impure" soil (*Manu-smṛti* 5.5).

Most Jain housewives are very scrupulous on these matters. In India the act of nutrition is religious and in Jainism it is governed by *ahiṃsā.* Despitethe fact that not all Jain families are so strict—although they are always vegetarian—it is quite normal for many women when cooking to abstain from using garlic, onions, potatoes, carrots and radish during the monsoon season, when ascetics interact a great deal with laity. These taboos also increase on *parvan* days. In this way they bring their diet in line with ascetics (Williams 1963: 177), for at least some days or months of the year. These dietetic restrictions give Jains a sharply focused social identity. Through these dietetic restrictions children learn about *ahiṃsā* and become aware of their distinguishing characteristics as Jains, and it is through the dietetic restrictions (which are simply an act of *tapas* via *ahiṃsā)* that the Jain laity bring ascetic values into their everyday lives.

Even without taking the vow of the *bhogopabhoga-parimāṇa-vrata* many pious Jains take personal vows to leave out certain food on specific days. They might abstain from salt, aubergines, and meals prepared with *ghī* (clarified butter). Rather than following a strict code of rules, what is entailed is aiming at a higher standard of virtues, and dietetic restrictions lay down a very high grade of compromise with the doctrine of *ahiṃsā.* Usually, these subjects become accentuated with age. James Laidlaw (1995: 169) gives us an example: a young man would not be censored if he included potatoes in his diet; but later on in his life he would be criticised for the same act. Most Jain merchants would eat onions when away from home, but never on a *parvan* day, if they are going to the temple or in the presence of an ascetic.

The vow includes not drinking water that has not been filtered. This point has extended to such an extent among the community that there is no need to take the vow to comply with it. Even though few Jains boil their water (which is the technically recommended procedure) it is filtered in all Jain homes. One could rightly protest, what difference is there between boiling or filtering the water if all the diminutive beings that inhabit it are going to die anyway, but what really counts is not so much the fate of the microscopic beings (which will perish anyway) but avoiding being the direct cause of their death. What is involved is an aesthetic sensibility that urges avoiding violent contact with all forms of life. In this way a Jain can drink water free of all life.

The vow obliges one not to cook or eat after sunset *(rātri-bhojana),* a practice about which women, once again, are more scrupulous than men. In the dim light one could inadvertently swallow diminutive *jīvas;* and if a lamp were lit, it would inevitably attract a multitude of lives that would perish in the flame or on the hot light bulb. Some Jain authors justify the *rātri-bhojana* with dietetic arguments: nocturnal digestion is bad (Nyāyavijayajī 1952: 145); or ayurvedic ones: night is a time of calamity when semi-demonic creatures feed, such as the *daityas* (Hemacandra, *Yoga-śāstra* 3.48). The model Jain should eat once a day, a less virtuous one twice a day; the idiot fringe, they who understand nothing, would eat day and night and, as Hemacandra sardonically says *(Yoga-śāstra* 3.62), would behave like an animal, though devoid of horns and a tail. As can be seen, this vow is at all events an intensification of the first *pratimā.*

8) THE VOW OF LIMITING HARM

The next vow consists of not wishing anyone harm or putting any life in danger *(anarthadaṇḍa-vrata).* It overlaps the previous vow along with the vow of non-violence. It provides a mandate against five malignant activities: wishing others ill, thoughtless conduct (gambling, cock-fighting, felling trees), facilitating destruction (selling arms), giving bad advice (leading to violence), and idle listening (to pornographic material, false doctrines).

The rationale remains constant: violent action and unnecessary passion must be avoided, as they favour the inflow of *karma,* but here one must underline a detail, in that nearly all masters recognise that certain harmful activities are legitimate and profitable *(artha)* if carried out for the good of Jainism (such as building a temple), and for the good of one's organism (such as eating and taking medicine), or for the maintenance of the family (such as growing food). These same actions, if carried out for other reasons, are in that case unfruitful *(anartha).*

Now we come to the last four vows, those known as *śikṣāvratas.* They are carried out daily, weekly or monthly, but once the vow has been taken, firmness must be the rule.

(9) THE VOW OF REDUCING THE RADIUS OF ACTION

The first of these vows, the ninth in our list, involves limiting even more one's radius of action *(deśāvakāśika-vrata).* It is an intensification of the sixth vow, even where it can only be kept up for some days. The vow also usually leads to an intensification of the seventh, in reducing worldly activity to a minimum.

(10) THE VOW OF MEDITATION

The 10th vow is that of equanimity *(sāmāyika-vrata).* In Jainism, equanimity means the process of centring oneself; that is, meditation [see page 460]. Usually, the *sāmāyika* consists of meditating daily for an Indian hour *(muhūrta):* 48 minutes. Such meditation usually includes reciting hymns to the *jinas* or the virtues of the Jaina path. As a rule, it is associated with worship *(pūjā).* Like ascetics, meditators will concentrate on their walking, speaking, moving things... always controlling physical, mental and verbal activity. Texts never cease to tell us that the lay and ascetic identities converge when meditating *(Śrāvakā-prajñāpti* 293; cited in Williams 1963: 134).

(11) THE VOW OF FASTING

The 11th vow concerns fasting *(poṣadhopavāsa-vrata).* It involves devoting the four *parvan* days in each month (roughly the 8th, 14th, 22nd and 30th, the days marking changes in the phases of the Moon) to fasting and meditating. This vow too has become part of everyday life in all Jain families.

Fasting can be partial (one meal, as insipid as possible) or total. But there are other spheres of application. For example, regarding care of one's body (also partial or total), sexual activity (likewise) plus occupations and everyday chores (likewise). Digambaras only accept the possibility of a vow being partial in the case of nutrition. This is another of the vows that has fostered the connection between the lay and renunciant sectors (Stevenson 1915: 217). During the hours or days of fasting lay people virtually become ascetics.

(12) THE VOW OF GENEROSITY

Lastly, there is the vow of generosity *(dāna-vrata).* It relates, above all, to the giving of food to mendicants, helping those in need, as well as giving donations for temples, images and monasteries. The vow is also fundamental in keeping the *saṃgha* together, even if the practice of generosity is so common [see pages 438-446] that the vow to practice it is scarcely necessary.

The stage of vows ends here. If the first five vows are rather general (not to lie, or steal, to be generous, and so forth), the remaining vows are more precise. In addition, since they are exclusively Jain, they provide a more solid sense of identity. Remember that the vows are for life and have to be reinforced by confessions, meditation practice, worshipping in temples, participation in religious sermons. With the path of the 12 vows, monastic asceticism enters fairly and squarely into the pattern of life of the lay community.

(13) THE VOW OF THE ENLIGHTENED DEATH

Although the vows consist of 12 stages, in some places the inclusion of a thirteenth supplementary vow or last rite *(anta-kriyā)* is recommended: voluntary death or the decision to commit euthanasia by fasting unto death *(sallekhanā-vrata, saṁlekhanā* or *samādhi-maraṇa).* This is the most sacred of all vows.

For Indians, the last moments of life constitute a crucial transition determining important aspects in their next reincarnation. A Jain *sūtra* (in Schopen 1995: 482) says concisely that just how the mind is at the moment of death, so will be its future reincarnation. Hence, one gathers that death while meditating or in a transcendental state is liable to generate of much karmic merit. With greater or lesser acceptance, Indian tradition has come to recognise different forms of voluntary death, the great journey *(mahāprasthāna),* as it is usually called. One of the classic ones is throwing oneself into the sacred river and letting oneself drown *(jalasamādhi),* or burning oneself to death *(agnipraveśa),* or self-sacrifice in war *(jahuar)* to avoid capture, or the immolation of the virtuous widow *(satī)* on the funeral pyre of her husband. All these forms of death are considered extremely sacred religious rituals. If other reasons come into play, which are not spiritual, Indian traditions condemn them severely.

However, Jainism considers these forms of voluntary death as varieties of suicide and are evaluated as other forms of violence, making them a good way of prolonging existence in the *saṃsāra (Vyākhyā-prajñāpti* 2.1 [118a]). What Jain voluntary death is about is reaching the moment of death in a state of clear consciousness, without senility or illness having led them to involuntarily or fatally break any of the foregoing vows or ritual ascetic obligations. For this reason, the *Sūtrakṛtāṅga* (1.8.15) recommends *sallekhanā* when one is incurably ill or extremely old, when one knows that one's life span is reaching its end. One's whole existence of religious observations and meditation could end up being in vain if through illness, weakness, senility or need, *dharma* is violated. Self-purification loses its meaning with the arrival of decrepitude. In contrast, if final moments are spent in serene meditation, even grave sins can be eradicated and annihilated. Since no one forces the devotee and it is done with dedication and surrender, Pūjyapāda *(Sarvārtha-siddhi* 7.22; cited in Singh 1975: 68) considers that the act cannot be called suicide. Thanks to a death under these conditions, the conscientious devotee is unquestionably assured of an ethereal rebirth.

The rite has to be performed according to clearly laid down recommendations. It is recommended that it should take place in a temple, a sacred *tīrtha,* or if this is not possible, at home. With the consent of the family and under the supervision of an ascetic (who will have to approve the aspirant as being sufficiently qualified to carry out the rite) the devotee will begin a gradual fast, aided in every case by meditation. Apart from fasting, all other forms of euthanasia are prohibited (Nyāyavijayajī 1952: 159). First, solid food is abstained from, later sustenance is obtained only from liquids, in meditation and with firm determination, murmuring the *namaskāra-mantra* or listening to companions recite it. No desire to reach the superior heavens, of gaining religious merit or having a swift death must obscure the rite, as this would only be another form of attachment, and therefore suicide. Confession of sins will be made and a general *pratikramaṇa* carried out. In due course, the practice of fasting leads to its logical conclusion and the devotee will completely stop taking sustenance. Finally, the hour of death will arrive while in deep meditation *(samādhi-marana),* which is what the act is preferably called in Jain writings. Possibly, the last words the dying person hears would be those of their *guru* whispering in their ear:

> "...By yourself see yourself within yourself [*ātmānam ātmanātmani paśya*]" (Āśādhara, *Sāgāra-dharmāmṛta* 8.69; cited in Williams 1963: 169).

Although epigraphs have revealed large numbers of laypersons (including not a few royalty) who committed *sallekhanā,* it is customary among laity to take the vow informally, postponing it for a future time. Meanwhile, the aspirants stay firm on the other twelve vows, and continue preparing themselves emotionally for their eventual voluntary euthanasia. In any event, it is quite common for laypersons When on the brink of their final hour, to ask to take the great vows *(mahāvratas)* of renunciants, and so, technically becoming ascetics in the last hours of their lives.

Sallekhanā, on the other hand, is a strongly recommended vow for ascetics. In fact, a very large number of dying ascetics choose to take this path in their final moments, but through epigraphs and mausoleums erected by faithful followers we know of thousands of absolute fasts carried out by ascetics who were in perfect health. This practice is more common among Digambaras. The recorded history of the 20th century provides eloquent instances of ascetics who chose this heroic vow. Not long ago, Muni Samanthabhadra (1891-1988), founder of the *gurukula* in Kolhapur, put an end to his long life through this pacific and controlled form [see FIG. 45].

The rite may sound harsh, especially to someone who has grown up in the Western culture, which traditionally never accepted voluntary death (since no one other than God has the right to give or take away life) and for whom finitude holds true terror. For Westerners, death is the extinction of our individuality; it is the terrifying door to *nothingness.* Therefore, Western culture, fed by Judaeo-Christian eschatology, has opted for the opposite way, for prolonging, at all cost, by all necessary means, the life of terminally ill people. But in India, and not least in the Jain community, the act of dying has other connotations and their attitude is different. For one thing, God does not enter into the matter. Given their conception of *karma* and the nature of the *jīva,* Jainism considers that one is responsible for one's own destiny. Their position in the face of issues such as the artificial prolongation of life is clearly that of non-interference. It is not that Indians are impassive in the face of death. Death always unchains *emotional* anguish; *existential* anguish, however, is absent. The loss of the ego is in any case what Jains actually aspire to. Jains, convinced of the inevitability of *karma* have no fear of death. On the other hand, India has always considered death as the entrance onto another plane, by which means there is no assimilation of the notion death = nothingness, but that is not all. We must bear in mind that the practice of fasting is very common among Jains. Those who have opted for this glorious end will have been through hundreds or even thousands of fasts beforehand. Not only will they be physically and psychologically prepared, but prepared spiritually and in terms of morale also, because, as Padmanabh Jaini (1979: 232) has written, the entire spiritual life of lay Jains, and even more clearly, mendicants, consists of preparation for such a sacred death. What we have here is a pacifying act of spiritual purification, an act of *tapas,* and it is logical that a tradition that has conceded so much value to the salutary power of *tapas* considers that in crucial moments—and what is more so than imminent death—*tapas* combined with *dhyāna,* bring about extreme purification. And so death presents itself as an opportunity to eliminate residues of past actions. For ascetics it will without a doubt mean the Upper World, cutting through hundreds of reincarnations in the *saṃsāra.* In few existences, they will be able to live in the presence of a *jina,* who will help them to complete the path they have so arduously journeyed.

* * *

These 12 or 13 vows of the second stage are much more than mere observances and prohibitions. They shape truly ways of life. Conforming to them is not a theoretical notion, but a commonplace, even if because of their nature only a small part of the community may be able to practice them in their entirety. The ideal mapped out by these 12 vows and eleven stages has totally permeated the forms and the spirit of this community.

Much of the contents of the vows is now a part of the everyday activities in the lay community. Although many laypersons only know the vows in broad outline (and may even be unable to enumerate them) the vow of *ahiṃsā,* adhered to overwhelmingly by most of the community, actually encapsulates all the rest. From infancy, Jain children are educated to respect all forms of life and to act with due care. On becoming adults, perhaps they may not be able to take the path of the vows as strictly as the Śrāvakācāras suggests, but invariably they will be scrupulous when it comes to eating, moderate with possessions, honourable in business, help the community at festivals, support the building of temples, fast regularly and rigorously avoid certain professions.

THE NEXT *PRATIMĀS*

The first two stages or *pratimās* form the heart of the ideal lay path. The path proceeds with another nine rules of virtue, in one way or another linked to these first two stages Basically, they involve making the vows already taken in the second *pratimā* more rigorous and, as we shall see, many of the following stages are just reinforcements of the previous vows. While medieval treatises view this as gradual progress, from stage to stage, in practice the sequence seems rather to be a theoretical model.

The third stage entails progressively increasing the periods of daily meditation *(sāmāyika-pratimā)* already taken in the *sāmāyika-vrata.* With this more intense dedication to meditation, laypersons will reach the minimum ascetic level of meditation and will progress in their internal purification. Digambara tradition at this stage urges daily worship.

The fourth stage progressively increases the periods of fasting *(poṣadha-pratimā)* to severed days and, if possible, progression to total fasting. It also requires the ceasing of all labour, social, and domestic activities on these days.

The fifth stage cultivates the virtue of not harming plants, and the purity of food taken *(sacittatyāga-pratimā).* It includes details of how not to pick fruit from trees and of how not to eat it until another person has taken the core out. It also places restrictions on eating salad, fruit, and tubers. Their basic diet will be mainly lentils, pulses and dried fruit. Liquids that contain salt will be avoided.

The sixth stage consists of limiting sexual activity *(rātribhakta-pratimā)* still further. This stage is an intensification of the vow of chastity, and basically implies limiting sexual activity to night-time, to a moderate form, and never on fasting days. For some Digambaras, it also means abstaining from eating at night.

The seventh stage is that of absolute continence *(brahmacarya-pratimā).* One will have to avoid one's partner and, progressively also the gods, human beings and animals of the opposite sex, even in one's thoughts. No fantasising or talking to people of the opposite sex. In its broadest meaning, this stage represents the almost total abstention from domestic activity. Manufactured clothes will not be worn, nor will the body be adorned with any jewel or perfume that enhances beauty. Those who have reached this stage are called *brahmacārin* or *svāmī,* titles of maximum respect in the community.

The eighth stage is the abstaining from all labour *(ārambhatyāga-pratimā).* The devotee still allows for his activities to be carried on via servants or employees, but will become completely dependent on the rest of the family, while totally dedicated to the study of texts and meditation.

The ninth stage is the formal abandonment of all possessions *(parigrahatyā-ga -pratimā).* This entails rooting out of the slightest trace of ambition. There will be no more servants or any indirect activity carried out by employees. All the burden of activity will be transferred to sons, daughters, brothers and sisters.

The 10th stage is the total abandoning of domestic activity *(anumatityāga-pratimā).* The layperson still living at home will totally abstain from worldly activity. He or she will go to the temple to study and pray.

Finally, we come to the 11th vow, which concerns devotees' total abstinence from all food that has been specially prepared for them *(uddiṣṭatyāga-pratimā).* They will only eat other people's leftovers. They may shave their head emulating ascetics, and may carry a begging bowl and a duster.

A NON-INITIATED RENUNCIANT

Possibly, at this time, the devotee will definitively abstain from the world and will ask to join a group of ascetics. They may at this time be very old and opt for the sacred death in meditation. Perhaps, they will do neither and keep on being a pious layperson. Until they take the great vows *(mahāvratas)* of renunciants, they will technically still be considered a layperson, but in practice those who have reached the last stage lead an identical lifestyle to ascetics. Step by step, their passion has subsided, neutralising their actions and they progress towards integration with the self.

In Śvetāmbara tradition those who have progressed to the 11th *pratimā* are given the honorific title of *Śramaṇabhūta.* Digambaras divide this last level into *kṣullakas* (who wear three items of clothing and have reached the 10th stage) and *ailakas* (who wear only one item of clothing and have reached the eleventh stage). *Kṣullakas* take their food in a bowl or their hands, while sitting down, and cut their hair and beard with scissors. They can also wear sandals. The second category, the *ailakas,* are virtual ascetics. Even though they have not been initiated and do not go naked, they eat out of their cupped hands, pull their hair out from the roots in tufts and carry the same whisk broom made from peacock feathers as ascetics. The only difference is in some of their prohibitions: the study of certain sacred texts, the classical form of begging observed by ascetics, asceticism beneath the Sun and immobile standing meditation for a whole day. For centuries, the *kṣullakas* and *ailakas,* having progressed to the last *pratimās,* have taken the position and place of the extremely scarce Digambara ascetics.

32. THE PATH TO *NIRVĀṆA*

THE PROBLEM

Jainism states that the bondage of the soul *(bandha)* is without beginning *(anādi),* but not necessarily without end *(anant).* Jainism, as soteriology, occupies itself with putting an end to the state of bondage. What is involved is the purification of the soul of all *karma,* of contingency, all that is *ajīva.* We return to the heart of the question: *karma.*

We have seen how Jain treatises take pains to describe meticulously all the forms that *karma* can infiltrate into the being *(āśrava)* and the consequences of the materialisation of action, and we know that *karma* penetrates by virtue of the action of the senses, the emotions, and the mind. Nonetheless, the texts themselves warn that it is not possible to divert the feelings from objects and eliminate the experiences of pleasure and pain. The problem is not to perceive, think, or feel, but rather:

> "Pleasant things [by themselves] do not cause indifference nor emotions [as anger, etc.]; but by either hating or loving them, a man undergoes such a change through delusion" *(Uttarādhyayana-sūtra* 32.101).

That is the problem: how to bring bondage to an end? How to transcend the passions (*kaṣāyas*), which produce the vibration whereby *karma* infiltrates and sticks on to the spirit? The solution to the problem and the answer to these questions is the *path of asceticism* (*tapas-mārga*), which lead to the Ultimate.

THE REJECTION OF *KARMA*

What Jain *yoga* seeks to do is to stop, to reject *(saṁvara)* the inflow of *karma.* This is the fifth fundamental principle *(tattva)* of Jainism. The rejection of *karma* is not achieved through non-action (although this possibility has never been forgotten in Jainism) but by complete dispassion in a framework of strict control and vigilance.

According to Umāsvāti *(Tattvārtha-sūtra* 9.2), there are six means by which to reject *karma:* control *(gupti),* carefulness *(samiti),* the observance of virtue *(dharma),* reflections *(anuprekṣās),* conquest of afflictions *(parīṣahas)* and conduct *(cāritra).* They represent perfectly the ascetic path of the renunciants, the third jewel of right conduct *(samyak-cāritra)* as ascetics understand it. This is what *sādhus* and *sādhvīs* understand by *yoga* in its strict meaning of both "yoking" and "unification"—of the soul.

CONTROL

In the first place, we need the control *(gupti)* of mental, verbal and corporeal activity. It is necessary to control all activity such that there is no agent (ego) directing any action. There is simply talking, thinking and acting. Only in this way will action be detached, and thus karmically innocuous. Step by step, the ascetic brings his activities to an end: staying still for long periods, concentrating in a single point and observing large periods of silence.

CAREFULNESS

Secondly, vigilance or carefulness *(samiti)* in five daily activities: (1) in walking; always slowly, never hurrying or leaping; (2) in speaking; only when necessary; (3) in receiving donations; watching that the right foods are received, and not seeking satisfaction; (4) in moving things; taking care not to hurt small *jīvas;* and (5) when carrying out bodily functions; always where there are no living creatures *(Uttarādhyayana-sūtra* 24.2).

To comply with these injunctions an ascetic might make a detour of many miles so as not to tread on a plantation (teeming with lives), or stay for days without eating in their cell, since going out under the rain to beg is prohibited and no layperson is permitted to take food to the monastic retreat. When ascetics walk, they do not raise their gaze more than two metres above the ground so as to lose sight of what they are treading upon. Frequently, they stop and gently brush the ground to avoid the accidental death of an insect or a tiny creature with one sense. When they sit down, they will first look very carefully to ensure there is no tiny creature that could be squashed before doing so. In other words, it is in interactions with the nonhuman world that the ascetics are most highly attentive, observant, and mindful—when they are quintessential ascetic (Vallely 2002: 199).

The three controls *(guptis)* and the five carefulnesses *(samitis)* are so important in transcending attachment that the *Uttarādhyayana-sūtra* (24.27) does not hesitate to say that they form the essence of the doctrine. And Hemacandra *(Yoga-śāstra* 1.34) likens them to the jewel of right conduct.

THE OBSERVANCE OF *DHARMA*

The third way of impeding the inflow of *karma* is observation *(dharma)* of ten moral virtues *(dharma):* (1) the observance of patience *(kṣamā);* (2) the cultivation of sweetness and humility *(mārdava);* (3) the cultivation of simplicity *(ārjava);* (4) the strict observance of veracity *(satya);* (5) self-control *(saṁyama)* of word, thought and deed; (6) the cultivation of righteousness and ascetic behaviour *(tapas)*; (7) the cultivation of purity *(śauca)* or the absence of covetousness; (8) the practice of voluntary poverty *(tyāga, nirlobhatā);* (9) the attitude of total renunciation and spiritual obedience *(akiṁcinatva, ākiñcanya);* and (10) the observance of continence *(brahmacārya),* as is stated in one of the great vows.

REFLECTIONS

These practices should be accompanied by a series of reflections *(anuprekṣās, bhāvanās)* intended to combat passionate attachment and designed to strengthen the spirit of non-attachment and renunciation. Normally twelve types of reflection are mentioned: (1) on the impermanence,(*anitya*) of the world; (2) on the vulnerability *(aśaraṇa)* of the *jīva* and the inevitability of death; (3) on the cycle transmigration *(saṃsāra);* (4) on the total solitude *(ekatva)* of all living beings; (5) on the difference and the separation *(anyatva)* between body and soul; (6) on the impurity and weakness *(aśucitva)* of the material body; (7) on the inflow *(āśrava)* of *karma;* (8) on how to reject *(saṃvara)* this inflow; (9) on how to extinguish *(nirjarā)* karmic material already acquired; (10) on the truths concerning the universe *(loka);* (11) on the rarity of fully attained consciousness *(bodhidurlabhatva)* and of the great number of creatures who have not become aware of their situation; and (12) on the immense benefit of Jain *dharma (dharmasvākhyātva).* Meditating on these truths [see below] the adept will understand them in all their fullness.

THE CONQUEST OF AFFLICTIONS

The next means of rebutting the inflow of *karma* is the conquest of twenty-two physical and moral afflictions *(parīṣahas).* For example: indifference to heat, indifference to cold, control of thirst, coping with hunger, indifference to dirt, immutability toward insect bites, lack of feelings or arousal when looked upon by women, victory over the vicissitudes of begging, over the lack of comfort, over the problems caused by going naked (in the case of the Digambaras) over illness, over fear of meditating in dismal places, in the face of insults, and so forth *(Uttarādhyayana-sūtra* 2.1). And all trace of pride over the overcoming these afflictions should in itself be overcome.

LITURGICAL PRACTICES

Lastly, the texts place importance on the observance of six rules of conduct *(āvaśyakas)* specifically for ascetics (even though they may also be, and commonly are, observed by lay men and women). The term *āvaśyaka* means "necessary", "obligatory". While these rules are imperative for ascetics, in the case of lay persons adherence to them would indicate dedication to the faith.

This behaviour probably became ritualised quite early on within the ascetic tradition, so that today what have here are a series of fundamentally liturgical practices. These rules taken as a whole may be considered the epicentre, so to speak, of the ritual monastic culture of Jainism. It finds its greatest expression in the *Āvaśyaka-sūtra* and its many commentaries (among the Śvetāmbaras) and the hymnological texts known as Bhaktis (among the Digambaras). These obligations not only permeate the life of the ascetics, but are also reenacted twice daily (at sunrise and sunset) in a communal rite *(āvaśyaka-kriyā),* which the Pandit Sukhalalji (1962: 129) compares to Christian prayers, and the rite of conjunction *(saṃdhyā)* of Vedic society.

The first ritualised act or *āvaśyaka* is the daily cultivation of equanimity *(sāmāyika).* In actual fact, the main act of the "lesser" initiation into the order is the taking of a vow of equanimity for life [see page 194]. What is involved here is the attaining of a mental and emotional disposition which is essentially contemplative. As Vaṭṭakera says:

> "*Sāmāyika* is that state in which the ascetic is the same towards himself and another, to his mother and to all other women, to pleasant and unpleasant things and to honour and disrespect" *(Mūlācāra* 521; cited in Dundas 1992: 147).

The whole of ascetic life is in any case the cultivation of this equanimity, the way to make the self impermeable to *karma.* Normally, ascetics practice equanimity at dawn and at dusk, with hymns and with concentration on the *tīrthaṅkaras*.

The second practice is the worship of the *tīrthaṅkaras (deva-pūjā).* This is the devotional element in the ascetic life of the monks, which in their case becomes internal worship *(bhāva-pūjā).* Normally, this takes the form of the "Hymn to the Twenty-four *Jinas",* which is repeated several times a day. Among the Digambaras and the Mūrtipūjaka Śvetāmbaras this practice is usually conducted in the temple, before the statue of the Jina. Among the Sthanākavāsīs and Terāpanthīs, this is performed in the retreat. Each hymn is accompanied by different gestures *(mudrās)* and postures *(āsanas).*

The third practice according to the rule is veneration and respectful salutation of the masters (*vandana).* Once the ascetic has received permission to approach the venerable one, the ascetic touches his or her right foot with their forehead and hands and ask them if they have had a good day (or night), if their inner journey is proceeding, with their senses under control and their soul free The dialogues employed are the same as those used by laypersons [see pages 454-455].

As with the lay Jains, this activity tends to be associated with the following, fourth action, which is that of repentance and confession *(pratikramaṇa),* a practice that may well go back to the earliest stirrings of Jainism. According to the *Āvaśyaka-sūtra,* repentance should be performed in the presence of the master twice a day, as well as every time one goes out into the outside world. Confessions are also timetabled according to the calendar (every four months, each year and before death in meditation). It is considered to be a very powerful inner purification practice. Normally, this is carried out communally, as part of the *āvaśyaka -kriyā.* Personal, private confession is termed *ālocanā.*

The fifth practice is the abandonment of the body *(kāyotsarga).* This is a very efficient type of *tapas.* Basically, it involves emulating one of the two main iconographic position: the ascetic sitting still *(padmāsana)* or standing *(kāyotsarga, jinamudrā)* with the arms hanging at the sides but without touching the body. An essential part of asceticism is silence *(mauna),* a particularly powerful form of purification. As the former Jain monk Satish Kumar (2004: 63) recalls, the very word for monk is *muni,* a person who keeps *maunam* or silence. At the same time, even though the monastic tradition has placed great emphasis in asceticism, mere mortification of the flesh is considered futile, and there are many stories in the *Āvaśyaka* literature (in Balbir 1990: 47) which teach us that not looking after the body is misguided and wrong. The object here is to stop the entry of more *karma* through the overcoming of the body. Thus, the immobile body posture should be accompanied by murmured *mantras.* The practice is obligatory, for example, after going out begging or after a journey on foot.

The last practice to be mentioned is known as abandon *(pratyākhyāna).* Essentially, this consists in avoiding a number of actions, beverages, and above all, foods. Besides fasts of various sorts, the pledge not to eat or drink from a little before nightfall until after dawn the next day is obligatory.

Thanks to these liturgies the practice of the monastic life of *sādhus* and *sādhvīs* took on considerable cohesion. Plus, and this is just as important, all these activities spread to the lay community to form part of their religious life too [see chapters 27 and 29]. It is even possible that many of these practices established themselves in monastic liturgy thanks to the influence of the lay community. These practices are not obligatory for lay Jains but are compulsory for ascetics.

* * *

With the practice of control, of carefulness, of reflection, observance of *dharma,* the overcoming of afflictions and hardships and the *āvaśyakas,* one attains a mode of being that is basically contemplative. The different varieties of *karma* are no longer able to infiltrate. As advances are made in spiritual mastery, ascetics raise a shield against the more subtle karmic material, until at last no karmic material can adhere to their souls. Whoever has mastered these practices is a true Nirgrantha, a Jain virtuoso.

THE EXTINCTION OF *KARMA*

Ascetics should not just resist the entry of *karma,* they should at the same time destroy the accumulated *karma* of the past, since this will otherwise continue to obscure the luminosity of the *jīva.* This step is known as the extinction *(nirjarā),* desintegration, elimination or annihilation of *karma,* This is the sixth fundamental principle of Jainism. The extinction can be voluntary, activated by asceticism. Equally, it can be involuntary, when for example a living being has to bear privations and calamities. Thanks to involuntary extinction, many tiny beings are able to evolve to higher stages in subsequent existences. The process is likened to a fruit that can ripen naturally or made to ripen artificially (Hemacandra, *Yoga-śāstra* 4.86-91). The interesting aspect of Jain asceticism is that ripening (*vipāka)* of the act can be consciously and prematurely brought on by the monk or nun. It is possible, Jainism teaches, to extinguish the karmic valencies and, in a theoretical framework, achieve liberation in that lifetime. The basic way to extinguish *karma* is the practice of *tapas.*

It is here that asceticism takes up a central position in practice since, as Umāsvāti says *(Tattvārtha-sātra* 9.3), *tapas* not only serve to reject *karma* but to actually extinguish it. Only with the *tapas,* emulating the example of Mahāvīra and the hundreds of ascetic stories that the tradition has recorded, is it possible to extinguish one's karmic burden. Two types of asceticisms are recognised: the outer *(bāhya-tapas)* and the inner types *(ābhyantara-tapas).*

OUTER ASCETICISM

Outer asceticism includes: (1) the practice of fasting *(anaśana*—the quintessential *tapas)*; (2) the vow to reduce the number of meals *(avamaudarya);* (3) the voluntary limitation of the number of homes visited to ask for alms *(vṛttiparisankṅyāna);* (4) the reduction of certain tasty foods *(rasaparityāga)*; (5) distancing oneself from others and withdrawing to unpopulated places *(vivik-taśayyāsana)',* and (6) the practice of mortification of the body *(kāyakleśa)* (Umāsvāti, *Tattvārtha-sūtra* 9.19), such as staying in difficult postures or standing still in the Sun for long periods of time.

Basically, the point is to control body activities and passions to achieve total indifference to the senses. Obviously, asceticism has no value if it does not express an attitude of inner equanimity. Recall that Jain practices are not conceived as aggressions against the body. The body is used to overcome the passions and the mind, much more subtle enemies to control. It would be completely erroneous, says James Laidlaw (1995: 242), to see Jainism in terms of an antagonistic dualism between body and soul. Only with a human body—not with a divine one, even—can the discipline be exercised that leads to liberation.

INNER ASCETICISM

For this reason, outer asceticism should be complemented with other practices, those known as inner asceticism. These include: (1) correct religious conduct *(vinaya)* in thought, word and deed; (2) the confession of weaknesses, transgression and the penitence suited to atoning for them *(prāyaścittas);* (3) the sense of duty and service to other members of the order *(vaiyāvṛtya),* especially to the elderly and the sick; (4) the study of the scriptures *(svādhyāya),* whether by memorisation, sessions of questions with the master or reflection on the text; (5) the renunciation of forms of possession *(vyutsarga);* and (6) concentration or meditation *(dhyānd),* the practice which, duly perfected [see below], will catapult the ascetic to the highest objective.

With these inner ascetic practices, the point is to bring one's indomitable mental activity under control. Ascetics who have mastered the body and the senses thanks to the outer ascetic practices, now attack the mind by means of inward practices. These are exercised in more than the achieving of non-attachment: Jain asceticism is also characterised by knowledge. An ascetic, who does not simultaneously cultivate love for all living beings, who has not understood the true solitude (and at the same time interaction) of the spirit, would be a mere fakir. In conceiving asceticism as a practice with its roots in correct knowledge of ethics and doctrines, Jains have been able to criticise the ascetic practices of certain Śaiva devotees, who may sometimes be most ostentatious.

JAIN MEDITATION

Of all the forms of external and internal ascetic practice, concentration and meditation (*dhyāna),* is what the philosophers and commentators are unanimous in thinking of crucial importance. Hemacandra has it that:

> "*Mokṣa* is achieved through the shedding of *karmas.* The *karmas* are destroyed through self-realisation. The realisation of self comes through meditation" *(Yoga-śāstra* 4.113).

Despite the importance given to it by the masters, the texts give scant information on Jain meditation. The basic recommendations do not differ from the practice of equanimity *(sāmāyika)* as a suggested practice for lay people and obligatory for monks and nuns. The recommendations are nothing if not general. It is clear that Jainism did not develop as structured and as deep an approach to meditation as the Buddhist or Yogic traditions. The reason, as Paul Dundas (1992:143) suggests, inheres in the fact that early Jain teachings were more concerned with the cessation of mental and physical activity than their transforming. During the medieval period the Jain contemplative culture all but disappeared. All emphasis was put in outer ascetic practices. Hemacandra himself, whose scheme for meditation became normative for Śvetāmbara Jainism, recognised that he taught the higher levels simply because they had came down to him through the tradition, and should not be lost *(Yoga-śāstra* 11.4). Despite that, since the end of the 19th century interest in Jain meditation has increasingly gained adepts, especially among the Terāpanthīs. The traditional Digambara description is to be found in Rāmasena's *Tattvānuśāsana* (10th century) or the *Jñānārṇava* by Śubhacandra (11th century); the Śvetāmbara counterpart being the *Dhyāna-śāstra* written by Jinabhadra Gaṇi (6th century) and the *Yoga-śāstra* by Hemacandra (12th century).

Jainism defines meditation *(dhyāna)* as the retention of thought and concentration in a single object *(ekāgratā).* This maxim is identical to that of Patañjali's classical Yoga. The postures *(āsanas),* breath control *(prāṇayāma),* withdrawal of one's mind from sense organs *(pratyāhāra),* and concentration *(dhāraṇā)* virtually replicate the recommendations in Patañjali's methodology (Hemacandra, *Yoga -śāstra* 5.1).

Normally, the point of concentration is the source or basis of life: the *jīva* or *ātman* (although as we shall see, yogis can visualise different points before concentrating on the *jīva).* The immediate effect of *ekāgratā* is suppression of all distractions and automatic mental ticks or habits which dominate and shape our ordinary state of consciousness. Thanks to this concentration on a single point, the two causes behind the generation of mental flow are controlled: that is, sensorial activity and the activity of the subconscious (Eliade 1975: 58). To practice concentration, certain postures *(āsanas)* are specifically recommended, such as the lotus posture, the hero posture or standing position, which in turn require good physical condition. Following Patañjali, Hemacandra *(Yoga-śāstra* 4.134) recommends that the yogi adopt the posture that will ensure the greatest mental and physical stability. Above all, tension should disappear, so that the body does not perturb the mind. As Mircea Eliade (1975: 65) says, *āsana* is *ekāgratā*; the body is "stable", "concentrated" on a single position. In the case of *prāṇayāma,* the aim is to make breathing more rhythmic and slower, so that the yogi can advance lucidly to other.states of consciousness. This will allow the freeing of the sensory activity from the influx of external objects *(pratyāhāra)* and facilitate concentration *(dhāraṇa).* To facilitate meditation, the yogi is helped by the murmured repetition of the *namaskāra-mantra* with intervals of silence. What the yogi imitates or recreates—thank's to the lack of gestures—is the way of being of the pure soul (Eliade 1975: 72). In all this, Jainism is quite unoriginal, in that it has availed itself of the techniques of Patañjali's Yoga. It is in the method of meditation itself that Jainism shows some new development, and according to the traditional norm, Jainism subdivides its meditation technique *(dhyānas)* into four types.

UNDESIRABLE MEDITATION

The first type of meditation focuses on disagreeable scenes *(ārtadhyāna)* such as envy, enmity, weapons, poisons, separation from one's loved ones, association with undesirables, and anxiety about overcoming pain or illness, or of freeing oneself from such images. This meditation is characteristic of negligent ascetics.

CRUEL MEDITATION

The second type is that known as "cruel" *(raudradhyāna).* In theory, the yogi should concentrate on all kinds of *hiṃsā,* especially the perverse pleasure of causing pain to others, lying, robbery, or the way of guaranteeing oneself pleasures. In other words, the ascetic concentrates on the opposite of the five great vows.

Being based on very negative emotions, these first two types, and especially the second, are inauspicious and need to be got rid of completely. They not only impede self-realisation, but they may bring on one rebirth in the Lower World, including the dreadful seventh hell. Seeing what they are, it is not easy to see why they were considered meditative states. Śubhacandra himself admits that only the next two types of meditation [see below] have to do with spiritual progress leading to liberation *(Jñānārṇava* 3.33). Perhaps the Jain theorists simply followed Patañjali *(Yoga-sūtra* 2.33-34) when he recommended that to eradicate doubt one should exercise discrimination over perverse actions.

VIRTUOUS MEDITATION

The third type of concentration is the one known as virtuous meditation *(dharmadhyāna).* It is here that Jain meditation, undoubtedly influenced by other Yogic traditions in India, truly begins. The *dhyāna* consists of the contemplation of different objects, normally the twelve subjects of reflection *(anuprekṣās).* For example, a yogi concentrates on the principles *(tattvas)* given by the Jina, or on the misery suffered by most of the rest of living beings. Or how others have strayed from the right path, or on the mysterious mechanisms governing the inflow of *karma,* or on the structures and future of the universe. With consciousness fixed on the doctrines and truths of Jainism, the yogi "penetrates" them and "apprehends" them directly, without mediation of the intellect. Although the meditator still has not achieved absolute control or mastered all passions *(kaṣāyas)* it is said that during the practice of these types of concentration the ascetic attains momentarily the seventh rung *(guṇasthāna)* of the ladder that leads to salvation. Constant practice of these concentrations will lead to the following type of trances.

PURE MEDITATION

The fourth and last type is pure concentration *(śukladhyāna),* the only type of meditation located within a truly soteriological context. It is said that to enter these extraordinary levels of concentration, knowledge of the Pūrvas is essential (Hemacandra, *Yoga-śāstra* 11.2), which in itself explains why liberation is not possible in these times. Within the range of pure concentration, Hemacandra speaks of four basic forms.

The first is concentration on imaginary objects *(piṇḍasthadhyāna).* This involves visualising different landscapes with the four elements (earth, water, air and fire) as well as a vision of the soul separated from the body. In the first four visualisations, yogis "enter" their mental landscape and sit on their throne, ready to eliminate all *karmas.* Then, with the fifth visualisation, the task for the yogi is to apprehend the transcendent nature of the soul and purify it meditatively.

The second type or class of pure meditation is based on certain sacred litanies *(padasthadhyāna).* Seated on the throne, ascetics imagine a lotus flower sprouting from their navel and concentrate on reordering the syllables of the *namaskāra-mantra* to form different mystic formulas. The more concentrated the *mantra,* the better. Alternatively, the names of the supreme ones will serve. The preferred form of concentration is the muttered repetition *(japa).* Once at this level, the yogi no longer uses sensory activity in order to know things. Such yogis can know everything by means of contemplation. The intellect *(citta)* simply mirrors objects without the intervention—or imposition—of the senses. Thanks to this, yogis are able to contemplate directly the essential nature of all things and develop supernatural faculties such as clairvoyance or telepathy. In fact, so luminous is the yogi in these meditative states that he or she becomes comparable to a divine being. Even where such yogis have distanced themselves from Tantric practices, a clear influence from esoteric *yoga* is detectable here, above all that of the influential Śaivism of Kashmir. The *mantras* become a meditation vehicle of incomparable efficiency, and this, according to Tantric Jainism, is because the mystic sound is the object it represents. The *mantra* is the seed of the supreme being and, when the mystic formula is repeated according to the right rules, the yogi takes on his or her ontological essence and assimilates the supreme being or the state of saintliness that the *mantra* represents, in a concrete and immediate way. Commentaries on Umāsvāti, dealing with the last aphorism *(Tattvārtha-sūtra* 10.7), state that these types of concentration produce extraordinary powers *(siddhis)* in the yogi. Nonethless, as Walther Schubring (1934: 316) already observed, the commentary seems rather to be an attempt to place these mythical powers, so frequently mentioned in the scriptures, in a soteriological context. The problem, perhaps, is that they have been inserted in an inappropriate place, for whoever reaches this level of spiritual development should be above such magic tricks. The *siddhis* have nothing to do with the path that leads to liberation. In any case, whoever renounces the *siddhis* (yet another form of renunciation and asceticism, notice) will be able to progress even more on their journey of purification.

Removed from the human condition, thanks to the control of the body and of breathing, lightened thanks to ascetic practice, with the inflow of *karma* impeded owing to their non-attachment, yogis at this level move on to concentration of the third kind, this time centred on the Jina *(rūpasthadhyāna)* seated in the sacred assembly. Here, *yoga* the science of *mantras* and iconography all come together. The image or picture is now the vehicle of the meditation. With their consciousnesses focused on the way of being of the omniscient, and their breathing quieted, yogis take on the nature of the omniscient one. In *rūpastha-dhyāna,* the meditator becames aware of his or her own omniscient potential. Although in fact the enlightened *jīva* has always been present, thanks to *dhyāna,* he or she who meditates wakes to a new awareness of this ontological truth:

> "By the practice of the material meditation, the meditating yogi, who identifies himself with the omniscient, finds himself to be an omniscient" (Hemacandra, *Yoga-śāstra* 9.11).

The yogi has identified to such an extent with the object of meditation, that all distinction between subject and object vanishes. This is what Patañjali *(Yoga-sūtra* 3.3) and the Yogic tradition call trance or enstasis *(samādhi).* It is here that the break in level takes place, the paradoxical transition from *being* to *knowing* (Eliade 1975: 84). Unmoving, without a trace of appetites, passions or emotions, beyond the ego, absolutely identified with the *jina* [see FIG. 47], the consciousness reveals itself as the unique *(kaivalya, kevala)* soul *(ātman, jīva).* This is a full awakening, right vision in all its amplitude, enlightened wisdom *(prajñā).*

The last type of pure concentration is that which transcends form *(rūpātīta-dhyāna),* or concentration on abstract qualities such as omniscience, pure bliss or infinite energy which characterises the liberated one. This type of meditation belongs, properly speaking, to the state of the omniscient one.

By means of these forms of meditation the yogi has gradually annihilated or eliminated an enormous quantity of destructive *karmas* and has ascended on the ladder from the eighth to the twelfth rung. On the 10th rung, they are beset by the most subltle passions which will necessarily have taken a short cut along the path of total eradication. Otherwise, if mere repression had been opted for, after a brief glimpse of the 11th rung, the yogi would have fallen to the lowest levels of all. Total erradication is only possible by means of mastery of yogic techniques for the unification of consciousness. With the total elimination of the passions via asceticism and pure meditation, the yogi will ascend to the 12th rung. Now, there is no longer any possibility of falling.

Śubhacandra *(Jñānārṇava* 33-35; in Ghoshal 1917: 241) and other authors provide variants, but in all instances the ascetic undertakes the destruction of the body on the level of imagination and concentrates on the stream of consciousness produced in the visualisations. All Jain soteriological practice consists of purifying oneself of corporeal, passion-derived and mental burdens. The yogi does not obtain, add or attain anything; all that is eliminated is the veil of ignorance revealing the *jīva* that is infinite consciousness. This realisation is the coinciding with one's self.

THE OMNISCIENT

Whoever has reached the 12th rung has succeeded in extinguishing all negative *karmas,* including the *mohanīyas,* which have bound the soul for millions of aeons. By destroying the passions, the *karmas* which obstruct vision, knowledge and energy are destroyed as well (Umāsvāti, *Tattvārtha-sūtra* 10.1). This is because all karmic material had existed in a state of complete interdependence (Jaini 1979: 258). All destructive *karmas* have been rejected and eliminated.

There is now no room for further efforts. Thoughts emerge, actions happen, sensations occur, but there is "nobody" who holds on to them, because there is only an awareness of self. It is not that the mind reaches itself, this is impossible, but once the mind (language, thoughts, emotions) and the body (sensations) have been transcended the source that remains is the single consciousness, the transpersonal witness.

In a spontaneous way, the yogi ascends to the thirteenth *guṇasthāna* or rung, that of the living omniscient, still with a material body. The *sayoga-kevalī* is the highest level that any living creature of the universe can attain. Not even the gods can be compared to such. In point of fact, a break of level has occurred on a cosmic scale: *the jīva* now has the knowledge, the perception, the bliss and infinite energy of the liberated. Imperturbable, like the *bodhisattvas* of Mahāyāna Buddhism or the *jīvamukta* of Hinduism, the omniscient remains suspended in a modality of existence and knowledge characterised—if indeed they can be characterised—by absolute equanimity. This coincides completely with the definition of *jñāna-yoga* in the *Bhagavad-gītā* (2.48). Now the yogi can be called one who is deserving of worship *(arhat)* or omniscient *(kevalin),* because no negative *karma* now adheres to the *jīva*.

The quality that best characterises this mode of being and experiencing is omniscience *(kevala-jñāna).* Knowledge without any disturbance from *karma.* All that exists *(sat),* the substances *(dravyas)* as well as its qualities *(guṇas)* and modes *(paryāyas),* are reflected simultaneously and spontaneously in the absolute knowledge, since all karmic dust has disappeared thanks to its rejection *(saṁvara)* and extinction *(nirjarā).* There is not an intention to know, nor mental activity, only pure perception. The *Kalpa-sūtra (Jina-caritra* 121) depicts Mahāvīra's omniscience:

> "When the Venerable Ascetic Mahāvīra had become a *Jina* and *Arhat,* he was a *Kevalin,* omniscient and comprehending all objects; he knew and saw all conditions of the world, of gods, men, and demons: whence they come, whither they go, whether they are bom as men or animals or become gods or hell-beings, the ideas, the thoughts of their minds, the food, doings, desires, the open and secret deeds of all the living beings in the whole world; he the *Arhat,* for whom there is no secret, knew and saw all conditions of all living beings in the world, what they thought, spoke, or did at any moment".

Such knowledge can perhaps be termed divine. Not for nothing do the theists describe their God with a kind of almighty knowledge of this sort. However, the Jain tradition has not been too concerned over whether or not the *arhat* or *jina* is able to know everything. He could be like the eye of the Cosmic Being, which penetrates and grasps every atom of the universe, but this aspect has not been much underlined. On the other hand, what is stressed is that such omniscient never identifyies himself with the objects that he knows; he is not their Soul or *brahman* (Amṛtacandra, *Laghutattva-sphoṭa* 15). The accent is always put on the fact that the omniscient soul fundamentally and essentially *knows itself.* Or more exactly, the *kevalin* does not know the *jīva,* but rather this non-dual knowledge *is* the *jīva.* There is no difference between the knower, knowledge and the known. Parallels with the Wisdom of *prajñā-pāramitā* of Mahāyāna Buddhism are clear *(Pañcaviṃśatisāhasrikā-prajñā-pāramitā-sūtra* 1.2.6-7).

Up until the moment of death, the *arhat* will stay on the thirteenth rung. According to the Digambaras, the omniscient ones reside in the glory of total isolation *(kaivalya).* According to the Śvetāmbaras, these sublime ones continue with their usual tasks, although none of their movements generate an inflow of *karma* nor are they mediated by the senses. Values are dispensed with. They do not experience joy or pain, gaiety or sadness, or anything of that sort, because this activity is *not theirs.* The fact is that, in the words of Mircea Eliade (1975: 38-39), when we understand that the soul is free, eternal and inactive, everything that happens to us (pain, feelings, desires, thoughts, and so on) *no longer belongs to us. The jīva* is simply the observer *(sākṣin),* the witness who apprehends everything directly and spontaneously. Even the experience of liberation is not attained or possessed. Hence, the absolute indifference of the *tīrthaṅkara.*

THE EXPLOSION

As only neutral *karma* keeps him alive, it is said that the *kevalin* is active *(sayoga).* Being of the same duration, the *karmas* that have to do with the *kevalin's* constitution, parentage and longevity will disappear in the last moment of life. Only the *karmas* that have to do with pain and pleasure *(vedanīya)* may entail one or two more incarnations. So that the last practice of the *kevalin,* the meditation or *dhyāna* so to speak worthy of a *kevalin* (and an impossible thing for those who have not attained this level of spiritual evolution), consists of lining up these *karmaṣ* with the other three, so that they too disappear at the time of death. This phenomenal process of equalisation is called "explosion" *(samudghāta).* By means of her or his yogic control, the *jīva* expands in mil-lionths of a second to the far confines of the universe and then contracts again to normal size *(Praśamarati-prakaraṇa* 213-274*).* In this event, the *kevalin* projects the last karmic atoms as peace is achieved. The doctrine of the Yogic "explosion", unique to Jainism, clearly shows the materialistic conception of *karma.* It might be the Jain response to the Upanisadic claim of realisation of the *ātman* or the Buddhist highest meditative trances. Once the omniscient one has thrown off the last particles of *karma,* the *kevalin's* pilgrimage in the ocean of *saṃsāra* has come to an end.

Before death, the *kevalin* enters into the last pure trances. All mental, verbal or physical activity ceases. All that remains is the heartbeat and breathing. With a last meditation, the pulse and the breathing also come to an end. The fourteenth rung has been attained, that of omniscience without activity *(ayoga-ke-valī).* This fourteenth rung only lasts for an infinitesimal moment, because when the *karmas* (all perfectly equalised) that maintained life vanish, the *jīva* abandons all subtle bodies and hurtles like a missile to the heights of the universe.

NIRVĀṆA

In a mere moment, the *jīva* ascends in a straight line up through the celestial levels to the Slightly Curved Place *(iṣatprāgbhāra)* or the World of the Perfect Ones. There to reside, totally liberated, for all eternity. The ascetic Keśīn asks Gautama, and the latter replies:

> "There is a safe place in view of all, but difficult to approach, where there is no old age nor death, no pain nor disease" *(Uttarādhyāyana-sūtra* 23.81).

Keśīn asks: "What is this place called?" Gautama made the following reply:

> "It is what is called *nirvāṇa,* or freedom from pain" *(Uttarādhyāyana-sūtra* 23.83).

Nirvāṇa is liberation *(mukti),* emancipation *(mokṣa),* the isolation *(kaivalya)* of the spiritual monad in its innate purity. It is endless saintliness, where even the danger of a celestial life has been overcome, since there is now no *karma,* which might lead to a new existence. Umāsvāti defined spiritual liberation as elimination of all types of *karma (Tattvārtha-sūtra* 10.3). *Nirvāṇa* is the total disconnection from matter. For that reason, this immaterial state can only be represented iconographically by the *Siddhapratimā-yantra* [see FIG. 48].

But liberation is not the extinction of existence. It is said that the infinite *jīvas* that dwell in the Abode of the Liberated Souls are two thirds the size they were in the previous incarnation, simply now the *jīva* occupies the whole of the bodily space. This expression, generally taken today metaphorically, serves to illustrate that while all souls are identical in nature, individuality persists even in the liberated state. Furthermore, the image places emphasis on the fact that the liberated one was previously a human being.

The truth, however, is that the Jain tradition has shown relatively little interest in speculating about *nirvāṇa.* The fact is, how to describe in words—

asks Amṛtacandra *(Laghutattva-sphoṭa* 599)—the state of omniscience? *Nirvāṇa* does not have, in truth, any cause. It is not the result of any action, for however good an action is, an action is *karma,* and *karma* cannot eliminate *karma.* Liberation has no cause, has no origin; it is simply what remains when the *jīva* has ceased to be obstructed by *karma. Mokṣa* or *nirvāṇa* is the soul in its pristine state: purely consciousness *(caitanya)* as Haribhadra said *(Yoga-bindu* 445; cited in Desai 1983: 66). Thus, it can be and usually is called supreme soul *(paramātman).* We should not be misled by the terminology. There is no absorption in *brahman* or union with the Divine. Within Jainism individuality is eternal. There is only one life *(jīva)* indifferent to mundane events, indescribable, transpersonal. Kundakunda *(Pañcāstikāyasāra* 28) defines *nirvāṇa* as the state of transcendental bliss, pure knowledge and infinite perception.

JAIN NON-DUALISM

Kundakunda is precisely the greatest exponent of the mystical tendency within Jainism. His writings, especially the *Pravacanasāra* and the *Pañcāstikāyasāra,* shaped the Digambara edifice philosophically. But Kundakunda deserves special mention for the mystic line of approach which he opened in the *Samayasāra,* a work that had immense repercussions, evident in enlightened laypersons such as Banārasīdāsa, Rājacandra, in movements that were clearly based on the lay community, like Kanjisvāmī-Panth and even in Śvetāmbara masters. It is clear that Kundakunda's work is not merely the work of a restless and somewhat unorthodox author, but rather the result of a line of probably very ancient Digambara thought. The fact that his commentators prolonged and extended this mystic approach without any hesitation, notably in the case of Amṛtacandra (9th-10th centuries), indicates that, while a minority trend within Jainism, there was a mystic path within it (parallel to the ascetic one), which was well defined and capable of neutralising the tendency to dualism characteristic of Jainism. I want to finish this volume with an exposition of Jaina mysticism, as conceived by Kundakunda and Amrtacandra and as subscribed to by an increasingly numerous Jains.

In many passages of his books, Kundakunda goes as far as to say that liberation is not reached as a result of the destruction of *karma,* but through the destruction of illusion *(moha)* and ignorance *(avidyā) (Pravacanasāra* 195). Gnosis eliminates the illusion. This declaration is highly subversive.

For Kundakunda, bondage ceases to be a physical problem, as in the Vedānta, a question of ignorance. *Karma* is not matter *(pudgala)* but rather a modification in states of consciousness *(bhāvas)* of the soul. It is certain that the orthodox position of Jainism states that the association of soul with matter is, so to speak, accidental. Hence, the description of the soul would be strictly non-material (consciousness, energy and bliss). But Kundakunda goes much further and affirms that soul and matter do not mutually effect each other. The position taken by Kundakunda and Amṛtacandra is easily on a level with the non-dualism of Vedānta Advaita or the eternalism of Sāṃkhya. Like the sages of the Upaniṣads, Kundakunda considers that the true liberated state is that of *knowing*. Once one has discerned between the soul *(jīva)* and that which is not the soul *(ajīva)* and is totally alien to it, all that remains is *knowing*. Once ignorance—concerning the *jīva* being associated with the *ajīva*—is eliminated by means of meditation, there can no longer be bondage nor rebirth. The person who meditates perceives that the body, mind and speech are substances other than the soul. If this perception becomes a *realisation* thanks to meditation, then neither speech, nor the mind, nor the body can do anything to stop the ascension towards liberation. Kundakunda sums this up apophatically:

> "I am neither the body, nor the mind, nor the speech, nor the cause thereof, nor the agent, nor the commissioner, nor the consentor of the doers" *(Pravacanasāra* 160).

Kundakunda is but a step away from concluding—as in Vedānta or in Yogācāra Buddhism—that bondage is really an illusion *(māyā)*. If the *jīva* has no connection with matter, then, what has asceticism to do with this realisation? The path of the mystic and that of the ascetic are bound up together by Amṛtacandra, when he praises the *jina* in these terms:

> "Although you were [already] endowed with internal control, which is independent [of external formalities such as becoming a monk, etc.], you still established yourself at first in the path of external control. Thus, you did not invalidate the imporance of the absolute interdependence of internal and external control" *(Laghutattva-sphoṭa* 53).

In other words, Amṛtacandra does not rule out the need to annihilate the passions *(kaṣāyas)* through asceticism *(tapas)*. For Kundakunda and Amṛtacandra, inner asceticism are to be seen as a public demonstration, a symbol *(liṅga)* of being on the right path. However, external asceticism is clearly outdone by inner asceticism, especially meditation *(dhyāna)*, since it is the only way to conquer ignorance *(mithyātva)*. For Kundakunda, the root of bondage is, as in Buddhism, ignorance and illusion *(moha)*, which impels us to act dominated by our passions and our attachment. External bondage is seen in our attachment to the things of this world; inner bondage is to be seen in our passions. It is no longer a question of eliminating the *karma* generated by killing a living creature, for example, but of rejecting the mental modification that such an act creates. In a sense, Kundakunda sets out to interiorise right behaviour. He does not seek physical inactivity, but rather inactivity of the passions; the reflecting of pure consciousness. The ideal behaviour is an attitude of calm and lack of passion, rather than asceticism and catalepsy.

While external asceticism becomes unnecessary, I agree with Will Johnson (1995: 223) in not underestimating the importance of the public and social display of any religion. This is an aspect that should never be underestimated or devalued. If modern Jainism were to renounce *tapas, ahiṃsā* and the insistence in renunciation, could it then maintain its identity vis-à-vis polymorphic Hinduism? Very probably the answer is no. For that reason, Kundakunda was quite capable of arguing for positions, which philosophically speaking are contrary to his own postulates. At all events, with his idea of interiorising right conduct, for Kundakunda there would be no need—at least logically—to become an ascetic. Will Johnson (1995: 228) has observed the more positive attitude toward the laity in this type of passage, which clearly implies different social conditions and perhaps even having a different audience in mind. It would not be surprising, that laypersons such as Banārasīdāsa, Rājacandra or Kanji Svāmī would praise this mystic way less anchored in monasticism.

However, in the *Samayasāra,* Kundakunda goes further and no longer makes any concessions. He says that from the conventional point of view *(vyavahāra),* which takes it that the soul interacts with that which is non-soul (and in this way creates *saṃsāra)* is unreal. In reality, he is not bothered about the reality or irreality of the *ajīva,* since this is irrelevant to liberation. In a way, Kundakunda ends up by rejecting philosophical pluralism in favour of a single point of view *(naya)* on reality: the absolute *(niścaya).* As William Johnson (1995: 245) says, Kundakunda seems in the end like an *ekāntavādin,* much in the style of the Vedāntin Śaṅkara. It seems as if Kundakunda were maintaining two different positions concerning the two realities. In the classical version, the conventional point of view considers that the soul acts and experiences the fruits of action. The higher vision, however, maintains that there is no action or experience. Both points of view become harmonised or compatible when seen from the standpoint of *anekāntavāda.* The first is to be seen from the modal point of view *(paryāya-naya),* the second from the substantial perspective *(dravya-naya),* but in his second position Kundakunda differs. Here, the conventional point of view is basically erroneous and illusory. The higher point of view, on the other hand, is not just another point of view, it is the *only* point of view, a mode of thinking which is incompatible with *anekāntavāda.* And this has it that the *jīva* has never been connected with matter. In which case, how can the situation of bondage *(bandha)* be explained? For Kundakunda, the *jīva* causes alterations in its psychic state *(bhāva)* by means of its own agency [see pages 389-390], and these alterations cause matter in its different states and processes to modify, in turn causing the *jīva* to transform its mental states. Simply put, Kundakunda replaces the passions *(kaṣāyas)* with mental states *(bhāvas)* to explain bondage. But:

> "When this discriminative knowledge, free from error, arises in the Self, then the nature of the Self, manifests in the form of pure *upayoga* [consciousness] and he does not cause any kind of impure psychic states" *(Samayasāra* 183).

The true cause of bondage is ignorance. The soul has nothing to do with bondage. The latter is a chain of mirages between ignorant mental states and *karmas* that produce more ignorance. The exact mechanism of this circular dance, however, is not explained. This is very reminiscent of the Sāṃkhya philosophy, which always maintained that soul *(puruṣa)* and nature *(prakṛti)* were never bound together. In stead of proclaiming the irreality of one of the two (the *ajīva* for example, as the Vedānta would do) what is emphasised is the illusory nature of the *relationship.* Metaphysical dualism is not eliminated, but becomes very devalued. Bondage is, in sum, a question of ignorance. It results from thinking that soul and matter interact. Instead, Kundakunda here puts forward the higher point of view *(niś-caya-naya)* not as a description of the liberated soul, but as a means by which the soul can attain liberation. It is not, just one more point of view among others, given that, unless one believes that it is the correct point of view, it is not possible to attain liberation (Johnson 1995: 265). Once one looks upon bondage as an illusion, karmic material ceases to have any effect. What is needed, in the end, is to apprehend the higher viewpoint, but in fact this is beyond any conceptual thought. This is liberation.

This is doubly subversive, because it does away with the problem of the loss of the Pūrvas. One can attain liberation in one's lifetime, realising the *ātman.* With the practice of discrimination—for which Kundakunda uses the characteristically Buddhist term *prajñā (Samayasāra* 296)—with the help of the higher point of view, one can *become aware* that the soul has never been—nor never could have been—attached. This is a tremendous conclusion that Kundakunda dares to formulate only implicitly. This position is the equivalent of saying that the soul has been, is, and always will be a *kevalin,* something fascinatingly similar to the Buddhist notion that all beings already possess (or are) Buddha nature, the theory of the *tathāgata-garbha.* Of course, Kundakunda does not take the final step of equating *saṃsāra* with *nirvāṇa,* but distances himself completely from the Jain ideal of burning *karma* through hardship and asceticism and adheres to the position of his contemporary Nāgārjuna. For the latter discriminating wisdom is the means by which one apprehends the higher truth *(paramārtha-satya).* Moreover, as in Mādhyamaka Buddhism, Kundakunda understands wisdom to be not just the intellectual and analytical means for realising discrimination, but as the realisation of liberation (Nāgārjuna, *Mūlamadhyamakakārikā* 24.10). *Prajñā* is the non-dual experience. Therefore, the only way to experience the soul is the gnostic-meditative way. Kundakunda repeats again and again:

> "Such a right knowing Self, of the nature of perception and knowledge entirely

> different from alien nature, contemplates upon his pure Self and very soon becomes identical with that Pure Self (*Samayasāra* 189).

As the mystic advances on the path towards integrating with the self, he or she develops an attitude of indifference towards all that is not soul. Instead of right conduct, meditation upon the soul is postulated *(ātmabhāvanā),* instead of renouncing external things, the renunciation of mental states *(bhāvas)* is postulated. Freedom from possessions and renunciation are interiorised. Even the signs of sectarian identity *(liṅga)* such as non-violence and asceticism should be relinquished according to the radical position taken by the *Samayasāra.* For how are those who continue attached to external signs to realise the soul? Clearly, the social impact of these doctrines must have been tremendous. Yet Kundakunda insists that it is not the external sign in itself that should be abandoned, but rather one's attachment to them. Monastic practice is valid, but for those who are close to the *kevala-jñāna,* confessions, concentration, purification, the pursuit of good and rejection of evil, are all nothing less than poison *(Samayasāra* 306). This thinking is extremely radical. William Johnson (1995: 301) compares them to the *kōans* of Zen Buddhism. It is as if they were intended to produce a shock in the advanced ascetics and take them beyond the daily round of religious practices, the excessive ritualisation of the Jain path. Apart from that, Kundakunda and Amṛtacandra remain faithful to the notion that the monks should continue with their ascetic practices as an external symbol, but only—and this is what is innovatory—because such practices reflect the degree of inner purity and wisdom attained.

Coincidence with the *jīva* is conceived in a way that is very similar to what the Yogic tradition of India called absorption, enstasis *(samādhi),* the state in which the object of meditation (the *jīva)* is apprehended directly, and where there is identification and real coincidence between knowing and the object of knowledge. The *kevalin* does not know that which exists as a result of its relationship with such, but because of its indifference, non-possession and strict separation, attained thanks to meditation. The soul *(jīva)* and gnosis *(jñāna)* are identical, and the *kevalin* does not have to do anything to know, since:

> "It is, from the practical point of view only, that the Omniscient Lord, perceives and knows all; from the real standpoint, the Omniscient perceives and knows his own soul only" (Kundakunda, *Niyamasāra* 159).

While metaphysics are not abandoned, it could be said that what we have here is the sort of non-dual epistemic experience that we also find in Advaita Vedānta, in Sāṃkhya, in Yoga, in Theravāda Buddhism, in Mahāyāna, in Zen and in Vajrayāna. Amṛtacandra *(Laghutattva-sphoṭa* 14) specifically states that perfect knowledge is non-dual *(advaita).* When it comes to explain the experience of non-duality, Jains maintain philosophical non-absolutism and opt for not overvaluing any of the poles (the *ātman,* impermanence), or they may opt, as Kundakunda does, for what is virtually a Vedāntic position, and affirm that the only thing that has existed, now exists, and will exist, is the enlightened *jīva.* But, in truth, any *explanation* that we decide to offer, will always be a necessarily dualist linguistic construct, and thus a limitation incapable of describing the non-dual experience, which seems to be beyond all language.

The isolation of the *jīva* from the rest of the *jīvas* reflects perfectly the isolation *(kaivalya)* of the *jīva* that has attained *kevala-jñāna* at the zenith of the universe (Johnson 1995: 181). Together with the other perfect monads, all un-moving, without changes, the limpid drops of life realise the fullness of life. Mahāvīra's words in one of the most ancient passages in Jainism, describe this in apophatic fashion:

> "All sounds recoil thence, where speculation has no room, nor does the mind penetrate there...
>
> [The liberated] is not long nor small nor round nor triangular... he is not black nor blue nor red nor green nor white... he is without body, without resurrection, without contact [of matter], he is not feminine nor masculine nor neuter; he perceives, he knows, but there is no analogy [whereby to know the nature of the liberated soul]; its essence is without form; there is no condition of the unconditioned" *(Ācārāṅga-sūtra* 1.5.0.3-4).

No form possesses the *jīva,* no tint colours the soul, no sex describes it, and no thought or prayer can alter it. This is the true nature of the soul, and it is through this realisation of one's own nature that the beatitude of liberation and perfection is attained, that is to say, *nirvāṇa, mokṣa,* the solitude that is known as *kaivalya.*

REFERENCES

Ācārāṅga-sūtra. English Translation and Introduction by Hermann Jacobi (1884) in: *Gaina Sutras,* Part I, "Sacred Books of the East", vol. 22. Delhi: Motilal Banarsidass, 1964.

Aitareya-Brāhmaṇa. English Translation and Introduction by Arthur Berriedale Keith (1920) in: *Rigveda Brahmanas. The Aitareya and Kausitaki Brahmanas of the Rigveda.* Delhi: Motilal Banarsidass, 1971.

Altekar, A.S. (1956). *The Position of Women in Hindu Civilisation.* Delhi: Motilal Banarsidass, 1959.

Amṛtacandra. *Laghutattva-sphoṭa.* English Translation and Introduction by Padmanabh Jaini (1978) in: *Amṛtacandrasūri's Laghutattvasphoṭa.* Ahmedabad: L.D. Institute of Indology, 1978.

—*Ātmakhyāti.* English Translation and Introduction by A. Chakravarti (1971) in: *Samayasāra with English Translation and Commentary based upon Amrtacandra's Ātmakhyāti.* New Delhi: Bharatiya Jnanpith, 1997.

Aṅguttara-nikāya. English Translation and Notes by F. L. Woodward (1932) in: *The Book of Gradual Sayings* (5 vols). London: PTS, 1995.

Āpastamba-dharma-sūtra. English Translation and Introduction by Georg Bühler (1879) in: *The Sacred Laws of the Āryas,* Part I, "Sacred Books of the East", vol. 2. Delhi: Motilal Banarsidass, 1965.

Āśvalāyana-gṛhya-sūtra. English Translation by Hermann Oldenberg (1886) in: *The Grihya Sutras,* "Sacred Books of the East", vol. 29. Delhi: Motilal Banarsidass, 1965.

Atharva-veda. English Translation and Introduction by R.T.H. Griffith (1895-1896) in: *Hymns of the Atharvaveda* (2 vols). Delhi: Munshiram Manoharlal, 1985.

Babb, Lawrence A. (1996). *Absent Lord. Ascetics and Kings in a Jain Ritual Culture.* Berkeley: University of California Press, 1996.

— (1998). "Ritual Culture and Distinctiveness of Jainism". In: J.E. Cort (ed.), *Open Boundaries.* Albany: SUNY, 1998.

— (1999). "Rejecting Violence. Sacrifice and the Social Identity of Trading Communities". In: V. Das, D. Gupta and P. Uberoi (eds.), *Tradition, Pluralism and Identity.* New Delhi: Sage, 1999.

— (2004). *Alchemies of Violence. Myths of Identity and the Life of Trade in Western India.* New Delhi: Sage, 2004.

Balbir, Nalini (1990). "Stories from the Āvaśyaka Commentaries". In: P. Granoff (ed.), *The Clever Adulteress & Other Stories.* Oakville: Mosaic Press, 1990.

Banārasīdāsa. *Ardhakathānaka.* English translation and Introduction by Rohini Chowdhury (2009) in: *Ardhakathanak (A Half Story).* New Delhi: Penguin Books, 2009.

Banks, Marcus (1991). "Orthodoxy and Dissent: Varieties of Religious Belief Among Immigrant Gujarati Jains in Britain". In: M. Carrithers and C. Humphrey (eds.), *The Assembly of Listeners.* Cambridge: Cambridge University Press, 1991.

Barnett, Stephen A. (1975). "Approaches to Changes in Caste Ideology in South India". In: B. Stein (ed.), *Essays on South India.* New Delhi: Munshiram Manoharlal, 1997.

Barz, Richard (1976). *The Bhakti Sect of Vallabhācārya.* New Delhi: Munshiram Manoharlal, 1992.
Basham, Arthur L. (1951). *History and Doctrines of the Ājivikas. A Vanished Indian Religion.* Delhi: Motilal Banarsidass, 1981.
— (1954, 1967). *The Wonder That Was India.* New Delhi: Rupa, 1981.
— (1989). *The Origins and Development of Classical Hinduism* [Edited by Kenneth Zysk]. Boston: Beacon Press, 1989.
Batchelor, Stephen (1994). *The Awakening of the West.* London: Aquarian, 1994.
Baudhāyana-dharma-sūtra. English Translation and Introduction by Georg Bühler (1882) in: *The Sacred Laws of the Aryas,* Part II, "Sacred Books of the East", vol. 14. Delhi: Motilal Banarsidass, 1965.
Bayly, Susan (1999). *Caste, Society and Politics in India. From the Eighteen Century to the Modern Age.* Cambridge: Cambridge University Press, 1999.
Bechert, Heinz (1995). "Introductory Essay. The Dates of the Historical Buddha. A Controversial Issue". In: H. Bechert (ed.), *When Did the Buddha Live?* Delhi: Sri Satguru, 1995.
Bhagavad-gītā. English Translation and Study by S. Radhakrishnan (1948) in: *The Bhagavad-Gita.* London: Aquarian, 1989.
Bhāgavata-Purāṇa. English Translation and Notes by Ganesh V. Tagare (1978) in: *The Bhagava-ta-Purana* (5 vols). Delhi: Motilal Banarsidass, 1989.
Bhattacharyya, Narendra N. (1975). *Ancient Indian Rituals and their Social Contents.* New Delhi: Manohar, 1996 (revised edition).
— (1976). *Jain Philosophy.* New Delhi: Munshiram Manoharlal, 1976.
Biardeau, Madeleine (1981). *L'hindouisme. Anthropologie d'une civilisation.* [English Translation: *Hinduism. The Anthropology of a Civilization.* Delhi: Oxford University Press, 1989.]
— (1993). "Le brâhmanisme ancien, ou la non-violence impossible". In: D. Vidal, G. Tarabout and É. Meyer (eds.), *Violences et non-violences en Inde (Collection Puruṣārtha 16).* Paris: École des Hautes Études en Sciences Sociales, 1994.
Biardeau, Madeleine and Malamoud, Charles (1976). *Le sacrifice dans l'Inde ancienne.* Paris: P.U.F., 1976.
Bilimoria, Purushottama (1998). "Indian Religious Traditions". In: D.E. Cooper and J.A. Palmer (eds.), *Spirit of the Environment. Religion, Value and Enviromental Concern.* London: Rout-ledge, 1998.
Bose, Ashish (1997). *Population Profile of Religion in India.* Delhi: B.R. Publishing, 1997.
Bossche, Frank van den (2007). *Elements of Jaina Geography.* The Jambdvīpasaṃgrahaṇī *of Haribhadra Sūri.* Delhi: Motilal Banarsidass, 2007.
Bouillier, Véronique (1993). "La violence des non-violents, ou les ascūtes au combat". In: D. Vidal, G. Tarabout and É. Meyer (eds.), *Violences et non-violences en Inde (Collection Puruṣārtha 16).* Paris: École des Hautes Études en Sciences Sociales, 1994.
Brand, Michael (1995). *The Vision of Kings.* Camberra: National Gallery of Australia, 1996.
Bṛhadāraṇyaka-upaniṣad. English Translation and Introduction by Max Müller (1884) in: *The Upanishads,* Part II, "Sacred Books of the East", vol. 15. Delhi: Motilal Banarsidass, 1965.
Caillat, Colette (1970).[Spanish Translation: "El jinismo". In: H-C. Puech (ed.), *Historia de las religiones* (vol. 4). Madrid: Siglo XXI, 1978.]
Caillat, Colette and Kumar, Ravi (1981). *La cosmologie jaïna.* Paris: Chêne, 1981.
Campbell, Joseph (1962). *The Masks of God.* [Spanish Translation: *Las máscaras de Dios* (4 vols). Madrid: Alianza Editorial, 1991.]
Carrithers, Michael (1991). "Community Among Southern Digambar Jains". In: M. Carrithers and C. Humphreys (eds.), *The Assembly of Listeners.* Cambridge: Cambridge University Press, 1991.
Carrithers, Michael and Humphrey, Caroline (1991). "Conclusion". In: M. Carrithers and C. Humphrey (eds.), *The Assembly of Listeners.* Cambridge: Cambridge University Press, 1991.
Chakrabarti, Dilip K. (1997). *Colonial Indology. Sociopolitics of the Ancient Indian Past.* New Delhi: Munshiram Manoharlal, 1997.

Chakravarti, Appaswami (1950). *Samayasāra with English Translation and Commentary based upon Amṛtacandra's Ātmakhyāti.* New Delhi: Bharatiya Jnanpith, 1997.
Chāndogya-upaniṣad. English Translation and Introduction by Max Müller (1876) in: *The Upan-ishads,* Part I, "Sacred Books of the East", vol. 1. Delhi: Motilal Banarsidass, 1965.
Chappie, Christopher Key (1990). "Karma and the Path of Purification". In: V. Hanson, R. Stewart and S. Nicholson (eds.), *Karma. Rhythmic Return to Harmony.* Wheaton: Quest, 1990.
— (1993). *Nonviolence to Animals, Earth and Self in Asian Traditions.* Delhi: Sri Satguru, 1995.
— (1996). "Monist (Ekatva) and Pluralist (Anekānta) Discourse in Indian Traditions". In: N. Smart and S. Murty (eds.), *East-West Encounters in Philosophy and Religion.* Long Beach: Long Beach Publications, 1996.
— (1998). "Haribhadra's Analysis of Pātañjala and Kula Yoga in the Yogadṛṣṭisamuccaya". In: J.E. Cort (ed.), *Open Boundaries.* Albany: SUNY Press, 1998.
— (2000). "Life Force in Jainism and Yoga". In: J. Runzo and N.M. Martin (eds.), *The Meaning of Life in the World Religions.* Oxford: OneWorld, 2000.
— (2002a). Introduction". In: C. Key Chappie (ed.), *Jainism and Ecology. Nonviolence in the Web of Life.* Cambridge: Harvard Divinity School, 2002.
— (2002b). "The Living Earth of Jainism and the New Story". In: C. Key Chapple (ed.), *Jainism and Ecology. Nonviolence in the Web of Life.* Cambridge: Harvard Divinity School, 2002.
Chattopadhyaya, Debiprasad (1990). *Cārvāka/Lokāyata.* New Delhi: Indian Council of Philosophical Research, 1994.
Chang, Garma C.C. (1971). *The Buddhist Teaching of Totality. The Philosophy of Hwa Yen Buddhism.* Delhi: Motilal Banarsidass, 1992.
Clémentin-Ojha, Catherine (1993). "L'initiation de la *devī.* Violence et non-violence dans un récit viṣṇuite". In: D. Vidal, G. Tarabout and É. Meyer (eds.), *Violences et non-violences en Inde (Collection Puruṣārtha 16).* Paris: École des Hautes Études en Sciences Sociales, 1994.
Conze, Edward (1951). *Buddhism. Its Essence and Development.* New Delhi: Munshiram Manoharlal, 1994.
Coomaraswamy, Ananda K. (1914). *Jaina Art.* New Delhi: Munshiram Manoharlal, 1994.
— (1928). *Yakṣas* (2 Partes). New Delhi: Munshiram Manoharlal, 1980.
— (1934). *The Transformation of Nature in Art.* [Spanish Translation: *La transformación de la naturaleza en arte.* Barcelona: Kairós, 1997.]
Cort, John E. (1991). "Mūrtipūja in Śvetāmbar Jain Temples". In: T.N. Madan (ed.), *Religion in India.* Delhi: Oxford University Press, 1992.
— (1992). "Śvetāmbar Mūrtipūjak Jain Scripture in a Performative Context". In: J. Timm (ed.), *Texts in Context.* Delhi: Sri Satguru, 1997.
— (1995). "The Rite of Veneration of Jina Images". In: D.S. Lopez jr. (ed.), *Religions of India in Practice.* Princeton: Princeton University Press, 1995.
— (1995). "Jain Questions and Answers: Who Is God and How Is He Worshiped?". In: D.S. Lopez jr. (ed.), *Religions of India in Practice.* Princeton: Princeton University Press, 1995.
— (1998). "Introduction: Contested Jain Identities of Self and Other". In: J.E. Cort (ed.), *Open Boundaries.* Albany: SUNY, 1998.
— (1998). "Who is a King? Jain Narratives of Kingship in Medieval Western India". In: J.E. Cort (ed.), *Open Boundaries.* Albany: SUNY, 1998.
— (2001). *Jains in the World. Religious Values and Ideology in India.* New York: Oxford University Press, 2001.
— (2002). "Green Jainism? Notes and Queries toward a Possible Jain Environmental Ethic". In: C. Key Chapple (ed.), *Jainism and Ecology. Nonviolence in the Web of Life.* Cambridge: Harvard Divinity School, 2002.
— (2004). Cort, John E. (2004). "Jains, Caste, and Hierarchy in North Gujarat". In: D. Gupta (ed.), *Caste in Question. Identity or Hierarchy?* New Delhi: Sage, 2004.
— (2006). "A Fifteenth-Century Digambar Jain Mystic and His Followers". In: P. Flügel (ed.), *Studies in Jaina History and Culture. Disputes and dialogues:* London: Routledge, 2006.

— (2007). [Catalan Translation: "Déu com a rei o asceta". In: J. Guy (ed.), *L'escultura en els tem ples indis. L'art de la devoció.* Barcelona: Fundadó "La Caixa", 2007.]
Cottam Ellis, Christine (1991). "Jain Merchant Castes of Rajasthan". In: M. Carrithers and C. Humphrey (eds.), *The Assembly of Listeners.* Cambridge: Cambridge University Press, 1991.
Couliano, loan P. and Eliade, Mircea (1990). *Dictionnaire des Religions.* [Spanish Translation: *Diccionario de las religiones.* Barcelona: Paidós Ibérica, 1992.]
Cullavagga. English Translation and Introduction by T.W. Rhys Davids and H. Oldenberg (1885) in: *Vinaya Texts,* "Sacred Books of the East", vols. 17 and 20. Delhi: Motilal Banarsidass, 1965.
Daniélou, Alain (1985). *La fantaisie des Dieux et l'aventure Humaine.* Monaco: Rocher, 1985.
Daśavaikālika-sūtra. English Translation and Notes by Kastur Chand Lalwani (1973) in: *Daśavaikālika-sūtra.* Delhi: Motilal Banarsidass, 1973.
Dasgupta, Surendranath (1922-1955). *A History of Indian Philosophy* (5 vols). Delhi: Motilal Banarsidass, 1975.
Davis, Richard (1995). "Introduction". In: D.S. Lopez jr. (ed.), *Religions of India in Practice.* Princeton: Princeton University Press, 1995.
— (1998). "The Story of the Disappearing Jains". In: J.E. Cort (ed.), *Open Boundaries.* Albany: SUNY, 1998.
Deo, S.B. (1955). *History of Jaina Monachism.* Pune: Deccan College Dissertation Series, 1956.
Desai, S.M. (1983). *Haribhadra's Yoga Works and Psychosynthesis.* Ahmedabad: L.D. Institute of lndology, 1983.
Dhammapada. English Translation, Introduction and Notes by Sarvepalli Radhakrishnan (1950) in: *The Dhammapada.* Madras: Oxford University Press, 1966.
Dīgha-nikāya. English Translation and Prefaces by T.W. and CAP. Rhys Davids (1899-1921) in: *Dialogues of the Buddha* (3 vols). London: PTS, 1995.
Dirks, Nicholas (1990). "The Original Caste. Power, History and Hierarchy in South Asia". In: M. Marriott (ed.), *India through Hindu Categories.* New Delhi: Sage, 1990.
— (2001). *Castes of Mind. Colonialism and the Making of Modern India.* Delhi: Permanent Black, 2002.
Dixit, K.K. (1971). *Jaina Ontology.* Ahmedabad: L.D. Institute of lndology, 1971.
— (1978). *Early Jainism.* Ahmedabad: L.D. Institute of lndology, 1978.
Drew, John (1987). *India and the Romantic Imagination.* Delhi: Oxford University Press, 1987.
Dumézil, Georges (1968, 1971, 1973) *Mythe et Epopée I, II, III.* Paris: Gallimard, 1995 (revised edition).
Dumont, Louis (1966,1*919). Homo Hierarchicus. Le systūme des castes* et *ses implications.* Paris: Gallimard, 1979.
Dundas, Paul (1991). "The Digambara Jain Warrior". In: M. Carrithers and C. Humphrey (eds.), *The Assembly of Listeners.* Cambridge: Cambridge University Press, 1991.
— (1992). *The Jains.* London: Routledge, 1992.
— (2002). "The Limits of a Jain Environmental thic". In: C. Key Chapple *(ed.), Jainism and Ecology. Nonviolence in the Web of Life.* Cambridge: Harvard Divinity School, 2002.
— (2003). "Conversion to Jainism. Historical Perspectives". In: R. Robinson and S. Clarke (eds.), *Religious Conversion in India.* New Delhi: Oxford University Press, 2006.
— (2004). "Beyond Anekāntavāda. A Jain Approach to Religious Tolerance". In: T. Sethia (ed.), *Ahiṃsā, Anekānta and Jainism.* Delhi: Motilal Banarsidass, 2004.
— (2006). "A Non-Imperial Religion? Jainism in Its 'Dark Age'". In: P. Olivelle (ed.), *Between the Empires. Society in India 300 BCE to 400 CE.* New York: Oxford University Press, 2006.
Eliade, Mircea (1972). *Le yoga. Immortalité et liberté.* [Spanish Translation: *El yoga. Inmortalidad y libertad.* México: F.C.E., 1991.]
— (1975). *Techniques du Yoga.* [Spanish Translation: *Técnicas del Yoga.* Barcelona: Kairós 2000.]
— (1976). *Histoire des croyances et des idées religieuses.* [Spanish Translation: *Historia de las creencias y de las ideas religiosas* (4 vols). Madrid: Ediciones Cristiandad, 1978.]

Farquhar, J.N. (1914). *Modern Religious Movements in India.* New Delhi: Munshiram Manoharlal, 1977.
Feuerstein, Georg (1989). *Yoga. The Technology of Ecstasy.* Los Angeles: Jeremy Tarcher, 1989.
Feuerstein, G., Kak, S. and Frawley, D. (1995). *In Search of the Craddle of Civilization.* Wheaton: Quest,1995.
Flood, Gavin (1996). *An Introduction to Hinduism.* Cambridge: Cambridge University Press, 1996.
Flügel, Peter (2006). "Demographic Trends in Jaina Monasticism". In: P. Flügel (ed.), *Studies in Jaina History and Culture. Disputes and dialogues.* London: Routledge, 2006.
Fohr, Sherry E. (2006). "Restrictions and Protection. Female Jain Renouncers". In: P. Flügel (ed.), *Studies in Jaina History and Culture. Disputes and dialogues.* London: Routledge, 2006.
Folkert, Kendall W. (1993). *Scripture and Community. Collected Essays on the Jains.* [Edited by John Cort]. Atlanta: Scholars Press, 1993.
Frank, Andre Gunder (1998). *ReORIENT. Global Economy in the Asian Age.* Los Angeles: University of California Press, 1998.
Frauwallner, Erich (1953). *Geschichte der Indischen Philosophie.* [English Translation: *History of Indian Philosophy* (2 vols.). Delhi: Motilal Banarsidass, 1983-1984.]
Frazer, Elizabeth (1940). "The Origin of Religion". In: M. Ratna-Prabha Vijaya (ed.), *Śramaṇa Bhagavān Mahāvīra. His Life and Teaching* (6 vols). Delhi: Parimal, 1989.
Fuller, Christopher J. (1992). *The Camphor Flame. Popular Hinduism and Society in India.* Princeton: Princeton University Press, 1992.
Fynes, R.C.C. (1998). *Hemacandra. The Lives of the Jain Elders.* Oxford: Oxford University Press, 1998.
Gadamer, Hans-Georg (1975). *Wahrheit und Methode.* [Spanish Translation: *Verdad y Método* (2 vols). Salamanca: Sígueme, 1977.]
Gandhi, Mohandas K. (1927,1929). *An Autobiography. The Story of My Experiments with Truth.* Boston: Beacon, 1957.
Gautama-dharma-sūtra. English Translation and Introduction by Georg Bühler (1879) in: *The Sacred Laws of the Aryas,* Part I, "Sacred Books of the East", vol. 2. Delhi: Motilal Banarsidass, 1965.
Ghoshal, S.C. (1917). *Dravya-Saṃgraha.* Delhi: Motilal Banarsidass, 1989.
Glasenapp, Helmuth von (1915). *Die Lehre von Karman in der Philosophie der Jainas.* [English Translation: *The Doctrine of Karman in Jain Philosophy.* Bombay: Bai Vijibhai Jivanlal Pannalal Charity Fund, 1942.]
— (1925). *Der Jainismus. Eine Indische Erlösungsreligion.* [English Translation: *Jainism. An Indian Religion of Salvation.* Delhi: Motilal Banarsidass, 1999.]
— (1958). *Die Philosophie der Inder.* [Spanish Translation: *La filosofía de los hindúes.* Barcelona: Barrai Editores, 1977.]
Gombrich, Richard (1988). *Theravāda Buddhism.* London: Routledge and Kegan Paul, 1988.
Gonda, Jan (1965). *Change and Continuity in Indian Religion.* New Delhi: Munshiram Manoharlal, 1997.
Granoff, Phyllis (1990). "Jain Biographies". In: P. Granoff (ed.), *The Clever Adulteress.* Oakville: Mosaic Press, 1990.
— (1992). "Jinaprabhasūri and Jinadattasūri. Two Studies from the Śvetāmbara Jain Tradition". In: P. Granoff and K. Shinohara (eds.), *Speaking of Monks.* Oakville: Mosaic Press, 1992.
Gros, François (1992). *Le livre de l'amour.* Paris: Gallimard, 1992.
Guṇabhadra. *Ātmānuśāsana.* English Translation by Jagmanderlal Jaini (1928) in: *Atma Anushasana.* Internet: http://www.aditi.net/Jain/Sacred/SacredHome.htm.
Gupta, Dipankar (2000). *Interrogating Caste. Understanding Hierarchy & Difference in Indian Society.* New Delhi: Penguin, 2000.
Halbfass, Wilhelm (1988). *India and Europe.* Delhi: Motilal Banarsidass, 1990.
—(1991). *Tradition and Reflection.* Delhi: Sri Satguru, 1992.

— (2000). *Karma und Wiedergeburt in indischen Denken.* [Spanish Translation: *Karma y re nacimiento.* Barcelona: Libros Cúpula, 2001.]
Hardy, Friedhelm (1990). "The Story of King Yaśodhara". In: P. Granoff (ed.), *The Clever Adulteress.* Oakville: Mosaic Press, 1990.
Hegel, G.W.F. (1837, 1840). *Vorlesungen über die philosophie der Geschichte.* [Spanish Translation: *Lecciones sobre la filosofía de la historia universal.* Madrid: Alianza, 1980.]
Hegewald, Julia A. (2006). "Architectural, Sculptural and Religious Change". In: P. Flügel (ed.), *Studies in Jaina History and Culture. Disputes and dialogues.* London: Routledge, 2006.
Heesterman, Jan C. (1985). *The Inner Conflict of Tradition. Essays in Indian Ritual, Kingship, and Society.* Chicago: The University of Chicago Press, 1985.
Hemacandra. *Pariśiṣṭa-parvan.* English Translation and Introduction by R.C.C. Fynes (1998) in: *The Uves of the Jain Elders.* Oxford: Oxford University Press, 1998.
— *Yoga-śāstra.* English Translation by A.S. Gopani (1989) in: *The Yoga Shastra of Hemchan-dracharya.* Jaipur: Prakrit Bharti Academy, 1989.
Hiriyanna, M. (1945). *Essentials of Indian Philosophy.* London: George Allen & Unwin, 1978.
Hopkins, E. Washburn (1898). *The Religions of India.* New Delhi: Munshiram Manoharlal, 1970.
Hudson, Dennis (1989). "Violent and Fanatical Devotion Among the Nāyanārs". In: A. Hiltebei-tel (ed.), *Criminal Gods and Devotees.* Albany: SUNY, 1989.
Humphrey, Caroline (1991). "Fairs and Miracles: At the Boundaries of the Jain Community in Ra-jasthan". In: M. Carrithers and C. Humphrey (eds.), *The Assembly of Listeners.* Cambridge: Cambridge University Press, 1991.
Iḷaṅkō Aṭikaḷ. *Cilappatikāram.* English Translation, Introduction and Postface by R. Parthasarathy (1993) in: *The Tale of An Anklet.* New York: Columbia University Press, 1993.
Inden, Ronald (1990). *Imagining India.* Bloomington: Indiana University Press, 2000 (revised edition).
Īśvarakṛṣṇa. *Sāṃkhya-kārikā.* English Translation and Study by Gerald J. Larson (1969) in: *Classical Sāṃkhya.* Delhi: Motilal Banarsidass, 1979 (revised edition).
Jacobi, Hermann (1884, 1895). *Gaina Sûtras* (2 vols), "Sacred Books of the East", vols. 22 and 45. Delhi: Motilal Banarsidass, 1964.
Jaffrelot, Christophe (1998). *La démocratie en Inde.* Paris: Fayard: 1998.
Jain, B.C. (1972). *Jainism in Buddhist Literature.* Nagpur: 1972.
Jain, H.L. and Upadhye, A.N. (1971). "General Editorial". In: A. Chakravarti, *Samayasāra with English Translation and Commentary based upon Amṛtacandra's Ātmakhyāti.* New Delhi: Bharatiya Jnanpith, 1997.
Jain, Jagdishchandra (1947). *Life in Ancient India as Depicted in Jaina Canon and Commentaries.* New Delhi: Munshiram Manoharlal, 1984 (ed. revis.).
— (1989). "The Medieval Bhakti Movement: Its Influence on Jainism". In: N.N. Bhattacharyya (ed.), *Medieval Bhakti Movements in India.* Delhi: Munshiram Manoharlal, 1989.
Jain, Jyoti P. (1951). *Jainism. The Oldest Living Religion.* Varanasi: P.V. Research Institute, 1988.
Jain, Kailash Chand (1974). *Lord Mahāvīra and His Times.* Delhi: Motilal Banarsidass, 1991 (revised edition).
Jain, Kamala (1983). *The Concept of Pañcaśila in Indian Thought.* Varanasi: P.V. Research Institute, 1983.
Jain, Sagarmal (1989). "The Jaina Spirit and Spirituality". In: K. Sivaraman (ed.), *Hindu Spirituality.* Delhi: Motilal Banarsidass, 1995.
Jaini, Jagmanderlal (1916). *Outlines of Jainism.* Indore: J.L. Jaini Trust, 1979.
Jaini, Padmanabh S. (1978). *Amṛtacandrasūri's Laghutattvasphoṭa.* Ahmedabad: L.D. Institute of Indology, 1978.
— (1979). *The Jaina Path of Purification.* Delhi: Motilal Banarsidass, 1979.
— (1991). *Gender and Salvation. Jaina Debates on the Spiritual Liberation of Women.* Berkeley: University of California Press, 1991.

— (1991). "Is There a Popular Jainism?". In: M. Carrithers and C. Humphrey (eds.), *The Assembly of Listeners.* Cambridge: Cambridge University Press, 1991.

— (1994). "The Jaina Faith and Its History". In: N. Tatia, *That Which is. Tattvārtha Sūtra.* London: Harper Collins, 1994.

— (2000). *Collected Papers on Jaina Studies.* Delhi: Motilal Banarsidass, 2000.

— (2002). "Ecology, Economics, and Development in Jainism". In: C. Key Chappie (ed.), *Jainism and Ecology. Nonviolence in the Web of Life.* Cambridge: Harvard Divinity School, 2002.

— (2004). "Ahiṃsā and 'Just War' in Jainism". In: T. Sethia (ed.), *Ahiṃsā, Anekānta and Jainism.* Delhi: Motilal Banarsidass, 2004.

Jamison, Stephanie (2006). "Women 'Between the Empires' and 'Between the Lines'". In: P. Olivelle (ed.), *Between the Empires. Society in India 300 BCE to 400 CE.* New York: Oxford University Press, 2006.

Jātakas. English Translation under the direction of E.B. Cowell (1895) in: *The Jātaka or Stories of the Buddha's Former Births* (6 vols). Delhi: Motilal Banarsidass, 1990.

Jinabhadra Gaṇi. *Gaṇadharavāda.* English Translation and Introduction by D.P. Thaker (1950) in: M. Ratna-Prabha Vijaya (ed.), *Sramaṇa Bhagavān Mahāvīra. His Life and Teaching,* vol. 3. Delhi: Parimal, 1989.

— *Nihnavavāda.* English Translation and Introduction by D.P. Thaker (1947) in: M. Ratna-Prab ha Vijaya (ed.), *Sramaṇa Bhagavān Mahâvīra. His Life and Teaching,* vol. 4. Delhi: Parimal, 1989.

Jinaprabha Sūri, *Vividhatlrthakalpa.* Partial English Translation by John Cort (1990) in: "Twelve Chapters from *The Guidebook to Various Pilgrimage Places".* In: P. Granoff (ed.), *The Clever Adulteress.* Oakville: Mosaic Press, 1990.

Jivanlal Doshi, M. (1948). "The Horoscope of Śramaṇa Bhagavān Mahāvīra". In: M. Ratna-Prabha Vijaya (ed.), *Sramaṇa Bhagavān Mahāvīra. His Life and Teaching,* vol. 2. Delhi: Parimal, 1989.

Johnson, William J. (1995). *Harmless Souls. Karmic Bondage and Religious Change in Early Jainism with Special Reference to Umāsvāti and Kundakunda.* Delhi: Motilal Banarsidass, 1995.

Jones, J. Howard M. (1991). "Jain Shopkeepers and Moneylenders". In: M. Carrithers and C. Humphrey (eds.), *The Assembly of Listeners.* Cambridge: Cambridge University Press, 1991.

Jordens, J.F.T. (1987). "Gandhi and Religious Pluralism". In: H. Coward (ed.), *Modern Indian Responses to Religious Pluralism.* Delhi: Sri Satguru, 1991.

Kalpa-sūtra. English Translation and Introduction by Hermann Jacobi (1884) in: *Gaina Sûtras* Part I, "Sacred Books of the East", vol. 22. Delhi: Motilal Banarsidass, 1964.

Kalupahana, David J. (1986). *Mūlamadhyamakakārikā of Nāgārjuna. The Philosophy of the Middle Way.* Delhi: Motilal Banarsidass, 1991.

Kapur, Nandini S. (2002). *State Formation in Rajasthan. Mewar during the Seventh-Fifteenth Centuries.* New Delhi: Manohar 2002.

Kauṣītaki-Brāhmaṇa-upaniṣad. English Translation and Introduction by Max Müller (1876) in: *The Upanishads,* Part I, "Sacred Books of the East", vol. 1. Delhi: Motilal Banarsidass, 1965.

Kauṭilya. *Artha-śāstra.* English Translation, Introduction and Notes by R.P. Kangle (1963, 1972) in: *The Kauṭilīya Arthaśāstra.* Delhi: Motilal Banarsidass, 1986 (revised edition).

Kelting, M. Whitney (2001). *Singing to the Jinas. Jain Laywomen, Maṇḍai Singing, and the Negotiations of Jain Devotion.* New York: Oxford University Press, 2001.

— (2009). *Heroic Wives. Rituals, Stories, and the Virtues of Jain Wifehood.* New York: Oxford University Press, 2009.

Khadabadi, B.K. (1992). *Śrāvakācāra. Its Significance and Its Relevance to the Present Times.* New Delhi: Sri Rajakrishna Jain Charitable Trust, 1992.

Kinsley, David (1982). *Hinduism. A Cultural Perspective.* Englewood Cliffs: Prentice-Hall, 1982.

Klostermaier, Klaus K. (2000). *Hinduism. A Short History.* Oxford: Oneworld, 2000.

Kolenda, Pauline (1978). *Caste in Contemporary India.* Menlo Park: Cummings Publishing, 1978.

Koller, John M. (2002). "Jain Ecological Perspectives". In: C. Key Chapple (ed.), *Jainism and Ecology. Nonviolence in the Web of Life.* Cambridge: Harvard Divinity School, 2002.
— (2004). "Why is Anekāntavāda Important?". In: T. Sethia (ed.), *Ahiṃsā, Anekānta and Jainism.* Delhi: Motilal Banarsidass, 2004.
Kosambi, D.D. (1965). *The Culture and Civilisation of Ancient India in Historical Outline.* New Delhi: Vikas, 1997.
Krishan, Yuvraj (1997). *The Doctrine of Karma.* Delhi: Motilal Banarsidass, 1997.
Kulkarni, V.M. (1952,1990). *The Story of Rāma in Jain Literature.* Ahmedabad: Saraswati Pustak Bhandar, 1990.
Kumar, Satish (2004). "Nonviolence for All". In: T. Sethia (ed.), *Ahiṃsā, Anekānta and Jainism.* Delhi: Motilal Banarsidass, 2004.
Kumārila Bhaṭṭa. *Śloka-vārtika.* English Translation and Notes by Ganganatha Jha (1900, 1908) in: *Ślokavārtika wiht the Commentaries "Kasika" and "Nyayaratnakar".* Delhi: Sri Satguru, 1983.
Kundakunda. *Niyamasāra.* English Translation by Uggar S. Jain (1931) in: *Niyamsara.* Internet: http://www.aditi.net/Jain/Sacred/SacredHome.htm.
— *Pañcāstikāyasāra.* English Translation and Essay by A. Chakravarti (1920) in: *Panchastikayasara.* Internet: http://www.aditi.net/Jain/Sacred/SacredHome.htm.
— *Pravacanasāra.* English Translation by A.N. Upadhye (1984) in: *Pravachansara.* Internet: http://www.jainworld.com/book/pravachansara/index.htm
— *Saemayasāra.* English Translation and Introduction by A. Chakravarti (1950) in: *Samayasāra with English Translation and Commentary based upon Amrtacandra 's Ātmakhyāti.* New Delhi: Bharatiya Jnanpith, 1997.
Laidlaw, James (1995). *Riches and Renunciation. Religion, Economy and Society Among the Jains.* Oxford: Oxford University Press, 1995.
Lamotte, Etienne (1958,1976). *Histoire du Bouddhisme Indien.* [English Translation: *History of Indian Buddhism.* Lou vain: Institut Orientaliste de Lou vain, 1988.]
Laṅkāvatāra-sūtra. English translation and Introduction by Daisetz T. Suzuki (1932) in: *The Laṅkāvatāra-sūtra. A Mahāyāna Text.* New Delhi: Munshiram Manoharlal, 1999.
Larson, Gerald J. (1994). "Are Jains Really Hindus?". In: P. Pal (ed.), *The Peaceful liberators. Jain Art from India.* New York: Thames & Hudson, 1994.
— (1995). *India's Agony Over Religion.* Delhi: Oxford University Press, 1997.
Lath, Mukund (1991). "Somadeva Suri and the Question of Jain Identity". In: M. Carrithers and C. Humphrey (eds.), *The Assembly of Listeners.* Cambridge: Cambridge University Press, 1991.
Laughlin, Charles (1994). "On the Relationship Between Science and the Life-World". In: W. Harman and J. Clarks (eds.), *New Metaphysical Foundations of Modern Science.* Sausalito: Institute of Noetic Sciences, 1994.
Lefeber, Rosalind (1990). "Hemacandra's Pariśiṣṭaparva. The Story of Cāṇakya". In: P. Granoff (ed.), *The Clever Adulteress.* Oakville: Mosaic Press, 1990.
Lewis, Martin and Wigen, Kären (1997). *The Myth of Continents. A Critique of Metageography.* Berkeley: University of California Press, 1997.
Lingat, Robert (1967). *Les Sources du droit dans le systūme traditionel de l'Inde.* Paris: Mouton, 1967.
Lorenzen, David N. (1972). *The Kāpālikas and Kālāmukhas.* Delhi: Motilal Banarsidass, 1991.
Loy, David (1988). *Nonduality. A Study in Comparative Philosophy.* New Jersey: Humanities Press, 1997.
Mahābhārata. English Translation by Manmatha N. Dutt (18%) in: *The Mahabharata* (7 vols). Delhi: Parimal Publications, 1994.
Mahāprajñā, Ācārya (1994). *Prekṣā Dhyāna. Theory and Practice.* Ladnun: Jain Viśva Bharati, 1994.
— (1998). *The Art of Positive Thinking.* New Delhi: B. Jain Publishers, 1998.

Mahāvagga. English Translation and Notes by T.W. Rhys Davids and H. Oldenberg (1885) in: *Vinaya Texts,* "Sacred Books of the East", vols. 13 and 17. Delhi: Motilal Banarsidass, 1965.

Maillard, Chantai and Pujol, Óscar (1999). *Rasa. El placer estético en la tradición india.* Varanasi: Indica Books, 1999.

Majjhima-nikāya. English Translation, Introduction and Notes by B. Ñaṇamoli and B. Bodhi (1995) in: *The Middle Length Sayings Discourses of the Buddha.* Boston: Wisdom, 1995.

Manu-smrti. English Translation and Introduction by Georg Bühler (1886) in: *The Laws of Manu,* "Sacred Books of the East", vol. 25. Delhi: Motilal Banarsidass, 1965.

Mardia, K.V. (1990). *The Scientific Foundations of Jainism.* Delhi: Motilal Banarsidass, 1996.

Marriott, McKim (1968). "Multiple Reference in Indian Caste Systems". In: J. Silverberg (ed.), *Social Mobility in the Caste System in India.* The Hague: Mouton, 1968.

Matchett, Freda (2001). *Kṛṣṇa. Lord or Avatāra?* Richmond: Curzon Press, 2001.

Matilal, Bimal K. (1985). *Logic, Language and Reality. An Introduction to Indian Philosophical Studies.* Delhi: Motilal Banarsidass, 1999.

— (1999). "Anekānta: Both Yes and No". In: N J. Shah (ed.), *Jaina Theory of Multiple Facets of Reality and Truth (Anekāntavāda).* Delhi: Motilal Banarsidass, 2000.

McCrindle, John W. (1926). *Ancient India as described by Megasthenês and Arrian.* New Delhi: Munshiram Manoharlal, 2000.

McGee, Mary (2004). "Saṃskāra". In: S. Mittal and G. Thursby (eds.), *The Hindu World.* Abingdon: Routledge, 2004.

Mehta, T.U. (1993). *The Path of the Arhat.* Faridabad: Pujya Sohanalala Smaraka Parsvanatha Sodhapitha, 1993.

Menski, Werner (1991). "Marital Expectations as Dramatized in Hindu Marriage Rituals". In: J. Leslie (ed.), *Roles and Rituals for Hindu Women.* Delhi: Motilal Banarsidass, 1992.

Merutuṅga. *Ṣaḍdarśana-nirṇaya.* English Translation and Study by Kendall W. Folkert (1985) in: *Scripture and Community. Collected Essays on the Jains.* [Edited by John Cort]. Atlanta: Scholars Press, 1993.

Mette, Adelheid (1995). "The Synchronism of the Buddha and the Jina Mahāvīra and the Problem of Chronology in Early Jainism". In: H. Bechert (ed.), *When Did the Buddha Live?* Delhi: Sri Satguru, 1995.

Monier-Williams, Monier (1899). *A Sanskṛit-English Dictionary.* Delhi: Motilal Banarsidass, 1970.

Mookerjee, Satkari (1944). *The Jaina Philosophy of Non-Absolutism.* Delhi: Motilal Banarsidass, 1978.

Mora, Juan Miguel de (2001). "Ecología jaina y Anekāntavāda". In: C. Maillard (ed.), *El árbol de la vida. La naturaleza y el arte en las tradiciones de la India.* Barcelona: Kairós, 2001.

Nāgārjuna. *Mūlamadhyamakakārikā.* English Translation and Essay by Jay L. Garfield (1995) in: *The Fundamental Wisdom of the Middle Way.* New York: Oxford University Press, 1995.

Nahar, P.C. and Ghosh, K.C. (1917). *An Encyclopaedia of Jainism.* Delhi: Sri Satguru, 1988.

Nārada-bṛhaspati. English Translation and Introduction by Julius Jolly (1889) in: *The Minor Law-Books,* "Sacred Books of the East", vol. 33. Delhi: Motilal Banarsidass, 1965.

Nemicandra. *Dravya-Saṃgraha.* English Translation, Introduction, and Essay by S.C. Ghoshal (1917) in: *Dravya-Saṃgraha.* Delhi: Motilal Banarsidass, 1989.

Norman, K.R. (1991). "The Role of the Layman According to the Jain Canon". In: M. Carrithers and C. Humphrey (eds.), *The Assembly of Listeners.* Cambridge: Cambridge University Press, 1991.

Nyāyavijayají, Muni (1952-1954). *Jaina Darśana.* [English Translation: *Jaina Philosophy and Religion.* Delhi: Motilal Banarsidass, 1998.]

Oguibénine, Boris (1993). "De la rhétorique de la violence". In: D. Vidal, G. Tarabout and É. Meyer (eds.), *Violences et non-violences en Inde (Collection Puruṣārtha 16).* Paris: École des Hautes Études en Sciences Sociales, 1994.

Olivelle, Patrick (1993). *The Āśrama System.* New York: Oxford University Press, 1993.

Pal, Pratapaditya (1994). "Introduction". In: P. Pal (ed.), *The Peaceful Liberators. Jain Art from India.* New York: Thames & Hudson, 1994.
— (1995). "Two Jain *Yantras* of the Fifteenth Century". In: R.T. Vyas (ed.), *Studies in Jaina Art and Iconography and Allied Subjects in Honour of U.P. Shah.* Vadodara: Oriental Institute-University of Baroda, 1995.
Pañcaviṃśa-brāhmaṇa. English Translation with Notes by W. Caland (1931) in: *Pañcaviṇśa Brāhmaṇa.* Delhi: Sri Satguru, 1982.
Pañcaviṃśatisāhasrikā-prajñā-pāramitā-sūtra. English Translation and Essay by Edward Conze (1975) in: *The Large Sutra on Perfect Wisdom.* Delhi: Motilal Banarsidass, 1979.
Pande, G.C. (1984). *Foundations of Indian Culture* (2 vols). Delhi: Motilal Banarsidass, 1984.
Pániker, Agustín (2005). *Índika. Una descolonización intelectual.* Barcelona: Kairós, 2005.
Pániker, Salvador (1987). *Ensayos retroprogresivos.* Barcelona: Kairós, 1987.
Panikkar, Raimon (1957, 1976). *The Unknown Christ of Hinduism.* [Spanish Version: *El Cristo desconocido del hinduismo.* Madrid: Grupo Libro 88, 1994 (revised edition).]
— (1966, 1983). *El silencio del Buddha.* Madrid: Siruela, 1996 (revised edition).
— (1981). "Presentation. A Treatise of Spirituality". In: N. Shāntā, *The Unknown Pilgrims.* Delhi: Sri Satguru, 1997.
— (1997). *La experiencia filosófica de la India.* Madrid: Trotta, 1997.
Paper, Jordan (1995). *The Spirits are Drunk. Comparative Approaches to Chinese Religion.* Albany: SUNY, 1995.
Parasher-Sen, Aloka (2004). "Introduction". In: A. Parasher-Sen, Aloka (ed.), *Subordinate and Marginal Groups in Early India.* New Delhi: Oxford University Press, 2004.
Parpola, Asko (1994). *Deciphering the Indus Script.* Cambridge: Cambridge University Press, 1994.
Parrinder, Geoffrey (1970). *Avatar and Incarnation.* Oxford: One World, 1997.
— (1976). *Mysticism in the World's Religions.* Oxford: OneWorld, 1995.
Parthasarathy, R. (1993). *The Tale of An Anklet. An Epic of South India.* New York: Columbia University Press, 1993.
Patañjali. *Yoga-sūtra.* English Translation, Introduction and Essay by B.K.S. Iyengar (1993) in: *Light on the Yoga Sutras of Patañjali.* London: Aquarian Press, 1993.
Peña, Ernesto de la (1992). *Kautilya o el Estado como mandala.* México: Pórtico de la Ciudad de México, 1993.
Peterson, Indira Viswanathan (1989). *Poems to Śiva.* Delhi: Motilal Banarsidass, 1991.
— (1998). "Śramaṇas Against the Tamil Way". In: J.E. Cort (ed.), *Open Boundaries.* Albany: SUNY, 1998.
Praśamarati-prakaraṇa. English Translation, Introduction and Notes by Yajneshwar S. Shastri (1989) in: *Prāśamarati Prakaraṇa.* Ahmedabad: L.D. Institute of Indology, 1989.
Quintanilla, Sonya R. (2004). "Exemplars of Anekānta and Ahiṃsā. The Case of Early Jains of Mathura in Art and Epigraphy". In: T. Sethia (ed.), *Ahiṃsā, Anekānta and Jainism.* Delhi: Motilal Banarsidass, 2004.
Qvarnström, Olle (2006). "The Jain-Mīmāṃsā Debate on Omniscience". In: P. Flügel (ed.), *Studies in Jaina History and Culture. Disputes and dialogues.* London: Routledge, 2006.
Radhakrishnan, Sarvepalli (1923, 1929). *Indian Philosophy* (2 vols). Delhi: Oxford University Press, 1940.
Rājaśekhara. *Ṣaḍdarśana-samuccaya.* English Translation and Study by Kendall W. Folkert (1985) in: *Scripture and Community. Collected Essays on the Jains.* [Edited by John Cort]. Atlanta: Scholars Press, 1993.
Ramanujan, A.K. (1991). "Three Hundred *Rāmāyaṇas".* In: P. Richman (ed.), *Many Rāmāyaṇas. The Diversity of a Narrative Tradition in South Asia.* Delhi: Oxford University Press, 1994.
Rankin, Aidan (2006). *The Jain Path. Ancient Wisdom for the West.* Winchester: O Books, 2006.
Ratna-Prabha Vijaya, Muni (1948-1950). *Śramaṇa Bhagavān Mahāvīra. His Life and Teaching.* (6 vols). Delhi: Parimal, 1989.

Reynell, Josephine (1991). "Women and the Reproduction of the Jain Community". In: M. Carrithers and C. Humphrey (eds.), *The Assembly of Listeners.* Cambridge: Cambridge University Press, 1991.

Ṛg-veda. English Translation and Notes by R.T.H. Griffith (1889, 1896) in: *The Hymns of the Ṛgveda.* Delhi: Motilal Banarsidass, 1973.

Richards, Glyn (1985). *A Source-Book of Modern Hinduism.* London: Curzon Press, 1996.

Ries, Julien (1989). [Spanish Translation: "El hombre religioso y lo sagrado". In: J. Ries (ed.), *Tratado de Antropología de lo sagrado,* vol. 1. Madrid: Trotta, 1995.]

Rizvi, S.A.A. (1987). *The Wonder That Was India, Part II.* Calcutta: Rupa, 1993.

Robert, Jean-Noël (1993). [Spanish Translation: "El budismo. Historia y fundamentos". In: J. Delumeau (ed.), *El hecho religioso.* Madrid: Alianza Editorial, 1995.]

Ross Reat, Noble (1996). "The Historical Buddha and His Teachings". In: K.H. Potter (ed.), *Encyclopaedia of Indian Philosophies,* vol VII. Delhi: Motilal Banarsidass, 1996.

Royston Pike, Edgar (1951). *Encyclopaedia of Religion and Religions.* [Spanish Translation: *Diccionario de religiones.* México: F.C.E., 1960.]

Ryan, James (1998). "Erotic Excess and Sexual Danger in the Cīvakacintāmaṇi". In: J.E. Cort (ed.), *Open Boundaries.* Albany: SUNY, 1998.

Said, Edward W. (1978). *Orientalism.* [Spanish Translation: *Orientalismo.* Madrid: Liber-tarias/Prodhufi, 1990.]

Śākaṭāyana. *Strinirvāṇa-prakaraṇa.* English Translation and Study by Padmanabh S. Jaini (1991) in: *Gender and Salvation. Jaina Debates on the Spiritual Liberation of Women.* Berkeley: University of California Press, 1991.

Salter, Emma (2006). "Rethinking Religious Authority. A perspective on the followers of Śrīmad Rājacandra". In: P. Flügel (ed.), *Studies in Jaina History and Culture. Disputes and dialogues.* London: Routledge, 2006.

Sangave, Vilas (1959). *Jaina Religion and Community.* Long Beach: Long Beach Publications, 1997 (revised edition).

— (1991). "Reform Movements Among Jains in Modern India". In: M. Carrithers and C. Humphrey (eds.), *The Assembly of Listeners.* Cambridge: Cambridge University Press, 1991.

Śaṅkara. *Brahma-sūtra-bhāsya.* English Translation by George Thibaut (1904) in: *The Vedānta-Sūtras with the Commentary by Sankarākārya,* "Sacred Books of the East", vols. 34 and 38. Delhi: Motilal Banarsidass, 1962.

Sarkar, Benoy Kumar (1917). *The Folk-Element in Hindu Culture.* New Delhi: Oriental Books Reprint, 1972.

Satapatha-brāhmaṇa. English Translation and Introduction by Julius Eggeling (1882) in: *The Shatapatha Brahmana,* "Sacred Books of the East", vols. 12, 26, 41, 43, 44. Delhi: Motilal Banarsidass, 1989.

Schopen, Gregory (1995). "Death, Funerals, and the Division of Property in a Monastic Code". In: D.S. Lopez jr. (ed.), *Buddhism in Practice.* Princeton: Princeton University Press, 1995.

Schubring, Walther (1934). *Die Lehre der Jainas nach den alten Quellen dargestellt.* [English Translation: *The Doctrine of the Jainas.* Delhi: Motilal Banarsidass, 1978.]

Schweitzer, Albert (1935). *Die Weltanschauung der indischen Denker.* [Spanish Translation: *El pensamiento de la India.* México: F.C.E., 1952.]

Sergent, Bernard (1997). *Genūse de Vinde.* Paris: Payot, 1997.

Seymour, Susan C. (1999). *Women, Family, and Child Care in India.* Cambridge: Cambridge University Press, 1999.

Shah, Umakant P. (1955). *Studies in Jain Art.* Varanasi: Jaina Cultural Research Society, 1955.

— (1973). *More Documents of Jaina Paintings and Gujarati Paintings of Sixteenth and Later Centuries.* Ahmedabad: L.D. Institute of Indology, 1976.

Shāntā N. (1985). *La voie jaina.* [English Translation: *The Unknown Pilgrims. The Voice of the Sādhvīs.* Delhi: Sri Satguru, 1997.]

Shastri, Yajneshwar S. (1989). *Praśamarati-prakaraṇa.* Ahmedabad: L.D. Institute of Indology, 1989.

Shendge, Malati J. (1977). *The Civilized Demons: The Harappans in the Ṛgveda.* New Delhi: Ab-hinav Publications, 1977.
Siddhasena Mahāmati. *Nyāya-avatāra.* English Translation and Essay by Satishchandra Vidyab-husana (1915) in: *Nyaya Avatara.* Internet: http://www.aditi.net/Jain/Sacred/SacredHome.htm.
Singh, Ram Bushan P. (1975). *Jainism in Early Medieval Karnataka.* Delhi: Motilal Banarsidass, 1975.
Singhi, N.K. (1991). "A Study of Jains in a Rajasthan Town". In: M. Carrithers and C. Humphrey (eds.), *The Assembly of Listeners.* Cambridge: Cambridge University Press, 1991.
Sircar, D.C. (1971). *Studies in the Religious Life of Ancient and Medieval India.* Delhi: Motilal Banarsidass, 1971.
Sivaraman, Krishna (1987). "Śaiva Siddhānta and Religious Pluralism". In: H. Coward (ed.), *Modern Indian Responses to Religious Pluralism.* Delhi: Sri Satguru, 1991.
Smith, Brian K. (1989). *Reflections on Resemblance, Ritual and Religion.* New York: Oxford University Press, 1989.
Smith, R. Morton (1973). *Dates and Dynasties in Earliest India.* Delhi: Motilal Banarsidass, 1973.
Smith, Vincent A. (1909). *The Edicts of Asoka.* New Delhi: Munshiram Manoharlal, 1992.
Smith, Wilfred Cantwell (1978). *The Meaning and End of Religion.* San Francisco: Harper & Row, 1978.
Snellgrove, David (1987). *Indo-Tibetan Buddhism.* London: Serindia, 1987.
Somadeva Sūri. *Nītivākyāmṛta.* Edited and Translated to English by Sudhir K. Gupta (1987) in: *Nitivakyamritam. 10th Century Sanskrit Treatise on Statecraft.* Jaipur: Prakrita Bharati Academy, 1987.
Sontheimer, Günther D. (1989). "Between Ghost and God". In: A. Hiltebeitel (ed.), *Criminal Gods and Devotees.* Albany: SUNY, 1989.
Sorman, Guy (2000). *Le génie de l'lnde.* Paris: Fayard, 2000.
Srinivas, M.N. (1996). *Village, Caste, Gender and Method. Essays in Indian Social Anthropology.* Delhi: Oxford University Press, 1996.
Staal, Frits (1975). *Exploring Mysticism. A Methodological Essay.* Berkeley: University of California Press, 1975.
— (1990, 1993). *Ritual and Mantras. Rules Without Meaning.* Delhi: Motilal Banarsidass, 1996.
Stcherbatsky, T. (1923). *The Central Conception of Buddhism and the Meaning of the Word Dharma.* [Spanish Translation: *Dharma. El concepto central del budismo.* Málaga: Sirio, 1994.]
Stevenson, Sinclair (1915). *The Heart of Jainism.* New Delhi: Munshiram Manoharlal, 1984.
Stietencron, Heinrich von (1989). "Hinduism: On the Proper Use of a Deceptive Term". In: G.-D. Sontheimer and H. Kulke (eds.), *Hinduism Reconsidered.* New Delhi: Manohar, 1997.
Strohl, Ralph (1990). "The Story of Bharata and Bāhubali". In: P. Granoff (ed.), *The Clever Adulteress.* Oakville: Mosaic Press, 1990.
Śubhacandra. *Jñānārnava.* English Translation by Ajit Prasada (1940-1941) in: *Gyana Arnava.* Internet: http://www.aditi.net/Jain/Sacred/SacredHome.htm.
Sukhalalji, Pandit (1962). *Jain Dharmno Pran.* [English Translation and Selection: *Essence of Jainism.* Ahmedabad: L.D. Institute of Indology, 1988.]
Sūtrakṛtāṅga. English Translation and Introduction by Hermann Jacobi (1895) in: *Gaina Sûtras,* Part II, "Sacred Books of the East", vol. 45. Delhi: Motilal Banarsidass, 1964.
Śvetāśvatara-upaniṣad. English Translation and Introduction by Max Müller (1884) in: *The Upanishads,* Part II, "Sacred Books of the East", vol. 15. Delhi: Motilal Banarsidass, 1965.
Swearer, Donald K. (1995). *The Buddhist World of Southeast Asia.* Albany: SUNY, 1995.
Taittiriya-saṃhitā ("Black" *Yajur-veda).* English Translation and Introduction by Arthur Berriedale Keith (1914) in: *The Veda of the Black Yajus School entitled Taittiriya Sanhita* (2 vols). Delhi: Motilal Banarsidass, 1967.
Taittiriya-upaniṣad. English Translation and Introduction by Max Müller (1884) in: *The Upanishads,* Part II, "Sacred Books of the East", vol. 15. Delhi: Motilal Banarsidass, 1965.

Tardan-Masquelier, Ysé (1999). *L'Hindouisme. Des origines védiques aux courants contemporains.* Paris: Bayard Éditions, 1999.
Tatia, Nathmal (1994). *That Which Is. Tattvārtha Sūtra.* London: Harper Collins, 1994.
Tatia, N. and Kumar, M. (1981). *Aspects of Jaina Monasticism.* Ladnun: Jain Viśva Bharati, 1981.
Teskey Denton, Lynn (1991). "Varieties of Hindu Female Ascetism". In: J. Leslie (ed.), *Roles and Rituals for Hindu Women.* Delhi: Motilal Banarsidass, 1992.
Tēvāram. English Translation and Essay by I.V. Peterson (1989) in: *Poems to Śiva. The Hymns of the Tamil Saints.* Delhi: Motilal Banarsidass, 1991.
Thapar, Romila (1978). *Ancient Indian Social History.* Hyderabad: Orient Longman, 1979.
— (1989). "Syndicated Hinduism". In: G.-D. Sontheimer and H. Kulke (eds.), *Hinduism Recon sidered.* New Delhi: Manohar, 1997.
— (1996). *Time as a Metaphor of History: Ancient India.* Delhi: Oxford University Press, 1996.
Tiruvaḷḷuvar. *Tirukkural.* French Translation of the *Kāmattupāl* and Introduction by François Gros (1992) in: *Le livre de l'amour.* Paris: Gallimard, 1992.
Titze, Kurt (1998). *Jainism. A Pictorial Guide To the Religion of Non-Violence.* Delhi: Motilal Banarsidass, 1998.
Tiwari, Maruti N. P. (1995). "Jaina Iconography: Evolution and Appraisal". In: R.T. Vyas (ed.), *Studies in Jaina Art and Iconography and Allied Subjects in Honour of Dr. U.P. Shah.* Vado-dara: Oriental Institute-University of Baroda, 1995.
Tobias, Michael (1991). *Life Force. The World of Jainism.* Berkeley: Asian Humanities Press, 1991.
Trautmann, Thomas R. (1997). *Aryans and British India.* New Delhi: Vistaar Publication, 1997.
Tulasi, Ācārya (s/f). "Anuvrat. A Way to Reconciliation and Tolerance". In: S.L. Gandhi (ed.), *Anuvrat Movement.* Ladnun: Jain Viśva Bharati, 1992.
Tull, Herman W. (1989). *The Vedic Origins of Karma. Cosmos as Man in Ancient Indian Myth and Ritual.* Delhi: Sri Satguru, 1990.
Umāsvāti. *Tattvārtha-sūtra.* Edited and Translated to English by Nathmal Tatia (1994) in: *That Which Is.* London: Harper Collins, 1994.
Uttarādhyayana-sūtra. English Translation and Introduction by Hermann Jacobi (1895) in: *Gaina Sûtras,* Part II, "Sacred Books of the East", vol. 45. Delhi: Motilal Banarsidass, 1964.
Vallely, Anne (2002). "From Liberation to Ecology". In: C. Key Chappie (ed.), *Jainism and Ecology. Nonviolence in the Web of Life.* Cambridge: Harvard Divinity School, 2002.
— (2004). "Anekānta, Ahiṃsā and the Question of Pluralism". In: T. Sethia (ed.), *Ahiṃsā, Anekānta and Jainism.* Delhi: Motilal Banarsidass, 2004.
Varma, Pavan K. (2005). *Being Indian. Inside the Real India.* London: Arrow Books, 2005.
Vāyu-Purāṇa. English Translation, Introduction and Notes by G.V. Tagare (1987) in: *The Vayu Purana* (2 vols). Delhi: Motilal Banarsidass, 1987.
Vidyabhusana, Satishchandra (1978). *A History of Indian Logic.* Delhi: Motilal Banarsidass, 1996.
Viṣṇu-Purāṇa. English Translation, Introduction and Notes by H.H. Wilson (1840) in: *The Viṣṇu Purana* (2 vols). Delhi: Nag Publishers, 1980.
Vyākhyā-prajñāpti. Abbreviated English Translation, Critical Edition and Introduction by Jozef Deleu (1970) in: *Viyāhapannatti (Bhagavaī).* Delhi: Motilal Banarsidass, 1996.
Vyas, R.T. (1995). In: R.T. Vyas (ed.), *Studies in Jaina Art and Iconography and Allied Subjects in Honour of UP. Shah.* Vadodara: Oriental Institute-University of Baroda, 1995.
Vyāsa. *Yoga-sūtra-bhāṣya.* English Translation by Bangali Baba (1976) in: *Yogasūtra of Patañjali with the Commentary of Vyāsa.* Delhi: Motilal Banarsidass, 1979.
Warder, A.K. (1972-1987). *Indian Kāvya Literature* (6 vols). Delhi: Motilal Banarsidass, 1992.
Watts, Alan (n/d). *Live in the Moment.* [Spanish Translation: *Vivir el presente.* Barcelona: Kairós, 1994.]
Weber, Max (1921). *Gesammelte Aufsätze zur Religionssoziologie.* [Spanish Translation: *Ensayos sobre sociología de la religión* (3 vols). Madrid: Taurus, 1987.]

— (1922). *Wirtschaft und Gesellschaft. Grundriss der Verstehender Soziologie.* [Spanish Translation: *Economía y sociedad. Esbozo de sociología comprensiva.* Mexico: F.C.E., 1964.]

White, Hayden (1973). *Metahistory. The Historical Imagination in Nineteenth-Century Europe.* [Spanish Translation: *Metahistoria. La imaginación histórica en la Europa del siglo XIX.* México: F.C.E., 1992.]

Whitehead, Alfred North (1925). *Science and the Modern World.* New York: Free Press, 1967.

Wiley, Kristi L. (2002). "The Nature of Nature: Jain Perspectives on the Natural World". In: C. Key Chapple (ed.), *Jainism and Ecology. Nonviolence in the Web of Life.* Cambridge: Harvard Divinity School, 2002.

Williams, R. (1963). *Jaina Yoga.* Delhi: Motilal Banarsidass, 1983.

Wijayaratna, Mohân (1993). [Spanish Translation: "El budismo en el país del Theravada". In: J. Delumeau (ed.), *El hecho religioso.* Madrid: Alianza, 1995.]

Winternitz, Moritz (1907-1922). *Geschichte der indischen Litteratur.* [English Translation: *History of Indian Literature* (3 vols). Delhi: Motilal Banarsidass, 1983.]

Xuanzang. *Da Tang xiyou-ji.* English Translation and Notes by Samuel Beal (1884) in: *Si-Yu-Ki. Buddhist Records of the Western World* (2 vols.). Delhi: Motilal Banarsidass, 1981.

Yasovijaya, Muni Shri (1974). *Tirthankara Bhagawan Mahavira.* Bombay: Jain Sanskruti Kala Kendra and Shri Parshwa Padmavati Trust, 1993 (revised edition).

Zaehner, R.C. (1962). *Hinduism.* London: Oxford University Press, 1962.

Zimmer, Heinrich (1935). *Indische Sphären.* [Spanish Translation: *Yoga y budismo.* Barcelona: Editorial Kairós, 1998.]

— (1951). *Philosophies of India.* [Edited by Joseph Campbell]. Princeton: Princeton University Press, 1969.

— (1955). *The Art of Indian Asia* (2 vols). [Edited by Joseph Campbell]. Princeton: Princeton University Press, 1983 (revised edition).

INDEX